D1391614

Twentieth-century accounting thinkers

Editorial panel

Twentieth-century accounting thinkers

Edited by John Richard Edwards

London and New York
Published in association with

First published 1994
by Routledge
11 New Fetter Lane, London EC4P 4EE

Simultaneously published in the USA and Canada
by Routledge
29 West 35th Street, New York, NY 10001

Reprinted 1995

Typeset in Times by LaserScript, Mitcham, Surrey
Printed and bound in Great Britain by
Antony Rowe Ltd, Chippenham, Wiltshire

British Library Cataloguing in Publication Data
A catalogue record for this book is available from the British Library

Library of Congress Cataloguing in Publication Data
A catalogue record for this book is available from the Library of Congress

ISBN 0-415-10283-9

Contents

Contributors

Kees Camfferman is Assistant Professor of Accounting at the Faculty of Economics, Vrije Universiteit, Amsterdam.

Arnaldo Canziani is Professor of Accounting at the Faculty of Economics and Commerce, University of Brescia.

Junichi Chiba is Professor of Accounting at the Faculty of Economics, Tokyo Metropolitan University.

Frank Clarke is Professor of Accounting at the Department of Commerce, University of Newcastle.

Bernard Colasse is Professor of Accounting at the Centre de Recherches Européen en Finance et Gestion (CREFIGE), Université de Paris-Dauphine.

Graeme Dean is Associate Professor of Accounting at the Department of Accounting, University of Sydney.

Romain Durand is Associate Professor of Accounting at the Centre de Recherches Européen en Finance et Gestion (CREFIGE), Université de Paris-Dauphine.

Michael Gaffikin is Professor of Accounting at the Department of Accountancy, University of Wollongong.

Jack Kitchen is Professor Emeritus of Accounting, University of Hull.

Kari Lukka is Associate Professor of Accounting at the Turku School of Economics and Business Administration.

Cheryl McWatters is Assistant Professor of Management at the Faculty of Management, McGill University.

Patti A. Mills is Professor of Accounting at the School of Business, Indiana State University.

Maurice Moonitz is Professor Emeritus, University of California at Berkeley.

Tetsuya Morita is Professor of Accounting at the College of Economics, Nihon University.

Michael J. Mumford is Senior Lecturer in Accounting at the Department of Accounting and Finance, Lancaster University.

Robert H. Parker is Professor of Accounting at the Department of Economics, University of Exeter.

Pekka Pihlanto is Professor of Accounting at the Turku School of Economics and Business Administration.

Erich Potthoff is Associate Professor of Auditing and Accounting at the University of Cologne.

Gary J. Previts is Professor of Accounting at the School of Management, Case Western Reserve University.

Thomas R. Robinson is Assistant Professor of Accounting at the School of Business, University of Miami.

Günter Sieben is Professor of Auditing and Accounting at the University of Cologne.

Geoffrey Whittington is Price Waterhouse Professor of Financial Accounting at the Faculty of Economics and Politics, Cambridge University.

Yasushi Yamagata is Professor of Accounting at the Faculty of Economics, Tezukayama University, Nara.

Stephen A. Zeff is Herbert S. Autrey Professor of Accounting at the Jesse H. Jones Graduate School of Administration, Rice University, Houston.

Foreword

The task of selecting entries for a collection on twentieth-century accounting thinkers must have been a difficult one, and I am glad that the responsibility lay with Professor Edwards and not with me. He has had to try to balance the claims of three or four generations of writers, from many countries, and of several different schools of thought. It would be naïve to expect his choices to meet with universal acclaim.

In a trivial sense, anyone who writes about any aspect of accounting qualifies as an accounting thinker. By what criterion are we to distinguish those who merit consideration for inclusion in a book of this kind? The test that I would use would be to ask: has the writer said something illuminating about the *nature* of accounting? It is not enough to have explored some particular accounting problem, unless that exploration also throws new light on the nature of accounting itself. As an example of such a work, I would cite Edwards and Bell's *Theory and Measurement of Business Income* (1961) which, though explicitly concerned with income measurement, sheds light on the nature of accounting measurement generally.

Such work has been out of favour with young accounting academics in recent years, so that with one exception to be noted later, Professor Edwards's exclusion of contemporary work from the present volume may not have sacrificed much of importance. The blight of 'positive accounting theory', which confines itself to the study of accountants' behaviour, driven, it is claimed, exclusively by self-interest, has left little room for the broad theorising about accounting (as distinct from accountants) that attracts accounting thinkers. Fortunately there are signs that the tide is turning. The twenty-first century may after all see its Patons and Schmalenbachs and Mattessiches.

Dennis Beresford had some trenchant things to say about this situation recently. Contrasting what he called 'before the fact' questions and 'after the fact' questions, he made the point that researchers like *ex-post* questions whereas standard setters need help with *ex-ante* questions:

> Academics tell us that sophisticated research tools cannot be employed if the requisite data are lacking, which often is the case with 'before the case' questions. But what then? Should academics do nothing? Or should they use the tools that are available, even if those tools are not as sophisticated as those

currently in favour? For example, if the best tools available for tackling a relevant question are thoughtful analysis and logical argumentation, should academic researchers not use them?

In an earlier age, prescriptive thinking about accounting was not the monopoly of academics. George O. May, Leonard Spacek, Eric Kohler, Kenneth MacNeal and Henry Sweeney in the US, and Sewell Bray and Harry Norris in the UK were not academics. Now, after a period of silence on the part of practitioners, they are being heard from again, but it is in a different guise from formerly. Now it is as standard setters or as commentators on the standard setting process. Dennis Beresford in the US has already been quoted, and the names of Donald Kirk and Reed Storey might be added. David Tweedie in the UK, Warren McGregor in Australia as well as Ross Skinner and Alex Milburn in Canada also merit mention in this connection. Unfortunately, my comparative ignorance of the literature in languages other than English prevents me from citing examples, if they exist, from other countries.

If one is looking for important contributors to accounting thought in this century (and even earlier), it would be a mistake to overlook the economists. In fact, it could be persuasively argued that most seminal contributions to account- ing have been the work of economists rather than of accountants. J. R. Hicks, Sidney Alexander and Edwards and Bell on income, J. M. Clark and Ronald Coase (and in an earlier age, Dionysius Lardner) on cost theory, James Bonbright on valuation and Basil Yamey on accounting history are outstanding examples. (I omit J. B. Canning from this list because I do not associate him with any particular contribution to accounting, and I omit Ronald Edwards because he was an accountant before he became an economist). A volume devoted to the contri- butions of economists to accounting thought would be a worthy companion to the present volume.

Looking through the list of thinkers covered by this book, one naturally asks who has been omitted. Again my lack of familiarity with the literature in languages other than English forces me to stay close to home when asking that question. The considerable space devoted here to European and Japanese authors will give most Anglophone readers a first acquaintance with writers not pre- viously encountered; but it has caused the exclusion of some writers in English who may have made a bigger contribution. I shall not attempt to name them; but I do regret that concentration on the first three-quarters of the century has resulted in the exclusion of a potentially important stream of thought, namely the so-called critical theorists Tony Tinker, David Cooper, Ruth Hines *et al.* To most of us brought up in a more orthodox tradition, what these writers have to say looks misguided, for their criticisms, overtly directed at accounting, seem really to be condemnations of society. Nevertheless, this school of thought, with all its excesses and defects, may be the most significant new turn in accounting thought as we approach the end of the twentieth century.

Accounting has come a long way since Hatfield delivered his famous

'Historical Defense of Bookkeeping' in 1923. He himself played down the progress that had been made in the previous four hundred years, for he says:

> Only two hundred years ago science – in the leading American college [he was referring to Harvard] – was a futile and ludicrous display of ignorance. More than four hundred years ago, in the very first book published on the subject, bookkeeping was outlined in a form which still prevails around the entire world.

Much of the progress we have made since 1923 is chronicled in this book. It fittingly marks Pacioli's quincentenary.

David Solomons

Introduction

The idea for this book arose from a discussion with Anthony Carey and Jan Latham in Autumn 1991 concerning collaboration between the Research Board of the Institute of Chartered Accountants in England and Wales and the Cardiff Business School's Business History Research Unit.[1] The outcome of these discussions were plans for two volumes to help celebrate the 500th anniversary of the publication of Luca Pacioli's *Summa de Arithmetica, Geometria, Proportioni et Proportionalita*. The other volume will appear as a special issue of *Accounting, Business and Financial History* edited by Basil S. Yamey and myself entitled 'From Clay Tokens to *Fukushiki-Boki*: Record Keeping over Ten Millenia'.

Luca Pacioli has been variously described as 'accounting's Renaissance man' (Weis and Tinius 1991: 54) 'the father of modern accounting' (Hatfield 1950: 3) and, perhaps most relevant for our purposes, 'the first academic accountant' (Nobes 1979: 66). His life and works have been the subject of extensive study, but not those of his successors. This anthology of biographies of accounting thinkers is therefore intended to help fill an important gap in the accounting literature. A number of short studies of *British* Accountants, who have been deemed important to business development, are of course contained in the *Dictionary of Business Biography* (Jeremy 1984–6), and it is possible to add to these from a scrutiny of the literature,[2] but the list is not long and the treatment of particular subjects varies a great deal.

In designing the present text, the first problem was to choose the subjects. Perhaps in an endeavour to avoid total responsibility for this onerous task, I consulted the editorial board members of *Accounting, Business and Financial History* for suggestions.[3] Then came the question of who should write, and would be willing to write, about a particular subject. Within a tight time-scale, this served as a significant constraint on subject coverage. There are inevitably some important omissions, and the geographical coverage is less comprehensive than one might have wished. In addition, the number of subjects covered for a particular country is not intended to imply a proportionate measure of its contribution to the development of accounting ideas. Also, I decided to confine the choice of subjects to those who had made their major contribution by about the 1970s in order to allow some space for the development of a consensus concerning the weight of their contribution.[4]

It was decided, as a general rule, to arrange for entries to be written by academics principally active within the country where the subjects lived and worked. The authors were given free rein to write their entries as they saw fit; had I been otherwise minded, I am sure my directions would have properly met with stubborn resistance from the authors. The only suggestion which I put forward, with the aim of achieving a small element of uniformity in approach, was that authors might consider giving attention to: a portrait of the person, dealing with family, background and education; career details; professional links; the subject's ideas and theories; an assessment of their impact on accounting theory and practice; major influences on the 'thinker', for example from other writers; and their leading publications.

In the main, contributors have written about individual theorists; the exceptions are Geoffrey Whittington, who has written on the 'LSE triumvirate', and Bernard Colasse and Romain Durand, who decided to study 'French Accounting Theorists'. Most of the manuscripts were sent out to one or more members of the editorial panel, for comment, and their help is gratefully acknowledged.

The entries are listed in alphabetical order by country. The United States and United Kingdom are best represented with four items each; there are three for Japan, six for continental Europe (Germany two, Finland, France, Holland and Italy, one each), and one each for Canada and Australia.

The earliest of the subjects to make his mark was Lawrence Dicksee. Indeed, probably his best-known book, *Auditing*, was written in 1892, which may appear to place a question mark against his inclusion in this anthology. However, he was a prolific writer, described by Kitchen and Parker as having created an accounting literature almost single-handedly, and was still writing material for publication in the fourth decade of the twentieth century. The most recently active (indeed a number of them still very active) are Ray Chambers, Ricco Mattessich, the LSE triumvirate and Edward Stamp.

Fifteen of the entries have been specifically written for the purpose of the present text; of the other four, three (de Paula, MacNeal and Blough) are reprints while the entry for Dicksee is based on earlier publications by the present authors but also contains new material.

Possibly reflecting the nature of accounting as a discipline, each of the subjects has been concerned to use accounting theory to help solve practical accounting problems. There is little evidence that they were interested in theory for its own sake, and it might be argued that certain of their other accounting contributions were more important than that to original accounting thought; for example, it is arguable that Stamp's most important contribution was as an agent for accounting change. All except Blough and MacNeal were academics; some were practising accountants either at certain stages or throughout their career (for example Blough, de Paula, Dicksee, and Schmalenbach). It is likely that some of them had an enormous influence not only on academic study but also on professional study (books by Dicksee, de Paula, Hatfield and Paton, for example, were widely used as preparation for professional examinations, while Limperg influenced professional study through teaching and involvement in the NIvRA) and professional pronouncements (for example de Paula, the LSE triumvirate, Stamp, Blough, Kurosawa, Iwata and Saario).

A number of the subjects seem to have been mainly influential in affecting developments within their own country, but some have clearly also had a major international impact. The latter group certainly includes Chambers, Dicksee, Hatfield, Paton, Schmalenbach and Schmidt. It is, however, the purpose of the book, not the Introduction, to illuminate the contributions of respective subjects in terms of their influence on the development of accounting thought and practice, the events and individuals who shaped their own ideas and attitudes, and the inter- and intranational impact of their life's work.

John Richard Edwards, Cardiff Business School

Notes

1 I am pleased to acknowledge financial support provided for this project by the Research Board of the Institute of Chartered Accountants in England and Wales.
2 A list would include: Bedford and Ziegler (1975); Bloom, Collins and Debessay (1990); Boutell (1979); Buckner (1975); Carsberg (1966); Cooper and Ijiri (1979); Edwards and Salmonson (1961); Forrester (1979, 1993); Gaffikin (1990); Hein (1959); Hirabayashi (1989); Jones (1988); Kitchen and Parker (1980); Mann (1978); Mautz and Previts (1977); Murphy (1947, 1953); Parker (1980a, 1980b); Previts (1975); Previts and Taylor (1979); Roberts (1975); Stabler (1975); Stevelinck (1972); Zimmerman (1967).
3 I am pleased to acknowledge their advice, though the responsibility for the final choice is mine alone.
4 It is hoped that this comment will not offend subjects who are still extremely active and engaged in work which builds significantly on their achievements to date.

References

Bedford, N. M. and Ziegler, R. E. (1975) 'The contributions of A. C. Littleton to Accounting Thought and Practice', *Accounting Review*, July.

Bloom, R., Collins, M. and Debessay, A. (1990) 'Gilman's Contribution to Accounting Thought: A Golden Anniversary Retrospect', *Accounting History* 2(2).

Boutell, W. S. (1979) 'Memorial: Lawrence Lee Vance, 1911–1978', *Accounting Review*, April.

Buckner, K. C. (1975) *Littleton's Contribution to the Theory of Accountancy*, Atlanta, Ga.: Georgia State University Research Monograph No. 62.

Carsberg, B. V. (1966) 'The Contribution of P. D. Leake to the Theory of Goodwill Valuation', *Journal of Accounting Research*, Spring.

Cooper, W. and Ijiri, Y. (eds) (1979) *Eric Louis Kohler: Accounting's Man of Principles*, Reston, Va.: Reston Publishing.

Edwards, J. D. and Salmonson, R. E. (compilers) (1961) *Contributions of Four Accounting Pioneers – Kohler, Littleton, May, Paton*, East Lansing: Michigan State University.

Forrester, D. A. R. (1977) *Schmalenbach and After*, Glasgow: Strathclyde Convergencies.

Forrester, D. A. R. (1993) *Eugen Schmalenbach and German Business Economics*, New York: Garland.

Gaffikin, M. J. R. (1990) *Accounting Methodology and the Work of R.J.Chambers*, New York and London: Garland.

Hatfield, H. R. (1950) 'An Historical Defence of Bookkeeping', in W.T. Baxter (ed.)

Studies in Accounting, London: Sweet & Maxwell, pp. 1–12. First printed in *The Journal of Accountancy*, April 1924.

Hein, L. W. (1959) 'J. Lee Nicholson: Pioneer Cost Accountant', *The Accounting Review*, January.

Hirabayashi, Y. (1989) 'Memorial to the late Emeritus Professor Kojima (1912–1989)', *The Accounting Historians Journal*, December.

Jeremy, D. J. (ed.) (1984–6) *Dictionary of Business Biography*, vols. i–v, London: Butterworths.

Jones, E. (ed.) (1988) Introduction to *The Memoirs of Edwin Waterhouse, A Founder of Price Waterhouse*, London: Batsford.

Kitchen, J. and Parker, R. H. (1980) *Accounting Thought and Education: Six English Pioneers*, London: ICAEW.

Mann, H. S. (1978) *Charles Ezra Sprague*, New York: Arno Press.

Mautz, R. K and Previts, G. J. (1977) 'Eric Kohler: An Accounting Original', *Accounting Review*, April.

Murphy, Mary E. (1947) 'Arthur Lowes Dickinson, Pioneer in American Professional Accountancy', *Bulletin of the Business History Society*, April.

Murphy, Mary E. (1953) 'Lord Plender: A Vignette of an Accountant and His Times, 1861–1948', *Bulletin of the Business Historical Society*.

Nobes, C. W. (1979) 'Pacioli – the first academic accountant?', *Accountancy*, September.

Parker, R. H. (1980a) 'Memorial: Frank Sewell Bray 1906–1979', *Accounting Review*, April.

Parker, R. H. (ed.) (1980b) *British Accountants: A Biographical Sourcebook*, New York: Arno Press.

Previts, G. J. and Taylor, R. F. (1979) *John Raymond Wildman (1878–1938)*, University, Al.: Academy of Accounting Historians.

Previts, G. J. (1975) Foreword to reissue of *Accounting Practice and Procedure*, by Arthur Lowes Dickinson, 1914, reprinted by Scholars Book Co., Houston, Tex.

Roberts, A. R. (1975) *Robert H. Montgomery: A Pioneer Leader of American Accounting*, Atlanta, Ga.: Georgia State University Research Monograph No. 63.

Stabler, H. F. (1975) *George O. May: A Study of Selected Contributions to Accounting Thought*, Atlanta, Ga.: Georgia State University Research Monograph No. 61.

Stevelinck, E. (1972) 'David Murray: Accounting Historian 1842–1928', *The Accountant's Magazine*, August.

Weis, W. L. and Tinius, D. E. (1991) 'Luca Pacioli: Accounting's Renaissance Man', *Management Accounting* (US), July.

Zimmerman, V. K. (1967) 'The Long Shadow of a Scholar', *The International Journal of Accounting*, Spring.

Acknowledgements

Extracts from 'Lawrence Robert Dicksee' by Jack Kitchen and Robert H. Parker in *Accounting Thought and Education: Six English Pioneers*, London: ICAEW, 1980, is reprinted with permission. Extracts from 'Lawrence Dicksee, Depreciation, and the Double-Account System' by Jack Kitchen in *Debits, Credits Finance and Profits*, edited by Harold Edey and B.S. Yamey, London: Sweet & Maxwell, 1974, is reprinted with permission. 'Frederic Rudolph Mackley de Paula' by Jack Kitchen and Robert H. Parker in *Accounting Thought and Education: Six English Pioneers*, London: ICAEW, 1980, is reprinted with permission. 'Carman G. Blough, 1895–1981' by Maurice Moonitz, *Accounting Review*, January 1982, is reprinted with permission. '*Truth in Accounting*: The Ordeal of Kenneth MacNeal' by Stephen A. Zeff, *Accounting Review*, July 1982, is reprinted with permission.

1 Raymond Chambers (b. 1917)

Determined seeker of truth and fairness

Michael Gaffikin

Abstract

Raymond Chambers has made an immense contribution to twentieth-century accounting thought. Although not all have accepted the substantive elements of the theory that he has developed, his insistence on rigorous and logical method in accounting research has provided an example of the progress of a true scholar. His early writings provided new insights into the processes of research and his criticism has sharpened the arguments of many.

There are various ways in which an assessment of someone who has significantly contributed to a discipline can be made. One of these is to examine the working life of the subject in order to determine the external factors that have shaped his or her ideas. For such an assessment of Chambers, it may well be that history is too young to know his true contribution to the development of accounting thought.

INTRODUCTION

Accounting, Raymond John Chambers has written, is 'a process of discovery, of getting at the facts which are pertinent to economic categories of actions'. As such, he has argued, 'it is no different to other empirical sciences'. And, for Chambers, this process of discovery is made possible by remaining consistent to 'observable realities'.

Chambers' life and work in his chosen discipline has been consistent with these sentiments. To him, the application of the principles of logic and rigour that he saw in use in other sciences would lead inevitably to the determination of the reliable basis of the financial information needed to enable sound economic decisions to be made.

Chambers entered an accounting world seemingly devoid of rigorously derived principles, where the order of the day was 'ad hocery and expediency'. He has sought to bring some order to this world, to draw attention to the need for sound principles, to demonstrate what these principles are and to provide the necessary accounting theory. Some have claimed that his work is the most complete and theoretically sound in the history of accounting (Gaffikin 1989), but this claim has been denied by others (for example, Grinyer 1992) and the major accounting model proposed by Chambers seemingly has failed to win acceptance by the accounting community.

If his work is theoretically sound, its non-acceptance is a perplexing problem and those who support it would have had to seek reasons for this apparent rejection. Such an enquiry could take several paths. Given that they have accepted the thesis that Chambers has presented a sound theory, they would have to look to other factors in the creation and establishment of a theory to explain its non-acceptance; factors that would include the behavioural, political, philosophical and sociological circumstances surrounding theory development. This essay represents such an attempt; one which does not examine the substantive components of the theory – Chambers remains the best exponent of his theory, so there would be little purpose served in merely being an echo – but which discusses some of the circumstances surrounding the person. It is hoped that through this process some light will be shed on the person and work of someone who has made an immense contribution to the development of the discipline of accounting and who is clearly one of the most important of the twentieth-century accounting thinkers.

THE WORKS

Chambers has made an enormous contribution to the accounting literature over a period of nearly four decades.[1] His first book was published in 1947 and was followed by several more monographs, hundreds of articles in academic and professional journals, published addresses and lectures, letters, submissions to committees, news media appearances, editorial comments and even accounting verse. In these works he has spanned a wide variety of areas of concern to the discipline. Although his major single work, *Accounting, Evaluation and Economic Behavior* (1966) contains the main argument for his theory of continuously contemporary accounting (CoCoA), it has been the mistake of too many critics to view it in isolation, away from the many other works that supplement, complement, clarify, modify and amend that argument. He has been accused of producing work without adequate empirical foundations (for example by Nelson 1973), yet as early as 1955, in his monograph *The Function and Design of Company Annual Reports*, he presented a survey and analysis of extant published company financial statements and, later, his *Securities and Obscurities* demonstrated his reliance on the current practice of external reporting in building his theory. It is important to note that throughout his work he was conscious of the need for any theory to be firmly rooted in the everyday world of accounting practice.

In the early 1950s Chambers was called upon by the profession to present a series of research lectures. There were three lectures: in June 1950, he lectured on 'The Relationship Between Accounting and Financial Management', at the University of Melbourne; in July 1951 his topic was 'Accounting and Business Finance', at the University of Queensland; and in September 1953, his subject was 'The Formal Basis of Business Decisions', at the University of Tasmania.

In each of these lectures the audience was exposed to a degree of assertive, rigorous and logical argument not previously encountered in accounting. The titles are fairly indicative of the content of each lecture and signal Chambers' vision of accounting as being the provision of information necessary but not sufficient for economic decision making. The lectures also signalled his intention not simply to accept the sacred cows of accounting but to seek some logical justification for accounting action. He argued that conservatism has no place in accounting: it cannot be theoretically justified and flies in the face of many other basic principles of accounting. He argued, contrary to what many other writers had suggested, that disclosure is a matter of policy, not a theoretical proposition. And he also argued that accounting is a fact-finding function, a belief that persisted throughout his subsequent work.

The international accounting community was exposed to this same degree of rigour with the publication of his article, 'Blueprint for Theory of Accounting' (1955) in which many of the doyens of accounting academe were shown to have provided works which fell far short of what would be regarded as rigorous theory in other, more established disciplines. Works described as being 'theories of accounting', he argued, were not theories but formulations of practices and as such were misleading, for it could be assumed from such a process that account-ing practices were sound, rather than being based as they were on the mass of contradictory sets of propositions. Even as formulations of practice they were incomplete – for example, overlooking cash flow accounting, a widely used practice but one that did not neatly fit the prescriptions of the theorists. Although some of the 'theories' appealed to history, 'antiquity is no criterion: in fact the history of other arts suggests that antiquity makes a practice suspect from the start' (1955: 18). The paper continues by describing what a theory should comprise and states the premises for a theory of accounting.

One of those criticised in the 'Blueprint' article, Littleton, took exception, and there followed an exchange which seemed to have done more to establish Chambers' intellectual credentials to the international community than vindicate the naïve empiricism of those he was criticising. Littleton responded to Chambers' criticism in his paper 'Choice Among Alternatives' (1956). Partly as a response to this (and some other criticism), Chambers reacted by publishing a series of articles, seminal in the accounting literature in their appreciation of the (then) accepted philosophical means for establishing theories. All argued for more rigour in accounting thinking. Once again their titles indicate the argument contained in them, for example, 'A Scientific Pattern for Accounting Theory', 'Detail for a Blueprint', 'The Influence of Economic Forces on Accounting', 'Measurement and Misrepresentation', and 'The Conditions of Research in Accounting'. His concern for methodological issues in accounting was not wasted, for in 1961 he produced a major work, *Toward a General Theory of Accounting*, in which he makes an attempt to present his own theory formulation.

Strong themes are found in all of these works. Chambers was calling for *scientific* rigour in uncovering the facts of accounting. The facts were economic and the challenge was to express them in numbers. Thus, to Chambers, any argument had to be expressed as a logical development, and in the 'General Theory' paper his argument is presented as a series of propositions syllogistically developed from basic premises. The propositions are developed from notions dominant in the current economic theory. Because accountants expressed these economic 'facts' in numbers it was important that they developed consistently from the theory of measurement. Accountants' numbers had to represent meaningful and measurable economic properties. Some propositions could be taken as already proven in economic theory. When combined with the observed and measured economic facts, a theory of accounting could emerge.

The 'General Theory' contained the kernel of what was to follow, and *Accounting, Evaluation and Economic Behavior* (*AEEB*) assumed a similar, although much more thoroughly developed, form. To Chambers, accounting was vitally linked to economic behaviour – it was economic behaviour which provided the *raison d'être* of accounting. The economic propositions on which the argument is based are clearly established in the first 100-odd pages. This was something which had not occurred in accounting before and many reviewers and commentators suggested that the 'book' really started after that (see, for example, Paton 1982).

During the period in which *AEEB* was being developed, other works significant in the development of accounting thought appeared, notably those by Edwards and Bell (1961), Mattessich (1964), Moonitz (1961) and Sprouse and Moonitz (1963). It is interesting to note that all these works were concerned with the same problems Chambers had noted. Edwards and Bell, as economists, attempted to provide economic wisdom for accountants. Mattessich had made earlier forays into the world of methodology and his work aimed at providing a strict methodological foundation for accounting measurements. The Moonitz and Sprouse and Moonitz studies were written to set out the fundamental premises or postulates on which an accounting theory could develop. On the surface, they would seem to have been providing the explanations Chambers was working hard to supply. Chambers reviewed (at length) each of these works; no doubt this was done to clarify his own thoughts as well as to demonstrate the weak- nesses in these other works. The conclusions of all these other works were very different to his own and he went to lengths to show they were defective.

For a period after the publication of *AEEB*, Chambers' work was concerned with defending it against critics, modifying it and marketing it. Some very fine works were produced. His paper, 'The Foundations of Financial Accounting' (1967) represents the first major extension of his theory and in which the expression 'continuously contemporary accounting' (CoCoA) is first used. Many of the notions in *AEEB* are further explicated and an appendix poses eighteen questions as to the requirements of a system of accounting; his theory is the only one that can satisfy these requirements. This is a technique that Chambers used several times in his efforts to win CoCoA's acceptance.

One of the largest single problems facing the accounting profession in the second half of the twentieth century has been that of changing price levels. The fact that conventional accounting could not solve this problem highlighted the weakness of the traditional model. A large number of Chambers' works have addressed the issue. Changing price levels is one of the problems CoCoA overcomes. With its use of current market selling prices, there is no need to make further adjustments as any price changes have been accounted for. In the minds of many, CoCoA became merely a method of catering for the effects of inflation. Chambers seems to have seen this as a 'selling point', and many of his works were designed to demonstrate the failures of the traditional model and the inadequacies of suggested alternatives, concluding that CoCoA was the only system that solved the problem. To some this was a source of frustration and disenchantment, for it seemed that Chambers 'twisted' the argument to suit a CoCoA solution. However, to see CoCoA solely as a method of accounting for inflation was most unfortunate, because it failed to expose the true strength of CoCoA as a system of providing relevant, up-to-date information for real economic decision making.

From about 1970 the research fashion in accounting changed. Starting in the US and then spreading to other Western countries, philosophical or methodical discourse gave way to large-scale data collection and manipulation. This, it was claimed, was the true empirical method of scientific research. Those who had made the largest contribution to accounting thought in the previous decades were dismissed as having failed to be empirical; Chambers was one of these (despite his earlier claim that accounting is 'fact finding'!). One of his reactions was to defend his methodology, attack being one of the best methods of defence, as, for example, in his 'Stock Market Prices and Accounting Research' (1974). Later, in a manner that seemed to suggest he had accepted the adage 'if you cannot beat them, join them', he chose to demonstrate CoCoA's obvious utility through a series of empirical (survey) studies (for example, *The Serviceability of Financial Information: A Survey*, 1984).

In addition to these empirical studies, in the last decade, Chambers has produced works which are more reflective and 'broad sweeping' in their examination of issues but which all arrive at the conclusion of the merits of CoCoA. Titles indicate the tone of the works. In 'Accounting – "One of the finest inventions of the human spirit"', the words of Goethe are used. 'Positive Accounting Theory and the PA Cult' is far more biting. And, in 'Metrical and Empirical Laws in Accounting' he returns to an earlier theme: the essential nature of and the need for accurate and theoretically sound measurement in accounting. All these works demonstrate his breadth of understanding of the great intellectual movements of the world, his command of expression and his desire to relate it all to *his* real world of economic affairs.

Currently Chambers is working on (and has been for some years) a *Thesaurus of Accounting*. The work is a highly ambitious project which seeks to trace the use of ideas relevant to accounting that have been used throughout its history. In so doing, he hopes to demonstrate the inconsistent and sloppy use of words and expressions in accounting and to point to their originally intended meanings. It is a gigantic project which, now near its completion, will show him to be one of accounting's greatest scholars.

THE PERSON

Chambers is a man of strong principles. He believes passionately in his work and his theory. Too often, his consistent avowal of his theory has been misinterpreted. It is not a stubborn and dogmatic assertion of faith but a belief in a carefully devised, rigorous and logical theory developed from a lifetime's work. To him, to accept anything else would be a denial of reason and observation. Such strength and commitment is rare. It arises not from self-interest, but from a genuine attempt to contribute a solution to some of the world's problems; to know Chambers is to know this is true.

Raymond John Chambers was born in Newcastle in New South Wales in Australia on 16 November 1917, the older, by two years, of two brothers. Newcastle was an industrial centre dominated by a steel mill. However, Chambers' father was a businessman, operating a small, family-run organisation. Much of Chambers' early non-school life was spent working in the business. After three years of secondary schooling Chambers left to take up a career in advertising and commercial art. However, the intervention of his headmaster saw him return to school, from where he matriculated with a university exhibition (scholarship) at the University of Sydney. Despite this, he was obliged to study part-time, working during the day first in the Attorney General's office and then with the Shell Oil Company as an accounts clerk. He graduated as a Bachelor of Economics in 1939 and, after other employment, worked for the Australian Prices Commission from 1943 to 1945. His work there involved the regulation of prices; it was to have a profound influence on his later thinking.

An economics degree did not entitle Chambers to be an accountant, so he then had to take the professional examinations necessary to qualify. Tuition was provided by correspondence with the Sydney Technical College. He was appalled at the standards of teaching and when he was appointed as a part-time correspondence teacher of auditing he was determined to change it from the 'arid, doctrinaire and unimaginative' learning process that he had endured.

Chambers' association with technical colleges was to continue and be a strong early influence on him. In the technical colleges of the principal cities of Australia in the early years of the Second World War, there had been set up departments of foremanship and industrial supervision, to speed up the process of supervisory responsibility. By the end of the war these departments were responsible for extensive educational and rehabilitation programmes in many subjects, including supervisory and managerial studies.

In 1945 he commenced his full-time teaching career, taking up an appointment at the School of Management of the Sydney Technical College. In this position he had to teach not only accounting but also a variety of management-related subjects that were offered in the above-mentioned programmes. One of his responsibilities was the programme in costing and cost control. However, he was disturbed to note that, despite the many management-related subjects being taught, there was not one in financial management. Not only did he manage to have such a subject introduced, there being no finance related textbooks, he produced, at the end of his first two years, his book, *Financial Management*. It was very different from other such books at the time in that he consciously related the everyday financial management skills to the everyday problems of managerial decision making. Three later editions, each substantially different from the previous, maintained and refined this notion.

In 1953 he was appointed Senior Lecturer, the first full-time accounting position in the Department of Economics within the Faculty of Economics of the University of Sydney. Although responsible for accounting teaching and research, he continually rubbed shoulders with economists, members of a discipline that had won intellectual acceptance many years previously. Even more important, it was an environment in which he was permitted to pursue his intellectual goals. To, in his words, 'cherish the independence of thought and inquiry that had contributed to the advancement of other learned professions'; to 'resort to the ideas of linguists, mathematicians, scientists, philosophers, lawyers and sociologists', but to also 'listen to the wise men of the profession' (Chambers 1991c).

In 1960 he was appointed Professor of Accounting and Chair of the new Department of Accounting at the University of Sydney. A year later he published his 'General Theory', which clearly indicated the direction in which he was headed. Soon after, he ventured overseas to Britain and the USA in search of others with similar aims, only to return disillusioned. His next step was to attempt to reconstruct accounting, to replace 'ad hocery and expedience in theory and practice with empirically and logically established principles' (1991c), to write *AEEB*. The book was awarded the American Institute of Certified Public Accountant's gold medal for contributions to the accounting literature.

In 1973 he was the first American Accounting Association (AAA) Distinguished International Lecturer to the United States. Since then he has received many awards and honours, which have included the AAA's Outstanding Educator Award and induction to the Accounting Hall of Fame. In 1976 he received the Alpha Kappa Psi Foundation Award for distinguished service and accomplishment in accounting. He was invited by the Academia Italiana di Economia Aziendale to be a member with the title Academico Ordinario. He has been named an Officer of the Order of Australia. He has also maintained his commitment to the profession and was for many years a Councillor and then National President of the Australian Society of Accountants (now the Australian Society of Certified Practising Accountants), subsequently being elected to Life Membership for his services to the profession. He has continued to serve on many advisory committees of the two major professional accounting bodies in Australia. He was the founding editor of *Abacus*, to which he still serves as consulting editor.

He has been a teacher and has been a visiting professor to a large number of universities in various parts of the world. He has contributed to academic and practitioner conferences and seminars in several institutions in Australia and around the world. He has always been selflessly willing to talk to students and staff at educational institutions (with no thought for pecuniary gain). He has lectured to many classes and supervised a large number of student research studies (including a large number of doctorates). He has always been willing to discuss and debate issues with colleagues and inspire in them the need for rigorous and logical argument. Many a junior colleague has been daunted at the prospect of such debates, but none has not appreciated this stern critic's concern and willingness to enter such discussion (even though they may not have agreed with his conclusions). It is difficult not to sound too adulatory when describing Chambers' approach to colleagues and students in assisting their intellectual endeavours, but it is all well-earned and deserved praise.

Chambers has been described as a loner (Gaffikin 1989), which he has resented (private correspondence). However, the description was not intended to describe a social disposition but rather a spirit of a true individual. Very few of his works have been collaborative efforts and there are few bibliographical references in his works. Some who have tried to work with him and in support of him have been disappointed, even disillusioned, at his lack of recognition of their efforts. He would be the first to deny that he has not learned from others, from those with whom he has been associated and with those whose works he has read and absorbed, agreed and disagreed. Yet he has doggedly maintained the energy of an individual in pursuit of a single goal – the advancement of knowledge in his chosen discipline. In these endeavours he has had to be 'alone'; very few could have matched his zeal and commitment. As is often the case in such circumstances, in his younger years, when his passion for his goal was more charged, he was accused of arrogance and intolerance. Older now, the same passion remains but it is mellowed and circumspect in its outward manifestation. He is at times frustrated and disappointed – frustrated by his inability to make others 'see the facts' and disappointed by the lack of resolve in some of his former colleagues and students. Yet, overall, he remains optimistic and cites many instances where it has taken societies a long time to accept new ideas.

THE METHODOLOGY

Almost before he started his journey to reconstruct accounting, Chambers was extremely conscious of his mode of travel. Many of his major early works are concerned with methodological issues.

> If a theory of accounting is to go beyond practice and if the historical development of the practice is to be disregarded, upon what basis, then may it proceed? Upon the same basis as any other theory; that is, by building up a series of relevant propositions from a few fundamental assumptions or axioms.
>
> (Chambers 1955: 349)

The Blueprint article was followed by 'A Scientific Pattern for Accounting Thought', 'Detail for a Blueprint', 'Conditions for Research in Accounting' and the General Theory paper. Thus, it seems that he was building the foundation on which to build his general theory. This theory (in the General Theory) is constructed consistently with his earlier statements on methodology. He was frustrated with the lack of rigour in earlier works. Earlier theorists were more concerned to rationalise the current practice of their time. This led to inconsistencies, contradictions and what he called 'doublethink'. Many of the earlier theorists had made significant and often novel contributions to accounting. They had pointed to the defects and deficiencies of accounting. However, in the end most resorted to the rationalisation of the expedients of practice.

In the Blueprint article Chambers suggests that while it is possible to build up a theory of accounting without reference to the practice of accounting, it does not mean that the theory will have no connection with reality (p. 19). An essential ingredient of a theory was its testing: the process of checking back is of the nature of scientific method (p. 19).

To Chambers, a theory was a series of propositions built up from a few assumptions or axioms. This methodology is clearly a statement of the hypothetico-deductive method accepted and described in the literature as *the* scientific method. In making this statement so early, Chambers is one of the first, if not the first (in the twentieth century) in the accounting literature to appeal for the use of the methods of science. To him, such method, if followed strictly, would remove the sloppy thinking in accounting, the doublethink and the doublespeak. It would remove the uncertainty and contradictions that had dogged earlier accounting writing. It would provide the basis for a soundly constructed accounting theory. This is the path he was to tread and, being a highly principled person, he followed closely the method of enquiry that he had described. It is the method of the General Theory and is found in its refined and more sophisticated version in *AEEB*. It is for this reason that the claim at the start of this essay was made. Chambers clearly listed his methodological predilection and followed it consistently. This methodology was that which he judged the most appropriate, based on his reading of the mainstream philosophical and economic literature. In the context of accounting he was ahead of his time. To him, the conditions of accounting research, as the prerequisite to accounting theory, comprised:

1 a belief that accounting could be studied scientifically;
2 a knowledge of the modes of communication, thought and action pertinent to economic action;
3 a readiness to re-examine prevailing presumptions or assumptions;
4 a willingness to explore all sources of relevant facts, transdisciplinary and transnational;
5 a recognition of the hierarchical structure of ideas;
6 a readiness to follow a line of argument to its conclusion;
7 a readiness to search for ways of testing conclusions;
8 a recognition of the difference and relationships between reasoned conclusions and rules of practice.

Most of these conditions are of the type found in conventional statements of the positivist hypothetico-deductive methodology. However, there is a greater emphasis on that aspect which most exponents of hypothetico-deductivism have avoided. That is, some of Chambers' earlier conditions are concerned with the context of discovery (for example see Broad and Wade 1982: 126–7). Adherents were usually more concerned with science as a logical structure than in science as a process. Chambers, however, in his second, third and fourth conditions, is suggesting that theories emerge from a process of observation and exhaustive study of extant knowledge. His fifth, sixth, seventh and eighth conditions are more typical of the then conventional wisdom: the structuring of hypotheses, the deductive reasoning and the testing of the conclusions.

The same methodology is found in current mainstream accounting research studies. One of the major differences is that assumptions are now presumed, rather than stated up front. Another difference is the systematic testing of the large data bases, employing techniques that were not available to Chambers at that time. The data now is no more empirical than that observed and incorporated by Chambers. However, by employing modern technology to 'massage the data', techniques have become more important than results. Whereas Chambers was concerned with workable solutions to improve the state of accounting, many contemporary mainstream researchers are merely seeking novel techniques for stating what they have already concluded before they started their investigation. They suffer from the positivist delusion – that theirs is the path to an objective revelation of the world. There is no critical challenge to extant practices, despite the obvious manifestations of them in the spectacular corporate collapses around the world. There is concentration on minutiae because that is better for demonstrating the efficiency of the techniques used. This sort of behaviour, to Chambers, is unethical in its unconscious waste of scarce resources and its ignorance of the real problems facing the economic and commercial environment.

Chambers was faithful to his conditions in constructing *AEEB*. Early in the book he confidently asserts that accounting can be studied scientifically. The first hundred pages are devoted to explication of the modes of communication, thought and action pertinent to economic action. In the remainder of the book the other conditions are well satisfied. Having thoroughly developed his theory it must have come as somewhat of a shock to then observe the criticisms in the reviews and review articles that appeared. Chambers today sees it all as the reaction to a challenge to the status quo, to someone that was presenting a new view of accounting, different to that in which the critics had been trained. This would certainly seem to be so.

It has always been important to Chambers that accounting should provide economic decision makers with the information that is most relevant and most reliable. The message in the title of his book is quite clear. It is economic behaviour that accounting assists. If it is to do this properly then it must employ methods of measurement that are theoretically and empirically sound. To these ends Chambers made detailed and full enquiries into what was held to be the basis of economic behaviour and to measurement theory. He selected those notions of economic behaviour which were held to be the dominant view according to economic theory and which he experienced and observed. Where conventional accounting contradicted this wisdom, it was rejected.

He had made a similarly detailed enquiry of measurement theory. In stating that accounting measurements must be based on observable common properties of the elements which they purported to represent, he was stating a truth of which everyone was aware but which they refused to accept. That is, in times of fluctuating price levels, historical cost accounting produces meaningless aggregations. Throughout his work, accurate measurement, observation and utility have been important precepts. The measures used by reporting accountants wedded to conventional accounting procedures gave rise to the communication of misleading and therefore useless information. His interest in measurement is significant, for his conclusion that current cash equivalents are the only reliable measures that accountants could provide users is based on his appreciation of measurement theory.

However, many of his critics seem to have missed the point, for they concentrated on what they perceived to be the practical problem posed by current market prices – the question of aggregation. That is, what would be the basic unit to measure? And they questioned the availability of current market prices, often completely missing the point that if there was none available then there was no market value. Chambers' defence of his theory has been strong, wide-reaching and sustained. He has worked hard to demonstrate that CoCoA was the only system that adhered to the principles of measurement theory. He has attempted to convince audiences that any theory must be constructed on the basis of reliable observations of practice and that CoCoA does this. He has attempted to prove beyond any doubt that CoCoA produces the information (numbers) that is most useful to managers and decision makers. He reviewed other works to point out their inadequacies, including those of contemporary accounting theories (for example, Edwards and Bell 1961, Mattessich 1964 and Ijiri 1967), of past purported theories (for example, Canning 1929), of economists (for example, Fisher 1906), of legal, official and quasi-legal professional pronouncements (for example, the Sandilands Committee Report in the UK, the Richardson Report in New Zealand, and Paul Grady's *Inventory of Accounting Principles* for the American Institute of Certified Public Accountants – the AICPA) and of many other works. He retained a sense of humour – the editor of one journal either missed or chose to ignore the acronym of the title of his review article of a previous paper: 'NOD, COG and PuPU: See How Inflation Teases' (*Journal of Accountancy*, September 1975).

In 1973 he published a major demonstration of the empirical basis of his work – *Securities and Obscurities* as well as other papers such as 'Observation as a Method of Inquiry – the Background of *Securities and Obscurities*' (*Abacus*, 1973). As suggested above, Chambers saw as a major selling point the fact that CoCoA solved the problem of accounting for inflation. From his very first ventures into the accounting literature, he had been concerned with the effects of inflation on accounting. Now, he produced a large number of works showing that CoCoA overcame the problem.

Chambers is still working to convince the world of the correctness of CoCoA. Initially, he must have believed that theories won acceptance through the rigour and logic of their construction. This is what the advocates of positivism (including hypothetico-deductivism) led people to believe. Chambers' rigour and logic has proved hard to fault. The world, however, it seems, does not operate in the manner the positivist purists would have us believe. Theory acceptance is subject to the vagaries of socio-political forces and fancies. Despite the fact that the problems for which Chambers was providing a solution have not been solved by any other more fashionable subsequent suggestion, CoCoA has not won significant acceptance. Despite the fact that, for some at least, CoCoA represents the most methodologically sound accounting, with few exceptions, it is overlooked by the professional community. Methodology is subservient to socio-political forces.

THE INFLUENCES

In most of Chambers' written work very few bibliographic references are provided so, on the surface, it is difficult to quickly determine the influences on him (but see Gibson 1991). He has resented being tied to any single source of influence, claiming that a vast amount of material that may have influenced him in one way or another has never been referred to by him in print. Some evidence tends to suggest that some influences were stronger than others, however. For example, his early university education was in economics and, because of his continual reference to the economic literature and commonly held economic notions, it seems that he has maintained an interest in the current economic literature. There is no doubt that his work has always had a strong economic foundation.

However, he has suggested (see Chambers 1971) that his earliest influences arose from his experiences with the Australian Prices Commission. What he observed there bore little relationship to what was described in the textbooks that first he studied and then, later, were available for him as teching aids.

His first full-time teaching responsibilities extended beyond accounting, so he read many of the general management texts of the time. He read and was exposed to works by Barnard and Simon (see Chambers 1971). Cannon's *The Wisdom of the Body* has been cited by him as having drawn his attention to the need for interaction between many disciplines to achieve effective management (1971). He was also drawn to the then foundling discipline of cybernetics, believing that it was the essence of management – steersmanship (1971). Beyond these more obvious sources it seems that Chambers read widely and has been truly eclectic in using those ideas that he believed useful to his aims. His reading included the current notions in the philosophy of science, measurement theory, economics and other social sciences. However, he was also very well-read in the accounting literature and has always believed that anyone working in accounting should be well aware of what has been said before. It may well be that had this approach had been taken by more people, the accounting literature would now be either briefer or more fruitful.

An analysis of his work shows that there have been many influences. Although he is likely to protest at any specific influence being suggested, it does seem that he was attracted to many aspects of the Austrian school of economists, and in particular the work of von Mises; similar views are found in the works of both scholars (for example, the notion of praxeology). In fact some ideas are only found in the works of both writers! Nevertheless, it would be only fair to point out that the work of many other economists has also influenced Chambers. For example, Hayek, Keynes and Machlup are also cited in *AEEB*; Hutchison, Knight and Robbins are alluded to several times in later works and in his teaching materials.

In his later work, reference sources are even harder to detect. Perhaps he had learned from experience that where he had made bibliographic citations, he found himself having to defend his work from charges laid against the cited work – for example, by Richard Leftwich's 'A Critical Analysis of Some Behavioural Assumptions underlying Chambers' *Accounting, Evaluation and Economic Behavior*' (Chambers 1969). Whatever the reason, it seems that he definitely preferred to 'go it alone'; to stand or fall by his own work (but perhaps not to fall). He has always strongly disliked being 'boxed' or categorised. Throughout his working career he has claimed that his source of inspiration has been his observations of the commercial and economic world; economic decisions are made on the basis of present resources with a few possible alternative courses of action. Thus, current market prices of currently held resources can be the only basis of determining economic actions.

THE POWER . . .

Chambers has had to work and survive in a professional world that has become increasingly aggressive and politically manipulated. Part of this was of his own making. When he entered the academic arena, intellectual matters were settled in a gentlemanly manner (this is not intended to be sexist, as there were very few women working in the field) with little attention to theoretical argument. What he saw was a discipline which had developed its practices with scant regard for logic and rigour. Theoretical expositions were poorly developed and were little more than justifications of the current practices. Chambers launched an intellectual attack on this, and it was through this attack that others were to become aware of him and his work. This attack was not a trivial matter, and Chambers accepted the responsibility for providing an alternative framework free of inconsistencies and the lack of philosophical and theoretical substance. In being critical of Littleton in the 'Blueprint' article (1955) he was questioning a doyen of accounting academe, a mentor to many in the profession and a symbol of the established order of accounting education and research. And he was doing this from outside the geographical boundaries of the established order. However, because fundamental issues were involved he was, after a while, accepted in the United States as having something to contribute to the discipline and this is evident in the many awards that have been accorded him. However, in Great Britain, where it could be claimed traditions survive stronger and longer, it seems that he has had little influence on accounting developments.

In Australia, in his early years, Chambers was forceful and outspoken in his chastisement of the profession for the direction it took. This was especially so for its response to the problems of inflation in the 1960s and 1970s. More recently, for the accounting standards it issued.

His reviews and criticism of the works of other academics has been equally forceful and direct; for example, his reviews of Moonitz, Sprouse and Moonitz, Mattessich, Edwards and Bell, and Ijiri.

Having chosen to live by the sword, Chambers had to be prepared to survive on the same basis. He challenged the established order in accounting on all fronts – the academics, the professional bodies and the regulators. These challenges arose solely because he believed that accounting had to have a more rigorously developed, intellectually sound foundation. But, as he had 'knocked the established order', many of the less enlightened have elected to 'knock' him and 'Chambers bashing' became a popular sport. This has only made Chambers more determined to establish the intellectual credentials of his theory. Intellectually, he has successfully withstood almost all the criticism levelled at his theory. However, accounting has never been a discipline in which problems are satisfactorily resolved. Rather, it is one which, from time to time, the winds of changing fashions sweep through. In the 1970s the approach to accounting research changed: and uncritical and naïve empiricism became the research order of the day. The work of the scholars who had been instrumental in establishing a more solid intellectual foundation for accounting – Chambers, Mattessich, Sterling and others – was now overlooked. Substantive issues became far less important than methods and techniques. Assumptions became presumptions and it was not *what* accounting produced but, on the basis of stock market data, how it seemed to be *used*. Chambers had always argued that accounting was necessary but not sufficient for economic decision making. The new researchers found they could only provide partial answers and very often it had to be *assumed* that changes in economic behaviour by actors were due to changes in accounting information.

Mainstream accounting research had changed. Ironically, the underlying economic assumptions of the new research and those employed by Chambers are essentially the same – they are conventionalist. So too are the underlying ontological and epistemological assumptions – realist and empirical. In both, economic facts are seen to exist independently of individuals and are there to be uncovered.

... AND THE GLORY?

One of the tenets of mainstream accounting research is that, according to good scientific research methods, research should be kept objective and value-free. Chambers would agree with this. However, some researchers see accounting and research in a different light. Scientism, the attempt to apply the methods of the physical sciences to all research, is rejected. The impossibility of objective, value-free research is accepted. In this spirit, this section is purposively reflexive in the belief that a personal response to knowing and working with Chambers can enlighten others.

I have found working with and knowing Chambers to have been an extremely valuable experience. He is a highly principled person and that has affected the way in which he sees the world. He has been missionary in his zeal to attempt to lift the intellectual standards of a discipline which, when he entered it, were near non-existent. Like all idealists he has had to pay the price of frustration. I believe the driving force for Chambers has been idealistic principles and not ego (although obviously ego will always play some part). My earliest experience as a colleague was to cautiously approach him for his opinion about some- thing I had written, only to find that he would immediately drop his pen (even halfway through a sentence), come around from the back of his desk and sit and discuss and debate with me the matter of concern. Other colleagues had similar experiences. The discussion and debate was rarely easy because you were expected to defend your position; if he disagreed with you, then that defence became difficult as he seemed to changed tack, bombarding you with questions from several angles. However, irrespective of the outcome, the discussion never became bitter or personal. I found these experiences extremely rewarding and I soon became aware of the need to have defensible positions. Nevertheless, not all colleagues reacted the same. Some became sycophantic, and some insecure and defeatist. To Chambers this must have been disappointing because it was obvious that his main aim was to help build the intellectual character of his colleagues in the manner he saw as best. The fact that many of his colleagues now hold positions of responsibility in many different institutions attests to at least some level of his success. He has said:

> But my greatest personal satisfaction has been in the academic and career achievements of students and colleagues in my home University. I have a firm belief that all who set their minds and hands to tasks of their choice can do better than they thought they could. It has been my privilege to encourage many to believe that of themselves.
>
> (1991c: 4)

Chambers works very hard, almost to the extent of being a workaholic. For many years he worked long hours, seven days a week. Later this was reduced to six, then five. Even in official retirement (from full-time employment) he works five full days on his academic pursuits. He has been ably supported by his 'patient and tolerant companion', his wife, a debt which he freely acknowledges (1991c: 5). To illustrate how hard he worked, consider his trip to the USA for a short period in 1966 where he travelled

> . . . out of San Fransisco severally to the universities of Alabama, New York, California at Los Angeles, Stanford, Michigan, Washington, Washington State, Alberta, Saskatchewan and Oregon. Between times in hotels, motels and faculty clubs I wrote publishable scripts of six papers, revised almost completely a 400-page book, wrote a critique of a current project of the American Institute of CPAs, presented a course of lectures to senior students at Berkeley – and carried on editing *Abacus*.
>
> (1991c: 4)

Through these efforts he has led from the front. Chambers has never left any doubt as to his preferred theoretical solution. He has been single-minded in his pursuit of its acceptance, and this has unsettled some of his detractors. To some this has been interpreted as intolerance and dogmatism. However, it can also be seen as confidence and a belief in his own theory. Logically it would seem inconsistent to develop a theory but then to defer to others. He has permitted others to hold their beliefs but reserved the right to disagree with their argument and conclusions (and has done so). It was the 'ad hocery and expedience' in theory and practice that drove him to develop his theory. This he did, as explained above, meticulously and through work over a large number of years. To have done otherwise would have been totally inconsistent. And Chambers is not that sort of person – he is highly principled and intellectually idealistic. He saw the acceptance of accounting into the rarefied intellectual atmosphere of universities as a chance to develop the discipline to a higher intellectual plain of empirically and logically established principles.

To those of us who have moved to less established universities, Chambers has always been available to assist, by visiting to present seminars, to talk to students and to serve in other advisory capacities. He is extremely generous of his time and energies in the pursuit of his intellectual aims.

This same generosity has been offered to other organisations. He never shirked his administrative responsibilities in his tenure at the University of Sydney, serving on committees and advisory bodies as well as assisting non-official bodies associated with the University. Similarly, with the professional bodies, practitioner and academic.

One of the most striking features of working with Chambers is his intellectual capacity. Supported by the knowledge obtained from his wide reading, his capacity to analyse situations and circumstances is awesome. Combine this with his determination and his debating style of frequently switching tacks makes argument with him a wearying task. This approach has not endeared him to many, especially when he was younger. Continually researching and writing, he would have been acutely aware of the need to defend his ideas and his work. Age and the frustration of continual battle have mellowed his manner (but not his wit). He has had the disappointment of seeing the 'school' he built around him dismantled by the new regimes. With retirement from a full-time position his working conditions have deteriorated. Yet he has doggedly persisted with his work; he is still travelling the road he chose to go down. He has also had rewards (awards and prizes) and it is natural to believe that this has assisted his resolve.

I believe the frustrations that he has had to bear would have made a lesser person resign. No doubt many of these frustrations have arisen from the environment which he created for himself, yet I believe that his spirit demonstrates a true commitment to the world's advancement. History is replete with stories of the non-acceptance of the contributions of many who later were considered great: philosophers, scientists, poets, artists, musicians and many others. Only time will tell the full extent of Chambers' work. Even if his CoCoA never wins full acceptance, there is little doubt that he has had an extremely significant influence on accounting thought. Not only has he influenced the way accounting researchers went about their work, he has instilled in the minds of many of his students and colleagues the need for the highest standards of intellectual argument and debate, in order that accounting can take its place alongside the other disciplines which have a longer history of academic acceptance – but not of practical significance.

Note

1 A full bibliography of Chambers' work to 1987 can be found in Gaffikin (1989).

References and select bibliography

Broad, W. and Wade, N. (1982) *Betrayers of the Truth*, Oxford: Oxford University Press.
Canning, J. B. (1929) *The Economics of Accountancy: A Critical Analysis of Accounting Theory*, Ronald Press.
Chambers, R. J. (1955) 'Blueprint for a Theory of Accounting', *Accounting Research* 6: 17–25.
Chambers, R. J. (1960) 'The Conditions of Research in Accounting', *The Journal of Accountancy*, December: 33–9.
Chambers, R. J. (1966) *Accounting, Evaluation and Economic Behavior*, Hemel Hempstead: Prentice Hall.
Chambers, R. J. (1967) 'The Foundations of Financial Accounting', *Berkeley Symposium on the Foundations of Accounting*, Berkeley: University of California.
Chambers, R. J. (1969) 'The Canons of Criticism', unpublished.
Chambers, R. J. (1971) 'The Development of the Theory of Continuously Contemporary Accounting', prepared for inclusion in the Japanese edition of *AEEB* (1966), 20pp.; revised (to 29pp.) for inclusion in the reprint of *AEEB* (1966) in the Accounting Classics Series, 1974.
Chambers, R. J. (1973) *Securities and Obscurities*, London: Gower Press.
Chambers, R. J. (1974) 'Stock Market Prices and Accounting Research', *Abacus* 10: 39–54.
Chambers, R. J. (1984) *The Serviceability of Financial Information: A Survey*, Canadian CGA Research Foundation.
Chambers, R. J. (1989a) 'Time in Accounting', *Abacus* 25: 7–21.
Chambers, R. J. (1989b) 'A True and Fair View of Position and Results: The Historical Background', unpublished, 17pp.
Chambers, R. J. (1991a) 'Accounting and Corporate Morality – The Ethical Cringe', Paper delivered to Sydney University Pacioli Society, May, 14pp.
Chambers, R. J. (1991b) 'An Academic Apprenticeship' (August 1990), *Accounting History* 3: 16–24.
Chambers, R. J. (1991c) 'Response', at a dinner to celebrate his achievements, University of Sydney, 27 July, unpublished.
Chambers, R. J. (1991d) *Foundations of Accounting*, Geelong, Victoria: Deakin University Press.
Chambers, R. J. (1991e) 'Metrical and Empirical Laws in Accounting', *Accounting Horizons* 5: 1–15.
Chambers, R. J. (1993a) 'Positive Accounting the PA Cult', *Abacus* 29: 1–26.
Chambers, R. J. (1993b) 'Historical Cost – A Tale of a False Creed', *Proceedings*, Swedish Doctoral Consortium, April, 29pp.
Chambers, R. J. and Wolnizer, P. W. (1990) 'A True and Fair View of Financial Position', *Company and Securities Law Journal*, December: 353–68.
Dopuch, N. and Revsine, N. (eds) (1973) *Accounting Research 1960–1970: A Critical Evaluation*, Center for International Education and Research in Accounting, Illinois.
Edwards, E. O. and Bell, P. W. (1961) *The Theory and Measurement of Business Income*, Berkeley, Calif.: University of California Press.

Fisher, I. (1906) *The Nature of Capital and Income*, New York: Ronald Press.

Gaffikin, M. J. R. (ed.) (1984) *Contemporary Accounting Thought; Essays in honour of Raymond J. Chambers*, Prentice-Hall of Australia.

Gaffikin, M. J. R. (1989) *Accounting Methodology and the Work of R. J. Chambers*, New York: Garland Press.

Gibson, R. (1991) 'Sources Cited by R. J. Chambers in Chambers on Accounting', *Accounting History* 3: 25–32.

Grinyer, J. R. (1992) 'Review of M. J. R. Gaffikin, *Accounting Methodology and the Work of R. J. Chambers*', *The British Accounting Review* 24: 292–3.

Ijiri, Y. (1967) *The Foundations of Accounting Measurement*, Hemel Hempstead: Prentice Hall.

Littleton, A. C. (1956) 'Choice Among Alternatives', *The Accounting Review* 31: 363–70.

Mattessich, R. (1964) *Accounting and Analytical Methods*, Homewood, Ill.: Richard D. Irwin.

Moonitz, M. (1961) *The Basic Postulates of Accounting*, Accounting Research Study 1, AICPA.

Nelson, C. (1973) 'A Priori Research in Accounting', in Dopuch and Revsine (1973).

Paton, W. A. (1982) Foreword (to Special Issue marking the retirement of Raymond J. Chambers), *Abacus* 18: iii.

Sprouse, R. and Moonitz, M. (1963) *A Tentative Set of Broad Accounting Principles for Business Enterprises*, Accounting Research Study 1, AICPA.

Staunton, J. 'Accounting Research: The Theorist and The Practitioner', in Gaffikin (1984) pp. 263–301.

2 A profile of Richard Mattessich (b. 1922)

Cheryl McWatters

Abstract

The contribution of Richard V. Mattessich (RVM) to twentieth-century accounting theory and scholarship underscores the need to learn from and to apply the insights of other disciplines in order for accounting to remain purposeful and current. Three main areas of RVM's scholarship are examined: foundational research in accounting, representational issues, and conditional-normative accounting theory.

In all three, RVM has championed the need for ontological and epistemological clarity within accounting, and the recognition of accounting as an applied science. While present-day accounting has become absorbed with complex statistical analyses, RVM's emphasis upon foundational issues and his theoretical approach provide an example to others, especially as the theory-practice gap continues to widen and as the expectations of our analytical models remain unfulfilled, due to their neglect of empirical realities.

INTRODUCTION

I was introduced to the work of Richard V. Mattessich (RVM) as a doctoral student when the first reading assigned was his research into the archaeology of accounting. I soon learned that this was just one side of a multi-faceted career and I continue to encounter his work with frequency as I now pursue my own researches. The magnitude of RVM's contribution to accounting theory can be demonstrated by enumerating the honours and awards granted to him by the academic community and by accounting practitioners. Though having the virtue of being succinct, this approach can do little more than provide a thumbnail sketch of his achievements. Perhaps this selective profile will whet the reader's appetite to delve into the original sources, or to pursue one of the many avenues which RVM has suggested as being fertile territory for accounting research and practice.[1]

Rather than a chronological enumeration of RVM's research, the focus here is upon a limited number of publications within three areas of RVM's scholarship which I believe to be the most indicative of its overall breadth: foundational research in accounting, representational issues, and conditional-normative accounting theory.[2] Beginning with a brief biographical outline, the remainder of this chapter is organised around these main ideas. An overall summary concludes the chapter.

A BRIEF BIOGRAPHICAL SKETCH

Although born in Trieste, Italy (on 9 August 1922) and holding Italian citizenship, RVM spent his childhood from 1923 in Vienna. RVM describes himself as 'ethnically Austrian' through three of his grandparents. RVM did not approach his academic accounting career directly, but first studied mechanical engineering. In 1940, he received his degree in engineering from the Engineering College of Vienna. After completing these studies, and coincident with his initial employment, RVM began studying business and economics, eventually registering as a full-time student.

This was not a carefree period, given the exigencies of wartime. Yet RVM has described these years as amongst his happiest, yielding the opportunity to pursue his quest for knowledge and to make many long-lasting friendships. Study conditions were less than optimal, with shortages of books, resources and time. None the less, RVM pursued his education and received the degree of *Diplom-kaufmann* (comparable to MBA) in 1944.

From 1943 to 1945, RVM was allowed to continue his education while serving as a cost accountant and front engineer with a large steel construction firm in Salonika, Greece. RVM has related his experience at the front in his own personal memoirs. Suffice it to say that the initial tranquillity of his arrival in Greece soon was replaced by the tumult of war. He returned from Greece in October 1944 on a journey best described as nothing less than horrific.

Upon his return, RVM wrote his doctoral dissertation, primarily at night in his family's cellar which served as an air-raid shelter. In March of 1945, his thesis filed with the Hochschule für Welthandel (now the Economic University of Vienna), he took his doctoral examination in economics and graduated Doctor of Economic Sciences (Dr. rer. pol) in April.

With the arrival of peacetime, RVM obtained employment with his original firm, but left in November of 1945 to accept a position as research fellow with the Austrian Institute of Economic Research. At this juncture, RVM's academic career truly began. He remained here for approximately four years. After a stay in Switzerland in the summer of 1947, he obtained an Instructor of Commerce position at Rosenberg College in St Gallen, a post which he retained until 1952.[3]

One advantage of working in Switzerland was the ability to earn hard currency, which enabled RVM to travel and to purchase the volumes with which to pursue his interest in philosophy. During one trip to visit his family, he met his future wife, Hermi, whom he married in April of 1952. Once married, RVM decided to find a more permanent position to eliminate the requirement for a yearly work permit. A few months prior to his thirtieth birthday, and married just one week, he emigrated to Canada, followed three months later by his new wife.

Determined to return to academia, RVM taught evening courses at McGill University while he and his wife both worked during the day in the Actuarial

Department of the Prudential Life Insurance Co. in Montreal. He sent his curriculum vitae to every Canadian university, but initially his quest for an academic position bore little fruit. In 1953, RVM joined Mt. Allison University in Sackville, New Brunswick, as head of the newly established Department of Commerce. Over the next five years he worked tirelessly to establish and build up the department.

RVM spent the 1958–9 academic year as Visiting Professor at the University of California at Berkeley.[4] This was followed by a tenured position from 1959 to 1967. RVM joined a prominent academic faculty, including (amongst others) eminent scholars such as M. Moonitz, R. T. Sprouse, G. Staubus, W. Vatter and J. Wheeler. He obtained great satisfaction from his students, a number of whom also became leading academics, including J. E. Butterworth, W. J. Bruns, G. A. Feltham, T. Mock and J. Ohlson.

While the environment at Berkeley was both animated and stimulating, especially the opportunities to meet with colleagues in related disciplines, RVM left Berkeley in 1967 to join the University of British Columbia.[5] At UBC, RVM considered that he had found 'the ideal collegiate atmosphere' (1992b: 42), and he has remained there ever since. However, the scope of RVM's recognition and contribution go far beyond the Canadian academic arena.

In 1970, RVM travelled to New Zealand as Distinguished Erskine Fellow and Visiting Professor at the University of Canterbury. In 1973, he was awarded the Gold Medal and Award For Notable Contribution to Accounting Literature by the American Accounting Association in conjunction with the AICPA. During the period from 1976 to 1978, he held a double professorship with UBC and the University of Technology of Vienna. He also was honoured by election into the national academies of both Italy and Austria.

RVM has received recognition within Canada, as Distinguished Arthur Andersen & Co. Alumni Professor from 1980 to 1987, and as Arthur Andersen Alumni Professor emeritus since 1988. Even in retirement, RVM has continued to be a prolific researcher. In 1988, his work on the archaeology of accounting received the 'Award For Best Paper' at the annual meeting of the Canadian Academic Accounting Association, while his collected papers earned him the Haim Falk Award For Distinguished Contribution To Accounting Thought in 1991. He received honorary membership in the Japanese Pacioli Society in 1992, along with honorary life-time membership in the Academy of Accounting Historians in recognition of his distinguished contributions to accounting theory and history.

RVM's career output could only be described as that of a true scholar who has combined his knowledge of accounting with an intense enthusiasm for, interest in, and comprehension of other disciplines. This has served to enhance not only his contributions to accounting, but also to the areas of administrative science and philosophy.

FOUNDATIONAL RESEARCH IN ACCOUNTING

While present-day accounting researchers increasingly have become absorbed with complex statistical analyses, the emphasis upon foundational issues distinguishes RVM as a major contributor to twentieth-century accounting theory. Throughout his lengthy academic career, RVM has not been afraid to counter prevailing trends, continually emphasising the need for accounting theories to have strong ontological and methodological foundations.

This commitment to methodological clarification has enabled RVM to differentiate clearly a number of issues that others have failed to grasp. 'The Constellation of Accounting and Economics' (1956) was RVM's first paper published in English. Portrayed as a follow-up to J. B. Canning's (1929) *Economics of Accountancy*, which had attempted to clarify the mutual interests and interdependence of economics and accountancy, the 'Constellation' article foreshadowed many of the theoretical issues which RVM has explored more deeply over the years.

First, RVM attributes much of the difference between accounting and economics to a discrepancy between the deductive methods of economic analysis and the inductive approach of accounting. Further, the economist's deductivism results in models which are valid only for limiting cases. In contrast, those items which economics tends to disregard, such as 'the minute regulation of many business affairs, the innumerable little details of everyday economic life, traditions and habits of business thinking, and the irrational element in man's behaviour' (1956: 553–4), forces accounting to adopt an inductive approach. This, declares RVM, keeps accounting much closer to reality.

None the less, RVM is emphatic that the two sides have much to gain by greater co-operation. Additionally, in RVM's ardent call for accounting to adopt the tools of economics, one can sense an effort to enhance the position of accountancy within the academic community. Indeed, RVM considers an ultimate goal to be the amalgamation of managerial economics with managerial accounting.

Second, RVM argues for conceptual clarification within accounting. The tendency to declare accounting 'an art' has led unnecessarily to the neglect of the benefits to be gained from an underlying axiomatic framework and the application of analytical methods. Such clarification would serve to reduce the parochial attitude within accounting, especially the tendency to equate accounting with financial accounting at the expense of fields such as national income accounting, government accounting and management accounting.

Yet not everyone has viewed such a merging in a positive vein; rather, some considered the entry of economics into the sphere of accounting as an unwanted intrusion. RVM (1956: 562) is more optimistic: 'When accountancy emerges as the incarnation of economics, the rational decision-maker will be able to take optimal advantage of the achievements of economic science.' It also seems that he has been both prophetic and realistic in his acknowledgement that the future accountant would require 'comprehensive training in economic analysis, social accounting and mathematics' (1956: 563) combined with university study in order to deal effectively with the complexities of the economic phenomena with which he works.[6]

The response to this article is noteworthy. Others, including J. P. Powelson, and R. J. Chambers who were pursuing similar approaches, received RVM's article favourably. The article initiated lengthy correspondence between RVM and Chambers. As their individual approaches to accounting theory (often compared and evaluated jointly) have diverged greatly, much contention resulted between them.

RVM expanded upon the axiomatic framework in a second article, 'Towards a General and Axiomatic Foundation of Accountancy' published in 1957. RVM (1980a) has indicated that this paper was to prove more influential and consequential to his personal career.[7] The paper provides a series of axioms and definitions from which eight accounting theorems can be derived and proven rigorously. RVM's advocacy of an axiomatic framework was reinforced by some intensive training in mathematical methods. As a Ford Foundation fellow in the summer of 1955, RVM was both inspired and influenced by prominent researchers in economics, mathematics and the social sciences – most notably, by G. Debreu.

Debreu's efforts to provide an axiomatic basis for both value and equilibrium theory, coupled with earlier exposure to Leontief's input–output analysis, evolved into RVM's own ambitious research programme. This comprised an analytical foundation of accounting, the axiomatisation of its basic assumptions and the general application of input–output analysis to micro- and macro-accounting systems. Today, it would require a Herculean effort to become proficient in the modern analytical methods necessary to undertake such wide-ranging research. Because of the knowledge explosion in every field, it is unlikely that someone with even the demonstrated determination of RVM could do so. The tendency, and often in the case of young scholars the necessity, to specialise in one area results in a certain tunnel vision. RVM's constant willingness and ability to remain current and to apply the insights of other disciplines, such as economics and philosophy, to accounting has been both an admirable and an exemplary achievement. I doubt that in the future we will often see such a 'Renaissance person' in accounting.

While RVM was developing a comprehensive axiomatic framework, it was only part of a growing interest in fundamental research by other theorists such as R. J. Chambers, M. Moonitz and R. T. Sprouse. In Germany, the development of postulates was undertaken by M. Schweitzer and E. Kosiol. Kosiol invited RVM to be Visiting Professor at the Free University of Berlin in 1965, which provided RVM 'the opportunity of getting closer acquainted with' the two German theorists and their work (RVM 1992b: 55). The lack of progress in this area resulted, in part, from the tendency of these individual researchers to work in isolation. While communications were more difficult compared to today, this does not explain totally the lack of co-operation amongst those searching for the basic postulates of accountancy. RVM was no different in this respect, and was quick to indicate the distinctiveness of his own efforts. This tendency to declare the validity of his own theoretical and philosophical position may have contributed to its lack of advocacy by other accounting academics.

The 1957 paper serves two main purposes. First, it provides a matrix presentation of an accounting system, which highlights the flow system inherent in every accounting system. Second, it introduces some much needed generality and rigour to the development of accounting models. This results in a certain efficiency and a stratification of accountancy in terms of the distinction between principles, standards, concepts, customs and mere convention. This view is similar to J. Ohlson's (1990, 1991) recent theory of clean surplus. Ohlson's significant research indicates a return to fundamentals; the balance sheet and its basic stock variables and the flow variables, which are derived from the former and which seek to explain changes in them under conditions of uncertainty.

The response to RVM's paper was enthusiastic at the time of its publication. It is still considered to be 'the first serious attempt to axiomatise the discipline.' (Willett 1987: 159) Yet the insistence upon methodological rigour and consistency upon which to build the foundations of our discipline has proven to be the most notable contribution of this paper, and not the axiomatic framework in itself.

According to M. Moonitz (1986: 56), it was this 'penetrating article' which brought RVM to the attention of many in North America. As mentioned previously, it also brought RVM an invitation as Visiting Associate Professor at Berkeley during 1957 to 1959, followed by a regular appointment until 1967. Interest in foundational research greeted RVM at Berkeley. Indeed, M. Moonitz cites RVM's paper, along with the work of R. J. Chambers, as seminal in this area. However, Moonitz (1982: 2) declared that his own study was 'not prepared to operate at the level of abstraction implied by the axiomatic method', due to the inability to sell this approach to practitioners. R. T. Sprouse and M. Moonitz (1962) also drew upon RVM's insights in their own subsequent monograph.

The research programme implied by these two initial papers was ambitious and would occupy much of the next few years. On a practical level, RVM recognised that he lacked the mathematical grounding for such an undertaking and attempted in 1961 and 1962 to acquire the necessary skills. These efforts culminated in the publication of *Accounting and Analytical Methods (AAM)* in 1964. The influence of P. Suppes is indicated by RVM's reliance upon the predicative form by means of which an axiom system can be represented as a logical structure. W. W. Cooper (1965), who reviewed the volume for *The Accounting Review*, declared it a seminal work. Perhaps not surprisingly, the lengthy review article by R. J. Chambers (1966) in *The Journal of Accounting Research* underscored their diametrically opposite views.

While RVM has sought to clarify the foundations of accounting by means of logical and mathematical rigour, Chambers has championed a behavioural point of view in which theory and interpretation are developed jointly. Thus, the instrumental and flexible nature of RVM's postulational approach, including the use of place-holder assumptions, has been misunderstood. Chambers began with the assumption that the objective of accounting is the representation of market prices, whereas RVM has emphasised valuation as the objective of accounting through the use of the pertinent valuation method. Moreover, RVM's theory remains either uninterpreted or semi-interpreted. An interpretation of the theory constitutes a model, such as Chamber's current cost model. In contrast, RVM leaves such interpretations to users, including standard setters.

Specifically, Chambers has disputed RVM's interpretation of accounting measurement and what he considers to be RVM's 'disregard' of the role of the price mechanism:

> the place where monetary measures enter into a great number of relations with other monetary measures is the market place; and the measures of the market place (money prices) are not at all the will of the measurer, or of any single buyer or seller. If price were arbitrary, if measures in the monetary scale were measures by fiat, business operations and planning would be impossible and economists who concern themselves with market processes would be wasting their time.
>
> (Chambers 1966: 183–4)

AAM is not without limitations. First, RVM's terminology does not distinguish clearly between axioms and definitions (*AAM*, 1964: 446) with the result that many of the proposed axioms are conditional definitions. The complexity of the framework lessens its mathematical rigour. Like the later work by Y. Ijiri (1965), the framework's usefulness resides more in its descriptive analysis of the basic elements of the accounting system. It is transaction-based, yet its use of numerical definitions results in the addition of values being assumed rather than determined by the axiomatic framework itself.[8]

While RVM considers *AAM* to be a monumental work, in many ways it expanded upon the issues set out initially in his earlier publications. It provides an in-depth evaluation of many of the accounting issues which have continued to elude clarification. Moreover, RVM's analytical framework has influenced later researchers (many of whom were his students), for example, J. E. Butterworth and G. A. Feltham. Nor can the international interest in this volume be dismissed. In Japan, RVM's approach has been both adopted and improved upon, especially by S. Saito who has indicated weaknesses in and clarified RVM's set-theoretical formulation. Similar interest in the axiomatisation of accounting has been seen throughout Europe. Most recently, renewed interest in matrix accounting is evident in the work of S. A. Leech (1986) and R. J. Willett (1987). As RVM has shifted his own attention to philosophical issues, the focus on an axiomatic basis for accounting has continued in his work with W. Balzer (1991c) which provides a reconstruction of the accounting model in terms of structuralist metatheory. This reconstruction indicates that, like other empirical theories, accounting consists of a core model and a theory-net of specialisations. While the core model is empirically empty, the physical and social dualities of accounting are empirical phenomena and assume a normative status in terms of accountability. Moreover, accounting is not merely an analytical tautology superimposed upon economic reality (1991c: 213–14).

More importantly, RVM's initial work in this area conditioned his thinking to perceive a vital accounting link in the archaeological research of Professor

D. Schmandt-Besserat. While *AAM* may not be declared a classic, RVM's insights into early record-keeping undoubtedly will have long-lasting influence upon the accounting discipline.

Counting, accounting and the input–output principle

The archaeological work of Professor Schmandt-Besserat emphasises Middle Eastern writing and counting; however, RVM has provided a valuable extension by demonstrating that these methods were the earliest systematic accounting systems.[9]

Mathematics divides the evolution of counting into three stages: counting by one-to-one matching, concrete counting, and abstract counting. The first stage may appear primitive as a counting procedure, yet it is quite effective as a method of record keeping and accountability. Current evidence also indicates that tokens did not represent numerals before 3200 BC. Thus accounting predates abstract counting.

Briefly, we are dealing with collections of plain, concrete tokens, the existence of which has been traced back over 10,000 years. Beginning around 3250 BC, these were sometimes enclosed within hollow 'clay envelopes'. The surfaces of the latter were marked to indicate their content. The impressions on the outside were credits, whereas the tokens on the inside were debits. RVM's analysis clarifies that these tokens represented commodities, such that every variety of token represented a specific type of account. In present-day accounting, we resort to different words to distinguish different accounts. In ancient Sumeria, these distinctions were made by different token shapes.

These tokens became more diverse with respect to shape, markings and perforations to string them together. RVM links these changes to the increased bureaucratisation of the Sumerian city state. He provides the following analysis:

> the multiplication of tokens coincided with the imposition of mandatory dues to the state and the control it entails. The complex tokens enabled the keeping track of a larger number of different commodities in a more specific way, but like the plain ones, each complex token still represented one unit of a particular good or service.

(1988: 205)

What is striking about RVM's conjectures is the accounting perspective which he brings to bear on the more general issue of counting and writing. First, each token represented one unit of a good or service. Each token shape represented a type of account. Second, receptacles or clay envelopes were accounts pertaining to stewards/debtors and inventories. The number of tokens (in an envelope/on a string) equalled the quantity of specific items, thus the sum identified the part of one's equity which a creditor lent to a debtor. Yet counting in the abstract sense was non-existent. Abstract counting was to emerge later, concurrent with writing. In this latter stage, numbers assumed an abstract existence such that they had universal application.

This may seem to be at first nothing more than an interesting reinterpretation of Schmandt-Besserat's initial research, but the key issue which RVM has recognised relates to the logical structure of transactions in terms of an input–output system. The ability to forge this link undoubtedly stems from his research into matrices and the axiomatisation of accounting, and the clear distinction which he has made between the duality of transactions and the dual-entry method.

How is this link made? Simple tokens represented commodities of agricultural communities, whereas complex tokens represented labour and manufactured commodities associated with increased urbanisation. Also, complex tokens were more complicated with respect to shape and markings, and this complexity paralleled that of accounting itself. RVM points out that the distinction between complex and simple tokens resembles that made in sixteenth-century Italy between cash and non-cash items. Moreover, according to RVM, the ancient system avoided the valuation issue that has continued to plague accounting theory, as it dealt with physical rather than monetary realities.

Yet we also see that the duality of the system is represented: in individual detail, in terms of individual assets; and in totality, in terms of equity or a part thereof. It is not surprising that this interpretation of Schmandt-Besserat's research strengthens RVM's (1957, 1964, 1984, 1987b, 1988) previous presentation of these ideas concerning the logical form of an accounting transaction. Specifically, accounting is not founded upon the double-entry technique, but rather upon the input–output structure whereby the empirical manifestation of economic events is conceptually represented by accounting transactions. As RVM recognises (1988: 38), this input–output structure was prevalent in what he describes as 'prehistoric data processing systems'. The crux of the issue is not the occurrence of the economic transactions whereby the actual transfer of services and commodities took place. The significance resides in the more fundamental insight that the token system provided for the conceptual representation/duplication of these transactions.

The issue of representation begs the question of what we understand and mean by reality. Here again, RVM has explored, in a unique way, territory which other accounting researchers often have disregarded. The philosophical issues addressed by RVM underscore that his contribution resides not solely within accounting, but also in the broader philosophical realm.

REPRESENTATIONAL ISSUES IN ACCOUNTING

Since the 1980s, RVM's research has taken a definite philosophical turn. Work by J. E. Butterworth and H. Falk (1986), based upon earlier research by Butterworth, spurred RVM's interest in recent trends in the philosophy of science. While Butterworth and Falk have described accounting in Kuhnian terms, RVM looks to the work of I. Lakatos, J. D. Sneed, W. Stegmüller, W. Balzer and M. Bunge.

In this recent examination of representational issues, RVM retains a systems approach, a primary facet of his earlier research. One sees here various influences, including that of K. E. Boulding and his socio-ecological system,

W. Churchman, one of RVM's colleagues at Berkeley, and M. Bunge. RVM illustrates the interconnectedness of accounting with all economic fields which rely upon the flow concept prevalent in systems thinking.

RVM asserts that it is first necessary to clarify the difference between ultimate reality and the realities of higher order, which RVM describes as enveloping the former like layers of an onion. The key concept, originally discussed by RVM in *Instrumental Reasoning and Systems Methodology* (1978a: 31), is that of emergent properties or 'those characteristics of a particular system that go beyond the qualities of individual system components'. As described by RVM:

> We are all aware that such atoms as hydrogen and oxygen, or sodium and chlorine, etc. can combine (in specific proportions) to generate substances like water, and table salt respectively. But those newly emerging entities possess *properties totally different from their constituents* . . . These so-called *emergent properties*, although usually taken for granted, are the key to a better understanding of total reality, because through their formation an immense hierarchy of different *empirical* realities (which make up *total reality*) is brought about.
>
> (1991a: 5–6)

Social reality, which is pivotal for accounting, is within this hierarchy. RVM's masterful comprehension of philosophy provides further clarifying insights into the representational questions which accounting theorists have continued to probe, often with little success.

RVM asserts that to dismiss the empirical content of social reality would contradict the basic premise of social science. This would reduce accounting to mere formalism and deny its status as an applied science. Specifically, RVM takes issue with the recent arguments of L. C. Heath (1987) and R. R. Sterling (1988, 1989) which assert that accounting does not represent real phenomena. Sterling's positivism and Heath's external realism differ greatly from RVM's own philosophical position, which has been influenced by the German language literature.[10]

Heath argues against the tendency to reify accounting concepts such as income. According to Heath, income is only a conceptual model which is determined by measuring certain attributes of a firm's assets and liabilities and then manipulating this data. He states bluntly:

> Although the accounting concept of income is a model of real-world events, income does not exist in the real world any more than a family of 1.6 children exists in the real world. Both exist only in our minds. They are intangible concepts or abstractions.
>
> (1987: 2)

RVM takes issue with this argument, although he confirms that there is a definite need to distinguish the real from the conceptual. However unlike D. B. Thornton (1988), who has responded to Heath by focusing upon accounting as metaphor and the tendency to literally interpret the latter, RVM is concerned with a different dimension. Much more importantly, Heath fails to differentiate not between concepts and reality, but rather between social and physical reality. These are issues with which RVM has dealt much earlier in *Instrumental Reasoning*.

RVM also revisits his examination of the fundamental question of dual-classification accounting. In his early research, and most recently in his study of pre-historic accounting systems, he has demonstrated that dual classification does not require a system of double-entry bookkeeping. Now, RVM (1991b: 7) offers us an additional insight generally overlooked by accounting theorists.

Double-classificational accounting integrates three separate relationships, each with two dimensions: the physical transfer of goods and services which demonstrates the input–output system and physical reality; the debt claim (social reality) which connects debtor and creditor in terms of a financial-legal relation; and the legal relation between a person and an object (social reality) through which an ownership claim connects the asset to an owner. Importantly, RVM has shown that the verifiability of the social reality behind debt and ownership claims has existed for many thousands of years. In a lighter moment, RVM (1991b: 6–7) explains the concepts as follows: 'Try to convince the banker who granted you the mortgage on your home that his debt claim is not real, and he will soon convince you of the contrary by supplying the necessary empirical evidence.'

Quite simply, if we accept the notion of an ownership claim as real, then we are bound to acknowledge the reality of income. Income is nothing more than a specific change in this property claim. It is equally real in that, as a social construct, it has real effects. However, according to RVM, confusion has abounded in accounting from two directions. First, the blurring of this ownership claim (a social object) with the asset or physical manifestation (physical reality) behind it. Second, the need to determine income in terms of a monetary or other valuation measure. The fundamental problem is the tendency to use the same designation for the conceptual, linguistic and reality levels of discourse. The failure to distinguish the object on the reality level from both the linguistic term and the pure concept has resulted in much accounting confusion. Moreover, it alludes to the neglect by most accounting researchers of basic philosophical questions, the non-resolution of which places our analytical methods on shaky ground.

RVM's analysis demonstrates that accounting concepts, such as shareholders' equity and income, are not empirically empty notions, but instead represent a verifiable social reality. However, it does not in itself resolve R. R. Sterling's (1988) contention that accounting values do not measure real phenomena, and RVM also explores this issue.

Measurement issues

Measurement issues extend beyond merely proving that there exists a social and physical reality behind ownership and income and their corresponding assets. More importantly, RVM has stressed the need to clarify the notions of measure and measurement within the social sciences. RVM takes issue with Sterling's (1988) position that there are no phenomena which correspond to most numerals on financial statements. While the reality issue has been examined above in terms of physical and social reality, there are additional questions. First, how is it possible to measure the particular temporary property or value related to the empirical referents of accounting concepts? Second, what cost–benefit alternatives exist for such measurement?

RVM underscores that values are the expression of subjective preferences; thus these derived values are properties of the specific situation and not of the thing in itself. When one speaks of exchange value, the latter is the result of the interaction between subjective preferences and the bargaining position of the parties to the transaction. This exchange value possesses only a social reality status. RVM (1991a: 17) suggests that both Heath and Sterling, along with other accounting theorists, have been blocked in their understanding, given their focus on physical reality and 'the common illusion that intangibles cannot be real.' RVM likens accounting's failure to conceptualise the measurement of value to the parallel problem in physics with respect to the measurement of time. As demonstrated by relativity theory, time as a physical property cannot be measured in an absolute way, yet this has not eliminated its practical measurement.

More importantly, RVM attributes much of accounting's inability to resolve measurement issues to the emphasis, especially in the case of Sterling, upon the positive traits of pure science. It is necessary instead to accept the normative aspects of accounting as an applied science. While one needs to perceive the reality behind the accounting numbers, one also must be pragmatic in terms of what can be expected from these numbers. Cost–benefit constraints ensure that no perfect measure will be forthcoming.

RVM has long argued that accounting is an applied science, thus it is necessary to consider the purpose of our measurements within a cost–benefit (social science) framework. This position has placed RVM clearly at odds with other theorists, notably R. R. Sterling and R. J. Chambers, who have championed the use of current exit values. As can be seen in *AAM* and RVM's use of 'place-holders', the users' consensus determines which measurement method ultimately meets the long-run cost–benefit requirement. RVM agrees with Sterling and Chambers that a particular method, such as the use of acquisition cost, may not meet the standards of scientific rigour, but it may be more than adequate in terms of the pragmatic needs of users. This does not imply that theorists should not strive for better measures and accounting-valuation models. It does suggest that we need to be aware that such models may not be utilised if they do not meet the decision-making needs of the intended users.

Thus the role of the academic researcher is first to develop the best models to meet the alternative needs and purposes of users; then to educate users as to their relevance. While value may be volatile in nature, this issue is distinct from the imperfection of the estimation and measurement methods used to determine this value. Moreover, there is no implication that no empirical phenomena are being measured, which appears to be Sterling's argument.

These measurement questions are imbedded within a much broader issue of the status of accounting as a normative discipline. This aspect of RVM's theoretical approach has been refined and clarified over the years and continues to provoke much debate in light of the volume of research in positive accounting theory which took place in the 1980s.

CONDITIONAL-NORMATIVE ACCOUNTING THEORY

When RVM initiated research into foundational issues, his objective was a general framework of accounting (as in *AAM*), rather than specific applications.[11] RVM has declared none the less the purpose-oriented interpretation required of accounting. Indeed, this shift to specific accounting models to meet specific objectives, in contrast to an undefined but general-purpose accounting model, has parallelled the evolution of accounting theory from what RVM describes as the traditional to the modern analytical approach.

While foundational research has been largely crowded out of journals by the growing domination of finance theory and the increasing reliance upon statistical methods, RVM has continued to explore these methodological issues. Neglected within accounting, RVM's approach has met with a more favourable response from other social scientists, including support for *Instrumental Reasoning* which summarises his earlier position with respect to the epistemology of applied sciences. This research has resulted in many contributions to systems theory and to the philosophy of science more generally. It is somewhat ironic that RVM's own axiomatic approach has served to stimulate the use of analytical models to the neglect of foundational issues.

RVM contends that normative theories have been discarded, in part, due to their unscientific nature – value judgements cannot be empirically verified. Instead of rejecting a normative framework, he has reformulated the issue: the underlying norms of a theory are stated such that the normative theory is conditioned upon these value judgements. Precise means–end relationships are formulated through which these norms can be achieved (1992c: 3–4). These two requirements demonstrate that the normative theory is objective, in that value judgements are revealed at the outset, and are admitted to be only one of many possible sets of norms. Additionally, the means–end relationship of each theory requires a specific analytical formulation, along with empirical testing, to confirm to what extent the end can be achieved in a satisfactory manner.

Like many others, RVM adopted a Kuhnian view to the philosophy of science in the attempt to place both the methodology and epistemology of accounting on a sound foundation. More recently, he has advanced a post-Kuhnian approach, especially in his application of the work of M. Bunge, J. D. Sneed, I. Lakatos, W. Stegmüller and W. Balzer to accounting theory. This has manifested itself in two areas: first, the refinement of RVM's insistence upon accounting as an applied science and the role of normative accounting theory; second, the categorisation of the evolution of accounting as a struggle between vying research traditions. This differs from the Kuhnian view in which accounting paradigms replace each other by revolutionary upheaval. Rather change is evolutionary whereby different research traditions both compete with and are connected to each other.

RVM's conditional-normative accounting theory (CoNAT) is a general framework by which accounting objectives can be related to the means for their attainment. It contains three essential elements. First, the relating of means and ends is accomplished through the use of instrumental hypotheses, i.e. the purpose for the theory is clearly stated. This is in contrast to the indirect link made in most current empirical research. Second, a hierarchy of objectives pursued by both individuals and society at large is formulated. Third, goals incorporate wealth and profit maximisation, but also externalities, including imperfect rationality. Here RVM relies upon the previous work of H. Hotelling, K. Arrow and I. Fisher (amongst others) in what is termed ecological economics.

Not surprisingly, RVM distinguishes his CoNAT from other normative theories.[12] CoNAT utilises different models conditioned upon specific norms, value judgement(s) and objectives, thereby not restricting itself to one goal, such as short-run profit maximisation, as the only objective worthy of pursuit. Importantly, empirical confirmation is possible to determine whether a specific means can achieve a specific end, but it is not possible to determine the veracity of a specific norm. In contrast, Sterling would argue that a one-to-one correspondence between accounting numbers and reality is required if we are to use accounting to accomplish any goal. RVM suggests that pragmatic-normative accountants

> should be encouraged rather than discouraged to sell their theories on the market of value judgments (provided their norms are clearly revealed, and their arguments are rigorous), as long as they recognize CoNAT as the overall frame for revealing that their own set of value judgments is but one among many competing ones.
>
> (1992c: 8, n. 8)

Second, CoNAT differs in the explicit formulation of means–ends relationships, not currently undertaken by traditional empirical theories which often fail to demarcate such relationships. Since RVM considers accounting to be an applied science, this purpose-orientation is necessary. Clearly RVM's approach places him in sharp relief against the dominant position currently claimed by positive accounting theory (PAT). In contrast to others who have criticised this received view in terms of its technical limitations, philosophy-of-science position and its perfect-market assumptions, RVM focuses upon the triviality of PAT's prescriptions.

Additionally, he faults PAT for its reliance upon statistical hypotheses without amplifying the latter through the use of a systems methodology, as in other applied sciences. CoNAT extends positive accounting theory and other traditional empirical theories through the inclusion of instrumental hypotheses. It recognises accounting as an applied or mission-oriented discipline, whereas PAT seeks to portray accounting research as pure science.

RVM does not consider his position to be a total rejection of PAT, but rather an extension of it. The R. L. Watts and J. L. Zimmerman view of PAT is limited to description and leaves no room for prescription. In contrast, CoNAT requires that instrumental hypotheses and their underlying value judgements be explicitly revealed; thus, not only are description and explanation possible, but also the required prescriptions to achieve the selected goals can be inferred. As stated succinctly by RVM (1992c: 21–2): '[A] positive theory alone can hardly fulfil the foremost goal of any applied science, namely supplying different ready-made models for different specific situations and purposes.' Unfortunately, RVM dismisses the more fundamental argument that PAT is positive in name only and needs to be revised or renamed in a more appropriate manner.

While the above summary constitutes RVM's most recent formulation of CoNAT, he has long espoused this view, beginning with *AAM*. Here the separation of accounting's basic assumptions from its purpose-oriented hypotheses is delineated. This separation is refined in 'Methodological Preconditions and Problems of a General Theory of Accounting' (1972) which appeals for greater recognition of accounting's purpose orientation. RVM's main message can be summarised as follows: The verification of a general theory of accounting must be related to specific empirical propositions. Non-empirical accounting theories cannot exist. Instead, uninterpreted calculi of accounting may exist, but these are devoid of meaning without (at least the provision for) interpretive rules. Testing of an accounting system seeks to determine if the system is the best for the purpose outlined. This testing can only be done empirically and can lead to the amendment or alteration of the basic assumptions and/or the specific hypotheses. Thus each test of a specific system constitutes a joint test of the general theory.

For example, RVM points to inflation accounting as acceptance by standard setters of his methodology. Yet it seems that the experiment has been abandoned or made voluntary in many jurisdictions. RVM's methodology allows for different possibilities for this apparent failure:

> What would be the implications [of] the [Canadian] findings that people generally did not accept the new accounting data? One possibility would be that it was a strictly 'positivist' finding, irrelevant to Mattessich's conditional-normative argument above . . . A second possibility would be that the theory had been inadequately worked out by standard setters before people tried to interpret it. Consequently, people eschewed the disclosures, pending clarification and improvement of the theory. A third might be that the standard setters' recommended interpretations of the theory (i.e. models) were not useful to decision makers in accomplishing their goals. Finally, perhaps the information and its interpretations would have been accepted if costlessly provided, but the costs of preparing and utilizing the information outweighed the benefits.
>
> (Thornton 1985: 129)

While some have concluded that it is a rejection of a normative framework, RVM interprets the evidence otherwise:

> The major reasons for this 'failure' seem to me to be the abating of inflation during the second half of the 1980s, and the resistance of management toward inflation accounting because of additional accounting costs, and the revelation of additional information not only to the public but also to the competition, and as well as the insufficient education (not only of the public but of financial

analysts and even accountants) concerning the subtleties of inflation account-ing. As a result of this last item, professionals as well as the public were often unable to interpret the resulting figures. In other words, the patient did not take the medicine because he already deemed himself to be cured, and partly because he had lost confidence in it, due to a lack of understanding as to the long-term benefits, as well as its working.

(1991a: 23)

Importantly, RVM (1992c: 16) has striven to demonstrate that CoNAT is not 'merely a vision without any roots in present-day academic research . . . CoNat possesses a long-standing tradition in related disciplines and even in accounting literature.' While CoNAT portrays accounting as a 'mission-oriented' science, accounting theory has not been particularly successful in meeting the needs or expectations of accounting practitioners. Thus the gap between theory and prac-tice continues to grow. On this point, RVM is in agreement with the positive theorists who claim that it is not the researcher or theorist who must choose the objective to be pursued, but rather the ultimate user. This differs from Sterling, for whom decision models, not makers, would be supreme.

However, while Watts and Zimmerman speak of conditional predic- tion, RVM prefers conditional prescription. The subtle difference resides in who is to formulate the prescriptions to achieve alternate ends. In RVM's view, the role of the theorist is to formulate alternative instrumental hypotheses such that the ultimate user is able to apply the theory to practice. However, RVM's call to reduce the theory-practice gap possibly could be misinterpreted by his implica-tion that the development of the desired instrumental hypotheses and normative inferences is too complex for practitioners. It may be more fruitful to emphasise that the formulation is a two-way process, in order that our theoretical hypotheses are truly pragmatic and useful. None the less, a return to a conditional-normative framework of an applied science would be a logical means to reduce the gap between practice and academia.

> After all, accountants make many choices that are as yet unexplained; and a conditional-normative theory not only could uncover hidden objectives, it would also be the most rational way to connect the means to those ends. This could bring us a long way towards finding out why practitioners do what they do.
>
> (1991b: 954)

The second facet of RVM's post-Kuhnian approach is his categorisation of accounting theory. This is a useful way to conclude the chapter as this cate-gorisation illustrates RVM's distinctive place within accounting theory.

Paradigms, theory nets and research traditions

Adapting the paradigms of accounting postulated by Butterworth and Falk, RVM examines this characterisation in the light of more recent developments in the philosophy of science. Butterworth and Falk frame accounting within six paradigms. RVM questions whether the disputes within the accounting discipline can be equated with those of rival paradigms in the Kuhnian sense. RVM (1993: 179) declares not and instead adopts a more current methodological position. We have in accounting not separate research paradigms, but a small number of research trends which exist within a more general unifying framework.

RVM combines Butterworth and Falk's three stewardship paradigms (historical acquisition cost theory, agency theory, theories of asymmetric information) into one stewardship research tradition. Similarly, the three valuation paradigms (present value and current cost theories, theory of risk sharing, theory of financial markets) are united into one valuation research tradition. The two research traditions are distinguished by their primary focus. The stewardship tradition considers the main objective of accounting to be the monitoring of stewardship, with income measured in terms of accrual accounting and the matching principle. In the valuation tradition, the primary function of accounting is the evaluation of assets, equities and income, with income measurement undertaken in terms of discounted net cash flows. Given that the two traditions fundamentally differ in terms of their emphasis upon allocation versus valuation, this dichotomy simplifies, but goes beyond this, by seeking to reduce the current fragmentation of accounting theory.

A research tradition comprises a network of theory elements. The latter compete with each other, but are based upon the same fundamental premise. As a result, the change within a research tradition is evolutionary and is not the result of one paradigm's replacement by another. It eliminates the incommensurability of different theory elements, as those within one research tradition stem from the identical core theory. It also eliminates the current trend to declare different accounting paradigms, since it is methodological and not theoretical approaches which are in dispute. Different empirical methodologies incorporated within one theoretical approach do not imply separate paradigms. A research tradition must be pursued, both analytically and empirically, in order that the two branches develop in a complementary fashion. RVM emphasises that while accounting has become increasingly concerned with analytical elegance, it is likely that advances in this area will be incremental at best. To be of practical significance, analytical frameworks must be related to specific empirical hypotheses.

To distinguish his own view, RVM declares the need for a third research tradition or theory net – the information-strategic research programme. This differs from Butterworth and Falk, who include RVM's research within the stewardship tradition. This third research tradition recognises that general-purpose systems are inherently adequate only in simplified settings. In contrast, theorists have tended to pursue exclusively either the stewardship or valuation tradition, seeking generality and blind to the fact that both are equally limited in this respect.

RVM equates the quest for accounting's foundation to Bertrand Russell's pragmatism in searching for the foundations of science. Instead of seeking accounting's absolute foundation, it may be more fruitful to formulate the basic assumptions which one accepts when applying an accounting system. There is no implication that present-day accounting is adequate, but it does suggest beginning with accounting practice to infer inductively these basic assumptions. However, the development of specific hypotheses for specific applications is the more arduous task and allows for possible dissatisfaction with current models and assumptions.

While much of the third research tradition reinforces RVM's long-held views, he does not claim to be the precursor of this tradition. Rather he points to the work of J. M. Clark (1923) and provides a lengthy list of researchers who have been concerned with accounting's purpose orientation. Classifications by nature are, to some extent, the choice of the classifier in terms of reinforcing the latter's thesis. Yet while RVM's classification of accounting theory and research will not necessarily prove satisfactory and may be discarded, the fundamental issue need not be rejected along with it. His underlying premise is that epistemological and ontological clarity within accounting are necessary if accounting is to maintain its status as an applied science.

CONCLUSION

As accountants, much of our work, both in theory and practice, deals with the question and process of evaluation. Yet how do we evaluate the contribution of individuals within our own discipline? I have attempted here to demonstrate the significance of Richard Mattessich to twentieth-century accounting theory and scholarship. While RVM's theoretical approach may not be accepted by other accounting theorists, there are certain aspects which I consider to be enduring.

First, accounting must not operate in isolation, but must be prepared to learn from and to apply the insights of other disciplines if it is to remain current and purposeful. Second, there is a need to retain one's convictions in the wake of countervailing trends, all the while being open to new ideas. RVM's career has exemplified both of these features. His continued concern for philosophical issues, the resolution of which will serve to advance and to sustain our discipline, should provide an example to others. This is especially important as the gap between theory and practice continues to widen, as increasing demands are made for accounting to play a role in ethical and policy issues, and as the expectations of our analytical methods remain unfulfilled due to their neglect of empirical realities.

Notes

1 I have not attempted to restate details of RVM's career which have been published elsewhere. The interested reader should consult Mattessich (1980a), and RVM's memoirs published serially in *Chuo Hyoron* (in English), beginning with the April 1992 issue.

2 The study is limited, in that I have not undertaken to evaluate RVM's research in other disciplines. Moreover, I have not studied his many publications in German which generally complement his English publications.

3 Rosenberg College offered various courses of instruction, including a Commerce Diploma and preparation for the entrance examinations at the University of St Gallen.

4   This invitation was prompted by RVM's early publications related to the axiomat-isation of accounting.
5   In 1966–7, RVM also held the position of Professor with Chair of Economics at the Ruhr University Bochum, while maintaining his position at Berkeley.
6   Economists were not exempt here, in that RVM (1956: 563) declared the need for this group to have contact with actual accounting practice before being 'qualified to pass judgment on the concepts, methods and conventions of accountancy.'
7   At this time, Canadian accounting academics mainly published in practitioners' journals. RVM's articles comprised 30 per cent of all articles published by Canadian accounting professors in academic journals during the 1950s.
8   An in-depth review of the work of Mattessich and Ijiri is provided in R. J. Willett, 'An Axiomatic Theory Of Accounting Measurement', *Accounting and Business Research*, Spring 1987: 155–71.
9   This research received the 'Best Paper Award' at the 1988 Conference of the Canadian Academic Accounting Association, and was reprinted in 1991 by the Academy of Accounting Historians in its monograph, *Collected Papers in Honor of Dean Emeritus Paul Garner*.
10 It is this access to works in German which has placed RVM apart from the main-stream, especially in North America.
11 A noteworthy exception was the application of this framework to budgeting and simulation. This has led to the recognition of RVM's work as the precursor of spreadsheet programs, such as Visi-Calc, Super-Calc and Lotus 1-2-3. This is one example where theory has had a noted impact (albeit with a time-lag) upon practice.
12 An in-depth review of these theories is provided in Mattessich (1992a).

Select bibliography of Richard Mattessich

Books

(1964) *Simulation of the Firm Through a Budget Computer Program*, Homewood, Ill.: R. D. Irwin, Inc.
(1964) *Accounting and Analytical Methods – Measurement and Projection of Income and Wealth in the Micro- and Macroeconomy*, Homewood, Ill.: R. D. Irwin, Inc.
(1978a) *Instrumental Reasoning and Systems Methodology – An Epistemology of the Applied and Social Sciences*, Doredrecht, Holland and Boston, USA: D. Reidel & Co.
(1984/92) *Modern Accounting Research: History, Survey, and Guide* (edited and co-authored by R. Mattessich), Vancouver, BC: Canadian Certified General Accountants' Research Foundation.
(1991a) *Accounting Research in the 1980s and Its Future Relevance* – Supplementary Volume to *Modern Accounting Research*, Vancouver, BC: Canadian Certified General Accountants' Research Foundation.

Contributions to Books and Proceedings

(1978b) 'Systems Methodology and Accounting Research', *Collected Papers of the American Accounting Association's Annual Meeting*, 1977, Sarasota, Fla.: AAA: 270–86.
(1979a) 'An Evaluation of the "Statement of Accounting Theory and Theory Accept-ance"', *Collected Papers of the American Accounting Association's Annual Meeting*, 1978, Sarasota, Fla.: AAA: 597–600.
(1979b) 'Instrumental Aspects of Accounting', in R. R. Sterling and A. L. Thomas (eds) *Accounting for a Simplified Firm Owning Depreciable Assets: Seventeen Essays and a Synthesis Based on a Common Case*, Houston, Tex.: Scholars Book Co.: 335–51.

(1982a) 'The Market Value Method According to Sterling', reprinted in M. Gaffikin and
M. Aitken (eds) *The Development of Accounting Theory: Significant Contributors to
Accounting Thought in the 20th Century*, New York: Garland Publishing: 226–45.

(1982b) 'Towards a General and Axiomatic Foundation of Accountancy', reprinted in
Stephen Zeff (ed.) *The Accounting Postulates and Principles Controversy of the
1960s*, New York: Garland Publishing.

(1985) 'Fritz Schmidt's Pioneering Work in Current Value Accounting in Comparison to
Edwards and Bell's Theory: Preliminary Results', in Tito Antoni (ed.) *Proceedings of
the 4th Congress of Accounting Historians*, Pisa, Italy: 489–521.

(1987a) 'An Applied Scientist's Search for a Methodological Framework: An Attempt to
Apply Lakatos' Research Programme, Stegmüller's Theory-Nets, and Bunge's Family
of Research Fields to Accounting Theory', in P. Weingartner and G. Schurz (eds)
Logic, Philosophy of Science and Epistemology, Vienna: Hölder-Pichler-Tempsky:
143–62.

(1988) 'Counting, Accounting, and the Input–Output Principle', *Proceedings of Annual
Meeting of the CAAA*, Windsor, Ont.: CAAA: 199–230. Reprinted in O. F. Graves
(ed.) (1991) *Collected Papers in Honor of Dean Emeritus Paul Garner*, Mississippi:
Monograph of the Academy of Accounting Historians.

(1990) 'Mario Bunge's Influence on the Administrative and Systems Sciences', in P.
Weingartner and G. Dorn (eds) *Studies on Bunge's Treatise*, Amsterdam: Rodopi:
397–420.

(1991a) 'Social versus Physical Reality in Accounting and the Measurement of Its
Phenomena', in B. Banerjee (ed.) *Contemporary Issues in Accounting Research* 1(1),
Calcutta: Indian Accounting Association Research Foundation: 1–30.

(1992a) 'On the History of Normative Accounting Theory: Paradigm Lost, Paradigm
Regained', in A. Tsuji (ed.) *Collected Papers of Sixth World Congress of Accounting
Historians*, Tokyo: Accounting History Association: 937–73. Reprinted (1992) in
Accounting, Business and Financial History 2(2): 181–98.

(1993) 'Paradigms, Research Traditions and Theory Nets of Accounting', in M. J.
Mumford and K. V. Peasnell (eds) *Philosophical Dimensions of Accounting: Edward
Stamp Memorial Volume*, London: Routledge: 177–220.

Articles in journals

(1956) 'The Constellation of Accountancy and Economics', *Accounting Review* 31(4):
551–64.

(1957) 'Towards a General and Axiomatic Foundation of Accountancy', *Accounting
Research* 8(4): 328–55.

(1958) 'Mathematical Models in Business Accounting', *Accounting Review* 33(3): 472–81.

(1961) 'Budgeting Models and System Simulation', *Accounting Review* 36(3): 384–97.

(1967) 'Accounting and Analytical Methods: A Comment on Chambers' Review',
Journal of Accounting Research 5(1): 119–23.

(1970) 'On the Perennial Misunderstandings of Asset Measurement by Means of "Present
Values"', *Cost and Management*, March/April: 29–31.

(1971) 'On Further Misunderstandings about Asset 'Measurement' and Valuation: A
Rejoinder to Chambers' Article', *Cost and Management*, March/April: 36–42.

(1971b) 'Asset Measurement and Valuation – A Final Reply to Chambers', *Cost and
Management*, July/August: 18–23.

(1971c) 'The Market Value Method According to Sterling', *Abacus*, December: 176–93.

(1972) 'Methodological Preconditions and Problems of a General Theory of Accounting',
The Accounting Review 47(3): 469–87.

(1980a) 'On the Evolution of Theory Construction in Accounting: A Personal Account',
Accounting and Business Research, 'Special Accounting History Issue', 37A: 158–73.

(1980b) 'The Canadian Current Cost Accounting Exposure Draft: A Flawed Approach', *Camagazine*, November: 48–52.
(1981a) Major Concepts and Problems of Inflation Accounting: Part I', *CGA Magazine*, May: 10–15.
(1981b) 'Major Concepts and Problems of Inflation Accounting: Part II, General Purchasing Power, Capital Maintenance, and the Canadian CCA Exposure Draft', *CGA Magazine*, June/July: 20–7.
(1982c) 'Axiomatic Representation of the Systems Framework: Similarities and Differences between Mario Bunge's World of Systems and my own Systems Methodology', *Cybernetics and Systems*, 13: 51–75.
(1987b) 'Prehistoric Accounting and The Problem of Representation: On Recent Archaeological Evidence of the Middle-East from 8,000 BC to 3,000 BC', *The Accounting Historians Journal* 14(2): 72–92.
(1991b) 'Social Reality and the Measurement of Its Phenomena', *Advances in Accounting*, 9: 3–17.
(1991c) (co-authored with W. Balzer) 'An Axiomatic Basis of Accounting: A Structuralist Reconstruction', *Theory and Decision*, 30: 213–43.
(1992b) 'Foundational Research In Accounting – An Autobiographical Sketch', *Chuo Hyoron*.
(1992c) 'Conditional-Normative Accounting Theory: Incorporating Value Judgments and Means-End Relations of an Applied Science', Faculty of Commerce and Business Administration, The University of British Columbia, Working Paper 92-ACC-005, 1992d: 1–44.

Other references

Butterworth, J. E. and Falk, H. (1986) *Financial Reporting – Theory and Application to the Oil and Gas Industry*, Hamilton, Canada: The Society of Management Accountants of Canada.
Canning, J. B. (1929) *The Economics of Accountancy*, New York: The Ronald Press Co., Inc.
Chambers, R. J. (1966) 'Accounting and Analytical Methods: A Review Article', *Journal of Accounting Research*, Spring: 101–18.
Clark, J. M. (1923) *Studies in the Economics of Overhead Costs*, Chicago, Ill.: University of Chicago Press.
Cooper, W. W. (1965) 'Accounting and Analytical Methods and Simulation of the Firm Through a Budget Computer Program' (Book Review), *Accounting Review*, September: 201–6.
Heath, L. C. (1987) 'Accounting, Communication, and the Pygmalion Syndrome', *Accounting Horizons*, March: 1–8.
Ijiri, Y. (1965) 'Axioms and Structures of Conventional Accounting Measurement', *Accounting Review*, January: 36–53.
Leech, S. A. (1986) 'The Theory And Development Of A Matrix-Based Accounting System', *Accounting and Business Research*, Autumn: 327–41.
Moonitz, M. (1982) 'The Meaning of 'Postulate' in Accounting Research Study No. 1', in S. Zeff (ed.) *The Accounting Postulates and Principles Controversy of the 1960s*, New York: Garland Publishing.
Moonitz, M. (1986) *History of Accounting at Berkeley*, Berkeley: University of California – Professional Accounting Program.
Ohlson, J. A. (1990) 'A Synthesis of Security Valuation Theory and the Role of Dividends, Cash Flows, and Earnings', *Contemporary Accounting Research* 6: 648–76.
Ohlson, J. A. (1991) 'The Theory of Value and Earnings, and An Introduction to the Ball-Brown Analysis', *Contemporary Accounting Research* 8: 1–19.

Sprouse, R. and Moonitz, M. (1962) 'A Tentative Set Of Broad Accounting Principles for Business Enterprise', *Accounting Research Study No. 3*, New York: AICPA.

Sterling, R. R. (1988) 'Confessions of a Failed Empiricist', *Advances in Accounting* 6: 3–35.

Sterling, R. R. (1989) 'Teaching the Correspondence Concept', *Issues In Accounting Education*: 82–93.

Thornton, D. B. (1985) 'Modern Accounting Research: History, Survey And Guide' (Book review) *Contemporary Accounting Research* 2: 124–42.

Thornton, D. B. (1988) 'Theory and Metaphor in Accounting', *Accounting Horizons*: 1–9.

Willett, R. J. (1987) 'An Axiomatic Theory of Accounting Measurement', *Accounting and Business Research*, Spring: 155–71.

3 French accounting theorists of the twentieth century

Bernard Colasse and Romain Durand

Abstract

During the 1940s, standardisation of enterprise accounting practices to conform to the newly issued accounting code (*Plan comptable général*) disturbed the natural evolution of French accounting theory. Although the beginning of the century had been a period of theoretical effervescence, marked by such thinkers as Jean Dumarchey, Gabriel Faure and Jean Bournisien, the 1950s and 1960s were years of stagnation, during which all but a few specialists devoted themselves to work on standardising and popularising the accounting code.

INTRODUCTION

The expression *théorie comptable*, a recent addition to the vocabulary of the French language, is a literal translation of the corresponding Anglo-Saxon term 'accounting theory'. The use of the term in French is still rather limited. When we speak of twentieth-century French theorists of accounting, we are referring to authors who, with the possible exception of the most recent among them, do not bear this title in their own country and do not, in fact, consider themselves to be such. It is thus preferable to describe them as 'thinkers'.

The simple fact that the expression *théorie comptable* is of such recent coinage is witness to the intellectual status traditionally assigned to accountancy in France – that is to say, an inferior one. Considered above all to be a discipline essentially practical in scope, accounting could only be, at best, a subject linked to technical training for bookkeepers. That is why instruction in accountancy developed outside the university, first in private professional schools and later in state-run technical institutions. Today, training in accountancy, even for public accountants, is still offered primarily outside the university setting. Among those establishments which have contributed most to the development of training in accounting, we should include the Conservatoire National des Arts et Métiers (CNAM), whose Institut des Techniques Comptables, later the Institut National des Techniques Comptables, was founded in 1931; and the Ecole Normale Supérieure de l'Enseignement Technique (ENSET), now located in Cachan and called the Ecole Normale Supérieure de Cachan. Among the private institutions, we should mention two *grandes écoles*, the Ecole Supérieure de Commerce de Paris (ESCP, 1820) and the Ecole des Hautes Etudes Commerciales (HEC, 1881).

Many of the theorists cited in this article were teachers in these institutions. It was only in 1975 that a master's programme in the science and techniques of accounting and finance, leading to a degree in public accounting, was created and offered at a small number of French universities. Thus official university recognition of accounting as an academic discipline came very late in France, which could explain the belated arrival of theoretical writing and research in the field.

The 'theorists' identified in this article were frequently rather marginal figures; they were often people whose training or work experience did not involve them directly in the accounting profession. Among them we find company directors, civil servants, engineers, members of the legal profession and economists, but very few 'pure' accountants. Unlike today, the accounting profession did not attract the best students, no doubt because of an earlier intellectual disdain towards the discipline. In addition, due to regulations dating from the Revolution forbidding professional associations, organisation within the accounting field remained at a restricted level for a considerable period of time.

The absence of solid professional organisations before the 1940s would remain a characteristic feature of the French context, as opposed to English-speaking countries, until the Second World War period. In 1942 the Ordre des Experts-Comptables et des Comptables Agréés (OECCA) was founded, gaining official recognition in an Ordinance of 1945. Many associations of accountants had existed prior to the creation of the Ordre, but their role in promoting accounting theory had been limited. One notable exception, however, was the Société de Comptabilité de France, which had organised several series of lectures, one of which dealt with the history of accounting. As for the Ordre itself, its primary function since 1945 has been to represent and advance the interests of its members and, to a lesser extent, to address matters of doctrine through its standing committee on standards and practices, the Comité Permanent des Diligences Normales, created in 1964 (later replaced, in 1991, by the Comité Professionnel de Doctrine Comptable). If this committee has played only a very modest role in the evolution of accounting theory, it is perhaps because it has no power to set officially recognised standards; power which has always been delegated to government agencies. Yet the issue of standardisation has stood at the very core of twentieth-century French theoretical ideas on accounting.

The concern with standardisation has primarily influenced French accounting thought in three ways.

1 The movement towards standardisation has drawn upon French theoretical works from the turn of the century and, to a certain extent, has emphasised their undeniable impact on accounting theory.
2 Standardisation, and especially the development of the *Plan comptable général* (General Accounting Plan), has been a focus of the attention of theorists, to this day. Such specialists would typically have been members of the successive organisations concerned with standardisation: the Commission de Normalisation des Comptabilités (1945–7); the Conseil Superieur de la

Comptabilité (1947–57) and, thereafter, the Conseil National de la Comptabilité.

Finally, it was precisely through concentrating the efforts of theorists that the issue of standardisation would create an ongoing link between theoretical and research work – if indeed 'research' is the proper term here – and the problems involved in developing, diffusing and implementing the General Accounting Plan. It is thus not altogether surprising that, during the 1950s and 1960s, the writings of French authorities on accounting were essentially of a doctrinal or pedagogical nature, aiming primarily at publicising and explaining the content of the *Plan comptable général*.

In the light of the major role that standardisation has played in France, and its impact on the evolution of accounting theory, the chronological examination of the French theorists which follows will hinge upon this issue.

We should make it clear that we have had to make choices as to which French theorists to include, and that these choices are, of necessity, subjective in nature. We have endeavoured to select those theoreticians who, either through the originality or the widespread acceptance of their work, have exerted the greatest influence.

THEORIES AND THEORISTS: 1885–1940

No study concerning French theorists of the twentieth century could fail to mention the first convincing effort made to systematise accounting, work which was carried out by Eugène Léautey and Adolphe Guilbault.

Two pioneers: Léautey and Guilbault

When it was first published in 1885, *La science des comptes à la portée de tous* opened up new orientations in French accountancy.[1] Adolphe Guilbault was a man of extensive practical experience in both accounting and engineering who had previously published the *Traité de comptabilité et d'administration industrielle* (Guilbault 1865), seen by Léon Gomberg as a major achievement in the areas of administrative, economic and cost valuation (Gomberg 1929: 33). Ronald Edwards would later corroborate this evaluation.[2] Guilbault's colleague Eugène Léautey can be described as a theorist determined to take accounting away from practical procedures and teaching.

This well-balanced partnership would help to achieve the difficult task of editing a readable and usable manual based on bold new assertions. Accounting, a branch of mathematics, was now seen as a *science*, consisting of the rational co-ordination of accounts concerning the output of the work-force and of trans-formations of capital, i.e. the accounts of production, distribution and the consumption of private wealth. Moreover, the science of accounts would allow the individual to know, at any moment, the changes that economic or social operations would bring in the value of the wealth they possessed or managed.

Consequently, Léautey and Guilbault would forcefully claim:

- to create precise accounting language and to establish its final form;
- to support this language with rational principles and a scientific theory;
- to create a nomenclature as well as a methodical and practical classification of accounts;
- to establish a uniform format and content for the balance sheet.

On these premises, clearly expounded in *La science des comptes,* French accounting theory would later give priority to theoretical perspectives emphasising:

- standardisation, as a vector of terminology, rationality and uniformity,
- the role of the account, as a central feature of economic valuation.

Gabriel Faure and Jean Bournisien

Gabriel Faure, Professor at the Ecole des Hautes Etudes Commerciales and President of the Comité National de l'Organisation Française (CNOF),[3] wrote prolifically from 1901 to 1908. His name is associated with a certain renewal of the Personality concept, understood as a pedagogical method. His *Traité de comptabilité générale*, published in 1905, was the basis of most accounting courses offered in French business schools.

Faure cannot be considered a genuine theorist, but as a prominent individual he had considerable influence on the development of French accounting ideas. He consistently presented accounting as a *language* and was keenly interested in terminology, a position later taken up by Pierre Lassègue and several other French specialists. Acting as a consultant, Faure devised valuable accounting charts and anticipated the linking of accounting to budgetary techniques as well as to a concept of financial management implying an equilibrium of relations (ratios) between balance-sheet items. Faure considered accounting to be a technique which should be placed in the service of the economy and used as a basis for economic discussion. He and many other French theorists consistently emphasised the usefulness of accounting for management purposes, but this notion was not widely accepted until the 1960s.

Jean Bournisien is known as an advocate of the Legal Theory, or 'Theory of Values and Rights'. Behind this rather complicated term, we find an attitude which is very similar to one generally observed in English-speaking countries at the same time. Bournisien would repeatedly declare that the aim of accounting is researching and assessing the wealth legally belonging to a company, measured and presented as demanded by the directors (Penglaou 1929: 12).

In 1917, Bournisien published his *Précis de Comptabilité Industrielle appliquée à la Metallurgie*, a textbook of industrial integrated accounting and a detailed manual of costing for iron works. Bournisien was well aware of American accounting methods and was interested in the work of F. W. Taylor. He believed in the capacity of accounting procedures to control technical and financial congruence to precise standards.

Considering the performance of commercial accounting to be poor – and in this he was not alone – he would often lash out against what he saw as the weaknesses in accountancy training, the lack of recruitment standards for accountants and the lack of co-ordination within companies as far as cost accounting was concerned. In short, Bournisien was a man who was both orthodox and factual.

The 1920s: Jean Dumarchey (1874–1946)

Jean Dumarchey can be considered the most important, if not the only, French theorist from the first half of the century. He is remembered primarily for his *Théorie positive de la comptabilité* (1914), *La Comptabilité moderne: essai de constitution rationnelle d'une discipline comptable au triple point de vue philosophique, scientifique et technique* (1925) and his *Théorie scientifique du prix de revient* (1926).

For Joseph Vlaemminck,[4] Dumarchey wrote masterfully on accounting theory in the twentieth century, opening up numerous avenues of research with a view to establishing a theory of accounting. Dumarchey's influence on future French attitudes towards accountancy was also acknowledged by Jean Fourastié (1944).

Dumarchey was eager to raise accounting up to a scientific level. To his mind, the reason that no one had been able to accomplish this goal previously lay in earlier thinkers' inability to avoid pragmatic considerations and outmoded theories such as Personalism, Proprietary theory, etc. The time had come to apply up-to-date scientific approaches. For a Frenchman, the example would most logically come from Descartes and Auguste Comte. It was time for accounting to leave behind the metaphysical age and enter into the age of positivism. For Dumarchey, thinkers such as Léautey, Guilbault, Cerboni and Faure were mere metaphysicians: they had not been able to separate the scientific aspects of accounting from its more trivial practical concerns.

Dumarchey's science of accounting was a social science which made use of mathematics and was related to philosophy, economics and sociology. He believed that the future of accounting lay in sociology. Accounting was, in turn, the core of economics, since economics is the science of society's accounts. Dumarchey believed that an effective link could be made between micro- and macroeconomics by means of accounting processes. With this notion, he anticipated the work of the next two decades.

Indeed, Jean Dumarchey acknowledged a great respect for a number of well-known economists, including Jean-Baptiste Say, Léon Say, Jean G. Courcelle-Séneuil and Pierre J. Proudhon. Jean-Baptiste Say transmitted the message of Adam Smith to the Continent and taught accounting as early as 1820; his grandson, Léon Say, was Minister of Finance under the Third Republic and an enthusiastic proponent of accountancy. Jean G. Courcelle-Séneuil, a tough-minded exponent of liberalism, wrote the first management book to appear in France,[5] the *Manuel des Affaires*, published in 1885. Pierre J. Proudhon, a genuine French socialist, was a former businessman and accountant whose contribution to economics should not be neglected.[6]

From J.-B. Say, Dumarchey learned that accounting was a tool for appraising fluctuations in individual wealth; from Léon Say, the use of accounting as a means of conveying information; from Courcelle-Séneuil, the goals assigned in accounting: acknowledging, following and recapitulating; from Proudhon, the relationship between accounting and economics. The goal Dumarchey himself assigned to accounting was that of recording a complex reality by means of accounts, arranged to constitute a balance sheet, in order to give concrete form to a subjective image of reality.

Dumarchey's account is a class of units of value, variable in space and time. This class is homogeneous and all-encompassing, comprehensive and extensive. It is a collection of values responding to one and only one well-defined idea. Any discourse, any thinking related to the value of things necessarily entails the creation of a class of units of value: the account.

Thus the aim of accounting should be to study and classify data, in order to develop series of increasing complexity. This approach applies to a *static* balance, transformed into a *dynamic* balance by the effect of time. Dumarchey, in fact, acknowledged two types of balance sheet:

1 A balance sheet which recapitulates the wealth of a certain number of individuals which should be envisaged as a new form of economic statistic 'to move from an anarchistic economy to a planned economy' (Dumarchey 1933).
2 A balance sheet for the private sector which combines three major factors: assets, liabilities and net worth.

Dumarchey envisaged a possible reconciliation of the two types at an unspecified future date.

The theory of values also applies to the manufactured product, which is represented in accounting by an accumulation of values. Cost is, in fact, a result of value incrementation, phased by definite milestones and hours spent. Starting from pure mathematics, Dumarchey rediscovers the classical views about assets valuation and maximising profits. He was absolutely convinced that his concepts would enable accounting to describe any possible situation accurately.

Although some eminent individuals, such as René Delaporte and Jean Fourastié, gave Dumarchey credit for much of the progress made subsequently in French accounting technique, most specialists did not. In leading business schools his theory of value is often put forth as a crucial concept by teachers who never mention Dumarchey's name. In the 1930s, he would see himself as a victim of a 'conspiracy of silence', conducted by men who regarded him as an 'abstracter of quintessences'.

In the preface to *La comptabilité moderne*, Dumarchey lambasted those whose science was limited to 'scholarly discourses about paper formats and ways of handling pens'. In the same book, Gabriel Faure was criticised in no less than fifteen pages. In July 1934, *La Comptabilité et les Affaires*, a well-known journal founded by the consultant Alfred Berran, had to forgo collaborating with Dumarchey, because 'his studies are far too erudite for the majority of our readers'. This attitude may explain why much of Dumarchey's important contribution to the field still remains, albeit unfairly, unknown.

The 1930s: René Delaporte, Charles Penglaou and Maurice Lucas

René Delaporte, a former civil servant, greatly contributed to improving *la science des comptes* in the 1920s and 1930s. In *Concepts raisonnés de la comptabilité* (1930), Delaporte defined accounting as a science whose purpose is (1) to follow economic processes, (2) to calculate costs and (3) to assess financial position, results of transactions and the valuation of assets.

Delaporte considered that an accounting system must be able to facilitate forecasting. It should be based on values of utility and exchange which are both consistent in nature and representative of facts and means, as well as collected, regrouped and classified in an expressive form. Such a system, therefore, needs to be supported by theory.

In 1936, Delaporte included the essence of Dumarchey's views in his *Méthode rationnelle de la Tenue des comptes*: 'Accounting is the science of accounts; its purpose is to fulfil practical, legal and tax goals. It orders and links continuous *series* of independent terms of increasing complexity'.

In October and November 1936, he wrote a paper entitled, 'No more uncertainty!' for *La Comptabilité*. After theoretical analysis, the author recommends dropping contingent theories and adopting uniformity and accounting charts: 'No more fiction', he said, 'but facts and accounting plans!' Delaporte became a theorist out of necessity; he preferred concrete facts and boldly supported all initiatives in this direction: uniform classification, standardised terminology and budgetary control.

Charles Penglaou was another strong observer of accounting. As Bank Inspector, he had the opportunity to criticise the deficiencies of commercial accounting in France. In 1929, he envisaged writing an entire encyclopaedia of accounting matters, but later limited his sights to a very interesting introductory work, *Introduction à la technique comptable*.

Penglaou said that:

> Accounting is a set of arrangements designed to find out, assess and control facts concerning companies (*lato sensu*) and able to suggest means capable of influencing those facts. The question is no longer to find in an account what we have decided to put in it, but to know how this account is constructed, how accounts can be coordinated within a system, how such a system is possible and how it responds to users' expectations.
>
> (Penglaou 1929: 162)

In 1933, Charles Penglaou was still concerned by the lack of any usable doctrine. Nevertheless, in 1947, he recognised that the theorists of the 1930s had, in fact, contributed ideas of some importance.

Maurice Lucas is known to only a handful of chartered accountants. He tried to reconcile theory and practice, accounting and administration. In 1927, he declared that it was necessary to establish an accounting theory; in 1931, he published his own proposals, which anticipate the characteristics of a conceptual framework:

- to set forth the goals of accounting;
- to establish common principles;
- to say how those principles should be attained;
- to specify how proper accounting methods should be implemented.

Lucas also published a useful accounting chart and an interesting attempt to combine administrative accounting charts with filing systems.

Some important contemporaries: the engineers

Many notable engineers from the Ecole Polytechnique[7] have considered accounting to be an important management aid and have criticised the lack of doctrine, the deficiencies of accountants and the insufficient awareness of most executives and directors. These engineers generally act as executives, consultants or heads of professional associations.

Among this group, Edouard Julhiet published a reputable *Cours de Finance et Comptabilité dans l'Industrie*. In 1924, Eugène de Fages wrote *Les concepts fondamentaux de la Comptabilité*. For him, 'Accounting is the science whose purpose is the numbering of units in motion'; the account is a group of identified units having a common characteristic at a given moment. Louis Rimailho was a well-known artillery engineer who had participated in preliminary studies for the famous 75mm field-gun and in mass-producing the Lebel infantry rifle. Soon after the First World War, he helped to organise the Bata shoe factories. Rimailho was also an expert in organisation and cost accounting. Auguste Detoeuf, founder of Alsthom, president of the Electric Industries Association and president of the CEGOS,[8] did much to encourage cost control and budgetary control. [9]

At the end of the 1930s, French accounting literature was relatively rich and consistent. It is remarkable that most of this thinking was inspired by the concepts of value, account and classification of accounts in a clear and comprehensive way. This is the basis of 'process accounting' that would soon expand towards accounting plans and nomenclature.

Yet this richness was not fertile. Theorists, teachers, authors, critics and propagandists were isolated and often divided. They could not gain support from public or private users. The business world, made up primarily of small companies, was not convinced of the supposed advantages of a *science des comptes* which seemed too theoretical and abstract.

In a book called *Logique et Comptabilité* another critic, Louis Sauvegrain, observed that accounting doctrines were badly presented and declared, in 1937, that modern theories offered no solutions to accountants' problems, but simply displaced the questions. Accounting was generally seen as a product of Mother Nature, antedating human developments. Sauvegrain argues to the contrary, asserting that accounting principles are derived from facts, that accounting is an instrument. Sauvegrain was speaking into the wind. In 1939, French accounting seemed to be a dead-end street. However, unexpected developments would soon change the course of events.

STANDARDISATION AND ACCOUNTING PLANS

Historical circumstances

The economic crisis and subsequent political turmoil of the 1930s had inclined many, if not most, influential people to believe that *technique et machinisme* had killed liberalism. A new breed of politicians, economists and civil servants were well aware of the 'solutions' worked out in Italy, Germany, the Soviet Union and Roosevelt's America, solutions based on nation-wide statistics, economic research, cost and price controls, and national economic plans.

French resources in this field were far from satisfactory. Too many small companies were unable to produce accurate figures, and large ones were commonly accused of hiding theirs. Since 1883, a score of technical drafts and bills concerning financial reporting alone had come before Parliament and been rejected for various reasons: breach of confidentiality, inaccuracy of accounts due to inflation, impossibility of recommending uniform methods for different kinds of businesses. No detailed profit and loss account and no production figures were required from enterprises. The official industrial statistics in 1939 were based on a pattern established in 1839. Decrees issued between 1935 and 1939 had produced no effect by 1940.

On 16 August 1940, two months after the fall of France, a new law instituted 'absolutely compulsory statistics' and gave power to the newly created *Comités d'Organisation* to create statistics for different economic sectors or 'branches'. The economist Alfred Sauvy, although politically opposed to the Vichy regime, could not resist the opportunity to launch the long-desired Institut National de la Statistique, backed by the Institut de Conjoncture.

We have seen that many French accounting theorists were attracted by a possible linkage between individual company accounts and national accounts. There was a touch of Cartesianism in this approach, and the fact that other countries, namely the Soviet Union and Germany, might be nearing success in this area made the concept credible.[10]

Jacques Chezleprêtre, from the Tax Administration, had thoroughly examined the German accounting directives promulgated by Grossreichmarschal Goering in 1937. In December 1940, he proposed a tentative plan which closely resembled the German plan.[11]

During this period, the French Tax Administration was the only structure capable of imposing practical accounting standards or procedures. Its agents were among the best-trained in France. They had a wide-ranging knowledge of accounting, finance and economics and were also aware of foreign practices. From this time on, we shall see decisive action by senior civil servants in France to modernise its accounting institutions and procedures.

The 'German Plan'

The question of the French accounting plan of 1942 has been widely discussed. Its purpose was essentially:

- to produce reliable financial reports;
- to make cost control easier;
- to facilitate the creation of professional statistics for consolidation into nation-wide statistics.

A number of additional objectives were expected, notably better training for accountants, managers, workers, shareholders and accounting teachers.

There is no doubt that the packaging of the French plan was rather 'Germanic' in appearance, but it had incorporated a number of seriously studied French concepts regarding terminology, accounting procedures and valuation norms, as well as an excellent cost concept developed by the CEGOS and published in 1937. The fact that the project to develop a national accounting code took only a few months to complete demonstrates that the actors had ready solutions for most issues.

With regard to national statistics, A. Sauvy remarked that the 1941 solutions were prepared too hastily to be satisfactory, but added that indirect German pressure had none the less been profitable, inasmuch as people had been compelled to act. This remark is in part applicable to the accounting plan. Pressure from the Germans has never been proven, but French authorities used this excuse to force a score of skilled experts to work together – something which had never happened before – and to work out clear solutions. André Brunet, the driving force behind the 1947 Plan, acknowledges that the skill developed in formulating the 1942 Plan explains why the next plan, published in 1947, could be developed quickly and efficiently.

The project leader for the 1942 Plan was without question Jacques Chezle-prêtre, but he was ably assisted by a large number of specialists. Several books have described this plan at length. In the entire history of accounting, it is difficult to imagine such a massive effort to present and explain a plan, which was, in fact, never used. A full range of tables, indices, definitions and dictionaries, schemes, sketches and charts was then set up, all of which are still very much alive in French accounting textbooks today.

The 1947 Plan

For several reasons, the 1942 Plan was never applied:

1 opposition from the larger firms;
2 the lack of expertise in small companies;
3 questionable technical criteria;
4 passive opposition to the policies of the Vichy government.

Starting in 1942, members of the CNOF, headed by Pierre Garnier, Professor at HEC, began to devise a counter-plan. In the last chapter of his 1940 *La Méthode Comptable*, Garnier seemed impressed by the new opportunities offered to accounting in a corporate or government-controlled economy. In 1942, he realised what could be done. He considered the various methods of classification proposed since Léautey to be unsatisfactory. For him, the Schmalenbach-style

German and French plans were also 'irrational'. The right classification should facilitate the articulation and, eventually, the separation of financial accounting, cost accounting and, later, budgetary accounting.

In France, as elsewhere, there was a strong feeling that financial accounting had little to do with cost accounting, and many specialists of each discipline would have been very pleased with a divorce granting everyone more freedom. Financial accounting was based on a simple recording of facts expressing relations with third parties and corresponding to legal definitions. Cost accounting, however, was twisted by contingent factors based on organisation, calculation and assessments of all sorts. Reason demanded a clean break. For Garnier, it would have been possible to use a balance sheet for management purposes and an 'operation account', made up of sales, expenses by type (natural expenses), and occasionally one-time inventories, all obtained from official entries. The link between financial and cost accounting was limited to period inventories and a reconciliation between natural expenses and cost, achieved through a *Tableau de Répartition*. Charles Brunet, Professor of Industrial Accounting at the Ecole des Hautes Etudes Commerciales, supported this approach.[12]

The 1942 Plan included purchase and natural expense accounts, as well as contra-accounts established according to the same breakdown and serving as control accounts for allocations to inventory and cost centres. Natural expense accounts were kept open until year end, offering the possibility of providing the overall figures required by national accounts, e.g. salaries and wages, taxes and purchased services. This was a great advantage compared with the procedures of integrated accounting, where such data were allocated and subsequently lost in the cost-calculation process.

Yet both large and small companies had strong objections concerning the administrative constraints derived from the computation and checking of this transfer from natural expense accounts to cost accounts. Large companies did not want to change procedures, deriving from integrated accounting systems, and small companies were far from being ready to bear the cost of further internal administration and control.

Other criticisms could be levelled at the 1942 Plan. First, the classification of accounts was not aligned with a satisfactory classification of balance sheet and profit and loss accounts. Second, the classification could not ensure a perfect consolidation at the branch level and on a nation-wide level to satisfy economic research requirements.

Some improvements were still possible, and they were included in the 1944 CNOF plan. But the most remarkable innovation of this final plan was its clear distinction between financial accounting and management accounting. Such an opportunity would not be neglected.

A new commission was set up in 1946 to design another accounting code.[13] As Pierre Lauzel put it in 1948 (Lauzel and Cibert 1969, II: 16), French standardised accounting practice had to produce, once and for all, a means of comparison in time and space, to be based on agreed terminology, logical classification, a standardised method for recording and procedures for dealing with evaluation.

Standardisation[14] required terms and definitions to express realities, concepts and interpretations relevant for the users of financial documents.

This was not exactly new compared with the declarations of twenty years earlier, but this time the task had to be completed. For the most part, the work had already been carried out. The only remaining questions dealt with technical choices. The government wanted a truly usable plan and was not prepared to accept excuses after such a long period of inconclusive debate.

André Brunet was appointed to co-ordinate the commission's work. He was a Finance Inspector and a teacher at the CNAM. He had reason to believe that accounting inadequacies had led to 'wrong information, insufficient in quantity, loosely collected, neglecting the qualitative aspect of phenomena, established without permanent methods'.

In *La Normalisation comptable*, written in 1951, he recalls the objectives: price control, competition control, control of the validity of government subsidies, transport policy, customs, social policy, efficiency improvements, action against the social evils expected from a technocratic civilisation.

To be more prosaic, the real goal was to produce, along Leontieff's lines, industrial input–output charts similar to those developed in the United Kingdom and the United States, by means of a *Comptabilité Nationale* able to consolidate all transfers of value absorbed by investment, public services, financial activities, domestic spending and foreign trade.

For this, it was necessary to obtain from all companies, large and small, and from all non-incorporated businesses, adherence to a uniform plan, which would properly identify sales and natural expenses. The only way to make this acceptable in the short run was to draw up a related profit and loss model favouring the eventual separation of the two.

This decisive move facilitated the adoption of the 1947 National Plan.[15] In the long run, the new plan brought numerous changes concerning national statistics, macroeconomic accounting and planning, industrial co-ordination, accounting education and tax assessment.

The only problem, and it was not a small one, was that internal accounting was supposed to live its own life and was largely underestimated, if not disregarded, by financial accountants. This circumstance has long had a negative impact on the promotion of management accounting in France.

THE 1950s AND 1960s: A PERIOD OF THEORETICAL STAGNATION

It is surprising that the post-war era gave rise to so few accounting theorists. Some of those who were well-known prior to this period continued to write and publish their work, but almost no new names emerged. Some experts attribute this phenomenon to the emphasis on standardisation itself and to the influence of the *Plan*, which was to absorb the energy and expertise of the most capable specialists. The 1950s and 1960s might be considered years of theoretical stagnation, as if the concern with standardisation had a sterilising effect on accounting theory. The literature of the period was, above all, pedagogical in orientation.

The number of accounting manuals produced during this period is considerable, but on the whole, they are of only mediocre quality. Designed to train future accounting technicians, they reduce accounting to bookkeeping. Authors limited themselves to teaching, or indeed plagiarising, the *Plan comptable général*, focusing on its most technical aspects, particularly the accounts chart and the rules for recording transactions set forth therein.

None the less, three authors are worthy of a more detailed examination: André Cibert, Pierre Lassègue and Claude Pérochon.

André Cibert

Born in 1912, André Cibert began his career as a civil servant in the Ministry of Finance, where, significantly, he carried out audits in industries doing business with the state. These audit assignments led to Cibert's interest in how firms go about calculating cost price, and it was in this way that he became a specialist in management accounting.

Cibert was able to use this experience of his work on standardisation when he became first an external examiner and later Secretary General of the Conseil National de la Comptabilité (National Accounting Council). He is thought to have been the principal author of the chapter on cost accounting found in the *Plan comptable général*.

During his tenure on the National Accounting Council, Cibert also undertook part-time teaching at the Ecole des Hautes Etudes Commerciales (1964–9). In 1968 he participated in the founding of the University of Paris-Dauphine, the first university in France where management science and the study of organisations were the focus of both teaching and research. He would subsequently devote all his time to the University, of which he was Dean in 1969 and 1970. At Paris-Dauphine, Cibert created courses in general accounting, management accounting and management control, which he directed until his retirement in 1981.

His two best-known works are manuals: one in general accounting, the other in cost accounting (both first published in 1968).

André Cibert's manual on general accounting continues in the same tradition as Jean Dumarchey. Like Dumarchey, Cibert developed a net worth approach to double-entry bookkeeping, but he attached greater importance than his predecessors to problems of valuation.

Cibert's manual on cost accounting presents a more elaborate version of the method of cost calculation developed in the 1930s by a task force under the supervision of Lieutenant-Colonel Rimailho. This method was known as the *méthode des sections homogènes*.[16] The author clearly shows that implementing this method presupposes a bipartite corporate structure, namely a techno-economic entity on the one hand, and a hierarchy of responsibilities on the other. According to Cibert, calculating costs is of no interest unless the cost can be attached to a precise responsibility; in other words, cost calculations should be seen as the special tool of management control. In his writings the author was likewise concerned with budgetary control; among his various publications in this field, we should cite his book co-authored with Pierre Lauzel in 1959: *Des ratios au tableau de bord (From ratios to management reporting)*.

André Cibert's ideas were particularly influential, inasmuch as he held several important positions: first as Secretary General of the Conseil National de la Comptabilité and then as Professor at the University of Paris-Dauphine. At the University of Dauphine, Cibert gathered together a group of young teachers, much as Pierre Lassègue did at the University of Paris (Panthéon-Sorbonne). Today, several of those brought in by Cibert are among the most prominent teachers and researchers in the accounting field. He was, moreover, a member of important commissions which, during the 1970s, revamped the course of study leading to the public accountant's diploma, giving it a more theoretical, interdisciplinary basis.

Pierre Lassègue

Born in 1922, Pierre Lassègue was to become a university professor. This fact is worth noting since, as we underlined in our introduction, accounting had traditionally been looked down upon by French universities.

University professors considered accounting to be unworthy of being included in a university-level course of study. It was only at the beginning of the 1960s that a course in accounting was made obligatory for the Master of Economics programme. Since no university lecturer was specifically trained to give such a course, the work was taken on by teachers schooled in economics. Among the latter was Pierre Lassègue who for many years, until his retirement, taught a course in financial accounting at the Sorbonne. This course was designed for first-year university students in economics, rather than for aspiring accountants.

Pierre Lassègue's best-known work, *Comptabilité et gestion de l'entreprise* corresponds to this course. As its title indicates, the book deals with both accounting and corporate management. Pierre Lassègue presents accounting through an economist's eyes. For him, accounting is secondary to economics; it is a 'form' whose content is economics. Consequently, he delivers his critical assessments of accounting concepts from an economic point of view, never hesitating to criticise anything which might endanger its relevance for economics, particularly the fiscal constraints involved. He was naturally very interested in valuation problems.

This book, as well as Lassègue's other writings, are the work of an astute observer of accounting: one of his articles, 'Esquisse d'une épistémologie de la comptabilité', brings to our discipline the discourse of a science in search of its subject, its very nature, its methods, its flaws, its affiliations and its future. In this article he refutes the notion of accounting as a science, presenting it as a technical process of modelling based on a certain number of conventions. He therefore underlines the highly contingent and controversial nature of the firm's image within accounting, which he calls the 'accounting model'.

Elsewhere in his writings Pierre Lassègue frequently criticises certain aspects of the *Plan comptable général* and, more generally, overly detailed standardisation, which he claims deprives firms of the freedom to keep their own books.

Confronted with the paucity of theoretical work on accounting available in the 1950s, it seems that Pierre Lassègue reacted by deliberately adopting a severely critical attitude to reductionist notions whereby accounting was no more than a recording mechanism. Retrospectively, this highly critical stance appears to have been the precondition necessary for a renewal of accounting theory and research in France, a renewal which would begin towards the end of the 1970s and reach its culmination during the 1980s. It is important to observe, too, that it was specifically his position within the university system, as opposed to the French *Grande Ecole* system, that enabled Lassègue to direct work on doctoral theses. Lassègue was, at this time, one of the rare university professors who would accept doctoral dissertations on accounting subjects.

Claude Pérochon

Claude Pérochon, born in 1933, was a student of the Ecole Normale Supérieure de l'Enseignement Technique (ENSET), where he received instruction essentially in law and economics. His professor of economics there was Jean Fourastié, who actively participated in the first major work on standardisation. Pérochon taught accounting in secondary schools until 1973, when he was appointed Professor at the Conservatoire National des Arts et Métiers (CNAM) in Paris.

Pérochon's 1971 doctoral thesis in economics, under the direction of Pierre Lassègue, was entitled *Comptabilité nationale et comptabilités d'entreprises* (*National accounting and corporate accounting*). In 1962, Pérochon had also qualified as a public accountant, but it would seem that he was never actually employed as such.

Pérochon's contribution to accounting theory was to introduce concepts and ways of reasoning from economics, and more especially from national accounting practices, into corporate accounting procedures. For him, accounting was 'a projection of the firm at the value level'. Pérochon thought that the primary objective of accounting was to describe the operation cycle from procurement to production, the latter being defined, as it is in (French) national accounting practice, as consisting of three elements: production sold (sales), production in stock, and production of fixed assets. This conception of accounting would lead him to abandon the net worth interpretation to double-entry bookkeeping for an approach more tightly linked to economics, seen in terms of flows. For him, the double-entry recording system fundamentally reproduced a relationship of exchange rather than the impact of this relationship on corporate net worth. This interpretation of recording methods in accounting, illustrated in diverse manuals, is the one to which the majority of French academics in accounting adhere today.

It was, above all, as the author of accounting manuals (more than twenty titles) that Pérochon exerted his greatest influence within the French accounting community. His first works, published in the early 1960s, were designed for training accountants and were especially popular among secondary-school teachers in collèges and lycées who consistently recommended them to their many students. It is estimated that, overall, Pérochon sold close to 3,000,000 copies of his works.

The most important of these, from a theoretical standpoint, is his *Comptabilité Générale*, a pedagogical presentation of material from his doctoral thesis.

Pérochon was also influential as a member of the Conseil National de la Comptabilité, the organisation in charge of standardising accounting practices in France. As a member of this body during the 1970s, Pérochon contributed to the preparation of the 1982 *Plan comptable général*, to which he published a practical guide (1979). His knowledge of French standardisation made him an international expert in developing accounting plans; as such, he participated in the design and implementation of the 1973 *Plan comptable* for the Organisation de Coopération Africaine et Malgache (OCAM) (the Organisation for African and Madagascan co-operation) and, more recently (1986), that of the Moroccan *Plan comptable*.

Finally, like André Cibert before him, Claude Pérochon was for many years President of the jury which awards the chartered accountancy diploma.[17]

Synthesis

We find in the works of André Cibert and Pierre Lassègue echoes of several major themes present in French accounting theory at the beginning of the twentieth century.

Thus, as we said earlier, André Cibert's presentation of general accounting is close to that of Dumarchey. Likewise, his ideas on cost accounting owe much to the work of Rimailho and the CEGOS engineers.

As a critical observer of the accounting scene, Pierre Lassègue closely resembles Charles Penglaou, his aim being less to perfect a tool than to improve his understanding of it. His essentially cognitive approach, like that of Penglaou, stems from a philosophy or epistemology of accounting.

The writings of Claude Pérochon are more difficult to link to authors prior to the standardisation period, yet they were profoundly marked by this period as well as by the development of a national accounting system in France.

CONCLUSION: AND NOW ...

It was almost the end of the 1970s before new authors began to appear, developing research in France along lines pursued in the English-speaking world.

It was only in 1980 that, on the initiative of younger university and *Grande Ecole* academics, the Association Française de Comptabilité (AFC) was formed, on the model of the American Accounting Association (AAA), but some sixty years later!

During the 1970s, French accounting theory began to come out of its self-imposed isolation and to develop an interest in what was happening elsewhere, particularly in the English-speaking countries. Young researchers who were well-informed on work being carried out in other countries began to emerge. Specialised research centres were created within universities and the *Grandes Ecoles*, and for the past several years the number of doctoral theses on accounting problems has been growing.

Yet France still has no academic journal of accounting. There are but two accounting periodicals: the *Revue Française de la Comptabilité*, published by the Ordre des Experts-Comptables et des Comptables Agréés (OECCA), whose content is essentially directed towards the professional issues in accounting; and the *Revue de Droit Comptable*, now published by a firm of chartered accountants, which draws upon the fields of law and accounting.

Can the renewal of French accounting theory and research, which has co-incided with a re-examination of standardisation *à la française*, endure? We can only hope and believe that it will, but only history will tell.

Notes

The authors would like to thank Evelyn Perry of Paris-Dauphine for her translation of this article. They gratefully acknowledge the insightful comments provided by Daniel Boussard, Peter Standish and Hervé Stolowy.
  1 Twenty-nine editions were to follow. In 1980, this book was reprinted by Arno Press, at the suggestion of Richard Brief. For further analysis, see Bernard Colasse (1982), *The Accounting Historians Journal* 9(1): 127–9.
  2 Edwards, R. S. (1978) 'A Survey of French contributions to the study of cost accounting during the 19th century', in B. S. Yamey (ed.) *The historical development of accounting*, New York: Arno.
  3 The Comité National de l'Organisation Française (CNOF) was created in 1920 to facilitate and extend rational methods and studies concerning scientific management as a factor in economic and social progress.
  4 Vlaemminck, J. (1979), *Histoire et Doctrines de la Comptabilité*, Vesoul: Edition Pragnos.
  5 Or the second, if we count *Le Parfait Négociant* by Jacques Savary (1675).
  6 All of these influences are well presented by J. A. Schumpeter in his *History of Economic Analysis*, vol. II.
  7 The most prestigious of the French *grandes écoles* for engineering, providing instruction of the highest scientific calibre. Founded in 1794, the institution has trained and continues to train a large proportion of French administrators for both the private and public sectors.
  8 The Commission d'Etude Générale d'Organisation Scientifique du Travail (CEGOS) was created in 1926 to help French industrial companies in improving their methods of organisation. Particular organisation departments have been set up since then in a number of French professional associations.
  9 There is much more that could be said about Rimailho and Detoeuf, both prominent figures during the 1930s, but this 'more' is not closely related to accounting.
 10 French economists of the eighteenth century, such as Maréchal Sébastien de Vauban, the physiocrat François Quesnay and the scientist Antoine Lavoisier had already envisaged nation-wide statistics.
 11 For a knowledgeable discussion of this subject, see Peter Standish (1990), 'Origins of the *Plan comptable général*: a study in cultural intrusion and reaction', *Accounting and Business Research* 20(80): 337–51.
 12 For further details see, Romain Durand (1992) 'La séparation des comptabilités: origines et conséquences', *Revue Française de Comptabilité* 240, December 1992.
 13 See Anne Fortin (1991) 'The French Accounting Plan: Origins and Influences on Subsequent Practice', *The Accounting Historians Journal* 18(2), December.
 14 'To standardise [*normaliser*] is to simplify, unify, specify' – definition taken from 'Définitions des termes les plus usités en matière d'organisation et de rationalisation',

Le Chef de Comptabilité, October 1934 (monthly publication of the accounting association la Compagnie et la fédération des Chefs de Comptabilité).

15 Nevertheless, we should not forget that the new scheme was widely discussed and strongly criticised, that it was not made compulsory until 1982 – except for tax reasons – and that it contained numerous erroneous details which have been corrected one by one, due to the vigilance of such organisations as the Conseil National de la Comptabilité, the Ordre des Experts Comptables et Comptables Agréés, the Commission des Opérations de Bourse and others.

16 This method was designed to determine a product's full cost. It is based on an original way of dealing with overheads. The latter are first recorded in what are commonly called the 'sections homogènes', by which we mean divisions in an enterprise whose activity can be measured by a single homogeneous unit. The overheads of each section are then divided among products according to the number of activity units assigned to each.

17 In France, the public accounting diploma is awarded by a state-appointed jury rather than by the accounting profession. The President of the jury must be a university professor.

References and select bibliography

1855–1940

Bournisien, J. (1917) *Précis de comptabilité industrielle appliqué à la Métallurgie,* 2nd edn, Paris: Dunod et Pinat.

Courcelle-Séneuil, J.-G. (1855) *Traité théorique et pratique des entreprises industrielles, commerciales et agricoles ou Manuel des affaires,* Paris: Guillaumin.

de Fages, E. (1924, 1926, 1933) *Les concepts fondamentaux de la comptabilité,* Paris: Eyrolles.

Delaporte, R. (1928) 'La Comptabilité, science des comptes. Ses caractères et ses fonctions', *La Comptabilité et les Affaires,* November and December.

Delaporte, R. (1930) *Concepts raisonnés de la comptabilité économique,* Neuilly: Delaporte.

Delaporte, R. (1931) 'La comptabilité est-elle une science?', *La comptabilité et les Affaires,* March.

Delaporte, R. (1936) *Méthode rationnelle de la tenue des comptes,* Paris: E. Malfère.

Dumarchey, J. (1914, 1933) *La théorie positive de la comptabilité,* Lyons: Rey.

Dumarchey, J. (1925) *La comptabilité moderne: Essai de constitution rationnelle d'une discipline comptable du triple point de vue philosophique, scientifique et technique,* Paris: Gauthier-Villars.

Dumarchey, J. (1926) *Théorie scientifique du prix de revient,* Paris: Experta.

Faure, G. (1921) 'Quelques points de théorie et pratique comptable', *La comptabilité et les Affaires,* June 1921.

Garnier, P. (1940) *La méthode comptable,* Paris: Dunod.

Gomberg, L. (1929) *Histoire critique de la théorie des comptes,* Geneva: Thèse.

Léautey, E. (1897) *Traité des Inventaires et des Bilans,* Paris: Librairie comptable et administrative.

Léautey, E. and Guilbaut, A. (1885) *La science des comptes à la portée de tous,* Paris: Guillaumin. (The second edition of 1889 received the Gold medal of the Exposition Universelle de Paris. Twenty-seven subsequent editions followed. Reprinted in 1980, New York: Arno Press.)

Lefort, R. (1926) 'Essai de didactique comptable', *La comptabilité et les Affaires,* May and June 1929.

Lefort, R. (1929) 'Parallèle critique des principales théories comptables françaises'. Paper presented at the Fifth International Congress in Brussels, July 1926, *La comptabilité et les Affaires,* May and June 1931.

Lucas, M. (1931) 'Fixation d'une doctrine comptable', *La comptabilité et les Affaires*, February.

Penglaou, C. (1929) *Introduction à la technique comptable*, Paris: PUF.

Penglaou, C. (1933) 'Réflexion sur les essais "doctrinaux" en matière de comptabilité', *La comptabilité et les Affaires*, March.

1941–60

Brunet, A. Y. (1947) *Rapport général présenté au nom de la commission de normalisation des comptabilités*, Paris: Imprimerie Nationale.

Brunet, A. Y. (1951) *La normalisation comptable au service de l'entreprise*, Paris: L'économie d'entreprise.

Comité National de l'Organisation Françaises (CNOF), (1946) *Plan rationnel d'organisation des comptabilités*.

Comptabilité et les Affaires (La) (1950) 'Le Plan comptable', special edition, July–August.

Dalsace, A. (1947) *Le bilan, sa structure, ses éléments*, Paris: Bibliothèque Française.

Fourastié, J. (1944) *Comptabilité générale conforme au plan comptable*, Paris: Pichon-Durand-Auzias.

Garnier, P. (1947) *La comptabilité algèbre du droit et méthode d'observation des sciences économiques*, Paris: Dunod.

Lauzel, A. and Cibert, A. (1959) *Des ratios au tableau de bord*, Paris: Editions de l'entreprise.

Lauzel, A. and Cibert, A. (1959, 1969) *Le Plan comptable commenté*, 5 vols, Paris: Foucher.

Lutalla, G. (1950) Mise en application du Plan comptable. Rapport au Conseil Economique, mars 1949. Etudes et travaux du Conseil Economique n°17, Paris: PUF.

Penglaou, C. (1947) 'De l'incidence des doctrines sur la pratique comptable', *Revue d'Economie Politique*, May–June.

Péricaud, J. and Calandreau, A. (1943) *Le plan comptable dans les entreprises*, Paris: Le Commerce.

Projet de cadre comptable général élaboré par la Commission interministérielle instituée par le décret du 22 avril 1941 (1943), Bordeaux: Delmas.

Projet élaboré par la Commission de Normalisation des Comptabilités, approuvé par arrêté du Ministre de l'Economie Nationale en date du 18 septembre 1947 et mis à jour des modifications proposées par le Conseil Supérieur de la Comptabilité, à la date du 1er janvier 1950. Imprimerie Nationale, 1950.

Retail, L. (1951) *Etude critique du Plan comptable 1947*, Paris: Sirey.

After 1960

Cibert, A. (1968) *Comptabilité analytique*, Paris: Dunod.

Cibert, A. (1968) *Comptabilité générale*, Paris: Dunod.

Cibert, A. (1968) *Les résultats comptables*, Paris: Dunod.

Lassègue, P. (1959) Comptabilité et gestion de l'entreprise, Paris: Dalloz.

Lassègue, P. (1962) 'Esquisse d'une épistémologie de la comptabilité', *Revue d'Economie Politique*, May–June.

Penglaou, C. (1962) 'Une épistémologie de la comptabilité est-elle possible et souhaitable?' *Journal de la société de statistique de Paris* 4.

Pérochon, C. (1971) 'Comptabilité nationale et comptabilité d'entreprise', doctoral thesis (Doctorat d'Etat ès Sciences Economiques), Université de Paris I.

Pérochon, C. (1974) *Comptabilité générale*, Paris: Foucher.

Pérochon, C. (1983) Présentation du plan comptable français (PGC 1982), Paris: Foucher.

4 Martti Saario (1906–88)

The developer of Finnish accounting theory

Kari Lukka and Pekka Pihlanto

Abstract

The scientific work of Martti Saario (1906–88), a Finnish Professor of Accounting, represents unique and original accounting thinking. His major contribution is the expenditure–revenue theory of financial accounting, first documented in his doctoral thesis (1945). This theory forms the core of accounting thinking in Finland, and is also the basis for Finnish accounting regulation. Saario's other important contribution, the theory of the priority order of costs (1949), has been greatly exploited in Finnish accounting research during recent decades. Each of these theories is, here, the subject of critical examination.

INTRODUCTION

The history of accounting – often in common with history generally – seems to be mainly about the achievements of individuals. In many cases a person may be promoted as a symbol of his times in the attempt to illuminate history by reference to that individual's deeds. As regards Finnish accounting, however, it is an indisputable fact that the input of a single researcher has had a decisive impact on its development. This person was Martti Saario.

If it is accepted that his effect on Finnish accounting actually started with the publication of his doctoral thesis (1945), his influence could be seen to have lasted for almost half a century, since the principles of his theory of expenditure–revenue accounting are still present in current Finnish accounting and tax legislation.

Saario completed the degree of Bachelor of Economic Sciences in 1928, his masters degree in 1929, and the degree of Licentiate in Economic Sciences in 1932. He also completed the degree of Associate in Laws at around that time. He taught at the School of Commercial Training in Vyborg, 1929–39 and worked for the government during the war as the chief auditor, 1942–4. Saario was a Lecturer, 1943–8, and Professor, 1948–71, of Accounting at the Helsinki School of Economics and an Acting Professor for the Turku School of Economics and Business Administration, 1964–73. In these posts he impressed his theories and views on both undergraduate and post-graduate students of accounting. He also influenced decision makers in business through a large number of journal articles and lectures.

It has been stated that Saario had an inborn gift for making haste with little speed, combined with a unique ability gradually to charge himself up mentally, and then be capable of translating this mental energy into noteworthy achievements (Honko 1966). This may be demonstrated by reference to the fifteen years preceding completion of his doctoral thesis (1945), during which nothing was published, and to the thorough and epoch-making nature of that dissertation.

The ability to see problems in places where they had usually not even been suspected has been seen as characteristic of Saario. This was linked with the skill of reducing problems to their essential features and of presenting original and even surprising solutions – often in a forceful fashion (Honko 1966). Saario described his working method as being closer to that of an inventor than that of a researcher. For instance, he was able to pin down the exact moment when the interpretation of the nature of the profit and loss account (later to form the core of the expenditure–revenue theory) dawned on him.

The improvement of business practice was a driving force in Saario's work, but this concern with practical matters did not stop Saario from aiming at theory formation or from criticising, for example, American researchers for the fact that they 'were practical and pragmatic, and without interest in problems which appeared purely theoretical, lacking in immediate practical application' (Saario 1945: 60).

Saario's theoretical yet simultaneously practice-based ontological thinking is portrayed by his criticism of Walb's view (1926) that the objective of income measurement is not to measure the actual, concrete result of financial management, but instead to present numerical calculations which have no actual equivalent in reality. For Saario, this actual equivalent was money, the earning of which was the purpose of the entrepreneur's operation.

From the outset, Saario's work focused on two of the interested parties of a company. The most important of these, according to Saario, was the owner or entrepreneur, who aims to make a profit through the company's operations. Saario believed it was wrong to assume, as some did, that the business itself would have such objectives. He questioned, jokingly, whether the business of a cabby should instead be examined from the viewpoint of the horse or the carriage (Saario 1945: 23). The second interested party consisted of the tax authorities, who were starting to play a more central role in profit sharing. Saario's interest in taxation arose early on, and is documented in both his master's thesis and early published articles.

It was typical of Saario to use a simple mathematical format, particularly in his later work, as the framework for presenting a problem together with his proposed solution. Another feature is the absence of references from all publications other than his doctoral thesis, probably due to the fact that Finnish accounting research internationalised rather slowly.

In this article, we shall examine Saario's work, which has not as yet been extensively evaluated, from today's methodological perspective. The effect of his charismatic personality lives on and, possibly because of this, assessments to date have consisted of relatively neutral descriptions of his theories and ideas (e.g. Lukka *et al.* 1984).

The remainder of this chapter concentrates on aspects of Saario's work which we consider most crucial. We first examine the realisation principle and the depreciation of fixed assets in income measurement (Saario 1945), and the expenditure–revenue theory based on these ideas (Saario 1959). We then move on to examine the theory of the priority order of costs (1945 and 1949). Finally, we summarise the results of the study.

SAARIO'S THEORY OF FINANCIAL ACCOUNTING

Doctoral thesis 'Realization principle and depreciation' (1945)

Saario started studying depreciation in the summer of 1938, apparently due to his observation that a considerable proportion of the tax complaints taken to the Supreme Administrative Court concerned this topic. He then realised that research into depreciation in business administration was casuistic, and incapable of offering general answers or of creating a universally applicable depreciation theory. He thus set out his research task as follows:

> as the objective for this study, the presentation of such a depreciation method which is simple and logical, yet applicable from the business administration viewpoint, which would supersede all previous ones, and would take simultaneously into account the real effect of all phenomena affecting depreciation. The objective here is a depreciation theory which is comprehensive, explanatory to all empiric observation, universally applicable, and relatively simple.
> (Saario 1945: foreword)

Saario's objective is thus to arrive at a comprehensive theory which is simultaneously both logical and applicable, and to explain existing accounting practice through the discovery of general rules. The construction aimed at appears to consist of features of both normative-deductive and inductive accounting theories (cf. AAA, 1977): formally it looks more normative-deductive, whereas in fact it contains an inductive, very practical element. The setting actually appears quite strange today. Perhaps Saario was concerned about this, because he acknowledges the inductive starting point for his study, whilst deciding to present it in a deductive form.

Saario's knowledge of the business administration literature of his time appears to have been relatively extensive, though somewhat slanted toward German material. Saario is relatively critical, especially of the ideas expressed by perhaps his most important contemporary, Eugen Schmalenbach. Indeed, it is perhaps because of the latter's prominent position that Saario attempted, wherever possible, to use Schmalenbach's work as the starting point for criticism and analysis. Saario does not seem to have a profound acquaintance with Anglo-American literature, and for some reason – perhaps because of wartime difficulties in obtaining material – nearly all his references to research in the English language are from the 1920s. This is unfortunate, inasmuch as kindred souls to his thinking may be found especially in this area (see Saario 1945: 25–7).

The objective specified for Saario's thesis was, with hindsight, over-ambitious. However, it contains all the elements developed in his later work. These are now considered.

The realisation principle and income measurement

The indisputable cornerstone of Saario's entire work is Part One of his doctoral thesis, entitled 'The Realization Principle and Income Measurement'. Paradoxically, its only role in the thesis is to outline the theoretical background, or to support the actual problem-solving function of the thesis (i.e. to aid in searching for the right depreciation method in Parts Two and Three of the thesis). Part One makes a full-bodied read today, since the text (typically Saario) proceeds fluently through concrete examples, is carefully written and at times is argued with genius.

Saario develops an axiomatic construction to explain the logical effect on income measurement when a 'private economic' perspective is adopted (i.e. the impact on the entrepreneur) in examining an enterprise. This term is the opposite of 'collective economic' view which, at the time, was prevalent especially in German business administration research. The collective economic perspective referred to the normative standpoint according to which the primary aim of business administration was to promote the general (e.g. national economic) benefit. This view was promoted by, for instance, Schmalenbach (1934). Saario argued that this was a fruitless and tenuous basis for research in business administration, since it appeared to lead inevitably to operations with various 'values'. He found support for his viewpoint from Anglo-American literature in which 'researchers still practically without exception have maintained a private economic or subjective research standpoint which has been condemned as out-dated in [Continental] Europe, and remained in favour of the old "profit doctrine"' (Saario 1945: 25).

A private economic perspective for Saario implied that the enterprise was seen as its owner's tool for profit seeking. The purpose of income measurement was to identify the amount of distributable profit defined at an interface between the enterprise (Saario's 'business') and the entrepreneur: 'The purpose of income measurement will thus not be to note how much profit the business has made, but rather, how much profit the owner has gained through his business' (1945: 23). Here, too, Saario seems to be particularly willing to break away from Schmalenbach: he emphasises the company's role as the entrepreneur's source of wealth, whereas Schmalenbach targets his examination on the company as a production unit, and on fluctuations in that company's well-being.

Because Saario generally equated profit-seeking with purchasing power, he linked profit calculation directly to money values based on historical cost and the firm's cash, which through this became a kind of 'absolute zero point' for examination.[1] Although he acknowledged the problems caused by, among others, fluctuations in the value of money, he saw it – because a fixed calculation point seemed necessary to him – as the best option for linking financial accounting to money.

The distance travelled from here to the central point of Saario's work, the realisation principle, was short:

> Only when purchasing power has been gained in money terms, and that power's increase is truly in the hands of the subject does profit exist, and only then can it be counted; its amount is of course = the purchasing power gained in the sale + the purchasing power lost in the purchase. We call this type of profit calculation or accounting method the realisation principle.
>
> (1945: 30)

Since in Saario's theory the item 'money' has been selected as the fixed starting-point for calculation, fluctuations in the value of money directed at this item must not effect the firm's result.[2] Instead, for items other than elements of cash, changes in the value of money are allowed to affect the realised result, freely, because such profits and losses are an essential part of business operation. Acknowledging the problems linked with money calculation, Saario emphasised that his theory was concerned only with the *calculation* of the result, not its *evaluation*:

> An evaluation of the size of the result and consideration for the conditions and viewpoints pertaining to it play no part in income measurement based on the realisation principle, the task of which shall remain only the objective statement and measurement of the amount of profit, not the statement of subjective evaluations of the results of the measurements.
>
> (1945: 37–8)

Saario was fully aware of the fact that he did not invent the realisation principle, and refers to business administration literature to support its choice as the cornerstone for his theory. However, most other researchers seemed to favour the realisation principle only because of the practical virtue of objectivity; no one other than Saario – apart from, perhaps, Fischer (1905, 1913) – paid it serious theoretical attention. Thus Saario's contribution was not the principle as such, but the demonstration of its logical consequences for an integrated financial accounting theory.

The key concepts of financial accounting based on Saario's realisation principle are money, expenditure and revenue. These concise concepts, and Saario's clear interpretation for their use, considerably simplify the heavy apparatus which was typical of the prevalent financial accounting approach of the time. 'Money' reveals the amount of purchasing power the firm has at a certain time. Transfers within the items of cash are irrelevant with regard to income measurement. 'Expenditure' and 'revenue' for their part do affect the result. Expenditure is recognised by the fact that it causes (via its counter entry) a decrease in the firm's money. Correspondingly, the characteristic of revenue is that it implies an increase in money. Saario's concepts are well-suited for the implementation of his central thesis – 'all accounting is only about money calculation' (Saario 1945: 53).

Proceeding to his actual theme, periodical income measurement *vis-à-vis* the realisation principle, Saario again logically endeavours to establish a solid axiomatic starting point from which it is possible to deduce everything else logically.

This starting point, in addition to the realisation principle, is the firm's total income, i.e. the firm's profit for its whole lifetime.

The total income is an important starting point for Saario because it can be defined objectively, independent of applied calculation principles. It is possible to calculate the total income consistently in two different ways: either in what Saario would call the 'traditional' way, as the change in cash-in-hand during the firm's lifetime (here again, Saario mainly refers to German sources only), or as the matching of revenue and expenditure.

Since according to the so-called congruence principle the total income is the sum of its periodical incomes and thus each periodical income is a part of this total income, each periodical income may correspondingly be determined in two ways that provide a consistent result. Saario's innovative change of viewpoint lay in his paying attention to the fact that, of these two ways, calculation via revenue and expenditure, based on the realisation principle, was much more fruitful from the point of view of periodical income measurement than was calculation via the aid of the change in cash.

Saario summarises the focus of his entire study:

> Since total income only exists at the point where all property has been changed into money or realised, and since its amount is = sales receipts + purchase outlay, no part of it can be calculated before a sale, i.e. before there are sales receipts with which the purchase outlay may be compared. In calculating total income, all expenditures (K) are subtracted from the revenue. In calculating a part of the total income, an annual income, there is naturally only one year's revenue (m), with the expenditure for the same year (k) as the subtrahend. If k however contains such investments of money to which no revenue has been accrued during that year, . . . These investment outlays . . . are eliminated from the income of their purchase year by not transferring them to the profit and loss account but instead, transferring them to the balance sheet as assets . . . In this fashion it is possible (from the total income) through following the congruence principle, to deduce the realisation principle in periodical income measurement.
>
> (1945: 63)

Again, the objective of a coherent and straightforward model typical to Saario is apparent here. From the realised revenue of a period, corresponding expenditures are deducted. Other expenditures are capitalised in the balance sheet, which in Saario's theory is a pure 'money balance', in that only money items in different forms are presented there: either in cash, as capitalised expenditure, or as investors' capital. All the assets in the end-of-period balance sheet are subjected to the same interpretation: they are expenditures from which no revenue has yet been attained, although it is expected that this shall happen at some future date. If we compare, today, Saario's streamlined theory with, for example, the so-called dynamic financial accounting model[3] presented by Schmalenbach (1933), the latter system seems incredibly complex.

The realisation principle and depreciation of fixed assets

Moving on to the primary research objective of his doctoral thesis – i.e. the development of a rational, simple and relevant depreciation theory in Part Two – Saario starts with the idea of a 'matching procedure' (Saario 1945: 105). This has the same meaning as the matching convention, long known in Anglo-American literature,[4] according to which income measurement matches revenue with the expenditure which caused this revenue. Saario's original input is that apparently no one else had aimed at developing an explicit depreciation theory from this basis.

Saario relates the idea of depreciation in accordance with the realisation principle to the general theory of income measurement formulated in Part One of his thesis. Depreciation is taken to mean the matching of long-term expenditure with the appropriate time period, by linking it with the revenue it has created. The process of capitalisation then makes it possible to transfer the expenditure to a future accounting period, provided there is anticipated future (related) revenue at the moment of capitalisation.

The weak point of Saario's depreciation theory lies where, in the light of current knowledge, it might be expected; namely his attempt to formulate a 'right theory' for allocating long-term expenditure between consecutive accounting periods. Saario was not unaware of this problem (Saario 1945: 130–1). While advocating the division of total expenditure exactly in proportion to the revenue, whereby the relative profit for each year and for each monetary unit received becomes equal,[5] he observes: 'Although this division cannot be proven any more correct than the second method for division described in the example, we shall however take it as the basis and starting point for the division of the depreciation' (1945: 131).

To provide a basis for matching long-term expenditure with related revenues, Saario develops the concept of 'realisation revenue' (t). This is the contribution arrived at by subtracting the current expenditure[6] (privileged) of a period (k) from the revenue of the period (m). [7] Depreciation, which is matched according to the distribution of the realisation revenue, is termed 't-depreciation' by Saario. He argues – again with the aid of examples – emphasising the central idea of his depreciation theory, that the actual creation of a separate depreciation fund (i.e. a sum of money set aside for the replacement of capitalised expenditure) and its mere calculation are two different issues – that depreciation is only possible where the subtraction m – k is positive (1945: 138–50).

The significance of Saario's depreciation theory, although original at the time, does not appear tremendously great in the light of current knowledge: all accounting researchers apparently accept the result of Thomas's (1969, 1974) analysis that no 'right' depreciation theory (and thus, no right depreciation method) can exist. Time has thus taken away the ground from under the normative-deductive part of Saario's research task, naturally leaving options open for meaningful inductive research that Saario reports on in the third part of his study. However, the principal limitation of research which describes and explains accounting practice from the viewpoint of establishing the 'right' depreciation method is already linked to the so-called Hume's law: how things should be cannot be deduced from the way they are. To make the issue even more complex, accounting practices *per se* are in the sphere of influence of norms and normative research, and thus, the analysis of practice is concerned more or less with the examination of realisations of various normative constructions.[8]

Saario's theory on depreciation is in one respect, however, highly commendable: Saario endeavoured to prove by deduction the implications, for depreciation, of following the realisation principle. In this limited environment, i.e. accepting Saario's previous axioms, it is possible to discuss the 'right' depreciation method. In addition, Saario's depreciation theory is significant from the viewpoint of subsequent Finnish standardisation of financial accounting practice.

Saario's own assessment of his depreciation theory

In the third part of his doctoral thesis, Saario presents an evaluation of his depreciation theory, on the one hand in relation to previous literature and on the other, with a view to the calculation of depreciation. At the outset, Saario acknowledges the fact that he has taken some unknown factors as known (total realisation revenue and its distribution over time): 'in order for the burden of reality not to be an impediment to the solution of questions of principle' (Saario 1945: 197). Saario continues in typical fashion to stress the significance of the practical functionality of theoretical constructions:

> It remains unexamined whether results have thus been achieved that bear significance to practice, and with the aid of which it is possible to explain phenomena of reality, since the scientific value of each theory is to be weighed in the light of what follows from each individual theory, in relation to experience.
>
> (1945: 197)

Saario stated, however, that in his research, he would persevere in purely theoretical examination, thus ignoring a problem that disturbs a cornerstone of his depreciation theory – objectivity and economic meaningfulness – by stating that in the theory's application, 'only known factors are to be utilised, or in addition to these, such factors which, with the aid of experience, can be adequately evaluated' (1945: 198).[9]

Saario crystallises his depreciation theory into two points for the purpose of his own analysis:

1 fixed assets must be depreciated entirely during the period in which they accrue realisation revenue;
2 capital expenditure is divided into periods as a series of depreciations in proportion to periodical realisation revenues (1945: 198).

Since his 'realisation revenue' concept was previously unknown, we have seen that he made the assumption that a t-depreciation in accordance with the realisation revenue would correspond approximately to depreciation in accordance with income after interests and taxes.

Saario points out that the opinion of financial accounting theorists, apart from Fischer (1905, 1909, 1913), is unanimously against a depreciation method in accordance with periodical income. On the other hand, he sees sufficient evidence to state that this method represents actual practice in depreciation. From this standpoint Saario concludes that t-depreciation offers a foundation for an explanation in all cases and conditions (Saario 1945: 214). Taken *literatim* this statement is not very adventurous. Saario's uncertainty about his conclusion is also reflected in his other argumentation. For instance, he ascribes a rather significant role to alternative bases of explanation, such as taxation, dividend policy and conservatism, ultimately however disparaging their power of explanation (1945: 212–14).[10] However, it appears as if Saario did in fact wish to claim that t-depreciation would be the best basis for explanation. Although this has been left mainly to the reader, Saario states rather far-reachingly: 'As it is that in this study t-depreciation has been reached, starting from the profit motive via logical deduction, and given the observed consistency with real-world experience, there may be no more necessity to present further viewpoints in support of the theory' (1945: 215).[11]

Summary

The method Saario utilises seems to be a combination of deductive and inductive methods of reasoning. As Saario progresses through alternate lines of deduction he appears continuously to make his choices in order to build a structure (apparently preset by him) for a depreciation method in accordance with revenue, by arguing with the aid of practical examples as if each choice were the only logical option. This method seems to be effective in developing a general theory of income measurement based on the realisation principle, but in the depreciation analysis it falters in places, partly due to a certain unfeasibility in the normative-deductive part of the research task.

Undoubtedly the most significant part of the study is in Part One, where Saario constructs an entire axiomatic theory of financial accounting, focusing on periodical income measurement. Its fine, clear profile was tremendously ahead of its time, and this part shows up the particular genius of reduction in its constructor. This theory forms the pith of Saario's entire scientific work.

The expenditure–revenue theory of financial accounting (1959)

Saario's textbook, published in 1959, is a more oft-cited presentation of his theory than the thesis itself. By 1959 the theory had also acquired its current name: the expenditure–revenue theory of financial accounting. The textbook demonstrates the contents of Saario's theory using examples based on day-to-day bookkeeping records and financial statements replete with run-of-the-mill problems. Saario explicitly presents the two core aspects of his theory:

1 The division of revenue into periodically allocated expenditure and profit.

2 The division of expenditure into the periodically allocated (income-effective) part and the residual balance sheet figure.

The dynamic nature of expenditure–revenue theory is emphasised, and it is made crystal-clear that the balance sheet merely contains residual items and serves no purpose in the process of income measurement.

Saario's textbook takes a more practical view than the thesis, and through this, stresses the different options available for the presentation of income, available for the disposal of management discretion, 'permitted' by the expenditure–revenue theory.

The following quotation is illuminating: 'An amount of expenditure is subtracted periodically from revenue, such that their difference, i.e. the profit, will correspond to that part of total income which is seen as accrued in that year or considered advisable to present' (Saario 1959: 126). Saario's examination of income smoothing follows the same pattern. The common denominator for Saario appears to be the minimising of taxes: 'income smoothing, which is right in principle and advantageous from the point of view of taxation' (1959: 127). Although this fits in well with the profit motive of the entrepreneur that Saario employs in his thesis, a question arises about the full effects of this normative viewpoint in Saario's work. It may be asked whether Saario's entire work – and especially the central theory of financial accounting – is best understood as a problem-solving construction, the aim of which is merely to minimise the amount of the entrepreneur's taxation (cf. Kasanen *et al.* 1991).

Saario pays a lot of attention to the differences between his own theory and the so-called balance sheet equation theory prevalent in Finnish accounting practice at that time. Perhaps the most crucial element of Saario's theory is highlighted in this comparison, namely its simplified concepts and a coherent and logical structure. The theory is systematically based on the realisation principle and three different kinds of accounts: money, expenditure and revenue. For this reason, its pedagogical superiority is obvious.

Saario's influence on legislation and practice

The expenditure–revenue theory succeeded rather swiftly (in the 1960s) in superseding the balance sheet equation theory in the curricula of Finnish Schools of Economics. By the 1970s, it had become the foundation of financial accounting thinking in Finland. Also it had become the basis of Finnish accounting legislation (Accounting Act, 1973) and, to a significant extent, taxation concerning the income of business operations (Act on Business Taxation, 1968). For a country's financial accounting regulation to be based squarely on a previously formulated accounting theory is extraordinary.

The increasing need for the harmonisation of accounting practices has, however, brought problems created by the income-centredness of the expenditure–revenue theory into focus during recent years. The fact that the theory legitimises the irrelevance of the balance sheet in financial statements conflicts with practical and current international needs, whereby the financial statement should provide correct and sufficient information about a company's financial situation; information which in Finnish financial statements is left mainly to notes to the accounts (cf. Leppiniemi 1992). However, despite many pressures, the expenditure–revenue theory has so far retained its position as the foundation of accounting thinking in Finland. This is apparent, for instance, in that in the recent significant reform of accounting legislation in Finland, which came into force at the beginning of 1993, it had not been seen as necessary to abandon the core principles of the theory.

In addition to the two books reviewed above (Saario 1945, 1959), Saario published a large number of articles, mainly in business journals, which focused on current accounting problems. The profit and loss account and related taxation problems remained prominent, but he also tackled other themes. He proposed a new form of company financing (Saario 1960), for example, and argued in favour of taxation legislation which would support investment in shares. Another method of tackling financing problems, investment calculations, emerged in the late 1950s.

Saario also developed the concept of 'tax authorities' contribution toward costs': when tax deductible expenditure is met from income, it means that the 'tax authorities pay their share of the costs'. This outcome is realised, however, only if a negative annual income can be compensated via the transfer of that result to be subtracted from positive annual results during later periods; an option unavailable in the taxation legislation of the time. Saario also explored the problematique of national economics, through his taxation theme, by pointing out the capriciousness of the taxation system and the obstacles it presented to economic growth. His solution was the introduction of a neutral taxation system. Undoubtedly Saario increased the tax awareness of businessmen, and also influenced legislation.

THE THEORY OF THE PRIORITY ORDER OF COSTS

The first version of the theory: priority order of expenditures

Perhaps the most often quoted of Saario's publications is his article entitled 'On The Priority Order of Costs' (Saario 1949; see also Saario 1950 and 1952). The ideas presented have been considered as indisputably the most significant in his scientific work (e.g. Honko 1966: 10; Näsi 1990: 81). It is not very well known, however, that Saario had already presented a basis for the theory in his doctoral thesis (1945), using the term 'priority order of expenditures'.

The idea of the priority order of expenditures matures gradually throughout Saario's thesis, and is grounded on the concept of depreciation based on revenue, or 'realisation depreciation', examined above. We have seen that the calculation of realisation revenue – which is the basis of realisation depreciation – requires the deduction of current expenditure from gross revenue, and therefore Saario suggests that current expenditure is 'privileged' in relation to the depreciation of fixed assets, i.e. to be recovered 'in priority' from gross sales revenue (Saario 1945: 121 and 152). As that part of revenue remaining after depreciation is profit, the entrepreneur's part is the last of the three items (current expenditure, depreciation and profit) in the priority order.

To justify the priority order, Saario draws attention to the different degrees of risk involved in current expenditure compared with fixed assets. The entrepreneur has accepted a certain risk as he trusts this spending on fixed assets to produce revenue in the long term. Therefore, fixed assets can 'wait' a longer period to be covered, compared to current expenditure. Saario also justifies his order of priority by reference to the current literature (Saario 1945: 162–3). He cites Grossmann (1925) and Mellerowicz (1933), according to whom depreciation is last in order and, where the sales price is insufficient, is not covered (Saario 1945: 163).

The priority order of costs

The main features of the priority order

The 1949 seminal article, which focuses on cost (or management) accounting rather than financial accounting, contains a greater number of cost items than covered in the priority order of expenditures. But, in common with the earlier work, he again argues that there is a certain order in which each production factor, i.e. each cost, is covered from sales receipts. Saario's thinking diverges from the common view expressed in foreign literature, stating that in relation to sales revenues all costs are homogeneous, that is, all costs together have produced (or will produce in the future) certain sales revenues. Saario (1949: 196) cites Paton to this effect: 'In their basic relation to revenue all costs are homogeneous; expenses are not recovered through earnings in preferential order.' (Paton 1941: 465).

Saario links priority order of a cost item to the point in time when the cost arises. The production factors presented uppermost in Figure 1 are as a rule linked to production later than those on the lower steps, and are prioritised on this basis.

PRIORITISED
Direct labour
Direct materials
Variable overheads
Organisation
Tools and machinery
Buildings
Land
Entrepreneur
NON-PRIORITISED

Figure 1 The priority order of production costs
Source: Saario (1949: 175)

Grounds for the priority order

Saario attempts to justify the priority order with the help of simple practical examples concerning investment decisions and, on the basis of these, comes to a generalisation: 'In making decisions in advance, *ex ante*, later costs are given a categorical preference in relation to previous ones.' (Saario 1949: 171). Since the examples illuminate some features of Saario's practical way of thinking, and perhaps also help us to understand how he discovered the idea of the priority order of costs, one of these examples is now critically discussed.

According to this example, the price paid for a forest area distant from transportation routes will not be the same as would be paid for one located in the close vicinity of advantageous roads for transport or place of consumption; the reason for this is that the buyer deducts estimated transport costs in advance from the timber revenue he expects to gain (Saario 1949: 170).

This is obviously correct: in searching for a tender price for an investment alternative and comparing the alternatives, any excess cost item under one alternative will reduce the price which the buyer would be prepared to pay. Thus the total sum of costs (and expected revenues) are relevant in the comparison of alternatives (or at least the items that are different in the alternatives). Of course, on the basis of this example, it is not possible to logically 'prove' the existence of the priority order.

Saario states, based on several examples like the above:

> It is deemed in advance that, of the total revenue which will be accrued from a commodity H + from the necessary extra costs K, these extra costs K take their share from the top, according to their priority, which means that from H is accrued only the remainder = total revenue – K.
>
> (Saario 1949: 171)

Judging from the examples, the purpose of calculating this remainder of income is to solve the 'break-even' price for the commodity from the point of view of a potential buyer.[12]

If we accept Saario's conclusion that there are certain 'natural' grounds behind the order in which costs are deducted, a possible behavioural explanation would be that the decision-maker selects his targets of attention (attentiveness) in a particular order, rather than examining the cost items simultaneously as an entity.[13] A question then arises as to whether this 'natural' order is linked to the decision-making situation rather than a universal principle, which leads to a universally grounded priority order. In the former situation it may be the case that the decision maker first selects the greatest and therefore the most significant cost item as a target for his attention, and therefore to be deducted in a preliminary calculation. It is possible that those items easiest to estimate or easiest to allocate (if not of little significance), also receive attention before other items.

This does not undermine the meaningfulness of the priority order of costs as a convention; yet it does draw attention to other possible, situation-dependent, principles for constructing an order in which costs are to be deducted from revenues.

Saario (1949: 176) presents two concepts as further arguments for the priority order of costs, particularly in relation to *ex-post* calculations. For these purposes, the priority order is extended to include all possible categories of costs in addition to the two broad categories (current expenses and depreciation) in the priority order of expenditures. First, he arrives at the 'period of circulation', or the period of time in which the production factor remains in the production process. In Figure 1, the production factors listed lower down (those usually acquired earlier) have a longer period of circulation than the prioritised items. For example, the period of circulation of direct labour and direct materials is the shortest, which gives rise to their priority to be covered first by the sales price (Saario 1949: 176–7).

Second, Saario presents the concept of the 'apportionment ratio'. The number of products/revenue items contributed by a certain production factor is called the apportionment ratio of this production factor or of the corresponding cost. Each production factor will in principle produce a part of the revenue accrued during its period of effect. Thus, for instance, the revenue accrued through the lowest production factor in the priority order, the 'entrepreneur', is in principle divided between all products, i.e. sales revenue items accrued during the total life cycle of the company. In contrast, the revenue accrued from the materials and wages per a certain product (in single-product manufacturing) is as a whole included in the sales price of this product. Because of this, these (direct) costs are termed mono-apportioned and others multi-apportioned. In Saario's view those costs with a smaller apportionment ratio or 'low-apportioned' costs are covered first out of the sales price and thus prioritised ahead of those with a higher apportionment ratio (Saario 1949: 177).

It must be noted that, even if they are interesting concepts, neither the period of circulation nor the apportionment ratio provide grounds for the priority order. Instead, they provide the criteria with which different types of costs can be distinguished from each other, at least in principle.

The actual nature of the priority order

Since it is not possible to accept Saario's case for the priority order of costs, it may help to reflect on the actual nature and basis for the priority order. If we imagine the decision-maker proceeding up the steps in Figure 1 as in the priority order of costs, it is normal at each step, when considering outlay for the next cost, to deduct the cost at the next step (but also all costs beyond that, to be spent later) from the expected gross revenue. Thus it can be established whether or not revenue will cover the cost (and those costs following it), i.e. whether it is viable to continue the chain of cost outlay.

Strictly speaking, however, the only 'priority' here is that the costs under consideration at any point in time are deducted from the expected revenue, which is obvious since the costs disposed earlier are, as sunk costs, irrelevant to this decision-making situation. Saario seems to apply this concept of sunk costs to consecutive decision-making situations (as his examples also indicate) and 'sums up' the disconnected priority orders to a total order.

The combination of consecutive disconnected priority orders into the total priority order is, however, a solution based on convention and purpose, although Saario does not consider it such. Thus, it may be stated that the theory of the priority order of costs must be seen as a normative construction. It is apparent that in Finnish accounting research the theory has been taken as such, and perceived as useful – at any rate, no attention has been paid to its argumentation.

Before moving on, it might be noted that Paton's (1941) idea of the 'equal division' of costs as an accumulator of revenue cannot be considered any more 'correct' than the idea of the priority order of costs. A calculation of this kind is, again, only conventional practice, based on an averaged approach, the usefulness of which is actually more limited than that of the priority order.

The relation of the priority order of costs to some other accounting ideas

The priority order of costs that Saario developed independently of other scholars fitted very well with other contemporary accounting ideas. For example, at that time, in Finland, there was a keen interest in industrial product costing (mainly due to price control and new accounting law), which is an area where Saario's theory had a natural application. Similarly, for short-term profit planning, the American (subtraction-type) profit and loss account (that resembles the priority order of costs scheme, apart from usually containing only a few sub-totals) came into general usage (Eskelä 1964, Näsi 1990: 162–5).[14]

The theory of the priority order of costs has been said to have been a forerunner of direct costing (Hautakangas 1966: 76), which at the time Saario's article was written, was not well known in Finland.[15] In examining the term 'contribution margin', for instance, and especially its form 'contribution to fixed assets' (e.g. Horngren 1964: 340), tracks of approaches similar to those of Saario are visible: 'contribution' means a portion and thus represents that part of revenue which, after the deduction of current costs, remains to cover fixed costs. In Saario's terminology this portion 'belongs' to the lower costs in the priority order.

In thus examining costs in variable/fixed categories, direct costing and the priority order of costs closely resemble each other: both ideas link variable costs (of a product) more closely to the revenues than fixed costs. In direct costing the grounds for this link are the 'functional relation', i.e. a causal relation of variable costs to revenues that is either missing or more distant for fixed costs.[16]

Despite similarities, the theory of the priority order of costs is not a derivative of direct costing but an independent theoretical construction. It deviates, for instance, from the 'orders' used in direct costing, short-term profit planning and the American profit and loss account, in both ontological and theoretical views. It endeavours to determine a principle concerning, first, the relation between revenue and costs related to its obtaining, and second, the mutual relation (order) between different types of costs. This principle is based on the assumed way of thinking of practical decision makers, i.e. profit-seeking.

There is a less theoretical, clearly analytical motive behind direct costing (and other subtraction-type statements used in accounting), and no general principle is presented that corresponds, for example, to an apportionment ratio or period of circulation. Thus the aim of direct costing is to facilitate the analysis[17] by separating those costs dependent on production volume from other costs.

The priority order thinking in Finnish accounting research

The idea of priority order has influenced the thinking of Finnish accounting researchers. Honko (1959: 184–5) for instance has connected priority order with coalition theory, stating that a profit and loss account drawn along the priority order of costs indicates how the different interested parties to revenue accrue their portion of the sales revenues (see also Honko 1955). Artto (1968: 54–70) linked the priority order of costs to financial planning, using the term 'order of financing'. The order he presents deviates from Saario's in parts, which is natural since Artto examined the order in which cash outlays are deducted from cash receipts in financial planning.[18]

Several researchers in the field of both financial and management accounting have also referred to the priority order of costs at a later date. In addition, the subtraction-type profit and loss account enacted in Finnish accounting legislation has been adopted very much due to the priority order of costs thinking developed by Saario.[19]

Furthermore, the aforementioned formal similarity between the priority order of costs and direct costing apparently expedited and facilitated the adoption of the latter in Finland. In their presentation of direct costing, some authors took the priority order of costs as their starting point (Ahola 1962; Hautakangas 1966).

SUMMARY AND CONCLUSION

Martti Saario represents uniquely original and even unconventional accounting thinking in the history of the subject in Finland. His impact on the research and practice of accounting in Finland has been greater than that of any other individual.

The undisputed cornerstone of Saario's work is his doctoral thesis. In this, he documents the theory of financial accounting which has since been entitled the expenditure–revenue theory. This theory is based on the assumption that the entrepreneur is a profit-seeker, and on the realisation principle deduced from that. Its advantages are its clear and simplified concepts and logical and concise structure. The pedagogical advantages of the theory are thus undeniable. The theory construction soon proved its functionality in other ways, and in the 1960s grew to be the foundation of accounting thinking in Finland. Despite strong international pressure toward harmonisation, Finnish accounting legislation and, in parts, also business income taxation legislation are still based on this unique theory.

The depreciation theory developed by Saario in his thesis may be seen as the 'weakest link' in expenditure–revenue theory, which is due to the essential difficulties of the problem area. It is to be noted, however, that Saario's depreciation theory is by no means worse than other logical theories on depreciation – its advantage lies, typically to Saario, in its uncomplicated and coherent structure.

The theory of the priority order of costs developed by Saario sprang from his thesis. It has been greatly exploited in Finnish accounting research, and has also influenced the profit and loss account format of Finnish accounting legislation. Despite the fact that it is difficult to agree with Saario's arguments for the priority order or its universal nature, it is however a normative construction which has proved useful. The meaningfulness of this construction is increased by its compatibility with more modern ideas which have become widespread, such as direct costing.

Notes

1 Saario understood the firm's cash (i.e. money) 'broadly' to consist of, in addition to clear monetary items, sales receivables and accounts payable (as a deduction item).
2 Because of this, Saario confines his theory to ordinary economic conditions in which too high an inflation rate does not make this choice meaningless (Saario 1945: 36).
3 However, Saario's theory of financial accounting is also dynamic, stressing the priority of the profit and loss account in comparison with the balance sheet; see, e.g. Lehtovuori (1972).
4 Unfortunately it is not apparent in the study whether Saario was aware of this, as he does not refer to Anglo-American sources where the convention was already known (e.g. Paton and Littleton 1940); neither does he refer to German literature here.
5 This solution forms the basis for the so-called realisation depreciation concept, which plays a significant role in Finnish accounting thinking of today – see Saario (1961) and e.g. Aho (1982).
6 This refers to expenditures such as wages, materials, salaries and energy. Saario regards the production factors behind these types of expenditure as 'short investments' compared to fixed assets. Also excluded from current expenditure are taxes, interest and dividends, which Saario sees as distributions of profit (1945: 171–5).
7 Cf. section below entitled 'The Theory of the Priority Order of Costs'.
8 Saario examines these questions with merit without, however, taking his inferences to their logical conclusion as regards his own research, see Saario (1945: 214–15).
9 Cf. Honko's review (1959: 177–8) of Saario's depreciation theory.
10 If we look at Saario's other work, we might conclude that he did not intend to imply Friedman's (1953) positive and limited concept of explanation, in which no aspect of a theory other than its predictability has significance. However, Saario's conclusion could be interpreted exactly in this sense, as the theory seems to predict the posting of depreciation quite reliably.
11 We should note that Saario's empirical evidence draws on other researchers' findings about how depreciation charges were made in practice.
12 By applying a certain kind of negative deduction, Saario also expands this principle to *ex post* situations.
13 On the concept of selective perception, see e.g. Parker *et al.* (1989: 12).
14 Net sales, gross profit, operational profit and net profit; e.g. Rautenstrauch (1939: 368; see also Paton 1941: 25), to whom Saario refers. Rautenstrauch (1939: 369) further notes: 'Gross profit . . . is the profit realized before administrative and sales expenses have been deducted'; an element of the priority order could be seen here.
15 The first signs of direct costing appeared in Finland in 1950 (Näsi 1990: 167–8); in the USA the first articles on direct costing were published at the end of the 1930s, yet it became rooted in practice slowly (Keller 1957: 122).
16 'Advocates of variable costing maintain that the fixed portion of factory overhead is more closely *related* to the capacity to produce than to the production of specific units. . . . This approach (direct costing) emphasizes the *interplay* of revenue, cost, and profits, because the contribution margin is highlighted . . .' (Horngren 1964: 340; our italics).

17 Direct costing is even called a technique: 'contribution margin or marginal income technique' (Horngren 1964: 43).
18 See also Kettunen and Mäkinen (1972: 15–19) and Majala (1974).
19 The profit and loss account scheme presented in the Report of a Committee concerning the reform of Finnish accounting legislation (1969) corresponds to a great degree with the one presented by Saario (1966).
20 References marked with an asterisk include an English summary.

References[20]

Aho, T. (1982) *Investointilaskelmat (Capital Budgeting)*, Vaasa: Weilin & Göös.
Ahola, P. O. (1962) *Katetuottolaskennan perusteet (The Principles of Direct Costing)*, Helsinki: Tammi.
American Accounting Association (AAA) (1977) *Statement on Accounting Theory and Theory Acceptance*, Sarasota, Fla.: AAA, Committee on Concepts and Standards for External Financial Reporting.
Artto, E. (1968) *Yrityksen rahoitus. Systematiikka ja mukauttamistavat (The Financing of the Firm: Conceptual Framework for the Adaptation of the Monetary Financial Process)*, Helsinki: The Helsinki School of Economics.*
Eskelä, O. (1964) 'Havaintoja liikelaskennan viime vuosikymmenien kehityksen vaiheilta' ('Observations on the Last Decade's Development of Accounting'), *Ekonomia* 5.
Fischer, R. (1905) *Die Bilanzwerte, was sie sind und was sie nicht sind I*, Leipzig.
Fischer, R. (1909) *Über die Grundlagen der Bilanzwerte*, Leipzig.
Fischer, R. (1913) *Buchführung und Bilanzaufstellung nach Handelsrecht*, Leipzig.
Friedman, M. (1953) *Essays in Positive Economics*, Chicago, Ill.: University of Chicago Press.
Grossmann, H. (1925) *Die Abschreibung vom Standpunkt der Unternehmung, insbesondere ihre Bedeutung als Kostenfaktor*, Berlin and Vienna.
Hautakangas, T. (1966) 'Realisointiperiaate käytännön laskentatyössä' ('The Realisation Principle in Accounting Practice'), in J. Honko and J. Lehtovuori (eds) *Suomalaista liiketaloustiedettä 1966 (Finnish Research on Business Studies 1966)*, Helsinki: Weilin & Göös.
Honko, J. (1955) *Koneen edullisin pitoaika ja investointilaskelmat. Taloudellinen tutkimus (The Economic Life of a Machine and Calculations Concerning the Economics of Capital Investments)*, Helsinki: The Helsinki Research Institute for Business Economics.*
Honko, J. (1959) *Yrityksen vuosItulos (The Annual Income of an Enterprise and Its Determination)*, Helsinki: The Helsinki Research Institute for Business Economics.*
Honko, J. (1966) Esipuhe (Introduction), in J. Honko and J. Lehtovuori (eds) *Suomalaista liiketaloustiedettä 1966 (Finnish Research on Business Studies 1966)*, Helsinki: Weilin & Göös.
Horngren, C. T. (1964) *Cost Accounting. A Managerial Emphasis*, Englewood Cliffs, NJ: Prentice-Hall.
Kasanen, E., Lukka, K. and Siitonen, A. (1991) 'Konstruktiivinen tutkimusote liiketaloustieteessä' ('Constructive Approach in Business Studies'), *The Finnish Journal of Business Economics* 4, 301–29.*
Keller, W. I. (1957) *Management Accounting for Profit Control*, New York: McGraw-Hill.
Kettunen, P. and Mäkinen, H. (1972) *Yrityksen rahavirtojen kokonaiskuvauksen alkeet (The Elements of the Description of the Cash Flows of the Firm)*, Jyväskylä: University of Jyväskylä, Department of Economics, Publications 5/1972.
Lehtovuori, J. (1972) *Tuloslaskenta, taseteoriat ja tilinpäätösinformaatio (Income Measurement, Financial Accounting Theories and Financial Reporting)*, Turku: Publications of the Turku School of Economics.

Leppiniemi, J. (1992) 'YAS – kirjanpitolainsäädäntö uudistuu' ('FAS – Financial Accounting Legislation is Reformed'), *Tilintarkastus-Revision* 6, 443–51.

Lukka, K., Majala, R., Paasio, A. and Pihlanto, P. (1984) 'Accounting Research in Finland', in A. G. Hopwood and H. Schreuder (eds) *European Contributions to Accounting Research. The Achievements of the Last Decade*, Amsterdam: Free University Press.

Majala, R. (1974) 'Rahanlähteiden ja käytön järjestyksistä' ('On the Orders of the Sources and Uses of Funds'), *The Finnish Journal of Business Economics* 2, 197–202.

Mellerowicz, K. (1933) *Kosten und Kostenrechnung I. Theorie der Kosten*, Berlin und Leipzig: Walter de Gryeter and Co.

Näsi, S. (1990) *Laskenta-ajattelun kehitys viime vuosisadan puolivälistä nykypäiviin. Suomenkieliseen laskentatoimen kirjallisuuteen perustuva historiantutkimus (The Development of Accounting Thought from the Middle of the Last Century to the Present Day)*, Tampere: Acta Universitatis Tamperensis ser A vol 291.*

Parker, L. D., Ferris, K. R. and Otley, D. T. (1989) *Accounting for the Human Factor*, Sydney: Prentice Hall.

Paton, W. A. (1941) *Advanced Accounting*, New York: Macmillan.

Paton, W. A. and Littleton, A. C. (1940) *Accounting Theory*, New York: Ronald Press.

Rautenstrauch, W. (1939) *The Economics of Business Enterprise*, New York: Wiley.

Saario, M. (1945) *Realisointiperiaate ja käyttöomaisuuden poistot tuloslaskennassa (Realization Principle and Depreciation)*, Helsinki: The Helsinki Research Institute for Business Economics.*

Saario, M. (1949) 'Kustannusten etuoikeusjärjestyksestä' ('On the Priority Order of Costs'), *Huugo Raninen 50 vuotta. Kauppatieteellisen yhdistyksen vuosikirja 1949 (Huugo Raninen 50 Years. The Annual Book of the Association of Business Studies)*, Helsinki.

Saario, M. (1950) 'Om prioritetsordningen för kostnader' ('On the Priority Order of Costs'), *Affärsekonomi* 1183–6, 1193–4.

Saario, M. (1952) 'Kostnadernas prioritetsordning och resultatredovisningen' ('The Priority Order of Costs and Income Measurement'), *Affärsekonomi* 1193–4, 1200, 1202, 1204.

Saario, M. (1959) *Kirjanpidon meno-tulo-teoria (The Expenditure–Revenue Theory of Financial Accounting)*, Helsinki: Otava.

Saario, M. (1960) 'Investointiluotto, puuttuva rahoitusmuoto' ('The Investment Loan, The Missing Form of Finance'), *Liiketalous* 54–5.

Saario, M. (1961) 'Poistojen pääoma-arvo ja oikea-aikaisuus' ('The Present Value and Timeliness of Depreciations'), *Mercurialia MCMLXI. Kokoelma kirjoituksia Kauppakorkeakoulun täyttäessä 50 vuotta (Mercurialia MCMLXI. A Collection of Writings as the Helsinki School of Economics Completed its 50th Year)*, Helsinki.

Saario, M. (1966) 'Verotettava liiketulo ja yritysten tavoittelema voitto' ('The Taxable Income and the Profit Aimed at by the Firm'), *Ekonomia* 5.

Schmalenbach, E. (1933) *Dynamische Bilanz*, Leipzig.

Schmalenbach, E. (1934) *Grundlagen der Selbstkostenrechnung und Preispolitik*, Leipzig.

Thomas, A. L. (1969) *The Allocation Problem in Financial Accounting*, Sarasota, Fla: American Accounting Association.

Thomas, A. L. (1974) *The Allocation Problem: Part Two*, Sarasota, Fla.: American Accounting Association.

Walb, E. (1926) *Die Erfolgsrechnung Privater und Öffentlicher Betriebe*, Berlin and Vienna.

5 Eugen Schmalenbach (1873–1955)

Erich Potthoff and Günter Sieben

Abstract

Eugen Schmalenbach was born in Westphalia in 1873. After practical experience and studies in Leipzig he took up teaching in 1904 at the Cologne School of Commerce. He was also active as a consultant, auditor and independent business-man. During the period of National Socialist rule he sometimes had to go underground. After the end of the Second World War he again took up his teaching duties at the University of Cologne, for a short time. He died in 1955 at the age of 81. His academic activity focused on the theory of the dynamic balance sheet, auditing, cost accounting, standard charts of accounts, the calculation of internal prices and the financing of firms. He also worked intensively on questions of company valuation, company organisation and economics.

SCHMALENBACH'S LIFE AND WORKS

Eugen Schmalenbach was born on 20 August 1873 in Schmalenbach, a suburb of Halver, Westphalia, where his father had a small iron foundry. Schmalenbach left the grammar school after the tenth year of schooling. He then spent a short time as unpaid trainee in a machine building firm and soon afterwards three years' apprenticeship as clerk in an ironmongery. Except for one year's military service he worked in his father's firm from 1894 to 1898, finally becoming manager of the main operation with responsibility for bookkeeping and cost estimating.

Schmalenbach was one of the first students of the new school of commerce in Leipzig, which opened in 1898. He was taught by Richard Lambert, a proponent of the new 'Handelswissenschaft'; among his fellow-students were Heinrich Nicklisch and Fritz Schmidt. He gained a good pass in the higher education examination in 1900 and went on to study national economy at the University of Leipzig under Karl Bücher, whose assistant he later became. In 1901 Schmalen-bach married Marianne Sachs; they had two children, a son and a daughter. At this period, to eke out his living he was a regular contributor and at one time acting editor of the *Deutsche Metall-Industrie-Zeitung*, Remscheid.

Schmalenbach wrote numerous articles for this journal, including several essays in 1899 on bookkeeping and costing in factories. In an essay on the distribution of costs, he examined the problem of fixed costs; later he was to treat exhaustively their effects on the individual firm and on the national economy.

At Bücher's suggestion, in 1903 Schmalenbach went to the School of Commerce in Cologne, which had been established in 1901. He qualified for a professorial post with his monograph 'Die buchhaltungstechnische Darstellung der Betriebsgebarung' ('The representation of business behaviour in accounting'). In 1904 he was appointed lecturer and in 1906 professor. In the same year the *Zeitschrift für handelswissenschaftliche Forschung* appeared; Schmalenbach was not only its editor but its keenest contributor. Up to 1933 he wrote about 100 articles in it, some of them forming the basis of his later standard works on commercial accountancy.

Research, teaching and the practice of auditing and advisory work were interdependent activities in Schmalenbach's career at this point. As a sworn auditor he audited the year-end accounts of a large store. In 1911 he acquired about half the shares in a trustee company, the Treuhand-Aktiengesellschaft, becoming chairman of its supervisory board, in which post he remained until 1933. His Treuhand Seminar at the University of Cologne became a nursery for the best auditors.

Schmalenbach was also in business on his own account: in 1912 he established a small metal products manufactory in his home town of Halver. Three patents for technical equipment, dating from 1912, 1919 and 1936, attest to his ambitions as an inventor and entrepreneur. Schmalenbach's developmental phase was ended in 1914 by the outbreak of the First World War; for one-and-a-half years he had to give up his research and teaching activities for home defence duties.

The 1920s saw him at the apogee of his success. They were the years of the rise of business management theory in Germany. In 1919 the University of Cologne was opened, the School of Commerce becoming its Faculty of Economic and Social Sciences. In the course of the following decade, his standard works on company accounting appeared.

Schmalenbach became a sought-after government adviser for the new Weimar republic and its economy as it recovered after the end of the period of hyperinflation in 1923. Of note are his membership of the National Economic Advisory Council, his appointment as expert in the matter of the initial balance sheet of the State Railways (when they were reconstituted in 1924 as an independent undertaking), and his chairmanship of the Lignite Mining and Coal Mining Commission.

Schmalenbach produced reports not only for state agencies, but to an even greater extent for commercial firms, often on questions of balancing of accounts and valuation or the organisation of accounting. In 1928 Schmalenbach gave the main paper at the traditional Whitsun meeting of the association of German university teachers of business management, in Vienna. This 'Vienna speech' aroused great attention. It contained the forecast that the result of the growing share of fixed costs in undertakings would be the end of the free economy and the dawn of a new constitution of the economy.

The rise of the German economy, which had begun after the defeat of inflation and which reached a climax in the summer of 1927, came to a turning-point in 1928. It was caught up in the maelstrom of the world economic crisis which had been set off in October 1929 by the 'Black Friday' collapse of share prices on Wall Street. There were many business failures and the number of unemployed rose rapidly, leading because of the economic crisis to the phenomenon of long-term unemployment. In 1931 the German banks had difficulty in meeting their commitments.

The accession to power in Germany of the National Socialists in January 1933 was soon followed by the persecution of the Jewish part of the population. Schmalenbach, whose wife was Jewish, soon decided to retire; perhaps he could foresee some of the terrible developments culminating in the holocaust of the Second World War.

At first, Schmalenbach and his wife were left alone, but later they were harassed by the National Socialist authorities, being forced into smaller flats and suchlike. After the assassination attempt on Hitler in July 1944, married couples in western Germany that included Jewish wives were deported eastwards. Eugen Schmalenbach fled with his wife to the home of a former student, Dr Ludwig Feist in Bad Godesberg, where they remained in hiding to the end of the war.

In these difficult years Eugen Schmalenbach by no means remained inactive. His institutional base was on the one hand the Treuhand-Gesellschaft; its auditing business was sold to the two directors, so that the company became a sort of study society with very few employees, involved in administration of property and some consultancies in company organisation. Another support was an association of former students and friends of Schmalenbach, founded in 1932, which by skilful manoeuvring was able to survive the National Socialist period.[1]

Schmalenbach had to keep himself in the background, but was the secret central motor of the association and informal editor of its publications. During the 1930s and 1940s, volumes published by the society on the basics of orderly accounting for individual items of the balance sheet became manuals for the auditing of company accounts. Schmalenbach initiated the establishment of committees within the association to consider contemporary business management themes.

In some cases he wrote the manuscripts on which advice was based. Other treatises on basic matters of the discipline were sent to all members of the association, or to a select committee, with requests for their reactions. Even when living underground in the last months of the war, he continued to work on a number of new manuscripts.[2]

Personal talks with former students, who did not hesitate to visit their teacher from time to time, also helped him to retain that closeness to practical matters which was important to him. Many of these students risked a great deal to help him to survive the threats of the National Socialist period and the war.

By 1945, at the end of the Second World War, Schmalenbach was seventy-two. He immediately put himself at the university's disposal. For two years he lectured on accounting and finance, but continued to conduct his seminar. At the same time, under the difficult conditions of the occupation period, he attempted to bring out a periodical. Two fresh publications rounded off his academic work of over half a century. He died of heart failure at the age of eighty-one on 20 February 1955. One of his oldest students, Professor Theodor Beste, a retired professor of business management, spoke at his graveside.

SCHMALENBACH'S CONTRIBUTIONS

The basic idea of efficiency

Alongside Friedrich Schär, Wilhelm Rieger and Heinrich Nicklisch, Eugen Schmalenbach is one of the fathers of modern German business management theory. Much in his research and university teaching activity only appears in its correct light when we see that the postulate of efficiency or macroeconomic efficiency is his lodestar. He pursued this aim consistently in almost all his writings, though without defining it closely – he was more concerned with putting his basic idea into practice in companies.

Cost accounting and financial accounting had a particular significance here. Together, they were to make it possible for the practitioner to reach decisions, on the basis of correct values, that would promise the optimum efficiency for his undertaking.

For purposes of cost accounting the businessman should attempt to determine the 'Optimale Geltungszahl', Schmalenbach's term for the optimal cost value in a firm. With the idea of the 'Optimale Geltungszahl' Schmalenbach – influenced by Carl Menger and the Austrian School – for the first time transferred the economist's marginal utility theory to matters of companies' cost accounting. Very early, Schmalenbach also developed concepts which are today discussed in companies under the head of 'Controllership'.

Schmalenbach saw another important instrument for steering the company in the periodic financial accounts, as reflected in the dynamic balance sheet. He considered *Wirtschaftsprüfer* (German chartered accountants) to be 'advocates of efficiency' (Potthoff 1973: 1609ff.). The duty of an auditor was to check the capacity of the management instruments to function properly and thus to guarantee that efficiency in the firm was constantly being improved.

Schmalenbach thought of business management theory as an applied science. Its customers were the practitioners. The tasks and functioning of company accounting were the main focus of his research, but the company as a whole was always at the centre of his interest. Thus he concerned himself greatly with questions of pricing policy, financing by shares or capital contributions, company valuation and company organisation. As a researcher in business management, right to the end of his life, he considered every slightest detail important if it was a matter of finding ways to greater efficiency or discovering causes of waste (Schmalenbach 1948a: 12).

As a teacher, Schmalenbach emphasised the specifically management-oriented training of the thought processes. For him, the essential thing was that his graduates should be able to recognise and eliminate inefficiency in concerns. Thus the study of business management should inculcate in the student a highly developed 'sensitivity to disturbances in efficiency'. He did not see business management as a discipline devoted to training fully fledged businessmen. His priority, to which he devoted his energies as a teacher, was to develop students' abilities to apply economic thinking in practice. This aim could, he thought, be attained only on a secure basis of theory.

The dynamic balance sheet

Schmalenbach's first independent publication, *Grundlagen dynamischer Bilanzlehre* (*Basic Theory of the Dynamic Balance Sheet*), appeared in 1919. With it, management-oriented theories of accounting began to dominate in Germany; besides the 'dynamic' theory of the balance sheet, one other important contribution was Fritz Schmidt's 'organic' balance sheet (Schmidt 1921). From the fourth edition (1926) on, Schmalenbach called his work simply *Dynamische Bilanz*. The concepts of statics and dynamics which he first formulated became classic criteria for categorising theories of accounting as they appeared.

According to the dynamic view, the main function of the balance sheet is the calculation of profits. In this process the outcome of a comparable period is taken as a measure of efficiency; profits are defined as the difference between expenses and revenues. The calculation of profits is seen as the primary task of the annual accounts; so the profit and loss account is given priority over the balance sheet.

Diverging from the established view, Schmalenbach interpreted the balance sheet as an auxiliary to the calculation of profits. He viewed the individual items of the balance sheet as a collection of transitory and anticipatory quantities. In his approach the assets include, as well as money, payments to be received and expenses to be incurred in later accounting periods ('advance performance'); the liabilities on the other hand, as well as the capital, comprise 'subsequent performance', i.e. money to be paid out and revenues of later periods.

In this perspective the assets are composed of the following items:

- cash outflows that are not yet expenses (e.g. plant bought and subject to depreciation);
- cash outflows that are not yet cash inflows (e.g. assets bought and not subject to depreciation);
- revenues that are not yet expenses (e.g. plant provided internally and subject to depreciation);
- revenues that are not yet cash inflows (e.g. stocks, claims for payment for goods and services).

Liabilities on the other hand include:

- expenses that are not yet cash outflows (e.g. reserves);
- cash inflows that are not yet cash outflows (e.g. loans taken out);
- expenses that are not yet revenues (e.g. reserves in respect of future work to be carried out internally for postponed maintenance);
- cash inflows that are not yet revenues (e.g. deposits from customers).

The totality of these items, which eventually expire as revenues and expenses, is a representation of the company's resources and obligations. Thus the balance sheet according to Schmalenbach is no more or less than an image of the firm's reservoir of forces. It connects the cash inflows and outflows, the revenues and expenses of different periods. Its aim is thus not to deliver an image of the state of the undertaking, but to make apparent the movements of values. Hence Schmalenbach called it a 'dynamic' balance sheet.

It was not to be the job of the balance sheet to calculate the asset value or total value of a company. This static aim is one that Schmalenbach believes it cannot attain. Rather, the 'correctly' calculated profit outcome is the decisive factor for him. In profit he saw the measure of the efficiency of the company, and only with these figures can the entrepreneur manage his undertaking. In this sense the balance sheet is a control mechanism for the entrepreneur.

The outcome shown by the balance sheet fulfils both an internal and an external information function. On the one hand it is a key datum for the entrepreneur, as an expression of the efficiency of the company's entire performance. On the other hand this information is also a basis for decisions on the part of the shareholders, creditors and employees.

Schmalenbach did perceive the danger that tactical considerations would lead to balance sheets not showing true profit, but for him it was more important that the businessman's financial statement should become an instrument of company policy-making. He formulated principles of accounting (conservatism, periodicity, continuity, comparability, etc.). The annual accounts prepared on this basis should allow the entrepreneur to discern the trends of development; they should be a compass.

Looking back it seems understandable that Schmalenbach's views were scarcely accepted in an economic world that was primarily committed to thinking of balance sheets in static terms. Yet the sheer amount of criticism that met the dynamic balance sheet is astonishing.[3]

Wilhelm Rieger wrote a whole book, whose critical attitude in its detail and harshness was something new for German business management studies (Rieger 1936). Unlike Schmalenbach he took the view that the correct profit of an undertaking is to be determined solely by an account of receipts and outgoings embracing the whole life of an enterprise. 'An intermediate accounting such as is represented by the year-end balance sheet is merely a fiction necessary for the realisation of certain practical aims' (Rieger 1927: 209).

Fritz Schmidt, whose 'organic' view of the balance sheet expressed a particular attention to matters of devaluation of money and the related problem of safeguarding firms' assets, also had a different theory. Unlike Schmalenbach, who also dealt at length with the nexus of these problems, he propounded valuation at replacement values. Schmalenbach, on the other hand, favoured an index-oriented revaluation of these items. Fritz Schmidt also diverged from Schmalenbach in thinking that a balance sheet can be an account of the assets as well as of the profits.

But alongside the many criticisms levelled at the dynamic balance sheet there were also many positive voices in contemporary writing, the representatives of the 'Cologne School' being the first to take up Schmalenbach's ideas. Walb and Kosiol developed his ideas in their own concepts of the balance sheet, and Münstermann and his students answered many individual critical questions about the dynamic balance sheet.

Auditing and trustee matters

As he thought the balance sheet and the calculation of profits vital, Schmalenbach also made intensive attempts to develop auditing.

For Schmalenbach, auditing was not a matter of just ticking items off. Formal orderliness in his view goes hand-in-hand with an evaluative assessment of the processes of the business. The audit is not a technical test, but an economic one, based on (but going beyond) commercial bookkeeping. In particular he demanded that the auditor should check the financial statements produced for internal use to ensure that it contained everything that was necessary for deciding company policy. These demands, however, found little echo.

He repeatedly refers to the significance of compulsory auditing, which he thinks is also important from an economic point of view. When one looks at the great crises of the past with an eye to 'what has happened thanks to misleading and fraudulent balance sheets, then one will be grateful for the chance of a good compulsory audit' (Schmalenbach 1943a: 18).

Schmalenbach himself was appointed a sworn auditor in 1904, and from 1905 to 1919 audited the yearly accounts of Leonard Tietz AG in Cologne, the present-day Kaufhof AG. In 1913 he set up courses in auditing and trustee work at the then School of Commerce in Cologne. This discipline is very closely linked with Schmalenbach's achievements. When in 1931 auditing was made compulsory for joint stock companies, and the profession of *Wirtschaftsprüfer* (German chartered accountant) came into being, he had already introduced many young people to this area of work. He was always closely interested in the profession.

Cost accounting

Alongside bookkeeping, cost accounting and profit calculation are the pillars of accounting, according to Schmalenbach. They serve to keep a check on efficiency. In Erich Gutenberg's view Schmalenbach, particularly in his book *Grundlagen der Selbstkostenrechnung und Preispolitik (Bases of Cost Accounting and Pricing Policy)*, introduced scientific thinking to this area, previously treated unconvincingly by management theory (Gutenberg 1984: 1152).

The concepts of costs and expenses must be strictly separated:

> That use of goods which arises in cost accounting through the provision of an economic service is called costs. That use of goods which appears in financial accounting is called expenses. Costs and expenses are largely, but by no means wholly, the same.
>
> (Schmalenbach 1927: 17)

The relations are shown in a diagram (Figure 2) which has become a classic of German business management studies (Schmalenbach 1927: 15).

Expenses: Financial accounting

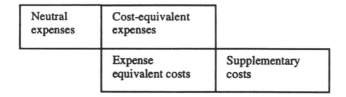

Costs: Cost accounting

Figure 2 Distinction of costs and expenses

Expenses that do not have the character of costs are called neutral expenses (e.g. donations; expenses concerning extraordinary events). When the amount of the costs does not appear in financial accounting (e.g. the cost of equity), we speak of supplementary costs. These distinctions in cost accounting, sketched by Schmalenbach, are still basic in German thought.

In thinking through the cost complex, Schmalenbach soon came upon the phenomenon of fixed costs – costs which are independent of the operating rate at any given time.

Reacting to his teacher Karl Bücher, particularly to his law of mass production, Schmalenbach made it clear that the main point is the degree of dependence of individual kinds of costs on the quantity produced; fixed costs have to be treated separately in estimating and pricing. Thus Schmalenbach laid the foundations in Germany for 'Deckungsbeitragsrechnung' ('contribution margin accounting, break-even analysis'), further developed particularly by Paul Riebel (Riebel 1959: 213). Rummel's 'Blockkostenrechnung' (Rummel 1949: 192, 211–15) and the 'Ertragskalkulationen' of M. R. Lehmann (Lehmann 1951: 151, 170ff.) were instrumental in this development. The concept of direct costing in the USA is a move in the same direction.

Schmalenbach saw dangers for the free market order in the continuous growth of fixed costs in firms caused by the striving to extend capacity so as to raise market share and profits. He was convinced (Schmalenbach 1949: 83ff.) that this leads to companies finding their plant underused and trying to drive each other from the market by offering special prices below their total costs. At this point entrepreneurs have no choice but to escape the ruinous competition by forming syndicates and cartels, eventually meaning the end of the free economy.

For all the importance Schmalenbach attached to cost accounting, he was quick to point out that it is not an end in itself, but that it has specific functions forward which it must be oriented. Thus it can be used to pursue divergent accounting aims. 'Checking business behaviour' and 'Price fixing' are in the foreground; later, Schmalenbach added 'Checking structural changes'. Determination of internal prices and support of the profit account, on the other hand, he reckoned to be among the subsidiary aims of cost accounting.

A particularly useful idea of Schmalenbach's was to transfer the concept of marginal utility from the macroeconomic sphere to cost accounting (Kilger 1972: 119). The right value within cost accounting was, according to his understanding, that sum at which goods are to be valued in order to be able to determine the most efficient choice. Simplified, this means that production factors that are unlimited in their availability are to be valued with reference to their marginal cost; production factors whose availability is limited, on the other hand, with reference to their marginal utility. This thesis was in opposition to the widespread expenditure accounting, in which only the expenditure actually incurred for the production process was included. Schmalenbach called the value he preferred 'Kalkulationswert', 'Betriebswert' and eventually 'Optimale Geltungszahl'.

Standard charts of accounts

Along with his publications on dynamic balance sheets and cost accounting, the work *Der Kontenrahmen* (*The Standard Chart of Accounts*) has influenced theory and practice of accounting in Germany to the present day. There were already many publications by individual authors and by different committees concerned with a systematic layout of accounts, but Schmalenbach's publications came as a breakthrough. This was presumably primarily because whilst trying to keep his standard charts of accounts close to practice, he at the same time laid down the theoretical model of the basic structure of the whole firm.

The arrangement of accounts in Schmalenbach's standard chart is dominated by the same principles seen in his work on profit calculation and cost accounting. These are (Schmalenbach 1935: 6ff.):

- the organic structure of accounting activity in the firm;
- exact cost accounting;
- reliable, quickly available monthly accounts;
- identifiability of causes of profit;
- separation of fixed and proportional costs;
- control of individual departments and cost centres;
- comparison of firms.

Didactic reasons played a large part in Schmalenbach's decision to use the principle of arrangement by *process* in his division of the accounts. Here he was guided by his familiar experiences in industry. But he did point out that the system was not suitable for all kinds of company. Even at the time of his first publication in 1927 he was clear that his concept would not survive unaltered. 'The discipline can of course not commit itself to a single chart of accounts', he writes in his second edition. 'Every new perspective demands new criteria for arrangement, and let us hope that new perspectives continue to appear'.

Indeed there has been no lack of these in the decades following. Schmalenbach's original idea of standard charts of accounts as a complete model of the concern has survived, in the sense that it is still seen as necessary to cover the whole concern with a single system. Schmalenbach saw this as the most important instrument of an undertaking's organisation and administration. With today's dangers of fragmentation through highly developed techniques, awareness of this holistic function of accountancy has been sharpened once more.

Regulatory prices

With *Pretiale Lenkung* (*Price Guiding*), Schmalenbach for the first time investigated the regulatory function of internal prices as a means of developing a firm. The regulatory price within the enterprise was the key concept of his theory, set out in 1948 (Schmalenbach 1948b). He starts from the idea that the market-economic regulation of supply and demand by price is transferable to value relationships within the company between different departments (Hasenack 1957: 308). Whether maximum utility is achieved is measured by the one-dimensional function of profit maximisation as an aim and norm of behaviour. At the same time, Schmalenbach pursued the idea that the individual responsible for a section of the firm should participate in the profit of the whole firm in proportion to the profit of his section (Hax 1981: cols. 1691ff.).

Today Schmalenbach's fundamentals have gained importance, with the divisionalisation of numerous companies. In 'Profit Centre' concepts the main idea is to make individual areas within the firm responsible for their own performance. Schmalenbach had the same intention: through price guiding in a firm the departmental managers were to become entrepreneurs. They were to be invested with considerable freedom of decision-making and were to be paid according to the profits of their departments. Instead of bureaucratic company direction, costs and services would become 'guide prices' by suitable valuation; in this context Schmalenbach has recourse to his concept of the 'optimale Geltungszahl' in the course of optimising the utilisation of scarce resources. This 'Geltungszahl' is the number which, when attained, signals the highest degree of efficiency in the production or the use of the goods. Using the economic theory of marginal utility as a basis, the idea of marginal value is transferred to the calculation of the optimal cost values. The optimal 'Geltungszahl' is in this context Schmalenbach's description of marginal costs as a value within the firm, that is as an internal price.

According to Schmalenbach, policy making in a firm is a continuous evaluation process. He differentiated between internal functional circles (personnel resource management, plant management, material management, production), external functional circles (purchasing, marketing), general functions (financing, accountancy) and the function of policy making. He discusses, by no means merely theoretically, the possibilities for managers of each section to reach optimal 'Geltungszahlen' in their sections. The removal of burdens from higher management is for Schmalenbach an important side-effect.

In newer management literature the idea of regulatory price in a firm is taken further in theory. Thus it has been possible by mathematical programming procedures to solve the difficulties previously encountered in dealing with the data needed to determine internal prices even where there are several bottle-neck factors (Hax 1981: cols. 1694ff.). Schmalenbach had solved the problem of calculating regulatory prices only for the case of a single bottleneck factor, by using marginal utility as the basis of calculation. The concept of regulatory prices can also be transferred to organisations with multiple aims, e.g. to hospital management (Sieben 1986: 539ff.). But it is already apparent that there are considerable complexities in this, as soon as one embarks on measurement of utility and aggregation of utilities.

Finance

Alongside accountancy Schmalenbach thought it urgent to improve the theory of money and capital movements. His book *Finanzierungen* (*Finance*) was published in 1915; eight further editions, some under a modified title, followed. In accordance with the state of financing theory at the time, Schmalenbach at first concerned himself with describing individual financing processes. On the basis of his personal experience from auditing and advisory practice he knew the problems of company financing; he was able to raise this branch of knowledge, which before his time was still a branch of 'business arithmetic', to independent status.

The amount of material later caused Schmalenbach to divide *Finanzierungen* into several books. The publication in 1933 of *Kapital, Kredit und Zins in betriebswirtschaftlicher Beleuchtung* (*The Significance of Capital, Credit and Interest for the Firm*) was to serve as a theoretical introduction for the series planned in the 1940s, *Die Finanzierung der Betriebe* (*Financing Enterprises*). Schmalenbach was in no doubt that with a book on capital, credit and interest he was moving in a controversial area of national economics. But, as he wrote in the foreword, he was not intending to take sides in the theoretical argument. 'It is rather a matter of finding and describing the kind of data that we as researchers in business management need in order to evaluate financing processes'.

The intended reader is the businessman who does not want to see things superficially, but desires to gain thorough, theoretical insights. Self-confidently, Schmalenbach continues by announcing that he will discuss with particular emphasis those subjects where he suspects the existence of distorted judgements, fed by commonplace clichés. Among these are: the great effect of unproductive consumption of capital, and opposed to this the major retro-effects of the transformation of idle capital into invested capital that is used for productive aims; the importance of interest as value as opposed to interest as price; the dangers of an interest rate that does not agree with the values of capital utilisation; the warning against mystical ideas about the possibilities of extending capital; the impact of the mobilisation of loans and capital investments, and the important transforming function of the lending institutions in reshaping short-term mass deposits into long-term credits.

The work is richly illustrated by examples from all areas of the economy, so that it is still worthy of attention. The ideas, however, found no acceptance in business management studies.

The great economic crisis, with numerous company collapses, set off by the collapse of share prices on the New York Stock Exchange in 1929, was the major impetus for him to publish in 1931 a monograph on finance plans. Here he emphasised the predictive nature of a finance plan as a means to avoid financial surprises. In this connection it is interesting that Schmalenbach describes budgeting as a modish trend of that time and a borrowing of the American love of making budgets, but also believes that budgetary matters are important in the German situation, too (Schmalenbach 1940: 44).

Valuation of businesses

Schmalenbach occupied himself intensively with the question of valuing whole companies, both academically and in his consultancy activities. As early as 1917 he published in the *Zeitschrift für handelswissenschaftliche Forschung* the essay 'Die Werte von Anlagen und Unternehmungen in der Schätzungstechnik' ('Estimating the value of fixed assets and enterprises'), an early example of work stressing the importance of capitalised value in valuation theory. From the second edition of his work on *Finanzierungen*, as early as 1921, he devoted a major section to the valuation of companies; this is the basis of modern theory of company valuation.

In this regard, Schmalenbach long ago propounded central principles of valuation, such as future-referentiality and holistic evaluation, which are today accepted in business management studies and by the auditing profession. 'The value of anything is determined only by the utility that it can bring; anything which is not in some way useful has no value' (Schmalenbach 1937: 29). Basically these considerations are the starting point for the two principles: for one, what matters is not the past utility of the business, but the utility it can bring in the future (future referentiality); and then, not the utility of the individual parts of the business is the basis of evaluation, but the total utility (holistic valuation).

In arguing against valuing whole firms on the basis of individual valuation of the component parts of their assets, he makes it clear with examples that the whole is not the same as the sum of its parts (Schmalenbach 1921: 6). Alongside the principle of holism and of future referentiality, there is a third principle that arises from the consideration that the value of a firm depends on its utility: that of the subject-dependence of the value of a business. One can only speak of a utility if there is a subject (person) to perceive the usefulness; so the value depends on the subject–object relationship in the particular case.

Here Schmalenbach can be reckoned neither among the adherents of the 'objective' theory of company valuation, which starts from the idea of a company value that is valid for everybody, nor among those of the 'subjective' theory, which starts from specific values according to the investment plans and expectations of a prospective buyer. Rather he assumes that the impartial trustee, to be appointed by the two parties acting together, will first determine the value for the vendor. After that he will calculate the value of the firm for the buyer. If the value for the vendor is higher than for the buyer, the sale should not take place. If it is lower, then the neutral trustee should suggest the average of the two, so that the parties can determine the price between themselves on the basis of this valuation.

Capitalised value was recognised by Schmalenbach as the nucleus of company valuation, as it expresses the firm's profitability. But it cannot be made the sole basis for calculations. Rather he starts from the general perception that the price of economic goods is determined by two characteristics, usefulness and scarcity. Therefore as well as capitalised value, he has recourse to reproduction value, which for him marks the scarcity threshold of the company. If the capitalised earnings value is lower than the reproduction value, the capitalised earnings value must hold. But if the reproduction value is lower, Schmalenbach is in principle in favour of halving the difference between the capitalised and reproduction values, in order to take account of, for instance, increasing competition. However, this combined valuation of substance and earnings, known today as 'Praktikerverfahren', is largely rejected in the more recent theoretical literature.

Other fields of work

Schmalenbach considered numerous other business management problems as well as the areas already mentioned. These can only be dealt with summarily.

In the first few decades of this century questions of company organisation were treated as marginal in the standard handbooks. Schmalenbach's contributions occupy a special place. He did not try to develop a theoretical concept of organisation, as he thought the time was not ripe for it; but he did deal with a large number of individual problems of organisation as no other management expert of the first half of the century did (Frese 1987: 9). Even before the First World War he presented the advantages of organising large banks on a decentralised basis and in a way oriented towards the customer. Questions of organisation were also treated in the books on regulatory prices and in some manuscripts from the Second World War period. His longer work on *Dienststellengliederung im Großbetriebe* (*Divisionalisation of Concerns*), written in 1941, appeared as a book after his death, in 1959.

Schmalenbach frequently expressed himself on economic matters. Certainly his time as assistant to Karl Bücher in Leipzig influenced his statements about the connection of management studies and economics: 'As the economist cannot avoid occupying himself with matters of the enterprise, such as wages, entrepreneurial profit etc., so the management student must ask how the economic organisation in which the firm is embedded and of which it is an agent looks' (Schmalenbach 1949: 11).

Here again, Schmalenbach is concerned with efficiency in practice. In his view the biggest inefficiencies in the economy are caused by 'distorted prices', that is, prices that do not reflect the scarcity of the goods. One of the main causes for distorted prices is in his view lack of stability in the value of money. He compares this with a nervous disease in a biological body (Schmalenbach 1943b: 2).

His sensitivity to disturbances, very marked in economic as well as in business matters, is shown for instance by this remark:

> Possibly those who are of the opinion that we can legitimately use the coal reserves of the earth without scruples and without thought of our descendants, since later, for instance by atomic fission, we shall probably discover agents of equal effectiveness for purposes of power, heating and chemical products, may be right. But it is only an expectation and not a guarantee. And if the expectation is not fulfilled, our generation will look irresponsible, light-headed and silly to our descendants.
>
> (Schmalenbach 1949: 48)

About thirty years before the Club of Rome – at a time when exponential economic growth was taken for granted – shook us into environmental awareness with its dramatic reports, Schmalenbach was already pointing to possible limitations and dangers of the unlimited consumption of raw materials.

Notes

The original text in German was translated by Alfred D. White of the University of Wales College of Cardiff.

1 The once informal association of students and friends today is known as the *Schmalenbach-Gesellschaft/Deutsche Gesellschaft für Betriebswirtschaft* (Schmalenbach Society), and can be considered one of the most important forums in Germany for fostering the dialogue between management theory and practice. Its activities range from editing books and the *Zeitschrift für betriebswirtschaftliche Forschung*, the former *Zeitschrift für handelswissenschaftliche Forschung*, to the organisation of lectures, meetings and study groups on current issues of business management. In 1993 there were more than 1,400 individual and 300 corporate members.

2 These included 'Entwurf einer Dienstanweisung für Finanzleiter nebst Begründung und einer Einleitung über allgemeine Organisationsgrundsätze' (1940), 'Über die Dienststellengliederung im Großbetriebe' (1941; later published by the Schmalenbach-Gesellschaft in 1959), 'Die Lagerverwaltung unter dem Gesichtsspunkt der Dienststellengliederung' (1943), 'Über die exakte Wirtschaftslenkung', (undated; completed early 1943), 'Handelsbilanzen und andere Bilanzen' (1943), 'Gedanken eines Betriebswirtschaftlers zum Wiederaufbau zerstörter Großstädte' (1943), 'Allgemeine Grundsätze ordnungsmäßiger Bilanzierung' (1944) and 'Über die zukünftige Gestaltung der Betriebswirtschaftslehre' (1944).

3 For the literary echo of 'Dynamische Bilanz', see the list by Otto von Kori (1971: 485ff.). A commentated overview of the most important contemporary German researchers is provided in Potthoff (1993: 660ff.).

4 A comprehensive listing of publications by Schmalenbach may be found by reference to Forrester (1977, 1993); Kori (1968, 1969); Kruk *et al.* (1984: 443–55).

References[4]

Forrester, D. A. R. (1977) *Schmalenbach and After*, Strathclyde.

Forrester, D. A. R. (1993) *Eugen Schmalenbach and German Business Economics*, New York: Garland.

Frese, E. (1987) *Grundlagen der Organisation* (*Bases of Organisation*) (3rd edn), Wiesbaden.

Gutenberg, E. (1984) 'Rückblick' ('Retrospect'), *Zeitschrift für Betriebswirtschaft*: 1151–68.

Hasenack, W. (1957) 'Maßnahmen des Rechnungswesens zur Gestaltung der Eigenverantwortlichkeit in der Unternehmung' ('Accountancy Steps to Shape Personal Responsibility in Companies'), *Zeitschrift für handelswissenschaftliche Forschung* 54: 307–15.

Hax, H. (1981) 'Verrechnungspreise' ('Internal Prices'), in E. Kosiol *et al.* (eds) *Handwörterbuch des Rechnungswesens*, Stuttgart, pp. 1688–99.

Kilger, W. (1972) *Flexible Plankostenrechnung* (*Flexible Planning Costs Accounting*) (5th edn), Opladen.

Kori, Otto von (1968) 'Verzeichnis der Arbeiten von Eugen Schmalenbach' ('List of the Works of Eugen Schmalenbach'), *Zeitschrift für betriebswirtschaftliche Forschung* 20: 473–88.

Kori, Otto von (1969) 'Verzeichnis der von Eugen Schmalenbach besprochenen Bücher und Zeitschriften' ('List of Books and Periodicals Reviewed by Eugen Schmalenbach'), *Zeitschrift für betriebswirtschaftliche Forschung* 21: 525–40.

Kori, Otto von (1971) 'Besprechungen zur Dynamischen Bilanz' ('Reviews on the Dynamic Balance Sheet'), *Zeitschrift für betriebswirtschaftliche Forschung* 23: 485–7.

Kruk, M., Potthoff, E. and Sieben, G. (1984) *Eugen Schmalenbach, Der Mann – Sein Werk – die Wirkung*, Stuttgart: 443–55.

Lehmann, M. R. (1951) *Industriekalkulation* (*Industrial Estimating*), (4th edn), Stuttgart.

Potthoff, E. (1973) 'Die Funktion des wirtschaftlichen Störgefühls' ('The Use of the Feeling for Economic Wrongness'), *Der Betrieb* 26: 1609–13.

Potthoff, E. (1993) 'Forscherpersönlichkeiten' ('Researcher Personalities'), *Handwörterbuch des Rechnungswesens* (3 vols), Stuttgart, pp. 660–78.

Riebel, P. (1959) 'Das Rechnen mit Einzelkosten und Deckungsbeiträgen' ('Accounting for Individual Costs and Contributions to Costs'), *Zeitschrift für handelswissenschaftliche Forschung*, Neue Folge 11: 213–38.

Rieger, W. (1927) *Einführung in die Betriebswirtschaftslehre* (*Introduction to Business Management*), Nuremberg.

Rieger, W. (1936) *Schmalenbach's dynamische Bilanz* (*Schmalenbach's Dynamic Balance Sheet*), Stuttgart.

Rummel, K. (1949) *Einheitliche Kostenrechnung* (*Unitary Cost Accounting*) (3rd edn), Düsseldorf.

Schmalenbach, E. (1899) 'Buchführung und Kalkulation im Fabrikgeschäft' ('Industrial Bookkeeping and Cost Estimating'), *Deutsche Metall-Industrie-Zeitung* 14: 98–9.

Schmalenbach, E. (1899) 'Was sind Generalunkosten?' ('What are General Costs?'), *Deutsche Metall-Industrie-Zeitung* 14: 393–4.

Schmalenbach, E. (1903) 'Die buchhaltungstechnische Darstellung der Betriebsgebarung' ('*The Representation of Business Behaviour in Accounting*'), unpublished.

Schmalenbach, E. (1915) *Finanzierungen* (*Methods of Financing*) (1st edn), Leipzig.

Schmalenbach, E. (1917) 'Die Werte von Anlagen und Unternehmungen in der Schätzungstechnik' ('Estimating the Value of Fixed Assets and Enterprises'), *Zeitschrift für handelswissenschaftliche Forschung* 12: 1–20.

Schmalenbach, E. (1919) *Finanzierungen* (*Methods of Financing*) (2nd edn), Leipzig.

Schmalenbach, E. (1920) *Grundlagen dynamischer Bilanzlehre* (*Basic Theory of the Dynamic Balance Sheet*) (2 vols), Leipzig. Later published as *Dynamische Bilanz*.

Schmalenbach, E. (1921) *Finanzierungen* (*Methods of Financing*) (2nd edn), Leipzig.

Schmalenbach, E. (1925) *Grundlagen der Selbstkostenrechnung und Preispolitik* (*Bases of Cost Accounting and Pricing Policy*) (2 vols), Leipzig.

Schmalenbach, E. (1927) *Der Kontenrahmen* (*The Standard Chart of Accounts*) (1st edn), Leipzig.

Schmalenbach, E. (1933) *Kapital, Kredit und Zins in betriebswirtschaftlicher Beleuchtung* (*The Significance of Capital, Credit and Interest for the Firm*) (1st edn), Leipzig.

Schmalenbach, E. (1935) *Der Kontenrahmen* (*The Standard Chart of Accounts*) (4th edn), Leipzig.

Schmalenbach, E. (1937) *Finanzierungen* (*Methods of Financing*) (6th edn), Leipzig.

Schmalenbach, E. (1940) 'Entwurf einer Dienstanweisung für Finanzleiter nebst Begründung' ('Reasoned Draft of Instructions for Financial Managers'), manuscript.

Schmalenbach, E. (1941) 'Über die Dienststellengliederung im Großbetriebe' ('On Divisionalisation of Concerns'), manuscript 1941; published in 1959 by Schmalenbach-Gesellschaft, Köln und Opladen.

Schmalenbach, E. (1943a) 'Die Handelsbilanz und andere Bilanzen' ('The Trading Account and other Accounts'), manuscript.

Schmalenbach, E. (1943b) 'Über die exakte Wirtschaftslenkung' ('Exact Economic Regulations'), manuscript.

Schmalenbach, E. (1943c) 'Die Lagerverwaltung unter dem Gesichtspunkt der Dienststellengliederung' ('Divisionalisation and Administration of Stocks'), manuscript.

Schmalenbach, E. (1943d) 'Gedanken eines Betriebswirtschaftlers zum Wiederaufbau zerstörter Großstädte' ('Thoughts of a Researcher in Business Management on the Reconstruction of Devastated, Large Towns'), manuscript.

Schmalenbach, E. (1943e) 'Handelsbilanzen und andere Bilanzen' ('Financial and other Balance Sheets'), manuscript.

Schmalenbach, E. (1943f) 'Über die exakte Wirtschaftlenkung' ('On Exact Guiding of the Economy'), manuscript, undated (completed early 1943).

Schmalenbach, E. (1944) 'Allgemeine Grundsätze ordnungsmäßiger Bilanzierung' ('Bases of Orderly Accounting'), manuscript.

Schmalenbach, E. (1944) 'Über die zukünftige Gestaltung der Betriebswirtschaftslehre' ('Shaping the Science of Business Administration in the Future'), manuscript.

Schmalenbach, E. (1948a) 'Einschränkung des Pfennigdenkens' ('Limitation of Taking Care of the Pennies'), *Betriebswirtschaftliche Beiträge* 3: 12.

Schmalenbach, E. (1948b) 'Die pretiale Lenkung des Betriebes' ('Price-guiding of Companies'), *Pretiale Wirtschaftslenkung*, Band 2, Bremen-Horn.

Schmalenbach, E. (1949) *Der freien Wirtschaft zum Gedächnis* (*In Memory of the Free Economy*) (1st edn), Cologne and Opladen.

Schmidt, F. (1921) *Die organische Bilanz im Rahmen der Wirtschaft* (*The Organic Balance Sheet in the Context of the Economy*), Leipzig.

Sieben, G. (1986) *Möglichkeiten und Grenzen pretialer Lenkung im Krankenhaus, Ökonomie des Gesundheitswesens, hrsg. vom Verein für Sozialpolitik* (*Potentials and Limitations of Price-guiding in Hospitals*), Berlin.

6 Fritz Julius August Schmidt (1882–1950)

Frank Clarke and Graeme Dean

Abstract

Challenges confronted Schmidt from the time of his first university appointment. Of Schmidt's numerous published contributions, his greatest was to view things systematically, looking for general propositions from observed day-to-day particulars.

There are more similarities than dissimilarities in the respective contributions of Schmidt's *Betriebswirtschaft* and Limperg's *Bedrijfseconomie*. Traditional Schmidt lore is that his theory did not address the general price level problem and that his accounting adjustment mechanisms were incident specific (hyperinflation), not an integral part of a theory of business economics. But, there is compelling counter-evidence. That evidence also suggests that development of Schmidt's ideas on current value accounting, especially in published form, predates Limperg, even in his own native Dutch.

EARLY LIFE AND INFLUENCES

Schmidt's early experiences were summarised in the Report of the Second (Het) International Accounting Congress in 1926:

> From 1906 till 1909 he studied at the Leipzig Handelschochschule [School of Economics] and at the Universities of Leipzig and Besançon. Between 1909–1910 he was teacher at the Höhere Handelsschule [College of Business and Commerce] in Dortmund. From August 1910 until April 1912 he was research assistant, till April 1913 lecturer of business administration and since then professor at the academy and later at the University [of Frankfurt am Main]. Visiting appointments: 1912 Cologne, 1922 Mannheim, 1925 Vienna.
>
> (Schmidt 1926: 379)

Clearly, educational challenges in the area of business management confronted Schmidt from the time of his first university appointment. He faced a traditional system, geared to regurgitation of current practice. There was a lack of systematic evidence to support the teaching of business administration. Schmidt was not lacking in business experience, having previously worked for nine years in the retail business, in wholesale, manufacturing, book selling, insurance, and overseas import and export. He also had formally studied and taught economics at several German universities and in 1920 had written a primer on economics, *The Fundamentals of Economics* (2nd edn 1922). A trained economist and an observer, he had participated and written widely on stock exchange and foreign currency activities (see Voigtlaender 1952). Thus, his writings drew upon, and not unexpectedly, included criticism of current economic thought, particularly price theory, marginalism and Irving Fisher's work on indexation. Perhaps less expected was his acknowledged indebtedness to the classical economists, Ricardo and Carey (see below). On Schmidt's reliance on economic theory the words of Schwantag (1951: 3) are instructive: 'The book [*Domestic Payment Transactions*, 1920] is complemented by the description of cash payment transactions [which] are covered and also questions of monetary theory are dealt with. Schmidt's criticism of the quantity theory of money is put forward here.' Schmidt's 'organic accounting' ideas also did not mirror the mainstream. As the noted Austrian accounting historian, Seicht (1982: 47) stated, they were the product of an extensive and systematic revision of the respective selling price-based ideas of Ciompa (1910) and the replacement cost-based ideas of Kovero (1911) and Fäs (1913).

Although Schmidt's work has received increasing attention in Anglo-American countries, it has been frustrated by language barriers. Reference to Schmidt has, until recently, been restricted primarily to his contributions in *The Accounting Review* (1930b and 1931) and *The Harvard Business Review* (1930a). Yet Schmidt has been described by those able to overcome the language barrier as the progenitor of the ideas underlying replacement value theory (MacDonald 1977: 246) and as the developer of the 'first, full-fledged theoretical framework dealing with inflationary accounting' (Mattessich 1982: 351). Perceptively interpreting Schmidt's organic notion, Mattessich (1982: 354) described Schmidt's theory as a 'genuine current cost system', and as having the aim of maintaining *relative* material values in the economy. It would also have the side benefit of mitigating the cyclical nature of economic activity.

In relation to price and price level accounting Schmidt considered indexation mechanisms such as *Indexbuchführung* and *Goldmarkbilanz* to be only partial solutions (1924: 80–121). In his opinion they failed to analyse firms and their related accounting in the context of the market economy, particularly in its depressed post-war state. In this respect they lacked an organic, holistic perspective. Clearly, Schmidt perceived accounting as an integral facet of any theory of economic equilibrium (1921: 36–7). Consider the following extract, attributed to 'Schmidt 1921':

> The firm does not operate in a void, but, is rather, part of the whole market economy . . . A business manager without a clear conception of the source of his values, profits and losses would be as inconceivable as a captain without any knowledge of the current or a pilot who knows nothing about wind and weather conditions.
>
> (Isaac 1950: 126)

The fundamental, organic nature of this part of Schmidt's accounting theory is well captured by Schwantag:

> The main [academic] result of [Schmidt's early] studies is the conception of organic current value accounting *as a theory of relations of values in business administration*, derived from the relations of values in the economy . . . Rather he wants to analyse the substance of the production process of the firm from an economic point of view. The starting point is the practical experience of the effects of inflation and the fall in productivity resulting from the war and post-war period, which had lead to the disruption of the currency, the wear and tear of the stock of fixed assets and to the weakening of physical and productive working capacities to an unprecedented extent. Against this background of the economic situation of the time it was obvious that the measure of economic figures formerly held to be fixed – the money unit – was flexible in reality and that this flexibility had to be taken into account when measuring . . . But to realise that money as a measure is not fixed in general and that this causes fundamental problems for the relations of values in business administration as the basis of the disposition of firms as units of production – like private households as units of consumption – and that the solving of these tasks of disposition is of critical importance for economic equilibrium, is the unparalleled achievement of Schmidt.
>
> (Schwantag 1951: 5–6)

This organic theme is apparent also in the extract from his *Das Prinzip der relativen Werterhaltung (The Principle of the Relative Maintenance of Value)*, reproduced at the end of Schwantag's (1951) biography. Schmidt's concept of the maintained firm entailed the retention of its relative capacity to satisfy consumers' needs, its relative share of the market for its production, its relative overall size in the productive fabric of the economy. Schmidt's firm was perceived of as 'a cell in a living organism which is a market economy' (De Motte Greene 1937: 77) and thus only one of the collection of economic means to an end. Schmidt thus proposed his organic current value accounting in a deliberate attempt to place the theory of the firm and accounting for a firm in the context of a dynamic economy.

Schmidt's published contributions are considerable in number and substantial in content. He published sixteen major books, the best known in accounting being his *magnum opus, Die organische Tageswertbilanz* (1929),[1] and over 120 articles on topics encompassing stock exchange, foreign exchange and banking practices, organic current value accounting, costs and pricing, theory of trade cycles, trusts and taxation theory, and matters to do with education and the economics profession (Voigtlaender 1952).

According to Schwantag, one of Schmidt's greatest contributions was to view things systematically, to look for general propositions from observed day-to-day particulars. Schmidt's publications cover three stages: (1) books and articles (1907–18), where he recorded observations of stock exchange and banking practices, resulting in the recording and classification of business forms and methods; (2) 1918–36 works, aimed at deriving theoretical breakthroughs with respect to accounting and business economics from observed particulars; and (3) thereafter works consolidating the efforts of the second stage seeking a consistent theory of business administration. Schmidt's works on accounting occurred during a shift in European business administration thought in the early decades of the twentieth century, from static, balance-sheet oriented theories to more dynamic, income-oriented theories.[2]

Unlike most of the current accounting theorists, Schmidt contributed widely to the business literature in general. This is to be expected, in so far as the development of accounting as a discrete discipline was far less so than now. But it might also be attributed to his perception of the systemic nature of business. Clearly his perception was of an integrated set of mechanisms: price theory, monetary theory, trade and trade cycle theory, international trade and exchange rate mechanisms, financing and the operation of securities markets, employment, money and banking (Schwantag 1951). Much of that was written without direct reference to accounting, but his explication of organic theory has the integrated flair which no doubt was the product of the catholicity of view of business activity and human endeavour in a commercial environment. In his time, perhaps only Limperg might have had such a universal perspective on business affairs, but he wrote little of a substantial nature about what he is reputed to have said. In contrast, Schmidt's written contributions leave no doubt as to the developed nature of his insights. Since his time, perhaps only Raymond Chambers could be claimed to have had such vision and understanding.

SCHMIDT AND THE EMERGING *BETRIEBSWIRTSCHAFTSLEHRE* IN 1920S EUROPE

Translated material confirms that Schmidt was cognisant of the views of classical economists, in particular Ricardo (1817) and Carey (1837), who suggested that the replacement costs of factor inputs were relevant for businessmen contemplating action. This is clearly evident in Schmidt's acknowledgement (1923 and 1926)[3] of his indebtedness to these classical economists. For instance, clearly Schmidt (1923) was aware that Ricardo held that the 'determinant for the price of any good is not the actual expenditure on behalf of that good, but the costs involved in the reproduction of that good'.

Schmidt was one of a number of German academics in the 1920s pursuing the theory of business economics or theory of the firm. Indeed, he was recognised as the intellectual leader of the theorists advocating an 'organic' theory of the firm. Schranz's (1930) overview of 'modern German accountancy' theories indicated the scope of the German modifications to conventional practice. It included descriptions of the static concepts of Schaer (1890), Hügli (1894), Nicklisch (1912) and Osbahr (1912) as well as explanations of the dynamic, monist approach (originating with Schmalenbach) which contrasted with Schmidt's organic, dualistic theory. With respect to the latter, Schranz noted:

The organic balance sheet of Schmidt and his adherents is, as a matter of fact, the balance sheet of inflation times. It endeavours, to establish principles which *obtain also in the time of diminishing currency value*, that is, in the time of inflation. The organicists emphasise the principle, that only the *value of objects* must be included in the balance. It is only permitted to distribute profit, if the distribution *does not disturb the substantial reserves of the enterprise*. For the determination of results . . . values on the day when the balance sheet is constructed must be employed . . . profit derived from the sales is given by the difference between this current replacement price and the selling price. The difference between the acquisition price and the selling price . . . is to be excluded from the calculation of the income, for this difference only causes a change in the value of the business assets. We carry over the difference – as a correcting item – to the account of the enterprise's own capital. In this way we have shown the fluctuation in the purchasing power of the enterprise's own capital. In preparing the balance sheet, *we must reckon with the same values*, viz, *the current values of the day of the statement*. In this way we obtain the correct figure for the profit arising from sale, and we can eliminate the acquisition price differences.

(1930: 166, emphasis added)

Schranz's explanations invite several observations. He seems to give Schmidt the role of leader in this field of thought, the others the role of 'adherers', as being attached as followers of his central theme.[4] Similarity between Schmidt's ideas and contemporary arguments for replacement prices is beyond dispute. 'Profit' can be distributed only if 'substantial reserves' are not disturbed, he explained; profit on sales is calculated as the difference between the current selling price and the measure of the current cost of inputs, the 'current replacement price' in Schmidt's scheme; and 'value changes' in fixed assets are not income. Each is a feature of modern current cost accounting (CCA) proposals, as the features catalogued below clearly illustrate.

A considerable portion of Schmidt's writings contrasts with the ideas contained in the works of some contemporary German business economics theorists, but also many of the French writers of the 1920s. His theory was operationalized into cost accounting as well as external financial accounting, a point seemingly overlooked by Edwards and Bell (1961); the French theories, we are told mainly were not (Wasserman 1931: 8–9, notes 26 and 27).[5] Schmidt's accounting was proposed as a means that would be for the good of the economy; in contrast the French did not, in the main, allude to macro considerations. In this regard, the impact of the post-war inflation on Schmidt's thinking should not be overlooked. Of particular significance were the immediate pressure of Germany's precarious economic state following the First World War, and the crippling prospect of war reparation payments to be exacted by Britain, the USA and France (Bresciani-Turroni 1937: 274–82 and Holtfrerich 1986). In contrast the French did not have the same kind of pressure – they were to be reparation recipients. Reparation payments were a means by which French industry would be restored. For

Germany, restoration and maintenance of industry presumably would be critical to the making of the reparation payments.

SCHMIDT'S ORGANIC ACCOUNTING

The essential features of Schmidt's organic theory are:

- Business or accounting theory should be consistent with the theory of economic equilibrium. The theory of the firm is integral to a theory of accounting, an approach described as *organic*. Specifically his theory was based on the 'principle of relative maintenance of value'.
- Assets are to be shown at their costs of replacement as at the balance date.
- Contrary to the received wisdom, Schmidt understood exactly the effects of changes in the general level of prices. His examination of this issue was extensive (1922a; 1922b; 1924: 80–149; 1926: 394–8; 1927; 1929b: 68–71; 1930b: 236–8). Schwantag suggests

   that Schmidt wants to analyse the substance of the production process of the firm from an economic point of view . . . [taking account of] the effects of inflation and falling productivity . . . it was obvious that the measure of economic figures formerly held to be fixed – the money unit – was flexible in reality and that this flexibility had to be taken into account when measuring

   (1951: 6)

   In essence his organic system is a form of stabilized accounting, a point not lost on Sweeney who described Schmidt as 'the German authority . . . [on] the subject [of stabilization]' (1935: 199).[6] Schmidt in fact suggested a type of gearing adjustment nearly fifty years before the 1975 Godley and Cripps UK proposal emerged.

- 'Business profit can only be that which exceeds the amount necessary for the maintenance of a firm's productive assets' (Schmidt 1926: 384). 'The leading principle of the current value accounting approach is the maintenance of the firm in its real [physical] state . . . the firm can only generate a profit if the sales proceeds . . . are higher than cost of either replacement or reproduction at the date of sale' (Schmidt 1926: 407). Schmidt was prepared to modify his replacement cost basis for capital maintenance in the case of speculative assets which were financed by loans. This issue is dealt with in Tweedie and Whittington (1984: 28–30) and Mattessich (1984: 496).
- Changes in the values of fixed assets are not regarded as profit; the increases or decreases in values are recorded in a special capital reserve account (*Wertberichtigungskonto*).[7] Again, this principle is modified in respect of speculative assets.
- Although Schmidt recognised the distinction between general and specific price changes and their differing impacts on a business, he rejected the incorporation in the accounts of general price changes in deference to specific

price changes. However, this has to be considered in the light of his suggestion that firms should match their monetary assets and liabilities, a strategy he described as the 'identity of values in the balance sheet'. Balancing amounts of monetary assets and liabilities would protect the entity against changes in the value of money. This could be achieved, he argued, by financing real assets from owners' equity and nominal assets from debt capital (for detailed discussion see Clarke and Dean 1986: 77).

- Schmidt's work introduced ideas not held by many of his contemporaries in the German *Betriebswirtschaftslehre*. A considerable portion of his work contrasts with the ideas of some of the contemporary European theorists as noted in the more recent evaluations of Schmidt (e.g. Coenenberg and Macharzina 1976, Mattessich 1982, 1984, Tweedie and Whittington 1984 and Filios 1985).
- Schmidt's terms 'Betriebsgewinn', or according to Mattessich 'Umsatz-gewinn' and 'Spekulationsgewinn' (1984: 521) or 'Konjunktur-or-Marktgewinn' (1982: 354), were synonymous, respectively, with Edwards and Bell's 'current operating profit' and 'holding gain'.
- Throughout Schmidt's works, argument and examples are couched in terms of economics applied to commodities, from the perspective of the wholesaler, retailer or consumer. This shows Schmidt's perspective of an integrated commercial environment in which his accounting was to function. Contrary to the view proposed by Limperg, it alludes to the integral part Schmidt perceived accounting to have in any complete theory of the firm and the economy.

Schmidt, along with the Dutch academic Theodore Limperg Jr (see contribution by Camfferman and Zeff in this volume), has been acknowledged in the Anglo-American literature as providing the theoretical antecedents of modern-day versions of replacement cost accounting. As noted in the Schranz commentary, Schmidt was one of a number of German academics in the 1920s pursuing the theory of business economics. Schmalenbach, Walb, Prion, Kalveram and Mahlberg were also prominent members of that group advocating a move from the *static* (balance sheet oriented) to the *dynamic* (income account oriented) perspective.[8] The *Betrieb-swirtschaftslehre* gained popularity following the dramatic economic decline in Germany after the First World War and the concomitant inflation. Seicht (1982)[9] lists the accounting alternatives proposed to overcome the consequential distortion of the financial information that emerged:

- Utilisation of the normal or base stock method of inventory valuation; resulting in absolute maintenance of values;[10] that is, retention of capital in terms of a *base* quantity of stock on hand, so that capital is not run down by virtue of sales revenue being insufficient to finance the replacement of the same quantity of stock sold.
- Indexed paper mark accounts correction procedures (*Indexbuchführung*) that provided surrogates for replacement costs (for pricing decisions); a better data base for investment decisions and evaluation, or both. Restatements of accounts data were made progressively forwards to recast them in terms of the

number of current paper marks having the equivalent general purchasing power of the paper mark at the time of the relevant transaction,

• Balance sheet stabilization procedures; e.g. *Goldmarkbilanz*, aimed at presenting balance sheet figures in comparable purchasing power terms. Restatements were made backwards to recast the data in terms of the number of 1914 gold marks having the equivalent general purchasing power of the paper marks at the time of the relevant transaction.

• Relative maintenance of values via use of replacement cost as at the sales date (for items sold) and replacement costs as at the balance date (for unsold items). Restatements were made in terms of current replacement costs so that the value of the firm's capital was retained in the same proportion to the value of the total capital in the economy, as it bore at the date of the transaction giving rise to the original transaction data.

Inflation, unemployment and industrial dislocation in Germany immediately following the First World War, encouraged pragmatism in accounting practice. Dean, Clarke and Graves (1990) describe how, in the immediate post-war period, replacement costs of factor inputs were proposed, to be followed shortly thereafter by systems of indexed based accounting which were put forward to rectify distortions in the accounts of German companies as inflation gathered momentum. They were implemented mainly by large companies (see Mahlberg 1923: 189). Main academic support for these indexed methods came initially from Mahlberg (1921), Prion (1921), Schmalenbach (1921) and Kalveram (1923).

Whilst there is dispute over to whom the original contribution might be attributed, we have argued elsewhere that Fritz Schmidt had the earliest and greatest impact on *Betriebswirtschaftslehre* developments (Clarke and Dean 1986 and 1990). Schmidt claimed that the same input data could be used to prepare an income statement and balance sheet. Hence, as noted, he was described as a 'dualist', in contrast to some other monist members of the *Betriebswirtschaftslehre*, who suggested it was impossible to use the same data for both purposes.

Schmidt's insights as to the functions of accounting are important. The link with economic action and measurement were essential in developing Schmidt's accounting theory. Whilst recognising that the unit of measure is variable, Schmidt did not incorporate general price level changes into the accounts. In contrast he opined that good managing required managers physically to match an entity's monetary assets and liabilities. This was referred to as his 'identity of values principle', which was widely criticised by Schmalenbach, Mahlberg and others at the time as being consistent with his totalitarian views. Arguably, this managerial policy of matching monetary assets and liabilities was the antecedent of the solution to which the gearing adjustments in the mid-1970s' UK CCA proposals were directed.

SCHMIDT'S INTERNATIONAL INFLUENCE, SPECIFICALLY ON THEODORE LIMPERG AND HENRY SWEENEY

Schmidt's works clearly gained international recognition. His ideas were exposed through international accounting conference presentations in 1923 and

1926, the 1934 translation into Japanese of his *Die organische Tageswertbilanz* and the acceptance of his trade cycle/accounting hypothesis by the recognised trade cycle authority, Gottfried Haberler. Further evidence of Schmidt's international influence comes from the transportation of his ideas through the works of the Dutch theorist, Theodore Limperg and the American, Henry Sweeney.

Schmidt and Sweeney

Schmidt's ideas are recognised to have had an impact on Henry Sweeney when the latter was developing his *Stabilized Accounting* mechanism. Sweeney's references indisputably link Schmidt to the inflation debate of the post-Second World War period in the English-speaking world. However, it is unclear to what extent Sweeney agreed with Schmidt's exclusion of an adjustment for changes in the general level of prices in his accounting calculations. It has to be recalled that Sweeney's first version of *Stabilized Accounting* entailed only the scaling of historical cost generated data by numbers drawn from an index of the changes in the general level of prices – the familiar current purchasing power (CPP) mechanism.

Understandably so, for it is most likely that Sweeney was attracted to that mechanism from his familiarity with the December 1923 Darmstadt legislation, which required the hyperinflation-racked German companies to scale-down their historical cost balance-sheets to reflect general purchasing power of an equivalent number of 1914 gold marks. Sweeney's avowed preference for a replacement-price-stabilized mechanism (Clarke 1976 and 1982) quite likely was more a politically correct response to Schmidt's comments disapproving of Sweeney's first-up affinity with stabilised historical cost, than an unequivocal change of heart. Sweeney's enthusiasm for the CPP type of mechanism as outlined in his Foreword to the AICPA's *ARS6* is suggestive of his deeper commitment to the CPP method.

None the less, Sweeney's role in changing the attention of western accountants on such matters forges a link between the debates over how to inject accounts with the financial effects of price and price-level changes and Schmidt's seminal contributions to accounting thought, particularly on those matters. From an epistemological perspective the Sweeney–Schmidt linkage reorientates the pervading reference to Limperg (and his Philips connection) being the dominant source of thought and practice in relation to replacement price valuation in the English-speaking world. Nothing need be taken from Limperg's masterly contribution to the discipline of accounting. His place in the history of accounting thought is well established and well-earned – though perhaps not exactly what it is claimed to be.

Unquestionably, Sweeney's personal contribution was to popularise methods of stabilising accounting data to account for the financial effect of price and price-level changes. Schmidt's influence on him, though open to speculation in respect to its translation into the mechanism explicated, provides a more direct linkage than the mainly folklore of what Limperg said and what he might have written had he been so inclined. The link with Limperg is now further addressed.

Schmidt and Limperg: an assessment

Many people in the Anglo-American literature and even the European literature have alluded to the significance of Theodore Limperg's ideas in the context of developing systematic CCA proposals (e.g. Goudeket 1952, van Seventer 1975, van der Schroeff 1959, and Camfferman and Zeff in this volume). However, Schmidt's influence has also been gaining recognition, especially in the Anglo-American literature, (Zeff 1976, Mattessich 1982, Tweedie and Whittington 1984, Graves 1985, Clarke and Dean 1986, 1989, 1990 and 1992 and Dean and Clarke 1989). Renewed interest in both authors' works, however, has produced contradictory evidence regarding the primacy issue and whether their respective theories differed. Some now even suggest that Schmidt's work not only predates Limperg's but that its theoretical structure is equally formidable (MacDonald 1977, Tweedie and Whittington 1984 and Clarke and Dean 1986 and 1992).

Schmidt published his 1923 article for the Dutch audience following lengthy periods of fluctuations in both prices and price levels in the Netherlands. The article, 'De winst van de onderneming', appeared in the first two issues of a *Bedrijfseconomie* journal, *De naamlooze vennootschap roermond* (15 February and 15 March 1923). It contained the major elements of his theory, based on his 1921 book, *Die organische Bilanz in Rahmen der Wirtschaft*. To our knowledge the first reference in the Anglo-American literature to this 1923 Dutch publication occurred relatively recently (Clarke and Dean 1986). Its subject matter, a thorough discussion of what constitutes business profit, essentially is a summary of Schmidt's organic theory, as initially developed and published in his 1921 classic. This 1921/23 organic theme was expanded subsequently to form the basis of his 2nd International Accountants Congress paper, 'Profit and Balance Sheet Value', delivered in German.[11] The International Congress was held in Amsterdam in October 1926.

The significance of this (1926) paper is evident from its reproduction, virtually verbatim, in Schmidt's 1929 third edition (pp. 54–90) of *Die organische Tageswertbilanz*; and also with the recognition that a little-referenced 1929 article by Schmidt appearing in *The Accountant* (1929b), also consisted primarily of a rearrangement of this 1926 paper. The existence of the 1923 Dutch publication, coupled to the consistency of Schmidt's ideas over time, lends added support for those arguing that Schmidt's theory was complete and accessible in Germany and Holland by as early as 1923. It is likely that MacDonald, an early speculator on those events, was unaware of the existence of the 1923 paper as he drew his controversial inference about the primacy of Schmidt's work, with reference only to the 1926 international congress paper (1977: 246).

On the basis of available translations of both authors' works, it appears that there are more similarities than dissimilarities in the ideas of Schmidt and Limperg. This proposition results in several myths being debunked, including the suggestion that Schmidt neither addressed changes in the general level of prices in his theory nor distinguished between price and price-level changes (see Zeff 1976); and that Schmidt's account adjustment mechanisms were incident-specific (hyperinflation) and not an integral part of a theory of business economics (Groeneveld *et al.* 1964: vol. I). We agree with the proposition of MacDonald (1977: 246) that it is Schmidt's work that was probably the primary antecedent of replacement cost accounting as we know it in the Anglo-American literature today. MacDonald concludes that it was Schmidt's system of accounting (expatiated upon by Dutch academics), that was subsequently applied by Philips. This proposition gains further credence when one considers the substance of Schmidt's 1923 paper, and the fact that prior to its publication Limperg had published nothing substantial in this area; a point recognised even by supporters of Limperg (e.g. van Seventer 1975: 68).

Schmidt's Replacement Value and Limperg's Replacement Cost

Dispute over primacy and the supposed differences between Schmidt's replacement prices and Limperg's replacement values also has added to the impression of a substantial theoretical rift between them. In *Bedrijfseconomie* (Groeneveld *et al.* 1964: vol. II) there is reference to the point made subsequently by Mey (1966: 14–15; Bloom and Debessay 1984: 138) that Limperg's replacement value and Schmidt's replacement cost concepts differ. The entrenched idea that the differences are significant comes through strongly, for example in the following extracts from Groeneveld *et al.* (vol. II):

- At page 62: 'Replacement value is nothing but the quantitative representation of the significance of a good, seen from the point of view of the *Sacrifices* which have to be made for its replacement'.
- At page 66 regarding sacrifices: 'it is not a matter of *replacement* but of *substitution* of the same capacity'.
- At page 72: 'It is fundamentally important that the significance of the difference [between replacement value and replacement cost] should be kept in mind: it being hidden in the varying conditions of the stock and of the market personnel for the price formation of the good which has already been produced and the good which still has to be produced.'

It is unclear just what Mey (1966) perceived to have been the differences between replacement cost and replacement value. Limperg was supposed to have proposed the latter and Schmidt the former. Mey's explanations at that point are less than satisfactory for distinguishing one from the other. This is especially disturbing, bearing in mind that he uses the allusion to those differences as a point of departure in distinguishing Limperg's theory of business economics from Schmidt's. Earlier in the same (1966) article, Mey had contrasted outlays (expenditures), with costs. The former, he explained, were 'derived from cash based accounting,' whereas the latter related to 'sacrifices, technically required and economically unavoidable . . .' (p. 4). Aggregating the current or replacement values of those factor inputs gave the value of the product (p. 5). It seems, according to Mey, that Limperg's notion of replacement value was equivalent to the dollar value of the current factor inputs, including the imputed value of administration (pp. 6, 9, 11 and 12). This integral unit cost '. . . measures the replacement value of a product to its producer', he explains (p. 6).

Mey's contrasting of the respective theories of Limperg and Schmidt might be seen in the context of those passages as a distinction between a variety of imputed current factor cost (supposedly Limperg's replacement value) and the actual current cost of replacing the good sold (Schmidt's replacement price).

Such a distinction is worth making, if that is what Mey intended. For it does distinguish between the notions of current cost or current value that Limperg and Schmidt were perceived to have been using. But there are problems with that interpretation of the distinction as Mey describes it. Certainly, that interpretation of Limperg's theory of replacement value would give little comfort to those who have alluded to his theory to draw support for their own variety of replacement price accounting (current cost accounting). Imputing a factor cost corresponding to Mey's description has not been part of the generic varieties of replacement price (or current cost) proposals which have alluded for theoretical support to what Limperg allegedly said. Mey's purpose was to illustrate how Limperg's value was objectively determined by recourse to current prices of those factor inputs as, usually, there are available market quotations (p. 15). But imputation of factor costs is likely to involve allocation of common costs, which is almost certain to be highly subjective, no matter how sophisticated one might be in devising the basis (or cost-driver). At this point it is worth noting that as early as 1923 Schmidt in his Dutch article had suggested the need to include the current costs of *all* factor inputs, including depreciation of fixed assets.

A further essential of Mey's explanation was to illustrate how Schmidt's notion of replacement price entailed the transfer of the confusion between outlays and values from the past, to the future, on the grounds that Schmidt's replacement price was an estimate of the future price that would be paid when replacement occurred. That seems at odds with Schmidt's explanation that his organic income calculation would inject the current prices for the goods sold and property consumed in the production process prevailing at the date of sale, those existing during the turnover cycle. That stands in stark contrast with Mey's description and interpretation of Schmidt's organic theory. It also appears to accord more with the CCA proposals of the 1970s and 1980s than Limperg's system, at least as Mey explains it.

This appearance of conflict between what Limperg and Schmidt are considered to have meant is indicative of the confusion which surrounds their contributions. No doubt some of this is due to the received wisdom that Limperg and Schmidt were miles apart in their thinking. Some of those perceptions must be rooted home to those who authored *Bedrijfseconomie* and reproduced their recollections of Limperg's criticism of Schmidt's work. But the fact remains that the thinness of Limperg's own written explanations of his theory has placed everyone who tries to reconstruct it at a distinct disadvantage. An extended discussion of this supposed rift appears in Clarke and Dean (1992, esp.: 295–6).

SUMMARY

The recent evidence now supports an inference that there are more similarities than dissimilarities in the respective contributions of Schmidt and Limperg. Sifting through recent translations, many provided in works by Clarke and Dean (1990 and 1992), opens to question much of the traditional Schmidt lore: the suggestions that Schmidt did not address the general price-level problem in his theory and that his accounting adjustment mechanisms were incident specific (hyperinflation) and not an integral part of a theory of business economics. There is also support for the suggestion that the so-called developments associated with modern CCA prescriptions, the value to the owner and the Hyde gearing proposals, were in fact contained in the proposals of Limperg or Schmidt.

Finally, there is compelling evidence to support the proposition that the development of Schmidt's ideas on current value accounting, especially in published form, predates Limperg, even in his native Dutch. Schmidt's works were undeniably extensive and impressive for their breadth and their systematic character and their impact on the development world-wide of replacement cost accounting.

Reassessments certainly suggest that Schmidt rightly holds the mantle of being one of the leading thinkers in twentieth-century accounting thought.

Notes

This account of Fritz Schmidt's life and works draws on a eulogy by one of his students, Schwantag (1951), and also on Voigtlaender's (1952) bibliography of Schmidt's works and an analysis of his contributions by Clarke and Dean (1986, 1990 and 1992). The first two items appeared in *Zeitschrift für Betriebswirtschaft*, a leading German business economics journal, founded by Schmidt in 1924 and edited by him till his death in 1950. They appeared in translation in Clarke and Dean (1986).

1 Schmidt, *Die organische Tageswertbilanz* (1929a). This was the third edition with the first appearing in 1921 and the second in 1922.
2 Forrester (1992) describes many aspects of the German *Betriebswirtschaftslehre*, including the differences between static and dynamic theories (esp. pp. 154–5, Fig. 5.25).
3 The latter was originally presented at the Second International Accounting Congress (Schmidt 1926); then published in *Zeitschrift für Betriebswirtschaft*, vol. 3 (1926: 813–25, 906–29), and eventually included (almost verbatim) in Schmidt (1929a: 54–90).
4 Schneider (1981: 137–8) confirms Schmidt as that movement's leader.
5 The ideas of French theorists in the mid-to-late 1920s need to be presented and analysed exhaustively in the Anglo-American literature. This would help historians better understand how *European* inflation accounting thought developed.
6 This point has been questioned by O. F. Graves (1991).
7 Schmidt used the following synonyms to depict this capital adjustment account: *Wertänderungskonto, Vermögenswertkonto, Wertberichtigungskonto*. The adjustment account corresponds to the more recent current cost adjustment reserve account, a feature of the CCA proposals in the 1970s and early 1980s.
8 See Schneider (1981) and Seicht (1982). Both publications appear in German only. De Motte Greene (1937) provides an extensive description of these German accounting theories in English, whilst a summary is contained in Schranz (1930).
9 This is a condensed version of his doctoral work (1970). Both appear in German only. Older summaries of these proposals abound, including Kalveram (1923), Mahlberg

(1923: 206–46) and Schmidt (1924: 80–121). For a critique of Seicht's work, see Schneider (1973). We thank A. Wagenhofer, Universität Graz, for this reference.

10 For a discussion of the use of this method, refer to Schmidt (1931: 292) and Sweeney (1936: 169–70).

11 The 2nd International Congress was also the venue of Limperg's 'now famous congress speech of 1926 about "The meaning of the Accountant's Certificate in Connection with the Accountants' Responsibilities"' (*Bedrijfseconomie*, 1964). It is of interest that his major address at this congress did not discuss business economics issues, but rather auditing issues. He did, however, comment on Schmidt's Business Profit paper and J. M. Clark's paper on Valuation.

References

Bloom, R. and Debessay, A. (1984) *Inflation Accounting: Reporting of General and Specific Price Changes*, New York: Praeger.

Bresciani-Turroni, C. (1937) *The Economics of Inflation*, London: Allen & Unwin.

Carey, H. C. (1837) *Principles of Political Economy: The Laws of the Production and Distribution of Wealth*, vol. I; reprinted by Augustus M. Kelley, 1965.

Chambers, R. J. (1966) *Accounting, Evaluation and Economic Behavior*, Englewood Cliffs, NJ: Prentice-Hall.

Ciompa, P. (1910) *Grundriss einer Oekonometrie und die auf der Nationalökonomie aufgebaute natürliche Theorie der Buchhaltung – Ein auf Grund neuer ökonometrischer Gleichungen erbrachter Beweis, dass alle heutigen Bilanzen falsch dargestellt werden*, Lemberg: C. E. Pöschel.

Clark, J. M. (1980) 'Valuation for the Balance Sheet and Profits': 369–77, *Proceedings, Het Internationaal Accountantscongres*, J. Muuses, Purmerend, 1926. Reprinted by Arno Press, New York.

Clarke, F. L. (1976) 'A Closer Look at Sweeney's Stabilised Accounting Proposals', *Accounting and Business Research*, Autumn: 264–75.

Clarke, F. L. (1982) *The Tangled Web of Price Variation Accounting*, New York: Garland.

Clarke, F. L. and Dean, G. W. (1986) 'Schmidt's *Betriebswirtschaft* Theory', *Abacus*, September: 65–102.

Clarke, F. L. and Dean, G. W. (1989) 'Conjectures on the Influence of the 1920s *Betriebswirtschaftslehre* on Henry Sweeney's *Stabilized Accounting*', *Accounting and Business Research*, Autumn: 291–304.

Clarke, F. L. and Dean, G. W. (1990) *Contributions of Limperg and Schmidt to the Replacement Cost Debate in the 1920s*, New York: Garland Publishing Inc.

Clarke, F. L. and Dean, G. W. (1992) 'The Views of Limperg and Schmidt: Discovering Patterns and Identifying Differences from a Chaotic Literature', *The International Journal of Accounting* 27(4): 287–309.

Coenenberg, A. and Macharzina, K. (1976) 'Accounting for Price Changes: An Analysis of Current Developments in Germany', *Journal of Business Finance and Accounting*, Spring: 53–68.

Dean, G. W. and Clarke, F. L. (1989) 'A Note: Graves, Sweeney and *Goldmarkbilanz* – Whither Sweeney and Schmidt's *Tageswertbilanz*?', *The Accounting Historians Journal*, June: 101–9.

Dean, G. W., Clarke, F. L. and Graves, O. F. (1990) *Replacement Costs and Accounting Reform in Post World War I Germany*, New York: Garland Publishing Inc.

De Motte Green, C. (1937) *The Dynamic Balance Sheet: A German Theory of Accounting*, Ph.D. thesis, UCLA. Published by Arno Press, New York, 1980.

Edwards, E. O. and Bell, P. W. (1961) *The Theory and Measurement of Business Income*, Berkeley, Calif.: University of California Press.

Fäs, E. (1913) *Die Berücksichtigung der Wertverminderung des stehenden Kapitals in den Jahresbilanzen der Erwerbswirtschaften*, Tübingen: H. Laupp.

Filios, V. (1985) 'Some German Financial Accounting Theories', Working Paper no. 17, University of Sydney Accounting Research Centre, May.

Fisher, I. (1911) *The Purchasing Power of Money*, London: Macmillan. German edition, *Die Kaufkraft des Geldes*, Berlin: Julius Springer, 1916.

Forrester, D. (1992) *Eugen Schmalenbach and German Business Economics*, New York: Garland Publishing Inc.

Goudeket, A. (1952) 'Fluctuating Price Levels in Relation to Accounts', *Proceedings of the Sixth International Congress of Accountants*, London: Gee & Co.

Goudeket, A. (1960) 'An Application of Replacement Value Accounting', *Journal of Accountancy*, July: 37–47.

Graves, O. F. (1985) 'Accounting for Inflation: German Theory of the 1920s; Schmidt, Mahlberg, Current Value Accounting' (unpublished Ph.D. thesis, Alabama).

Graves, O. F. (1987) 'Accounting for Inflation: Henry Sweeney and the German Gold-Mark Model', *Accounting Historians Journal*, Spring: 33–55.

Graves, O. F. (1989) 'Walter Mahlberg's Valuation Theory: An Anomaly in the Development of Inflation Accounting', *Abacus*, March: 7–25.

Graves, O. F. (1991) 'Fritz Schmidt, Henry Sweeney and Stabilised Accounting', *Accounting and Business Research*, Spring: 119–24.

Groeneveld, G. L., Haccon, J. F., Kleerekoper, S., Limperg, E. and Misset, H. A. J. F. (1964) *Bedrijfseconomie: verzameld werk van Prof. Dr. Th. Limperg, Jr.*, Deventer: A. E. Klewer, vol. I, 1964; II, 1968; III–VII, 1965.

Guttmann, W. and Meehan, P. (1975) *The Great Inflation*, London: Saxon House.

Holtfrerich, C. L. (1986) *The German Inflation: 1914–1923*, Berlin: de Gruyter.

Hügli, F. (1894) *Die konstante Buchhaltung*, Berne.

Isaac, A. (1950) 'Fritz Schmidt, Forscher und Persönlichkeit', *Zeitschrift für handelswissenschaftliche Forschung*, New Series, vol. 2.

Kalveram, W. (1923) *Die kaufmännische Rechnungsführung unter dem Einfluss der Geldentwertung*, Berlin: Spaeth und Linde.

Kindelberger, C. P. (1982) *A Financial History of Western Europe*, London: Allen & Unwin.

Kovero, I. (1911) *Die Bewertung der Vermögensgegenstände in den Jahresbilanzen der privaten Unternehmungen mit besonderer Berücksichtigung der nicht realisierten Verluste und Gewinne*, Berlin, 1912; Helsinki.

Limperg, T. (1926) 'The Accountant's Certificate in Connection with the Accountant's Responsibilities', *Proceedings, Het Internationaal Accountantscongres*, Purmerend: J. Muuses, pp. 85–104. Reprinted by Arno Press, New York, 1980.

Limperg, T. (1937) 'De gevolgen van de depreciatie van de gulden voor de berekening van waarde en winst in het bedrijf', *Maanblad voor Accountancy en Bedrijfshuishoudkunde*, January: 14–31.

MacDonald, E. B. (1977) Postscript, in W. Baxter and S. Davidson (eds) *Studies in Accounting*, London: ICAEW.

Mahlberg, W. (1921) *Bilanztechnik und Bewertung bei schwankender Währung*, Leipzig: G. A. Gloeckner, 1921; 2nd edn 1922; 3rd edn 1923a.

Mattessich, R. (1982) 'On the Evolution of Inflation Accounting', *Economia Aziendale* 1(3): 349–81.

Mattessich, R. (1984) 'Fritz Schmidt (1882–1950) and His Pioneering Work of Current Value Accounting in Comparison to Edwards and Bell's Theory', *Proceedings of Fourth International Congress of Accounting Historians*, Pisa: Editrice.

Mey, A. (1966) 'Theodore Limperg and his Theory of Costs and Values', *Abacus*, September: 3–23.

Nicklisch, H. (1912) *Allgemeine kaufmännische Betriebslehre als Privatwirtschaftslehre des Handels und der Industrie*, Stuttgart.

Osbahr, W. (1912) *Die Bilanz vom Standpunkt der Unternehmung*, Berlin and Leipzig: G. A. Gloeckner, 1912, 1st edn; 1923, 3rd edn.

Prion, W. (1921) *Die Finanzierung und Bilanz wirtschaftlicher Betriebe unter dem Einfluss der Geldentwertung*, Berlin: Julius Springer.

Ricardo, D. (1817) *On The Principles of Political Economy and Taxation*; reprinted by Cambridge University Press in 1953.

Sandilands Committee (1975) *Inflation Accounting: Report of the Inflation Accounting Committee*, Cmnd, 6225, London: HMSO.

Schaer, J. R. (1890) *Versuch einer wissenschaftlichen Behandlung der Buchhaltung*, Basle.

Schmalenbach, E. (1921) 'Geldwertausgleich in der bilanzmässigen Erfolgsrechnung', *Zeitschrift für handelswissenschaftliche Forschung*, October: 401–17.

Schmidt, F. (1921) *Die organische Bilanz in Rahmen der Wirtschaft*, Leipzig: G. A. Gloeckner 1921; 2nd edn, *Die organische Tageswertbilanz*, 1922; 3rd edn, 1929a.

Schmidt, F. (1922a) 'Gewinn und Scheingewinn der Unternehmung', *Zeitschrift für Aktienwesen*: 50–6.

Schmidt, F. (1922b) 'Bilanzberichtigung durch indexziffern (Goldmarkbilanz)', *Zeitschrift für Aktienwesen*: 484–92.

Schmidt, F. (1923a) *Der Wiederbeschaffungspreis des Umsatztages in Kalkulation und Volkswirtschaft*, Berlin: Spaeth und Linde.

Schmidt, F. (1923b), 'De winst van de onderneming', *De naamlooze vennootschap roermond*, 15 February and 15 March: 301–4 and 332–4.

Schmidt, F. (1924) *Bilanzwert, Bilanzgewinn und Bilanzumwertung*, Berlin: Spaeth und Linde.

Schmidt, F. (1926) 'Profit and Balance Sheet Value': 378–436, *Proceedings, Het Internationaal Accountantscongres*, Purmerend: J. Muuses. Reprinted by Arno Press, New York, 1980.

Schmidt, F. (1927) 'Die Industriekonjunktur – Ein Rechenfehler!', *Zeitschrift für Betriebswirtschaft* 4: 1–29, 87–114 and 165–99.

Schmidt, F. (1929a) *Die organische Tagesuertbilang* (3rd edn), Leipzig: Gloeckner.

Schmidt, F. (1929b) 'The Valuation of Fixed Assets in Financial Statements', *The Accountant*, 16 November: 616–29.

Schmidt, F. (1930a) 'The Basis of Depreciation Charges', *The Harvard Business Review*, April: 257–64.

Schmidt, F. (1930b) 'The Importance of Replacement Value', *The Accounting Review*, September: 235–42.

Schmidt, F. (1931) 'Is Appreciation Profit?', *The Accounting Review*, September: 289–93.

Schneider, von D. (1973) 'Renaissance der Bilanztheorie', *Zeitschrift für betriebswirtschaftliche Forschung*, pp. 29–58.

Schneider, von D. (1981) *Geschichte betriebswirtschaftlicher Theorie*, Munich and Vienna: R. Oldenbourg.

Schranz, A. (1930) 'Modern German Accountancy', *The Accounting Review*, June: 165–7.

Schwantag, K. (1951) 'F. Schmidts wissenschaftliches Werk', *Zeitschrift für Betriebswirtschaft*, January: 1–9.

Seicht, G. (1970) *Die kapitaltheoretische Bilanz und die Entwicklung der Bilanztheorie*, Berlin: Duncker und Humblot.

Seicht, G. (1982) *Bilanztheorien*, Vienna: Physica.

Sweeney, H. W. (1927), 'Effects of Inflation on German Accounting', *Journal of Accountancy*, March: 178–91.

Sweeney, H. W. (1928) 'German Inflation Accounting', *Journal of Accountancy*, February: 104–16.

Sweeney, H. W. (1935) 'The Technique of Stabilized Accounting', *The Accounting Review*, June: 185–205.

Sweeney, H. W. (1936) *Stabilized Accounting*, New York: Harper and Brothers. Reprinted by Arno Press, New York 1980.

Sweeney, H. W. (1964 reprint) *Stabilized Accounting*, New York: Holt, Rinehardt and Winston.

Tweedie, D. and Whittington, G. (1984) *The Debate on Inflation Accounting*, Cambridge: Cambridge University Press.

van der Schroeff, H. J. (1959) 'Limperg's Theorie van de Vervangingswaarde', *Maanblad voor Accountancy*, December: 557–61.

van Seventer, A. (1969) 'The Continuity Postulate in the Dutch Theory of Business Income', *The International Journal of Accounting, Education and Research*, Spring: 1–9.

van Seventer, A. (1975) 'Replacement Value Theory in Modern Dutch Accounting', *The International Journal of Accounting, Education and Research*, Fall: 67–93.

Voigtlaender, Dr (1952) 'Bibliographie: Das wissenschaftliche Werk von F. Schmidt', *Zeitschrift für Betriebswirtschaft*, January: 182–5.

Wasserman, M. (1931) 'Accounting Practice in France During the Period of Monetary Inflation', *The Accounting Review*, March: 1–32.

Whittington, G. (1983) *Introduction to the Debate on Inflation Accounting*, Cambridge: Cambridge University Press.

Zeff, S. A. (1976) *Asset Appreciation, Business Income and Price-Level Accounting, 1918–1935*, New York: Arno Press.

7 The contributions of Theodore Limperg Jr (1879–1961) to Dutch accounting and auditing

Kees Camfferman and Stephen A. Zeff

Abstract

Limperg's influence on Dutch accounting and auditing should be understood against the background of both his experience as a prominent practising auditor and his attempt to construct, as an academic, an integrated theory of *bedrijfseconomie*. This chapter describes the context, rather than the detailed contents, of his two most important contributions, current value accounting and the theory of the social role of the auditor. These descriptions are followed by an assessment of the reception and influence of Limperg's views in The Netherlands and abroad.

LIFE AND CHARACTER[1]

Theodore Limperg (1879–1961) was born in Amsterdam, where he was to live and work throughout his life. His father was a civil engineer working for the municipal department of public works. After primary school, Limperg followed the five-year curriculum at the Amsterdam Commercial School (Openbare Handelsschool). This was a quite select secondary school which prepared students for functions in business by offering practice-oriented courses in such subjects as foreign languages, law, bookkeeping, economics and statistics. By the middle 1920s, many of its graduates occupied key positions in business and commerce. Of the twenty-two men who graduated with Limperg in 1897, by 1925 thirteen were listed as managing directors of companies, including one bank, or as partners in trading firms.

It is unclear how Limperg earned a living between 1897 and 1900. What is known is that, in 1898, he passed an examination in bookkeeping organised by the Rotterdam association of trade apprentices known as Mercurius, which, according to the association's terms, implied that he was in fact employed in business. Late in 1900, he obtained the government-sponsored qualification for teaching bookkeeping in secondary schools, the so-called Acte Boekhouden M. O. KXII. This degree was usually taken after part-time study or evening classes and functioned to a certain extent as a general benchmark in accounting education. Many holders of the degree worked in accounting practice; a number of them became prominent members of the auditing profession.[2]

In the spring of 1900, Limperg was made an assistant auditor, presumably in the same Amsterdam firm of which he became a partner in July 1901. He was to remain an audit firm partner, in a succession of changing partnerships, until 1922. From 1916 until 1922 he was in partnership with his brother, L. Limperg (1881–1949), who is not known to have played a significant role in the organised Dutch auditing profession.

In 1901, Limperg had neither legally come of age (at the time, the legal age was twenty-three) nor completed any programme of study in auditing. Yet, despite this lack of formal qualifications, Limperg's astonishing precociousness allowed him to play, almost from the start of his career, a dominating role during the formative years of the Dutch auditing profession.

Limperg obtained his credentials as an auditor in 1904 by passing the examinations of the Dutch Institute of Auditors (Nederlandsch Instituut van Accountants,[3] or NIvA), which was founded in 1895. The auditing profession in The Netherlands during the first years of the twentieth century was still very loosely organised. Those who called themselves auditors had grouped themselves in four or five rival organisations, or were not members of any organisation at all. Among members of the NIvA, the senior and largest organisation, the quality of work varied considerably, and professional examinations were still at an experimental stage. In the next few years, Limperg devoted himself to but one goal: to improve the standard of performance by the auditor and thus to raise the auditor's professional status. In 1903, he became the editor of a monthly journal, *Accountancy*, which he used, until 1924, as a platform for venting his views on auditing technique, professional education, ethics, and the organisation and legal recognition of the auditing profession. The high standards he advocated brought him into conflict with senior members of the NIvA, who were comfortable with the less demanding ways of accepted practice. In 1906, Limperg and a few like-minded auditors broke away from the NIvA after a quarrel, insignificant in itself, on a point of honour with the NIvA's management board. They founded their own Dutch Association of Auditors (Nederlandsche Accountants Vereeniging), which, in its Code of Professional Conduct, its examination system and its disciplinary boards, was moulded according to Limperg's strict ideals. In 1919, the Association merged, on Limperg's terms, into the NIvA. As a result of the merger, the NIvA established itself as the most prominent among a still considerable number of rival organisations, and it also became a stronghold of Limperg's views.

At about this time, Limperg's life entered a second phase. In 1922, the Municipal University of Amsterdam established a department of economics. Limperg had for many years advocated the establishment of such a department and had used the society of alumni of the Amsterdam Commercial School, of which he was a prominent member, as a means for organising support for this idea. It was therefore not surprising that Limperg was offered and accepted the chair of *Bedrijfshuishoudkunde*[4] at the new department. He was to remain a full-time professor until 1950.

In the university curriculum, *bedrijfseconomie* and *algemene economie* ('general economics', which would simply be described as 'economics' in English) were the two core subjects, considered to be of equal importance. This made Limperg a key figure in what was, initially, a very small department. The broad scope of *bedrijfs-economie* (see note 4) meant that he lectured on a wide range of topics. During the 1930s, Limperg began to be assisted by lecturers who used his notes. In 1929, the department added a post-graduate course in auditing in which Limperg was also involved. Finally, he supervised seven out of the twenty-five doctorate theses completed in the department over the period 1922–50.

During these years, Limperg's efforts were directed not only at developing the organisational life of the new department. He also attempted to reshape the subject of *bedrijfseconomie* itself. Hence, his ongoing struggle to bring order to the nascent auditing profession was complemented by equally tenacious attempts to impose theoretical rigour on what was then an ill-defined academic discipline. During the years of his professorship, he produced a large body of systematic theory on *bedrijfs-economie*, including his theory of current value accounting and his views on auditing, which are discussed in more detail in the following sections.

Although a professor, Limperg did not limit himself to purely academic pursuits. He continued to play an active role in the NIvA. Until 1929, he chaired the NIvA's Examinations Bureau. Afterwards, he continued to serve as an examiner until 1948. From 1931 to 1947, he presided over an important committee charged with reformulating the NIvA's Code of Professional Conduct.

He also served on a number of committees, commissions and advisory boards, both in government and in the private sector, dealing with a wide range of topics, such as the introduction of accounting requirements in the Dutch Commercial Code in 1929, the legal regulation of the auditing profession and issues relating to Amsterdam commerce, old-age pensions and post-war reconstruction. He was active in the Dutch Institute for Efficiency and in the Conseil International de l'Organisation Scientifique, of which he was president from 1932 to 1935 and honorary president until 1953.

In the 1930s, he contributed to the public debate on government economic policy during the Depression (e.g. Limperg 1938). Politically, he would probably have to be described as a moderate socialist, but he was careful to separate this aspect of his life from his academic work. During the Second World War, his outspoken support for the student resistance movement meant that he had to go into hiding from 1943 onwards. Throughout and after his professorship, he served in an advisory capacity to his former auditing firm, until advancing age forced him to cease all professional activities. Regarding his private life, Limperg married in 1906 and had three children.

Both as an auditor and as an academic, Limperg single-mindedly dedicated himself to the pursuit of perfection. Dogged self-confidence in his ability to meet his own high standards gave him an unshakeable conviction of the superiority of his views which seldom failed to provoke strong reactions in his audiences. Limperg found it difficult to countenance dissent or to admit the relativist nature of his insights, and the intransigence displayed in conflicts with his many opponents often earned him epithets like 'dogmatic' and 'rigid'. At the same time, those whom he managed to win over to his convictions formed a circle of loyal adherents who only half in jest spoke of him as 'the great master' and of themselves as his 'disciples'. And many, whatever their views on Limperg's theories, have paid tribute to his kindness, his warm interest in others and his concern for social issues that were as much part of his character as his occasionally off-putting rigour.

THEORY[5]

Bedrijfseconomie[6]

At the start of Limperg's professorship in 1922, he was charged with teaching a subject that was still hardly defined. At the time only Rotterdam had, since 1913, a School of Economics. By the example of this other university, instruction in *bedrijfseconomie* consisted of inculcating a sense of pragmatism and of teaching students to solve loosely connected practical business problems by common sense and *ad hoc* reasoning. This approach to *bedrijfseconomie* was epitomised by Rotterdam professor J. G. Ch. Volmer, who had been the leading partner of the firm that Limperg had joined in 1901. It would surely not have been difficult for Limperg to follow the example of his close associate. His experience as an auditor over the previous twenty years presumably had provided him with an ample store of case material, rules of thumb and knowledge of the way in which problems were solved in practice. That Limperg nevertheless was to choose an entirely different course became evident in the inaugural lecture given, in accordance with Dutch custom, at the start of his professorship in 1922. Here he showed his conviction that, being called to give academic instruction, it was his duty as a professor to impart the results of sound scientific research. Since academic *bedrijfseconomie* was still in its infancy, Limperg saw it as his responsibility to take a fundamental starting point by beginning to define the nature of 'research' in the context of *bedrijfseconomie*.

In Limperg's view, the science of *bedrijfseconomie* was inseparable from the science of economics in general. It was merely a matter of a convenient division of labour that some economists would specialise in the study of the management and operation of enterprise. The closed and complex nature of modern businesses made their affairs difficult for most economists to observe and understand. Only those trained in practice to use the peculiar instrument suitable for observing the enterprise, the accounting system, could usefully participate in this kind of study.

But this use of specialised techniques for gathering data did not mean that there was a fundamental difference in analysis between the two spheres of economics. Once having accepted that *bedrijfseconomie* is a branch of economics in general, Limperg took what he regarded as the proper scientific approach to economics, and applied it with unflinching rigour to *bedrijfseconomie*. In accordance with prevailing notions of science, Limperg took causes, not phenomena, as the starting point of his research. A proper division of labour among sciences required that each science concern itself with the explanation of phenomena on the basis of a single primal force or cause. For economists, the primal force was the rational striving towards greater welfare, towards a lessening of the gap between wants and means. This force he called the 'economic motive' (BE, I: 31).

Economic motive was applied by Limperg as a latter-day Occam's razor in developing economic theory: an analysis based on anything but economic motive should not be allowed, and, consequently, the economist should refrain from studying phenomena that could not be explained by economic motive. In a similar way, an economist occupied with *bedrijfseconomie* should not try to explain enterprise phenomena in their entirety, but only in so far as they were explicable by economic motive.

This approach gave Limperg's theory of *bedrijfseconomie* its two salient characteristics:

1 The theory was presented as 'normative-deductive'. In fact, it was a rather strict form of deductive reasoning, because the theory allowed for only one explanatory factor: everything that was in accordance with it was sound, while everything that departed from it was not. Clear prescriptions could be derived with compelling logic from one source that could not contradict itself. When practice was found to deviate from a properly deduced theoretical norm, there had to be an error in practice. Empirical work was therefore never a characteristic part of the work of Limperg. The practical experience of Limperg that underlay his careful choice of the definitions to be used in reasoning lent credibility to this primacy of reason over observed facts and prevented *bedrijfseconomie*, as taught by Limperg, from becoming a barren theoretical construct (Van de Woestijne 1959: 740–1). On the whole, it had an aura of irresistibility, enhanced by the strong personality of its founder.

2 The strict confinement of the theory to economic motive meant that a host of phenomena in and around enterprise that could not be traced to this simple, originating principle were, on the whole, left out of consideration. This defining conception gave Limpergian *bedrijfseconomie*, even though it dealt with most areas of the enterprise, such as finance, organisation, accounting and marketing, a characteristically narrow focus. This constraint was knowingly accepted by Limperg as part of his conception of science, and did not prevent him addressing a truly impressive array of subjects.

The extent to which Limperg, in developing his *bedrijfseconomie*, drew upon, or was aware of, other theorists, can only be assessed in general terms on the basis of published material. From late 1901 until the middle of 1905 he edited a section 'Foreign Books and Journals' in the NIvA's journal. The scope of the section leaves little doubt that he was as aware as anyone in The Netherlands of accounting and auditing developments in the UK, the US, France and Germany. It is difficult to establish the full extent of his reading, but his continuing interest in developments abroad may perhaps be deduced from the fact that the journals of which he was the editor-in-chief, *Accountancy* and *Maandblad voor accountancy en bedrijfshuishoudkunde*, featured systematic and extensive reviews of domestic and foreign literature on accounting, auditing and other subjects related to *bedrijfseconomie*.

In his lecture notes, the nature of the references to the works of others varies with the subject matter. His notes on *bedrijfseconomie* and on its relation to economics in general give the impression that he acquired his knowledge of the economics literature in the early 1920s, but did not systematically keep up with new developments thereafter. The most frequent references are to the Germans and Austrians C. Menger, F. von Wieser, E. von Böhm-Bawerk and G. Cassel, and to the Americans H. C. Carey, J. B. Clark, and F. W. Taussig. References to works from the 1920s (Keynes) or 1930s (von Mises) are made only in passing.

Limperg's notes on finance contain very few references to foreign works, but in his notes on industrial relations and business organisation the dates and numbers of the references show that he kept up very well with the literature, especially on scientific management.

In the remainder of this chapter, only the two parts of his theory that have made a major impact in The Netherlands, namely, current value theory and auditing theory, will be discussed. The theories on these two subjects were developed in the first decade of Limperg's professorship, and were substantially complete by the beginning of the 1930s.

VALUE AND INCOME *(WAARDE EN WINST)*[7]

Value theory

Given Limperg's emphasis on economic motive, it is not surprising that value theory became a cornerstone of his *bedrijfseconomie*: since all relevant decisions are concerned with welfare, they need to be made on the basis of a trade-off between properly evaluated benefits and sacrifices. Limperg devoted much effort to showing that his theory of value was logically derived from the originating principle of economic motive. True to his vision of *bedrijfseconomie* as a branch of economics rather than a separate discipline, Limperg developed a concept of value that was, in his view, applicable to the field of economics as a whole.

That Limperg attempted to construct a complete value theory did not mean that he paid no attention to achievements already attained in this area. Rather, he took existing theory, primarily that of the Austrian school of economics, as his starting point. As will be seen, Limperg's resulting value theory anticipated the notion of 'value to the owner', or 'deprival value', as developed and refined between the 1930s and the 1960s by North American, Australian and British theorists.

As a first step, Limperg defined the value of a good as its contribution to the welfare of its owner, or, conversely, as the welfare forgone upon loss of the good. Limperg acknowledged (BE, I: 149–54) that this value concept owed its origin to Carl Menger (1840–1921) (see Menger 1871, I: 78). Following the reasoning of one of Menger's students, Eugen von Böhm-Bawerk (1851–1914) (see von Böhm-Bawerk 1921 I: 230–1), Limperg further elaborated this value concept by stating that, for every economic actor, value had to be the lower of (1) the value associated with the good when used, retained or sold (*opbrengstwaarde* or 'beneficial value'[8]) and (2) its current cost[9] (*vervangingswaarde*). For if the current cost of a good were to be higher than its 'beneficial value', the owner would not replace it when lost, and value would equal 'beneficial value'. If the opposite were true, the value of a good would not be its 'beneficial value' since, upon loss of the good, the owner's former position could be restored by expending its current cost, which would therefore equal the decrease in welfare occasioned by the loss.

From this general concept of value, Limperg went on to consider valuation in the context of a business, a subject more appropriate to *bedrijfseconomie*. And here he parted company with the Austrians, who had accorded a dominant role to subjective preferences in the determination of 'beneficial value'. It was clear to Limperg that general concepts such as 'beneficial value' and current cost might have different meanings to consumers and producers. For instance, consumers could base their valuations on their subjective preferences, which a firm, especially if it were collectively owned, could not be assumed to possess. The next step, therefore, was to define what was the quintessence of being a firm (or a producer), so that the general value concept could be applied to this more specific type of economic subject.

In developing a theory of the firm, Limperg followed the classical economists and took it for granted that the division of labour increased the yield of resources used in production. But though the originating principle of economic motive dictated that division of labour, or specialisation, was preferable from the perspective of society as a whole, individuals and firms could be expected to concentrate on specific aspects of production only if they could be sure that their production could be exchanged with that of others. Although Limperg did not elaborate on the mechanisms by which this result came about, he noticed that economic life was based on a tacit agreement, apparently not unlike Adam Smith's 'invisible hand', that all economic agents would continue to participate in specialised production and the resulting exchange. Furthermore, the force of economic motive would assure that this specialisation would reflect the economies of scale associated with the current state of technique, the size of the market, etc., so that the allocation of resources would produce the optimal output. The resulting organisation of production was sufficiently stable for Limperg to state that production was guided by what he called a 'law of continuity'.

Limperg viewed society as a series of interlinked 'industrial columns', composed of enterprises active in the various branches and stages of production and connected by markets, through which goods moved in an uninterrupted flow from the primary producers to the final users. Each enterprise knew that its place, size and operations were for the time being fixed by the relevant 'quantitative proportions' of nature, technique and costs. The only reason for incurring the costs of changing its position in the intricate social network of production was that changes in the relevant 'quantitative proportions' made the benefits of doing so exceed the costs. Such changes in 'quantitative proportions' could include the effect of new technologies and shifts in the subjective valuations of end users that provided the 'pull' that kept the flows going (BE, II: 30–1, 47).

This emphasis on continuity allowed Limperg to apply his general concepts of value to the firm, for it explained why a firm would be interested at all in comparing 'beneficial value' with current cost, given its absence of subjective preferences. In the case of a tradable good, the usual case would be that the 'beneficial value' would equal net realisable value and would exceed current cost. This positive difference served as an indicator to the firm that it was economically rational to continue operations. The consideration that, if it were deprived of the good, the firm would suffer a loss equal to current cost (the lower of the two values) was therefore based not merely on a hypothetical replacement, but on a replacement made virtually mandatory by economic rationality as expressed in the 'law of continuity'.

In the case of non-tradable goods, such as machinery, the concept of 'beneficial value' needed a little extension. Such goods would usually not be kept for the purpose of trading, but rather for productive purposes, at least as long as their own selling price was exceeded by the value of their output. Their 'beneficial value' was therefore set equal to the higher of:

1 'Net realisable value' (*directe opbrengstwaarde*, or 'direct beneficial value'): the proceeds to be obtained by selling the productive assets themselves, and
2 'Present value' (*indirecte opbrengstwaarde*, or 'indirect beneficial value'): the net proceeds from the sale of the products made with the productive assets.

For practical purposes, the complementarity of productive assets implied that 'present value' could be determined only for a productive complex as a whole. According to Limperg, when the 'present value' of the enterprise as a whole, equal to the present value of expected earnings, exceeded the aggregate current cost of the assets, it was rational to continue operations. In that case, the only relevant value concept for individual productive assets was their current cost (BE, II: 63–71). It can now be seen that it is not entirely correct to refer to Limperg's value theory as a theory of current cost. What he propagated was a composite value concept that has come to be designated as 'current value' (*actuele waarde*).

It is evident that Limperg's composite value concept closely resembles the notion of 'value to the owner'. This latter concept began to be developed in the English-speaking world about a decade after Limperg formulated his value theory. Both developments took their starting point in Austrian economics, especially as formulated by von Böhm-Bawerk, and should probably be regarded as independent derivations of the latter's work.[10]

Income theory

From this conception of value, it was but a small step to develop a notion of income. Income for the producer, or profit, as seen by Limperg was the reward for keeping a particular firm in working order as part of the national productive network. Given the capitalistic ordering of society, income consisted of the residual benefits accruing to the producer as long as he maintained a continuity of operations that was, from the point of view of society as a whole, economically rational. These residuals had to be calculated on the basis of continuity: the demand for continuity was such that the act of selling created the necessity to replace the factors consumed in the production of the good sold. In an alternative formulation, income was the amount that could be distributed to the owners for consumption without impairing the physical capital required for continuous production. So, income resulting from a sale was the difference between sales proceeds and the current value of the good sold, determined on the basis of current factor values at the moment of sale. Related to the idea of continuity was Limperg's strong conviction that income could accrue only through exchange. Since the economic purpose of each enterprise was to maintain the flow of goods from primary producers to final consumers, there could be no reward for the entrepreneur before he had achieved his ultimate objective of exchanging his goods with the next agent down the line towards final consumption (BE, VI: 295). Holding gains, whether realised or unrealised, achieved in the course of con- tinuous production, could therefore never be part of income.

Limperg would, however, recognise all holding losses. In effect, he introduced a dual capital maintenance criterion, according to which income could be said to exist only when both physical and nominal capital were kept intact. Curiously, he did not offer clear arguments for this position, a deficiency recognised even by his students (Van Seventer 1975: 75–7). Although Limperg denied this himself, it is possible that his experience with contemporary business policy led him to attach more value to conservatism than was strictly called for by his theoretical framework (BE, VI: 301). The general rule that neither realised nor unrealised holding gains could ever be included in income did not apply when the enterprise engaged in purely speculative trading. The very nature of such trading – the exploitation of incidental price differences in a single market – meant that the enterprise was not committed to the continuous movement of products from primary producers to consumers. In that case, even unrealised holding gains could be recognised as disposable income (BE, VI: 322–4).

Relation to other theorists

Limperg took great care to distinguish his theory of value and income from those of others. In pure value theory his main contention was with the Austrian school. Although his value definition owed much to Menger, it was not adopted without modification. Limperg's fundamental criticism of the Austrians was that their reliance on subjective preferences made economics subservient to psychology, something that was unacceptable under his rigid separation of the sciences. Against subjective valuation, Limperg advocated his concept of 'current value' which was essentially a 'social value' derived from the organic place of the business in society (BE, I: 158–68).

A contemporary theorist in the field of accounting with whom Limperg had to contend was F. Schmidt.[11] At first sight, Schmidt's 'organic' income theory, first expounded in 1921, which placed the enterprise in the middle of a flow of values in which it had to maintain its position relative to the economy as a whole, appears to be identical to Limperg's derivation of value and income from the 'law of continuity'. Schmidt's ideas had become well-known in The Netherlands before 1925, well before those of Limperg were made accessible beyond the circle of his students in the early 1930s,[12] and this encouraged the view that Limperg had built on foundations laid by Schmidt (e.g. Sternheim 1934, and, more recently, MacDonald 1977). Limperg always rejected suggestions that similarities between the two theories were more than superficial (BE, I: 223), and claimed that he had already developed the basis for current value accounting between 1910 and 1920. Indeed, publications like Limperg (1917a, 1917b, 1917c, 1918) and Polak and Limperg (1918/1919) show that at the time Limperg opposed strict adherence to historical costs in costing products. At one point (Limperg 1918: 3), he claimed to have been advising clients to separate, in effect, holding gains from trading income by transferring raw materials at current market prices from inventory account to the manufacturing account. But these discussions were confined to methods of costing, an interest also reflected in his inaugural lecture (Limperg 1932). There are no indications that Limperg had, at the time, particular views on balance sheet valuation, capital maintenance and the calculation of disposable income. Therefore, it is evident that, with respect to these latter issues, Schmidt published his work earlier than did Limperg.

Schmidt's primacy made it necessary for Limperg to show in what way the two theories differed. Limperg's main argument, which might not have been convincing to practical minds, was that Schmidt had developed his theory as an *ad hoc* response to the German hyperinflation, and that he had not attempted to link his proposals with an economic value theory. For Limperg, this alone was apparently sufficient to dismiss Schmidt as a theorist, although he conceded that application of Schmidt's recommendations would confer many of the benefits that would follow from application of his own theory (BE, I: 223–6; II: 124–9). In fact, in some cases the results would be identical (Limperg 1937: 3). Despite these similarities, Limperg and his students maintained that the two theories were fundamentally different. This was supported by pointing out Limperg's tripartite conception of 'current value' as opposed to Schmidt's 'monistic' stress on current cost only, and by claiming that Schmidt's theory was mainly applicable to price increases rather than to price changes in general.

Views on accounting practice

Although Limperg is often referred to as an exponent of current value accounting, one should recognise that his theory of value and income was not primarily an accounting theory. It was an economic value theory that would, in the course of practical application, have some implications for accounting. In expounding the theory, Limperg gave but an outline of the record-keeping required for its application, and he did not claim that the theory provided answers to every accounting question. That Limperg perceived a difference between theory and accounting practice may further be inferred from his belief that bookkeeping and accounting practice were not proper subjects for a university curriculum in *bedrijfseconomie*, since they offered no scope for scientific enquiry (Trompert 1988: 33).

One must therefore distinguish between the following two categories.

Accounting questions on which the theory of value and income had a direct bearing As has been suggested above, Limperg's interest in current value accounting started with cost accounting, and cost accounting continued to interest him throughout his career. For both his inaugural and valedictory lectures, he chose 'costing' as his theme (Limperg 1932, 1950).

Most of the normative implications of the theory of value and income amounted to a proper determination of costs, whether they were individual product costs or the sum of all costs to be expensed in the annual income statement.

Product costs, to be used in pricing decisions, were governed by the necessity to ensure the continuity of the enterprise. In Limperg's view, this implied that the selling price had to cover full costs on the basis of current value. Consequently, Limperg had great reservations about the use of marginal costs in pricing decisions (Limperg 1950; BE, II: 78, 109). Limperg's contributions to standard costing and to cost allocation on the basis of causality might be mentioned here.

In income determination, the main questions were the determination of cost of goods sold and depreciation. These were governed by the assumption that the basic, if not the only, function of the financial statements (balance sheet and income statement) was to serve as a guide to rational dividend policy on the basis of a report of net income. A rational dividend policy implied that only so much income was distributed to owners as would leave the firm intact as a source of future income. But whether this implied a maintenance of financial or physical capital was an ambiguity in Limperg's theory (Burgert 1967: 166). Although this approach meant that it was imperative that the costs of goods sold and depreciation in the income statement were based on current value, there was no similar theoretical imperative for showing assets in the balance sheet at current value. Nevertheless, the practice he described in his lecture notes is such that, at the balance sheet date, all assets were to be valued at a proportion of current value commensurate with their remaining life. Any revaluations were to be credited to a 'reserve for pricing differences' that would be excluded from the category of income so long as the firm continued in operation, and would therefore consist of both realised and unrealised holding gains.

Accounting questions that were not directly related to value and income theory Limperg recognised that, especially in financial accounting practice, there might be considerations and priorities that were not covered by his economic theory (BE, VI: 284). And although these practical issues were indeed interesting to him, their treatment in his published works is much less systematic and complete than is true of issues related to value and income theory. Indeed, throughout his career, although mainly between 1900 and 1920, he published a number of articles dealing with practical accounting and bookkeeping questions (e.g. Limperg 1904, 1908, 1909, 1917a). Yet, Limperg commented more extensively on some issues than on others. For example, there seems to be no recorded utterance by Limperg on the subject of consolidated financial statements.

Limperg was less than enthusiastic on expanding the scope of the legal regulation of financial reporting. In 1912, he stated his opposition to a general requirement that listed companies publish their income statement, arguing that reliance should instead be placed on pressure brought by shareholders and creditors (Van Slooten 1912). In 1929, a government commission of which Limperg was a member proposed a set of skeletal requirements for published balance sheets. The law incorporating the commission's proposal, which was in force until 1971, was considered at the time of its passage as a cautious if not inadequate response to criticisms made of company financial reporting (Zeff *et al.* 1992: 59–62).

Given his strong views on income determination, Limperg might have been expected to be an opponent of secret reserve accounting. In fact, his position was in tune with the prevalent thinking of the time. On the one hand, Limperg conceded that secret reserves would hide the true amount of income from shareholders, but on the other hand he acknowledged that such reserves might be a necessary political tool in running a business (BE, III: 232). Limperg also defended, in 1946, the inclusion of a clause in the NIvA's Code of Professional Conduct that allowed a clean opinion to be given on a set of financial statements containing secret reserves, so long as income was not increased by undisclosed transfers. At the occasion, Limperg expressed his sympathy with opponents of secret reserves within the NIvA, but argued that the auditing profession could not, of its own accord, declare an end to a practice that was still widespread (NIvA, 1946: 90–3).

AUDITING[13]

In 1929, Limperg started an academic training programme for auditors at the Municipal University of Amsterdam. To Limperg, the link between auditing and his chair in *bedrijfseconomie* was natural: on the one hand, a knowledge of *bedrijfseconomie* would give the auditor a deeper insight into his client's business that not only might help to detect audit risks, but also might make the auditor a better general adviser. On the other hand, none would be better suited than auditors with their broad and intimate acquaintance with business to carry out research in the academic discipline of *bedrijfseconomie* (Limperg 1924).

Limperg himself set an example by incorporating his views on auditing into the body of *bedrijfseconomisch* doctrine. These views can in some measure be found in his journal articles dating from the first decade of the century (notably Limperg 1905a, 1905b) and were thus conceived long before the development of the complete theory of *bedrijfseconomie*. It is useful to keep this historical development of Limperg's views in mind and to distinguish two levels in his theory of auditing. The first part, which might be called the substructure, is made up of his views on the actual practice of auditing, formed during his years as a public accountant. On to this he grafted, in the course of his academic career, a superstructure that formed the link with *bedrijfseconomie* and that dealt not with concrete norms for the conduct of the audit, but rather with the significance of auditing and the role of the auditor in society.

Starting with the substructure, one might say that its main feature was Limperg's belief in the logical or objective nature of auditing. Auditing ought to be characterised by the application of intellectual effort and expert insight into each specific client's situation, rather than by thoughtless reliance on established routine. The type of reasoning required of the auditor involved having a clear view of the purpose of an assignment in order to determine the work necessary for achieving that particular purpose.

To understand the significance of this position, one should keep in mind that, at the start of Limperg's auditing career, it was not at all unusual for the auditor to confine his enquiry to checking the correspondence between the financial statements and the ledger accounts, and perhaps to see whether the latter were kept in an orderly manner. To Limperg, this was pointless, since internal consistency of the administrative records did not imply their correspondence with reality. Audits of this kind could therefore not serve their apparent purpose, which was to give assurance to third parties with respect to the reliability of the reported figures. If this was indeed the purpose of the audit, it followed that the auditor had to take economic reality, not the records, as his starting point. To look at the economic reality of an enterprise usually meant that the enterprise should be seen as a coherent whole, organised to maintain a steady flow of goods starting with purchases, followed possibly by productive activity and ending with sales. This implied that a systematic audit could and should be structured around the resulting regular patterns of payments, movements of goods, stocks, receivables and payables. A comprehensive reconstruction of this economic reality had to be the basis for ascertaining whether the records reflected the underlying reality accurately and completely. In short, it was

> the duty [of the auditor] to investigate the business of which the figures are being verified in all its details, including an investigation of the completeness of the accounting of all goods purchased and produced; judging the causes of the results of the concern, therefore also a judging of the manner in which the business is being managed; and lastly the duty to judge the value of the assets including everything connected with it, namely an investigation of the solvency of the debtors, taking of stocks of merchandise and investigating the value of these goods.
>
> (Limperg 1926: 95)

This approach to auditing came to be known as the 'sufficient audit' (*volkomen controle*): the audit embracing all that was, according to the expert judgement of the auditor, logically necessary to serve a rational purpose.[14] According to this definition, 'sufficient audit' did not refer to any particular audit programme. Rather, in a given situation it might be possible that a number of different programmes might meet the criteria of completeness and interrelatedness, and might therefore all be qualified as 'sufficient'.

As far as can be reconstructed, it was with this preconceived idea about auditing that Limperg started to develop the superstructure that put this norm for auditing in a wider context. Specifically, the superstructure addressed the question of who was to determine the 'rational purpose' to be served by the 'sufficient audit'.

This more general part of the theory of auditing is usually referred to as 'the theory of inspired confidence' and was first made public at the International Congress of Accountants of 1926. This theory, in harmony with the main body of *bedrijfseconomie*, was based on the notion of division of labour.

According to Limperg, specialisation and differentiation, both within and among enterprises, almost always necessitated a certain delegation of authority and therefore a concomitant rendering of an account by those to whom authority had been delegated. Theoretically, those using the rendered accounts to supervise the work of their delegates might themselves perform the necessary task of verification. But the growth of enterprises and the rise of the limited liability company with broad shareholder interests, which created the need for a greatly expanded scope of accountability, had made it economically rational to have this function of verification performed by specialised individuals or firms. Within enterprises, this gave rise to the internal auditor. But, more importantly, the relations between firms and their shareholders and creditors led to the development of a whole specialised industry of external or public auditing, taking its place among other specialised industries. The output of this industry is essentially 'confidence': by his signature, the independent and expert auditor adds to the trustworthiness of representations made by management, and therefore renders practicable the use of productive and financial arrangements such as the large, public limited liability company with anonymous shareholders.

Limperg's emphasis on the economic background of the auditing function was in accordance with his attempt to incorporate auditing theory into *bedrijfseconomie*. The dominance within that context of the originating principle of economic motive prevented him from explaining the existence of an audit function by other than economic reasoning. Auditors were therefore seen to produce 'confidence' as an intermediate good, rather like machine tools, because it was an essential ingredient in an optimal pattern of resource allocation, productive organisation and output. Limperg would undoubtedly have regarded it as morally reprehensible for the auditor to be remiss in fulfilling the reasonable expectations of the reader of an auditor's report concerning the reliability of certified financial statements. But such a moral consideration could not be used to construct an economic theory of auditing. When Limperg presented maintenance of confidence as an imperative, he used the argument that the disappearance of a trustworthy auditing profession would result in an overall economic loss to society.

In the same way, Limperg presented his two main demands on the auditor, independence and expertise, not as lofty ideals but as technical requirements indispensable to the production of 'confidence'.

Since 'confidence' was thus seen as the essence of the auditor's function, rather than an accompanying feature, maintenance of confidence was to be the primary consideration in determining the actual work to be done in an engagement. This relation between confidence and audit work was formulated by Limperg in a simple, almost tautological, way:

> If the [audit] function is to achieve its objective, then no more confidence may
> be placed in its fulfilment than is justified by the work carried out and by the
> competence of the accountant, while, conversely, the function must be ful-
> filled in a manner that justifies the confidence placed in its fulfilment.
>
> (Limperg 1985: 16)

This dual formulation might suggest either that an equilibrium has to be found
with a simultaneous solution for 'confidence inspired' and 'work carried out and
competence of the accountant', or, worse, that the formulation is a form of
circular reasoning. That neither is true is due to the fact that 'confidence' was
determined exogenously, a further result of placing the theory in the economic
framework outlined earlier. This framework, which presents auditing as an
industry among others, suggests that an audit does not occur in isolation, but
amidst many similar audits. This recurring nature of audits enables the readers of
audit reports to form reasonable expectations concerning the purpose and significance of audit reports in general. These expectations are formed in what
Limperg called the 'economic and social climate' (*maatschappelijk verkeer*).
'Economic and social climate' is a general Dutch phrase, not coined by Limperg.
It is used to designate in a general manner the environment in which specific
activities, such as financial reporting, take place. The phrase evokes the image of
an ordered society in which individuals transact their public business in a
common, well-understood but not necessarily static framework of institutions,
norms and traditions.

The element of 'tradition', or 'usage', endows the phrase 'economic and social
climate' with a rather vague normative content. In the case of auditing, though,
Limperg was able to specify much more precisely the normative implications of the
fact that audits occur in the context of the 'economic and social climate'.

In the 'economic and social climate' a particular auditor's report would not be
considered on its own, but as another instance of a familiar phenomenon. The
significance attached to a specific report would therefore largely be determined by
experience with other reports. Now Limperg claimed in a final hypothesis that, based
on this experience, the 'economic and social climate' would form its expectations
concerning the audit report in a rational manner, and this brought him in a convenient
way back to his starting point. If the 'economic and social climate' was rational, it
would in due course learn to expect a 'sufficient audit' (Limperg 1985: 21).

It is this final step, in which Limperg in fact attributed his own views on
auditing to the 'economic and social climate', that saved the theory of inspired
confidence from becoming an indeterminate user-oriented approach to auditing.
While at first sight the establishment of auditing standards was referred to the
amorphous outside arbiter of the 'economic and social climate', this referral was
tightly constrained by binding this arbiter to the technical norm of the 'sufficient
audit'. The practical result was that the actual formulation of auditing norms was
carried out by debate within the profession, following the lines of deductive
reasoning implied in the concept of the 'sufficient audit' (Schilder 1992: 32–40).
At the same time, the invocation and rather passive involvement of the 'eco-

nomic and social climate' endowed this norm of the 'sufficient audit' with a sense of objectivity that norms, perceived purely as the common point of view of the auditing profession, could hardly achieve.

Limperg presented his theory of 'inspired confidence' as a framework for developing auditing norms rather than as a coherent collection of norms themselves. His insistence on the professionalism of the auditor and his realistic assessment that in the 1920s and 1930s neither the 'economic and social climate' nor the auditing profession had yet fully understood the concept of the 'sufficient audit' made him reluctant to present detailed directions for auditing. Such auditing standards might stifle further progress in a profession that to him had not yet reached its full technical potential (BE, VI: 56–7).

It is for this reason that, despite his repeated calls for systematic audits, there are no passages in his published work discussing the drafting of audit programmes. Nevertheless, especially through its tie with the 'sufficient audit', the theory of inspired confidence led Limperg to air his views on a number of practical auditing issues.

One of his most important conclusions was that, once an audit function was to be standardized, that is, once clear expectations were formed about it in the 'economic and social climate', it could not in any way be modified on request of the client in a specific assignment. Specifically, a client asking an auditor to 'audit our financial statements' could in no way impose limitations on the work of the auditor. The auditor, as an independent expert, had to determine what work was required in the particular assignment to meet his responsibilities to the 'economic and social climate'. This conclusion was at variance with the contemporary practice of auditors accepting quite arbitrary restrictions, mainly intended to reduce the cost of the audit, and of disclaiming responsibility for the resulting deficiencies in the audit by notes in the audit report stating which checks had been omitted. In this way, management might stipulate, for instance, that the auditor refrain from taking stock of inventories (Tempelaar 1952: 132). According to Limperg, readers of audit reports could be expected to attach a correct meaning to unqualified reports in general, but, not being auditors, they lacked the expertise to assess the significance of any departures from standard auditing procedure that might be mentioned in the audit report. These considerations were the basis for Limperg's scepticism concerning the scope and opinion paragraphs in audit reports. His 'ideal' report consisted of the mere signature of the auditor below the financial statements. Limperg insisted that the auditor would never be able to formulate the wording of his report with sufficient clarity as to inspire the precise degree of 'confidence' that might be intended (BE, VI: 43).

Another characteristic point was Limperg's strong bias against reliance on internal controls. If the 'economic and social climate' expected an audit that was independent, it would not do for the auditor to rely for vital elements in his conduct of the audit on affirmations made by the client or its employees. And since the audit was to be a systematic and interrelated whole, every element would be as vital as the others (BE, VI: 82–5).

Finally, Limperg's critical attitude to sampling should be mentioned. Limperg was vehement in his rejection of the unsystematic sampling used by many of his contemporaries, since this evidently conflicted with his views on 'sufficient audits'. And since, in Limperg's days, the Dutch auditing profession lacked the proper mathematical tools for taking systematic samples, sampling was for most practical purposes ruled out.

RECEPTION OF LIMPERG'S VIEWS

General

The strength of Limperg's convictions meant that, in the main, those who came into contact with his views did not react with indifference. Indeed, they became either disciples or opponents.

As to favourable reception, there gradually came into existence a circle of graduates from the Municipal University of Amsterdam that was so distinctly recognisable that it has been named the 'Amsterdam School'. Although this name was first associated with adherents to Limperg's views on auditing, it was later used to refer to those who accepted his particular approach to *bedrijfs-economie* as a whole.[15]

The visibility and coherence of the Amsterdam School have apparently led many foreign observers to fail to appreciate the diversity of views held by Dutch academics during this period.[16] From the middle 1930s until shortly after Limperg's retirement as a professor in 1950, the Municipal University of Amsterdam enrolled between a fifth and a quarter of all Dutch university students in economics, whereas about one-half were enrolled at The Netherlands School of Economics at Rotterdam. For this reason, it was not unusual to contrast the Amsterdam School with a 'Rotterdam approach' to *bedrijfseconomie*, but the adjective 'Rotterdam' should really be read as meaning 'anything but Limpergian'. Limperg was only one member of a generation of professors who developed the originally *ad hoc* approach to *bedrijfseconomie* into a more mature academic discipline. Prominent among Limperg's contemporaries were N. J. Polak and J. Goudriaan at Rotterdam and M. J. H. Cobbenhagen at Tilburg. In fact, Polak's inaugural lecture (Polak 1922), which was delivered a few months before that of Limperg, showed the same desire of transforming *bedrijfs-economie* from mere description of practice to a higher level of analysis on the basis of economic reasoning. 'Rotterdam' academics developed the same devotion to careful scientific enquiry as their Amsterdam colleagues, but did not seek to produce the kind of comprehensive, normative and enduring theory that was characteristic of Limperg. This meant, in effect, that the Amsterdam School formed a tightly-knit and militant group within a much larger, but loosely structured academic community.

Over the last twenty-five years, the Amsterdam School has gradually declined in importance and eventually disappeared. Likely explanations for this reversal were the death of Limperg in 1961 and the fact that, without the dominating presence of their master, his disciples were not capable of transmitting his vision to the next generation of adherents. But this inability seems to have stemmed also from the inherent limitations of the Limpergian approach. Van der Schroeff, an early Limperg disciple, described in 1970 how he gradually lost his belief in the possibility of constructing an enduring, normative theory as he came to realise that the questions to be addressed by *bedrijfseconomie* were continually changing and constantly required new approaches (Van der Schroeff 1970: 9–10). Moreover, Limperg's meticulous care not to go beyond his narrowly defined boundaries of deductive economic reasoning failed to address many problems that were tackled by the more pragmatic, *ad hoc* Rotterdam approach. This latter approach was also more in harmony with the American literature that began to make an impact in The Netherlands during the 1950s and 1960s.

In short, work on the construction of the all-embracing normative-deductive edifice of *bedrijfseconomie* has been abandoned. In some areas, like finance, organisation theory and labour relations, Limperg's views have fallen into obscurity. Most of his work in these areas has simply been forgotten, rather than consciously rejected.[17] Only his value and income theory and auditing theory have shown themselves capable of an existence independent of the grand theoretical framework.

Beyond the University of Amsterdam, Limperg's views influenced the courses for the preparatory examinations offered by the NIvA. Limperg chaired the Association's (later the NIvA's) Examination Bureau from 1909 to 1929, and, perhaps owing to this influence on the main avenue into the profession, the NIvA has always displayed considerable loyalty to his views.[18] As in the academic community, though, there were sufficient independent-minded individuals within the NIvA to prevent a one-sided dominance by Limperg. A narrow focus on the Amsterdam School was also prevented by the fact that Rotterdam academics, including N. J. Polak, served with Limperg in the corps of the NIvA's teachers and examiners, and by the inclusion, at least during the 1930s, of a considerable amount of foreign literature in the required reading.[19]

Current value theory

When the first published accounts of Limperg's current value theory appeared in the 1930s, they did not go without criticism (as in Bakker 1935, de Langen 1937). Nevertheless, following their gradual dissemination, they found acceptance, not only among Limperg's students and within the NIvA, but also in business. Attention for the theory increased with the devaluation of the guilder in 1936, following the abandonment of the gold standard. Limperg used the occasion to present his views in print for the first time (Limperg 1937).[20]

Following the war, and increasingly during the 1950s and 1960s, a number of companies began to adopt one form or another of current value accounting (in the income statement only, or integrally in both income statement and balance sheet). As in the case of Philips, which led the way in this development, the reasons for adopting current value accounting may have transcended purely accounting considerations (Zeff *et al.* 1992: 77–8). Van Rietschoten (1950) has pointed out that cost figures based on current value could be used to justify price increases under the post-war regime of controlled prices. But whatever the reasons for adoption, current value accounting showed itself to be practicable, and acquired a definite place in Dutch thinking on financial and management accounting. The publications on Philips' adoption of current value by its chief internal auditor, A. Goudeket, helped to form a foreign perception in which Dutch accounting was firmly associated with current value (see Goudeket 1960). The status of current value accounting was further enhanced by its espousal in influential reports on financial reporting issued in 1955 and 1962 by the co-operating Dutch employers' associations (Zeff *et al.* 1992: 101–2, 132–3).

Although it is undeniable that current value accounting came to occupy a prominent place in The Netherlands, it is likely that many non-academic accountants accepted it as a generic concept rather than as an idea specific to Limperg. Since much attention had been devoted to Schmidt in The Netherlands during the 1920s, it is not unlikely that the advocacy of current value accounting by Limperg and his students in the 1930s was perceived by some as a revival, rather than as the introduction of something completely new. Even those who were aware of, and who rejected, Limperg's own theoretical justifications for current value accounting, could support current value accounting in general as a useful part of the common body of accounting knowledge.[21]

While current value accounting acquired a foothold in practice, the academic world had not sat idly by. Although Limperg had been largely inactive in this field between his retirement in 1950 and his death in 1961, his adherents continued to refine his theories in response to increasingly effective criticism. In the late 1950s, a discussion in the journals gathered pace on what were called, with deference to Limperg, 'blemishes' rather than errors in the theory of current value. Following protracted and convoluted arguments, current value emerged in the late 1960s with its theoretical foundation severely shaken. By then it had become clear that the imposing structure of deductive theory showed some fundamental flaws. Among these were uncertainty about the 'maintenance criterion' (real or financial capital), and the fact that Limperg had not been able to demonstrate convincingly why, according to his theory, holding losses were to be treated differently from holding gains.[22]

Despite these acknowledged defects, current value accounting continued to be propagated as a system leading to more useful information than historical cost accounting. In the course of the theoretical debates during the 1950s and 1960s, modifications were suggested that, while never formally part of Limpergian theory, helped to solve some practical issues. One of these modifications was a gearing adjustment that acknowledged that capital maintenance could in part be achieved by additional borrowing (Van der Schroeff 1969). Another was the acknowledgement that the revaluation account represented in part a tax liability, given that the tax authorities would not accept the calculation of income on the basis of current value (Ten Doesschate 1959).

In the course of the 1970s, when accounting for inflation became an international issue, individual Dutch auditors and the NIvRA[23] enthusiastically propagated current value accounting as an alternative to general price level accounting (Zeff *et al.* 1992:

229–31). Yet this advocacy, which descended from Limperg's formulations, was presented in non-Limpergian terms, without its full theoretical underpinnings. Whereas Limperg would have argued in principle against the use of price-level adjusted figures, the NIvRA advanced a pragmatic argument that current value data for non-monetary items were more accurate than historical cost figures adjusted by general price-level indices. And where Limperg thought in terms of a simple one-purpose income figure, the NIvRA advocated a composite income statement from which the user could construct the relevant figure.[24]

Current value accounting has clearly occupied a prominent place in Dutch accounting research and teaching. When specific valuation rules were introduced in Dutch financial reporting legislation in 1983, the tripartite Limpergian current value concept was recognised as an alternative to historical cost. Nevertheless, one assumes that its role in practice, though certainly not inconsiderable, has disappointed its advocates. Despite expectations in the 1960s that current value accounting would ultimately become the prevailing method, publicly listed companies adopting some form of current value accounting have always remained a minority.[25] Most of the more prominent adopters – such as Hoogovens and Philips – have reverted to historical cost in the main body of their financial statements.

Auditing theory

The fate of Limperg's auditing theory seems to present a marked contrast with that of value and income theory. The latter is presently in abeyance for purposes of financial reporting but is still seen as a staple of Dutch accounting by some foreign observers (e.g. Kieso and Weygandt 1992: 21, Horngren *et al.* 1993: 727). The former is still the professed foundation of Dutch auditing practice. Limperg's 1932/33 articles on the 'theory of inspired confidence' are still in use as instructional material in the education for the profession, and his concepts still pervade current professional regulations. Nevertheless, Limperg's thought on auditing has received little attention abroad, even though it was presented in English to a foreign audience as early as 1926. One reason for this may be that academic attention for auditing in English-speaking countries is by and large a recent phenomenon. Another reason may have been that Limperg's auditing theory did not find an international advocate of the stature of Goudeket backed by the Philips organisation.

The long-standing popularity of the inspired confidence theory in The Netherlands might obscure the fact (1) that its acceptance did not come about without opposition and (2) that, over the years, its practical meaning has undergone some changes.

Following its acceptance in circles of the NIvA during the 1930s, the theoretical structure of 'inspired confidence' has remained basically unchanged. However, meanings attached to the 'sufficient audit', which, as has been shown, was the key to the practical implications of the theory, began to shift. It is important to note that this shift in meaning was in conformity with Limperg's dynamic conception of the 'sufficient audit'. Since an audit meeting this requirement was to contain all that was 'reasonably necessary', it was not only to be expected but also to be encouraged that, by improvements in internal accounting systems and in auditing techniques, more efficient and effective auditing practices could be developed. During Limperg's active years, and even more so after the Second World War, one could see a gradual increase in reliance on more global auditing techniques, such as reliance on internal controls and sampling.[26]

CONCLUDING REMARKS

By any measure, Limperg was a formidable figure during the first half of the century. His pioneering work in the development of the field of *bedrijfseconomie* and his unceasing and successful efforts to elevate the practice of auditing to a professional level left an imprint on Dutch accounting and auditing that is still clearly visible today. Limperg's influence still appears in small details and in important issues alike: the title of today's Dutch research journal, *Maandblad voor accountancy en bedrijfseconomie*, which was founded by Limperg in 1924, shows his view of the close relation between auditing and *bedrijfseconomie*; to implement the clauses in the EC's Fourth Directive referring to current cost, the Dutch law used Limperg's tripartite current value concept; a number of universities and the NIvRA jointly sponsor a research foundation known as the Limperg Instituut; and until recently, the limited review of financial statements (i.e. an investigation amounting to significantly less than a full audit) was ruled out in The Netherlands on the basis of purely Limpergian arguments.

Since Limperg's influence is so pervasive, few who are active in accounting in The Netherlands today would deny his greatness. But, at the same time, the sheer scope of his influence makes it difficult to reach agreement on a more specific characterisation of his importance.

Reasons for differing assessments of Limperg in The Netherlands include the following:

- Limperg's significance cannot be reduced to his contributions to the literature. He did write numerous articles, and his published lecture notes do convey his thoughts to posterity, but a summary of his concepts and theorems does not capture all of Limperg. Limperg's importance was not just theoretical, it was also practical and inspirational. As to the practical, one might, for instance, argue that his founding of a rival accountancy body in 1906 did as much to further Dutch auditing as did his theory of 'inspired confidence'. Inspiration was provided by the rigour and the unflinching quest for perfectionism that he infused into all that he did. Colleagues in the profession were made to see that professional issues might have to be treated as matters of high principle, even though there might be disagreement over the principles themselves. This intangible context should be kept in mind when assessing the mark left by Limperg.
- Looking at his theoretical contributions only, one must recognise that not all of them have stood the test of time. Most conspicuously, his comprehensive

theory of *bedrijfseconomie* was not a realisation of his ideal of an all-embracing and rigorous theoretical system. The audacity and novelty of Limperg's conception of *bedrijfseconomie*, together with Limperg's force of expression, may have caused him and his disciples to fail to distinguish the promise from the fulfilment, giving the extant parts of *bedrijfseconomie* a brighter aura of perfection than was warranted by closer inspection. That such bold claims were made for the theory made it harder for his adherents to distance themselves from his views when these came in need for revision, and made the theory an easier target for detractors. To determine which of Limperg's observations on individual topics have retained their value despite the loss of the broader framework is a complex task that necessarily gives rise to differing interpretations.

- The many independently viable elements of Limperg's theories have in a natural way been used as a basis for further development. As a result, Limperg's work has receded somewhat into the background, in the sense that his views are no longer as dominant as they once were. In 1959, it was still possible to write that 'one can still, on the basis of notes of Limperg's original lectures, take part in a scientific study of problems in *bedrijfseconomie* in The Netherlands without running the risk of being considered hopelessly out of date' (Van de Woestijne 1959: 749). This is no longer true, at least not for *bedrijfseconomie* as a whole. Hence, those who are currently active in *bedrijfseconomie* and auditing may have only an imperfect awareness of the Limpergian strain that is intermingled with other influences in today's theory and practice.

Given these reasons for the varying appreciation of Limperg within The Netherlands, it is hardly surprising that those who have no access to Dutch sources tend to be unclear about the nature of his work and legacy. This lack of clarity was exacerbated by an imbalance in the way Limperg's views have been presented abroad.

Limperg's followers took a clear lead over his opponents in presenting Limperg's views abroad, with the apparent result that Limperg's name, and especially his current value theory, was more firmly associated with Dutch accounting as viewed in other countries than might have been justifiable by Limperg's domestic standing. This association was only reinforced by the initiatives of the leaders of the Dutch auditing profession, during the wave of interest in inflation accounting in the 1970s, to bring current value accounting to the fore in international accounting circles. But the increased availability of facts about accounting in The Netherlands following in the wake of this revivalist advocacy gave observers from overseas an opportunity to learn something about the lack of solidarity within The Netherlands itself for a method of accounting that had long been associated with the country's auditing profession. It became known that only a sprinkling of Dutch companies actually used current value accounting in their published financial statements, and that its theoretical underpinnings were not free from criticism in the Dutch literature. The resulting adjustment in the foreign appraisal of Limperg must have been hindered by another imbalance in views of Limperg held abroad: until recently, the English-language literature has paid little attention to the fact that much of Limperg's standing in The Netherlands derives from his contributions to auditing rather than to accounting.

Today, Limperg is honoured for his undeniable contributions during a distinct historical phase in Dutch accounting and, above all, auditing. At the same time, it is acknowledged that, as is only natural, these contributions either have been superseded by, or gradually have taken a more modest place among, the growing body of subsequent experience and insights.

Notes

The authors express their gratitude to Philip W. Bell, Willem Buijink, Graeme Dean, Jan Klaassen, J. W. Schoonderbeek, David Solomons and A. van Seventer for their valuable comments on earlier drafts.

1 A profile of Limperg in English can be found in Muis (1980). Bak and Schoonderbeek (1979) contains an important series of personal reminiscences about Limperg in Dutch by former colleagues and students, many of which have been used in preparing this section. Other personal views and assessments of Limperg are contained in Reesink (1947), Hennipman (1966), I. Kleerekoper (1969), Van der Schroeff (1961) and the unpublished speech by N. J. Polak, made when Limperg was awarded an honorary doctorate at the Netherlands School of Economics at Rotterdam (8 May 1947). Other sources consulted are Van Sloten (1987) and Trompert (1988) for biographical details; Knapper (1897) and *Gedenkboek* (1925) on the Openbare Handelsschool and its society of alumni, and Vanthoor (1992) on the University of Amsterdam. Metzemaekers (1983: 79–87) contains further details on the auditing firms Limperg served with; Mey (1960) has an overview of Limperg's committee-work, and De Vries (1985) is the most important single source, in Dutch, on the Dutch auditing profession during the first decades of the century. Limperg (1903) gives, in English, an outline of Limperg's view of the Dutch auditing profession.
2 The years in which Limperg took his examinations are derived from the regular reports on examination results in *Maandblad voor het Boekhouden*, vols 1898 and 1901. De Vries (1985: 33) contains particulars on the Acte Boekhouden M. O. KXII.
3 In Dutch, the English words *accountant* and *accountancy* are generally used to refer to auditor and auditing, respectively.
4 *Bedrijfshuishoudkunde* is a synonym for *bedrijfseconomie*, although the former is no longer current. Both have often been translated literally as 'business economics', but since that rendering does not convey the wide scope of *bedrijfseconomie*, the Dutch word will be used in the text. As used today in The Netherlands, *bedrijfseconomie* is the collective name for such subjects as accounting, finance, marketing, organisation theory, management science and industrial organisation, all of them studied or taught with a background in economics. In general, *bedrijfseconomie* is seen as the twin of *algemene economie* ('general economics'), which includes macro- and micro-economics, public finance, etc., and which would simply be called 'economics' in English. Although Limperg's influence has been important in bringing about the general usage of the word *bedrijfseconomie* in the sense outlined above, the word as generally used does not refer exclusively to Limperg's approach to *bedrijfseconomie*. Further notes on *bedrijfseconomie* can be found in Klaassen and Schreuder (1984: 113–16).
5 Limperg's views are accessible from two sources. One is *Bedrijfseconomie, Verzameld werk van Prof. dr Th. Limperg Jr.*, 7 volumes (Limperg 1964–8). This edition of collected lecture notes was issued posthumously by some of Limperg's students

and purports to present the theoretical system of *bedrijfseconomie* in its entirety as it appeared to Limperg at the end of his academic career. Despite the unfortunate fact that the editors' objective was to produce an up-to-date textbook rather than a scientific edition of the manuscript originals, the collection is indispensable in studying Limperg. References to this work will take the form of (BE, I: 1), in which roman numerals indicate the volumes and arabic numbers the pages.

The second source is formed by Limperg's numerous articles in professional publications. There is currently no complete published bibliography, but a reasonably complete listing of publications (eighty-one items spanning the period 1903–54) can be found in *Bedrijfseconomie* (BE, VII: 495–8, reproduced in Van Sloten 1981).

6 Source material for this section includes Limperg's inaugural lecture mentioned in the text. This lecture, entitled 'Eenige beschouwingen over kostprijs en prijsvorming als bedrijfshuishoudkundig probleem' ('Some Observations on Product Costs and Pricing as a Problem in *Bedrijfseconomie'*) was given on 8 May 1922 and has been published as Limperg (1932). Polak (1934) and Bindenga (1990) characterise *bedrijfseconomie* before Limperg with specific reference to Volmer. Discussions of Limperg's views on economic research can be found in Klant (1979) and Van Sloten (1987). Klaassen and Schreuder (1984) provide some materials on *bedrijfseconomie* in English. Perridon (1956) is an interesting discussion in French that attempts to capture the spirit of Limperg's teaching as well as its more concrete details.

7 Materials in English on Limperg's value and income theory include: Klaassen and Schreuder (1984), Mey (1966 and 1988), Van Seventer (1969 and 1975) and Van Sloten (1981). A translation into English of a section of the relevant material from *Bedrijfseconomie* (BE, II: 49–140) is included in Clarke and Dean (1990: 75–166).

8 Since Limperg began his analysis by positing an unspecified economic actor, it was necessary for him to refer to a generalised concept of 'beneficial value' that might be applied both to the case of a consumer, where it would equal utility value, and to the case of an enterprise, where it might refer to present value or net realisable value.

9 Although many Dutch authors use the term 'replacement value' for *vervangingswaarde* when writing in English, the term 'current cost' is preferred by the present authors, as being more in line with usage in the English-language literature.

10 An important modern exposition of 'value to the owner' is provided in Solomons (1966: 122–5). If one bears in mind that Solomons does not have a direct equivalent to 'beneficial value', it can be readily seen that Limperg's other value concepts are equivalent to the components of Solomons' 'value to the owner', as presented in Parker and Harcourt (1986: 29–30).

On the development of 'value to the owner', it can be noted that Solomons (1966) referred to the work of James C. Bonbright (1891–1985) as a principal source, and may well have been inspired to do so by the work of R. S. Edwards, as in Edwards (1938). Bonbright himself (1937: I, 95–7) acknowledged a debt to von Böhm-Bawerk.

11 An extensive comparison of the theories of Limperg and Schmidt can be found in Clarke and Dean (1990). Passages in Schmidt that might call to mind Limperg's 'law of continuity' include Schmidt (1929: 28–32, 79–81, 126). Mey (1931) and Van der Schroeff (1947: 7–8) are critical discussions of Schmidt by Limperg students.

12 Evidence of knowledge of Schmidt in The Netherlands in 1923–4 is abundant and includes, merely as the most prominent examples, Van Overeem (1923), Polak (1924) and Renaud (1924). As early as 1925, the examination programme for the Boekhouden M. O. KXII degree mentioned in the text included knowledge of 'static, dynamic and organic balance sheet conceptions'. Against this attention for Schmidt, the first published outline of Limperg's views came as late as Mey (1931), while Kleerekoper (1934) may be considered as the first full published discussion of Limperg's theory.

13 Sources include the first public exposition of Limperg's complete auditing theory at the 1926 International Congress of Accountants (Limperg 1926). A more developed version of the theory appeared in 1932 and 1933 as a series of articles in the Dutch

journal *Maandblad voor accountancy en bedrijfshuishoudkunde* (Limperg 1932–3). An English translation of the journal articles has been published as Limperg (1985). Finally, the theory is also included in Limperg's collected notes (BE, VI: *passim*). Further international presentations of the theory occurred at the international congresses of Berlin (Keuzenkamp 1938) and Amsterdam (de Lange 1957). Flint (1985, 1988: 106–7, 120, 152–3) is an exception to the general silence in the English-language literature on Limperg's auditing theory.

Discussions in Dutch of the development and reception of Limperg's auditing views are Tempelaar (1952), Diephuis (1959), De Vries (1985: 104–8), Dassen (1989) and Van de Poel and Schilder (1991:12–21).

14 A literal translation of *volkomen controle* would be 'perfect audit'. But Limperg's notion suggested the element of adapting the audit to the circumstances of each case, omitting what was not reasonably required. To the authors, 'sufficient audit' more aptly captures the spirit of Limperg's conception. On the other hand, one should remember that, when Limperg propagated the 'sufficient audit' during the 1930s, it was seen by those who opposed it as an intolerably high standard, rather than as a minimum on which one might fall back.

15 Among the more prominent Limperg disciples one should count A. Mey (1890–1971), S. Kleerekoper (1893–1970) and H. J. van der Schroeff (1900–1974), all professors at the Municipal University of Amsterdam, and G. L. Groeneveld (1904–89), professor at the Catholic University at Tilburg. A. Goudeket (1903–69), chief internal auditor of Philips, is well known as an advocate of current value accounting, but since he was not a graduate of the University of Amsterdam he is not usually included in the Amsterdam School. Van Rossum (1979) gives a detailed analysis of the membership and coherence of the Amsterdam School.

16 See, for instance, Scott (1971) who sees Limpergian *bedrijfseconomie* as the basis of *the* Dutch approach to accounting.

17 Gans (1979), after a comparison of Limperg's views with modern textbooks on finance, concluded that, in the light of developments since Limperg, 'hardly any current significance' can still be attributed to Limperg's theory of finance. It should be noted that Gans' rare attempt to rescue this aspect of Limperg's work from oblivion was commissioned for a memorial volume on Limperg, and might not have appeared otherwise at all.

18 Before 1940, graduates from the three academic auditing programmes at Amsterdam, Rotterdam and Tilburg provided but a small minority of new NIvA members. During the 1950s, the number of academic auditing programmes rose to five, but in the early 1960s their combined annual output of students was still far exceeded by the 90 to 100 graduates produced annually by the NIvA's own programme (De Vries 1985: 151, Kleerekoper 1964: 244). Acknowledgements of Limperg's influence on the NIvA's programme include Keuzenkamp (1949) and Van Rietschoten (1959).

19 An unusual publication in *De Accountant* (1931: 141–6) contained a list of books and articles used within the courses offered by the NIvA, presumably reflecting circumstances at the time when Limperg gave up his chairmanship of the Education Board. The list contains more than seventy books, and teachers in each of the courses were apparently expected to make a selection covering all of the relevant areas. About half of the list consists of non-Dutch literature and includes such well-known works in German as Kovero (1912), Schmalenbach (1922, 1930, 1931), Schmidt (1929) and Osbahr (1923), and in English as Clark (1923), Dicksee (1928), Montgomery (1927), Pixley (1922), Spicer and Pegler (1923, 1930). (Since the original list did not mention specific editions, the references in this note have been based on the assumption that the most recent editions would have been used.)

20 An English-language translation of this article is included in Clarke and Dean (1990: 55–71). Expositions of the theory by Limperg's students had appeared earlier (Mey 1931, Kleerekoper 1934).

21 See de Langen (1937), Sternheim, quoted in Limperg (1936), Polak (1940).
22 The fundamental objections raised against Limperg's theory during this period are summarised in Burgert (1972). This article also stands out as the first indication to overseas readers that current value accounting might not be as generally accepted in The Netherlands as might have been supposed abroad. Burgert, a Rotterdam professor, has been prominent in bringing to the attention of practising auditors the academic arguments against Limperg's theory. Further notes on developments in current value accounting since Limperg can be found in Van Offeren (1986) and Van Seventer (1984: 358–61). A useful study in Dutch on developments since Limperg by a Limperg disciple is Groeneveld (1979).
23 On the occasion of the legal regulation of the auditing profession in 1967, the NIvA and three other organisations of auditors were amalgamated into the NIvRA (Nederlands Instituut van Registeraccountants), which became the sole professional organization of Dutch auditors.
24 A good example of the way in which current value accounting was advocated at the time is a memorandum presented to the Institute of Chartered Accountants in England and Wales in regard to ED, 8 (NIvRA, 1974).
25 The biennial surveys of financial statements issued since 1973 by the NIvRA give some information on the application of current value. Owing to changes in the survey questions, the series allows only general inferences about trends. Apparently, the proportion of listed companies using current value for all applicable items has varied between 4 per cent and 8 per cent over the period 1971–86, out of a total of 120 to 135 companies. During the same period, approximately one-half of the listed companies gave at least some form of current value information, either in the financial statements or in the notes. In general, the provision of current value information peaked around 1980, after which a slow decline set in (NIvRA, 1973–87).
26 Notes on developments in Dutch auditing since Limperg, especially as a result of influences from overseas, can be found in Wallage (1991).

References

Bak, G. G. M. and Schoonderbeek, J. W. (eds) (1979) *Herinneringen aan Limperg*, Amsterdam: Limperg Instituut.
Bakker, O. (1935) 'Beschouwingen over de theorie van de vervangingswaarde', *Maandblad voor accountancy en bedrijfshuishoudkunde* 12: 67–71.
Bindenga, A. J. (1990) 'De Rotterdamse School', *De accountant* 96: 578–87.
Bonbright, James C. (1937) *The Valuation of Property*, New York: McGraw-Hill Book Company.
Burgert, R. (1967) 'Bedrijfseconomisch aanvaardbare grondslagen voor de gepubliceerde jaarrekening', Appendix to *De accountant* 74: 153–92.
Burgert, R. (1972) 'Reservations about "Replacement Value" Accounting in the Netherlands', *Abacus* 8: 111–26.
Clark, J. M. (1923) *Studies in the Economics of Overhead Costs*, Chicago: The University of Chicago Press.
Clarke, F. L. and Dean, G. W. (1990) *Contributions of Limperg and Schmidt to the Replacement Cost Debate in the 1920s*, New York: Garland Publishing.
Dassen, R. J. M. (1989) 'De Leer van het Gewekte Vertrouwen: Agency avant la lettre?', *Maandblad voor accountancy en bedrijfseconomie* 63: 341–52.
de Lange, A. T. (1957) 'Principles for the Accountant's Profession', *Proceedings of the Seventh International Congress of Accountants 1957*, Amsterdam.
de Langen, W. J. (1937) 'De inkomsten- en vermogensbelastingen en de depreciatie van de gulden', *Maandblad voor accountancy en bedrijfshuishoudkunde* 14: 124–9.

de Vries, J. (1985) *Geschiedenis der Accountancy in Nederland, aanvang en ontplooiing, 1895–1935*, Assen/Maastricht: Van Gorcum.

Dicksee, L. R. (1928) *Auditing: A Practical Manual for Auditors*, London: Gee & Co.

Diephuis, G. (1959) 'Functie en verantwoordelijkheid (als grondslagen voor de taakbepaling van de openbare accountant)', *Maandblad voor accountancy en bedrijfshuishoudkunde* 33: 471–8.

Edwards, R. S. (1938) 'The Nature and Measurement of Income', *The Accountant* 99: 45–7, 81–3, 121–4.

Flint, D. (1985) 'Professor Limperg's Audit Philosophy: The Theory of Inspired Confidence', *The Social Responsibility of the Auditor*, Amsterdam: Limperg Instituut.

Flint, D. (1988) *Philosophy and Principles of Auditing*, Basingstoke: Macmillan.

Gans, M. P. (1979) 'De financieringstheorie van Limperg', in J. W. Schoonderbeek and G. G. M. Bak (eds) *Reflecties op Limperg*, Deventer: Kluwer.

Gedenkboek van 'Hou' en Trouw' *Vereeniging van oud-leerlingen der openbare handelsscholen te Amsterdam 1885–1925* (1925) Amsterdam, privately published.

Goudeket, A. (1952) 'Fluctuating price levels in relation to accounts', *The Sixth International Congress on Accounting*, London, 73–9.

Goudeket, A. (1960) 'An Application of Replacement Value Theory', *The Journal of Accountancy* 110: 37–47.

Groeneveld, G. L. (1979) *Limperg/Groeneveld: Waarde, winst en jaarrekening*, Deventer: Kluwer.

Hennipman, P. (1966) 'Bedrijfseconomie: Verzameld werk van Prof. dr. Th. Limperg Jr.', *TVVS* 9: 235–8.

Horngren, C. T., Sundem, G. L. and Elliott, J. A. (1993) *Introduction to Financial Accounting* (5th edn), Englewood Cliffs, NJ: Prentice Hall.

Keuzenkamp, T. (1938) 'Thema 3 "Prüfung des Jahresabschlusses', Nationalbericht 10, Niederlande', *Kongress-Archiv des V. Internationalen Prüfungs- und Treuhand-Kongress*, vol. B, Berlin.

Keuzenkamp, T. (1949) *Enige beschouwingen over het onderwijs in de accountancy*, inaugural lecture Rotterdam, 1 December 1949, Purmerend: J. Muusses.

Kieso, D. E. and Weygandt, J. J. (1992) *Intermediate Accounting* (7th edn), New York: Wiley & Sons.

Klaassen, J. and Schreuder, H. (1984) 'Accounting Research in the Netherlands', in A. G. Hopwood and H. Schreuder (eds) *European Contributions to Accounting Research*, Amsterdam: Free University Press.

Klant, J. J. (1979) 'Grandeur en zwakte van een systeem', in J. W. Schoonderbeek and G. G. M. Bak (eds) *Reflecties op Limperg*, Deventer: Kluwer.

Kleerekoper, I. (1964) 'Terugblik op 70 jaar opleiding en examens', *De accountant*, 71: 238–45.

Kleerekoper, I. (1969) '"Bedrijfseconomie' – Verzameld werk van Prof. dr. Th. Limperg Jr.', *De accountant* 75: 324–6.

Kleerekoper, S. (1934) *Bedrijfseconomie*, Amsterdam: De Arbeiderspers.

Knapper, C. (1897) 'Amsterdam's Handelsschool', *De accountant* 2: 1–4.

Kovero, I. (1912) *Die Bewertung der Vermögensgegenstände in den Jahresbilanzen der Privaten Unternehmungen*, Berlin: Heymanns.

Limperg Jr, T. (1903) 'Accountants abroad', in G. Lisle (ed.) *Encyclopaedia of Accounting*, Edinburgh: William Green & Sons, 17–19.

Limperg Jr, T. (1904) 'Theorie en practijk inzake afschrijvingen', *De accountant* 9: 14–17.

Limperg Jr, T. (1905a) 'Oude en nieuwe richting', *Accountancy* 3: 2–3.

Limperg Jr, T. (1905b) 'Onze verantwoordelijkheid', *Accountancy* 3: 65–6, 77–9, 101–2, 125–6.

Limperg Jr, T. (1908) 'Leidende beginselen der Inrichtingsleer', *Accountancy* 6: 68–70.

Limperg Jr, T. (1909) 'De Kameralistische methode', *Accountancy* 7: 81–3, 133.

Limperg Jr, T. (1917a) 'Kostprijsberekening en Kostprijsboekhouding', *Accountancy* 15: 42–4, 55–8, 63–6, 87–9, 104–5.

Limperg Jr, T. (1917b) 'De kostprijs als grondslag voor prijsovereenkomsten', *Accountancy* 15: 90–1.

Limperg Jr, T. (1917c) 'Prijsregeling en prijsovereenkomsten in vereenigingen van nijverheidsondernemingen', *Accountancy* 15: 111–13.

Limperg Jr, T. (1918) 'Kostprijs', *Accountancy* 16: 2–4.

Limperg Jr, T. (1924) 'De beteekenis der bedrijfshuishoudkunde voor den accountant', *Maandblad voor accountancy en bedrijfshuishoudkunde* 1: 161–4.

Limperg Jr, T. (1926) 'The Accountant's Certificate in Connection with the Accountant's Responsibility', *Het Internationaal Accountantscongres*, Purmerend: J. Muusses.

Limperg Jr, T. (1932) 'Eenige beschouwingen over kostprijs en prijsvorming als bedrijf-shuishoudkundig probleem', *Bedrijfseconomische Studiën*, Haarlem: De Erven F. Bohn.

Limperg Jr, T. (1932–3) 'De functie van den accountant en de leer van het gewekte vertrouwen', *Maandblad voor accountancy en bedrijfshuishoudkunde* 9: 17–20, 151–4, 173–7; 10: 193–7.

Limperg Jr, T. (1936) 'De gevolgen van de depreciatie van den gulden voor de bepaling van waarde en winst', *De accountant*: 422–87.

Limperg Jr, T. (1937) 'De gevolgen van de depreciatie van de gulden voor de berekening van waarde en winst in het bedrijf', *Maandblad voor accountancy en bedrijf-shuishoudkunde* 14: 1–8.

Limperg Jr, T. (1938) 'Het tekort op de rijksbegroting voor 1939', *Economisch-Statistische Berichten* 23: 959–62.

Limperg Jr, T. (1950) *De gevaren van de leer der marginale kostprijs-calculatie*, Purmerend: J. Muusses.

Limperg Jr, T. (1964–8) *Bedrijfseconomie – Verzameld werk van Prof. dr. Th. Limperg Jr.*, 7 vols, Deventer: E. E. Kluwer.

Limperg Jr, T. (1985) 'The Function of the Accountant and the Theory of Inspired Confidence', *The Social Responsibility of the Auditor*, Amsterdam: Limperg Instituut.

MacDonald, E. B. (1977) postscript to A. Goudeket, 'An Application of Replacement Value Theory', in: W. T. Baxter and S. Davidson (eds) *Studies in Accounting Theory* (3rd edn), London: The Institute of Chartered Accountants in England and Wales: 246–9.

Menger, C. (1871) *Grundsätze der Volkswirthschaftslehre*, Vienna: Wilhelm Braumüller.

Metzemaekers, L. A. V. M. (1983) *Een eeuw in balans, De wordingsgeschiedenis van Moret & Limperg, 1883–1983*, Amsterdam: privately published.

Mey, A. (1931) 'Eenige critische beschouwingen over de leer der organische winstcalculatie', *Maandblad voor accountancy en bedrijfshuishoudkunde* 8: 1–6, 22–5, 65–72.

Mey, A. (1960) 'Limperg tachtig jaar', *Tijdschrift voor Efficiency en Documentatie* 30: 5–6.

Mey, A. (1966) 'Theodore Limperg and his Theory of Value and Costs', *Abacus* 2: 3–23.

Mey, A. (1988) 'Replacement Value Theory: The 'Circular Flow' and the Calculation of Value', *Advances in International Accounting* 2: 3–21.

Montgomery, R. H. (1927) *Auditing Theory and Practice*, New York: The Ronald Press Company.

Muis, J. W. (1980) 'Wie was Limperg? Outcast Who Blazed the CCA Trail', *Accountancy* (UK) 91: 69–70.

NIvA (1946) *Verslag van de buitengewone algemeene vergadering van 22 juni 1946*, Amsterdam: Nederlandsch Instituut van Accountants.

NIvRA (1973–87) *Onderzoek Jaarverslagen 1971–1986*, Amsterdam: Nederlands Instituut van Registeraccountants.

NIvRA (1974) 'Some Notes on Inflation Accounting and Actual-value (Replacement-value) Accounting', *De accountant* 80: 406–9.

140 Twentieth-century accounting thinkers

Osbahr, W. (1923) *Die Bilanz vom Standpunkt der Unternehmung* (3rd edn), Berlin: Paschke.

Parker, R. H. and Harcourt, G. C. (1986) 'Introduction to the First Edition', in R. H. Parker, G. C. Harcourt and G. Whittington (eds) *Readings in the Concept and Measurement of Income* (2nd edn), Oxford: Philip Allan Publishers.

Perridon, L. (1956) 'Les problèmes économiques du coût et du prix de revient dans la doctrine de l'école d'Amsterdam', *Revue Française de Comptabilité*: 178–83, 187–94; 1957: 3–9.

Pixley, F. W. (1922) *Auditors, Their Duties and Responsibilities*, London: Pitman.

Polak, J. and Limperg Jr, T. (1918/19) 'Kostprijs', *Accountancy* 16: 37–41, 85–8; 17: 22–3.

Polak, N. J. (1922) *Het huidig stadium en de naaste taak der bedrijfsleer*, Haarlem: F. Bohn.

Polak, N. J. (1924) 'Waarderings – en balansproblemen', *De Economist* 74: 683–99, 787–97.

Polak, N. J. (1934) 'Volmers beteekenis voor de bedrijfsleer', in M. J. H. Cobbenhagen, J. Goudriaan and N. J. Polak (eds) *Van boekhouden tot bedrijfsleer*, Wassenaar: Delwel.

Polak, N. J. (1940) 'Goed koopmansgebruik in verband met de winstbelasting', *De Naamlooze Vennootschap* 19: 33–5, 161–3, 192–4, 221–4, 258–61.

Reesink, M. (1947) 'Meesters en leerlingen', *Jaarboek Studievereeniging der Economische Faculteit 1947*: 86–7.

Renaud, A. J. W. (1924) *Invloed der waardeveranderingen van het geld op de balans*, Wassenaar: G. Delwel.

Schilder, A. (1992) 'The Struggle for Independence: A Historical Sketch of Dutch Audit Research', *MARC Research Memorandum 010*, Maastricht: Maastricht Accounting and Auditing Research Center.

Schmalenbach, E. (1922) *Finanzierungen* (3rd edn), Leipzig: G. A. Gloeckner.

Schmalenbach, E. (1930) *Grundlagen der Selbstkostenrechnung und Preispolitik* (5th edn), Leipzig: G. A. Gloeckner.

Schmalenbach, E. (1931) *Dynamische Bilanz* (5th edn), Leipzig: G. A. Gloeckner.

Schmidt, F. (1929) *Die organische Tageswertbilanz* (3rd edn), Leipzig: G. A. Gloeckner.

Scott, G. M. (1971) 'A Business Economics Foundation for Accounting: The Dutch Experience', *Accounting and Business Research* 1: 309–16.

Solomons, D. (1966) 'Economic and Accounting Concepts of Cost and Value', in M. Backer (ed.) *Modern Accounting Theory*, Englewood Cliffs, NJ: Prentice-Hall.

Spicer, E. E. and Pegler, E. C. (1923) *Audit Programmes*, London: H.F.L. (Publishers).

Spicer, E. E. and Pegler, E. C. (1930) *Practical Auditing*, London: H.F.L. (Publishers).

Sternheim (1934) 'Bedrijfseconomie', book review, *De Kroniek van Dr. Mr. A. Sternheim* 12: 43–4.

Tempelaar, A. F. (1952) 'Leer van het gewekte vertrouwen', in A. Mey and A. F. Tempelaar (eds) *Beknopte encyclopedie der accountantscontrôle*, Utrecht: W. de Haan.

Ten Doesschate, J. F. (1959) 'Enige moeilijkheden bij de praktische toepassing van de vervangingswaarde', *Maandblad voor accountancy en bedrijfshuishoudkunde* 33: 479–84.

Trompert, K. (1988) *Een Amsterdamse lente, Honderd jaar Limperg 1879–1979*, Delft: Eburon.

van de Poel, J. H. R. and Schilder, A. (1991) *Normen voor accountants, Nivra geschrift 59*, Amsterdam: Nederlands Instituut van Registeraccountants.

van de Woestijne, W. J. (1959) 'Limperg tachtig jaar', *De Economist* 107: 737–49.

van der Schroeff, H. J. (1947) *De Leer van de Kostprijs*, Amsterdam: Kosmos.

van der Schroeff, H. J. (1961) 'In memoriam Prof. dr. Th. Limperg Jr.', *Folia Civitatis* 16 December: 1–2.

van der Schroeff, H. J. (1969) 'Winstbepaling en vermogensstructuur', *Maandblad voor accountancy en bedrijfshuishoudkunde* 43: 50–72.

van der Schroeff, H. J. (1970) *Verleden, heden en toekomst van de bedrijfseconomie*, valedictory lecture, 24 October 1970, Amsterdam and Antwerp: Kosmos.

van Offeren, D. H. (1986) 'Replacement Value Accounting: Theory and Practice', *Advances in International Accounting* 2: 23–50.

van Overeem, M. (1923) 'De invloed van de valuta-veranderingen op de balans en verlies- en winstrekening', *De Bedrijfseconoom* 1: 9–14, 25–37.

van Rietschoten, A. M. (1950) *Enkele beschouwingen over de functies van het accountantsberoep*, inaugural lecture 20 November 1950, Amsterdam and Antwerp: Kosmos.

van Rietschoten, A. M. (1959) 'De opleiding tot het accountantsberoep', *Maandblad voor accountancy en bedrijfshuishoudkunde* 33: 546–9.

van Rossum, W. (1979) 'Wetenschappelijke ontwikkeling als een sociologisch probleem met speciale aandacht voor ontwikkelingen in de Nederlandse bedrijfseconomie', University of Amsterdam, unpublished thesis.

van Seventer, A. (1969) 'The Continuity Postulate in the Dutch Theory of Business Income', *The International Journal of Accounting* 4: 1–19.

van Seventer, A. (1975) 'Replacement Value Theory in Modern Dutch Accounting', *The International Journal of Accounting* 11: 67–94.

van Seventer, A. (1984) 'Accounting in the Netherlands', in H. P. Holzer (ed.) *International Accounting*, New York: Harper & Row.

van Slooten, G. (1912) 'Wettelijke regeling der verplichte openbaarmaking der balans en winst- en verliesrekening van naamlooze vennootschappen', *Accountancy* 10: 148–51, 11: 4–7, 19–20.

van Sloten, P. J. (1981) *The Dutch Contribution to Replacement Value Accounting Theory and Practice*, ICRA Occasional Paper no. 21, Lancaster: University of Lancaster, International Centre for Research in Accounting.

van Sloten, P. J. (1987) 'Theodore Limperg, Systeembouwer en pragmaticus', in A. J. Vermaat, J. J. Klant and J. R. Zuidema (eds) *Van liberalisten tot instrumentalisten*, Leiden and Antwerp: Stenfert Kroese.

Vanthoor, W. F. V. (1992) 'Zeventig jaar Economische Faculteit binnen de Universiteit van Amsterdam 1922-1992', in M. M. G. Fase and I. van der Zijpp (eds) *Samenleving en economie in de twintigste eeuw*, Leiden: Stenfert Kroese.

von Böhm-Bawerk, E. (1921) *Kapital und Kapitalzins II, Positive Theorie des Kapitales* (4th edn), Jena: Gustav Fischer.

Wallage, P. (1991) 'Een onderzoek naar de methodiek van accountantscontrole in Nederland', *Maandblad voor accountancy en bedrijfseconomie* 65: 443–55.

Zeff, S. A., van der Wel, F. and Camfferman, K. (1992) *Company Financial Reporting: A Historical and Comparative Study of the Dutch Regulatory Process*, Amsterdam: North-Holland.

8 Gino Zappa (1879–1960)

Accounting revolutionary

Arnaldo Canziani

Abstract

Applying Kuhn's concepts of evolution–revolution, the last phase in the development of Italian accounting owed much to Gino Zappa. Building on the heritage of Fabio Besta, and renewing the methodology of scientific research according to the critical positivism of Mach, Poincaré, Enriques and others, Gino Zappa wholly renewed accounting studies by (1) basing them on the study of income (1920–9) and (2) including accounting in a larger branch of knowledge called Economia Aziendale which refers to any production and consumption of wealth (1926ff.). Gino Zappa dedicated the second part of his life to the development of the Economia Aziendale and gave (also through the contributions of a group of scholars who followed his methods and proposals) a new imprint to Italian business studies.

EVOLUTION AND REVOLUTION IN ITALIAN ACCOUNTING, 1796–1922

From Fibonacci to Cinquecontisti

Although some critics define Kuhn's concept of evolution-revolution as merely descriptive and inconclusive, it nevertheless seems to be profitably applicable to the evolution of social science, particularly economics. New problems spring every day from new events or from innovative ways of looking at old ones, and new hypotheses or models or theories are designed to interpret them, to propose or – perhaps – to impose the author's opinion on the academic community. This is true of economic policy, and particularly true of the accounting field, where the old controversies of current values vs. historical costs, of primary vs. secondary measures, of entity vs. the proprietary theory in consolidated accounts are mainly stories of alternate revolutions.

As for the newcomers in oligopolistic industries, new ideas are anyway rejected, accepted, or even put aside, depending on how strong are the old paradigms (and how widespread and self-defensive) and depending, at the same time, on the inner validity of innovations: which take years (or decades) to become paradigms in their turn, not to mention the cases of refuted or forgotten truths.

Could we use the evolution-revolution model to illuminate the history of modern Italian accounting, ignoring for a while the bloody debates as well as the unsolved problems which disappeared with no apparent conclusion due to changes in fashion or to effective revolutions, we could begin by defining the following five accounting periods (Canziani 1980):

- empirical double entry, from the late Middle Ages to the end of the eighteenth century;
- the Cinquecontisti revolution, from Napoleon to Cerboni (first half of the nineteenth century);
- the Cerboni revolution, from the middle to the end of the nineteenth century;
- the Besta revolution (the Venice School), from 1880 to the Second World War;
- the Zappa revolution, from 1922 to the present day.

The circumstances surrounding the origin of double-entry bookkeeping is still a debated and unsolved topic in Italy. Some authors attribute its origins to the activities of Italian maritime states during the Middle Ages (Venice and Genoa in particular), others underline instead the role of non-maritime states such as Lombardy and Florence. The primacy of Italy in this field is well-known also from a theoretical point of view; early double-entry theorising can be attributed to Fibonacci and others; also to a follower of them, whose name is widespread in the Anglo-Saxon world: Luca Paciolo.

According to our present knowledge, the centuries following the fifteenth were a period of economic and socio-political decadence, with both private and business accounting following old and semi-mechanical paths. Only public accounting in Italy – but we are now referring to the regions which came under Austrian domination in the eighteenth century – registered the practical and theoretical innovation of the cameralist accounting (*Kameralistik*).

Perhaps the first paradigm to imprint both theory and practice in a larger way was the French Cinquecontisti (five-accounts school), proposed by the two Louis Degranges: this method was diffused from France with Napoleon at the beginning of the nineteenth century and was dominant during the first fifty years of this period, especially in Northern Italy.

From Cerboni to Besta

Giuseppe Cerboni's basic idea was to restore such an absolute personality in double-entry accounts as to addressing them always and only as *persons*, no matter whether physical or juridical. Assets and liabilities were immediately attached to rights and obligations, with special columns for differences – i.e. results; the whole building process gave life to a sort of 'accounting law' to Cerboni (1873). This innovation – a revolution in fact, quality and complexities apart – would have also permitted a general accounting unification and, once applied to state accounts, the international unification of accounts; its founder gave it the name of *Logismografia*.

Cerboni's revolution, which took place broadly speaking after 1870, gradually eliminated French influence. In the history of Italian accounting of the nineteenth century, it is of overwhelming importance for three special reasons. First, and due to the public role of its founder, *Logismografia* was diffused (and later imposed) to public accounts; second, it was regarded as a purely Italian contribution, a way of reaffirming the nation's recovery in sciences and techniques, as had happened in the political field passing from regional states to the State, which was unified in 1860; third, the theory tried over the years to enlarge and deepen itself becoming a comprehensive, self-contained theory of the firm. The latter development, 'a necessary step' in the evolution, occurred in the years which followed the acceptance and triumph of *Logismografia*, when Besta's revolution – the last but one – was approaching.

The passage from accounting to the economy of the firm (i.e. the interface of business economics and business administration) was to be based on the following principles (Cerboni 1894):

* Accounting is composed of four branches, i.e. calculus, theory of double entry, accounting and organisation, the study of managerial functions.
* Accounting is the science of business administration.
* In every economic entity, from the family to the State, there is a general similarity of administrative functions, i.e. starting, managerial, and concluding phases and processes (from profitability forecasting to income distribution, accounts presentation, audit and so on).

The difficulty of reconciling existing theory with new practices is one of the most important causal factors in the formation of new theories. This was true also for the *Logismografia*: the passage to a comprehensive theory of the firm was but a step in the right direction; the inner bureaucratic complications of Cerboni's system of double entry were developing rapidly as a result of the increasing complexity of firms during this period of Italian economic development.

The first real scientific revolution was accomplished by Fabio Besta, who gave accounting a new theoretical base, building on philosophical premises as well as historical researches masterly conducted. Joining the historical method of analysis (as regards bookkeeping and administration) with Spencerian epistemology (as regards the object, the methods and the contents of accounting and auditing), Besta gave life to a general theory of accounting which found its own place within the general system of sciences of his age. In particular, building also on the theories of G. B. Vico and A. E. Schaeffle, Besta proposed to include accounting within the sciences – an equal to law, economics, and mathematics – studying the same phenomena, that of wealth (Besta 1880, 1922).

He distinguished the pure science and its practical side (the art) by stating – echoing John Stuart Mill – that they are strictly connected, the art representing the imperative mode of the science, which is the indicative; the art, in its turn, is a system of pieces of knowledge ranked and interconnected, oriented to practice.

Consequently the field of accounting is not mere bookkeeping, but concerns the whole control of the wealth of the firm: control is achieved in fact by both accounting and management, the former measuring and orienting the latter.

Besta was appointed in 1880 to the chair of accounting at the Upper School of Commerce of Venice (established in 1872, and one of only four upper schools of commerce in Italy, together with Genoa, Naples and Bari) and, over the years, his efforts helped to put the School in the top rank. As accounting was not taught at university level in Italy prior to the 1920s and 1930s, Besta's theories exerted a dominant influence – at the scientific, practical, and academic levels – from the end of the nineteenth century to the Second World War.

The phenomena Besta dealt with can be summarised as follows (Besta 1922, vol. I: 3–35):

• Even if the ultimate goal of working activity is the satisfaction of human needs and the improvement of the single person, men are motivated to work by the search for a 'subjective' goal (Aristotle): for this reason, common things become economic goods once they serve subjective goals.
• Gaining wealth is the most important part of economic activity; furthermore, the very result of working (Cossa's 'production of wealth'), and wealth is represented by the exchangeable goods.
• Through the investment process, the saved share of wealth later in time becomes 'working wealth' (Ferrara, Say), or 'intermediate utility' (Schaeffle) to produce new wealth once more. Due to the complexity of production, people cannot obtain by themselves the largest part of the goods they need: that is why they form societies for 'gathering of reciprocal utilities' (Vico), nowadays meaning also production, exchange, consumption and so on.

The economic activities allowed and implied by the gathering of people in human society to attain the economic objectives, require, as a basic element, administration i.e. 'wise governance'. This means personal actions tending to guide, to manage, to govern for the utility of any subject, and the process can be subdivided into three main elements: (1) the owners and their authority, (2) the managers, who are the group of persons who have the duty of governing every administrative activity according to the directives of the owners; (3) the organisation, which includes the attitudes and strengths to undertake the administrative work. The object of administration is the *azienda*, which is not a physical or juridical subject, but the sum of facts, relations and affairs concerning a given set of capital goods belonging to a person, a family or to any other subject, from the single (limited) company to the State.

Administration is different from *azienda* to *azienda* but, as it always makes use of goods and wealth, it reveals in any case some similarities of functions and processes which permit the identification of its three common features:

• Governance, which seeks to aim every action at pursuing the firm's goals in the most effective way.
• Management, i.e. the general actions aimed at regulating and giving direction to every kind of specific technical action.

- Control, i.e. audit, accounting and control of economic effects and results in order to aim at the predefined goals and to improve both governance and management by increased awareness.

Within this system, accounting is an applied or concrete science in a Spencerian framework. From the theoretical point of view, it studies and defines the laws of economic control within every kind of *azienda*, also deducing the rules that have to be followed to get an effective, complete and convincing control. From the practical side, it is nothing but the correct applications of those rules.

The Venice School and Gino Zappa

Fabio Besta had many important followers, including Alfieri, D'Alvise, De Gobbis, Ghidiglia, Rigobon and many others, who dominated university accounting in Italy from the beginning of the twentieth century. This cultural and sociological domination was reinforced after the 'truce' with the Cerboni schools, broadly speaking from about 1905. From the accounting point of view, the years that followed were evolutionary in the worst sense: repetitions, imitations, practical applications of Besta's theories to different kinds of firms, long and useless monographs to try to combine the results of Besta's and Cerboni's revolutions.

From the economic point of view, however, those very years saw initial signs of various turning points of the twentieth century (among them J. M. Keynes' *Indian Currency and Finance*, J. A. Schumpeter's, *Die Theorie des Wirtschaftliche Entwicklung*), as well as the enrichment or the completion of some reputed pillars of economic thought (among them Boehm-Bawerk 1909–12, and Fisher 1906 and 1911).

It was at this time that a brilliant and highly promising student of professor Bellini of Milan, Gino Zappa, the son of an entrepreneur in the field of international trade, was sent to Fabio Besta to complete his training, becoming in this way the youngest among Besta's assistants. In this way Bellini – a reputed accountant whose most important success had been the individuation of the 'off-balance sheet' elements – succeeded in exposing Zappa to the most reputed Italian scholar in the field of accounting.

Zappa's approach – up to his early thirties – was the classical one of a 'brilliant assistant' – a 'top pupil', in Kalecki's words: clean, clear, crisp, scholarly documented, deep and complete; but lacking originality. This is specially true of *Le valutazioni* (1910), an important book (it sold out rapidly) which examines the evaluation criteria for annual accounts (including a critical analysis of the choice between historical costs and current values), but which was totally framed within Besta's system of thought.

Towards new epistemic foundations after 1911

Advances in the field of accounting largely depend on the interpretation of its field as an epistemic one, or not. Accounting theories had already advanced: (1)

as they accepted the double reality of accounting problems – a mixed nature, jointly practical and theoretical, and (2) as they treated it with adequate scientific methods which succeeded in combining these two aspects.

The confirmation of these propositions comes from both epistemology and historical reflection: Cerboni, Besta, and especially Zappa were soundly grounded in a single philosophical way of thinking which was at the same time a clear-cut way to knowledge.

Cerboni was rooted in concepts of organism and system, while Besta was rooted in the classical positivism of his era, that of Spencer-Comte. While the former imagined a larger field than accounting in which to interpret the economy of administrative bodies, the latter reserved this role for the economy, but at the same time raised accounting to the same scientific level (as for law and mathematics) as 'the science of economic control', thus giving it a specific role 'within the general tree of sciences'.

Younger than Besta by some forty years, Gino Zappa himself was grounded within that positivist tradition which dominated the social sciences world from around 1870 to 1910. A somewhat mysterious turning point occurred in his scientific life between 1910 and 1920; broadly speaking, a complete overturn in his way of learning, knowing, and conceptualising. No one knows the 'shock factors' of this change, although two or three such have been proposed, on an inductive basis. In any event, we are approaching this change, which has been termed 'the making of the Revolution' (Canziani and Rondo Brovetto 1992).

Undoubtedly the contrasts between Cerboni and Besta – basically unresolved – represented the initial point of departure for a consideration of the nature of accounting's potential, its goals and contents. Second, there was the still unresolved issue of *value* in business and economics, stemming from Ricardo (and before) and persisting – evident or hidden – throughout the nineteenth and twentieth centuries. Third, there was the nature of income and its relation to wealth. *Le valutazioni* (Zappa 1910) had been close – maybe too close – to the Anglo-Saxon debate of 1900–8 about the nature of income, and to the works of Irving Fisher, so a well-grounded reflection on that topic would have been possible only *after* 1910. The reality of income – particularly during inflation and with reference to firms – became a topic of troubled speculation in those very years, 1912–20, when firms themselves revealed more and more their true understanding of 'systems of prices' (i.e. the interplay of cost prices and revenue prices in space and time). Finally, the (relatively) new epistemic theories, the 'critical positivism' of about 1900–20 which taught different paths for knowledge, in particular the scientific one. This was of overwhelming importance for Zappa who, reading Enriques, Vailati and others, found himself disappointed by the same positivism in which he had previously believed.

This tentative list does not provide a full explanation. Heidegger once asked 'Where do ideas come from?', and still nobody knows, especially as regards scientific concepts. Maybe the environment, maybe the sum of books, theories, lessons and conversations one has been exposed to in life, maybe – last and not least – the continuous search for solutions to scientific problems by the scholar, indifferent to scientific novelties and fashions but determined to master still unsolved topics. We should never forget the unending desire for understanding on the part of the scientist, the unlimited capacity for solving problems (and creating new ones) of the genius. As it has been said, it is not the (inductive-deductive) method which resolves, but the spirit: 'the Genius and the mortal instruments', in Shakespeare's words.

BEFORE THE METHODOLOGICAL TURN-ROUND FROM EMPIRICISM TO IDEALISM

The years 1900–20 in social sciences

During the second part of the nineteenth century, Europe experienced the development and the triumph of positivism, a philosophical approach attributing an overwhelming importance to facts. 'Scientific' was the adjective attached to a branch of knowledge once it had established a close attention to actual facts: so there was a 'scientific' medicine, a 'scientific' psychology, sociology, and so on. In those early years a blind attention to facts seemed to be a self-sufficient solution to any scientific (and methodological) problem. One of the most important Italian philosophers of the present century gave the following sketch of that situation:

> The philosophy of positivism is the product of the historical development of sciences: it has the same objects as all the other positivistic sciences from mathematics to sociology (it is simply the sum of them all) and the same method: 'facts and experience are the very base of the positivistic philosophy'.
>
> This position seems nowadays to have no sense; it is not even worth criticising. But we must remember the meaning it had in the period of empirical intoxication we faced in Italy for nearly twenty years between 1870 and 1890. In those days everyone believed facts existed as such, and that it was enough to have open eyes to perceive their presence, to see them as they really are – one by one as a whole – and to build from them a science driven by material things. Anyway, that epistemology was so comfortable! It said: *quot capita, tot sententiae*, as many systems as there are heads. So let's cut all the heads off and leave – what? – facts and experience! This was the answer of thousands of positivistic scholars of every positivistic science.
>
> (Gentile 1948: 297–8)

From the beginning of the twentieth century, however, the idea developed that *no fact exists without a subjective consideration* (this being especially true for scientific facts), and that every science had to become metaphysical in order to be able to explore the problems *beyond* the facts. Through the years, therefore, not to mention Kuhn's theories once more, the total blind attention given to facts began to face stronger and stronger opposition. This was due in general to the discontent increasingly associated with every scientific revolution as it progressively wins, dominates and becomes dogmatic; in particular to the excess of pragmatism, the massive *a posteriori* reasoning and the development of 'scientific' theories even when the facts are ordinary, fuzzy, badly defined or even wrong (Canziani 1986).

Due to this development, we can say that the last phase in the evolution of positivism took place in the period 1900–20, before the massive return to Idealism (Croce and Gentile in Italy), Subjectivism (Prichard, Josep, Joachim in England), and Ontology (Heidegger in Germany).

That evolution was, as usual, as multi-directional as lava, with the conflicting and overlapping mixture of (1) the continuation of the story in a pure positivistic fashion, (2) the *internal* criticism of positivism, and (3) the bluntly anti-positivistic ways of reasoning, i.e. those leaning again towards the *a priori* within theory-building processes.

The continuation of the story is common to every evolutionary process, where old theories under attack are defended, strengthened and even improved. This process involved emphasising once more the role of facts, the declared impossibility of defining any *a priori* framework, the exclusive focus on empirical research and – at the end – a purely inductive degeneration. The scholars within this framework, determined to have no methodology but facts, were actually followers – most of them unconsciously – of that peculiar epistemological stream called integral empiricism (or pan-inductivism).

On the opposite side, we can now easily understand why the final reaction to positivism, to empiricism, and to induction, could have produced nothing but the return to idealism, to *a priori*, and to deduction. This switch back could have occurred in a number of ways, and in fact did. The common ground was the existence of *a priori* principles, *a priori* judgement schemes, and the action of the subject in building thoughts, theories and facts. The scholars connected themselves, generally, to Hegel (the neo-Hegelism of Bradley in Britain, of Croce in Italy, of Royce in the US) or Kant (the neo-criticism of Renouvier and others in France, of Cohen and Natorp, of Windelband and Rickert, of Husserl in Germany) or both.

The 'critical positivism' of Zappa

The above influences – although concentrated in two nearly neglected decades today commonly perceived like a minor step between Marshall and Keynes – were of great importance for the evolution of economics in general, as the true scholar is always questioning himself on methodological problems and in those very years two incompatible epistemic streams were fighting each other – empiricism and idealism.

The average scientific mentality of that time (or better the *Zeitgeist*) gradually led to the demise of integral positivism and – year after year – to the rapid emergence of 'critical positivism' and 'neo-Kantism'. This phase, only an intermediate stage in the path towards subjectivity in science, was also a critical one from the point of view of studies of business and of the firm, especially in Germany and Italy.

The practical contents of these sciences remained obviously large, but the definition of their relationships with theory remained problematic. The interpretation of business disciplines as nothing but techniques – thus approaching the concept and contents of art in the Renaissance sense (Schmalenbach 1911–12) – was at its sunset, in favour of abstraction-based frameworks of the Kant-Hegel type (Nicklish 1932). The intermediate phase of 'critical positivism' – brief but powerfully widespread in economics and law – is of overwhelming importance, as it appears to have been for some years – and for long in the case of scientific schools – a junction between the two, mixing positivism and idealism, *a posteriori* and *a priori* in renewed if not original ways.

Gino Zappa belonged to this particular stream of thought, to which he remained faithful up to the end of his life, urging his followers to read Enriques above all. As a result of his controversial speculative period, he adopted the suggestions of 'critical positivism' as regards the method, which is the mixed or the simultaneously deductive-inductive method. According to this, general hypotheses are used to select special, *scientific* facts (not casual nor common, but similar to each other in space and time and belonging to series), the analysis of which allows the researcher to correct, modify and specify the hypotheses themselves.

The critical positivism of Gino Zappa goes back to Bacon and Descartes and brings together empiricism and rationalism up to Kant and beyond. It recalls the last contributions of John Stuart Mill on the mixed *a priori* method of 'induction reasoning' (*On the definition of Economic Policy*) as well as Ricardo, and concludes with the active role of the scholar and his hypotheses according to Spencer, Mach, Poincaré, Le Roy and others. By applying his renewed methodology to the study of the core problems of accounting – i.e. capital and income, the value of money, production and distribution of wealth – Zappa realised (and stated) that *income* is the most important phenomenon in the firm's economy, and that whatever notion of capital one has, it has to be related in some way to income (Zappa 1920–9) (see below).

In this conception, Zappa was partly influenced by the economic debate of the period 1900–10, including Fisher's work (1906), but he was also challenged by the economic consequences of the First World War (including hyperinflation) as well as by German advances in the field. The same influences led Zappa to underline not only the relevance of income, but also the necessity – both for its calculation and in more general terms – of a deep knowledge (a 'scientific' one) of the economy of the firm in its dynamics, structure and composition. In conclusion, a renewed concept of accounting must be based on an overall, self-contained science concerning the analysis of the firm as a whole, the *Economia Aziendale* (see below).

INCOME (1920–9), OR THE MAKING OF THE REVOLUTION

The long-lived interest in income, and its direct measurement

Some forty years ago, a leading US accounting scholar wrote:

Fifty years ago the principal interest of those concerned with the financial data of business enterprises centred on the periodic display of assets and liabilities (balance sheet) . . . at the present time the principal attention of investors, financial analysts, and the general public is focused on the statement setting forth the periodic net income or earnings of the business, with the balance sheet being viewed ' . . . as the connecting link between successive income statements.'

(Hepworth 1953)

Such a shift was probably brought about by the dramatic change in price stability that occurred in the US during and after the Second World War. A similar situation was faced by European accountants, businessmen and scholars after the First World War, when a period of economic disorder followed the sound international stability of 1871–1911. During the previous long period of stability (with fixed exchange rates based on the gold standard), there was no problem of distinguishing monetary from real variables, no dramatic change in prices, no foreign exchange variations: uncertainty problems were minor, if any, except for those that were firm-related. In that situation the following ideal definition could have been accepted as fully valid: 'A company is organised to purchase an asset whose life is known. The asset will produce known revenues each year and will require known outlays each year' (Storey 1960). Equally, in such frameworks, the Boulding-Hicks definition of capital and income is acceptable: as fixed-value assets produce a stable income flow, income is the dividend that could be paid yet leaving the firm as well off at the end as at the beginning of the period (Hicks 1946). Due to the stability of prices on one side and the certainty of the income flow on the other, the system is logically determined: capital produces income, income is the difference in the value of capital between two subsequent measurements, the twins are now congenial for a while.

It is debatable whether these conditions ever really existed but, if they did, variations in prices dramatically altered the equilibrium after 1914, and separated economic theory from accounting, in a way, perhaps indefinitely (Boulding 1962).

The income-production process remains unaltered (assets transform input into output and costs into revenues as they did before), but two major changes occur as far as the measurement processes are concerned, which can be summarised as follows:

- The entry values of assets diverge more dramatically from their current values, even though the so-called 'historical' cost paid out retains its significance for the overall financial situation of the firm.
- The income-stream volatility increases, giving rise to alternate net profit or losses stemming from the very same assets and liabilities.

Both income and wealth are changing under these conditions, and the notion of income as 'the difference in financial situation between two subsequent measurements' – rather idealistic in any case – is no longer viable.

The post-First World War reaction of European countries to these problems varied, though it must be admitted that conditions differed from one to another. The conclusion of the Pigou vs. Hayeck debate is that Great Britain failed to respond to the need for change, but in two countries – namely Germany and Italy – innovative (and somewhat controversial) accounting ideas were developed, which tried to cope with the new theoretical and practical problems which inflation (and renewed epistemologies) had given rise to. The standard authors in the field are Eugen Schmalenbach for Germany (*Dynamische Bilanz*, 1919) and Gino Zappa for Italy (*Il Reddito*, 1920–9), who arrived at similar conclusions along different paths.

Two major problems, among others, troubled Schmalenbach and Zappa:

1 how to be able to measure annual income, as its bases of measurement are no longer static;
2 how to attribute to assets a value in circumstances where they helped to give rise to annual results which were variable in sign (positive or negative) and size.

These questions raised the further question of the causal link – from the value-attribution point of view – between income and wealth. As turbulent prices meant turbulence within the economic system, the idea was presented of the value of capital being dependent upon the amount of income it was able to produce.

From the logical standpoint, this concept would seem to invert the capital → income link, into a new income → capital relationship. This notion would have required, to become operational, the direct measurement of income as the only way to achieve this goal (Canziani 1982).

Such a notion implied a revolution in the interpretation of the economic nature of income and wealth. Under the new hypotheses, partly connected to Irving Fisher's considerations about the importance of income in (turbulent) economic times, the role of assets in transforming inputs into outputs remained unchanged, but the value-attribution process centred upon the flow values (income) instead of stock values (capital).

From the operational point of view, it was the attention paid to income to underline the importance of the income statement, as the true statement by which (1) to understand the sign, amount and composition of income, and (2) to give a proper valuation to assets and liabilities (expressed in 'historical' values) which were considered as multi-annual costs to be transformed into revenues (the assets) and into financial revenues to be repaid (the liabilities).

The role of primary measures

From the business economics point of view, a firm's life is a continuous interplay of costs and revenues, of monetary variations of both signs: under this light, income is the core of the firm's activity, assets and liabilities being interpretable – in a sense – like the mere result of the interplay between costs and revenues.

According to Zappa's interpretation, the only possible way of measuring costs and revenues with the highest possible methodological correctness is to look at the relative monetary magnitudes at the exchange transaction moment. The negotiated cost (revenue) expresses the value produced by the input (output) of a firm's operations (see Table 1). Obviously, periodic income determination is no longer a process of assets evaluation, except for the need to allocate 'values common to two, or more, periods', i.e. mainly stocks and plant.

In this way we can define the following steps – which are some of the most important among Zappa's conclusions – practical and methodological at the same time:

- The inductive-deductive method is of basic importance in every science, in order (1) to select 'scientific' facts only, i.e. the common, constant, repeated, regular ones, (2) to gather them in groups, series, relationships and hierarchies, and (3) to attain to abstraction-generalisation, which represent the truly scientific knowledge expressed by principles.
- In practical sciences both the general framework and particular facts are of importance. Within business studies – as firms are (1) complex and systemic combinations of factors of production, and (2) autonomous but 'disturbed' going concerns – accounting theories must be able to show the unity of interdependent facts belonging to previous, present and future moments in the life of firms. In addition, they must show both the relationships in space and time among administrative facts and their own connections with the overall economy of the firm.
- Whatever the notion of capital, its interpretation depends on income as 'the most important fact within a firm's life'. For this reason, accounting systems must represent the formation of income, which is related both to every administrative fact and to the firm's overall dynamics. The accounts are now designed to achieve a new goal, measurement of income. They are established on exchange transactions as the 'critical event'. The monetary magnitudes which stem from these transactions are presented so as to reach higher and more systematic knowledge; above all, they give origin to economic values which are certain (or not uncertain) in nature. Accounting systems of this kind are fully related to the dynamics of the firm: income is generated in time, capital is continuously modified. In such a way:
  - the whole double entry system is based on external transactions (cost and revenues certain in nature), while dynamic processes (e.g. stocks) are often evaluated outside double entry through statistical methods;
  - balance-sheet values represent only accounting values in one moment – the end of the period – of their continuous change.
- Facts are self-contained and perfectly related to precedent and subsequent facts, while measurements, on the contrary, are partial and in this respect abstract. Common accounting operations are limited and imperfect, tending to abstract from reality according only to monetary variations. This way they need to be enlarged and completed: as accounting has a set of multiple objects and goals, so it has to rely on multiple accounting measurements, statistical ones in particular.

Under these hypotheses the problem of allocating the 'lifetime income' to accounting periods emerges. The need to split a firm's life into a succession of administrative periods (financial years) gives rise to no problems only where every operation is concluded *within* the administrative period. But this special case apart, the problem of determining the yearly income immediately emerges. According to the nature of economic processes and operations (ended vs. going), the profit and loss account for the period n will be composed as in Table 1.

Table 1 Profit and loss account for the period (n)

Negative elements	Positive elements
Initial work in progress (costs sustained to $n-1$)	Sales
Costs measured by money transactions	Expected revenues or final work in progress (costs for $n+1$)
Amortisation, depreciation, provisions	

In this way, operations which start and end within the administrative period give rise to no problem of measurement, as they derive from a couple of monetary variations, i.e. exchange transactions as primary measures. The operations which start within the administrative period and continue pose, on the contrary, valuation problems of a monetary type (the *ex ante* uncertainty, Shwayder 1967). Every profit and loss account mixes – as the financial year puts them together – costs and revenues of a certain vs. uncertain nature depending on their proximity to transactions: they are determined by the double entry system (labour costs, purchases, sales and so on) or through statistical methods (depreciation, work in progress, stocks). The former are named quantità economiche; the latter – the true critical path of the model, 'values common to two (or more) periods' – are called secondary measures and distinguished between (1) *stime* (estimations), if they meet a proof in time like inventory or provisions for taxes or bad debts and (2) *congetture* (conjectures) if they cannot meet any specific proof in time but only a judgement about their consistency (like yearly depreciation allowances) (VV. AA – i.e. various authors – 1982).

From the theoretical point of view, according to Zappa's system:

• The gross margin of the year should have represented the 'fairly allocable income' related to the cost-revenue dynamics of both the closing period and the incoming one, averaged by the analytical evaluation of profits and risks in progress.
• The interfacing balance sheet should have represented – though based on 'historical' costs – secondary measures expressing the expected evolution of the income stream.

Such an accounting system naturally faced substantial opposition from previously accepted theories, as evaluation criteria, the nature of the annual accounts, and double entry systems seemed to be challenged. Moreover, one major problem arose in relation to the role and value of assets. Zappa's system – as to an extent with Schmalenbach's – seemed to reduce the role of depreciable-depletable assets and the importance of 'historical' costs. According to its pure version, the system of assets was worth the contribution that could be made to future income streams. If the problem was solved – as regards inventories – by the attribution of a value oriented by the expected sale prices, with relation to depreciable-depletable assets, the new system could have given rise to a 'circular causation link' (Swan 1962), as their value is connected to income streams, and these in turn depend on depreciation allowances.

From the practical point of view the implementation of such a measurement system was also difficult: above all, it contravened civil law prescriptions, which were generally based on 'historical' costs as well as the prudence principle.

In most cases, a mixed system was implemented, respectively based:

- on monetary magnitudes as primary measures;
- on the prudence principle as far as secondary measures were concerned (this meant historical costs in most cases, or even the lesser of historical costs and market values);
- on fiscal regulations in every permitted 'grey area', the filed balance sheet being also the basis for taxation.

Although, as a result, the annual accounts resulted in a combination of historical costs, current values and expected values (when not ruled by the principle of prudence) the two revolutions of Besta and Zappa had a substantive role in suggesting the modifications – and final substance – of the book of the Civil Code containing company laws.

The Royal Codes of 1942 – still under Besta's influence – prescribed the principles of truth, self-evidence, precision, minimum disclosures for assets and liabilities, and definite criteria for the valuation of plant, machinery and stocks (debtors and creditors being generally governed by the principle of prudence). The reform of 1974, this time under Zappa's influence, prescribed minimum disclosures for both costs and revenues and the report by the board of directors, as well as the inclusion of additional material, such as interim reports for listed companies and the results of subsidiaries.

As a result, and thanks to these two representatives of the Venice accounting school, the annual accounts of Italian companies were highly comparable even before adoption of the Fourth EC Directive.

THE *TENDENZE NUOVE* (1927) OR THE *ECONOMIA AZIENDALE* AS THE SCIENTIFIC BASIS OF ACCOUNTING

The nature of the firm in its larger boundaries

Gino Zappa became a full professor at Genoa University in 1919, and succeeded Fabio Basta at Venice University in 1921. However, it was not until about the 1940s that his view of accounting's aim and role become almost entirely dominant in Italy. We must remember, of course, that an innovative conception of the firm formed the basis of his accounting revolution. The firm was interpreted not as a set of assets and liabilities, nor as a nexus of contracts among the various factors of the production (Coase-Williamson), but as a set of contracted prices. Within the firm's overall life, costs and revenues cross and follow each other, and global income is at the same time the result of these variations and the goal the firm has to achieve.

This new concept of the firm, also defined as the 'going economic concern' (Zappa 1927), produced a new science, the *Economia Aziendale*: a general theory of the economy of the firm designed to study with new methods the laws of equilibrium and development of every kind of firm. *Economia Aziendale* was presented in the academic year 1926–7 at Venice University (Zappa 1927). Since those years also saw the publication of the *Reddito*, we can easily see that they were the common fruits of the same revolution.

Income – no matter whether we refer to global or periodic income – has no meaning outside the firm in which it is realized. In addition, it is at the same time the firm's goal and a measure of its efficiency as well as the critical profile of its dynamic economy. Therefore, to study the formation of income, we need a deep knowledge of both the economic processes of firms and the effects their dynamics bring into present and future costs and revenues; i.e. the new science of *Economia Aziendale*. Designed to achieve 'a synthesis of accounting, organisation science and management', the *Economia Aziendale* has the goal of defining 'the dynamic conditions of life' of the *azienda* (see below).

The steps which brought Zappa from the critical positivism and the revolution of income to the *Economia Aziendale* can be summarised as follows:

- Sciences, building groups and series of facts go from the heterogeneous to the homogeneous, to systems of facts useful in that truth is a quality of the whole rather than of its individual parts.
- In applied sciences we need the study of both general schemes and the specific; as the firm is a complex organic unit, the accounting system must represent the whole structure of the connected and interactive economic phenomena, including their relationships.
- Income – the most important fact in the life of the firm – has to be represented in accordance with every other phenomenon of the firm in a systemic way.
- Not every administrative fact being an accounting one, and every non-monetary fact getting lost in accounting, accounting measurements have to be integrated with statistical measurements.
- To build a sound integrated system of accounting and statistical information we need the new *Economia Aziendale*, as method and content cannot be separated.
- The task of accounting is (1) to separate the elements of the organic and unitary life of the firm, (2) to define values, and (3) to rebuild the system of the firm according to both wealth and organisation (that is why accounting, management and organisation enlighten each other and give a synthesis of the dynamics of the firm).

Economia Aziendale as a self-contained economic system

When we speak of the innovative power of the genius, we should remember that he will have absorbed numerous ideas, authors, models, facts and contributions over years as the basis for his inspiration. As far as Zappa is concerned, we should mention among his sources all the Italian (and also European and Anglo-Saxon) accounting tradition from Cerboni to Besta, from Gomberg to Paton; the whole galaxy of economists, from the classical ones to the German followers of the historical method to Mill, Pareto and Keynes. Last but not least, the whole group of the *Betriebswirtschaftslehre* scholars who proposed the unitary study of the business field – from families to firms to households in the pure empirical way (Schmalenbach 1911–12) or according to an absolute *a priori* method (Nicklish 1932; see also Canziani and Rondo Brovetto 1992).

Some sixty years later, one could point out that Zappa's fundamental contributions were the reference to the economic nature of the firm and his proposal of a synthetic branch, a unitary perspective to study the firm. Along the way, Zappa differentiated himself from both economists and accountants. The former would have studied the 'theory of the firm' but in a neo-classical way. The latter – business studies apart – would have studied mainly the firm's functions (accounting, finance, marketing), thus atomizing its economic nature.

Over the years, the studies by Zappa and his assistants were extended to markets and industries, to look into how markets, exchange structures and competition could influence the economy of the firm over time. Further fields were explored afterwards. Starting from income, firms and the market, the investigations led to the study of consumption and demand, investment, financing, loans and savings, interest rates, bank deposits and stock exchange behaviour.

Approaching the end of his life, Zappa tried – maybe due to the crisis of economics as well as some heritage from Cerboni, Besta, and the French sociologists of the 1930s – to develop the *Economia Aziendale* into an enquiry into the economic system as a whole, carried out through its components (families, enterprises, public administration) and their interrelationships. The processes of production and consumption were interpreted as special ones in firms, but similar in all entities, be they families or public authorities.

In this last stage, proposed by Zappa in his unfinished *Le produzioni* (1955–7), the *Economia Aziendale* is seen as a global economic science, an integration – or almost a substitution – for economics.

GINO ZAPPA AND HIS SCHOOL: THE EVOLUTION OF ACCOUNTING, MANAGEMENT AND *ECONOMIA AZIENDALE* STUDIES

In the master's steps

In social sciences, there are revolutions with and without disciples. But in contemporary scientific and academic revolutions, disciples are frequent (very frequent at the end) and also generally necessary. This is particularly so because, at the outset of the revolution, there is a whole system of thought – i.e. of teachers, textbooks, tenures, grants – which is functioning according to previous and antiquated paths.

One cannot evaluate here the moral and cultural motivations – frequently hidden – of innovators. We can remember that the faster revolutions defeat scientific hegemonic systems the more closely innovations answer the scientific questions of the time and the more they are defended and propagated. A substantial role in the dynamics of both Zappa's revolution and business studies in Italy is represented by Zappa's disciples as well as by his rivals and contemporary (or younger) colleagues, as all of them were impressed by his basic innovative statements.

A basic step in the process of revolution – extensions and applications apart – is the institutionalisation of the 'Great Work' in academic form, didactically viable and more easily accessible to the public. Hicks' role in relation to Keynes and the *General Theory* was filled – as regards Zappa and the *Reddito* – by Pietro Onida.

Professor at the Catholic University of the Sacred Heart in Milan and later in Turin and Rome Universities, Onida was perhaps the strongest treatise-writer among the disciples of Zappa. He wrote extensively in both the theoretical and the practical field, and brought his activity also to the international level: in English-speaking countries by the debate with R. J. Chambers. Onida's most important contributions are expressed by the twin books on finance (1931a, 1931b), by the two monographs on annual and special accounts (1935, 1944), by a book dealing with the new accounting logic stemming from Zappa's ideas (1947), and an historical recon- struction of the development of business and firm studies in Italy since the nineteenth century, also covering the innovative role of Gino Zappa as well as the discontinuities, with Giuseppe Cerboni (1951). His scientific life was concluded by the (still adopted) treatise *Economia d'Azienda* (1965).

To sketch the completion of Zappa's revolution, we must mention at least six more *mousquetaires*, representing the first generation of the scholars (they all were born in the period 1895–1915) who later on were called *zappiani*.

Ugo Caprara who, in his last years, recalled having suggested to Zappa the very name for the new branch of economics ('we have the economia *sociale*, the economia *pura*, this is economia . . . *aziendale*!'), was the first to mention the world 'school' while introducing the new concepts of double entry in a book published in 1923. He taught at Turin, Florence and Bocconi Universities, and he wrote deep studies on the functioning of markets (1926, 1928–31) – providing a sort of starting point for marketing studies in Italy – and the blueprint book, *La banca* (1946).

Giordano Dell'Amore, professor in Venice, at the Catholic University of Milan and later at the Bocconi University (Rector 1967–73) as well as a banker (chairman, at the height of his career, of the World Banks Federation), wrote first on industrial economics (1934, 1938–42, 1949), later moving on to write extensively on money, political economy, international trade and banking.

Giorgio Pivato, a professor at Genoa University and Bocconi, also an official stockbroker, dedicated himself in his early years to the service industry (1939), to move later to the economics of manufacturing firms, of industries and markets (1965) and to finance at the end of his career (1983).

Carlo Masini was a business manager and, later, professor at Venice, Parma and Bocconi Universities as well as a director of some leading companies. The starting phase of his career was along pure Zappa routes, with monographs published in 1947 and 1963. He ended his career with a treatise in the field of employment and saving (1971), designed to develop Zappa's ideas according to ways partly similar, partly different from Onida's *Economia d'Azienda*.

The last two, professors Guatri and Azzini, followed radically different paths. The first – a professor at Parma and then Bocconi University (Rector 1984–9) – studied such problems as productive efficiency (1950), multiple pricing (1951), manufacturing costs (1954, 1955) in his early years, to move definitely to the economy of industrial firms and especially marketing after 1964. Lino Azzini continued the pure Zappa tradition and helped revitalise it. He deepened the literature on such problems as investments, productivity, and the inter-temporal equilibria of the firm (1954, 1957). He then collaborated with Gino Zappa and Cudini to write textbooks for upper technical schools (1949, 1951, 1952, 1956). His later publications include the monograph *I Gruppi* (1968, which sees the entity concept as fundamental, with income and wealth only meaningful at group level, and the group as representing the firm from the economic point of view) and a treatise (1978), where the *Economia Aziendale* is strongly supported by the system theory.

One final scholar has to be remembered, who after graduation studied privately in Venice with Gino Zappa in the last years of Zappa's life while performing his academic career with Giordano Dell'Amore. Tancredi Bianchi, professor in Venice, Pisa, Rome, Bergamo and Bocconi Universities as well as a banker (chairman of the Italian Bankers' Association since 1992). From his early contributions in the field of finance (1958, 1963a, 1963b) he moved to banking (1967, 1975). His masterly work is notable for two reasons: (1) for extending the Zappa concept of (yearly) income to the annual accounts of banks, suggesting that profit and losses are *not* represented by positive and negative interests (they are secondary measures in fact) but rather by the whole positive and negative capitalisations inasmuch they are the very primary measures (the same for bonds and foreign currencies); (2) for having interpreted banks – the Central Bank included – as a system of prices and interdependent quantities (e.g. deposits, credits) which can be analysed using Zappa's concepts of economic combination and lucrative (or paying) co-ordinations.

Field advances over the years

We will now examine the contributions of the *zappiani* scholars specifically in relation to accounting. Across these different authors, periods and contributions, we can place the global renewing of accounting (and management) studies into interpretative categories, although such a global reconstruction should obviously also take account of different authors' contributions (e.g. the Tuscany School with Ceccherelli and Giannessi, the Naples School with De Minico).

First, the transition from capital to income implies a significant revolution in the double entry system as well as in the entire logic by which it is applied to the construction of annual accounts. After the early (or anticipatory) contribution by Caprara (1923), and the explicit (or implicit) applications stemming from the different editions of the *Reddito*, the first global and systemic exposition is Onida (1947); while a technical manual, both theoretical and empirical is Zappa, Azzini and Cudini (1949–56).

The general treatise on annual balance sheets – a classical approach like Paton – is Onida (1945), where the new economic logic imprints the general framework and technical solutions, while also referring to most categories of industrial and commercial company. This book puts forward the idea, dishonestly applied by some companies, of smoothing net income through special provisions in (highly) profitable years to be drawn upon in difficult years in order to permit the so-called 'dividend stabilisation'. Onida is widely referenced for specialised forms of balance sheets, and this theme was further developed by other disciples of Zappa.

The economy of deposit banks, interpreted as 'systems of prices' which have to be represented by their annual accounts, has been masterly analysed by various followers including Bianchi (1967) and Dell'Amore (1965–76).

The problem of inflation was a relevant topic in the formative phase of Zappa's revolution, and subsequently received masterly treatment from Masini (1963) (but their solution was never adopted for the purpose of Italian law). The essence of Masini's treatise – which rejected both the adoption of indexed accounts and the replacement-cost method due to their internal inconsistencies – was that it proposed the general restatement of annual values through the integration of the annual evaluation criteria with the 'revaluation technique' (the revaluation possibly producing either an increase or a decrease of values). It is required that, during inflation, past values be represented as well as new values resulting from changes in profit expectations. A general restatement of plant, machinery, and stocks is therefore suggested (as well as of depreciation and reserves), summarised within liabilities by provisions and the adjustment of equity.

Of overwhelming importance also were the studies of the dynamics of income, as they were able to make clearer the firm's operations (and profitability) as well as the nature of balance sheet values. Most of Zappa's followers treated this problem, including Azzini (1964).

A topic relatively set apart was cost (and managerial) accounting, due to the two following reasons: (1) the accent had been on income, that is to say on the external operations: production costs were in this way secondary measures and made outside the double entry system; (2) Zappa (1955–7) had made the firm statement that costs *per se* were impossible to know due to the fact that too many hypotheses and conventions were involved in their calculation. This clear-cut and rather dogmatic position, at the theoretical level, was mollified from the practical viewpoint as both Zappa and his followers were perfectly aware of the relevance of adequate costing in the decision-making process. But the concern with purely mechanical or un-reflected ways for cost measuring, and the desire to renovate financial accounting and to build *Economia Aziendale 'ex nihilo'* subordinated and postponed the studies of that area. However, cost accounting received closer attention with the works of Teodoro D'Ippolito (1935) (where costs are always linked to selling prices, and vice versa), Guatri (1955) and others.

Three more branches of accounting registered lesser contributions, obviously reflecting the emphasis Zappa had introduced into accounting. One was the study of markets, at the interface of industrial economics and marketing, intending to investigate the cross-relations of markets and firms, and the multiple ways by which they were reciprocally influenced (and, in addition, the rather mysterious interplay of costs, quantities and revenues in the formation of income). Besides the studies of Caprara, Dell'Amore, Guatri and others, we must mention Borroni (1930), Zunino (1938) and Marcantonio (1939). The last of these authors is almost the only author to have tackled the problems of public accounting, a discipline perhaps not easily theorised from the economic point of view in those years, due to its large juridical imprint (with Zappa 1954).

Finally, there is the historical perspective, never adopted by Zappa in his own studies. It is to Tommaso Zerbi (1937, 1939) that we are in debt for the only two historical books accepted within Zappa's series.

CONCLUSION AND CONTINUING PROBLEMS AT THE END OF THE TWENTIETH CENTURY

The evolution after the revolution

Looking back on the halcyon days of the high theory, we realise that Zappa's revolution was two-fold, at the same time both internal and external to account-ing. As far as this field is concerned, the transition was accomplished from wealth to income, from stock to flows, from positivism (naturalism) to a critical approach. Zappa achieved for Italy what Schmalenbach did for Germany and Saario for Finland.

In addition, for (nearly) the first time the firm was regarded, following a pure economic approach, as a self-contained reality: this fact was of seminal import-ance in the building of accounting theories (from double entry systems to annual accounts formats, evaluations and revaluations including the so-called 'account-ing for inflation') which were independent from the civil law regulations.

Subsequent events saw the deepening, improving and bringing to perfection of Zappa's theories. It is possible to argue that the disciples over-emphasized two or three points which Zappa obviously held dear, but these were used to stress differences of method and diversities in conclusions. Among them: (1) the large (absolute?) contrasts with the civil law regulations; (2) the originality of every firm and of its economy, i.e. the autonomy of every balance sheet, incompatible with 'common principles' regulations; and (3) the inconsistency of any absolute attribution of results to administrative periods, as operations and processes are interwoven and any disjunction (the so-called 'scission') must be arbitrary. From the same point of view, also in managerial studies, some interesting trends were facilitated: (1) the residual attention paid to finance, as interest was on the so-called 'typical operations' (exchanges, hence costs and revenues), and (2) the near impossibility of theorising in the fields of planning and control due to both a turbulent environment and the 'impossibility' of getting meaningful figures for costs and partial results.

Too much stress on the matters which preoccupied Zappa brought about:

- In the accounting field, the ideas of eternal independence from legal regulations (internal vs. external annual accounts); of subjectivism in valuations; of smoothing of income in order to achieve the goals of the firm (or of directors?). It seemed in some cases that measures designed to enable a better evaluation of a firm's economy opened the door to accounting subjectivism which was exploited to justify figures related to the personal interests of shareholders or directors.
- In the field of business, the rejection of managerial-oriented and functional studies, whether relating to the areas of cost accounting, marketing, strategy, etc.

There followed two developments which are typical evolutionary consequences of scientific revolutions: (1) the progressive seclusion of theory from practice and in some cases its sterile repetition, (2) its progressive substitution by different theoretical frameworks, respectively Anglo-Saxon (with their empirical methods) or juridical, which is the story of the 1970s and 1980s. These, incidentally, reinforced the still surviving capital-based theories heritage of Fabio Besta, and increasingly found themselves in line with new regulations such as the Fourth EC directive.

Economia Aziendale: institutionalized or not accomplished?

Proposing a new, self-contained branch of knowledge to study the *azienda*, perhaps Zappa felt in the risky situation acknowledged by Fabio Besta, namely that it is very dangerous to define a new science before accomplishing it. An attempt was subsequently made to apply *Economia Aziendale* to every kind of *azienda* which, by abstraction, is the economic profile of every institution, whether it be a family, a firm, or a community (from the district to the State). As it enlarged its scope, it become more and more indeterminate – its field being as large as economics but its history (and instruments) shorter – while in the 1970s and 1980s it was largely (even excessively) affected by Anglo-Saxon contributions – especially for the management of industrial firms – from writers such as Kotler, Ansoff, Porter, Williamson.

Some observers claim that *Economia Aziendale* is now an unaccomplished or mainly tentative science; others take the view that – accomplished or not – it has become institutionalised, as we now have in Italy courses, textbooks and Laurea degrees in *Economia Aziendale*. This aside, a much more substantial problem lies at the basis of this field, which can be expressed in the form of a question. Has

Economia Aziendale to be defined by its methods – systemic approach, income analysis, cost–revenue relationships, economic processes, formulation of (descriptive and normative) judgements about equilibrium, profitability and development of every kind of *Azienda* – or should it be referred to as a clear-cut defined field of analysis?

Should the former be the right approach, it could enlighten every kind of economic problem – from family consumption, to a firm's flow of funds, to the politics of state deficits – with clearer approximations than economics, confused by its excess of abstractedness and modelling.

According to the latter view, however, *Economia Aziendale* should be restricted to 'homogeneous universes', in particular to the study of firms (banks, insurance and services included), following the suggestion of Giannessi, a reputed Tuscany scholar and an independent thinker if not a rival of Zappa. This would also permit – as a first step at least – the limiting of study to 'phenomena which can be described by laws' (Husserl 1900: 5).

References

Azzini, L. (1954) *Investimenti e produttività nelle imprese industriali*, Milan: Giuffré.

Azzini, L. (1957) *Le situazioni d'impresa investigate nella dinamica economia delle produzioni*, Milan: Giuffré.

Azzini, L. (1964) *I processi produttivi e i rischi di andamento dei prezzi nel tempo*, Milan: Giuffré.

Azzini, L. (1968) *I Gruppi*, Milan: Giuffré.

Azzini, L. (1976) *Flussi di valori, reddito e conservazione del capitale nelle imprese*, Milan: Giuffré.

Azzini, L. (1978) *Istituzioni di economia d'azienda*, Milan: Giuffré.

Besta, F. (1880) *La Ragioneria*, Venice: Coletti.

Besta, F. (1922) *La Ragioneria*, 3 vols, Milan: Vallardi

Bianchi, T. (1958) *Mercato finanziario e borsa valori*, Milan: Giuffré.

Bianchi, T. (1963a) *Gli aumenti di capitale nelle imprese*, Milan: Giuffré.

Bianchi, T. (1963b) *L'autofinanziamento*, Milan: Giuffré.

Bianchi, T. (1967) *Costi, ricavi e prezzi nelle banche di deposito*, Milan: Giuffré.

Bianchi, T. (1975) *Le banche di deposito*, Turin: Utet.

Boehm-Bawerk, E. V (1909–12) *Positive Theorie des Kapitals*, 3rd revised edition in three vols, Innsbruck: VWUB.

Borroni (1930) *Il commercio dei cotoni. I cotoni americani*, Milan: Giuffré.

Boulding, K. E. (1962) *Economics and Accounting: the Uncongenial Twins*, in W. T. Baxter and S. Davidson (eds) *Studies in Accounting Theory*, London: Sweet and Maxwell: 44–55.

Canziani, A. (1980) *Concern economics and business policy in Gino Zappa's thought*, in VV.AA. 1980: 211–32.

Canziani, A. (1982) 'Measurements and Calculations in Accounting: a Note on Continental v. Anglo-Saxon Methodology', *Economia Aziendale* 1: 57–71.

Canziani, A. (1986) *Sulle premesse metodologiche della rivoluzione zappiana*, in VV. AA. 1987: 183–248.

Canziani, A. and Rondo Brovetto, P. (1992) *The emergence of the economics of the firm in continental Europe during the twenties: Betriebswirtschaftslehre and Economia Aziendale as methodological revolutions*, in VV.AA. 1992.

Caprara, U. (1923) *La partita doppia nella concezione della nostra scuola*, Milan: s.i.

Caprara, U. (1926) *Le negoziazioni caratteristiche dei vasti mercati*, Milan: Instituto Editoriale Scientifico.
Caprara, U. (1928–31) *Il commercio del grano*, Milan: Stucci.
Caprara, U. (1946) *La banca*, Milan: Giuffré.
Cerboni, G. (1873) *Primi saggi di logismografia*, Florence: La Minerva.
Cerboni, G. (1894) *La ragioneria scientifica*, 2nd vol., Rome: D. Alighieri.
Dell'Amore, G. (1934) *La lana*, Milan: Giuffré.
Dell'Amore, G. (1938–42) *Il commercio dei prodotti agrari in Italia*, 2 vols, Milan: Giuffré.
Dell'Amore, G. (1949) *I mercati a termine di borsa delle merci*.
Dell'Amore, G. (1965-76) *Economia delle aziende di credito*, 3 vols, Milan: Giuffré.
D'Ippolito, T. (1935) *Costi e prezzi nelle aziende industriali*, Milano: Giuffré.
Fisher, I. (1906) *The nature of capital and income*, New York: Macmillan.
Fisher, I. (1911) *The purchasing power of money*, New York: Macmillan.
Gentile, G. (1948) *Storia della filosofia italiana*, 2 vols, Florence: Sansoni.
Guatri, L. (1950) *I rendimenti*, Milan: Giuffré.
Guatri, L. (1951) *La diversificazione dei prezzi*, Milan: Giuffré.
Guatri, L. (1954) *Il costo di produzione*, Milan: Giuffré.
Hepworth, S. R. (1953) 'Smoothing periodic income', *The Accounting Review* 1: 32–9.
Hicks, J. R. (1946) *Value and Capital*, Oxford: Clarendon Press.
Husserl, E. (1900) *Logische Untersuchungen*, Halle: Niemeyer.
Marcantonio, A. (1939) *Legnami. gestioni forestali e gestioni mercantili*, Milan: Giuffré.
Masini, C. (1947) *Economia delle aziende industriali e rilevazioni d'azienda*, Milan: Giuffré.
Masini, C. (1957) *I bilanci*, Milan: Giuffré.
Masini, C. (1961) *L'ipotesi e l'economia d'azienda*, Milan: Giuffré.
Masini, C. (1963) *La dinamica economica nei sistemi dei valori d'azienda. Valutazioni e rivalutazioni*, Milan: Giuffré.
Masini, C. (1971) *Lavoro e Risparmio*, Turin: Utet.
Nicklish, H. (1932) *Die Betriebswirtschaft*, Stuttgart: Poeschel.
Onida, P. (1931a) *Costituzioni ed emissioni finanziarie*, Milan: Giuffré.
Onida, P. (1931b) *I 'finanziamenti' iniziali d'impresa*, Milan: Giuffré.
Onida, P. (1935) *Il bilancio delle aziende commerciali*; later published as *Il bilancio d'esercizio nelle imprese*, 1945, Milan: Giuffré.
Onida, P. (1944) *Le dimensioni del capitale di impresa. Concentrazioni, trasformazioni, variazioni di capitale*, Milan: Giuffré.
Onida, P. (1945) *Il bilancio d'esercizio nelle imprese*, Milan: Giuffré.
Onida, P. (1947) *La logica e il sistema delle determinazioni quantitative d'azienda*, Milan: Giuffré.
Onida, P. (1951) *Le discipline aziendali: oggetto e metodo*, Milan: Giuffré.
Onida, P. (1965) *Economia d'Azienda*, Turin: Utet.
Pivato, G. (1939) *Le imprese di servizi pubblici*, Milan: Giuffré.
Pivato, G. (1965) *Il mercato mobiliare*, Milan: Giuffré.
Pivato, G. (ed.) (1983) *Trattato di finanza aziendale*, Milan: Giuffré.
Schmalenbach, E. (1911–12) 'Die Privatwirtschaftslehre als Kunstlehre', *Zeitschrift fuer Handelswissenschaftliche Forschung*: 304–16.
Schmalenbach, E. (1919) *Dynamische Bilanz*, Cologne and Opladen: Westdeutscher Verlay.
Schumpeter, J. A. (1912) *Die Theorie des wirtschaftliche Entwicklung*, Leipzig.
Shwayder, K. (1967) 'A critique of economic income as an accounting concept', *Abacus* 8: 23–35.
Storey, R. K. (1960) 'Cash moments and period income determination', *The Accounting Review* 3: 449–54.
Swan, T. W. (1962) 'Circular causation', *Economic Record*, December: 421–6.

VV.AA. (1980) *Gino Zappa founder of concern economics*, Bologna: AIDEA.

VV.AA. (1982) *La determinazione del reddito nelle imprese del nostro tempo alla luce del pensiero di Gino Zappa*, Padua: CEDAM.

VV.AA. (1987) *Saggi di economia aziendale per Lino Azzini*, Milan: Giuffré.

VV.AA. (1992) *Perspectives in the History of Economic Thought*, London: Elgar.

Zappa, G. (1910) *Le valutazioni di bilancio con particolare riguardo alle società per azioni*, Milan: Società Editrice Libraria.

Zappa, G. (1920–9) *La determinazione del reddito nelle imprese commerciali. I valori di conto in relazione alla formazione dei bilanci*, Rome: Anonima Editoriale Italiana.

Zappa, G. (1927) *Tendenze nuove negli studi di ragioneria*, Milan: Istituto Editoriale Scientifico.

Zappa, G. (1955–7) *Le produzione nell'economia delle imprese*, Milan: Giuffré.

Zappa, G. and Marcantonio, A. (1954) *Ragioneria apllicata alle aziende pubbliche*, Milan: Giuffré.

Zappa, G., Azzini, L. and Cudini, G. (1949) *Ragioneria applicata*, Milan.

Zappa, G., Azzini, L. and Cudini, G. (1951) *Ragioneria generale*, Milan.

Zappa, G., Azzini, L. and Cudini, G. (1952) *Complementi di ragioneria*, Milan.

Zappa, G., Azzini, L. and Cudini, G. (1956) *Esercitazioni di ragioneria*, Milan.

Zerbi, T. (1935) *La banca nell'ordinamento finanziario visconteo*, Milan: Giuffré.

Zerbi, T. (1936) *Il mastro a partita doppia in un'azienda mercantile del trecento*, Milan: Giuffré.

Zunino, G. (1938) *Il mercato italiano degli oli d'oliva*, Milan: Giuffré.

9   Iwao Iwata (1905–55)

Tetsuya Morita

Abstract

Iwao Iwata made a major contribution to the reform of statutory accounting requirements, especially in relation to auditing in Japan after the Second World War. This chapter, however, focuses principally on his major academic contribution, which involves the development of 'the dual structure of income determination system'. Under this system income determination is seen to comprise two different models which Iwata extracted, in their pure theoretical form, from prevailing accounting practice. In addition, he demonstrated how the two models were combined with one another in practice.

INTRODUCTION

The name Iwao Iwata is little known among academic accounting circles outside Japan. This is partly because he was active at a time when international academic exchanges were less developed than is the case today; also, all his works were written in Japanese. Notwithstanding his relatively early death, he became one of the leading scholars of accounting in Japan and established an original theory which bears his name. When he died, most Japanese accounting journals issued a memorial number for him. His publications are at present regarded as classics in Japan. Therefore, it is very gratifying that Iwata has been chosen for inclusion in *Twentieth-Century Accounting Thinkers*, and we greatly appreciate the opportunity to introduce his theory to accounting academics all over the world.

CAREER

Iwata was born in 1905 in Tokyo. He started to study accounting at the Tokyo College of Commerce (today Hitotsubashi University) after graduating from the same college in 1930. His undergraduate course had focused on the methodology of economics and the young Iwata studied the value judgement discussion (*Werturteildiskussion*) that took place between Max Weber and Gustav von Schmoller in the early twentieth century. Post-graduate study of accounting took place under the direction of Professor Tetsuzo Ohta, who was a leading scholar at that time. Iwata then became lecturer of accounting at his *alma mater* in 1933. Later on, he was promoted to the position of assistant professor and then professor. He died in the early spring of 1955, just before his fiftieth birthday.

Iwata's activities can be divided into two parts. One is the study of accounting as a science and the other is the contribution to the reform of the legal accounting systems in Japan after the Second World War. In this chapter I will present, of course, the former of his activities as an academician or accounting theorist. However, his contribution to the reform of statutory accounting requirements was also substantial and will first be briefly considered.

After the Second World War Japanese statutory accounting requirements were completely reformed; based on the American model, the Securities and Exchange Act was enacted, the CPA profession was established, and a statutory audit of financial statements of listed companies by CPAs was introduced. For the new accounting system to work well, it was first necessary to introduce accounting and auditing standards in place of the defective body of accounting provisions contained in the Commercial Code at that time. Because an audit by CPAs was unprecedented, it was also necessary to educate both the CPAs themselves and the firms whose financial statements were to be audited concerning the nature of their respective roles.[1] Kurosawa and Iwata together played a leading part in bringing about the necessary changes.

Iwata's distinguished service related particularly to the establishment of the audit system in Japan in his position of chairman of the third committee (in charge of auditing) of the Business Accounting Deliberation Council of the Ministry of Finance. His colleagues, including Kurosawa, were deeply impressed by Iwata's knowledge of the development of the audit system in the United States, since most of his pre-war publications had been based on studies of the German accounting literature. Iwata died before the new audit system became firmly established in Japan, but he is widely recognised as the founder of both the CPA profession and the audit system in Japan. Indeed there is widespread agreement that no one else could have matched his achievements.

It is because Iwata devoted almost all his energies to institutional accounting reforms that he took a long time to develop his theory on the structure of income determination and, indeed, his work remained unfinished at the time of his death. Naturally this is a matter of considerable regret, and it might be argued that his work in the institutional area was an unfortunate digression for an academic. That is, however, a superficial conclusion, and the reason for his action will become apparent in the course of this chapter.

PUBLICATIONS

Iwata's academic works are divided into two fields: auditing and income determination. Until the last years of his life, his writings took the form of journal articles. This reflects partly his reluctance to publish his ideas in book form until they were fully developed, and partly because of his preoccupation with practical matters. When he finally decided to write books, he was hampered by being confined to bed with serious illness. He nevertheless succeeded in developing his earlier articles on auditing theory and practice in a book entitled *Kaikeishi-kansa (Audit by Public Accountants)*, at the end of 1954. A second book, *Kaikei-gensoku To Kansa-kijun (Accounting Principles and Auditing Standards)* is a study of the historical development of accounting principles and audit practice in the United States, and was published in the summer of 1955 just after his death.

Iwata's life-work, the explication of the structure of income determination, never reached book form because of his untimely death. However, his work was progressing steadily and almost the full picture of his ideas appeared in a series of articles published one year before his death (Iwata 1954a). These, together with other related articles, were worked up into a book *Rijun-keisan-genri (Principles of Income Determination)*, in 1956, by his disciple Toshio Iino who is now President (Vice Chancellor) of Surugadai University in the suburbs of Tokyo. The following is my own interpretation of Iwata's theory.[2]

IWATA'S THEORY – THE DUAL STRUCTURE OF INCOME DETERMINATION SYSTEM

Problems involved

Iwata started to study accounting in 1930 soon after publication of Schmalenbach's *Dynamische Bilanz* (1925). Static accounting theory, which is mainly concerned with the presentation of assets and liabilities and the determination of net worth, seemed to be superseded by Schmalenbach's new interpretation, which attached importance to the income determination process itself. However, as the result of studying the dynamic theories of Schmalenbach and his successors Walb (1926), Mahlberg (1925), etc., and the static theories of Simon (1910), Gerstner (1912), etc., Iwata identified what he saw as the differences between their underlying income determination models and the implicit purposes of accounting, especially in relation to the role of the balance sheet. Iwata doubted whether the income determination model of static theory was inconsistent with the dynamic theory, even if it is accepted that the static view of the purpose of the balance sheet is false.

Iwata arrived finally at the following idea. First, that the business accounting system is composed of two different income determination models, one underlying the dynamic theory and the other underlying the static theory. Second, that each model functions separately from but complementarily with the other. Based on this idea, Iwata analysed the accounting procedures found in practice and extracted from them two income determination models in their pure theoretical forms. He called them *Zaisan-ho* and *Son-eki-ho*, and tried to make clear in what manner both models combined with each other in the income determination system of business accounting. This is his theory of 'the dual structure of income determination system'.

The terms *Zaisan-ho* and *Son-eki-ho* could be literally translated as 'net worth method' and 'revenue and expense method'. However, I will use the Japanese terms without translation because, as will be shown later, Iwata gave these terms his own special meanings.

Zaisan-ho – income determination model underlying static accounting theory

In double-entry bookkeeping, all account balances in the general ledger put together in the adjusted trial balance are divided into two groups: revenues and expenses, and assets, liabilities and capital. The former group is transferred to the income statement, where income is computed as the difference between revenues and expenses. The latter is transferred to the balance sheet where income may be seen as the difference between net worth at the beginning and at the end of the year. Both income figures agree with each other. This is the popular explanation of the income determination process in double-entry bookkeeping. Iwata says, however, that this process is made up of two different income determination models.

Under the balance sheet approach, according to Iwata, income is determined by the actual amounts of the assets and liabilities ascertained by inspection or other means, and not by the bookkeeping records themselves. Today, of course, the values of the assets and liabilities are not always ascertained in this way, although such procedures are, of course, adopted in the case of most current assets. Aware of this fact, Iwata tried to develop an income determination model using the capital comparison method (*Kapitalvergleichsmethode*) and captioned it *Zaisan-ho*.

If income can be determined by the comparison of net worth at the beginning and at the end of the year ascertained by inspection of the assets and liabilities, full double-entry bookkeeping records are not necessary to determine income under *Zaisan-ho*. It is necessary, however, to keep records of additional capital paid in and/or dividends withdrawn during the year, even in *Zaisan-ho*. These amounts must then be added to or deducted from the net worth at the beginning of the year and such an adjusted beginning net worth amount must be compared with the year-end net worth ascertained by inspection.

The opening net worth adjusted for additional capital paid in and/or dividends withdrawn gives the amount of net worth which must remain at the end of the year in order to break even. Iwata calls this the *required amount* (*Sollbestand*) of the year-end net worth. The year-end net worth, ascertained by inspection of assets and liabilities, is instead captioned the *actual amount* (*Istbestand*) of the year-end net worth. Thus Iwata defines *Zaisan-ho* as an income determination model by the comparison of *Istbestand* and *Sollbestand* of the year-end net worth, and not by the comparison of net worth at two different points of time, the beginning and the end of the year.

The most important issue in *Zaisan-ho* is therefore to determine the *Istbestand* of the year-end net worth. It is accordingly necessary to set up the bases for the recognition of assets and liabilities on the balance sheet (*Bilanzfähigkeit*) and for the valuation of them (*Bilanzbewertung*).[3]

Zaisan-ho can determine the reliable actual amount of income, assuming that the year-end *Istbestand* of assets and liabilities can be properly ascertained by inspection or other means. Iwata places emphasis on the importance of *Zaisan-ho* in business accounting. He believes that it is dangerous for accounting to rely too much on the records, because these tend to depart from the reality. On the other hand, *Zaisan-ho* has a serious defect, in that it cannot make clear the sources of income. A model which cannot account for the sources of income is not an accounting system. This defect is therefore fatal to *Zaisan-ho* as an independent accounting model.

Iwata concluded that accounting was able to overcome the defects of *Zaisan-ho* by developing another model of income determination, that of *Son-eki-ho*.

Son-eki-ho – income determination model underlying Schmalenbach's dynamism plan

Iwata's *Son-eki-ho* is a model of income determination based on the relationship (revenues – expenses = income) which we see in the income statement. The distinctive feature of Iwata's approach is that he tries to formulate a theoretical model which excludes every element of *Zaisan-ho*.

Iwata defines *Son-eki-ho* as an income determination model in which all positive and negative elements of income are recognised and recorded as they occur; income is computed, directly, by recognising the causes of changes in the net worth. The issue here therefore is how the revenues and expenses can be recognised and measured directly when they occur.

In the accrual basis of accounting, revenues and expenses are recognised, as far as possible, on the basis of the supply of goods and services and consumption of resources when they occur. In cases where the supply and the consumption cannot be recognised when they occur, some assumptions or judgements are applied to enable their recognition at the end of year. As the supply of goods and services and the consumption of resources are recognised in terms of the physical quantity, the recognition of revenues and expenses is a physical quantity computation (*Mengenrechnung*).

On the other hand, all revenues result in receipts and all expenses result in payments in the money economy. Revenues are, in the accounting sense, receipts as the consideration for goods and services supplied (*Leistung*), and expenses are payments as the consideration of resources consumed for the accomplishments (*Aufwand*). For the purpose of income determination the recognition of revenues and expenses is, therefore, a process of discriminating the receipts and payments which are the revenues and expenses of the year from others. This is the process of monetary measurement of recognised revenues and expenses by matching of monetary computation (*Geldrechnung*) and physical quantity computation (*Mengenrechnung*).

Son-eki-ho is therefore an income determination model made up of the physical quantity computation and the monetary computation.

To measure revenues and expenses recognised on the basis of supply and consumption, the monetary computation must be expanded to include the future receipts and payments, otherwise the revenues and expenses which are not accompanied with cash flows on or before their occurrence are excluded from the monetary computation and a proper matching of the monetary and physical quantity computations is disturbed.

Function of bookkeeping records in Son-eki-ho

The daily records of revenues and expenses are indispensable to *Son-eki-ho*, and we might suppose that Iwata would find them as the output of double-entry bookkeeping. However, he regards the records of double-entry bookkeeping as the records of receipts and payments and not as the records of revenues and expenses. He explains this as follows.

The account balances of double-entry bookkeeping are put together in the unadjusted trial balance at the end of the year. The trial balance is originally prepared to confirm the mathematical correctness of accounts; under *Son-eki-ho* it also serves as the monetary computation, receipt and payment accounting. All of the accounts except cash in the debit side of the trial balance show the causes of payments and those in the credit side the causes of receipts. Some accounts in the trial balance are not, of course, cash flow items in the strict sense, but they can be regarded as the receipts or payments by using some analogy. For example, a transaction 'purchase on credit' is broken up to 'purchase for cash' and 'borrowing of money'. Then the purchase account in the trial balance is regarded as a payment and the accounts payable account as a receipt. Thus we can find in double-entry bookkeeping two types of receipt and payment accounting: one is on the cash account itself and the other in the trial balance.[4]

We will need to explain why Iwata does not try to find the revenues and expenses of *Son-eki-ho* in the account records of double-entry bookkeeping. According to him, they cannot be found there. Some debit accounts in the general ledger at the end of the year show definitely the amount of asset or expense and some credit accounts show the amount of capital, liability or revenue, but others show only the mixed amount of asset and expense or liability and revenue undivided. Consequently, the accounts in the general ledger except cash can show as a whole only the payments and receipts classified by the causes.

The unadjusted trial balance is nothing but a type of receipt and payment accounting, but it provides the data from which most revenue-receipts and expense-payments can be prepared. The criterion of the selection is, as stated above, the physical quantities of the goods and services supplied and the resources consumed for the supply during the year. Most of these physical quantities are recognised when the supply and consumption occur during the year and the recognised quantities, together with the receipts and payments, provide the bases of bookkeeping records. However, the recognition is not final for the determination of revenues and expenses of the year. Final recognition takes place in *Son-eki-ho* theoretically at the end of the year by re-examining the physical quantities actually supplied and consumed apart from the account records. On this final recognition, the account records are adjusted to show the revenue-receipts and expense-payments correctly. That is, the revenue-receipts and expense-payments for the accruals, together with the corresponding accrued assets and liabilities, are added to the bookkeeping records.

For example, the purchase account showing payment is divided into expense-payment (cost of sales) and the closing stock based on the quantities ascertained from the perpetual inventory records. The amount of interest revenue for the year is computed on the accrual basis and the account showing the receipt is divided into the interest revenue-receipt and the unearned receipt; alternatively, an amount accrued is added to the account.

Such adjustments of accounts are not based on the assets or liabilities at the end of the year, ascertained by inspection, but on the physical quantities supplied and consumed ascertained directly. This is the year-end adjustment in *Son-eki-ho*.

Balance Sheet in Son-eki-ho

Iwata's explanation for the balance sheet in *Son-eki-ho* is essentially similar to, but more refined than, that of Schmalenbach.

From the comparison of the receipts and payments in the trial balance with the revenues and expenses in the income statement, such suspended items (*schwebende Posten*) come out as [receipts, not yet revenues], [payments, not yet expenses], [revenues, not yet receipts] and [expenses, not yet payments]. Since these items are the necessary data for the income determination in the following years, they are put together in a sheet along with other suspended items, such as [receipts, not yet payments] and [payments, not yet receipts]. This sheet is the balance sheet in *Son-eki-ho*. It is prepared automatically from the receipt and payment items in the trial balance and the revenue and expense items in the income statement. It differs in essence from the balance sheet in *Zaisan-ho*, which is prepared from the assets and liabilities ascertained by inspection or other means apart from the records.

Iwata's explanation described above is the same as Schmalenbach's. Iwata answers further questions that Schmalenbach either did not or could not make clear in his *Dynamische Bilanz*. They are:

- On what grounds are the suspended items referred above allocated to the debit and credit side of the balance sheet?
- Why is cash placed on the debit side of the balance sheet?
- Is income shown or not shown in the balance sheet?

According to Iwata, it is not a logical explanation of the *Son-eki-ho* balance sheet to say, for example, that the item [payments, not yet expenses] is placed in the debit side because capital assets belong to the item. This explanation would assume the balance of *Zaisan-ho*. He instead explains how the balance sheet items arise in *Son-eki-ho* and answers the questions set out above by using the trial balance equation and the income statement equation.

The receipt and payment accounting in the trial balance is shown by equation (1).

[receipts] − [payments] = [cash] (1)

The revenue and expense accounting in the income statement is shown by the equation (2).

[revenues] − [expenses] = [income] (2)

We derive equation (3) from equations (1) and (2).

([receipts] − [payments]) − ([revenues] − [expenses]) = [cash] − [income] (3)

We obtain the following differences from the mutual relationship of the four terms in the left side of equation (3).
From the relationship of [receipts] and [revenues]:

[receipts] = [revenues] · · · · · → nothing
[receipts] > [revenues] · · · · · → + [receipts, not yet revenues]
[receipts] < [revenues] · · · · · → − [revenues, not yet receipts]

From the relationship of [payments] and [expenses]:

[payments] = [expenses] · · · · · → nothing
[payments] > [expenses] · · · · · → − [payments, not yet expenses]
[payments] < [expenses] · · · · · → + [expenses, not yet payments]

From the relationship of [receipts] and [payments]:

[receipts] = [payments] · · · · · → nothing
[receipts] > [payments] · · · · · → + [receipts, not yet payments]
[receipts] < [payments] · · · · · → − [payments, not yet receipts]

By replacing the four terms in the left side of equation (3) with the six inequalities above, we get equation (4):

[receipts, not yet revenues] − [revenues, not yet receipts] − [payments, not yet expenses] + [expenses, not yet payments] + [receipts, not yet payments] − [payments, not yet receipts] = [cash] − [income] (4)

We get equation (5) by transforming equation (4):

[payments, not yet expenses] + [revenues, not yet receipts] + [payments, not yet receipts] + [cash] = [receipts, not yet revenues] + [expenses, not yet payments] + [receipts, not yet payments] + [income] (5)

Equation (5) can be set forth in the account form as follows. This is the *Son-eki-ho* balance sheet.

Balance sheet

(payments, not yet expenses)	(receipts, not yet revenues)
(revenues, not yet receipts)	(expenses, not yet payments)
(payments, not yet receipts)	(receipts, not yet payments)
(cash)	(income)

The *Son-eki-ho* balance sheet is thus prepared automatically from the receipts and payments in the trial balance and the revenues and expenses in the income statement. The central issues in *Zaisan-ho*, such as Bilanzfähigkeit $\times 0$ and Bilanzbewertung $\times 0$, are not the subjects of discussion here. The central issue in *Son-eki-ho* is to set up the bases for the recognition and measurement of the revenues and expenses.

Defectiveness of Son-eki-ho $\times 0$

Since *Son-eki-ho* recognises the revenues and expenses on the basis of the supply of goods and services and the consumption of resources, it can make clear the sources of income. This function is a merit of *Son-eki-ho* as an income determination model.

On the other hand, *Son-eki-ho* has a serious defect: some revenues and expenses cannot be recognised without regard to the amounts of the year-end assets and liabilities ascertained by inspection, which is the procedure of *Zaisan-ho*.

The cost of sales, for example, can be obtained directly from the perpetual inventory records, but the inventory shrinkage and the loss from write-down of inventories cannot be recognised without a physical count and valuation of the inventories at the end of the year. In manufacturing enterprises, the defect of *Son-eki-ho* is more serious. In the process cost system, the measurement of the ending inventory of work-in-process is indispensable to determine product costs, but the measurement depends on the physical inspection of the ending inventory, which is the procedure of *Zaisan-ho*. Consequently, *Son-eki-ho* alone cannot determine even the cost of sales.

As mentioned earlier, Iwata agrees that it is dangerous to rely too much on the records, because they depart from reality. He calls the income of *Son-eki-ho* 'income in the records' and that of *Zaisan-ho* 'actual income', and insists that 'income in the records' must be compared with 'actual income' and adjusted to agree with the latter. This conviction leads Iwata to conclude that the models of *Son-eki-ho* and *Zaisan-ho* should be combined within the accounting system.

Dual structure of income determination

Combination of Zaisan-ho and Son-eki-ho

Zaisan-ho and *Son-eki-ho* each has both merits and demerits, and the demerits of one model are compensated by the merits of the other. While *Zaisan-ho* cannot make clear the sources of income, *Son-eki-ho* can. *Son-eki-ho* cannot recognise some revenues and expenses, and the income determined there is defective, but *Zaisan-ho* can determine the 'actual income', which includes all changes in the net worth. The models therefore complement each other and together comprise what Iwata calls 'the dual structure of income determination' in business accounting.

According to Iwata, *Zaisan-ho* and *Son-eki-ho* are combined with each other in the following manner.

In the *Son-eki-ho* model, the books are considered to be the records of receipts and payments. However, they include the record of supply of goods and services and the consumption of resources which are recognised during the year as the sources of the receipts or payments. This means that the revenues and expenses are recorded in the accounts to the extent that they are recognisable. The *Son-eki-ho* model tries to adjust these records of revenues and expenses at the end of the year by its own procedures of year-end adjustment.

However, most of the year-end adjustment procedures actually applied in the real world are not those of *Son-eki-ho* but of *Zaisan-ho*. For example, the physical count and valuation of inventories, the measurement of bad debts, and the valuation of securities are all *Zaisan-ho* procedures. As to interest revenue and interest expense, it is possible to measure their amounts for the year on the accrual basis and then to adjust the account records, which is an application of *Son-eki-ho* procedure. In the practice, however, the prepaid interest or accrued interest payable and the unearned interest or accrued interest receivable are measured on the accrual basis first and then the account records are adjusted to show the proper amounts of the revenue and expense. This is an application of *Zaisan-ho* procedure.

As will be stated later, it is impossible to apply exclusively *Zaisan-ho* procedures in the year-end adjustment, but they should be applied as much as possible.

In short, *Son-eki-ho* and *Zaisan-ho* are combined in the accounting practice to the extent that the accounting records of *Son-eki-ho* are adjusted by the procedures of *Zaisan-ho* at the end of the year. It necessarily means that the balance sheet in the accounting practice is that of *Zaisan-ho* and the accounting income is determined ultimately by the procedures of *Zaisan-ho*.

Here we encounter a serious question. If the accounting income is determined ultimately by *Zaisan-ho* procedures, it cannot be a proper income in the sense of the dynamic accounting theory, because *Zaisan-ho* is considered to be an income determination model which is compatible with the static theory. In Iwata's 'the dual structure of income determination', where two models are combined in the above manner, the static purpose becomes dominant. This does not accord with business accounting today, where the determination of the proper income is the most important purpose. Iwata's idea of 'the dual structure' then does not explain business accounting today. We must hear his answer to this question.

Two types of Zaisan-ho: dynamic theory and static theory

In *Zaisan-ho*, the income is determined on the balance sheet. The assets and liabilities are recognised by inspection or other means apart from the accounting records. The issues in *Zaisan-ho* are, as stated above, what should be recognised as the assets and liabilities and how they should be valued. The bases of the recognition and valuation of the assets and liabilities depend on the interpretation of the purpose of the balance sheet.

In the static theory, where the purpose of the balance sheet is to present a true position of net worth, the assets and liabilities are recognised and valued in line with that purpose. The amount of the income, which is determined as the difference between *Istbestand* and *Sollbestand* of the net worth at the end of the year, depends on the amount of the net worth which is determined consistently with the static purpose of the balance sheet. The main issue there is to present the net worth properly from the static viewpoint and not to determine the true or reasonable amount of income itself. The amount of income therefore is regulated by the static theory of *Zaisan-ho*.

On the other hand, we can conceive another type of *Zaisan-ho*: *Zaisan-ho* in the dynamic theory. The main purpose of the balance sheet is considered there to be the determination of the reasonable amount of income, and the assets and liabilities are recognised and valued in line with this purpose. The presentation of the net worth is only a secondary purpose of the balance sheet and it is regulated by the main purpose, the determination of reasonable income.

The difference in the recognition and valuation of assets and liabilities between the static and dynamic theories of *Zaisan-ho* could be seen in the following cases.

Assume that the specific purpose of the balance sheet in the static theory is to show the entity's ability to pay debts. Only those assets which enable debts to be repaid are recognised in the balance sheet, and they are valued at the amounts of their debt-paying ability. Therefore, both current assets and capital assets are valued at their net realisable value, and the resultant valuation gains or losses are included in income.

However, from the dynamic viewpoint, it is unreasonable to include all valuation gains or losses in income. Those assets, giving rise to valuation gains or losses which should not be included in income under the dynamic theory, are valued at cost. On the other hand, certain items having no realisable value can and must be recognised as assets in the dynamic theory of *Zaisan-ho* in order to compute reasonable income on the balance sheet. Iwata refers to Mahlberg's theory of neutralisation (*Neutralisierung*) (1925) as a typical dynamic theory based on the concepts of *Zaisan-ho*. Mahlberg asserted, for example, that the amount of original valuation of the base stock or the minimum level of inventories should be maintained in the balance sheet year by year to eliminate from income the effects of its price changes.

Iwata states that the difference between the dynamic and static theories relates to the purpose of accounting, especially of the balance sheet, and not to the income determination model. *Zaisan-ho* in the static theory is incompatible with *Son-eki-ho*, because *Son-eki-ho* is a model necessarily based on the dynamic viewpoint and it aims at the determination of reasonable income. It is therefore clear that *Zaisan-ho* in Iwata's idea of 'the dual structure of income determination' is *Zaisan-ho* in the dynamic theory. As such, it is compatible with and can be combined logically with *Son-eki-ho* within an accounting system.

Rise to dominance of *Son-eki-ho*

In Iwata's theory, dynamic *Zaisan-ho* is an indispensable component of the income determination structure. However, cases where the procedures of *Zaisan-ho* were technically inapplicable or economically impractical increased as the scale of businesses was enlarged, the capital assets increased, and the accounting standards were refined. Iwata admitted the inapplicability of *Zaisan-ho* above all to the depreciable assets.

Depreciation is, in Iwata's opinion, the accounting procedure of *Son-eki-ho*, because it determines the expense amount based on the acquisition cost or the beginning book value of the asset. The procedure of *Zaisan-ho* for a depreciable asset is to ascertain its actual amount at the end of the year (*Istbestand*) by physical inspection and to compare this value with its initial book value (*Sollbestand*). It is technically impracticable as well as economically impractical to inspect all depreciable assets physically and to value them separately from the records. In principle, therefore, the procedure of *Son-eki-ho*, is applied to the depreciable assets.

In the inventory accounting, cases are increasing where the original procedure of *Zaisan-ho* is not applied. Where the perpetual inventory records are kept, the physical inventory counts are not always taken at the year end. The counts are usually taken at times of low stock and the ending quantities themselves are not determined by the physical count.

Cases where the procedures of *Zaisan-ho* are technically inapplicable increase as the income determination accounting is refined. For example, the year-end balances of deferred charges such as the organisation costs and the costs of developing new markets cannot be ascertained by inspection apart from the records. Only the procedures of *Son-eki-ho* can be applied there.

Iwata admitted that items treated exclusively with *Son-eki-ho* are increasing in accounting practice and *Son-eki-ho* has become increasingly dominant over *Zaisan-ho*. However, his theory of 'the dual structure of income determination' would no longer be tenable if *Zaisan-ho* was eliminated from the accounting system.

Role of CPA audit in income determination system

Iwata was convinced that a daily record of transactions is necessary to reveal sources of income, but was equally convinced that they tend to depart from reality and periodically require adjustment. The income determined in *Son-eki-ho* must therefore be collated with that of *Zaisan-ho* to ensure the reliability of accounting income under 'the dual structure of income determination'.

The method of income determination, in practice, does not correspond with Iwata's theoretical structure. This was a matter of considerable anguish to Iwata, who saw *Zaisan-ho* being pushed into the background. His remaining hope was that the reliability of accounting income could instead be fulfilled by *Zaisan-ho* in the CPA audit. I will quote passages of his explanation (1956: 167–8), translated here as literally as possible, because they are essential parts of his theory.

> In today's business accounting system, which is mainly composed of *Son-eki-ho* procedures, the CPA audit takes the place of *Zaisan-ho*. The CPAs are in charge of *Zaisan-ho* which the business accounting has left out of the system.
>
> Main procedures of auditing, such as physical inspection, confirmation, observation, and enquiry, fulfil the functions of checking on the accuracy of accounting records by ascertaining the realities and adjusting the accounting records to agree with them.
>
> These procedures are nothing but those of *Zaisan-ho* . . . *Zaisan-ho* which was left out from the business accounting system of firms has developed outside of the system in the form of audit by the CPAs . . . Therefore the audit by CPAs is an integral part of the business accounting system. It is not too much to say that the business accounting which is not audited by CPAs is fully defective.
>
> I should explain in detail that the audit by CPAs is another form of *Zaisan-ho*. I should also make clear the situation that the firms are getting back *Zaisan-ho* in the form of the internal audit system and that the function of the audit by CPAs is changing from carrying out the part of *Zaisan-ho* to checking on the fairness of accounting judgements inherent in *Son-eki-ho* procedures. However, I would like to close the interim report of my study thus far with mentioning only the accounting significance of the CPAs' audit.

ASSESSMENT OF IWATA'S THEORY

Iwata's attempt to find the functions of *Zaisan-ho* in the audit by CPAs is unique; he places the audit by CPAs *inside* the accounting system. It serves as an integral component of his structure of income determination system in circumstances where *Zaisan-ho* in the original form is no longer practicable. We may assume that this is why he devoted all his energies to the establishment of the audit system of Japan in the post-war period.

From a common viewpoint which sees the CPA audit as checking financial statements from outside, Iwata's idea to place it inside the accounting system might seem rather strange. Iwata stresses, however, the role of the CPA audit as teaching (guidance) of accounting in business as well as checking of financial statements; the role of CPAs is not only to check the fairness of financial statements but also to advise and lead the business to prepare the financial statements fairly (1954b: 3–22). Such a view of the CPA audit might underlie his unique idea to place it inside the accounting system.

Nevertheless, his explanation, 'the audit by CPAs is another form of *Zaisan-ho*', is not necessarily clear enough to satisfy us. He died without submitting a 'final report' of his study.

It is true that we can identify many auditing procedures with those of *Zaisan-ho*; as Iwata states, but he admits also the fact that cases where the procedures of *Zaisan-ho* are technically inapplicable are increasing. It means that even the audit by CPAs cannot play the part of *Zaisan-ho* in his dual structure of income determination.

He says, 'the function of the audit by CPAs is changing from carrying out the part of *Zaisan-ho* to checking on the fairness of accounting judgements inherent in *Son-eki-ho*'. The precise meaning of this sentence is not clear, but it seems to suggest that the function of the CPA audit is changing to one of checking on the truthfulness of *Son-eki-ho* from the viewpoint of *Son-eki-ho* itself. Such a check certainly increases the reliability of accounting, but the reliability must be essentially different from that provided by *Zaisan-ho*. Then the combination of *Son-eki-ho* and the audit by CPAs will not be a dual structure but a simple structure of income determination system. Unfortunately we could not hear Iwata's answer to this question from himself.

After Iwata's death, the income determination system of business accounting seems to have become more and more refined as the model of *Son-eki-ho*. However, we can discern a tendency to reconsider such a trend of development. For example, the revival of assets and liabilities view which is seen in the Statement of Concepts by FASB (1985) and the change in standards for the tax effect accounting from APB Opinion (AICPA, 1967) to SFAS (FASB, 1992) could be regarded as the outcome of such a reconsideration. This new tendency means in a sense to attach importance to the procedures of *Zaisan-ho* and reassesses Iwata's theory in which *Zaisan-ho* is an integral component of the income determination system. We should remember and recognise the significance of *Zaisan-ho* and try to find a logic to restore its place in the income determination system of business accounting today.

Notes

1 The details of what happened are given in Chapter 10 of this volume, by Junichi Chiba.
2 The technical terms in Iwata's sentences are rather Germanic because his theory is based on the study of German accounting literature. I will use some German terms with English equivalents where necessary.
3 The bases for the recognition and the measurement of the revenues and expenses do not become a subject of discussion under *Zaisan-ho*.
4 Receipt and payment accounting in the unadjusted trial balance is not the monetary accounting itself which is a component of *Son-eki-ho*, because it does not include future receipts and payments for the accrued revenues and expenses. They are added, together with corresponding accrued assets and liabilities, to the receipt and payment accounting by the year-end adjustments.

References

AICPA (1967) APB Opinion No. 11, *Accounting for Income Taxes*.
FASB (1985) Statement of Financial Accounting Concepts No. 6, *Elements of Financial Statements*.

FASB (1992) Statement of Financial Accounting Standards No. 109, *Accounting for Income Taxes*.

Gerstner, P. (1912) *Bilanzanalyse*, Berlin.

Iwata, I. (1954a) 'Rijun-keisan no Nigenteki-kozo' ('Dual Structure of Income Determination'), *Sangyo-keiri* 14 (1–4 and 6).

Iwata, I. (1954b) *Kaikeishi-Kansa (Audit by Public Accountants)*, Tokyo.

Iwata, I. (1955) *Kaikei-Gensoku to Kansa-Kijun (Accounting Principles and Auditing Standards)*, Tokyo.

Iwata, I. (1956) *Rijun-keisan-Genri (Principles of Income Determination)*, Tokyo.

Mahlberg, W. (1925) *Der Tageswert in der Bilanz*, Leipzig.

Schmalenbach, E. (1925) *Dynamische Bilanz*, (3rd edn), Leipzig.

Simon, H. V. (1910) *Die Bilanzen der Aktiengesellschaften und der Kommmanditgesellschaften auf Aktien*, (4th edn), Berlin.

Walb, E. (1926) *Die Erfolgsrechnung privater und öffentlicher Betriebe*, Vienna and Berlin.

10 Kiyoshi Kurosawa (1902–90)

An intellectual portrait

Junichi Chiba

Abstract

Kiyoshi Kurosawa was a flagbearer for the modernisation of Japanese accounting in the twentieth century. He established a sociological method of accounting
research which bordered on the disciplines of sociology, economics and law,
while trying to integrate Franco-German accounting ideas and Anglo-American
accounting thought. The issues which interested Kurosawa were of national
importance in Japanese economic affairs. Kurosawa also sought the modernisation of Japanese civil indigenous and autonomous accounting principles and
regulations. Indeed, one might say that Kurosawa's life and works are representative of the accounting history of twentieth-century Japan.

INTRODUCTION

Kiyoshi Kurosawa was an academic scholar who undertook responsibility for the
twentieth-century development and modernisation of Japanese accounting
theories and regulations. Irrespective of their intellectual standpoint, Japanese
academic and professional accountants are, without exception, familiar with
Kurosawa's work.

Kurosawa is well known, not only as the author of more than sixty books and
640 articles on accounting theory, accounting regulation, accounting history and
business administration, but also as Chairman of the Board of Directors and
President of the Japan Accounting Association (1964–75), Chairman of the
Business Accounting Deliberation Council of the Ministry of Finance (1966–80),
and a Member of the Science Council of Japan (1948–60). Kurosawa was the
President of Yokohama National University (1959–65), the President of Dokkyo
University (1970–4) and an important member of various official councils, such
as the Legislation Deliberation Council, the Taxation System Deliberation
Council and the National Railway Arbitration Committee. The Japan Accounting
Association elected Kurosawa as its Honorary Life President in 1982.

Kurosawa was not, of course, the first pioneer in the world of Japanese
accounting academics. The Japan Society of Accounting[1] was established in
1917, and in the next year it published a monthly journal, *Accounting (Kaikei)*,

and gained nearly 1,000 members, including more than ninety academics at universities and commercial colleges; the remainder were internal auditors or company accountants. Ryozo Yoshida, Sekigoro Higashi, Naotaro Shimono and Tetsuzo Ota were the central and leading academics of this Society. A youthful Kurosawa first made an appearance in this Society in the late 1920s, and soon gave full play to his academic gifts thereafter.

Kurosawa's main interest was the modernization not only of Japanese accounting but also of Japanese civil society. It appears that Kurosawa was always strongly interested in the degree of maturity of Japanese civil society. Japanese society in the early twentieth century was not a civil society separate from the political state, but rather a national or state society. Kurosawa also perceived an important need to establish an autonomous civil society in Japan, where self-regulations of external accounting would function.

What did the twentieth century hold for Kurosawa? What were the academic contributions of Kurosawa? And, how did Kurosawa's academic activities gain legitimacy with accounting academics and practitioners?

JAPAN IN THE TWENTIETH CENTURY: HISTORICAL BACKGROUND

During the twentieth century, the global strategies of western nations came to encompass the rest of the world. Therefore, the modernization of Japan, not only after the Meiji Restoration (1868) but also into the twentieth century, inevitably and continuously meant westernization under the direction of the Meiji state and leading technocrats (from above), and under the external pressures of western nations (from outside) (Norman 1940). From the dawn of Japanese history, it was of course China that had most affected Japan in matters of polity, bureaucracy, the humanities and culture (Beasley 1990). However, with China thoroughly subjugated by western powers over the course of the nineteenth century, what would be the future of a small country like Japan?

The answer was the rapid conversion of Japan into a strong military nation, culminating in the Japanese Empire's 'miracle' victory in the Russo-Japanese War (1904–5). Alexander Allan Shand,[2] manager of Parr's Bank, played an important role in helping Japan to raise great amounts of foreign loans in the London market (Tsuchiya 1969). After the First World War, Europe permitted Japan to expand its political empire in Asia, and no more that half a century after the Meiji Restoration, Japan appeared on the world stage of the Versailles Peace Conference in 1919 as one of the main military and industrial nations of the world. This gave Japan official recognition as one of the 'Big Five' of the new international order (Reischauer 1964).

However, in contrast to the glory of the Japanese Empire, there were many problems in Japanese civil society at the beginning of the twentieth century. In the second half of the Taisho period (1912–26), which followed the Meiji period (1868–12), the gulf between rich and poor grew deeper. During the First World War, while Japanese and American (rather than European) commodities were exported to all parts of Asia, and the Japanese heavy and chemical industries were founded, the dual business structure – characterised by a small number of large enterprises and a large number of small and medium subcontractors – was established (Morishima 1982, Allen 1981).

In those days, the embryonic socialist or anarchist movements were severely oppressed by the Japanese state. In 1923, for example, a famous anarchist, Sakae Osugi, and his wife, Noe Ito, were slaughtered by a military policeman in the headquarters of the military police. The despotism of militarists who were elated by their victories in the Sino-Japanese War (1894–5) and the Russo-Japanese War (1904–5) became more and more evident.

The shift to heavy and chemical industries in Japan did not progress greatly in the 1920s, on account of post-war inflation, the establishment of naval arms limitations resulting from the Washington Disarmament Conference (1922), the great earthquake of Kanto (greater Tokyo) (1923), the financial crisis (1927) which occurred relating to misuse of earthquake bonds issued by the government for the reconstruction of greater Tokyo, and the world depression (1930). However, the heavy and chemical industries of Japan did develop more rapidly during the Japanese war with China (1931–45).

These were the socio-historical circumstances in which Kurosawa began his academic career.

EDUCATION AND EARLY CAREER: SOCIOLOGY

Kurosawa was born in Nakaminato, Ibaraki Prefecture, Japan, in 1902, the first of six children. Kurosawa's father, Yoshinosuke Kurosawa, was a middle-level postmaster, while his mother, Setsuko Kurosawa, came of the Inaba family, a samurai family of the domain of Mito (*Mito-han*). Setsuko's grandfather, Togaku Inaba, was a famous scholar. In 1910, Kurosawa's father was transferred to Tokyo, and in 1915 Kurosawa entered Seikei Gakuen, a five-year private school, the founder of which was Haruji Nakamura. In his own words, Kurosawa selected Seikei Gakuen on account of its privileges, such as free tuition and scholarship (Kurosawa 1982). At any rate, it appears that Kurosawa's early life was on the whole quite free and modern by contemporary standards, and that Haruji Nakamura's spirit of practical learning had a strong influence on the young man (Kurosawa 1962, Tanaka 1990).

Kurosawa entered the Imperial University of Tokyo (presently the University of Tokyo) in 1923. At first, he enrolled in the Department of Sociology,[3] within the Faculty of Literature and Humanities, under the supervision of Teizo Toda. In those days there were seven Japanese imperial universities from which were recruited the graduates who became the top élite of the political and bureaucratic world. Political science and law were the traditional subjects for study by aspiring leaders, while sociology (a new subject) was sometimes branded as socialistic or anti-establishment. Kurosawa nevertheless decided to study sociology rather than political science or law.

Many important works by German and French sociologists had already been introduced and translated into Japanese during the second half of the Taisho period. Indeed, in those days, sociology and social thinking in Japanese imperial universities were dominated by German sociology. It was therefore natural for Kurosawa to study German and French sociology, such as Georg Simmel's *Über soziale Differenzierung* (*The Social Differentiation*, 1890), Alfred F. Vierkandt's *Gesellschaftslehre* (*Phenomenological Sociology*, 1923), Emil Durkheim's *Les règles de la méthode sociologique* (*The Rules of Sociological Method*, 1895), and also the works of Karl Marx. Less usual, and under the guidance of Teizo Toda, Kurosawa studied the positivism of Anglo-American sociology, such as Thorstein Veblen's *The Theory of the Leisure Class*, 1899, and *The Theory of Business Enterprise*, 1904, and William McDougall's works (Kurosawa 1982). However, the highlight of Kurosawa's 'sociology age' was his chance meeting with Emil Lederer (1882–1939), a German professor of Heidelberg University who was invited by the Imperial University of Tokyo to lecture from 1923 to 1925. Lederer introduced Japanese academics and students to the social science methodology of Max Weber. A few years after Weber's death, thanks to Lederer, Kurosawa was therefore introduced to the interpretative sociology of Weber. Moreover, Lederer's own view of Japan surely influenced the young Kurosawa.

Lederer drew attention to the implications of European arrogance for the Far East in *Japan-Europa, Wandlungen im Fernen Osten* (1929) written with his wife, E. Lederer-Seidrer. Japan had become westernised in the process of its modernisation, which inevitably had demolished a large part of its irreplaceable traditions. Lederer criticised Europe, which had never had the experience of having another culture forced upon it, for forcing Japan to westernise. The questions he posed included the following. Why were Europeans still continuing to preach to Japan? Did Europeans have any qualifications to do so? Is this kind of European arrogance the opposite of the real European spirit of self-critique? (Lederer and Seidrer 1929, 1938; see also Mizunuma 1978).

Lederer stressed that Japanese pre-modern factors, such as totalitarianism and family-ism, on which Europeans were apt to set a negative value, were stronger than European individualism in aiding the rapid growth of Japanese industrialisation from below after the Meiji Restoration. Moreover, Lederer stated that such a spirit of family-ism, which compelled the patriarch to support his family, would eventually function as a critical factor by reason of its strength, when the socio-economic depression hit civil society, and neutral and unsentimental (*sachlich*) European-style rationalisation would inevitably be demanded from above and from outside. If Japan fell into such a crisis, she would be obliged to move against Asia in order to obtain a new colony or market. Clearly, Lederer foresaw and warned of the Japanese crisis and aggression in Asia as a means of resolving of the internal contradiction between industrialisation and maintenance of the patriarch's responsibilities in the early Showa period.

After taking note of Lederer's ideas, Kurosawa began to prepare his graduation thesis. Kurosawa's main interest was in the formation process of modern civil society. He saw that modern British civil society had developed with a minimum of state intervention; moreover, that the internal order of the civil society was maintained by an invisible and autonomous hand, without the protection or direction from the state. One of the important issues with which Kurosawa was involved (Chiba 1991a, 1991b) was, therefore how it was that the order of the civil society was not destroyed by internal struggles of the populace.

In order to recognise the essence of social phenomena, Kurosawa turned his attention to the phenomenon of sympathy and co-operation. He came to think that the concepts of 'sympathy' and 'co-operation' were more important than the concept of 'imitation', like Jean Gabliel Tarde, or 'collective representation', like Emil Durkheim. After that, under the guidance of Albion Small's *Adam Smith and Modern Sociology*, Kurosawa was absorbed in reading Smith's *The Theory of Moral Sentiments*, and *A Treatise of Human Nature in the Philosophical Works of David Hume*, edited by Thomas Hill Green (Kurosawa 1982).

After six months Kurosawa submitted his thesis, entitled 'A Sociological Study on the Theory of Moral Sentiments of Adam Smith to Teizo Toda'. In those days, half of the graduation theses by students in the Department of Sociology were rejected. However, Kurosawa's thesis was awarded a pass classification.

EDUCATION AND EARLY CAREER: ECONOMICS AND ACCOUNTING

In 1926, I graduated from the university. My only desire was to be a scholar, so I did not ask my university or anyone else to find me a job. However, in the circumstances of the late Taisho period, to become a scholar or a staff member of a university was quite difficult. No university or college could hire academic staff in the relatively new field of sociology . . . Sociology is a discipline of the methodology of all individual social sciences. I think that to make one's livelihood by teaching sociology in university would be a piece of good luck or a calling assigned to only a few exceptional people. Therefore, I did not dare to think about being an academic of sociology. Rather, I was going to make the most of my sociological methodology in individual scientific discipline. Now, I am sure that my desire was realized.

(Kurosawa 1982: 197–8)

After graduation, through the kind offices of Tetsuzo Ota, Kurosawa became a full-time lecturer at Chuo University in Tokyo, an institution which took its name 'Chuo' (middle) from Middle Temple in London. Also, at the kind request of Ryozo Yoshida, Kurosawa was engaged in editing the monthly journal, *Accounting (Kaikei)*. Yoshida and Ota were established accounting academics who were to influence Kurosawa's life course and career (Kurosawa 1962, 1982). Kurosawa had already listened to their lectures in a special course at Seikei Gakuen.

As a full-time lecturer at Chuo University, Kurosawa had to pursue studies in economics, management and accounting. At the same time, as a graduate of the Department of Sociology in the Faculty of Literature and Humanities, he was allowed to enter the Faculty of Economics of the Imperial University of Tokyo as an undergraduate. Kurosawa attended the seminar of Alfred Amon, who had recently been invited to replace Emil Lederer, and the seminars of Moritaro

Yamada and Yoshitaro Omori. Yamada and Omori were important members of the Marxian Economists School (*Koza-ha*). However, it appeared that neither of their seminars influenced Kurosawa much at this stage. While giving lectures on Leopold von Wiese's *Allgemeine Soziologie* (*General Sociology*, 1924–9), Werner Sombart's *Der Moderne Kapitalismus* (*Modern Capitalism*, 1916), and the works of Veblen to students of Chuo University, Kurosawa diligently studied management and accounting.

Soon after graduating from the Faculty of Economics, Kurosawa became a professor of management and accounting at Chuo University, in 1928, at the age of 26. It was in the same year that Kurosawa's work first made an appearance in *Accounting*. In 1936, Kurosawa transferred to Yokohama Commercial College (presently, Yokohama National University) as a professor of management and accounting.

RATIONALISATION OF INDUSTRY

There was a financial crisis in Japan, in 1927, and two years later the country began to suffer from the world depression. As a young academic Kurosawa was therefore thrown into the severe reality of Japanese economic society. The prevailing situation was not, in Kurosawa's judgement, conducive to the modernisation of the autonomous external accounting system along the lines of that found in British civil society. Kurosawa concluded that the reform of Japanese external accounting practices was indeed a long way off.

Kurosawa's problem in his early works was to establish his own discipline of accounting as opposed to the traditional theory of bookkeeping and the legal theory of accounting. Kurosawa contended that the accounting discipline was not mere bookkeeping theory or legal theory, but a branch of *Betriebswirtschaftslehre* or managerial economics. In those days, there were two ways for reconstructing accounting as a branch of *Betriebswirtschaftslehre*. One way, which was adopted by Torao Nakanishi, stressed that accounting is a methodology for critically assessing the logic or the value-law of 'individual capital' in modern capitalism (Nakanishi 1931). This approach was formulated under the strong influence of Marxian economists.

The other approach, adopted by Kurosawa, stressed that the central object of accounting was not the individual capital of the enterprise itself, but the individual capital which is 'recognised' by the 'capital account' (Kurosawa 1934). Here a distinction between the concept of capital, enterprise or profitability and that of '*Betrieb*' (management, economic establishment or economic organisation) was very important (Otsuka 1965), and accounting was recognised as a discipline of '*Betrieb*' by Kurosawa. It appears that these two ways, which were represented in two important books: Torao Nakanishi's *Betriebswirtschaftslehre* (*Keiei-keizaigaku*) in 1931 and Kiyoshi Kurosawa's *Accounting* (*Kaikeigaku*) in 1933, symbolised two themes for reconstructing Japanese civil society in the early Showa period. Further, Kurosawa's *Principles of Bookkeeping* (*Boki-Genri*) was published in 1934. In this book, Kurosawa examined the socio-historical meanings of double-entry bookkeeping, which was the most highly developed bookkeeping system from the viewpoint of formal rationality, quoting from *Wirtschaft und Gesellschaft (Economy and Society)* by Max Weber, and investigated the intellectual history of Franco-German, Italian, and Anglo-American accounting thoughts according to readings of German and English original texts. Kurosawa had of course already studied German accounting and management thoughts exhaustively.

For Kurosawa, accounting was a means for making order in civil society. His arguments confronted not only the critical school mentioned above but also the legal theorists of accounting. Kurosawa proposed a legal sociological approach, as opposed to the pure legal approach to accounting research. In later years this seed of argument sparked Kurosawa's interesting criticisms of the theory of accounting laws proposed by Kotaro Tanaka, who later became the Chief Justice of the Supreme Court of Japan.

Kurosawa's fundamental knowledge of sociology is not immediately apparent in his early published works. So far as we can judge today, it appears that Kurosawa's modern approach was only presented to the society of Japanese accounting academics. Kurosawa's individuality was expressed in real earnest, however, when he criticised the Working Rules of Financial Statements, released by the Temporary Bureau for the Rationalisation of Industry in the Ministry of Commerce and Industry. The Exposure Draft of the Working Rules was released in 1931, and finally promulgated in 1934. The aim of these Working Rules was to co-ordinate legal accounting requirements regulated by the Commercial Code and accounting practices, and to standardise the form and content of balance sheets.

> In the present circumstances of Japanese economic society, the balance sheet does not mean only that which will be prepared by executives for reporting to owners. There should be at least three types of balance sheet required:
> (1) a balance sheet which satisfies the required conditions of bookkeeping,
> (2) a balance sheet which satisfies the required conditions of *Betriebswirtschaft* or managerial economics, and
> (3) a balance sheet which satisfies the required conditions of law and society.
> A standard balance sheet should be one which satisfies the required conditions of society. The real function of a standard balance sheet is to be a tool for controlling social industry, while simultaneously being a means for harmonizing business with economic morals as far as the law permits.
> (Kurosawa 1932: 343–4)

Kurosawa stated his opinion not from the legal and micro-economics viewpoint, but from the sociological viewpoint. Clearly, Kurosawa's interest was transferred from accounting as a branch of *Betriebswirtschaftslehre* to accounting as a tool of social control or social institution. It appears that Kurosawa had already acquired knowledge of trends in the US, Great Britain and Germany. 'Verification of Financial Statement' (American Institute of Accountants 1929) in the US and *Aktiengesetz* (Stock Corporation Law, 1931) in Germany were both promoting the standardisation of balance sheets. In the UK, the 1929 Companies Act aspired to greater disclosure of the accounts. Kurosawa continued his critical comments on the Draft of the Working Rules (1931). These rules aimed to cover the accounts of every trader and company, except for special companies regulated by special laws. Kurosawa criticised the fact that the Exposure Draft of Working Rules created a sanctuary (*sei-iki*) for the banking companies' and insurance companies' accounts, and he emphasised that a general standard of balance sheet, including balance sheets of banking companies and insurance companies, had to be presented not by law but by accounting principles as a social norm.

> In the Exposure Draft of the Working Rules, there is a provision, which says that these forms of the accounts were made excluding the accounts of banking companies, insurance companies, because the accounts form of each category of business was subject to each special law, such as the Banking Law Insurance Law. This provision imprudently suggests that the Working Rules intends to make standard balance sheets for each category of business, separately or individually. However, this intention of the Working Rules was not necessarily realized . . . Rather, I think that this provision has to be eliminated and that it would be more reasonable to make and to present a general standard of balance sheet including balance sheets for banking companies, insurance companies, first of all.
>
> (Kurosawa 1932: 346–7)

Eventually, as a result of the criticisms of Kurosawa and others, the final draft of Working Rules (1934) was intended to apply to all industries. However, these Working Rules were not enacted in legislation and could not break through the wall of sanctuary (*sei-iki*) created by the special laws. It appears that Kurosawa had an insight into an important problem concerning Japanese modernization, wherein each key industry or each important category of business was protected by a special law and competent governmental authority, according to the differential economic structure created by the policy of promoting particular industries, and the singluar logic of traditional vertically structured Japanese society (*tate-shakai*).

ECONOMIC CONTROL AND THE TRANSFORMATION OF METHODOLOGY

The Working Rules (1934), which were the first accounting principles of Japan introduced for general trading and manufacturing companies, were promulgated as a part of the policy of economic rationalisation after the depression, mirroring corresponding developments in the US and Germany. However, the currency of the Working Rules was unfortunately very short (Kurosawa 1990). After 1935, Japanese society became subject to national policies for economic control. The policy of the Japanese government changed from economic rationalisation to economic control, or statism.

Kurosawa's attention was also transformed from accounting as a tool of social control into accounting as a means of state control, or from the standardisation of accounts to the unification of accounts. It appears that Kurosawa especially displayed his overall individuality at this phase. It was in those days that Kurosawa made an earnest and critical enquiry into the works of D. R. Scott and W. H. Schluter.

> Scott classified the development stages of economic organization of a society by making clear which persons or organizations were in charge (bearers, *Träger*). When the bearer of control is the market, the economic organization would be called the age of free market economy. When the bearer of control is the state, it would be called the age of controlled economy. According to Scott's view, the economic organization develops from the stage of free market economy into the stage of controlled economy. Along the line of such a development scheme, Scott tries to interpret the cultural meanings of accounting and accounting research and recommends that the bearer of control of future economic organizations should be an accounting system or organization, and that the age of accounting control should be realized . . . Nevertheless, although he foresees that an accounting system or organization will replace the old economics along with the loss of automatic economic control of a competitive market, his accounting theory is still subject to the market theory.
>
> (Kurosawa 1936: 805–13)

The controlled economy was, for Kurosawa, an economic organisation where all knowledge of economic life was mobilised and organised in order to realise a socio-economic rebirth, and accounting should be considered as part of such 'organised knowledge' to form the dynamic order of national society as a whole. Kurosawa was interested in W. H. Schluter's ideas, in which an independent institute of accounting should be established under the command of the national economic council, which was the top body of economic control, for co-operation between accounting information of individual companies and policy making of the national economy.

> An important point to be remembered is that modern business accounting is now restricted by internal circumstances which are governed by motives of the pursuit of business income and the avoidance of loss, and therefore accounting records are kept under lock and key as secret information available for competition by each individual company . . . In order to establish the institution of economic control, the present accounting concepts and the present accounting functions should be drastically reformed . . . to harmonize internal accounting with the external environment of individual companies and the national economic policy . . . Accounting, as a lasting system for adjustment of interests, is no longer a means of business administration, but is rather a tool for control of business enterprises from the viewpoint of the national economy.
>
> (Kurosawa 1938: 826–44)

Kurosawa's ideas on institutional accounting were a development of the socio-logical ideals of Veblen, Sombart, and others. Kurosawa presented these ideas before the Uniform Financial Regulations Committee of the Planning Council in 1939, in compliance with the invitation and wishes of Torao Nakanishi, who was the leader of the Committee. Even though Nakanishi had resigned from his position as professor at the Imperial University of Tokyo,[4] after the promulgation of the National Mobilisation Law (1938), all human, material and financial resources were mobilised by the Japanese government for the purpose of preparing for a full-scale war, and this included Nakanishi's appointment. Thus, in 1940, Kurosawa also became a member of the Temporary Bureau for the Rationalisation of Industry in the Ministry of Commerce and Industry, alongside Ryozo Yoshida and Tetsuzo Ota.

From 1939 until the 1980s Kurosawa participated, directly or indirectly, in almost all important Japanese accounting regulation decisions. From the pre-war age to the post-war age, the ideological position of Kurosawa was, in a sense, quite close to that of progressive-minded bureaucrats or economic bureaucrats. As one of the rationalists, Kurosawa insisted on the importance of decision-making on the basis of neutral and impartial (*sachlich*) accounting information, in opposition to the views of the ultra-nationalist fanatic spiritualists.[5] At this stage, Kurosawa's methodology was transformed from that of interpretative sociology to the problem-oriented approach for reformation of accounting discipline as a social institution for the purpose of economic order. Kurosawa thought that an institutional system was not a concrete structure, but rather a complex of functions which would be created by the identity of peoples having a certain problem in common. From the viewpoint of recent sociology, this approach is quite similar to the methodology and the view of systems of Niklas Luhmann (Chiba 1991a).

As to the theoretical phase, Kurosawa put forward a new discipline of 'political accounting' or *Rechnungswirtschaftslehre* (*keisan keizaigaku*) as opposed to the discipline of traditional political economy, which was prevalent between the wars. Kurosawa thought that the role of 'political accounting' would be to solve the problems of cost control and price control within a controlled economy. Indeed, according to Kurosawa, the role of 'political accounting' was to make calculation order as a part of a dynamic social order. It appears that after the war, the discipline of 'social accounting' partly gave way to Kurosawa's notion of 'political accounting'.

ACCOUNTING DISCLOSURE SYSTEM AND THE INDEPENDENT INSTITUTE

Kurosawa's attempt to rationalise and modernise Japanese accounting before the war was thwarted by the atmosphere of ultra-nationalism at that time. In Japan, 'rationalisation' meant not to reform the traditional establishment but only to increase efficiency within the scope of a given purpose and a given organisation. Therefore, the formation of an independent accounting profession responsible for the development of accounting practice carried over into the post-war age as an unresolved issue.

After the Second World War, under strong US influences the Japanese external accounting system was drastically transformed from the 'accounting reporting system', where the availability of accounts was restricted to existing shareholders, to the 'accounting disclosure system', where the accounts were made available to the public. However, with regards to this historical phase, two important points should be remembered.

First, this transformation was not a direct consequence of occupation by the Allied Forces. The US had of course established the advanced accounting disclosure system on the basis of the Securities and Exchange Commission regime, and Kurosawa, Iwao Iwata and a few Japanese accounting academics knew about these developments. We now know, however, that there were no accounting experts in the Allied Forces, except for Hessler and a few officers who were Certified Public Accountants, but they were not so well acquainted with US accounting principles (Kurosawa 1980). As the core members of the Investigation Committee on the Business Accounting System in the Economic Stabilisation Board, Kurosawa together with Iwata worked hard to establish the Business Accounting Principles, including the US-style accounting disclosure system, and the Working Rules for Financial Statements. This transformation was therefore a largely Japanese initiative. Moreover, from a modern viewpoint, the formation of the Business Accounting Principles was not the starting point but the end result of the formation movement of accounting principles in Japan, which had begun in the 1930s. It appears that at this stage Kurosawa and Iwata realised the fruits of their research between the wars.

Second, the accounting disclosure system of Japan was established under the authority of the newly created Japanese Securities and Exchanges Commission. The establishment of a new securities administrative office similar in many respects to the SEC of the US was one of the central requisite conditions for reopening Japan's stock exchanges, which were direly needed for Japan's post-war economic recovery. Under the Securities Exchanges Law (1947), the Securities Transaction Commission was established. In the following year, the Securities Exchanges Law was amended in line with the US Securities Act (1933) and the Securities Exchange Act (1934) of the US. This Commission became an Attached Bureau of the Ministry of Finance and the power of this Commission was strengthened, while the (English) name was changed to the Securities and Exchanges Commission. In the same year (1948), the Certified Public Accountants Law was also promulgated. This provided for the establishment of a Japanese body of certified public accountants to carry out external audits.

It was during this historical phase that Kurosawa argued strongly, in *Accounting*, for an independent Business Accounting Law based on regulations issued by an independent institute. However, the Working Rules (1949) of the Economic Stabilisation Board instead received legal authority by means of the promulgation of Regulation Concerning Terms, Formats and Preparation Methods of Financial Statements of the Securities and Exchanges Commission (Regulation, No. 18 of Japanese SEC) in 1950. We might therefore conclude that the Japanese SEC was not the independent accounting institute favoured by Kurosawa, but that, in the current circumstances, it was the best type of organisation for accounting regulation that could be achieved.

The Japanese Securities and Exchanges Commission was abolished in July 1952, three months after the enforcement of the Peace Treaty between the Allied Forces and Japan, as a link in the chain of administrative reform. The administration of securities and accounting disclosure was transferred to the First and the Second Department of Securities, in the Finance Bureau of the Ministry of Finance. However, no critical comments of Kurosawa can be found concerning this important historical phase (Chiba 1990, 1991a). From that time on, Kurosawa continued to strive as a central member of the Business Accounting Deliberation Council, which was merely a consultative board of the Minister of Finance, for the establishment or revision of accounting principles. Where was the plan of an independent accounting institute as envisioned by Kurosawa? In the pre-war age of economic control, Kurosawa had said the following:

> Criticism of the bureaucracy is related to the socio-historical nature of the Japanese. A dual characteristic of the Japanese, an extreme worship of bureaucracy on one side and a deep-rooted criticism of bureaucracy on the other side, is representative of the psychology of the average Japanese. In other words, there is a split in the Japanese personality between a nature which makes self-regulation impossible while desiring it on one side, and embracing the bureaucracy while criticizing it on the other side. Therefore, popular criticism of the bureaucracy is out of the question in a strict sense, except as a political issue . . . At the beginning of the political issue on the reformation of the Price Committee, I proposed a new discipline of 'political accounting'. However, my aim is not to solve the political issue at all. I think that with this proposal as a start, I would like to insist on the reformation and the transformation of accounting itself.
>
> (Kurosawa 1939a: 308–9)

There was an important and critical problem in the political control structure of bureaucracy in Japan. It appears that Kurosawa's ideological position against the bureaucracy did not change from its first stage at all. Kurosawa thought that, because of the underdeveloped accounting profession, the accounting regulations of Japan had to be enforced by a technocrat who would mediate between the political state and civil society. In the situation in 1952, it appears that Kurosawa's interest lay not with the political issue directly, but rather with continuously reforming and transforming the discipline of accounting. However, Kurosawa's asceticism, simultaneously, kept at a distance the realisation of his 'political accounting' and his plan of an independent accounting institute. Kurosawa's academic plan was, in a sense, a far-reaching but unfulfilled ambition.

OTHER WORKS

In 1954, the Business Accounting Principles were revised and the Annotations on the Business Accounting Principles were newly established. In the latter, several surpluses, such as government subsidy for capital expenditure, contribution in aid of construction, donated surplus for supplying a capital deficit, gain on insurance claims, and profits on treasury stock were enumerated as examples of capital surplus. In contrast, the Commercial Code treated them as profit reserves and the tax laws treated them as income. In this period, Kurosawa, as a flag-bearer of the Business Accounting Principles, strongly stressed that these sur-pluses should be treated as capital surpluses (Kurosawa 1951). Of course, not a few critical comments were made on this issue. The year 1954 was a take-off point for the first high-growth period of the Japanese economy. What effect did Kurosawa's opinion of capital surplus have on the socio-historical condition in this period? At any rate, it appears that the high growth of the Japanese economy was another problem for Kurosawa to deal with in the 1950s and 1960s.

Kurosawa tried hard to co-ordinate the Business Accounting Principles with the Securities and Exchanges Law, the Commercial Code and tax laws. For example, regarding the publication of consolidated financial statements, Kuro-sawa insisted on their introduction at an early stage of the Business Accounting Principles (1949). However, it was not until 1975 that the Principles for Pre-paration of Consolidated Financial Statements were promulgated by the Business Accounting Deliberation Council as a result of serious disputes after a chain of cases of window-dressing in the first half of the 1960s.

While busy taking up many posts, such as that of President of Yokohama National University, and a member of various deliberation councils, Kurosawa energetically published many academic books and papers. From the 1950s to the 1980s, Kurosawa published each year, on average, one or two books, including revised editions, and nearly sixteen papers. In particular, *The Theory of Balance Sheet* (*Taishakutaishohyo-ron*, 1947), *Modern Accounting* (*Kindai-kaikeigaku*, 1951), *The Theory of Modern Accounting* (*Kindai-kaikei no Riron*, 1955) and *The Theory of Fund Accounting* (*Shikinkaikei no Riron*, 1958) are well-known. In countless papers, Kurosawa always paid close attention to current issues, such as public corporations accounting, public utilities accounting, labour unions accounting, social accounting, accounting information systems, accounting as a behavioural science, human resources accounting, accounting for decision making, ecological accounting, and accounting for organisational development.

As for Kurosawa's favourite subject, his methodological or intellectual interests were transferred, after the 1960s, from interpretative sociology or social thoughts to behavioural science, the system theory, scientific philosophy or logical positivism. Also, it was Kurosawa who introduced the general theory of accounting measurement into Japan in the 1960s (Tanaka 1990). Since then, the accounting measurement theories also came into bloom in Japan in the 1970s. The establishment of a scientific basis of accounting discipline was an important and continuous problem for Kurosawa.

Unfortunately, the numerous works of Kurosawa remain unknown to overseas academics, reflecting a language barrier which remains largely impenetrable, even in the twentieth century.

KUROSAWA'S CONTRIBUTIONS

Kurosawa was undoubtedly a key figure in the modernisation of Japanese accounting in the twentieth century. Kurosawa had to pursue his aims while, at the same time, complying with national demands. This was because Kurosawa's interests – the standardisation of accounting for the rationalisation of industry in the age of economic crisis, the unification of accounting for a controlled economy in the age of a war regime, the accounting disclosure system for economic democratisation in the age of post-war rehabilitation, and the revision of accounting principles for economic growth and social control in the high-growth period – were all national problems in each crucial age of Japanese economic development. It appears that the alternative ideas of accounting regulations were defeated by reason of this kind of legitimisation process which permeated the whole of Japanese national society.

> It is often said desultorily that purely Japanese accounting theories have to be established . . . However, the road to isolation of Japanese accounting from the accounting research theories, accumulated as intellectual properties in overseas countries, is not the road to the establishment of Japan's own accounting theories at all . . . An important point to be remembered is that we have to make clear the real accounting theories which could respond to the social problems to be solved in Japan. In this way, the resulting accounting theories could be indeed called Japan's own unique accounting theories in a legitimate sense.
>
> (Kurosawa 1939b: 587–8)

The man who carries a national issue on his shoulders and makes good use of the intellectual properties of overseas countries to solve the problem might be called an international scholar. Kurosawa's academic works and his life's journey have shown us such a man.

Kurosawa was a 'marginal' man who lived in a boundary discipline of sociology, economics and law, and became an important symbol of accounting. Kurosawa always desired the maturing of Japanese civil society, where indigenous and autonomous accounting principles and regulations would be produced and would function, continuously. Kurosawa saw that Japanese accounting even in the late twentieth century was still in the process of modernisation. He entrusts this crucial issue to us and to the twenty-first century.

Late in his academic life, Kurosawa tried earnestly to bring the history of Japanese accounting to a conclusion. It appears that Kurosawa's methodology drifted away from a historical approach, and that this work represented more a locus of Kurosawa's own academic life. However, his last work was pregnant with much hidden meaning. After Kurosawa's death in 1990, and in the same year, his last unfinished work was published as *The History of Japanese Accounting Development* (*Nihon Kaikei-seido Hatten-shi*).

Notes

The author wishes to acknowledge the kindly and helpful advice of the editor.

1 The Japan Accounting Association was established in 1937, when it separated from the Japan Society of Accounting. The leading founders of the Japan Accounting Association were Ryozo Yoshida, Tetsuzo Ota, Kinzo Minabe, Seiichi Okada, Yoshio Watanabe, Yasubei Hasegawa, Gen Murase and Kiyoshi Kurosawa. Their ardent wish was that a pure academic society of accounting should be established (Japan Accounting Association 1987). As of 31 March 1992 membership of the Japan Accounting Association numbered more than 1,650 academics at universities and commercial colleges.

2 Shand's connections with Japan stretched back to the 1870s when he was called in to the Ministry of Finance's Bureau of Bank Notes, by the Japanese government, for the purpose of installing uniform accounting methods in the national (commercial) banks.

3 It was in 1893 that an independent chair of sociology was established in the Imperial University of Tokyo. In 1919, a department of sociology was also established in the same university.

4 As the Sino-Japanese dispute and war (1931–45) became prolonged, expressions of liberal views increasingly became the subject of severe oppression by the Japanese state. In October 1938, the sale of four books written by Eijiro Kawai, who was a professor of social policy in the Faculty of Economics at the Imperial University of Tokyo, was prohibited by the Home Minister by reason of his criticisms of fascism. This provided the trigger for a serious confrontation between the supporters (including Professor Torao Nakanishi) and critics of Kawai in the Faculty of Economics. As a result of this confrontation, thirteen professors and associate professors from both sides presented their resignation in 1939.

5 The fanatic spiritualists did not believe in statistical and accounting data, and were convinced that the Japanese spirit could overcome any problems. This attitude is referred to as the 'unbeatable myth' (*fuhai shinwa*).

References

Allen, G. C. (1981) *A Short Economic History of Modern Japan* (4th edn), London: Macmillan.

American Institute of Accountants (1929) 'Verification of Financial Statement', *The Journal of Accountancy* 47: 321–54.

Beasley, W. G. (1990) *The Rise of Modern Japan*, Tokyo: Charles E. Tuttle.

Chiba, J. (1990) 'A Statement of Business Accounting Principles under the Scheme of Japanese SEC after World War II' ('Sengo Wagakuni Shoken Torihiki Iinkai Koso to Kigyo Kaikei Gensoku'), Tokyo Metropolitan University, *Economy and Economics (Keizai to Keizaigaku)* 66: 1–41.

Chiba, J. (1991a) 'Modernization Process of Accounting and Accounting Theory in Japan, A Socio-Historical Meaning of the Theories of Kiyoshi Kurosawa' ('Nihon ni okeru Kaikei to Kaikeigaku no Kindaika-katei', *Accounting*: 31–49.

Chiba, J. (1991b) *A History of British Financial Accounting* (Eikoku Kindai Kaikei Seido), Tokyo: Chuo Keizaisha.

Durkheim, E. (1895) *Les règles de la méthode sociologique*, Paris: Presses Universitaires de France. Translated by Sarah H. Solovay and John H. Mueller, *The Rules of Sociological Method*, New York: The Free Press, 1966.

Japan Accounting Association (1987) *A 50 Years History of Japan Accounting Association (Nihon Kaikei Kenkyu Gakkai 50 nen-shi)*, Japan Accounting Association.

Kurosawa, K. (1932) 'On the Meanings of Standardisation of the Balance Sheet' ('Taishakutaishohyo Hyojunka no Igi ni tsuite'), *Accounting*: 340–66.

Kurosawa, K. (1933) *Accounting (Kaikeigaku)*, Tokyo: Chikura Shobo.

Kurosawa, K. (1934) *Principles of Bookkeeping (Boki Genri)*, Tokyo: Toyo Shuppansha.

Kurosawa, K. (1936) 'The Accounting Theory of DR Scott', *Accounting*: 441–51, 795–814.

Kurosawa, K. (1938) 'Theory of Controlled Economy and Accounting', *Accounting*: 59–68, 173–8, 479–88, 679–88, 821–44.

Kurosawa, K. (1939a) 'The Price Committee and the Cost Committee' ('Bukka-iinkai to Genka-iinkai'), *Accounting*: 305–18.

Kurosawa, K. (1939b) 'A Type of Critique of Accounting' ('Kaikeigaku-Hihan no ichi-Tenkei'), *Accounting*: 587–98, 751–68.

Kurosawa, K. (1947) *The Theory of Balance Sheet (Taishaku-taishohyo-ron)*, Tokyo: Tokyo Shokan.

Kurosawa, K. (1951) *Modern Accounting (Kindai-Kaikeigaku)*, Tokyo: Shunjusha.

Kurosawa, K. (1955) *The Theory of Modern Accounting (Kindai-kaikei no Riron)*, Tokyo: Hakuto Shobo.

Kurosawa, K. (1962) 'My Personal History' ('Waga Oitachi no Ki'), *Bulletin of Kurosawa Society*, 11, in Celebration of Kurosawa's 60th birthday.

Kurosawa, K. (1980) 'Dissolution of Zaibatsu and Democratization of Securities' ('Zaibatsu Kaitai to Shoken Minshuka'), *Accounting Journal (Kaikei Journal)*, January, JICPA: 10–17.

Kurosawa, K. (1982) *Beyond the Clouds, My Life's Journey (Kumo no Kanata-ni Waga Tabi no Ki)*, Tokyo: Chuo Keizaisha.

Kurosawa, K. (1990) *The History of Japanese Accounting Development (Nihon Kaikei-seido Hatten-shi)*, Tokyo: Zaikei Shohosha.

Lederer, E. and Lederer-Seidrer, E. (1929) *Japan-Europa, Wandlungen im Fernen Osten (Japan-Europe, Transition in the Far East)*, Frankfurt am Main: Frankfurter Societäts-Druckerei GmbH.

Lederer, E. and Lederer-Seidrer, E. (1938) *Japan in Transition*, London, Humphrey: Yale University Press.

Mizunuma, T. (1978) 'Memorandum on E. Lederer's Japan-Europa' ('E. Lederer Nihon-Yoroppa Oboegaki'), in Takahito Saki *et al.* (eds) *Japanese Capitalism: Its Development and Logic*, Tokyo: University of Tokyo Press.

Morishima, M. (1982) *Why Has Japan 'Succeeded'? Western Technology and the Japanese Ethos*, Cambridge: Cambridge University Press.

Nakanishi, T. (1931) *Betriebswirtschaftslehre (Keiei Keizaigaku)*, Tokyo: Nihon Hyoronsha.

Norman, H. (1940) *Japan's Emergence as a Modern State, Political and Economic Problems of the Meiji Period*, New York: Institute of Pacific Relations.

Otsuka, H. (1965) '*Betrieb* to Keizai-Gori-Shugi' ('*Betrieb* and Economic Rationalism') in Japanese, in *The Works of Otsuka, Hisao* (1969), Tokyo: Iwanami Shoten.

Reischauer, E. O. (1964) *Japan, Past and Present* (3rd edn), Tokyo: Charles E. Tuttle.

Securities and Exchanges Law (translated by Ministry of Finance) (1947) February 18, in *Records of the Ministry of Finance*, Z-526-28-2.

Securities and Exchanges Law (1948) April 13, in *Official Gazette*, English Edition, Government Printing Bureau.

Simmel, G. (1890) *Über sociale Differenzierung, Sociologische und psychologische Untersuchungen (Social Differentiation, A Sociological and Psychological Inquiry)*, Leipzig: Duncker & Humblot.

Sombart, W. (1916) *Der moderne Kapitalismus (Modern Capitalism)*, I, II, Leipzig: Duncker & Humblot.

Tanaka, A. (ed.) (1990) *Development of Accounting Researches in Japan (Nihon ni okeru Kaikeigaku-kenkyu no Hatten)*, Tokyo: Dobunkan.

Tsuchiya, T. (1969) *Employed Foreigners, Finance (Oyatoi Gaikokujin, Zaisei-Kinyu)*, Tokyo: Kashima Shuppansha.

Veblen, T. (1899) *The Theory of the Leisure Class*. Reprinted by Viking Penguin, New York, 1979.

Veblen, T. (1904) *The Theory of the Business Enterprise*. Reprinted by Transaction Publications, New Brunswick, NJ, 1989.

Vierkandt, A. F. (1923) *Gesellschaftslehre, Sociology*, Leipzig: Duncker & Humblot.

von Wiese, L. (1924/29) *Allgemeine Soziologie (General Sociology)*, Leipzig: Duncker & Humblot.

Weber, M. (1925) *Wirtschaft und Gesellschaft (Economy and Society), Grundriss der Verstehenden Soziologie* (2nd edn), Tübingen: J. C. B. Mohr.

11 Wasaburo Kimura (1902–73) and modern accounting theory

Yasushi Yamagata

Abstract

Wasaburo Kimura viewed accounting as a science in a process of continuous change, responding to changing business circumstances. Kimura's accounting theory therefore stresses the importance of the historical analysis and the prevailing social and economic background; he was also convinced of the need for theoretical explanation of accounting activities to be founded on economic thought. This chapter identifies Kimura's concerns with views expressed in Paton and Littleton in *An Introduction to Corporate Accounting Standards* (1940) and outlines Kimura's own version of accounting theory.

PERSONAL HISTORY AND PERSONALITY

Professor Wasaburo Kimura was born in Osaka on 3 February, 1902. He had an eventful career. Although born into wealth, he had to find employment after primary school because of the death of his father. He worked during the day and continued his education by night. After three years of business experience, he became a regular student. At that time Kimura worked in a small company which he helped to develop into a large business; he possessed inherent management ability.

Kimura entered Kobe Higher Commercial School in 1923 and graduated in 1925, before moving on to enrol as a graduate student at the School of Economics, Kyoto University, completing his studies in 1928. He was awarded a doctorate in Economics in 1951, although during the Second World War, Kimura had been purged from university by the militarists, for he was a liberal.

Kimura's first job was as Professor at Wakayama Higher Commercial School in 1928, moving on to Osaka Higher Commercial School in 1929, and Osaka University of Commerce in 1942 (renamed Osaka City University in 1949). At the last named institution Kimura was Professor from 1949 to 1965, Dean 1951–3, and Emeritus Professor from 1965 until his death.

When he was fifty years old, Kimura lost his eyesight but he continued his research and studies and was able to overcome all difficulties with the help of his wife. He died on 30 January 1973.

Kimura liked to play tennis, had an appreciation for music and enjoyed

Rakugo (a national Japanese story ending with a joke). There was a touch of irony in his lecturing style which made his lectures popular with students. His lectures were witty and informative, but he was severe when it came to grading. Kimura was a popular figure, both at the university and in the academic associations. His clear thinking, sharp theory and warm heart with regard to a large range of topics made him popular. He was well-informed and had a retentive memory. His lecture room was often overflowing with eager and earnest students.

Kimura lived in Takarazuka, about 20 miles north-west of Osaka, which was famous for the young girl's opera, 'Hot Spring'; he himself was fond of taking hot baths and travelled to many hot springs for that purpose.

Kimura had a son and two daughters and was a devoted father and husband. He was also a pious believer in Buddhism; every morning he offered a prayer before the shrine of his ancestors. He took much interest in the science of divination; the guiding principle in his self-control.

He was fond of beer and was a gourmet. He liked Japanese food and visited many fashionable Japanese restaurants in order to sample a delicious dish. He always said that he was a glutton, but I believe that he was a glutton, not for food, but for books and work.

FEATURES OF THE KIMURA THEORY

Kimura took much interest in the wide field of accounting theory. He was the author of eleven books (all in Japanese) and translated several accounting books into Japanese. He was the author also of approximately one hundred articles concerned with the issues of bookkeeping, accounting, cost accounting, management accounting, and auditing. This demonstrates the wide range of his interests in accounting.

Accounting is a science that is subject to continuous change. This is because accounting is concerned with business activities which are themselves ever expanding, developing and changing in nature. The content of accounting theory has, therefore, to evolve in line with developing business activities. It is for this reason that Kimura's accounting theory stresses the importance of the history analysis of accounting: 'all science is the outcome of historical developments, so we must see accounting in the process of historical development' (Kimura 1972: 7).

Kimura believed that modern accounting theory was initially developed in the early part of the twentieth century, beginning with H. R. Hatfield's *Modern Accounting*, which saw the balance sheet as its key subject. In the 1930s, the emergence of dynamic accounting theory emphasised the income statement and measurement of business income. W. A. Paton and A. C. Littleton's *An Introduction to Corporate Accounting Standards* was considered a great work at this time. Kimura highly appreciated their book and his interpretation and criticism of their message is the main subject of this chapter.

The second feature of Kimura's approach to accounting theory was that he emphasised the importance of the social and economic background. Kimura thought that the theory should address the environment of which accounting is a product. Since accounting symbolises business activities in quantitative terms, it is logical that accounting studies should research such measures, with consideration being given to the social and economic conditions of the time. In particular, the modern joint-stock company, securities exchange, mass production and so forth, are important to the social and economic background of accounting study.

Kimura tried to understand how accounting theory was connected to social and economic developments and thought that accounting theory mirrored economic conditions of the times. In England, Garcke and Fells' *Factory Accounts* (1887) had been an eminent work, depicting the advanced manufacturing process in England at that time and showing the need of cost accounting practice. Paton and Littleton's work is a reflection of 1930s American company accounting and the Securities Exchange Commission system. In Germany the commercial law had a great influence on accounting theory, where E. Schmalenbach's *Dynamische Bilanz* (1919) was most famous.

Each of these cases illustrates the fact that the social and economic background is the most important element of accounting study, and we will see that this theme is the foundation of Kimura's theory.

The third feature of Kimura's theory is the economic view. Kimura regarded accounting as a branch of economics, so that the theoretical explanation of accounting activities must be founded on economic thought. Trying to explain the act of accounting without economic theory is dismissed as superficial, on the grounds that it does not clarify that which is the essence of accounting. This conviction may be illustrated by reference to the following observations made by Paton and Littleton: 'Broadly defined, cost is the amount of the bargained-price of goods or services received or of securities issued in transactions between independent parties' (1940: 24) and 'Revenue is the product of the enterprise, measured by the amount of new assets received from customers' (1940: 46).

Kimura pointed out that this represents a confusion between cost and revenue. According to Paton and Littleton, cost is the concept of the buyer's side and revenue is the concept of the seller's side – cost and revenue become the same. If we view a transaction from the buyer's side, the amount of bargained-price of goods is cost and the same amount is revenue from the seller's side. Kimura says that if cost and revenue are the same concept in terms of any transaction, we cannot explain the source of income. If the same goods are seen as cost from the buyer's side and as revenue from the seller's side, there is nowhere for income to occur. In order to explain the origin of income, there must be a value theory. Activities that add to the value produce income, which is evidence of the social usefulness of produced goods. In a capitalist society, produced goods do not always sell out, that is goods are produced by private companies and are subject to the uncertainty of the market-place. This means that goods left unsold are not acceptable in the market-place. As cost is a private activity and revenue is a social event, cost and revenue have to be distinguished in accounting.

From the point of view of business management, such thinking does not occur. Economic view and economic theory teach the difference of cost and revenue. That is the reason why Kimura stressed economics, and the value theory. Price is not the main object of accounting. Value is the most important object of accounting study, because it shows the origin of income and the essence of accounting.

THE FRAMEWORK OF THE KIMURA THEORY[1]

Kimura assumed a critical attitude towards the popular accounting theory and thought the subject of accounting theory should be approached using a social scientific method of research.

According to this view, the subject of accounting is the method of recording, reporting, and interpreting. The research method of accounting is analysis and synthesis. In accounting studies, as in other social sciences, we must analyse the accounting method of recording and reporting, then reach an area which cannot be further analysed and that is what is called a transaction. Our research study begins the other way, that is a synthesis which begins with one area which is built on, to become the framework for accounting theory. The capital cycle is the earning process of business which is the object of accounting recognition, measurement and reporting. In this process the most important point of view is that of the researcher. In accounting research, Kimura stressed economic and historical analysis. The subject of accounting research is the method of recording, reporting, and interpreting, which includes:

- the historical development of double entry bookkeeping;
- establishment of the periodic earnings measurement system;
- accounting measurement and valuation method;
- accounting standards and principles;
- accounting conventions, basic concepts, and basic postulates.

In Kimura's view, the study of accounting needs only two postulates, which are the accounting unit and the accounting period. The accounting unit is the subject of accounting research and the accounting period is a technical feature of the accounting calculation. Kimura believed that no other postulates were necessary for accounting study.

Kimura commences his accounting research from the starting point of the business entity. The business entity is equivalent to the capital cycle. The business entity has to continue its economic activities, and accounting symbolises these activities as a cycle of business capital. As is generally known, capital repeats its cycle indefinitely. However, the capital cycle periods are different for fixed capital and current capital, so accountants have to know the different cyclical forms of fixed capital and current capital. Current capital changes to other forms of capital or expense at one cycle and fixed capital gradually transfers its value to other objects. Typically, depreciation is the process of this value transfer. In bookkeeping, this process is recognised as a recording from one account to another. These transactions are conventionally recorded at the price level which symbolises the value of the goods when the transaction first took place.

Kimura believed, however, that transactions of the business entity have to be seen at the level of value. Generally, price is the monetary expression of value;

however, price and value are quite different concepts. In order to see the substance of business activity, it must be analysed at the value level; the investigation of the price level is dismissed as superficial research. Embedded in this analysis is Kimura's conviction that the true substance of matters cannot be recognised by observing only the external appearance.

Begin with the value analysis and go to the price level, then to the capital cycle – this is the process and sequence of Kimura's study. At the level of value analysis, Kimura sees the essence of value as the social usefulness which creates the profit of the business. The business entity must therefore produce socially useful goods or services. These are the objects of social consumption and at the same the origin of business profit. Accounting theory has to recognise these processes of business activity as a recording of the capital cycle; for this purpose we must know the value theory and price level. The capital cycle takes various forms and in a concrete way appears as money, goods, machines, land and so on. Kimura thinks they are temporary forms and that they possess a value flow which must be recognised as the object of the study of accounting. For instance, machines have value, so they will depreciate, but land will not. The price of land is that of the right of ownership and such a right does not depreciate in value, consequently, it has a price but no value. If the recognition of business activities is correct, the capital cycle of the business entity can be followed. Otherwise the measurement of the business's financial condition and income cannot be achieved.

That is the reason why Kimura stresses value analysis and capital cycle in accounting.

In his framework, Kimura attaches importance to the category of capital which has two meanings. One meaning is the common one where the value flow of capital is evident. The other meaning is fictitious capital, that is the share market price of the business entity. Fictitious capital comes into existence through the share price of the business entity in the share market, thus bringing capital surplus to the enterprise. So Kimura points out that research into the price of shares and the securities exchange market is the most difficult and the final object of accounting theory.

KIMURA VERSUS PATON AND LITTLETON

Kimura thought highly of Paton and Littleton's book, *An Introduction to Corporate Accounting Standards* (1940) and discussed it fully in *Accounting Theory Research* (Kimura 1954). In order to understand Kimura's way of thinking, his analysis of Paton and Littleton's book must be set out in detail.

According to Kimura's view, Paton and Littleton's *Introduction* has nine theoretical features, as follows:

1 *Objectivity of profit measurement* Income measurement in business accounting must have objectivity, which means accounting income is not the result of subjective valuation.
2 *From valuation to measurement* Accounting measurement must have the same character of physical measurement which can be recognised by everybody.

3 *From valuation principles to measurement standards* Measurement standards means a basis of income measurement in objective and reliable accounting practice. Subjective valuation must be removed from accounting.

4 *'Verifiable, objective evidence'* This phrase is used by Paton and Littleton and emphasised by them as an important feature of accounting records. Account- ing records must be supported by verifiable objective evidence.

5 *Foundation of auditing* Verifiable, objective evidence is also emphasised in auditing.

6 *Price aggregate, that is, cost* Price aggregate is broad enough to designate the basic subject matter of accounting and possesses the attributes of verifiable, objective evidence. So Paton and Littleton used this term rather than cost.

7 *Recorded cost as the standard* As recorded cost is objective, the consistent use of recorded cost in accounting brings to the accounting records reliability and objectivity. It has become stronger as complex business activities have increased and as business management and financial investment have drawn further apart.

8 *Matching cost and revenue* Assigning costs to revenues is crucial from the standpoint of periodic income measurement; it likewise comprehends most of the difficult problems of accounting analysis. In accounting, costs are con- sidered as measuring effort, revenues as measuring accomplishment. The concepts of recorded price aggregate, of cost attaching, of matched cost and revenue, and of income as a difference are fundamental to accounting.

9 *Periodic matching of costs with revenues* As the business activities are continuing events, the process of measuring periodic income involves the division of the stream of costs incurred between the present and the future, and periodically matches costs to revenues with the relevant time interval.

The above-mentioned features are the backbone of Paton and Littleton's account- ing theory, and Kimura pointed out that they can be resolved into the following two points: the historical (recorded) cost basis, and income measurement. As a result, (1) the current cost basis is excluded, (2) there is no possibility of subjective valuation – objective measurement takes the lead in accounting theory, and (3) business income measurement becomes objective and reliable. Kimura asserted that the above three points have been the framework of Paton and Littleton's accounting theory.

Kimura criticised the three points as follows:

• Paton and Littleton do not absolutely rule out valuation in accounting. Especi- ally in the case of plant and equipment, if their prices have advanced or decreased remarkably, book prices have to be written up or down. That is, Paton and Littleton's idea of accounting boils down to the fact that the measurement of income should be based on cost as much as possible, and we must not depart from conservatism unless there is an unavoidable need for a valuation to be made. Paton and Littleton did not explain exactly the role of accounting valuation, as their theory was based on the original prices paid rather than value theory.

- According to Kimura, the most important problem of accounting valuation is radical changes in the price of assets. Paton and Littleton admit the need for revaluation in times of rapid inflation, and also see a case for the publication of supplementary data which take account of movements in the general price level. Kimura states that inflation is accompanied by unequal price changes for different items, so a general price level adjustment should not be applied. Unequal price change is a problem whereby the debtor profits occur and wages are reduced. As governments and big business are debtors and labour are the creditors, inflation has good effects for the former and bad effects for the latter. Kimura wanted us to see economic reality in inflation accounting, and did not favour applying either of the methods given consideration by Paton and Littleton.
- Paton and Littleton's opinion of objective income measurement contains some highly problematic points. Of course, price aggregates in transactions between independent parties are objective, but, costs as price aggregates turn to the stream of costs incurred in the process of business management and the accountant divides them between the present and the future. This cannot be done objectively; the accountant must make a subjective judgement which leads to a subjective income measurement and an inevitable problem in accounting measurements. The relevance of the accounting measurement depends on the accountant's judgement. Kimura therefore draws our attention to the fact that we cannot escape from subjective income measurement in accounting because of the need for subjective cost allocation. Here we can find the necessity for accounting standards to provide guidance for the accountant's actions.

CONCLUSION

Kimura had a sharp mind and was a warm person. He was both an excellent research worker and an honourable professor. He wrote numerous works and gave lessons in many Japanese universities. His lectures contained advanced theories, full of interesting substance. Kimura attained fame and served as a member of the Business Accounting Deliberation Council of the Ministry of Finance in Japan. Kimura believed that truth is eternal and devoted his life to find truth in accounting and, thereby, establish a theoretical framework of accounting which would serve as a relevant guide to accounting practice.

Kimura's theory begins with value analysis, moves to discuss cost flow and ends with the capital cycle. All accounting events arise at the level of market price; however, they should also be viewed at cost level and capital level to find truth in accounting events. The form of accounting events could be misleading. The most important point in Kimura's accounting theory is that a scientific, analytical view is always necessary. Music by famous composers will always attract large audiences and good accounting theory will exist for ever. This is what Kimura sought.

The three features of Kimura's accounting theory – historical development research, the study of the socio-economic background and the importance granted to economics – demonstrate the fact that he had an extensive knowledge, that he was a profound scholar and possessed a retentive memory. In his later days, when he had lost his sight, his work, continued unabated.

Kimura often said that he should write articles in English, for he thought it to be an international language and wanted his ideas to be appreciated internationally by accounting researchers. During his student years he wrote his diary in English and in German, and had intended after his retirement to write his articles in English, but the loss of his eyesight prevented him fulfilling his wish. Therefore, it is a great honour for me that on behalf of Kimura I have this opportunity to introduce his accounting theory. I sincerely hope that my understanding and recounting of it is correct.

Note

1 See Kimura (1954: 131–205, 1972: 7–14, 20–32, 92–6).

References and select bibliography

Garcke, E. and Fells, J. M. (1887) *Factory Accounts; Their Principles and Practice*, London.
Hatfield, H. R. (1918) *Modern Accounting*, New York.
Kimura, W. (1935) *Bank Bookkeeping*, Yuhikaku.
Kimura, W. (1936) *Study of Rice Distribution Cost*, Iwanamishoten.
Kimura, W. (1938) *Japan Bookkeeping*, Dainihontosho.
Kimura, W. (1938) *Principal Bank Bookkeeping*, Dobunkan.
Kimura, W. (1943) *Studies in Depreciation*, Nihonhyoronsha.
Kimura, W. (1947) *Studies in Cost Accounting*, Nihonhyoronsha.
Kimura, W. (1954) *Accounting Theory Research*, Yuhikaki.
Kimura, W. (1972) *Accounting as a Science*, vols 1 and 2, Yuhikaku.
Kimura, W. and Kojima, O. (1955) *A Primer of Bookkeeping*, Moriyamashoten.
Kimura, W. and Kojima, O. (1960) *A Primer of Industry Bookkeeping*, Moriyamashoten.
Paton, W. A. and Littleton, A. C. (1940) *An Introduction to Corporate Accounting Standards*, Sarasota, Fla.: American Accounting Association.
Schmalenbach, E. (1919) *Dynamische Bilanz*, Cologne and Opladen: Westdeutscher Verlag.

12 Lawrence Robert Dicksee (1864–1932)[1]

Jack Kitchen and Robert H. Parker

Abstract

Besides being the most prolific of the early British writers on accounting, following the establishment of the new profession, Lawrence Robert Dicksee is distinguished among them as having been the first to carry his teaching into the universities.

CHILDHOOD AND FAMILY BACKGROUND

Lawrence Dicksee was born in London in 1864 at 27, Howland, St., W. The house no longer stands, but its site is only a hundred yards or so from the present London School of Economics' Hall of Residence (Carr-Saunders Hall) in Fitzroy Street, adjacent to Fitzroy Square and two minutes' walk from the Post Office Tower. The Dicksees were a large, talented and united family of successful and distinguished artists. Lawrence's father, John Robert Dicksee (born in 1817) and his uncle, Thomas Francis Dicksee (born in 1820) lived and worked as artists in close association throughout their lives. They had shared premises in Soho in their twenties (at 36 Gerrard Street, and 53 Old Compton Street) and both had moved to Howland Street at or about the times of their marriages: Thomas first, to 23 Howland Street, and John later, to 27. John already had enjoyed modest success and some reputation as a portrait painter, but Thomas was perhaps rather the more successful of the two as a painter and illustrator.

Thomas had four children at Howland Street and John five, of whom Lawrence was the youngest. These nine children (six boys and three girls, all born between 1852 and 1864) must have made a lively group. The two households included other relatives from time to time and each had at least two domestic servants living on the premises. Both households later moved to Fitzroy Square (Thomas's to No. 2 and John's to No. 6) and when the children came in due course to set up house for themselves, they moved to addresses in the area of St John's Wood and Hampstead, where the close family associations seem to have continued.

In Lawrence's childhood, the families might have been described as at least 'of modest means' or 'comfortably off'. When the nine youngsters grew up they seem generally to have maintained and improved upon their parents' living standards and position. Most of the nine followed their fathers' professions in some field of art or architecture, with Lawrence's cousin Frank (who was eleven years his senior and had early success as a painter) shining the brightest.[2]

Possible influence of family environment on Dicksee's development

We do not know how it came about that with a family background rooted so firmly in the arts, Lawrence should have been launched into accountancy in 1881 at the age of seventeen, but he had been educated at the City of London School where his father had been teaching since 1852.[3] John Robert Dicksee was also first curator of the City of London Corporation's works of art, and it may be that these links with the City, and the developments in accountancy then current, brought to notice the possibilities for Lawrence of a career in the new profession.

We can discern something of Lawrence's family environment in his work. His colleague and friend Stanley W. Rowland wrote at the time of Lawrence's death in 1932:

> He was intimate with few of his professional associates. To those few he revealed a man cast by nature for the life of an artist, although accounting translated his love of beauty into a desire for neatness and precision in all things.
>
> (*The Accountant* of 27 February 1932: 284)

Certainly it was natural for a man with Lawrence Dicksee's background to turn readily to teaching. On the other hand, it is interesting to speculate whether the thought processes of the artist, with which Lawrence necessarily lived constantly during his formative years, may have worked against the full success of his important contribution to the development of accounting thought and ideas.

Like most other early writers in the field, Lawrence Dicksee lacked formal training as a scholar, at any rate beyond school years, and though his consideration of accounting and accounting problems was extensive and deep, there is evidence that he lacked in some measure the stamina, determination, and power of analysis (to reject some inadequate conclusions and to persist in the elimination of some important loose ends) which might have been available to a mind of comparable quality well trained in the thought processes of science or the law.

Stanley Rowland, writing in love and admiration after Dicksee's death of his mode of working, said (in *The Accountant* of 27 February 1932):

> Dicksee's was a very remarkable brain. He had a power of rapid assimilation which gave him the material for confidence in his own knowledge. But he was able to pass everything through the processes of his own mind in such fashion that his teaching bore the impress of his individual minting. Consequently, he was rarely seen to consult other men's writings before delivering himself on any particular subject. For him the writing of an article was a matter for intense mental concentration, in course of which he called his forces to his command, and at the blast of his trumpet difficulties appeared to vanish. His dictating machine was his constant companion, and he could put into it long stretches of dictation which would transcribe with hardly the correction of a word.

Of course, the 'other men's writings' which Dicksee might have been more frequently 'seen to consult' were, at the time of his early work, sparse and often of indifferent quality. It was, indeed, Dicksee's strong independence of mind and his confidence in his own grasp of his subject which enabled him to play his important pioneering role in providing single-handed so large a portion of the accounting literature of his day. Inevitably, however, his lonely working style, in which writing followed swift on meditation, inclined him to miss (or to under-estimate) some invaluable references, occasionally in *The Accountant* in the years following his entry into articles, and later in some judicial opinions and judgements, the bases for which he might with advantage have weighed more patiently and assiduously.

1881–92: DICKSEE'S EARLY CAREER

Lawrence Dicksee was conscious that, unlike many early leaders of the profession, he qualified by examination for membership of the Institute of Chartered Accountants in England and Wales. Following its incorporation by Royal Charter, the Institute had a membership in 1880 of rather under 600, including (to quote from Dicksee's Presidential Address to the Birmingham Chartered Accountants' Students' Society in 1904) 'practically every practitioner worthy of . . . serious attention' (*The Accountant*, 19 November 1904: 627). By the time Dicksee became an articled clerk in 1881 the membership had grown to nearly 1,200, about half having been admitted 'by virtue of their previous membership of existing Societies', and the remainder 'admitted by the Council' (*The Account-ant*, 10 June 1882, 392: 6). When Dicksee was admitted in 1886, there were about 1,400 members (*The Accountant*, 7 May 1887: 265). It may well be that Dicksee's early experience of the professional examinations was among the factors which awakened his interest in writing and teaching.

Dicksee's principal was George Norton Read, FCA (G. N. Read, Son & Co., chartered accountants, of 51 Queen Victoria Street, London, EC). He had been admitted to membership of the ICAEW in June 1880 and Lawrence Dicksee was his first articled pupil. There quickly came to be established between them the strong bond which Dicksee forged with a small number of his professional colleagues and friends. When Dicksee published his *Auditing* in 1892, it was 'affectionately dedicated' to G. N. Read.

After Dicksee's admission to membership of the Institute in November 1886, he set up in practice straight away, first at 6 Fitzroy Square, and later at 57 Moorgate Street, EC. However, his early venture into professional practice was 'only moderately successful' (*The Accountant*, 1 January 1921: 3) and after three years Dicksee joined Mr Peter Price in practice in Cardiff at 21 High Street under the style of Price & Dicksee. At the same time Mr Price's elder son was articled to Dicksee.

Dicksee was to practise for five years in Cardiff. Price & Dicksee kept on Dicksee's London office for a time, but this did not attract sufficient business to justify its continuance. Dicksee was admitted to Fellowship of the ICAEW in

November 1891. Three occurrences during his sojourn in Cardiff are notable: first, he began to work as a lecturer on bookkeeping at the 'Technical Schools of the County Borough of Cardiff' as was to be stated, in due course, on the title page of *Auditing*; second, following a change of responsibilities resulting from Dicksee's entry into the partnership, a fraud was discovered in the accounts of the Cardiff Building Society of which Mr Peter Price was Secretary; and third, Dicksee prepared and published in 1892 his first book, *Auditing*.

The building society fraud was a simple one, perpetrated over a period of years by a clerk with access to cash, and successfully concealed by him, despite recurrent audit by unqualified auditors. His main method of concealment (which called for some skill in timing and execution) was to alter individual mortgage account balances after they had been listed and checked by the auditors, but before they were added to provide the total for mortgage debtors. After the addition had been checked, the falsely inflated individual account balances were altered back again (with the 'total' left unchanged) so that any later references to individual balances would raise no suspicion. In all, the defalcations amounted to some £8,600 and the Building Society's directors and Mr Peter Price made up the whole of the deficiency between them, with Mr Price contributing:

> nearly half of the total sum required (he giving up nearly the whole of his property), a fact the more remarkable as he was by no means a rich man or possessed of the means which some of the other officials could command.
>
> (From *The South Wales Daily News*, quoted in *The Accountant*, 15 October 1892: 776)

In 1890 frauds of the kind discovered at the Cardiff Building Society were common, and the Cardiff case received notice in *The Accountant*. The paper's readers were told in January 1890 that:

> It is the old tale of blind confidence in a clerk, and it is extremely doubtful whether the frauds would have been discovered even now, but for the fact of the Secretary having entered into a partnership which rendered the defaulter's services as his clerk unnecessary from that time.
>
> (18 January 1890: 28)

Subsequently, a correspondent asked for 'Details of the *modus operandi*', and on 19 April *The Accountant* published a long leading article (pp. 193–5) in explanation, introduced as follows:

> we have been furnished with the recently issued accounts of the Cardiff Building Society, and also have been favoured with a detailed account of the mode by which the late clerk of the society managed to abstract a sum of nearly £8,600 before he was detected.

The leading article recorded that 'Messrs. Read, Son & Co., of London' had been called in by the directors to make an independent investigation, 'and from their report, which is a plain and concise statement of the work done, and the position of the Society, it is clear that the concern now stands on a sound basis'.

We may discern Lawrence Dicksee's hand in all this. The incident made a deep impression on him, as *Auditing* was to show. *The Accountant* had earlier noted (18 January 1890: 28): 'there is not the slightest doubt that for an expenditure of a few guineas per annum for an audit by Chartered Accountants, [the amount of the defalcation] would have been saved.'

Peter Price was sixty-five when Dicksee joined him as a partner, and was well-known and respected in Cardiff for an unstinting, though unostentatious, contribution to public life in that City, particularly in relation to the establishment of the Cardiff Free Library. Price was a governor of the University College of South Wales and Monmouthshire in Cardiff, and was similarly associated with other organisations and also a magistrate. The shock and the heavy cost of the building society fraud was a severe blow to him. He died in 1892. Lawrence Dicksee carried on the Cardiff practice until 1894 when Price's son's articles were successfully completed. He then returned to London, and in September 1894 joined Arthur Sellars FCA in partnership at Copthall House, 48 Copthall Avenue, EC. Together they practised as Sellars, Dicksee and Co. Dicksee was to head the firm from 1898 until he died in 1932.

MARRIAGE

Lawrence Dicksee took another important step in 1894. On 31 July at St Andrews Church in St Marylebone he married Nora Beatrice Plumbe, the daughter of an architect. The bride's 'residence at the time of marriage' was 13 Fitzroy Square. The couple lived for a while in Townshend Road, St Johns Wood, and later in Antrim Mansions, Hampstead. Some time in 1908 or 1909 they moved to 153 Haverstock Hill, Hampstead, which was to be the family home for the rest of Dicksee's life. The house no longer stands. They had one child, a boy; he was a casualty of the 1914–18 war, and his death was a tragedy of particular poignancy for a man of Dicksee's warm and sensitive nature, the product of an environment in which children and family had such importance.[4]

DICKSEE'S *AUDITING*

Dicksee signed the preface to his first book, *Auditing*, in Cardiff on 13 July 1892, and Gee & Co. published it later that year. Dicksee was twenty-eight. *Auditing* was well described by its sub-title as 'A Practical Manual for Auditors' and Dicksee placed his emphasis on identifying, elaborating, and explaining the methods to be adopted by auditors to achieve the objects of the audit, which he saw as:

The detection of fraud;
The detection of technical errors; and
The detection of errors in principle.

Dicksee also sought to consider and convey 'the leading principles that should guide an Auditor in the course of his investigations' and he aimed his work to a substantial degree at accountant students, while expressing in the Preface the

hope that it would be 'also of some utility to practising members of the profession
. . . [especially] when they find themselves face to face with the accounts of a
business with which they have hitherto been unfamiliar'. For this latter purpose
he included a long chapter on special considerations in different classes of audits.
He regretted that lack of space had prevented 'a more full discussion of the
various legal decisions that affect the duties and responsibilities of the profession'; in this, he was probably yielding to advice, as well as to inclination,
since Pixley's *Auditors. Their duties and responsibilities* already dealt substantially with such aspects. Dicksee nevertheless included two principal appen-
dices, one comprising extracts, for reference, from a number of relevant statutes
(mainly those dealing with corporate bodies registered otherwise than under the
Companies Acts) and the other, extracts from Law Reports of decisions of
interest to auditors. The extracts from statutes were similar to, though less
extensive than, those provided in Pixley's book.

Dicksee's introductory chapter opened with a discussion of audit notebooks,
instructions and programmes, the extent to which complete or test checking of
transactions recording should be undertaken, and the rival merits of 'continuous'
and 'completed' audits. There was an echo of the Cardiff Building Society
incident in his reference to

> the extreme importance of *completing* each item of the audit as soon as
> possible after it is begun. Extensive frauds have escaped detection because the
> Auditor checked the balances of a Ledger one day, and the additions of such
> balances on the next – some of the items having been altered in the meantime.
> (1892: 10)

Auditing was an immediate success. Fourteen British editions were published
during Dicksee's lifetime, the fifteenth was in preparation when he died. The
book found a market also in the United States, and a first 'Authorized American
Edition' was published in 1905. It was edited by Robert H. Montgomery, who
had opened a New York Office for the Philadelphia firm of Lybrand, Ross Bros,
and Montgomery some while before. Montgomery published his own *Auditing
Theory and Practice* in 1912. It has been said that Montgomery's adaptation of
Dicksee's text to American needs in 1905 marked the beginning of American
literature in accounting. The American edition of 'Dicksee' was reprinted three
times in 1907 and 1908. A second American edition was published in 1909.

ASSET VALUATION, DEPRECIATION, AND INCOME

Auditing was Dicksee's first, and also his most important, book. To those reading
it in the late twentieth century, over one hundred years after it was first drafted,
it is most of all distinguished for a real attempt (in Chapter 5) to work out an
acceptable and rational basis for asset valuation, depreciation, and income. For
this, Dicksee recognised and considered the double-account system which had
increasingly come into use during the nineteenth century and which was prescribed under statutes of 1868 and 1871 for railway and gas companies, and being

widely used for other similar undertakings such as docks and water companies. His basic attitude towards depreciation is set out in the first edition of *Auditing* (1892), written soon after the decision of the Court of Appeal (February 1889) in *Lee v. Neuchatel Asphalte Co.* which had taken the accountancy profession aback. There was a relationship between the *Lee* judgement and the logic underlying the double-account system which Dicksee must have been aware of, though he does not seem to have seen it very clearly.

Dicksee introduced his discussion with the warning that 'As the points now about to be discussed are the most important, so are they also the most debatable, accountants of the highest repute being by no means agreed as to the principles involved.' At the same time, he seems to have felt impelled to assert that 'the acute observer' would be able to discern that 'much of this apparent difference is . . . merely verbal,' adding that 'it is . . . not unreasonable to suppose that, in any particular case . . . there would not exist among our leading practitioners any radical difference of opinion as to what the profit of a company had really been' (1892: 117)

Dicksee went on to consider the 'Principle in Valuation of Assets' in the following terms:

> It being the primary object of most ordinary undertakings to continue to carry on operations, it is but fair that the assets enumerated in a Balance Sheet be valued with that end in view; before this subject is pursued any further, however, it is well to acknowledge two *essentially different features* obtaining to different classes of accounts. Certain Parliamentary Companies, constituted for the purposes of undertaking certain definite public works are, on account of the peculiar circumstances under which they were called into existence, required to render their accounts in a manner radically different from that of all other undertakings: the system they are required to adopt is called the DOUBLE-ACCOUNT SYSTEM. It being required that all capital raised by these companies shall be expended in the construction of the public works (for the construction of which they were called into existence), care was taken by the Legislature to see that this provision is duly complied with: hence a special form of account, in which all monies expended in the construction of the works is separated from the General Balance Sheet. Now, in order that this account (the Capital Expenditure Account) might perpetually show that – and how – the capital authorised to be raised had actually been spent only upon the authorised purposes – except a small margin for working capital or contingencies – it was necessary that the actual amount expended on the works alone be debited to the account, regardless of any fluctuations in value that might afterwards occur. It would, of course, have been easy for the Legislature to have provided that any fluctuation that might occur should be duly allowed for in the General Balance Sheet; but, having regard to the fact that no such fluctuation could in any way practically affect the company, so long as it carried on business, and bearing in mind also the fact that it was contemplated that the company should *permanently* carry on business, it would appear that

all consideration of these fluctuations was considered superfluous. With an eye to the future, however, and doubtless also with a view to – so far as possible – insuring the business being permanently carried on, it was provided that the company's works (which were required to be kept perpetually at the amount of their initial cost, regardless of their after value) be continuously kept in a state of efficiency, and that the cost thereof be borne out of Revenue. It will thus be seen that the *form* of the Double-Account system arose from the statutory requirement that all capital raised should be used for the carrying out of the works for the execution of which the company was created; and that the principle that, so long as the works were maintained in a state of efficiency their actual value need not be periodically reconsidered, arose from the circumstance that it was contemplated that the work authorised would be permanently carried on.

How far – if at all – these considerations need affect one's judgement concerning the valuation of the assets of undertakings not specifically covered by [such statutes] it will now be necessary to enquire; but it may be mentioned that, inasmuch as Auditors are not compelled to regard the Legislature as the highest possible authority in the matter of accounts, they are still free to discuss the principles involved upon their merits, even if a sense of logic compels them to admit an analogy between the accounts of Parliamentary companies and those of other undertakings.

(1892: 117–18)

Dicksee then turned to the case of private traders, 'whether *sole* or firms', noting that 'as no man can ... hope to live for ever, the business of such an one is ephemeral ... compared with that of a parliamentary company'. None the less, since such businesses often outlived their founders, a revaluation of assets was likely to be involved upon a change of proprietorship, and it must be expected that the basis of valuation in such case would be 'as a going concern'. To this term, Dicksee attributed a somewhat 'elastic meaning' implying 'at such a value as [the assets] would stand in the books if proper depreciation had been provided for' – the term 'depreciation' being taken to represent 'the amount by which the value of an asset has become reduced by effluxion of time or wear'. Having also commented that it was 'not really practicable so to maintain the efficiency of assets that no depreciation' should 'ever exist', and that private firms were 'under no statutory requirement to *retain* the whole of their undertaking intact', Dicksee concluded that the double-account system did not apply to the accounts of private traders.

Considering registered companies, Dicksee noted that they had a perpetual succession and 'consequently the Double-Account system of stating values might be employed'. But he argued that it should not, because companies in practice were generally shorter-lived than private businesses; because registered companies were under no obligation to retain any particular one of their assets; and because in any case it was impracticable to divide the assets into two balance sheets on the basis that some were permanent and others not. Dicksee concluded: 'The amount, therefore, at which *all* assets are stated in Balance Sheets, except where a special statutory provision to the contrary obtains, should be regulated by the value of such assets' (1892: 120).

However, it is not certain that Dicksee was able to dismiss the influence of the double-account system (with its emphasis on different treatment for capital and non-capital items) as readily from his mind as his arguments above might lead us to suppose. Thus, he turned almost immediately to consider the 'valuation of so-called Permanent Assets,'[5] arguing:

> The points to be borne in mind here are that wasting may reduce their value, and that fluctuation may increase or reduce their value. So far as wasting is concerned, inasmuch as it has directly contributed to the profit earned, it is clearly an expense with which profit may be fairly charged. On the other hand, fluctuation is something altogether apart from profit and loss, being merely the accidental variation (owing to external causes) in the value of certain property owned, but not traded in: to carry the amount of such variation to Profit and Loss Account would be to disturb and obscure the results of actual trading, and so render statistical comparison difficult if not impossible. On no account, therefore, should the results of fluctuations affect the Profit and Loss Account.
>
> (1892: 121)

A few pages later Dicksee repeated the same point and added:

> The author is not prepared to admit that this distinction is contrary to the various legal decisions that have occurred from time to time; but in any case, he would remind readers that, whatever deference or obedience is owing to the Courts, they cannot be regarded as indisputable authorities upon matters of account.
>
> (1892: 126)

As to depreciation methods and individual asset values, Dicksee's consideration proceeded for about a dozen categories, from freehold buildings to furniture. Fixed instalments, and fixed percentages on reducing balances (with or without interest adjustments), were based specifically or by implication on original cost (1892: 126–8).[6] Obsolescence received appropriate treatment, but Dicksee clearly thought much plant and general machinery ran 'comparatively little risk of becoming obsolete'. For assets like plant or furniture and fittings, Dicksee thought 'an occasional revaluation [would] be desirable' (1892: 130)[7]

Dicksee mentioned two other categories which should be noted:

> Investments need not be depreciated unless of a wasting nature, such as shares in Single Ship Companies.
>
> Mines undoubtedly depreciate in direct proportion to the amount of mineral extracted. By a singular inconsistency of the law, however, no depreciation need be provided for by a mining company before declaring a dividend.
>
> (1892: 128–9)[8]

If we are to reckon it a measure of the failure of Dicksee and the other account-ants of his generation that they effectively abandoned the attempt to erect a better basis than original cost for the valuation of fixed assets in accounts, we must see to it that in our generation we achieve the needed improvement. At least we are well aware of what is unsatisfactory in our present situation.

That Dicksee was satisfied, by and large, with original cost we need not doubt, though he did not announce his unqualified adherence to it as did some of his contemporaries and immediate successors. We need to bear in mind the general experience relative to price level changes during the latter half of the nineteenth century and up to the First World War. It does seem possible, however, that Dicksee and his generation were further influenced in favour of original cost, even than they might otherwise have been, as a result of the emphasis placed upon it by the double-account system.

Overall, we may note that Dicksee's views changed comparatively little between 1892 and 1928 when the fourteenth edition of *Auditing* appeared. Dicksee did, however, insert some additional material under the heading of 'Principle in Valuation of Assets' before turning to the 'Valuation of Fixed Assets' in the fourteenth edition of *Auditing*, e.g.

> In the great majority of cases there can be no doubt that the position of affairs can be more readily and clearly disclosed by a single Balance Sheet than by accounts kept upon the Double-account System.[9] In the case of companies, however, there is a further point to be considered, namely that there are increases which are not divisible profits, and losses which (as a matter of law) need not be made good before dividing profits in the form of dividend. The Profit and Loss Account must obviously be framed so as to show the divisible profits, and the question thus remains . . . how profits and losses that do *not* affect Revenue – or, to put it another way, capitalised fluctuations – are to be treated . . . [It] is clear that two courses are open. Either the capitalised items must be disregarded in the Balance Sheet by misstating the value of an asset or a liability, or some account must be raised to record the profit or loss that is not taken to Revenue . . . If, however, a profit has been made which is not available for distribution, it is often considered unnecessary to modify the accounts so as to disclose the circumstance . . . As a general rule, the amount at which *all* assets are stated in the Balance Sheet – except where a special statutory provision to the contrary obtains – should be regulated by the realisable value of such assets on the basis of a going concern.
>
> (1928: 196–8)

The 'general rule' was, however, plainly vulnerable, for in the next paragraph (anxious to register the distinction between realisable value in a forced sale and the balance sheet's normal concern with the affairs of a continuing business) Dicksee asserted that the function of the balance sheet was:

> chiefly to prove the reasonableness of the apportionment of income and expenditure as between one year and another, and also to show the financial position of the business – *i.e.* the resources it has available to meet its current liabilities . . . [So] far as [fixed] assets are concerned, so long as it is

reasonable to assume the continuity of the business, the correct thing is not to attempt to show the realisable value (which may be considerably more, or very considerably less, than the original cost) but rather to show such expenditure *as* expenditure, subject to the fact that in so far as it will not last for ever its cost must be apportioned as fairly as possible, and charged against the profits earned in successive years, in order to arrive at the true working expenses and the true net profit of each year.

(1928: 198)

The similarity is marked between this latter statement and the view conveyed at the time of its issue by (e.g.) paragraphs 3 and 4 of *Recommendation N. 18* (Presentation of balance sheet and profit and loss account) published by the Council of the Institute of Chartered Accountants in England and Wales in 1958.

LOCAL AUTHORITIES[10]

At the time Dicksee was writing, one of the pressing contemporary issues was the accountability of municipal corporations. The larger of these took on responsibility for the supply of a range of trading services – water, gas, electricity and transport – as well as the provision of civic amenities. This naturally involved the obligation to account for vast amounts of money, at a time when the level of capital expenditure in many industries remained relatively modest. The appropriate method of accounting for capital expenditure loomed large in such entities.

There were both similarities and differences between municipal corporations and companies supplying similar services in the private sector. An important similarity was the use by each type of entity of the double-account system; a difference was the reliance of municipal corporations on debt finance which they were obliged to repay from revenue over periods of time laid down by statute. The burning question was whether municipal corporations in particular and local authorities generally should be obliged to make any further charges against revenue in respect of the diminution in value of fixed assets over time. Dicksee became closely associated with this debate.[11]

A wide range of schemes received enthusiastic support from different quarters. These included the conviction that it was enough to charge only the loan repayment against revenue (new capital expenditure could then be financed by raising fresh debt capital) and the alternative view that repaying debt and maintaining assets intact were separate questions which necessitated a 'double charge'. Dicksee moved between both these extremes over the years. In 1903 Dicksee wrote:

There is, however, absolutely no connection whatever between paying off liabilities and earning profits, and under no possible circumstances can the payments of liabilities, as such, be a charge against Revenue *per se*. Clearly, therefore, it cannot be such a charge against Revenue as to absolve these undertakings from any ordinary customary charges which are absolutely essential to enable true profits to be determined.

Four years later, in a lecture presented to the Chartered Accountants Students' Society of London, Dicksee observed that

> the charge against revenue in respect of the sinking fund may, under these peculiar circumstances [where the life of the asset approximated to the period of the loan, which he considered to be government policy], be regarded as being the statutory equivalent for, and as taking the place of, the ordinary businessman's charge for depreciation of assets.
>
> (1907: 484)

J. W. Forster, Borough Accountant, Tunbridge Wells commented:

> One of the most significant and important signs of the altered state of opinion . . . is to be found in the present attitude of Professor Dicksee, the very able Professor of Accounting in the University of Birmingham, who at the present time occupies an important position in the War Office in connection with the re-organisation of that Department on business lines.
>
> (1907: 128)

When confronted with this inconsistency, Dicksee replied that he 'did not know that any useful purpose would be served by attempting to reconcile [his present views with] the statement quoted, which was made four years ago' (1907: 131). We can therefore at least conclude that Dicksee was familiar with all the arguments when reaching his later assessment.

However, Forster does not do Dicksee full justice. Dicksee's paper also advocates a compromise solution designed to achieve the maintenance of capital, namely that an additional charge should be made where the loan repayment period was more than the estimated asset life. The need for such a charge could arise in the case of an individual asset but, more likely, in the following two situations: because of premature obsolescence, particularly in the case of electricity and tramways, and to deal with the inclusion of short-lived items among the total range of assets financed by a single loan equal to the average life of the concern's assets – called the 'equated' loan period. Dicksee illustrates this latter point by reference to capital expenditure on an electric lighting undertaking whose constituent assets varied from twelve years in the case of meters, to eighty years in the case of the buildings (1907: 485).

It seems that it was practical experience that caused Dicksee to revise his views. At Bristol Corporation, following the establishment of the electricity department in 1893, small amounts were written off in respect of depreciation, and modest transfers were made from profit to build up a reserve fund and depreciation fund of £10,000 and £6,000 respectively by 1905. In the following year the method of accounting for fixed assets was altered on Dicksee's recommendation. The depreciation charge was written back to profits, while the other two amounts were credited to the newly created 'reserve (for renewals) fund account'. Also credited to this account, from revenue, was £2,500 described as the 'difference between the provision for renewal of assets recommended by Professor Dicksee and the amount of the statutory repayment of loans' (1906 accounts: 140). We can therefore see that what might be described as the 'topping-up' system was adopted, with the rates used possibly those set out in Dicksee's paper published in *The Accountant* in the following year (1907: 485).

OTHER PUBLICATIONS

Even before Lawrence Dicksee left his Cardiff practice, he was delivering occasional lectures to Chartered Accountants' Students' Societies in London, Leeds and elsewhere. After his return to London in 1894, these activities multiplied and he produced a steady output of lectures, articles and unsigned contributions to periodicals including *The Accountant*.

Beside *Auditing*, Dicksee's publications included: *Bookkeeping for Accountant Students*, first published 1893; *Comparative Depreciation Tables* (1895); *Bookkeeping for Company Secretaries* (1897); *Goodwill and its Treatment in Accounts* (1897, with Frank Tillyard); *Bookkeeping Exercises for Accountant Students* (1899); *Depreciation, Reserves and Reserve Funds* (1903); *Published Balance Sheets and Window Dressing* (1927). Dicksee also published *Advanced Accounting* in 1903, an important book, associated with his university courses at Birmingham and London, which ran to seven editions during his lifetime.

Dicksee wrote several books on accounts for different classes of organisations, including: *Auctioneers' Accounts* (1901); *Gas Accounts* (1902); *Solicitors' Accounts* (1902); *Hotel Accounts* (1905), *Mines Accounting and Management* (1914) and *Garage Accounts* (1929). He also developed an interest in business organisation and Longmans Green brought out a book for him with that title in New York in 1910. Dicksee published *Business Methods and the War* (1915); *Office Machinery, a handbook for progressive office managers* (1917), and *The True Basis of Efficiency* (1922), part of a series for the London School of Economics edited by Sir William Beveridge and Professor A. J. Sergeant. Earlier, with H. E. Blair (Sir Herbert Blair) he had published a book on *Office Organization and Management* which was already in its third edition by 1914 and continued to appear in successive editions into the 1950s. If we take his published lectures and articles into account, it is not unfair to say that he provided a literature for accounting single-handed.

In 1932, the obituary for Dicksee in *The Accountant* (20 February 1932: 236) recorded that 'for nearly thirty years he [had been] a constant and most valued contributor to our columns' adding that Dicksee had been 'obliged through pressure of work to give up writing regularly for us' about eleven years previously. Stanley Rowland in his own obituary article for Dicksee (*The Accountant*, 27 February 1932: 283) noted that 'There must be thousands of columns of *The Accountant* where those with eyes to see can detect the authentic and confident notes of his style'.

We need to bear in mind the work involved in Dicksee's output of published material, and the labour of revision for later editions of his books, along with his university teaching at London and (to 1906) at Birmingham; and we need to recall that throughout, he continued to lecture outside the university, and (with everything) to fulfil the role of senior partner in a sizeable accountancy practice. The load he carried was a formidable one.

UNIVERSITY TEACHING

Lawrence Dicksee was appointed to the Chair of Accounting at the University of Birmingham in 1902, the first appointment to such a Chair in any British university. He was to become the first holder of a Chair of Accounting in the University of London, and he was also to be the first teacher of Accounting at the London School of Economics.

After his return from Cardiff, Dicksee had run the coaching classes of the London Chartered Accountants' Students' Society. The University of Birmingham announced in 1901 that they proposed to set up a Faculty of Commerce, and they advertised a part-time Chair of Accounting. The advertisement appeared in *The Accountant* of 21 June 1902. The part-time post was to carry a stipend of £300 a year – from the third year. Because the duties in the first and second years would be 'comparatively light', the stipends for those years were set at £150 and £225 respectively. Dicksee's appointment was announced in *The Accountant* of 2 August 1902 with the following comment:

Professor Dicksee's name will be so well known to our readers that it is unnecessary for us to enlarge here upon his qualifications for this important post. He has been one of the largest contributors to the literature of the profession, and the value of his works is shown by the fact that they are not merely sold extensively wherever the English language is spoken but are also in demand upon the Continent. Readers of *The Accountant* to which paper he has been a frequent contributor will regret the necessary severance of his connection. It is his intention to continue his practice in London, however.

A few months later, when the London School of Economics issued its sessional programme for 1902/3 it included an optional course of sixty lectures over two years on 'Accountancy and Business Methods' for the London Bsc(Econ). Dicksee was named as the lecturer. He was to teach at LSE for the next twenty-five years.

Dicksee continued to live in London and he limited his visits to Birmingham to one day a week during term time, though his work for the Birmingham courses occupied much of his time. The M.Com. which he was awarded at the Birmingham Degree Congregation in 1903 seems to have been granted in recognition of his published work and his membership of Senate.

In 1906 Dicksee found it necessary to resign the Birmingham appointment in order to give more time to his work at LSE, which had been increased following the introduction there in 1906/7 of the so-called annual 'Army Class', a War Office scheme for the training in Business Methods and Business Administration of a limited number of serving officers, which ran successfully for many years. Dicksee was made Reader in Accounting in 1912, and given the title of Professor of Accounting and Business Organization in 1914. This title he held to 1919, when the London Commerce Degree was introduced and he was appointed to one of the newly established Chairs as Sir Ernest Cassel Professor of Accounting and Business Methods in the University of London.

Dicksee was Dean of the Faculty of Economics in the University of London in 1925/6. He retired in 1926 and was awarded the title of Emeritus Professor of Accountancy and Business Methods in the University in recognition of his work. He continued to give occasional lectures at LSE for another year or so, and to lecture elsewhere and to write into the last months of his life.

PUBLISHED BALANCE SHEETS AND ACCOUNTS

Under this title, Lawrence Dicksee gave an important public lecture at the London School of Economics on 7 October 1920. It was one of a short series of public lectures given at the School by the newly appointed occupants of the Sir Ernest Cassel Chairs. The lecture is notable because Dicksee took the opportunity to declare his position on secret reserves and what were sometimes called 'condensed balance sheets'. Dicksee said *inter alia*:

> Shareholders, in the nature of things, . . . prefer uniform dividends. They are . . . willing that distributions out of profits should . . . increase, but they are . . . inclined to be disappointed, . . . when the rate of dividend falls. Accordingly, those . . . responsible for the preparation of accounts, and for the successful conduct of a business, very naturally adopt in the main a procedure that tends in the direction of avoiding large distributions of profits which they know it will be impossible to maintain in the future . . . Accordingly, we commonly find that where the dividend . . . proposed . . . is markedly less than the amount of the . . . profits available to be divided, pressure is brought to bear by the shareholders for the dividend to be increased, and directors as a rule endeavour to resist that pressure where in their opinion the standard of distribution proposed is too high to be maintained. To assist them in resisting that pressure, it is a very common thing to transfer a . . . part of the profits actually earned to a reserve, thus reducing the amount of undivided profits shown . . .

Dicksee continued:

> Instead of transferring profits to a reserve that is clearly shown upon the face of the balance sheet . . . the practice has grown up, and during recent years appears to be decidedly upon the increase, of piling up what are sometimes called 'internal reserves', sometimes 'undisclosed reserves', and sometimes 'secret reserves'. The term 'secret reserve' does not seem to be much used save by those who oppose this particular kind of policy and regard it as being highly undesirable.
>
> The effect of the policy is to withhold from those to whom the balance sheet may be sent the fact that the undertaking has made certain profits which have not yet been divided. The directors do not 'account' to the extent of such reserves. On the face of it that might seem to be entirely improper and highly

unjustifiable, but it has been held that there is nothing whatever illegal about such a practice so long as it is not contrary to the regulations of that particular company.

Dicksee complained of the burden falling on the auditor required to decide whether he should make disclosure to the shareholders, and where he did not, to satisfy himself that the directors were acting in good faith for the benefit of the company and the shareholders. He added:

> We cannot, and ought not to, complain, but rather to congratulate [the directors] if their general policy is always to be on the safe side, and to aim at disclosing a position in their published balance sheets that is certainly not better than the true position . . . In spite of all this we must draw the line somewhere, or we shall find that we are driven to the conclusion that the balance sheet may mean little or nothing.

Dicksee followed these remarks with a reference to a shipping company 'having total assets amounting to £1,305,000 odd' which explained £1,073,811 of that amount simply as 'Stock in steamships and investments, book value at 31 December 1918, after deducting depreciation previously written off.'

Dicksee continued:

> At the annual meeting . . . the chairman was asked whether he would state how much of that figure represented steamships and how much represented investments, and he said that it was not in the interests of the company to give that information. At that time, the £10 shares of the company stood at about £45. A little later the ships were sold and the company was wound up, and the return to the shareholders is now expected to be about £130 per share. One wonders whether it really was in interests of the company that shareholders should have no information which would suggest to them that their shares were worth a very great deal more than the current market price.

Dicksee also complained of another practice, which was common in 1920, and which continued to be widely followed through the 1930s, of 'condensing' information on asset holdings by grouping together a number of items under one head, thereby disclosing and at the same time concealing information. Dicksee observed:

> The balance sheet should show in reasonable detail the grouping of its assets. Most balance sheets do that. Some certainly do not; and as an illustration of one that does not, I should like to read you an extract from a balance sheet of a well-known company. Explaining an outlay of upwards of 5¾ millions sterling, it does it in five lines of print, as follows: 'By land, water rights, reservoirs, effluent works, buildings, plant, machinery, office furniture, goodwill, designs, engraving, and sampling, as per last account, £5,776,212 19s 8d. Further capital expenditure at cost (less sales) for the two years ended 26th June 1920, £14,922 16s 11d, making a total of £5,791,135 16s 7d'. I suggest that this is not an ideal way of disclosing to interested parties what the main resources of the undertaking consist of.

The experience of the 1920s and 1930s was to show that there would be no real advance in the standard of disclosure in the published accounts of companies until the setting-up and use of secret reserves had ceased to command the wide approval of businessmen. For this the necessary change of attitudes had to await the catalyst of the Kylsant case.

DICKSEE'S CONTRIBUTION

In his day, Lawrence Dicksee's contribution to education and ideas in accounting was an enormous one. And he won affection as well as reputation. There is a genuine ring about Stanley Rowland's introductory sentences in the Preface to the fifteenth edition of *Auditing*, which had been in preparation in the last months of Dicksee's life and was published soon after his death:

> Since the fourteenth edition of this work was published its distinguished author has been removed by death. The profession has lost a man of very singular ability, and I have been deprived of teacher, partner, and friend.

Notes

1 This paper is based on Kitchen and Parker (1980) and Kitchen (1974). See also Kitchen (1979).
2 Sir Francis Bernard (Frank) Dicksee: elected President of the Royal Academy (1924), knighted (1925), given the honorary degree of Doctor of Civil Law of Oxford University (1926) and created KCVO (1927). He was amongst many other things a Trustee of the British Museum and of the National Portrait Gallery. His death (in 1928, when he was 75) was followed by a splendid funeral service in Westminster Abbey, with representatives present from HM the King, the Prince of Wales, and other Royal personages, the Prime Minister and the Lord Mayor of London and a large congregation (British and foreign) of corresponding distinction.
3 John Robert Dicksee continued in his post as head drawing master at the City of London School until 1897, when he was already 80. He continued to paint, and exhibited his last picture at the Royal Academy's 1905 exhibition, a few months before his death. He was followed as head drawing master at the City of London School by his third son, Herbert, who at that time and for many years afterwards lived at Oak House, Kidderpore Avenue, Hampstead. When John Robert died in September 1905, his address was Platts Lane, Hampstead, where another son, Bernard, had a house at No. 4.
4 Dicksee's son was buried near Sunderland in County Durham. Dicksee's Will, made in 1925, includes the following, instruction: 'after my death my body shall be cremated or buried in the grave belonging to me wherein the body of my only son is buried and wherein my wife also desires . . . [to] . . . be interred'.
5 Dicksee called these 'fixed assets' in later editions of *Auditing*.
6 Prices in general had fallen steadily from about 1873 to 1886, whereafter a less noticeable decline in prices continued to about 1896.
7 In the first edition of *Depreciation* (1903), Dicksee said of shafting that 'within reasonable limits it may perhaps be said that there is practically no risk of [its] becoming obsolete' (p. 31), though he included a caveat about light machinery and small electric motors. These observations remained unchanged into the fifth edition of *Depreciation* (1926).

8 The 'singular inconsistency' must refer to the *Lee v. Neuchatel Asphalte* case of 1889.
9 It may be interpolated here that Dicksee had, from 1903, continually stressed that the difference between the double-account and the single-account need be no more than one of form only. But the difference of form did invite a different attitude to depreciation.
10 This section is based on Coombs and Edwards (1993).
11 Dicksee was also interested in other aspects of local authority accounting. He wrote further on the topic in 1910 and, in *Auditing* (1892: 94–103), reproduced with approval the very detailed audit programme used by F. R. Goddard FCA for the purpose of auditing the accounts of the Newcastle Corporation.
12 For an extensive bibliography of Dicksee's work, see Brief (1980: 16–22).

References[12]

Brief, R. P. (1980) *Dicksee's Contribution to Accounting Theory and Practice*, New York: Arno Press.
Coombs, H. M. and Edwards, J. R. (1993) *Accounting Innovation. Municipal Corporations 1835–1935*, a report for the Research Board of the ICAEW.
Dicksee, L. R. (1892) *Auditing: A Practical Manual for Auditors*, London: Gee. Reprinted by Arno Press, New York, 1976.
Dicksee, L. R. (1893) *Bookkeeping for Accountant Students*, London: Gee. (Eight editions published during his lifetime.)
Dicksee, L. R. (1895) *Comparative Depreciation Tables*, London: Gee. (Three editions.)
Dicksee, L. R. (1897) *Bookkeeping for Company Secretaries*, London: Gee. (Six editions.)
Dicksee, L. R. (1899) *Bookkeeping Exercises for Accountant Students*, London: Gee. (Four editions.)
Dicksee, L. R. (1901) *Auctioneers' Accounts*, London: Gee.
Dicksee, L. R. (1902a) *Gas Accounts*, London: Gee.
Dicksee, L. R. (1902b) *Solicitors' Accounts*, London: Gee.
Dicksee, L. R. (1903a) *Advanced Accounting*, London: Gee. Reprinted by Arno Press, New York, 1976. (Seven editions.)
Dicksee, L. R. (1903b) *Depreciation, Reserves and Reserve Funds*, London: Gee. Reprinted by Arno Press, New York, 1976. (Five editions.)
Dicksee, L. R. (1905) *Hotel Accounts*, London: Gee.
Dicksee, L. R. (1907) 'Depreciation: with special reference to the accounts of local authorities', *The Accountant*, 13 April.
Dicksee, L. R. (1910a) 'Auditing with Special Reference to the Accounts of Local Authorities', *The Accountant*, 13 August.
Dicksee, L. R. (1910b) *Business Organisation*, London: Longmans Green.
Dicksee, L. R. (1914) *Mines Accounting and Management*, London: Gee.
Dicksee, L. R. (1915) *Business Methods and the War*, London: Gee.
Dicksee, L. R. (1917) *Office Machinery, a handbook for progressive office managers*, London: Gee. (Three editions.)
Dicksee, L. R. (1922) *The True Basis of Efficiency*, item in series for the London School of Economics edited by Sir William Beveridge and Professor A. J. Sergeant.
Dicksee, L. R. (1927) *Published Balance Sheets and Window Dressing*, London: Gee. Reprinted by Arno Press, New York, 1980.
Dicksee, L. R. (1929) *Garage Accounts*, London: Gee.
Dicksee, L. R. and Blair, H. E. (1914) *Office Organization and Management* (3rd edn), London: Gee.
Dicksee, L. R. and Tillyard, F. (1897) *Goodwill and its Treatment in Accounts*, London: Gee. (Four editions.)

Forster, J. W. (1907), 'Sinking Funds and their Relation to Depreciation Funds', *Report of Proceedings of the Annual Meeting of the Institute of Municipal Treasurers and Accountants*: 126–67.

Kitchen, J. (1974) 'Lawrence Dicksee, depreciation and the double-account system' in H. C. Edey and B. S. Yamey (eds) *Debits, Credits, Finance and Profits*, London: Sweet & Maxwell.

Kitchen, J. (1979) 'Fixed asset values: ideas on depreciation 1892–1914', *Accounting and Business Research*, Autumn: 281–91.

Kitchen, J. and R. H. Parker (1980) *Accounting Thought and Education: Six English Pioneers*, London: ICAEW: 51–63. Reprinted by Garland Publishing, New York and London, 1984.

Montgomery, R. H. (1912) *Auditing: Theory and Practice*, New York: The Ronald Press Company. Reprinted by Arno Press Inc., New York, 1976.

Pixley, F. W. (1881) *Auditors. Their Duties and Responsibilities*, London: Effingham Wilson. Reprinted by Arno Press, New York, 1976.

13 Frederic Rudolph Mackley de Paula (1882–1954)[1]

Jack Kitchen and Robert H. Parker

Frederic de Paula brought charm and an exceptional capacity to a remarkably wide span of activities ranging from the centre to the perimeter of the accountancy profession and beyond it. In all of these he achieved distinction: as student, teacher, practitioner, and author; as war-time administrator in two World Wars; as university lecturer and professor, albeit part-time; as accountant and financial manager in industry; as standard-bearer in the movement for fuller disclosure and greater comprehensibility in financial reporting; as the first non-practising member of the Council of the Institute of Chartered Accountants in England and Wales (ICAEW); as a main progenitor of the ICAEW's important *Recommendations on Accounting Principles* which began to appear under his Vice-Chairmanship and Chairmanship of the ICAEW's Taxation and Financial Relations Committee early in the 1940s (and which brought to fruition a sufficient revolution in professional attitudes to transform within a few years both accounting practice and legislation on financial reporting); as successful industrialist and director of important companies; and as educationist. It was a minor personal tragedy that, at the end of his career, his fresh mind and forward thinking on education for the accountancy profession isolated him from some old friends and respected colleagues. His 'fault' was that he thought and spoke in advance of his time. Had Frederic de Paula lived another dozen years, he would have seen the kind of educational reforms he advocated well on the way to acceptance as the new orthodoxy. De Paula's ideas were influential well beyond Britain, and brought him a circle of friends around the world.

FAMILY

Frederic Rudolph Mackley de Paula was born on 23 July 1882 at Avenue House, Tenterden Grove, Hendon. Frederic's grandmother had come over from Germany to settle in Britain, and her son, Friedrich Moritz Alphonse Felix de Paula (Frederic's father) became a solicitor and partner in a City solicitors' practice (Carey, Warburton and de Paula) at 3 West Street, Finsbury Circus, EC from about 1876. The firm moved to 16 Finsbury Circus some twenty years later. Friedrich Moritz de Paula died in Greece in October 1902, leaving a widow (Ellen Harriet de Paula, nee Mackley), another son besides Frederic (Waldemar

Max de Paula, who was to become a respected City stockbroker) and three daughters.

In 1912, Frederic de Paula married Agnes Smithson Clark in Street, Somerset. She was the daughter of Francis Joseph Clark, boot and shoe manufacturer of that town. The Clarks were a well-known Quaker family, and the marriage was solemnised at the Friends' Meeting House in Street according to the usages of the Religious Society of Friends. The Quaker influence was to be a lasting one. Without doubt it supported Frederic's own strong independence of mind, and it revealed itself in small matters also; at his death, Frederic's will included the express wish 'that no mourning shall be worn by anyone'. There were two sons of Frederic's marriage to Agnes Clark: Hugh Francis Mackley de Paula, and Frederic Clive de Paula.

After her husband's death, Frederic's mother lived for a time in North Finchley, and later at 'Netherdale', Nether Street, Church End, Finchley. That address was Frederic's home at the time of his marriage. Frederic and Agnes were to live for many years in Radlett, Hertfordshire, where they are remembered at the Porters Park Golf Club (they became Captain and Lady Captain respectively); and there was a London house at 49 Eaton Terrace, SW1 from about 1921, and later flats in Kensington and Knightsbridge. Frederic was aged seventy-two when he died in December 1954. His wife, who survived him, was seven years his junior.

EARLY YEARS IN THE PROFESSION

Frederic de Paula was articled in 1901 to C. F. Cape (Charles F. Cape & Co.) of 12 Coleman Street, EC. In later years, Frederic was heard to allege that he had had to learn quickly because of Cape's taste for hunting in the winter, when he left his clerks to do the work of the practice. Frederic took his Intermediate examination in December 1903, and his Final in December 1905, being placed fifth in order of merit in the first (out of 162 candidates) and seventh in order of merit in the second (out of 195 candidates). At each of these examinations, the first place in order of merit was taken by Gilbert Garnsey, who had been articled in Walsall to N. G. Harries, of Harries and Higgison, chartered accountants, who practised in Walsall with offices also in Birmingham and Wolverhampton. Garnsey was a few months younger than de Paula. He was to have a career of exceptional brilliance, with a partnership in Price Waterhouse & Co. from 1913, a knighthood in 1918, and a reputation thoroughly established by the early 1920s as favouring increased disclosure in the published accounts of companies, especially holding companies. He died in 1932 at the early age of 49.

After qualifying, de Paula remained for a time as clerk with C. F. Cape & Co. He went into practice on his own account in 1909, beginning modestly at 12 Coleman Street. He had already developed an interest in teaching, and in October 1908 was providing the Auditing lectures for the Finals students of the Chartered Accountants Students' Society of London. Lawrence Dicksee (lately resigned from his part-time Chair at Birmingham, and already into his seventh academic year as part-time lecturer at LSE) was still, in 1908/9, giving the Bookkeeping and Accounts lectures for the Chartered Accountants Students' Society of London finalists. De Paula was to take on Dicksee's Bookkeeping and Accounts lectures, in addition to his own Auditing course, in October 1910.

De Paula's work as a practitioner began to show promise, and he was joined in practice in 1910 by Edgar John Turner. They worked together as de Paula, Turner & Co., at 58 Leadenhall Street, EC, until 1913, when they were in turn joined by John Strickland Lake and the firm's name was extended to de Paula, Turner, Lake & Co., then of 56a Leadenhall Street. Frederic de Paula resigned his partnership in 1929 (see below).

De Paula's teaching work in auditing left him increasingly dissatisfied with the texts available, then mainly Pixley's, Dicksee's, and Cutforth's books. He decided to write his own, and did so in the spring and summer of 1914. Pitmans published the first edition of *Principles of Auditing* later that year. Despite the upheaval of the war, the book was successful: a second edition appeared in 1917 and a third in 1920. Frederic de Paula undertook his last major revision of the text for the eleventh edition in 1951, three years before he died.

Principles of Auditing, like Cutforth's *Audits*, was written primarily for students. De Paula said as much in his Preface to the first edition, adding that his object had been to produce a book of convenient size at a reasonable price. To shorten the book, de Paula, like Cutforth, eliminated reprinted sections of Acts of Parliament (apart from sections of the Companies Act); but unlike Cutforth, he also omitted certain matters, such as the particular problems arising in audits or investigations for different classes of undertakings and specialised companies, to which both Cutforth and Dicksee made extensive, though rather superficial, reference. De Paula's aim was to provide a deeper foundation and to

cover the whole of the ground-work with which every student of auditing must be familiar, . . . to explain the principles and reasons underlying each subject dealt with . . . [and] adequately to discuss the important root-principles that apply to every audit.

A hundred examination questions set out 'in order with the text of the book' were included in an appendix.

De Paula had put much preliminary thought into two lectures on auditing (stressing the need to supplement 'routine checking' with intelligent enquiry and research) which he had delivered to a number of Chartered Accountants Students' Societies in 1911 and 1912, beginning with the Chartered Accountants Students' Society of Hull (de Paula, 1912, 1913). He had presented an earlier, more specialised, lecture in 1909 on 'The audit and investigation of the accounts of Executors and Trustees' (*The Accountant*, 9 April 1910).

Robert H. Montgomery, who had edited the first and second authorised American editions of Dicksee's *Auditing*, in 1905 and 1909, had published his own *Auditing Theory and Practice* in 1912 on the grounds that Dicksee's book no longer met the needs of the profession in the USA where 'much more work [was being done] in audits than was called for' in 'Dicksee'. In Britain, by 1915, when Dicksee's tenth edition was published, *The Accountant*'s reviewer (amongst many favourable observations) was noting that

> The book has now passed through so many editions that parts of it have assumed a slightly patchwork appearance, and we would suggest that those portions dealing with matters which have been subject to changing conditions should be completely rewritten before the book again goes through the press.
>
> (*The Accountant*, 10 July 1915: 54)

When de Paula's *Principles* appeared, Dicksee's book was already more than twenty years old. De Paula had said in his 1913 Student Society lecture: 'nowadays far more is expected from an auditor and a far greater knowledge is required than was the case in years gone by'. De Paula's views were justified by the success of his book.

THE FIRST WORLD WAR: EXPERIENCE OF LARGE-SCALE ADMINISTRATION

When William Cash gave his Presidential Address at the ICAEW's Autumnal Meeting in London in 1921, he noted that the previous Autumnal Meeting had been that of 1913. Speaking of the war, he said (*inter alia*)

> perhaps the most important work undertaken by members of our body was in connection with the new Government Departments, organised to meet war exigencies, and at the War Office and the Admiralty, at the Ministry of Munitions, and in the Government Trading Department in food, timber, sugar, etc., by advice, in organisation in financial control, in regulation of contracts, there were found most of the leaders of the profession, and a very large number of the younger members also, whose training and capabilities were invaluable in setting in motion and carrying on the enormous undertakings that were created for the necessities of the war.

Frederic de Paula was amongst the younger practicioners who left their firms for such work. He was first employed at the Ministry of Munitions in the Gun Ammunition Filling Department under Sir Eric Geddes. De Paula was concerned with organising the statistical section of the Department, first under George Beharrell, and later, when Beharrell went to France, as Director of that section in his stead. At the beginning of 1917, de Paula was commissioned and joined the staff in France of Sir Eric Geddes, at that time Director-General of Transportation at General Headquarters. De Paula became an Assistant Director-General of Transportation with the rank of Lieutenant Colonel. He was gazetted OBE (military division) and twice mentioned in despatches. De Paula was demobilised in September 1919, whereafter he returned to his practice.

His war-time experience of large-scale organisation and administration made a deep impression on him. It was to work again with Sir Eric Geddes and Sir George Beharrell that de Paula went in 1929 to the Dunlop Rubber Company as Chief Accountant, and later as Financial Controller.

THE LONDON SCHOOL OF ECONOMICS AND POLITICAL SCIENCE

Reference has been made above to Lawrence Dicksee's appointment in 1919 to the then newly created Sir Ernest Cassel Chair of Accountancy and Business Methods in the University of London, tenable at LSE. The 1919 appointment was to an established Chair and Dicksee had, at that date, already held a personal appointment as Professor at LSE for five years. The Sir Ernest Cassel foundations in 1919 included Chairs in Banking and Currency, and International Relations, as well as in Accountancy, which along with three Readerships and three Lectureships, were to assist the University to establish its new degree in Commerce at LSE.

By the beginning of the 1920 academic year, provision has been made for the full Commerce curriculum to be offered to students, and Frederic de Paula had joined Dicksee at LSE as Lecturer (part-time) with him in the courses on Accounting and Business Methods. Dicksee himself gave the courses in 'Business Organisation' and 'Cost Accounts and Efficiency Methods' as they were called. In the early 1920s, many of the students taught by Dicksee and de Paula at LSE were demobilised officers. These sustained the interests of both men in general problems of large-scale administration and in the particular problems facing returning servicemen. In 1924 the institution of a Readership in Accounting and Business Organisation was announced and de Paula was appointed to the post, again on a part-time basis.

When Dicksee retired in 1926, Frederic de Paula followed him as Professor of Accountancy and Business Methods, holding that appointment (part-time) until December 1929, when he resigned his Chair and his position as senior partner in de Paula, Turner, Lake & Co., to join Dunlops.

INTERESTS AND IDEAS IN THE 1920s

In addition to his work at LSE, Frederic de Paula continued in the 1920s to give formal lectures to outside groups, such as 'The Detection of Fraud in Accounts' to various CA Students' Societies in 1920 and 1921, and 'The Interpretation of Accounts' to the Institute of Bookkeepers in March 1926 (republished, with other similar material, in de Paula's *Developments in Accounting* 1948a). Broadly, these followed his general approach in *Principles of Auditing* (1914): the former stressed that to discover fraud, 'an auditor must go behind the actual books of account, and examine original records and make intelligent inquiries'; the latter ended with a reference to changing attitudes to disclosure in published accounts thus,

> in my opinion there is room for improvement in the form in which published Balance Sheets are presented, and evolution upon these lines would greatly assist in the interpretation of the accounts of commercial concerns. The policy of secrecy has been overstressed.

We may presume that de Paula had been present in October 1925 at a London Members' lunch chaired by Sir Gilbert Garnsey, at which Sir Josiah Stamp had given (in an address reproduced in *The Accountant* of 31 October 1925) what he called an 'outsider's reflection' on 'Accountants' Problems of Today', in particular on information presented in balance sheets. Sir Josiah was known to be strongly antagonistic to secret reserves, and Garnsey in 1925 had lately come under criticism from within the profession for his championship of consolidated balance sheets and consolidated profit and loss accounts for holding company groups.

Speaking in 1921 to the Annual Conference of the Incorporated Accountants in Liverpool, Sir Josiah Stamp had said, *inter alia*:

> deliberate upon the sorry figure that is cut . . . by . . . a 'safe' or 'sound' balance sheet, which lies in almost every line and yet is approved . . . because it overstates no assets and understates no liabilities . . . prudence . . . is just as possible without departing from what a balance sheet ought to be – a faithful record of the employment of the total capital invested in the business

That there were important and widely held views to the contrary may be judged from the Memorandum of Evidence submitted by the Council of the ICAEW in July 1925 to the Greene Committee on Company Law Amendment. This took a strong line against further disclosure by prescription. Thus:

> The conditions under which companies carry on their business are so numerous, the nature of the business so varied and the places at which the businesses are carried on so spread over the world that to attempt to prescribe either a statutory form of balance sheet or what a balance sheet must disclose or that there should be in addition a profit and loss account is considered likely to do more harm than good.
>
> Shareholders have the remedy to a large extent in their own hands. They can and do ask questions at the annual meetings. The business done by limited companies is, on the whole, transacted by directors and managers who are honest, and if in some cases they disclose in the published accounts less than some people desire the absence of detail is in most cases wise and is generally supported by the shareholders.

On 'secret reserves' the Memorandum of Evidence said, *inter alia*:

> Secret Reserves or Inner Reserves are in certain cases desirable and in many cases essential . . .
>
> If businesses carried on by joint stock companies are to be as successful in the future as in the past, too much disclosure should not be insisted on and the greatest possible freedom should be allowed to those responsible.
>
> It is always open to the auditors to report to the shareholders any exceptional reserves which are made or written back or other special matters dealt with in the accounts if the directors do not disclose them on the face of the accounts or in their report to the shareholders.

The ICAEW Memorandum of Evidence took a similar line as regards the accounts of holding companies and their subsidiaries, thus:

> It is considered undesirable to prescribe by legislation any rule for dealing in the accounts of Holding Companies with their subsidiaries. The circumstances under which such holdings arise are so varied and the places where such businesses are carried on are in some cases so spread over the world that to lay down any hard and fast rule would do more harm than good.
>
> In the opinion of the Council the form of the balance sheet should as at present be left to the directors and shareholders. To prepare a consolidated balance sheet would not show the true position of the company, so long as the subsidiaries are separate entities. If the accounts of subsidiary companies had by legislation to be made up to the same date as the parent company and incorporated in that company's published accounts, by the time the details were received by the parent company for incorporation, the accounts of the parent company would in some cases be ancient history.
>
> The question of whether or not what has been described as the legal balance sheet should be supplemented by other balance sheets is a matter entirely for the directors and shareholders.

At the October 1925 lunch, Sir Josiah directed his main attention to the disadvantages of secret reserves, though he did not, on that occasion, condemn them in such strong terms as in 1921. He also declared himself firmly in favour of consolidated accounts for holding company groups, thus:

> The consolidated balance sheet is familiar enough in America, but is only beginning to be known in this country. It can be developed with appropriate public education to understand it, and it is at any rate better than giving a sheaf of subsidiary accounts without nexus which bewilder the average shareholder
> . . .
>
> It seems to me that there can be nothing to be said against the publication of consolidated balance sheets in conjunction with the legal balance sheet, and everything to be said for it. Only in time will its full significance be appreciated. I am not pleading for wholesale legal action. It will grow by the establishment of the best as a practice, and the best is not necessarily what is oldest until it is shaken up by some abuse in a law court.

Six years afterwards in 1931, the Kylsant case was to remind many of these words.

Sir Josiah Stamp's remarks provoked a leading article in *The Accountant* (31 October 1925) and a little flurry of correspondence. Three weeks later, *The Accountant* presented two contributed comments on Sir Josiah's address, one by Mr Jonas Hambley (who represented, broadly, what might be termed 'traditional' reactions) and the other – a rather longer one, which appeared in short parts over three weeks – by Frederic de Paula, who offered what we might call a more notably 'progressive' response. It is worth recalling a few sentences from de Paula's comments:

The arguments in favour of the secret reserve, the condensed balance sheet, and the legal balance sheet of the holding company, are well-known to all accountants, but are these arguments really sound? If all reserves were shown openly in the balance sheet and reverses were charged thereto, would the public credit of the concern be shaken? If a full balance sheet were published what use could competitors . . . make of the information revealed?

My own view is that the arguments in favour of secrecy are exaggerated, and that from the point of view of the community the policy is a mistaken one, as it is creating a feeling of distrust. However, it is only by the weight of public opinion that this policy will be abandoned, but in my opinion more open methods will have to be adopted in the future and Sir Josiah Stamp is right in asking accountants to face these problems now, with a view to using their influence in the direction of changes of method which are inevitable.

(1925: 802)

Later in his comments, de Paula offered an observation which has a distinctly modern ring:

To my mind the peculiarity of the legal position [of the auditor of a company] is that the value of the auditor's advice and opinions is available to the management, whom he does not represent, but is not fully available to the shareholders, whose agent he is.

(1925: 888)

THE ACCOUNTANT IN COMMERCE AND INDUSTRY

Frederic de Paula's most important public lecture in the 1920s was delivered at LSE on 14 October 1926 shortly after his appointment to the Sir Ernest Cassel Chair of Accountancy and Business Methods vacated by Lawrence Dicksee upon his retirement in July 1926. Dicksee had been granted the title of Emeritus Professor and it was he who acted as chairman at de Paula's lecture, 'The Place of Accountancy in Commerce' (de Paula 1948a: 135–47).

De Paula was concerned to stress that the importance of Accounts Departments in commerce and industry had long been growing, but that, in his view, there were great possibilities for further development, in which he saw the professional accountant as being in a position to play an important part. However, de Paula expressed the opinion that substantial further progress would not be possible until the commercial world was convinced as to 'the great possibilities of accountancy and the great help which it can give to the management of every business concern'.

De Paula looked to reorganisation upon the lines of:

raising the whole status of the accounts department, which should rank equally with the principal executive departments. The chief accountant should not be merely the head book-keeper but he should be the chief financial officer of the concern, being responsible to the general manager for the whole of the finances of the business and its financial control . . . The chief accountant should . . . have a wide knowledge of business organisation, business generally and finance, and further, it would be necessary for him to have a highly trained staff under him.

The chief accountant . . . should represent finance, it being his duty to report upon the financial aspects of every proposition under consideration.

De Paula listed the principal functions of the accounts department of a manufacturing concern under eleven heads, as under:

1 The control of the whole of the bookkeeping records, which should be organised upon modern time-saving methods.
2 The control of the stores and costing system.
3 The control of a statistical system the objects of which are to record and focus all information of use to the management.
4 The preparation of weekly and monthly statistical summaries, including monthly revenue accounts and balance sheets.
5 The chief accountant should be responsible for the preparation of forecasts of the future requirements – for example: materials, labour, equipment, and capital.
6 The accounts department should supply the various executive departments with the accounting and statistical information required by them.
7 The preparation of the annual manufacturing and profit and loss accounts and balance sheet of the concern and reporting thereon to the management.
8 The settlement with the Revenue of the taxation liabilities of the concern.
9 The control of the financial administration of the business and the reporting upon the financial aspects of every proposal under consideration by the management.
10 The chief accountant should act as financial adviser to the managing director and should report to him the important factors revealed by the accounting and statistical records.
11 The accounts department should be constantly engaged upon research work and should report upon the present position, future prospects and suggestions as to improvements in the organisation with a view to the economical and efficient conduct of the business.

De Paula developed each of these heads in his lecture, concluding:

I do not wish to give the impression that I am suggesting that the accounts department is the most important of all and that it should be responsible for the practical management of the concern. The accounts department should be the servant of management and its purpose should be to watch and advise upon the financial aspect of affairs, and in this way to assist the management in the control and administration of the concern.

When, three years later, de Paula moved to Dunlops, it was to fulfil just such a role. At his lecture he was speaking primarily to future Commerce graduates, the bulk of whom could be expected to enter employment in industry and commerce. He set an exciting prospect before them.

De Paula presented another lecture with a similar title ('Accounts as an aid to Management') in 1927 to the Office Machinery Users' Association. It is of interest because it stressed the need of management to look ahead, and it was de Paula's argument that the accountant in industry or commerce must do the same. Accordingly, his lecture developed the practical advantages to be obtained through a system of budgetary control.

EDUCATION FOR THE ACCOUNTANCY PROFESSION

A couple of months after his October 1926 lecture at LSE, de Paula responded to a short series of letters in *The Accountant* dealing more or less directly with education for the accountancy profession. His name had been among several mentioned in the correspondence (including those of Sir William Plender and Sir Josiah Stamp) as possibly suitable to consider a scheme in which accountancy might be given a place among the honours degrees of universities and thereby form a part (as did the LLB for lawyers) of the accountants' professional education and training. De Paula's letter (dated 22 December 1926) was brief; he referred to the suggestions of the correspondent concerned, saying:

> in my opinion the present system of education is far from satisfactory.
>
> The practical work of the average articled clerk is mainly devoted to routine checking, which is of little educational value, and the theoretical studies of the great proportion of students are conducted by the professional 'crammers'. No doubt the results are satisfactory from an examination point of view, but from the point of view of the education of the future members of a great profession the present position, in my opinion, is capable of considerable improvement.
>
> I do not think that any change can be effected until the Councils of the Institute and the Society take a direct interest and concern in the methods of education of their future members.
>
> Considerable progress in the study of accountancy has been made in recent years by the modern universities, and I would suggest that the accountancy profession should take an active interest in this work, as, for example, the legal profession does in the faculty of law.
>
> Those who appreciate the great possibilities for the future development of accountancy, realize that there is a real need in this, as in other branches of human effort, for sustained academic study and research. The commercial world has realized the value and possibilities of this work and the developments to date have been initiated and financed to a considerable extent by such men as the late Sir Ernest Cassel; but so far as I am aware, the Institute and the Society have not directly concerned themselves with the academic study of accountancy or research work, and apart from the setting of examinations and financial support given to Students' societies, they have not concerned themselves directly with the educational methods in force within the profession itself.

Frederic de Paula's letter appeared in *The Accountant* of 1 January 1927. No further correspondence followed upon it. Mr Ernest Evan Spicer gave a lecture on 'The Articled Clerk in relation to Education' to CA Students' Societies in Manchester, Birmingham and Cardiff in December 1926 and January 1927, and this was published in *The Accountant* of 26 March 1927. It proposed wide-ranging (and drastic) reforms: a number of letters followed the lecture, but in 1927 the education issue did not prosper.

THE DUNLOP RUBBER COMPANY LTD

Sir Eric Geddes had become a director of the Dunlop Rubber Company in 1922, and its Chairman in 1924. Sir George Beharrell, knighted in 1919, had been appointed Managing Director of Dunlops in 1923. In the later 1920s, Geddes, Beharrell and the Dunlop board were interested in de Paula and in his ideas on the contribution which an accountant could make to the management of a large industrial undertaking such as theirs, which was suffering from financial problems. Frederic de Paula resigned from his practice and from his Chair at LSE, and joined the Dunlop Company on 1 January 1930, in the first instance as Chief Accountant, and shortly afterwards with the title of Controller of Finance. The appointment gave him a splendid opportunity to put his ideas into practice. He grasped it with both hands and his efforts proved immensely successful.

In his preface to *Developments in Accounting* (1948a), Frederic de Paula refers to his having 'persuaded the board of a public company, of which [he] was the auditor, to present its accounts in accordance with [his] ideas' for improved disclosure and comprehensibility. This was Temoh Tin Dredging Ltd, and de Paula records (though he does not name the Company) that the accounts 'were reviewed favourably in *The Accountant, The Economist, The Times,* and *The Financial Times'*. *The Accountant* printed out the Temoh Tin balance sheet at 30 June 1929 and the year's profit and loss account (*The Accountant*, 9 November, 1929: 393–4). The level of detail in the balance sheet was well ahead of prevailing legal requirements and contemporary practice (see Edwards 1981). In the balance sheet, for example, the company provided a breakdown of creditors, fixed tangible assets and stocks, rather than simply a single figure for each. The contrast between the Temoh profit and loss account and contemporary practice, where rarely was more than an appropriation account published, was even more striking. Temoh gave the make-up of sales, by product, and detailed each major head of expense deducted to arrive at 'Net Profit for the year'. The inclusion of a dividend provision in the profit and loss account, rather than merely referring to it in the directors' report, was another important innovation much canvassed by de Paula eventually to be universally adopted.

De Paula subsequently persuaded the Dunlop board to present their 1929 accounts in the general form worked out for Temoh Tin. When the 1931 accounts for Dunlops appeared they again attracted favourable comment, at least in part because they included comparative figures for 1930.

In 1931, the Kylsant case startled the City and the business world. It was widely reported in newspapers and periodicals. Full-length books on the subject included C. Brooks (ed.) *The Royal Mail Case*, and H. B. Samuel, *Shareholders' Money*, both of which appeared in 1933.

The case turned on the use of secret reserves to bolster the reported profits of the Royal Mail Steam Packet Company (RMSP), of which Lord Kylsant was Chairman. The auditor was Mr H. J. Morland, a senior partner in Price Waterhouse & Co. They were charged with publishing annual accounts of the Company for 1926 and 1927 which they 'knew to be false in a material particular . . . with intent to deceive' Both were acquitted, though Lord Kylsant was found guilty and imprisoned on another charge concerning a prospectus, with which Mr Morland was not associated.

As regards the RMSP accounts, the reference to profits for 1926, which was alleged to be misleading, ran:

> Balance for the year, including
> dividends 2 – on shares in allied and
> associated companies, adjustment
> of taxation reserves, less
> depreciation on the fleet, etc.　　　　£439,212: 12:1.

The words 'including . . . adjustment of taxation reserves' had been written in by Mr Morland on his own initiative when the accounts were in draft. In 1926, the Company had in fact been running at a loss, and the 'profit' was arrived at after crediting £750,000 out of the tax reserves. The issue was whether Mr Morland had acted in accordance with accepted practice, and expert evidence (which was not challenged) was successfully submitted to show that he had.

The response of the Council of the ICAEW to the Kylsant case was to encourage individual members to raise disclosure standards. The case made a deep impression on de Paula. His preface to the sixth edition of *Principles of Auditing* (which appeared in 1933) is worth quoting in full:

> Since the fifth edition of this book was published, the accountancy profession has been shocked by the *Royal Mail Steam Packet Case*. There is no single event in my memory that has made so profound an impression upon the accountancy world, and that case, in my opinion, is destined to influence accountancy practice in a marked degree.
>
> For these reasons I have dealt with this case at some length in this edition, and I have quoted considerable portions of the judge's summing up, as in my view every accountant should study this case most closely.
>
> The questions involved are of great importance, and this case brings to light vividly the vexed question of the creation and utilisation of secret reserves. In the previous edition, upon this subject I wrote: 'The attitude of auditors as regards secret reserves is being challenged; the whole subject therefore is one which merits serious consideration and upon which some form of uniform practice should be adopted by the profession.
>
> When I wrote those words I had little idea that challenge would come so swiftly and in such a serious form.

Upon this subject, collectively, the profession has not made up its mind, nor has it upon many others, e.g. the form in which the accounts of holding companies should be presented and the basis upon which they should be prepared; how the profits and losses of subsidiary and sub-subsidiary companies should be dealt with in the accounts of the holding company; what information should be disclosed in the published Profit and Loss Accounts of companies; the basis of calculation of depreciation of Fixed Assets; the basis of valuation of Stock in Trade and how forward contracts should be dealt with in accounts.

The individual practitioner and the executives of companies responsible for the framing of their accounts naturally turn to the accountancy profession for guidance upon these important points, but though there are many individual opinions – my own are given in this book – there are no accepted and established principles governing these several matters.

It does seem to me to be of urgent importance that the profession should make up its mind upon these questions. That it has not done so may be due to the fact that the profession has grown so rapidly and, individually, we have been so busily engaged upon our day-to-day tasks that the profession has not yet had time to pause, think these matters out, and collectively to make up its mind as to the correct principles that should govern these questions.

De Paula was to continue to canvass his ideas about the development of a professional view on important and controversial aspects of accounting practice, and a move towards uniformity. The preface to the sixth edition was dated February 1933: the fifth edition, to which it referred, had been brought out after the 1928–9 companies legislation, in respect of which it incorporated necessary revisions. It is a tribute to de Paula's work, and to the interest shown in his writing, that a seventh edition of *Principles* was quickly called for. De Paula dated the preface to his seventh edition 17 April 1934. It referred to the rapid growth and development of the profession all over the world, and continued:

In fact, this trend has been one of the most notable evolutions in industry and commerce during the past generation. At the same time the outlook of accountants has, in some directions, entirely changed. Perhaps no event throughout the whole period has had so profound an effect on the views of the profession as the Royal Mail Steam Packet case, which undoubtedly will be regarded in the future as an outstanding landmark. That case has completely changed the views of accountants as to their responsibilities in respect of the Profit and Loss Account and as to the creation and utilisation of Secret Reserves.

The preceding edition of this book was revised in the early part of 1933 under the shadow of that all-important case. Later in the same year there was held in London the International Congress of Accounting, which gave the profession an ideal opportunity to take stock of the position as regards this and other vital matters.

In my opinion, the proceedings of that Congress represent a contribution of the first importance in the world of Accountancy. They reveal clearly that the profession is moulding definite principles in regard to the important problems involved in the Royal Mail Steam Packet Company case.

The necessity of bringing out a new edition of this book has given me an opportunity to revise it in the light of these events. I have endeavoured to reflect the latest views of the profession by quoting from and referring to the most important and representative papers given at the recent Congress and elsewhere, thus enabling my readers to obtain a clear view of the opinions held by the leaders of the profession upon the problems that are perplexing all of us.

In particular I have expanded the text dealing with the Profit and Loss Account, Secret Reserves, Holding Companies, and the treatment of dividends and depreciation. Wherever I feel my own views to be unorthodox I have called attention to the fact, and have endeavoured clearly to state the traditional view as well as my own.

From the point of view of the accountancy profession, de Paula's most important contribution during his years at Dunlops was the design and preparation of the company's 1933 accounts, which for the first time included consolidated statements. After the lean years of the Depression, the Dunlop board in their 1933 accounts were able to report increased profits and to recommend an increased dividend. Following Kylsant, the policy of the Council of the ICAEW had been to look to reform in accounts through the influence of individual members. Their policy was triumphantly vindicated in de Paula's work on the Dunlop accounts for 1933 (reproduced in Kitchen and Parker 1980: 99–107), which had a rapturous reception in the financial press. *The Daily Telegraph* is worth quoting:

> The 1933 accounts of the Dunlop Rubber Co. will be a joy to its own shareholders and the envy of all others . . . Detailed balance sheets, classification according to liquidity, comparative figures and even 'consolidated' statements are now, happily, familiar features of many accounts, though in all these improvements Dunlop has led the way. But no other company has yet had the courage so far to break with tradition as to give what may be called a 'consolidated' profit and loss account, revealing the precise treatment of all subsidiary earnings and segregating all special credits; or to state plainly that all reserves are now disclosed. All these details now appear, and in the most unambiguous terms, with comparative figures in each case. The shareholder can hardly ask for more. It is no doubt too much to hope that all holding companies will speedily follow the Dunlop example, but, now that tradition has once been broken, it is probable that really frank inter-company statements will become more and more common. If so, Dunlop will earn the lasting gratitude of all discerning investors.

The Economist responded similarly, adding:

> The document embodies nearly all that the *Economist* and other critics of obscurantism have advocated, in season and out of season, for years past, and gives the lie to the familiar assertion that a large holding company cannot

afford to go beyond the meagre disclosure laid down by law, for fear of giving away valuable information to its competitors.

The Accountant's review (12 May 1934) included the following:

> The shareholders are now presented with a consolidated statement of the assets and liabilities of the company and of its subsidiaries, together with a very clearly compiled statement of profits for the year, showing exactly how the amount available for dividend has been built up. It is perhaps worthy of note that the consolidated statement has been reported on by the auditors to the effect that it has been 'correctly compiled from the balance sheets after giving effect to necessary adjustment in respect of foreign exchange, so as to exhibit a true and correct view of the consolidated position of the companies'. With regard to the legal balance sheet of the company, we should like to remark that we think it is an excellent model. The grouping is good, and the headings are logically arranged so that even the inexpert shareholder may get a clear idea of the financial situation. Not least amongst the merits of this publication, in our view, is that it has boldly adopted the practice of eliminating shillings and pence from the figures. Much space is thereby saved, and a greater sense of proportion is achieved. We wish that the practice were more general. The name of Mr F. R. M. de Paula does not appear on the accounts, but most Chartered Accountants will recognise his influence on the publication. We should like to congratulate Mr de Paula and all those associated with him in the financial management of the company on a very excellent production, which is likely to rank as a model.

In its 'Finance and Commerce' section in the same issue, *The Accountant* noted, *inter alia*:

> This is also the first occasion for the issue of a Consolidated Statement of the Assets and Liabilities of the Dunlop and subsidiary companies. In this we must certainly commend the directors for including sub-subsidiary companies, the point of consolidation being where the Dunlop Company owns 50 per cent of the ordinary capital or voting control of the subsidiaries or sub-subsidiaries. This practice of stating the point of consolidation should be generally adopted. The essential aim in this account has been to make the fullest disclosure that is possible. This has resulted even in the disclosure of a reserve for obsolescence previously deducted from 'Shares in Subsidiaries', by transferring it to the reserve for contingencies. Such complete frankness may not find approval in some quarters, but it is a policy which we feel can only produce good. Its adoption by such an important concern as the Dunlop Company cuts the ground completely from under those arguments which inevitably end with 'not in the interests of the company'. The strength of the position as shown by the combined statement is immense, current assets representing 38½ per cent of the capital employed and showing a surplus over current liabilities of £8 million. The capital structure is interesting. Debentures, mortgages and loans represent only £3,125,884 out of a total of

£29,420,625. In the facility with which these facts can be read off from the accounts is a practical example of the advantages of a suitable grouping of balance sheet items. May we presume that comparative figures will be given next year in the Consolidated Accounts.

De Paula put together a lecture on the 1933 Dunlop accounts ('The Form of Presentation of the Accounts of Holding Companies', reprinted in de Paula 1948a) which he delivered to CA Students' Societies of London and Birmingham and also to the Sussex Branch of the South Eastern CA Students' Society in November 1934. He made a tremendous impression on his audiences. Nevertheless, inertia in the business world and in the profession was such that general adoption of consolidated statements was delayed into the 1940s, despite a ruling by the Council of the London Stock Exchange in March 1939 requiring all holding companies seeking a new quotation to publish consolidated accounts.

The Dunlop Company's reputation benefited, and, to use a term unfamiliar in 1934, its 'image' was considerably enhanced by the much-lauded 1933 accounts. Nevertheless, from the company's point of view, Frederic de Paula's main contribution lay in his work in developing budgetary control within the company and in financial planning and control generally. De Paula gave a number of lectures in these areas (reproduced in de Paula 1948a). They included 'The Role of Finance and Accountancy in the Management of large Business Combines', presented to the British Association for the Advancement of Science in 1933; 'The Principles and Practice of Budgeting in Modern Business', delivered to CA Students' Societies in 1936 (with Lord Plender in the chair at the London lecture); 'The Valuation of Stock-in-Trade or Inventories', presented to the Chartered Accountants Students' Society of London in February 1937; and 'Financial Planning: Insuring for Future Profits', a public lecture given at the Regent Street Polytechnic in 1939. In 1939 also, de Paula gave a further lecture on 'The Form of Presentation of the Accounts of Holding Companies' in an address to the Birmingham and District Society of Chartered Accountants.

THE SECOND WORLD WAR

When war became imminent, de Paula was lent by Dunlops in June 1939 to the War Office, where he held the appointment of Deputy Director-General of Progress and Statistics, and where he worked until he was recalled to Dunlops in March 1940. In 1940 and 1941, he had a long period of serious illness, and at the end of 1941 retired from the Dunlop Company, going as Vice-Chairman and Joint Managing Director to Harding, Tilton and Hartley Ltd (later to be known as the British Van Heusen Co). De Paula became chairman of that Company, and served also on the boards of other important companies.

In 1942, de Paula presented a paper on 'Government Contract Cost Investigations' to the London Members of the ICAEW, opening his talk with an outline of the negotiations lately completed between the Federation of British Industries and the Treasury which had resulted in an agreed statement of guidance. De

Paula had been chairman of the sub-committee of the FBI which had dealt with the matter (de Paula 1948a: 245–61).

THE ICAEW'S TAXATION AND FINANCIAL RELATIONS COMMITTEE AND THE RECOMMENDATIONS ON ACCOUNTING PRINCIPLES

As the 1930s drew to a close, there had been evidence among members of the ICAEW of some uneasiness with regard to the membership and role of the Council. In 1941, there was a move to open the Council to younger members, and particularly to members directly employed in industry and commerce, whose numbers had been steadily growing for well over a decade. One idea canvassed at the time was, in due course, to enable returning servicemen to participate more fully. The Council was ready to respond to such pressures in 1942, and set up in that year a Taxation and Financial Relations Committee, with the main intention that it should serve as an instrument to promote liaison on business and financial problems with provincial members, and especially between members in practice and in industry. Regional sub-committees were established in the District Societies. The move was timely, for in the autumn of 1942 the ICAEW and the Society of Incorporated Accountants and Auditors were both under attack in papers like *The Economist* for being out of touch with their members in industry.

The ICAEW's Taxation and Financial Relations Committee (forerunner of the present Technical Advisory Committee) met for the first time in July 1942: H. M. Barton (later Sir Harold, and President of the ICAEW 1944–6) was elected Chairman, and Frederic de Paula Vice-Chairman. At the July meeting it was unanimously agreed that Stanley W. Rowland (a partner in Dicksee's firm since 1924 and for many years Lecturer in Accounting at LSE) should be approached to act as Secretary of the Committee. At its second meeting, in August 1942, the Taxation and Financial Relations Committee set up a General Advisory Sub-Committee 'to consider, *inter alia*, general questions of accounting principles and procedure'. The Council's first *Recommendations on Accounting Principles* (nos. I and II, dealing respectively with tax reserve certificates and war damage contributions, premiums and claims) were published on 12 December 1942. Three more *Recommendations* (dealing with the treatment of taxation – including special war-time taxation – in accounts, the treatment in accounts of income tax deductible from dividends payable and annual charges, and the inclusion in accounts of proposed profit appropriations) were published on 13 March 1943.

Harold Barton resigned as Chairman of the Taxation and Financial Relations Committee on 18 March 1943, and was replaced by Kenneth Arthur Layton-Bennett. In Layton-Bennett's absence at the next meeting (his health was deteriorating) de Paula as Vice-Chairman took the Chair, and he chaired the subsequent meetings until elected to the Chairmanship of the Taxation and Financial Relations Committee on a regular basis on 18 November 1943. Publication of the important *Recommendations* on reserves and provisions (no. VI) and on the disclosure of the financial position and results of subsidiary companies in the accounts of holding companies (no. VII) took place on 23 October 1943 and 12 February 1944. No. VIII, on the form of the balance sheet and profit and loss account, followed on 15 July 1944. *Recommendations* IX and X (on the depreciation of fixed assets and the valuation of stock-in-trade) appeared in January and June 1945.

Recommendation VI (reserves and provisions) was unequivocally in favour of the disclosure of all reserves in the balance sheet. For provisions, the *Recommendation* was that

> Only in circumstances where disclosure of the amount of a particular provision would clearly be detrimental to the interests of a company should it be included under another heading, for example 'Creditors'; the fact that such heading includes 'Provision' should then be indicated in the narrative.

The *Recommendation* concluded:

> Subject [as above] in regard to provisions the disclosure of which would be detrimental to the interests of a company, where reserves and provisions are created or increased, the amounts involved, if material, and the sources from which they have been created or increased, should be disclosed in the accounts. In all cases the utilisation of reserves, and of provisions proved to have been redundant, should be disclosed in the accounts.

This *Recommendation*, of October 1943, sounded the death knell of the secret or undisclosed reserve. The principles it incorporated were to be included in the 1947/8 legislation as a main plank in the new structure of requirements for disclosure. It is interesting to note that the subjects of the *Recommendations* VI to X, published between October 1943 and June 1945, followed exactly the list of subjects identified by de Paula in his 1933 preface to *Principles of Auditing* (except that the *Recommendations* did not yet deal with forward contracts) as those on which, in 1933, 'the profession [had] not made up its mind' and with regard to which 'some form of uniform practice should be adopted by the profession' or which should at least be the subject of 'accepted and established principles'.

Frederic de Paula retired from the Chairmanship of the Taxation and Financial Relations Committee in 1945. He was under heavy pressure and dividing his time between Taunton (Harding, Tilton & Hartley Ltd) and London. He held a number of important directorships, and the shadow of his illness of 1940/1 still lay upon him.

THE FIRST NON-PRACTISING MEMBER OF THE COUNCIL

In December 1943, Frederic de Paula had been elected to the Council of the ICAEW as its first non-practising member. The move created considerable interest in the financial press. Inside the profession, *The Accountant*'s 'Weekly Note' of 11 December 1943 was indicative of widely shared views:

> At its meeting held on 1st December, which is reported in another part of this issue, the Council of the Institute and Mr F. R. M. de Paula together made

history. Through the election of Mr de Paula to a seat on the Council, the Institute now has for the first time in the 63 years of its existence a direct representative of the large and growing number of members engaged in industry. In addition to the recognition of Mr de Paula's individual wisdom and experience, it is a general indication that the Council Chamber is not a closed room to those who, while not publicly practising the profession of accountancy, have an increasingly valuable contribution to make to the corporate life of the parent body, and it may well be regarded as a very important first step towards closing a gap which was a weakness in the ranks of the profession. There will be general satisfaction that the choice has fallen upon one who has had so distinguished a career and whose opinions are so widely respected.

EVIDENCE TO THE COHEN COMMITTEE (1943–5)

Frederic de Paula took the rather unusual step of submitting a personal Memorandum of Evidence to the Cohen Committee on Company Law Amendment which had been appointed in June 1943 to consider amendments to the 1929 Companies Act. He reprinted his Memorandum in 1948 in *Developments in Accounting* (de Paula 1948a). It ran to about 7,000 words and covered a wide range of matters, giving primacy to the issue of secret reserves (looking to 'full disclosure of all reserves and their utilisation') and much weight to financial disclosure by holding companies through consolidated statements ('A reasonably clear view of the financial position and trading results of a group of companies can, in my view, be obtained only by the preparation of a consolidated balance sheet together with a consolidated statement of earnings').

De Paula's Memorandum was dated 14 September 1943, and we may presume that he prepared it during the summer of that year while the draft *Recommendations* VI and VII (on reserves and provisions, and on the disclosure of the financial position and results of subsidiary companies in the accounts of holding companies) were in their late stages and before the Council of the ICAEW for final acceptance. In the end, *Recommendation* VI (published on 23 October 1943) must have met de Paula's requirements as a statement of 'best practice', and he must have been very satisfied, similarly, with *Recommendation* VII despite its listing three methods of disclosure, namely:

(1) To submit copies of the accounts of each of the subsidiary undertakings . . .
(2) To submit statements of the consolidated assets and liabilities and of the aggregate earnings of the subsidiary undertakings as distinct from those of the holding company . . .
(3) To submit a consolidated balance sheet and a consolidated profit and loss account of the holding company and of its subsidiary undertakings treated as one group.

The *Recommendation* (when it was published on 12 February 1944) said of Methods (1) and (2) that 'The first and second methods are suitable only in special cases' and of Method (3) that 'This method is the most suitable for general application'.

The ICAEW's own Memorandum of Evidence to the Cohen Committee was dated December 1943, and was less positive in its recommendations in favour of consolidated statements than was de Paula in his Memorandum or, indeed, than was *Recommendation* VII itself by the time it was published. The Cohen Committee's 1945 Report, which formed the basis for the 1947/8 legislation, followed de Paula and *Recommendation* VII. The ICAEW's representatives (Sir Harold Howitt, President of the ICAEW in 1945–6, and Thomas Buston Robson, President in 1952–3 and later Sir Thomas) gave oral evidence to the Cohen Committee on 25 February 1944. Frederic de Paula gave oral evidence to the Committee on 19 May 1944 (de Paula 1944).

REFRESHER COURSES FOR RETURNED SERVICEMEN

In 1942, de Paula canvassed the idea amongst accountants serving in the Forces, and in 1943 was among the first to raise the proposal that when the war ended the ICAEW might provide 'Refresher Courses' in some suitable form for young qualified men returning from war service. Later, in 1943 and in 1944, the ICAEW was seeking advice and help to this end from District Societies and public and private sector educational institutions, considering ways in which the work might be done, and asking members to assist, especially in preparing notes under a range of headings which could be published and form the basis for such courses or for use by discussion groups.

De Paula's initial proposal had been that an ideal form of refresher course would be residential (for up to four weeks) involving a group of twenty-five to thirty returned servicemen and held either in a residential centre to be specially established in a country location or possibly in one of the Oxford or Cambridge colleges during vacation. The suggestion was that prominent members of the profession should visit the course to introduce topics of importance and to take part in discussions, getting to know the course members and spending a day and a night with the course.

The ICAEW pursued the proposal for the establishment of a residential centre, but the difficulties involved at that time eventually proved insuperable. Residential courses were held, however, in colleges from 1945 and they proved immensely successful. De Paula was Director of Studies at the first course at Emmanuel College, Cambridge in August and September 1945. Stanley Rowland was among the visiting speakers. In the spring of 1946, courses were held at three Cambridge colleges (Downing, Pembroke, and Jesus) and at The Queen's College, Oxford. All were of three weeks' duration. De Paula was again Director of Studies for the first week of the Pembroke course and the last week of the course at Jesus. Members of the Taxation and Financial Relations Committee were prominent among the visiting speakers. In the summer of 1946, five more courses were held in Oxford and Cambridge, with de Paula and Rowland again Directors of Studies. These courses were the precursors of the ICAEW's Summer Schools.

Altogether, according to the President's Address at the 1947 Annual Meeting of the ICAEW (*The Accountant*, 17 May 1947: 280) ten refresher courses were held in Oxford or Cambridge colleges and, in addition, the District Societies, including London, arranged afternoon or evening lectures and discussion groups for over 1,000 members returned from war service.

After a short illness, Stanley Rowland died on 31 October 1946 when he was still comparatively young. He had willingly shouldered a heavy extra burden in his work for the Taxation and Financial Relations Committee and the Refresher courses. He had for years had a reputation for hard work, and through the war years had continually accepted additional responsibilities. He was sadly missed.

RISING PRICE LEVELS

Frederic de Paula gave a wide-ranging lecture in March 1943 (reprinted in *The Accountant* of 5 May 1943 and in de Paula 1948a) on 'The Future of the Accountancy Profession'. In it, he included the following paragraph:

> A most important problem that may arise after the war is whether the items in balance sheets will require re-valuation if the price level moves by reason of inflation. This vital problem urgently requires thinking out for the benefit of industry and our profession.

Not surprisingly, de Paula was not able in 1943 and in the years that followed to 'think out' any satisfactory solution to this problem. Indeed, it is apparent from part of his 1944 evidence to the Cohen Committee that his grasp of value concepts for balance sheet assets was not always strong.

Nevertheless, he recognised a major problem area and returned to the issue more than once. He spoke in May 1948 (de Paula 1948b) to a joint meeting of the professional accountancy bodies in Brighton. There he did not clearly disentangle the consequences of a change in general price levels from the consequences of changes in the prices of specific assets (buildings, plant, stock) but talked of a general replacement value approach to income and asset values, linking this with what he termed 'the view of the economists' that 'the purpose of an industrial undertaking should be to preserve intact for all time the original production capacity'. On this basis, the economists argued, in times of rising prices, that the cost of the increased amount of money capital required 'to replace fixed assets and augment working capital . . . should be provided for . . . out of revenue'.

As de Paula saw it, and, indeed, as many economists certainly saw it at the time:

> The reason why the economists are pressing this matter . . . is that they wish to measure accurately the national income and the national investment in durable goods. If, therefore, accounts were all prepared on the foregoing basis, they contend that their published accounts would enable these vital national statistics to be compiled.

De Paula continued:

> The important matter we have to consider is whether it is practicable and correct to prepare accounts on this basis and whether published accounts can serve the purpose desired by the economists.

De Paula foresaw many practical difficulties, and in particular the issue as to what purpose(s) accounts were intended to serve and whether they could usefully be prepared on a 'multi-purpose basis'. He saw a fundamental question in 'whether provisions for increases in the capital requirements of a company represent a charge against earnings or an appropriation', adding, 'if the latter it is obviously a matter of financial policy with which the auditor is not concerned'.

This was, in fact, his conclusion, though he stressed that he put it forward very hesitantly. He came down in favour of the 'financial policy' argument, stressing that all prudent boards of directors ploughed back profits. But he emphasised the importance of '[making] clear what has been done and what is the true position of affairs . . . An ideal would be for the board to make an estimate and disclose the total extra capital required and also state the aggregate amount that had been set aside for this contingency'.

De Paula spoke again on 'The Effects of the Price Level on Accounting' in a lecture to the Chartered Accountants Students' Society of Edinburgh in October 1952, after the ICAEW's *Recommendation* XII of January 1949 (rising price levels in relation to accounts) and *Recommendation* XV of May 1952 (accounting in relation to changes in the purchasing power of money) had both appeared, and after the subject had some debate at the 1952 International Congress on Accounting in London. However, he did not take significantly further his arguments and conclusions of 1948, except to recognise the possibilities of publishing one or more supplementary statements along with the legal accounts of companies.

THE CARR-SAUNDERS REPORT ON EDUCATION FOR COMMERCE

In June 1946, the then Minister of Education (the Rt. Hon. Ellen Wilkinson) set up a Committee on Education for Commerce with the following terms of reference:

> To consider the provision which should be made for education for commerce and for the professions relating to it, and the respective contributions to be made thereto by universities and by colleges and departments of commerce in England and Wales.

Sir Alexander M. Carr-Saunders, Director of the London School of Economics since 1937, and co-author of an important book on the professions, was appointed Chairman. A distinguished group of educationists and others including Sir Arnold Plant, Sir Ernest Cassel Professor of Commerce at LSE, and Professor J. G. Smith, OBE of the Faculty of Commerce, Birmingham University, was brought together on the Committee. Frederic de Paula was asked to serve as a member and agreed to do so.

In 1946, de Paula was at the zenith of his career in terms of his place in the profession and the regard in which he was held. He had been a member of the Council of the Institute for three years and was, of course, himself a former Sir Ernest Cassel Professor at LSE, having resigned his Chair in Accountancy and Business Methods at the end of 1929. He was a natural choice for membership of the Committee.

The Carr-Saunders Committee reported in the autumn of 1949. The Rt. Hon. George Tomlinson, the then Minister of Education, noted in a foreword to the Report that the enquiry had 'been exacting . . . because it was concerned with a very wide field which had never before been fully surveyed'. This is not the place to consider the content of the Report, save in so far as it affected de Paula's relations with the Council of the ICAEW. Sir Harold Howitt in his *History of the Institute of Chartered Accountants in England and Wales: 1870–1965* deals with it at pp. 109–10 and 189–90. Professor David Solomons deals with it in greater detail in *Prospectus for a Profession* (1974: 22–6).

Because of the generality of their terms of reference, and because the Committee were anxious not to get into difficulties in attempting to distinguish between education for commerce, and education for particular professions operating in the commercial field, they chose a very wide definition of the word 'profession' in interpreting their terms of reference, thus:

> we understand by the word 'profession' in our terms of reference any body of persons, using a common technique, however meagre in content and however little related to fundamental study, who form an association one purpose of which is to test competence in the technique by means of examinations.

As David Solomons was to observe in *Prospectus for a Profession* (1974: 23) this was not a definition 'calculated to win friends for the Committee', yet they had been understandably anxious not to have to decide 'where to draw the line between vocations which can properly be called professions in the traditional sense, and those which cannot be so denominated' (Report, Chap. 1).

Moreover, the Carr-Saunders Committee's Report included the following (amongst other things) in its Summary and Recommendations under a heading 'Professional Examinations':

> Professional associations in the field of commercial education should be invited to give consideration to the following proposals of this committee:
> > At the stage of the intermediate examination only general commercial subjects should be prescribed, vocational training being introduced only at the final stage.
> > Entry upon vocational training at too early an age should be discouraged and recruits to the professions under the age of eighteen should be advised to take national certificate courses. Unnecessary variation in syllabuses in common subjects should be eliminated.
> Courses in technical colleges for professional examinations should be extensively developed. Day-time facilities for training should be available, and day

courses on the part-time or the 'sandwich' principle, giving preparation for the intermediate and final examinations of the main professional bodies and associations, should be organised on a regional basis.

Solomons comments (1974: 24):

The Committee's conclusions were dramatically opposed to the views presented to it in evidence by the Institute's spokesmen and the Institute's reaction to the report, embodied in a 50-page report by the Council, can fairly be described as explosive.

The Council's report was dated March 1951, though it had originally been drafted at least a year earlier, but had not been issued:

as it was not then known what action, if any, the Minister of Education would take after consideration of the report of the Carr-Saunders Committee. It is now evident that the Minister is anxious to implement some of the recommendations of the Carr-Saunders Committee and it has therefore become important that the views of the Council should be available to everyone who may be concerned.

Earlier the Council's Report had noted:

All evidence given on behalf of the Institute was contrary to the recommendations now made by the Carr-Saunders Committee, although the Committee's report gives no hint of that fact.

It should be mentioned that although Mr F. R. M. de Paula, CBE, FCA, was a member of the Carr-Saunders Committee and was at that time a member of the Council of the Institute, his appointment to the Carr-Saunders Committee was a personal one and not in any way as a representative or nominee of the Council. Nor do the views expressed in the report which he signed agree with those of the Council.

The present report by the Council has been prepared to show why the Council is unable to support any move which may be made with the object of applying the recommendations of the Carr-Saunders Committee to the method of qualifying for membership of the Institute.

The first section of the report concluded:

The Council would offer the strongest opposition to the disintegration of the Institute's examinations or the system of training under articles. Whatever merits the recommendations of the Carr-Saunders Committee may have in relation to other occupations – a matter with which the Council of the Institute is not concerned – the Council considers that they can have no place in the education and training for membership of the Institute.

Clearly, Council members were gravely concerned and seriously displeased with de Paula, though within a few years they were to appoint their own Committee on Education and Training (the Parker Committee 1958). When that

Committee's Report was published in 1961, its general tenor appeared to be firmly in favour of the status quo. It did, however, recommend a reduction in the period of articles to four years for candidates who had both remained at school until the age of seventeen-and-a-half and obtained passes in two subjects at Advanced Level, and it left the door open for various further reviews and enquiries, including the feasibility of arranging for the provision of full-time courses by local educational bodies to be given in the periods before the intermediate and final examinations. In the event, developments in education and training for ICAEW after 1961 proceeded faster than a reading of the Parker Report might have implied and in 1966 the Council decided to introduce nine months' (Foundation) courses on a voluntary basis 'as a first step towards a new approach to education and training', recognising that short-term practical considerations made it necessary in the first instance for the period of the course to be within articles. These nine months' courses were the forerunners of the present Foundation Courses provided by the higher education sector for non-graduates wishing to enter training contracts. From 1971, entry requirements for trainees were raised to a two 'A' Level standard, and thereafter the acceptance of applications for training contracts by school-leavers with 'O' Level qualifications alone was steadily reduced.

De Paula was much affected by the strength of the Council's disagreement with the Carr-Saunders Committee's Report, which it seems clear that he had not adequately foreseen. Already, in 1947, his load of other work and the general state of his health had inclined him to resign from the Council of the ICAEW, though he had been dissuaded. At the end of 1949, however, he tendered his resignation on grounds of health and other commitments and in January 1950 it was accepted. It seemed a sad end to an association he had greatly valued, but he retained many friends on the Council and on Council Committees.

CLOSING YEARS

In 1950 also, Frederic de Paula resigned from the Taxation Committee of the Federation of British Industries, of which he had been a member since 1932 and Chairman since 1941. He was appointed CBE in the Civil List in the New Year Honours of 1951, in part following his work on a Government Committee appointed to review the organisation and administrative methods of the Inland Revenue Department. (His OBE was in the Military List and by custom was retained.) In 1951 also, he brought out the eleventh edition of *Principles of Auditing*. In 1952, at the Sixth International Congress on Accounting, held in London, de Paula was chosen to present the first paper in the section on 'The Accountant in Industry' (de Paula 1952). Rehabilitation was by then well advanced.

No argument is needed to establish that de Paula was a man of wide-ranging interests and achievements. Perhaps we cannot end this chapter better than by quoting from an obituary note written in 1954 by P. M. Rees, MC, FCA, Chief Accountant of Unilver and Lever Bros Ltd, and an old friend and colleague:

[Frederic de Paula] had an exceptional clarity and simplicity of expression in his numerous publications and lectures and a lively sense of humour, coupled with a great strength of character in adhering to his opinions which at times were in advance of his day. Many members now in practice must look back with appreciation to his initiative and endless trouble in establishing and running the residential courses at the universities after the last War which will always be remembered as the forerunners of the annual Summer Courses which are now so popular.

Many of us have lost a personal friend, but in mourning our loss we must be thankful that he fulfilled what I know was his ambition – to promote the welfare of our students and generally to raise the prestige of the Institute and of its members in practice and in industry and commerce.

Note

1 This chapter is a reprint, with minor revision, of Kitchen and Parker (1980). See also Kitchen (1979).

References

Brooks, C. (1933) *The Royal Mail Case*, Toronto: Canada Law Book Company. Reprinted by Arno Press, New York, 1980.
de Paula, F. R. M. (1910) 'The audit and investigation of the accounts of executors and trustees', *The Accountant*, 9 April.
de Paula, F. R. M. (1912) 'A few notes on auditing', *The Accountant*, 15 June.
de Paula, F. R. M. (1913) 'Some further notes on auditing', *The Accountant*, 22 March.
de Paula, F. R. M. (1914) *The Principles of Auditing*, London: Pitman. (Eleven editions in Frederic de Paula's lifetime.)
de Paula, F. R. M. (1925) 'Accountants' problems of today', *The Accountant*, 21, 28 November, 5 December.
de Paula, F. R. M. (1944) *Parliamentary Paper*. Evidence to the Company Law Amendment Committee, 1944 (1945) Cmnd 6659.
de Paula, F. R. M. (1948a) *Developments in Accounting*, London: Pitman. This is a collection of his major papers written between 1910 and 1948.
de Paula, F. R. M. (1948b) 'The effects of rising price levels upon the capital requirements of a business', *The Accountant*, 5 June.
de Paula, F. R. M. (1949) *Parliamentary Paper*. Special Committee on Education for Commerce (Sir Alexander M. Carr-Saunders, Chairman) – Report signed by de Paula as member of Committee – October.
de Paula, F. R. M. (1952a) 'The accountant in industry', *The Accountant*, 19, 26 July.
de Paula, F. R. M. (1952b) 'The effects of the price level on accounting' in *Proceedings of The Sixth International Congress on Accounting*, London.
Edwards, J. R. (1981) *Company Legislation and Changing Patterns of Disclosure in British Company Accounts, 1900–1940*, London: The Institute of Chartered Accountants in England and Wales.
Kitchen, J. (1972) 'The accounts of British holding company groups: development and attitudes to disclosure in the early years', *Accounting and Business Research*, Spring: 114–36.
Kitchen, J. (1979) 'Fixed asset values: ideas on depreciation 1892-1914', *Accounting and Business Research*, Autumn: 281–91.

Kitchen, J. and R. H. Parker (1980) *Accounting Thought and Education: Six English Pioneers*, London: ICAEW: 51–63. Reprinted by Garland Publishing, New York and London, 1984.

Samuel, H. B. (1933) *Shareholders' Money*, London: Pitman.

Solomons, D. and T. M. Berridge (1974) *Prospectus for a Profession. A Report of the Long Range Enquiry into Education and Training for the Accountancy Profession*, Advisory Board of Accountancy Education.

14 The LSE Triumvirate and its contribution to price change accounting

Geoffrey Whittington

Abstract

This chapter examines the contribution to price change accounting made by the 'LSE Triumvirate', William Baxter, David Solomons and Harold Edey. The development of their individual ideas in this field is traced through time. Their separate contributions are compared and found to be distinctive, although complementary. They are also considered in the context of a wider LSE tradition of business economics and accounting.

INTRODUCTION

At the end of the Second World War, there were no full-time professors of accounting in the United Kingdom,[1] all chairs in the subject to that date having been occupied on a part-time basis by practitioners, and consequently there was little academic research in the subject. In 1947, Professor William Baxter was appointed on a full-time basis to the Chair of Accounting at the London School of Economics (LSE) which had been vacant since 1930. He joined David Solomons, who became a Lecturer in 1946, and a Reader in 1948, until moving to the newly created Chair at Bristol (only the third Chair of Accounting in England and Wales) in 1955. Harold Edey became a Lecturer at the LSE in 1949, subsequently becoming a Reader in 1955, and a Professor in 1962. These three scholars, subsequently referred to as the 'LSE Triumvirate', can be regarded as the founders of the LSE school of academic accounting. This has had a profound impact on British accounting thought since the Second World War, through three distinct means.

1 Through published research papers, the Triumvirate developed ideas which, despite individual characteristics, had a distinctly common 'LSE' flavour. As we shall see, this applied to David Solomons even after he emigrated to the USA in 1959.

2 The Triumvirate influenced accounting thought through teaching a new generation of students, who populated both the accounting profession and academe. Baxter and Edey remained in full-time chairs at the LSE until their retirement (in 1973 and 1980 respectively), and until the expansion of

universities in the mid-1960s the LSE had the largest undergraduate honours programme in Britain and pioneered taught Masters courses in the subject. When the teaching of accounting in universities expanded in the late 1960s and early 1970s, the former students and members of the LSE accounting school were the largest source of recruitment to the academic profession. It also provided a high proportion of the accounting graduates entering the accountancy profession, and many of these have achieved eminence, thus providing a means of disseminating academic ideas into the world of practice.

3   Through direct participation in professional affairs. This is most obvious in David Solomons' two reports on education and training for the accountancy profession (Solomons 1974) and on guidelines for accounting standard-setting (Solomons 1989), and in Harold Edey's long service as a member of the Council of the Institute of Chartered Accountants in England and Wales (1969–80) and of the Accounting Standards Committee (1970–82). However, Baxter, Edey and Solomons have all maintained an active interest in the affairs of professional bodies which, although more diffuse, has probably had no less important an impact on professional thought. Indeed, one common theme in their theoretical writings on accounting has been to develop theoretical insights into problems which have potential relevance to accounting practice. William Baxter's forthright (and controversial) paper for the Institute of Chartered Accountants of Scotland (Baxter 1988) states this view very clearly.

We have identified the Triumvirate as a group which deserves distinct treatment, but it is important also to note that this group was part of a wider LSE tradition in business economics and accounting. In 1919 the LSE had become the second university institution in England and Wales to have a Chair of Accounting (following the University of Birmingham, which founded a Chair in 1902). Moreover, it had developed a strong school of commerce and business economics in the 1930s, under the leadership of Professor (later Sir) Arnold Plant. The younger members of this group included Ronald Coase (subsequently a Nobel Laureate in Economics) and George Thirlby, who helped to develop the LSE opportunity cost tradition (Coase 1938, Thirlby 1946),[2] and also Ronald Edwards, an accountant who subsequently became an economist and was thus in a uniquely strong position to apply economic theory to accounting practice in such areas as cost accounting (Edwards 1938a) and income measurement (Edwards 1938b).[3] A later member of this group was Basil Yamey, who developed a serious scholarly interest in the history of accounting, in addition to a wide range of interests in economics, and has published extensively in this field.[4]

Thus, the Triumvirate were partly the product of an existing school of thought, and they in turn trained a new generation to continue and develop the tradition of critical thinking about accounting which had a strong infusion of economic theory, as well as a concern for practical business problems and a strong sense of the historical development of ideas. Each member of the Triumvirate exhibits these characteristics, and each has therefore contributed to a wide range of accounting research topics, including cost and management accounting, financial accounting (particularly price change accounting), and accounting history. This is not to say that they form a tightly defined school of thought which exhibits total uniformity on all subjects. On some issues they have distinctly different views, a notable example being accounting standard setting, about which Baxter is a sceptic (Baxter 1953) whereas Edey and Solomons are both advocates (Edey 1977 and Solomons 1986), albeit with distinct views as to the form which standards should take. However, the members of the Triumvirate do share a common intellectual background and, if they reach different conclusions, it is often because they disagree on the empirical facts, rather than on the analytical framework which they apply to the facts.

It is impossible within a single essay to discuss the whole of the broader LSE tradition or even the collective contribution of the Triumvirate. The rest of this essay will therefore concentrate on the contribution of the Triumvirate to a particular field, accounting for changing prices. This has been a particularly controversial issue, both in academe and in practice during their careers, and it is an issue to which they have all contributed substantially. As we shall see, their contributions are each distinct, but they have in common four characteristics:

1 It is recognised that there is a distinction between changes in the general price level (inflation) and changes in specific prices (the valuation problem). Thus, the problem is price change accounting, not inflation accounting.
2 Non-monetary assets and liabilities (i.e. those not of fixed monetary value) should be expressed in current values, reflecting changes in their specific prices since acquisition.
3 General price level adjustment is applied to opening capital for a period to enable real profits to be separated from nominal (money terms) profits, which may be fictitious in periods of inflation.
4 The preferred method of valuation for obtaining current values (point 2 above) is deprival value (a phrase invented by Baxter), otherwise known as value to the owner or value to the business, and usually associated with Bonbright (1937).

ORIGINS OF PRICE CHANGE ACCOUNTING

Price change accounting has origins much earlier than its adoption by the LSE group. In the English-speaking world, the USA was the main source of ideas. Paton (1918 and later)[5] was the first to recognise the importance of price changes in accounts, and particularly the importance of separating the effects of general inflation from specific price changes. Paton and most other early writers on the subject refer to the economist Irving Fisher's book, *The Purchasing Power of Money* (1911), as their source of reference on the concept of general inflation and its measurement. Later, in the USA, Canning (1929) and Bonbright (1937) derived valuation rules of the deprival value variety.[6] Bonbright is the usual source of reference for members of the LSE school,[7] but F. K. Wright (1964), in his classic paper on depreciation, derived his opportunity value principle (which is identical with deprival value) from

Canning's concept of 'opportunity differences'. A third seminal contribution to price change accounting to emerge from the USA before the Second World War was Henry Sweeney's book, *Stabilized Accounting* (1936). This not only distilled the continental European (particularly the German) experience of general index adjustment of accounts (the constant purchasing power or CPP System) but also showed (in Chapter 3) how this could be combined with revaluation of non-monetary assets on a current value basis (replacement cost being the method preferred by Sweeney). Thus Sweeney anticipated some of the central features of the systems subsequently put forward by Edwards and Bell (1961) in the USA and by Baxter (1971) in the UK.[8]

On the continent of Europe, the hyperinflation following the First World War led to the development of constant purchasing power (CPP) systems of accounting designed to correct for the declining purchasing power of the monetary unit. In Germany, such systems were developed and refined by Schmalenbach (1919) and Mahlberg (1923), among others. A number of French writers also explored this type of accounting method, and much of the accumulated knowledge of these continental writers was distilled and published in English by Sweeney. Another German author of great significance was Schmidt (1921), who was a pioneer of replacement cost accounting systems and who also developed a gearing adjustment (to deal with the gain on borrowing in a period of inflation) similar to that subsequently adopted in current cost accounting in the UK (Schmidt 1931, Coenenberg and Macharzina 1976). Schmidt (1927) also developed the idea that historical cost accounting can have adverse economic effects by magnifying the trade cycle, an idea subsequently expounded by Baxter (1955). Finally, in The Netherlands, Limperg developed a system of replacement value accounting, which bore some striking similarities to Schmidt's system, but which was based on replacement value, a concept more akin to deprival value rather than (as in Schmidt's system) replacement cost. Limperg never published a comprehensive account of his system and it was left to his followers, such as Goudeket (1960), to expound it, but it did have a practical effect in that a significant number of leading companies in The Netherlands adopted forms of replacement value accounting for reporting purposes.[9]

Thus, most of the basic ideas and techniques which were discussed after the Second World War and were debated fiercely in the English-speaking world during the inflation of the 1970s (Tweedie and Whittington 1984) had their origins in the pre-war period. One country in Europe which seems to have avoided extensive discussion of price change accounting in this earlier period was the United Kingdom, possibly because it had avoided hyperinflation following the First World War, although Fells (1919) did point out the consequences of inflation for the measurement of cost.

THE LSE CONTRIBUTION TO PRICE CHANGE ACCOUNTING

Although the United Kingdom did not have a debate on price change accounting in the 1930s, the foundations of the LSE school's contribution to the subsequent debate were laid in this period (Baxter 1991). Baxter, Solomons and Edey all studied at the LSE at some time in the 1930s and thus were brought into contact with the ideas of Plant and his followers, and particularly that of opportunity cost. Deprival value can be expressed as the loss which would accrue to the owner of the asset in the event of his being deprived of it. Thus, deprival value can be interpreted as a form of opportunity cost,[10] and it would be likely to appeal to anyone trained in the LSE school of the 1930s. The single most striking achievement of the LSE Triumvirate in their later development of price change accounting was to graft deprival value on to the constant purchasing power/replacement cost system suggested by Sweeney (1936).

The Triumvirate also subsequently explored the theoretical basis of price change accounting, particularly in the context of income measurement. The foundation of this process was also laid in the 1930s, notably in a seminal series of papers by R. S. Edwards (1938b) on 'The Nature and Measurement of Income', which contrasted the accountant's conventional income measure, based upon accrued historical cost, with the economist's forward-looking view of income as change in net worth, where net worth is based upon discounted present values of future cash flows. Edwards concluded that the accountant should attempt to provide information which was relevant to assessing the economic net worth of a business, although the assessment would have to be made by the user of the accounts rather than by the accountant.[11] Edwards' analysis provided an argument for introducing more current values into financial reports.[12] However, this paper was written on the eve of the Second World War, during which Edwards became increasingly involved in the economics of industry, and he never returned to financial accounting theory. Moreover, the traditionally minded head of the Accounting Department at the LSE, Stanley Rowland, had expressed disapproval of the young Edwards' radical ideas. In the period following the Second World War, it was left to Baxter, Solomons and Edey to build on the earlier foundations. We shall consider the contribution of each, in turn.

WILLIAM T. BAXTER

Professor Baxter was trained as a Scottish Chartered Accountant in Edinburgh between 1924 and 1930, and also took a B.Com. degree at the University there. He was taught by William Annan, a distinguished Edinburgh practitioner who was the part-time Professor of Accounting and Business Method at Edinburgh University from 1927 to 1945. An entertaining and informative autobiographical account of the development of William Baxter's ideas and of his career is given in Baxter (1978). After qualifying he spent two years on a Harkness Fellowship at the Wharton School in Philadelphia and at the Harvard Business School, where he used his accounting skills in business history research. Returning to Britain, he spent a year as a part-time student at the LSE, where he attended Plant's undergraduate seminar and first recognised the potential of applying economic theory to accounting problems. He then lectured at Edinburgh University from 1934 to 1936, where his interest in economics was sustained by Kenneth

Boulding, then a young colleague, and later a leading economist in the USA. During this period, he published his first book, a textbook on income tax (Baxter 1937), which reflected the professional basis of the curriculum at Edinburgh. In 1937, he became Professor of Accounting at Cape Town, where G. F. Thirlby was a colleague and provided further contact with the ideas of the LSE business economics school. In 1947, Baxter became Professor of Accounting at the LSE where he remained until (and beyond) his retirement in 1973. He has always acknowledged his intellectual debt to the LSE business economists of Plant's group and to Bonbright (whose work came to his attention through a review by R. S. Edwards). With characteristic clarity, he summarises the essence of the LSE opportunity cost approach to costing and valuation in the simple question, 'What difference does it make?' (Baxter 1978: 15) (and with characteristic honesty and modesty he has subsequently, in private correspondence, attributed the authorship of this question to Harold Edey, 'who probably got it from Paish').

One of Baxter's first substantial papers after moving to the LSE was his 'Accountants and the Inflation', a paper read to the Manchester Statistical Society in 1949. This laid the foundations of the Baxter approach to price change accounting. The essential framework is general index adjustment, to translate all items in the accounts into common dated currency units, i.e. current pounds. Thus, the core of the paper expounds the constant purchasing power system (CPP), as developed by Sweeney and others in the 1930s. Baxter acknowledges Sweeney's work, but criticises its complexity and offers a simplified exposition. In this early paper he makes the assumption that replacement cost is equal to general indexation of historical cost and does not discuss the possibility of reporting current market values of specific assets. The paper also develops the idea that historical cost accounting can amplify the trade cycle, by over-stating profits in periods of inflation and under-stating them in periods of deflation.

These themes were developed further in subsequent papers. In 1951, in partnership with his former pupil, Basil Yamey, Baxter explored the foreign branch account analogy, which provides one method of expounding the CPP principle of translating all figures in the accounts into measurement units of common purchasing power. This analogy was mentioned in Baxter's 1949 paper, but it owes its origins to accounting practice in the 1920s (e.g. the German gold mark basis of accounting). In 1952, Baxter (in his Westminster Bank Review paper) once again advocated a CPP system, asserting that, for financial reporting purposes, general indexation of historical cost was an appropriate measure of replacement cost. In this paper, he advocated CPP adjustments as a basis for company income taxation and also developed further his view that historical cost accounting can amplify the trade cycle. The latter theme was the subject of a further paper, 'The Accountant's Contribution to the Trade Cycle' (1955), which provided algebraic formulations and more elaborate numerical and diagrammatic illustrations. This was subsequently the basis of an appendix in Baxter's book on *Accounting Values and Inflation* (1975).[13] A later paper in a similar vein, exploring an economic distortion which can be caused by historical cost accounting in periods of inflation, was Baxter's 1962 paper on 'Inflation and Partnership Rights'.

In 1956, a paper on 'The Inadequacy of Financial Accounts' included a section on changing price levels. This proposed three price change adjustments to the profit and loss account: for stocks, monetary assets and liabilities, and fixed asset depreciation, respectively. The preferred method was still general price level adjustment: there is a mention of the possibility of special indices being applied to specific types of asset, but the idea is not developed. This changed in 1959 with the publication of 'Inflation and the Accounts of Steel Companies'. This paper applies price change adjustments to the accounts of seven UK steel companies, in the manner of R. C. Jones' earlier works on US steel companies (Jones 1949). The object, which was achieved, was to demonstrate the materiality of price change adjustments. However, from a theoretical standpoint, an interesting feature was that specific replacement costs of stocks and fixed assets achieved serious attention, for the first time in Baxter's work. Replacement costs were still presented as optional additions to a basic CPP system, but they were treated as useful additions both to the balance sheet and to the profit and loss account, and statements of cumulative real valuation gains were presented (Tables 3c and 5c).

The latter innovation was carried further in a later paper Baxter (1964), which adopted the Edwards and Bell (1961) format for presenting real gains (including unrealised gains, due to assets appreciating more rapidly than the inflation rate) on an annual basis.[14] One of these authors (Bell) had spent a post-doctoral year (1956/7) at the LSE and had discussed his work with Baxter, whose help is acknowledged in the preface to Edwards and Bell (1961: x). In a 1967 paper, 'General or Special Index?', the Edwards and Bell approach was again adopted with approval, but the special index approach to capital maintenance, as adopted by Professor Gynther (1966) was strongly criticised. Baxter regarded the Gynther approach as being unsuited for reporting to equity shareholders, who are likely to judge their gains by reference to the general price level rather than the prices of the specific assets used by the accounting entity. However, Baxter has always been cautious and sceptical in his adoption of new ideas, and it is notable that in this paper he did not discuss fixed assets, preferring to expound the Edwards and Bell approach using an example which only contained stocks. It is, of course, much easier to accept the recognition of unrealised holding gains on stocks, which are likely to be realised within a relative short time, than it is to accept the recognition of such gains on fixed assets, which are likely to be realised by use over a number of periods, affecting the accounts by means of a depreciation charge.

Clearly, Baxter had not settled his view of depreciation, and it was to this that he turned next. The result was several papers and a book (Baxter 1971) which summarised the results of his researches. An earlier indication of his evolving view on the valuation of fixed assets was his 1967 review of Chambers' *Accounting Evaluation and Economic Behavior* (Baxter 1967b), in which Baxter advocated deprival values in financial reports. The 1971 book on depreciation also recognised the relevance of deprival value as a method of measuring the decline in an asset's value through time (Chapter 4 and 12). It also discussed changing price levels and depreciation cost (Chapter 11), advocating general index adjustment of the historical cost depreciation charge in the profit and loss account but specific revaluation of fixed assets in the balance sheet (with a corresponding credit to a revaluation reserve).

The scene was now set for the publication of *Accounting Values and Inflation* (1975),[15] which Baxter has described as 'my main effort of recent years' (Baxter 1978: 21). This brought together all the ingredients which had been carefully selected and developed in the previous thirty years or more. The central problem of price change accounting was seen as the 'time-lag error' which should be dealt with by general index adjustment. Thus, the profit figure was based essentially on pure CPP, i.e. historical cost adjusted by a general price index, with a degree of ambivalence about whether the inflationary gain on borrowing should be included in profit or left 'below the line' as an unrealised real gain. The balance sheet should show non-monetary assets and long-term fixed interest liabilities at current value, which would be deprival value (derived from Bonbright and Canning, with some further help from F. K. Wright's 1964 paper on depreciation).[16] However, unrealised real gains on these assets would be shown 'below the line' as gains credited to a revaluation reserve during the period in which they accrued. When such real gains were subsequently realised by use or sale, they were debited against the revaluation reserve and credited to the profit and loss account by reducing replacement cost of goods sold and depreciation to their indexed historical cost equivalents. Thus, Baxter combined some quite radical proposals (constant purchasing power measurement units and current valuation of non-monetary assets) with the traditional prudence of the professional accountant (in avoiding recording unrealised real holding gains in the profit and loss account). He also expressed his ideas with characteristic elegance and simplicity.

Since 1975, Baxter has studied the operation of CPP accounting in Latin America (1976), reviewed the Sandilands Report (1975) produced a radically revised version of his book, retitled *Inflation Accounting* (1984), and generally continued to contribute to the debate on price change accounting. He has been particularly critical of the physical capital maintenance concept embodied in current cost accounting. However, the first edition of the book was undoubtedly the most complete statement of his position, and we now turn to the work of his two colleagues, which in many important respects complemented his in the field of price change accounting.

DAVID SOLOMONS

David Solomons was born and educated in London and was an undergraduate studying for the B.Com. in Plant's department at the LSE, graduating in 1932. He thus was exposed at an early stage to the LSE business economics school. Following graduation, he trained as a chartered accountant in London, qualifying as a member of the Institute of Chartered Accountants in England and Wales (ICAEW) in 1937. During the Second World War, he joined the armed forces, became a prisoner-of-war, and, in the unlikely setting of a prisoner-of-war camp, developed a taste for teaching accounting and economics (Solomons 1984: xiv). After the Second World War, he returned to accounting practice, but also became a part-time teacher at the LSE. In 1946 he became a lecturer and in 1948 a Reader in Accounting at the LSE. In 1955, he became the first Professor of Accounting at Bristol University (in the Department of Economics), and in 1959 he emigrated to the USA, where he became a Professor in the Wharton School, Pennsylvania (to which Baxter had been briefly attached as a Harkness Fellow, more than a quarter of a century earlier). He remained at the Wharton School for the remainder of his academic career (retiring in 1983) and became a prominent figure in American accounting circles, serving *inter alia*, as a member of the Wheat Committee which carried out the AICPA's Study on Establishment of Accounting Principles (1972) and as President of the American Accounting Association (1977–8). He has also made important contributions to British accounting, notably through his study on education and training (Solomons 1974) and his guidelines for accounting standard-setting (Solomons 1989).

Despite his long absence in the USA, Solomons' work bears strong marks of his formative experiences as a student and teacher at the LSE. He refers to Ronald Edwards as 'one of my principal mentors during my LSE period' (Solomons 1984: xv). Like Edwards, he is centrally concerned with applying economic analysis to accounting problems. For example, in his classic 1966 paper, he writes: 'For most of the bricks, the economists have to be thanked. The accountants have been bricklayers rather than brickmakers . . .' (Solomons 1966a: 139). Also like Edwards, two of his central concerns have been with measuring cost and income. He has, to a much greater degree than Baxter, contributed to cost and management accounting, his first major contribution being his edited volume, *Studies in Costing* (Solomons 1952), and another of his substantial achievements in this field being his prize-winning book on *Divisional Performance: Measurement and Control* (Solomons 1965). More recently, he has contributed substantially to the literature of accounting standard setting (much of his thinking in this field is summarised in Solomons (1986)). Thus, his contribution to price change accounting is merely one aspect of a much more substantial contribution to accounting thought.

Solomons' concern with the economic analysis of cost and income measurement led him in an early paper ('Income – True and False', 1948) to advocate replacement cost accounting. He demonstrated how replacement cost adjustments, reflecting the costs of the specific assets concerned, could be applied to both the cost of sales (stocks consumed) and depreciation (fixed assets consumed) in the profit and loss account. He did not adjust balance sheet values to replacement costs, although he mentioned the possibility: his central concern was with income measurement. He was also, at this early stage, somewhat ambivalent about general price level adjustments: at one stage in the paper he seems to suggest that replacement costs are a proxy for these. Thus, in this period, Solomons and Baxter were approaching price change accounting from opposite perspective, Solomons starting from specific price changes and Baxter from changes in the general price level.

This initial contribution by Solomons to the price change accounting debate was quite influential and widely cited; for example, it was reprinted in the well-known collection of papers edited by Baxter (1950), and it was cited in the Association of Certified and Corporate Accountants' report *Accounting for Inflation* (1952) which advocated a replacement cost method. However, as Solomons himself records (Solomons 1984), he became deeply involved in management accounting, as part of the division of labour with his colleagues, Baxter and Edey, at the LSE, and apart from a paper on the use of accounting rates of return by the Monopolies Commission (Solomons and Silberston 1952) his interest in price change accounting did not manifest itself again in the public domain until 1961, when he published 'Economic and Accounting Concepts of Income'. This was inspired by his revision of Alexander's monograph on business income (subsequently published in Baxter and Davidson 1962). It is strictly an exploration of the theory of income measurement, rather than price change accounting, but the two issues are closely related (See Edwards, Kay and Mayer (1987) for a more recent exploration of the relationship). In this paper, Solomons examines the economist's concept of income as change in net present value of future cash flows, as advocated by Alexander (1950) and by Solomons' mentor, R. S. Edwards (1938b). He provides a useful schematic reconciliation of economic income with accounting income, which was subsequently adopted by Parker and Harcourt (1969). He concludes that uncertainty makes economic income an impractical concept for financial planning and control and predicts that 'so far as the history of accounting is concerned, the next twenty-five years may subsequently be seen to have been the twilight of income measurement' (Solomons 1961: 383). In this conclusion, he anticipated the critique by Beaver and Demski (1979) and others, who have suggested that accounts should provide a set of information which helps users to assess economic values, rather than attempting a direct provision of such values.

Solomons then turned to the theoretical analysis of the valuation basis of accounts, first in his paper on 'The Determination of Asset Values' (Solomons 1962) and subsequently in two important papers published in 1966. In 'Economic and Accounting Concepts of Cost and Value' (1966a), he provided an economic analysis of these two concepts and reached the conclusion that deprival value was the most useful single method of measurement for accounting purposes. His reasoning reflected that of the LSE opportunity cost school, and he provided the ingredients for the well-known exploration of deprival value in the form of inequalities between Present Value (PV), Replacement Cost (RC) and Net Realisable Value (NRV), which was adopted subsequently by Parker and Harcourt (1969). In the same year, Solomons (1966b) reviewed Chambers' book, *Accounting, Evaluation and Economic Behavior* and criticised Chambers' reliance on selling prices, rather than value to the owner (an alternative description of deprival value), as did Baxter's subsequent review of the same book. Thus, the LSE opportunity cost tradition, with the further influence of Bonbright, had brought Baxter and Solomons to virtually identical views on asset valuation by the mid-1960s: Solomons' advocacy of value to the owner was restated in 1971, when he made the revealing statement:

... it is value, not income, that is primary. The real investment problem, and the managerial problem, is to maximise present value: and income is the growth in present value which is achieved in this process of maximisation

(Solomons 1971)

This statement of the nature of income is entirely consistent with that of his mentor Ronald Edwards (1938b), and shows the influence of Solomons' LSE training. Later in the same paragraph, he writes, of income:

By seeking perfection in its measurement, we forgo the opportunity to make presently attainable advances. For my part, I am prepared to settle for something less than perfection, to get material improvements which are already within our grasp.

This pragmatic approach is similar in spirit to that adopted by Baxter in his approach to practical income measurement.

The complete development of Solomons' view on price change accounting appears in his book *Making Accounting Policy* (Solomons 1986, Chapters 7 and 8). In this (as part of a much wider statement of his views on financial reporting and its regulation) he summarises the alternative models of price change accounting and expresses a preference for what he describes as Current Cost Constant Purchasing Power Accounting (CCCPPA). This is a system which uses value to the owner (now renamed value to the business) as the valuation base but constant purchasing power (i.e. general index adjustment) as the capital maintenance concept for income measurement. This is, of course, essentially the same system as that advocated by Baxter (1975), although Solomons, unlike Baxter, is strongly critical of pure CPP systems (on the ground that their valuation basis is misleading) and is more favourably disposed to the disclosure of holding gains in a comprehensive income statement, in the style of Edwards and Bell (1961). A similar system is advocated in Solomons' *Guidelines for Financial Reporting Standards* (1989: Chapter 6).

Thus, Solomons and Baxter ultimately converged on a similar preferred system for price change accounting, but they arrived there by strikingly different routes, despite their common background in LSE business economics. Solomons' interest in cost accounting and economic analysis led him initially (1948) to replacement cost accounting and later to deprival value concepts (1966). It was only in the final stages of completing a system of price change accounting (1986) that he advocated general index adjustment, and that was for capital maintenance purposes only. Unlike Baxter, Solomons has always regarded general purchasing power adjustment of historical costs as an unsatisfactory basis for valuation. However, the conclusion was harmonious: 'On most topics, and especially on the deficiencies of historical cost accounting, Professor Baxter's views and his conclusions are close to my own' (Solomons 1986: 181).

We now turn to the work of the third member of the Triumvirate, who also shared these views and made the most strenuous effort to translate them into professional practice.

HAROLD C. EDEY

The youngest member of the Triumvirate is Harold Edey; he was also the last to join the staff of the LSE. Harold Edey followed the traditional training of an English chartered accountant in the 1930s. Leaving school at the age of sixteen, he served articles with a small firm of accountants in London, qualifying as a chartered accountant in 1935. After a brief period with a larger professional firm he joined S. Pearson and Son, the financial group, and also enrolled as a part-time undergraduate student at the LSE. Following service in the Royal Navy during the Second World War, he rejoined Pearsons as an investment analyst and completed his part-time degree, graduating in 1947. He became a part-time teacher at the LSE, and later, in 1949, a full-time lecturer, subsequently becoming a Reader (in 1955), a Professor in 1962, and pro-Director (1967–70), retiring in 1980.

His early career gave Edey a traditional professional training, which shows in the orderliness, care over detail and concern with practicality which marks his work. His contact with the LSE added to this the range of ideas associated with the LSE school of business economics and accounting: he pays particular tribute to Edwards, Coase, Baxter, Solomons and Yamey, as well as to other colleagues and teachers at the LSE (Edey 1982). A third influence of his formative years was his relatively brief period as an investment analyst: his writings on financial accounting are all marked by a particular concern that accounts should serve the needs of the investor. These strands were synthesised into a decision-oriented view of accounting, which Edey himself summarises as follows:

> One cannot usefully determine accounting procedures by a vain search for a 'correct' meaning of the words 'profit' and 'income'. A useful definition of these words can be found only in the procedures used to find the numbers in question, and then only in a particular context. The choice of procedures should emerge from the answer to the question; what is our objective in this particular context?
>
> (Edey 1982: Preface)

Edey's early writings addressed legal and historical aspects of accounting, particularly the development of company law and also taxation.[17] They show a respect for institutional constraints, but also a concern to adapt them to meet economic needs. These early writings do not confront the price change problem directly, although when price change problems do occur, Edey's judgement favours the reflection of current prices whenever that is practical, his central concern (from his first paper, Edey 1950, onwards) being that the investor should be aided in the assessment of prospective future cash flows, particularly dividends. This reflects the influence of Edwards (1938b). His 1960 evidence to the Jenkins Committee, for example, advocates the supplementary disclosure of insurance values of fixed assets. His interest in the taxation implications of alternative methods of measuring accounting income is reflected in his 1962 paper 'Income and the valuation of stock in trade' (Edey 1962).

The concern with predicting future cash flows was reflected in a book on business budgets (1959) and a paper 'Accounting Principles and Business Reality' (1963), which was presented to an annual conference of the ICAEW. This was a remarkably radical paper for a professional audience at that time, although many of the principles were derived from Edwards' much earlier work (1938b). It suggested that the discounted value of future cash flows was the essential concern of the shareholders, and suggested a variety of supplementary disclosures such as, ideally, cash budgets, and more practically, current values of assets, which might aid the process of assessing future prospects.

This radical approach apparently did not frighten the Council of the ICAEW because in 1964 Edey became a member of both the Research Committee and the Education Committee, and in 1969 he was co-opted to the Council, retiring in 1980. He also became a member of the Accounting Standards Steering Committee, (ASSC, subsequently the Accounting Standards Committee, ASC) from when it was set up in 1970 until 1982 and served on the Inflation Accounting Steering Group (IASG) which the ASC established in 1975. In these capacities, Harold Edey made a substantial contribution to the practical development of price change accounting in the UK.

His first contribution of this type was to the development of *Accounting for Stewardship in a Period of Inflation*, published by the ICAEW Research Committee, of which he was a member, in 1968. The principal author of this paper was the late Sir Edmund Parker, then President of the ICAEW, but it was scrutinised and approved by the Research Committee, which also did the preliminary work. This advocated a simple general index adjustment of historical cost accounts, i.e. pure CPP of which Baxter, but not Solomons, would have approved. This system formed the basis of the ASSC's Exposure Draft 8 (ED8, 1973) and Provisional Standard (PSSAP7, 1974), which were produced when Edey was a member. It should be noted that the title of 'Accounting for Stewardship' is consistent with one of Edey's fundamental precepts (as, for example, expressed in Edey 1970), that accounting methods should be selected with specific purposes in mind (in this case, stewardship). This paper and ED8 and PSSAP7 proposed CPP disclosures as supplementary to the main accounts, and this too is consistent with Edey's view of financial reporting (for example, Edey 1963). The pure CPP approach of 'Accounting for Stewardship' did not embrace current values (replacement costs or deprival values) which Edey had advocated earlier, although it did not preclude them, and PSSAP7 was at some pains to explain that the CPP system could encompass specific asset revaluations.

The next stage of Harold Edey's contribution to the professional debate came with his membership of the IASG, a sub-committee of the ASC, formed specifically to develop a price change accounting standard in the wake of the Sandilands Report, the report of a government committee which came down in favour of pure current cost accounting, with value to the business as the valuation basis but no general index adjustments to show the effect of inflation in eroding capital. Edey was an active member of the IASG and chaired the working party on the treatment of monetary items, i.e. how the inflationary gain on borrowing and loss on holding money should be reported. He was largely responsible for the insertion into the ill-fated ED18 (1976) of a supplementary statement of the real gains and losses of equity. This reflected what the IASG described as the 'ideal system', and is the real terms system preferred by the LSE Triumvirate: value to the business as valuation basis and general indexation to reflect the effects of inflation on capital. Unfortunately, ED18 was withdrawn.[18] Edey continued to labour for a workable system which, although not ideal, would represent an improvement on contemporary practice. To this end, he served on the group which prepared the simple and relatively successful Hyde Guidelines (1977), and continued to serve on the IASG while it produced ED24 (1979) and the standard SSAP16 in 1980. The standard incorporated the monetary working capital adjustment and the gearing adjustment to deal, respectively, with the inflationary loss on holding money and gain on borrowing. These were based upon specific index adjustment rather than the general index adjustment of the 'ideal method' preferred by Edey, but Edey was able to accept SSAP16 as being an improvement on existing practice:

> In the end no practical *ex post facto* measure of profit can be perfect or 'right' in an absolute sense as there is no obvious way of bringing all the intangibles into the accounting measurement . . . It is perhaps enough that if there is good understanding of the methods used, conclusions – or at least conjectures leading to further enquiry or consideration – can be drawn in the knowledge of their limitations.
>
> (Edey 1979: 198)

This quotation summarises the view which Edey shares with Baxter and Solomons, that accounting should provide information relevant to the measurement of value and income but cannot aspire to provide precise measures of those concepts.

Although Edey's major contribution to price change accounting was, during this period, substantially concealed behind the closed doors of standard-setting committees and working parties, some tips of the iceberg did appear in public view in his published papers. In 1970, his paper on 'The Nature of Profit' spelled out his fundamental theoretical position on profit measurement in accounts: 'The function of the accounts is best conceived as that of raising in the minds of those who study and read them useful *conjectures* about the company's state and progress' (Edey 1970: 55).

The paper examined a number of purposes for which profit measures might be used and was supportive of adjustments for inflation. Subsequently, in a paper which directly addressed the issue of inflation adjustment (Edey 1974a) he gave a clear public statement of his preference for a system of price change adjustments which incorporated both current values and general index inflation corrections, i.e. what was referred to above as 'the ideal method', as advocated also by Baxter (1975). In the same year, he published a careful analysis of deprival value (or value to the business), which explored the aggregation problem, and which also indicated his preference for deprival value as the basis upon which current values should be introduced into accounts (Edey 1974b). His 1979 paper, which has already been referred to, explored the difficult transition from the Sandilands current cost system to that recommended by ED24 (and subsequently implemented in SSAP16). This paper analyses the problems faced by Edey's monetary assets and liabilities working party and indicates a preference for the logic of the 'ideal' general index method, whilst accepting the ED24 gearing and monetary working capital adjustments as a necessary compromise. He has maintained this position in subsequent publications: 'One must not ask too much too quickly. The best is the enemy of the better. If the economic logic of CCA is better than that of HCA, the CCA figures will be of more use' (Edey 1980: 18).

In summary, Harold Edey's thinking is fundamentally based on the need to inform economic decisions. It is therefore very much in sympathy with that of David Solomons, and both Edey and Solomons acknowledge the influence of R. S. Edwards. Like Solomons and Baxter, Edey prefers a system of current deprival value combined with general index inflation adjustments, to deal with the effects of changing prices. Like Baxter, but unlike Solomons, he has been willing to advocate a pure general index (CPP) system as a first step towards his ideal. Above all, Edey has striven to be practical and has hoped to influence policy in the direction of improving practice rather than hoping for perfection.

SUBSEQUENT LSE CONTRIBUTIONS

This paper has been concerned with the work of the LSE Triumvirate: Baxter, Solomons and Edey. However, it is appropriate to note that the Triumvirate not only had predecessors (such as R. S. Edwards), whose contributions have been recorded, but also successors. Here, we can only briefly note the continuity of the Triumvirate's work by mentioning the work of two of their successors at the LSE, Michael Bromwich and Bryan Carsberg.

Michael Bromwich is currently a Professor at the LSE and is an LSE graduate from the school founded by Plant, which also included Edwards. In many respects, he is an intellectual successor to David Solomons, dealing in both management accounting and financial accounting, and basing his analysis firmly on economic theory. His work in the field of price change accounting has focused on asset valuation in imperfect and incomplete markets, e.g. his influential paper (Bromwich 1977) which concludes that the measurement of NPV is an inappropriate ideal for accountants to aim at, in many realistic market settings. Bromwich has also followed the LSE tradition of practicality and of participation in the standard-setting process, e.g. he was a prime mover in the ICMA[19] paper (ICMA 1984) which was addressed to the ASC and advocated a 'real terms' price change accounting system. He has also served as a member of the ASC and has been President of his Institute (CIMA).

Professor (now Sir) Bryan Carsberg qualified as a Chartered Accountant before becoming a student at the LSE (as did Harold Edey). He subsequently became a Professor at Manchester (1969–81) and the LSE (1981–6), before becoming the first Director-General of Telecommunications (OFTEL) and then (currently) Director-General of Fair Trading. He has made some notable contributions to price change accounting. He served as an Assistant Director of Research at the US Financial Accounting Standards Board and was responsible for the drafting of FAS 33 (1979), the standard which imposed a form of price change accounting in the USA which was consistent with the LSE Triumvirate's approach (i.e. combining current values, on a value to the business basis, with general price level adjustment). Returning to the UK, he became Research Director of the ICAEW and was responsible for a notable survey of the empirical evidence on the effectiveness of SSAP16 (Carsberg and Page 1984). His intellectual framework, emphasising the value of financial statements for predicting future cash flows can be regarded as a natural extension of the work of Edwards (1938b) and Edey (1963). Equally, his concern with and participation in the making of accounting policy is very much in the LSE tradition. He continues this as (currently) Deputy Chairman of the Accounting Standards Board.

These are but two examples (albeit prominent ones) of how the ideas of Baxter, Solomons and Edey have been adopted and developed by subsequent generations. Although we have concentrated on price change accounting, the influence of the Triumvirate extends to many other areas of accounting, and the intellectual framework is probably more important than specific policy prescriptions, such as the 'real terms' accounting system. Indeed, price change accounting has currently (and probably only temporarily) become a less important topic for standard-setting bodies in the UK and USA, as inflation rates have fallen and both FAS 33 and SSAP16 have been withdrawn.

CONCLUSION

In the specific area of price change accounting, the LSE Triumvirate converged, from different starting points but with the aid of a common LSE intellectual background, on a common prescription. This had three central propositions:

1 Assets (and liabilities) should be measured at current values.
2 The basis of current valuation should be deprival value, otherwise known as value to the business or value to the owner.
3 For income measurement purposes, opening capital should be adjusted by the change in a general price index over the period, to reveal real income, where 'real' is used in the economist's sense of implying constant command over goods and services, undistorted by inflation.

The intellectual framework, which enabled these conclusions to be reached, had, in turn, three components:

1 Accounting should be decision-oriented, i.e. the information should meet the needs of users in making particular decisions.
2 Economic theory provides a suitable framework within which to analyse these decisions and needs. The LSE opportunity cost concept was regarded as being particularly important.
3 Accounting measurement is, in practice, not a precise process, because of the inevitable uncertainty as to the future and the imperfections of markets.

Accounting is a practical activity, and proposals for accounting systems should take account of practical difficulties, in addition to being consistent with theory.

The policy conclusions derived by the Triumvirate were always tempered by a knowledge of practical constraints, arising from their professional training and connections.

The result has been a substantial contribution to the refinement and clarification of the theory of price change accounting and to the development of practice. It would be wrong to suggest that the LSE Triumvirate had a monopoly of ideas in this field: some other contributions were outlined earlier in this paper and there were many more which were not mentioned.[20] However, the LSE group did make a sub- stantial and distinctive contribution to this field, and it was the dominant intellectual influence on the price change accounting debate in the UK. It has also made notable contributions to other fields (e.g. accounting history, a field in which Basil Yamey has featured prominently). Our objective has been to show how the individual ideas of Baxter, Solomons and Edey developed through time and relative to one another. It is hoped that it has been demonstrated that it is reasonable to group them as members of a common school of thought. However, like all the best schools, it has been liberal in its thinking and eclectic in its sources of ideas. The three developed in harmony, but neither played exactly the same tune. Indeed there is no instance of the three (or any pair of them) having written a book or published a paper together.[21] Perhaps it would have been better to have characterised them as a musical trio, rather than a triumvirate.

Notes

This chapter is based partly on a lecture given at the London School of Economics as part of the celebrations to mark the fortieth anniversary of Professor Baxter's appointment to the Chair of Accounting. Helpful criticisms and suggestions on an earlier draft were received from the two referees (Professors Ted French and Bob Parker) and from Will Baxter, Phil Bell, Harold Edey, David Solomons, David Tweedie and Steve Zeff.

1 Solomons (1974: 39–42) gives an account of the early development of Accounting as an academic subject in Britain. In Scotland, accounting developed more rapidly in universities than in England and Wales, but on the basis of part-time chairs held by accounting practitioners. The Chair in Edinburgh was founded on a part-time basis in 1919 and the first full-time incumbent was the late Professor Edward Stamp, who was appointed in 1967 (Lee 1983).

2 Gould (1974) provides a survey and critique of this literature.

3 Professor Sir Ronald Edwards left academic life later, ending his career as Chairman of the Beecham Group.

4 It is interesting to note that Yamey was a graduate of the University of Cape Town, where he was taught by William Baxter (see Baxter 1978: 20). Thirlby also taught at Cape Town when Baxter was there, and earlier Arnold Plant had been Professor of Commerce at Cape Town (1923–30, see Coase 1987).

5 Zeff (1979) provides an analysis of the development Paton's views on accounting for changing prices.

6 Deprival value can be summarised as replacement cost or recoverable amount, whichever is the lower, where recoverable amount is the higher of value in use (the

discounted present value of anticipated future net cash receipts) or value in disposal (net realisable value). Solomons (1966a) provides a classic justification of the method, by a member of the Triumvirate.

7 Baxter's inaugural address at the LSE (Baxter 1948) cites both Bonbright and Canning, although not specifically in relation to deprival value.

8 Sweeney (1964) cites Baxter, with approval, as one of his intellectual successors in developing price change accounting, and Baxter cites Sweeney on many occasions, including his first paper on the subject (Baxter 1949) and his book (Baxter 1975).

9 Zeff, van der Wel and Camfferman (1992) give an account of the development of Dutch accounting practice, and of the work of Limperg (particularly Chapter 1). A fuller history of the development of price change accounting before the Second World War is given in Tweedie and Whittington (1984), Chapter 2. A more recent account of some aspects of the German School is provided by Graves (1991).

10 This can be seen very clearly in the exposition by Solomons (1966a).

11 This theme was taken up many years later by Bromwich (1977), Peasnell (1977) and Beaver and Demski (1979).

12 He produces an argument that aggregate replacement cost of the assets of a business provides an upper bound on their value and net realisable value provides a lower bound. This is closely related to the deprival value concept. Bonbright (1937) is referred to in the paper, but not in the context of deprival value.

13 In the 1955 paper, Baxter also refers to the work of Lacey (1952), an economist based in London. Lacey, however, advocated replacement cost accounting, in the sense of specific replacement cost, rather than CPP.

14 However, in another paper, 'Inflation and Accounts' (Baxter 1962a), a CPP system was proposed, although the numerical examples contained specific price change adjustments to fixed asset values.

15 An extended review of this book is Whittington (1975).

16 In the case of long-term liabilities, Baxter derives a deprival value rule which he describes as Relief Value. He has recently, in an unpublished paper, criticised this concept.

17 He also co-authored a well-known textbook on national income accounting (Edey and Peacock 1954).

18 Tweedie and Whittington (1984: Chapters 4 to 6), provides an extended account of the British debate on price change accounting.

19 The ICMA was the Institute of Cost and Management Accountants; following the award of a Royal Charter, it is now the Chartered Institute of Management Accountants (CIMA).

20 Whittington (1983) provides a survey of the subject up to the early 1980s.

21 I am grateful to Ted French for pointing out this remarkable fact.

References

Accounting Standards Committee (ASC) (1976) *ED18, Current Cost Accounting*, London: ASC.

Accounting Standards Committee (ASC) (1977) *Inflation Accounting – an Interim Recommendation by the Accounting Standards Committee* (The Hyde Guidelines), London: ASC.

Accounting Standards Committee (ASC) (1979) *ED24, Current Cost Accounting*, London: ASC.

Accounting Standards Committee (ASC) (1980) *Statement of Standard Accounting Practice No. 16, Current Cost Accounting* (SSAP16), London: ASC.

Accounting Standards Steering Committee (ASSC) (1973) *ED8: Accounting for Changes in the Purchasing Power of Money*, London: ASSC.

Accounting Standards Steering Committee (ASSC) (1974) *Provisional Statement of Standard Accounting Practice No. 7, Accounting for Changes in the Purchasing Power of Money* (PSSAP7), London: ASSC.

Alexander, S. S. (1950) 'Income Measurement in a Dynamic Economy', 1–97 of Study Group on Business Income (1950).

Association of Certified and Corporate Accountants, Taxation and Research Committee (1952) *Accounting for Inflation, a Study of Techniques under Conditions of Changing Price Levels*, London: Gee & Co.

Baxter, W. T. (1937) *Income Tax for Professional Students*, London: Pitman.

Baxter, W. T. (1948) 'Accounting as an Academic Study', *The Accountant*, 6 March.

Baxter, W. T. (1949) 'Accountants and the Inflation', *Proceedings of the Manchester Statistical Society*, 9 February: 1–19.

Baxter, W. T. (ed.) (1950) *Studies in Accounting*, London: Sweet and Maxwell.

Baxter, W. T. (1952) 'Inflation and Accounting Profits', *Westminster Bank Review*, May: 1–8.

Baxter, W. T. (1953) 'Recommendations on Accounting Theory', *The Accountant*, 10 October.

Baxter, W. T. (1955) 'The Accountant's Contribution to the Trade Cycle', *Economica* 22: 99–112.

Baxter, W. T. (1956) 'The Inadequacy of Financial Accounts', *The Accountant's Magazine*, February 1957: 80–95. (Read to the Institute of Chartered Accountants of Scotland Summer School, September 1956.)

Baxter, W. T. (1959) 'Inflation and the Accounts of Steel Companies', *Accountancy*, May: 250–7 and June: 308–14.

Baxter, W. T. (1962a) 'Inflation and the Accounts', *The Investment Analyst*, December: 3–11.

Baxter, W. T. (1962b) 'Inflation and Partnership Rights', *The Accountant's Magazine*, February.

Baxter, W. T. (1964) 'The Future of the Accountant: Dilemmas Facing the Profession', *The Accountant*, 11 July: 32–5 and 18 July: 67–70.

Baxter, W. T. (1967a) 'General or Special Index? – Capital maintenance under changing prices', *Journal UEC*, July: 172–81.

Baxter, W. T. (1967b) 'Accounting Values: Sale Price versus Replacement Cost', *Journal of Accounting Research*, 5: 208–14.

Baxter, W. T. (1971) *Depreciation*, London: Sweet and Maxwell.

Baxter, W. T. (1975) *Accounting Values and Inflation*, London: McGraw-Hill.

Baxter, W. T. (1976) 'Monetary Correction: Adjustments to inflation in three South American countries', *Bank of London and South America Review* 10: 184–94.

Baxter, W. T. (1978) *Collected Papers on Accounting*, New York: Arno.

Baxter, W. T. (1984) *Inflation Accounting*, Oxford: Philip Allan.

Baxter, W. T. (1988) *Accounting Research – Academic Trends versus Practical Needs*, Edinburgh: The Institute of Chartered Accountants of Scotland.

Baxter, W. T. (1991) 'Early critics of costing: LSE in the 1930s', in O. F. Graves (ed.) *The Costing Heritiage*, Harrisonberg: Academy of Accounting Historians.

Baxter, W. T. and Davidson, S. (eds) (1962) *Studies in Accounting Theory*, London: Sweet and Maxwell; 2nd edn (1977), London: Institute of Chartered Accountants in England and Wales.

Baxter, W. T. and Yamey, B. S. (1951) 'Theory of Foreign Branch Accounts', *Accounting Research* 2: 2.

Beaver, W. and Demski, J. (1979) 'The Nature of Income Measurement', *The Accounting Review* 54: 38–46.

Bonbright, J. C. (1937) *Valuation of Property* (2 vols), New York: McGraw-Hill.

Bromwich, M. (1977) 'The Use of Present Value Valuation Models in Published Accounting Reports', *The Accounting Review* 52: 587–96.

Canning, J. B. (1929) *The Economics of Accountancy: A Critical Analysis of Accounting Theory*, New York: Ronald Press.

Carsberg, B. and Page, M. (1984) *Current Cost Accounting: The Benefits and the Costs* (4 vols), London: Prentice-Hall.

Chambers, R. J. (1966) *Accounting, Evaluation and Economic Behavior*, Englewood Cliffs, NJ: Prentice-Hall.

Coase, R. H. (1938) 'Business Organisation and the Accountant', *The Accountant*, 1 October–17 December 1938. Reprinted in Solomons (ed.) (1952): 105–58.

Coase, R. H. (1987) '"Plant", Arnold (1898–1978)', in J. Eatwell, M. Milgate and P. Newman (eds) *The New Palgrave Dictionary of Economics*, New York: Holt, Rinehart & Winston, p. 891.

Coenenberg, A. and Macharzina, K. (1976) 'Accounting for Price Changes: An Analysis of Current Developments in Germany', *Journal of Business Finance and Accounting* 3: 53–68.

Edey, H. C. (1950) 'Published Accounts as an aid to Investment', *The Accountant*, 18 February: 163–8.

Edey, H. C. (1959) *Business Budgets and Accounts*, London: Hutchinson.

Edey, H. C. (1962) 'Income and the valuation of stock in trade', *The British Tax Review*, May/June: 164–72.

Edey, H. C. (1963) 'Accounting Principles and Business Reality', *The Accountant*, 24 and 31 August, and *Accountancy*, November: 998–1002 and December: 1083–8.

Edey, H. C. (1970) 'The Nature of Profit', *Accounting and Business Research* 1: 50–5.

Edey, H. C. (1974a) 'Some Aspects of Inflation and Published Accounts', *Omega* 2: 723–31.

Edey, H. C. (1974b) 'Deprival Value and Financial Accounting', Edey and Yamey (1974: 75–84).

Edey, H. C. (1977) 'Accounting Standards in the British Isles', Baxter and Davidson (1977: 294–305).

Edey, H. C. (1979) 'Sandilands and the Logic of Current Cost', *Accounting and Business Research* 9: 191–200.

Edey, H. C. (1980) *The Logic of Financial Reporting*, the Deloitte Haskins and Sells Lecture, Cardiff: University College Press.

Edey, H. C. (1982) *Accounting Queries*, New York: Garland.

Edey, H. C. and Peacock, A. T. (1954) *National Income and Social Accounting*, London: Hutchinson.

Edey, H. C. and Yamey, B. S. (eds) (1974) *Debits, Credits, Finance and Profits*, London: Sweet and Maxwell.

Edwards, E. O. and Bell, P. W. (1961) *The Theory and Measurement of Business Income*, Berkeley, Calif.: University of California Press.

Edwards, J., Kay, J. and Mayer, C. (1987) *The Economic Analysis of Accounting Profitability*, Oxford: Claredon Press.

Edwards, R. S. (1938a) 'The Rationale of Cost Accounting' in A. Plant (ed.) (1937: 277–99) *Some Modern Business Problems*, London, reprinted in Solomons (1952: 87–104).

Edwards, R. S. (1938b) 'The Nature and Measurement of Income', *The Accountant*, July–October, reprinted in Baxter (1950) and in abridged form in Baxter and Davidson (1962) and (1977: 96–140).

Fells, J. M. (1919) 'Some Principles Governing the Ascertainment of Cost', *Incorporated Accountants Journal*, November.

Financial Accounting Standards Board (FASB) (1979) *Statement of Financial Accounting Standards No. 33 (FAS 33): Financial Reporting and Changing Prices*, Stanford, Conn.: FASB.

Fisher, I. (1911) *The Purchasing Power of Money*, New York: Macmillan.

Goudeket, A. (1960) 'An Application of Replacement Value Theory', *The Journal of Accountancy*, July 1960, reprinted in Baxter and Davidson (1977: 234–79).

Gould, J. R. (1974) 'Opportunity Cost: The London Tradition', in Edey and Yamey (1974: 91–108).

Graves, O. F. (1991) 'Fritz Schmidt, Henry Sweeney and Stabilized Accounting', *Accounting and Business Research* 21: 119–24.

Gynther, R. S. (1966) *Accounting for Price-Level Changes: Theory and Procedures*, Oxford: Pergamon.

Institute of Chartered Accountants in England and Wales (ICAEW), Research Committee (1968) *Accounting for Stewardship in a Period of Inflation*, London: ICAEW.

Institute of Cost and Management Accountants (ICMA) (1984) *Accounting for Changing Prices . . . an ICMA View*, London: ICMA.

Jones, R. C. (1949) 'Effect of Inflation on Capital and Profits: The Record of Nine Steel Companies', *Journal of Accountancy*, January: 9–27.

Lacey, K. (1952) *Profit Measurement and Price Changes*, London: Pitman.

Lee, T. A. (ed.) (1983) *Professors of Accounting at the University of Edinburgh – a Selection of Writings 1919–1983*, Edinburgh: Department of Accounting and Business Method.

Mahlberg, W. (1923) *Bilanztechnik und Bewertung bei schwankender Währung*, Leipzig: Kapitel III.

Parker, R. H. and Harcourt, G. C. (eds) (1969) *Readings in the Concept and Measurement of Income*, London: Cambridge University Press.

Paton, W. A. (1918) 'The Significance and Treatment of Appreciation in the Accounts', 34–49 of *Twentieth Annual Report* of the Michigan Academy of Science.

Peasnell, K. V. (1977) 'A Note on the Discounted Present Value Concept', *The Accounting Review* 52: 186–9.

Sandilands Committee (1975) *Inflation Accounting: Report of the Inflation Accounting Committee*, London: HMSO Cmnd. 6225.

Schmalenbach, E. (1919) *Dynamische Bilanz*, Cologne and Opladen: Westdeutscher Verlay.

Schmidt, F. (1921) *Die Organische Bilanz in Rahmen der Wirtschaft*, Leipzig: Gloeckner.

Schmidt, F. (1927) *Die Industriekonjunktur ein Rechenfehler*, Berlin.

Schmidt, F. (1931) 'Is Appreciation Profit?', *The Accounting Review* 6: 289–93.

Solomons, D. (1948) 'Income–True and False', *The Accountants Journal*, October: 363–70.

Solomons, D. (ed.) (1952) *Studies in Costing*, London: Sweet and Maxwell.

Solomons, D. (1961) 'Economic and Accounting Concepts of Income', *The Accounting Review*, 36: 374–83.

Solomons, D. (1962) 'The Determination of Asset Values', *The Journal of Business*, January: 28–47.

Solomons, D. (1965) *Divisional Performance: Measurement and Control*, New York: Financial Executives Research Foundation.

Solomons, D. (1966a) 'Economic and Accounting Concepts of Cost and Value', in M. Backer (ed.) *Modern Accounting Theory*, Englewood Cliffs, NJ: Prentice-Hall.

Solomons, D. (1966b) Book review of Chambers (1966), *Abacus* 2: 205–9.

Solomons, D. (1971) 'Asset Valuation and Income Determination: Appraising the Alternatives' in R. R. Sterling (ed.) *Asset Valuation and Income Determination*, Lawrence, Kan.: Scholars Book Co.

Solomons, D. (1974) (with T. M. Berridge) *Prospectus for a Profession, the Report of the Long Range Enquiry into Education and Training for the Accountancy Profession*, London: Advisory Board of Accountancy Education.

Solomons, D. (1984) *Collected Papers on Accounting and Accounting Education* (2 vols), New York: Garland Press.

Solomons, D. (1986) *Making Accounting Policy: The Quest for Credibility in Financial Reporting*, New York: Oxford University Press.

Solomons, D. (1989) *Guidelines for Financial Reporting Standards*, London: ICAEW Research Board.

Solomons, D. and Silberston, A. (1952) 'Monopoly Investigation and the Rate of Return on Capital Employed', *The Economic Journal* 62: 781–801.

Study Group on Business Income (1950) *Five Monographs on Business Income*, New York: American Institute of Accountants.

Sweeney, H. W. (1936) *Stabilized Accounting*, New York: Harper and Brothers.

Sweeney, H. W. (1964) 'Forty Years After: Or Stabilized Accounting Revisited', in *Stabilized Accounting*, new edn, New York: Holt, Rinehart & Winston, pp. 17–39.

Thirlby, G. F. (1946) 'Subjective Theory of Value and Accounting Cost', *Economica* 13: 32–49.

Tweedie, D. P. and Whittington, G. (1984) *The Debate on Inflation Accounting*, Cambridge: Cambridge University Press.

Wheat Committee (1972) *Establishing Financial Accounting Standards: Report of the Study on Establishment of Accounting Principles*, New York: American Institute of Certified Public Accountants.

Whittington, G. (1975) 'Baxter on Inflation Accounting', *Accounting and Business Research* 5: 314–17.

Whittington, G. (1983) *Inflation Accounting: An Introduction to the Debate*, Cambridge: Cambridge University Press.

Wright, F. K. (1964) 'Towards a General Theory of Depreciation', *Journal of Accounting Research* 2: 80–90.

Zeff, S. A. (1979) 'Paton on the Effects of Changing Prices', in S. A. Zeff, J. Demski and N. Dopuch (eds) *Essays in Honor of William A. Paton*, Ann Arbor, Mich.: University of Michigan.

Zeff, S. A., van der Wel, F. and Camfferman, K. (1992) *Company Financial Reporting: A Historical and Comparative Study of the Dutch Regulatory Process*, Amsterdam: North Holland.

15 Edward Stamp (1928–86)

A crusader for standards

Michael J. Mumford

Abstract

Eddie Stamp was born in Liverpool, read Natural Sciences at Cambridge, and qualified in Toronto as an accountant. A naturalised Canadian, he became an academic in New Zealand, returning to Britain in 1968 to professorships at Edinburgh and then at Lancaster University, where he founded (and directed until his death in 1986) the International Centre for Research in Accounting. The only Professor of Accounting Research in Britain, he became widely known to accountants worldwide, less for the originality of his ideas than for his robust campaigns to raise standards of corporate reporting, auditing, and open administration.

EARLY LIFE

Eddie Stamp was born on 11 November 1928, the only child in a solid middle-class Liverpool home. Liverpool was a city still wealthy from its heyday as a great commercial seaport, and his father held a secure office post with Liverpool City Council. Eddie's childhood seems to have been safe if unspectacular; however, the pace quickened with his scholastic success at Quarry Bank High School, where he won an Open Scholarship to Cambridge to read Natural Sciences. This academic success shaped his destiny, but not in the most obvious direction. He wrote many years later that he had dreamed from the age of twelve of becoming a scientist; as it turned out, he became an accountant instead. He was thus a forerunner of hundreds of bright British mathematicians, scientists and engineers over the next forty years, who have turned away from a career in industry in favour of a more genteel existence in a professional accounting office.

Eddie Stamp went up to Cambridge in 1945, rather young for university entrance and in youthful contrast to the large group of ex-servicemen newly returned from the war, who were taking up places won some years earlier. They treated him well, enjoying his youthful exuberance and exciting him in turn with their mature ideas on science, learning, and the new society they hoped to see follow the devastation. In common with much of British life, Cambridge was changed by new patterns of thought and behaviour amongst this cohort of mature undergraduates, who were much less pliant than earlier and more youthful generations, less rigid in class attitudes, and less willing to defer to the authority of their dons and tutors.

This was an ideal milieu for the young Liverpool scholarship boy, whose contempt for pomposity and detestation of arrogance, whether of class or office, were to become powerful and lasting motivators throughout his life. In the classroom his work thrived. Out of class he took up rowing. St John's College was a large one, and its boat club boasted very good rowing teams. It may seem surprising that Stamp was so keen on this particular sport, in which team-work is of supreme importance. After all, his later reputation was as an iconoclast, a maverick, very much a lone campaigner; indeed, even his closest colleagues would admit that he could be thoroughly difficult. Yet he won, and held, his place in one of the college's Eights, and all his life he expressed delight in boats and the navy (particularly the Canadian Royal Naval Reserve, in which he served). One of the principal characteristics of life at sea is a high level of team-work, amongst a group of people whose membership is fixed, at least for the duration of the voyage. Strong individualist though he was, Stamp was a sociable person, an extrovert, loving company (particularly if it was disputatious).

He was duly awarded his science degree with first class honours, followed by a post-graduate fellowship, and a Fulbright Scholarship to do research in America. It seemed that the career he had chosen as a boy was now open to him; but soon after his arrival in America he decided against spending his life in science. He made enquiries about various other occupations, and decided to train as an accountant in Toronto. Clarkson, Gordon & Co. was one of the largest Canadian practices, affiliated to firms outside Canada that were later to form Arthur Young, McLelland Moores internationally (now part of Ernst & Young).

CANADA

Stamp could hardly fail to be aware that he was unusually bright – his whole career to date had underlined the fact. Now, as a trainee chartered accountant, he began to write papers and articles on the concepts of accounting. A volume of his collected works (Stamp 1984a) contains one of these, presenting an algebraic approach to double-entry bookkeeping, published in the professional journal of the Canadian Institute of Chartered Accountants in 1953 when Stamp was still a second year student in his firm. What is interesting is not so much the argument (which is sound enough, but does little to advance the subject), but the fact that within so few months of starting accountancy he believed he had new insights to offer. He has written (Stamp 1984a: xvii) of being prohibited by his firm from publishing other articles too, one on LIFO because 'it might upset one of the firm's clients who used LIFO', and one on statistical sampling because the proposals were thought to be 'in advance of their time'.

In spite of these slight set-backs to his ambition, it seemed obvious, once again, that the future offered him success and fortune, not now as the scientist he used to dream of but as a partner in what was probably Canada's leading accountancy firm. He qualified, was appointed as a manager three months later, and married a Toronto woman, Peggy Higgins, whose intelligence, charm and education suited her ideally for the future role of partner's wife. Eddie himself spent some months in the management consulting arm of the firm, and was then seconded to Gulf Oil, a major client, to work for several months in their long-range planning department. On rejoining the firm from Gulf Oil, he was moved to Montreal, where in 1961 he was made a partner.

Stamp was by this time encountering some interesting professional issues, such as the problems of applying a suitable inflation accounting treatment to the accounts of a major public utility, the Quebec Hydro-Electric Commission, which was a client. Here was an issue which interested him for many years thereafter.

It was clear that this business needed to be able to convince its public regulators to allow it to charge prices which would enable it to maintain its highly specialised assets in good condition. If it charged prices higher than this, it would be exploiting its position as a monopoly; if it charged too low a price, its services would decline and, while its existing customers might benefit, this could only be at the expense of the company's stockholders or of its customers in future years. The problem was (and still remains, in various utilities world-wide) to find a means of defining the conditions under which such highly specialised assets are indeed maintained intact, rather than declining or increasing. It must have been obvious that many of the assets used by the company were, if not unique, then very rare, so the extent to which their replacement costs were increasing or falling was not to be discerned by reference to any published price list or trade journal. Meanwhile, technical improvements were being developed which might well serve to reduce the cost of replacing plant that was either wearing out from usage or becoming technically obsolete. One task that Stamp put in train was to have the economic life of the assets of Quebec Hydro re-estimated 'on a scientific basis'.[1]

Defining and estimating what has since become known as 'productive capability' (Sandilands 1975) presented problems that few practising accountants up to that time had been forced to confront with such immediacy. Despite the research work done in America in the 1930s (for example, Sweeney 1936; Mason 1937), accountancy training for the profession made little reference to any academic literature on inflation accounting. The basic ideas were not new. For example, Limperg and Schmalenbach (each discussed elsewhere in this volume) had been developing the concepts in detail some forty years earlier in Europe, and it was possible to access their ideas in English through the major American academic journal, *The Accounting Review*. But the material was scattered widely, and the arguments were generally regarded as unorthodox, even heretical, amongst many American accounting practitioners who were used to the absolute refusal of the Securities and Exchange Commission to accept anything except historical cost figures for filed accounts.

Stamp himself was closely involved in the Quebec Hydro audit, and was able both to see and appreciate the issues; but in the absence of any guidance to the scholarly journals he had to reinvent for himself many of the concepts involved. (His personal library contained the research monographs on inflation accounting by R. C. Jones

1955 and 1956; it is not clear whether these were acquired during his time with Clarkson Gordon, or later when he was an academic in New Zealand.)

Moving Eddie Stamp to Montreal was not a happy decision on the part of his firm. He was already chafing at the restrictions of professional life, partly as a result of hearing Professor Harry Johnson demolish the economic arguments of Walter Gordon, autocratic senior partner of Clarkson Gordon, at a major policy conference of the Canadian Liberal Party. Johnson was an inspiration to Stamp, particularly for the independence of thought and expression that he clearly enjoyed. By contrast, Stamp was experiencing with rising exasperation the diplomatic inactivity of his firm, as he brought to the attention of his reluctant colleagues more and more evidence of bribery and corruption within the business and political circles of Montreal. Within 18 months of achieving partnership, Stamp resigned.

NEW ZEALAND

A new life as an academic beckoned, in a new country. New Zealand was a good choice. The academic community was quite small, but it was capable of exerting significant influence on public affairs, in particular on the nation's administration. The Victoria University of Wellington was a lively place for a new senior lecturer, who was full of ideas about accounting and about the way in which the business world should be conducted. Here it was possible to begin the crusades that were to combine Stamp's passion and intellect throughout the rest of his life. He started to develop political talents, not in party politics but in waging campaigns against what he perceived as dishonesty, apathy and the abuse of power. It became evident that he could be a difficult colleague. For example, he outraged his English-born head of department, Roy Sidebotham, by vigorously and persistently encouraging the New Zealand profession to look to America, rather than Britain, for intellectual leadership; and he greatly annoyed directors of some major New Zealand companies with his robust criticisms of their accounting disclosure practices.

One major friendship from this period in what he delighted to call 'perhaps the most beautiful and certainly the friendliest country in the world' was with Ivor Richardson, then in the Crown Law Office in Wellington. Eddie had worked with Richardson on the New Zealand government commission on taxation in 1966, and persuaded him to join the University, where Richardson played a major role until he returned to legal practice as an Appeal Court Judge (later becoming a member of the Privy Council). Richardson became Chairman of the New Zealand Inflation Accounting Committee, and mastered the technical details of the subject, writing the first draft of the report himself (Richardson 1976).[2] Stamp also came to know, and greatly admire, Ray Chambers, of the University of Sydney, and he soon became a member of the editorial board of the Australian academic accounting journal *Abacus*, which Chambers edited.

In spite of the charm and beauty of New Zealand, there was not sufficient challenge in his current occupation to absorb all Stamp's enthusiasms. When he was invited to apply for a chair in Britain, he was ready for new campaigns.

BACK TO BRITAIN: THE CAMPAIGN FOR EDUCATIONAL STANDARDS

Eddie Stamp was appointed in 1968 to be the first full-time occupant of the Chair of Accounting and Business Method at the University of Edinburgh, following a line of practitioners who had held the post on a part-time basis. Right from the start, it was clear that he would continue the campaign he had begun in New Zealand to raise professional standards, both in education and professional practice, to American levels. However, now the targets were Scotland, which prided itself greatly on the age and dignity of its own professional body, and England. It took very little time for Stamp to make an impression in Britain, even though he was unknown when he first arrived back.[3]

In June 1968 Stamp joined a number of senior British accountants, including Peter Bird and Bob Parker, in a meeting at the University of Kent to revive the moribund Association of University Teachers of Accounting. The AUTA (later to become the British Accounting Association) had been formed in the late 1940s by a small group of accounting academics based in the London School of Economics. (At the same time, an Association of University Accounting Students had been created; this had been wound up in Leeds in 1962.) Stamp's plenary address (reprinted in Stamp 1984a: A3) is forthright and highly critical:

> Please do not be deceived by my Cambridge degree or by my North Country accent. I have spent the last eighteen years in North America and Australasia, I am a Canadian citizen, and I am still using the eyes of an outsider when I look at the condition of British accountancy. Like virtually everyone else in North America or in Australasia, I have not been very impressed by what I see. British academic accountancy is moribund by comparison with its counterparts in Australasia or in the United States, and – perhaps because of this – the intellectual quality of the British profession suffers very badly in comparison with these countries, especially with America.
>
> (Stamp 1984a, A3: 1–2)

Such criticisms were documented in some detail in this and subsequent papers. Stamp laid much of the blame at the door of those who previously claimed to lead British academic accounting. He was particularly critical of those at the LSE, who, despite apparent advantages in terms of location and tradition, had seemingly failed for 30 years to make an impression on the profession. Indeed it was true that much of the intellectual impetus that had started to build up at the LSE in the 1930s had been lost. F. R. M. de Paula's chair of accounting had been taken over in 1930 by Arnold Plant as a chair of business administration; then de Paula's successor and protégé, Stanley Rowland, broke with some of the ablest scholars (such as Coase, Fowler and R. S. Edwards) and, apparently playing to a gallery of the most intransigent backwoodsmen on the Council of the English Institute, began publicly to disparage them and also the newly formed Accounting Research Association which Edwards had founded with Cosmo Gordon and Eric Hay Davison. Coase, David Solomons and Edwards subsequently left the accounting group (Coase to America, Solomons to America by way of Bristol, and Edwards to business administration). For thirty years, academic accounting in Britain survived as a small and sickly plant, a small LSE fiefdom only broken up in the late 1960s.

Accounting at the universities was given little nourishment by the accounting profession, which vetoed, for example, the 1954 McNair Report which sought to enhance accounting as a university subject and to encourage, by means of exemptions from professional examinations, those who took an approved undergraduate degree. To make matters worse, only five years after its inception, the only British academic journal in accounting, *Accounting Research*, was discontinued following the merger of the Society of Incorporated Accountants with the English Institute in 1957. (It was revived in 1970 as *Accounting and Business Research*.)

One of Stamp's particular ambitions was to see a review of education and training for accountancy established in Britain. He began to press for this in June 1968 (Stamp 1984a, A5: 5), but it was not for six years that the resulting Solomons Long-Range Enquiry appeared (Solomons 1974), and it was clear that the proposals contained in this report fell far short of Stamp's aspirations for it. If he was disillusioned, this was in part because his plans were over-ambitious. He had hoped to see, if not outright merger, then at least harmonisation of the educational policies of the six major UK professional accounting bodies.[4] He saw the current divisions as wasteful, ineffective and divisive. He thought that a common professional syllabus could be devised, with a little imagination and goodwill. As he commented in early 1972: 'I calculate that in the past four years, since I came to Britain, I have spent over 50 full days of my time attending meetings of intra-professional committees dealing with the subject' (Stamp 1984a, A5: 3). Alas, little progress was made in this area, either then or indeed in subsequent years.

Eddie had little success either in persuading the British accountancy profession to raise its entry standards, which in his view needed to be at graduate level. He also urged the profession to adopt a strong core of accounting theory within the professional examination syllabuses. Then (as now) most accountants regarded accountancy as a set of techniques to be learned, rather than a discipline with a body of theory of its own that requires to be understood. Until they began to appreciate the theoretical principles involved, argued Stamp, British accountants would never begin to reform accounting practice so that it would keep pace with the changing demands of business life, let alone take a part in leading new thinking internationally.

Finding it impossible in Edinburgh to raise the resources he regarded as necessary to expand his department, Eddie Stamp was glad to accept in 1971 another invitation to move, this time to the new University of Lancaster, to join his friend John Perrin who had founded Lancaster's Department of Accounting and Finance in 1968. (Perrin's Chair was widely rumoured, when it was first created, to be open only to applicants who were *not* members of any of the British accountancy bodies – so low were held the academic credentials of British accountants at the time.)

Stamp's move was associated with the creation of the International Centre for Research in Accounting (ICRA). The main purpose of this was to create a research institute that would both be, and be seen to be, entirely independent in its goals, policies and conduct. To appreciate the significance of this, it is valuable not only to recall Stamp's earlier brushes with authority in Canada and New Zealand, but also to note his second major campaign on arrival in Britain, which was designed to raise the quality of published accounts by a programme of accounting standards.

THE CAMPAIGN FOR ACCOUNTING STANDARDS IN BRITAIN

The opening blast of this campaign took the form of a letter in *The Times* Business News on 11 September 1969. This was followed by a response on 22 September from Mr R. G. Leach (then President of the Institute of Chartered Accountants in England and Wales, later Sir Ronald Leach). A rejoinder from Stamp appeared on 26 September. (These are all reprinted in Stamp 1984a, G3.) Stamp accused the British accounting profession of lax standards of theory, principles, training and practice. His forthright arguments were received with more sympathy than he had dared to expect.

Public opinion had already been stirred up by two well-publicised events. The first was the withdrawal, by the American company Leasco, of a takeover bid for Robert Maxwell's Pergamon Group, following discovery by the bidder that much of the value of inventories had been seriously overstated. The second was the disclosure, following the takeover of AEI by GEC, that a forecast by the victim company (published in response to the bid and ten months into its financial year) of profits of £10 million for the year was replaced just a few weeks later (after the takeover) by a reported loss of £4.5 million for the same period. Public opinion was shocked, and accountants were exposed to ridicule. Stamp happened to be the right person in the right place to translate public concern into action.

Nevertheless, as Stamp was later to acknowledge:

> the really remarkable feature of the exchanges between Ronnie Leach and myself in late 1969 was the fact that he paid any attention to me at all . . . it was the first time that an academic had ever had any serious attention paid by the Establishment to his criticisms.
>
> (Leach and Stamp 1981: 236; also in Stamp 1984a, G6)

Within a few months of the exchange of letters with Leach, Stamp published a book, written jointly with Christopher Marley, financial editor of *The Times*, detailing the need for reform of the regulatory mechanisms of the City of London (Stamp and Marley 1970). This book was detailed, knowledgeable and persuasive. It was also highly influential in stimulating the creation of the Accounting Standards Steering Committee (ASSC, later renamed the Accounting Standards Committee, ASC). Nevertheless, some important elements of the English Institute's 'Statement of Intent' which heralded the ASSC were not pursued. In particular, there was little sign of the theoretical framework being developed that the Statement promised, and that Stamp argued was necessary to support the weight of accounting standards. He was himself to spend much of the rest of his life working on such frameworks, first specifically on inflation accounting and then on the development of a general conceptual framework for financial reporting, although it has to be said that he never completed a theoretical framework of his own. However, his attention was more urgently taken up just at that time with the problems of accounting for inflation.

ACCOUNTING AND INFLATION

The late 1960s saw the revival of general price inflation. This was intensified greatly after 1971 by the rise in oil prices generated by the producers' cartel, the Organisation of Petroleum Exporting Countries, (OPEC).

Inflation was not widely regarded as inevitable up to this time, or indeed even as typical. In the decades since the middle of the nineteenth century, prices had fallen in nearly as many years as they had risen. There was reason to suppose that the general price level tended to rise and fall in cycles, in association with the trade cycle. The major cause of rising prices was war, mainly conducted between the larger European powers. The period of inflation between 1900 and 1920 had seen pressure for new inflation accounting techniques to deal with financial reporting, management accounting, and taxation. These pressures were renewed when price rises became conspicuous again in the 1940s. In each of these periods, wartime administrative arrangements were devised to address the special requirements of military procurement, massive demands for labour and transportation, and the economic dislocation that ensued. By contrast, falling prices in the 1920s and 1930s, and stable prices in the 1950s gave rise to pressures to dismantle state regulatory machinery and return to 'market forces'.

By the time inflation resumed in the late 1960s, there was a substantial literature (in several languages), addressing the distinctions between general and specific price rises, real and monetary returns on capital employed, and the need to distinguish between operating results arising from productive activities and the consequences of rises in the general level of prices.

By 1970, Eddie Stamp had been an academic for nearly ten years, during which time he had read and thought a great deal about inflation accounting, even though during the 1950s and 1960s rates of price inflation had been relatively low (less than 3 per cent a year most of the time, and virtually static at some stages). As it happened, the year of his return to Britain was also the year in which a booklet on inflation accounting was published by the English Institute at the instance of Sir Edmund Parker (ICAEW 1968), explaining how the method of general price level accounting worked.[5] This method had been developed in America, and publicised in particular by a 1963 book from the American Institute of Certified Public Accountants (AICPA). The technique became known in Britain as CPP accounting, the letters sometimes referring to 'Current Purchasing Power' and sometimes to 'Constant Purchasing Power' (although Whittington 1983: 73 points out that the former is really only a subset of the latter, which is really the appropriate use of the initials CPP).

The literature on inflation accounting tends to divide into two groups. There are those studies which are principally concerned with maintaining the capital of the business entity before profits are calculated for taxation, distribution or retention (the 'entity' view). Then there are those which are designed mainly to show proprietary shareholders whether their investments are producing a return which keeps pace with the general price level (the 'proprietary' view).

Entity systems, usually based on the replacement costs of the specific assets used by the firm, have tended to be supported by the management of the companies, including their salaried engineers and those accountants who identify with the interests of the entity. CPP systems have tended to be favoured by those taking a proprietary view, whether as investors or as auditors who see themselves as agents for the shareholders. It is, of course, possible to reconcile the two viewpoints, and in fact the hybrid system of Current Cost Accounting, or CCA, which developed in Britain during the 1970s sought to report separately on the operating profits of the entity and on the real return to share investors.

Stamp's position in this debate was interesting. Since he had trained as an auditor, it might have been expected that he would take the proprietary viewpoint of the shareholders, favouring a relatively objective and verifiable set of procedures by which to restate the historical cost accounts in current purchasing power units at the year end. In fact, perhaps as a result of his experiences with Quebec Hydro, he saw matters from an entity perspective.

From 1970 onwards he began to advocate the CCA system of inflation accounting, already set out by R. H. Parker (in his 'Introduction' to Parker and Harcourt 1969), which drew upon what Stamp saw as best both in the replacement cost system and in the CPP alternative. In a 1971 paper for the Scottish Institute (Stamp 1971), he argued from first principles in favour of the CCA system, based on what he termed 'Value to the Firm'. While being fully aware of the CPP system as set out in AICPA (1963) and ICAEW (1968), he rejected the CPP concept as being 'not enough':[6]

> general price-level adjustments will not result in balance sheet values being expressed in terms either of current replacement cost, or net realisable values. Nor will they ensure that the 'costs' being matched in the income statement are in any sense a representation of the current cost of obtaining the equivalent inputs of goods or services.
>
> (Stamp 1971: 284)

On the other hand, 'pure' replacement cost (RC) would not do either. It would be excessive in those cases where assets would not be replaced at current prices. We might describe these as being 'obsolete', whether as current assets (having a net realisable value above their economic value) or as fixed assets if their value in use were higher than their resale value. Stamp argued that RC would usually be the appropriate value to use in the accounts, except for what we call obsolete assets, when the higher of net realisable value (NRV) and economic value (EV) would be the relevant value instead. Stamp later came to modify his valuation rule, on the grounds that 'there are insuperable problems in determining objective and verifiable measures of economic value'; he then recommended using just the lower of RC and NRV (Stamp 1979: 169).

His views on income measurement differed from those of Edwards and Bell (1961), in that he specifically excluded from income the 'holding gains' that arise from revaluing assets as their current replacement costs increase. All in all, he presented a case that was much more sympathetic to the business entity (since it would retain productive capital intact) than to the investor (whose purchasing power might or might not be maintained). The arguments were not new: they had been discussed at length in Australia, for example, during the 1960s whilst Stamp was still in New Zealand, and he knew several of the protagonists well. Nevertheless, his views were sought and valued when the Australian and New Zealand professions were debating new standards on inflation during the 1970s (e.g. in the preparation of the Richardson Report, 1976). He was to become a prominent advocate of CCA in Britain.

Stamp's advocacy of CCA became all the more significant with his appointment to the Accounting Standards Steering Committee's working party which produced *The Corporate Report* in August 1975 (ASSC 1975). Stamp (aided by Ken Peasnell, whose Ph.D. was now completed under Stamp's supervision) was the academic consultant to the project, and he undertook a major part of the drafting of the report. Following the lead of the American 'Trueblood Report' (Study Group on the Objectives of Financial Statements, 1973), *The Corporate Report* took the definition of 'user needs' as its starting point, and it was primarily addressed to the question of identifying the purposes of the published reports of business entities. Corporate reports should be required not only of companies, friendly societies, banks and so on (all of which were already compelled to publish accounts), but of charities and large partnerships (such as the large auditing firms) as well.

Indeed, *The Corporate Report* addressed the need for public disclosure of far more than just the familiar accounting statements; it sought an employment report and statements of corporate objectives and future prospects as well as financial data. It also made a strong call for the use of CCA to prepare the accounts, even though valuation issues were little discussed in the body of the report.

It was a matter of some gratification to Stamp to discover that the government's own Committee on Inflation Accounting, the 'Sandilands Committee' (after its chairman, F. E. P. Sandilands), came in September 1975 to recommend the CCA system which he preferred, rather than the CPP system that the British accounting profession had only just adopted in Statement of Standard Accounting Practice No. 7 (ASSC 1974). The UK profession hastily modified its stance on the matter, and set up a series of committees to work out an acceptable Statement of Standard Accounting Practice based upon CCA principles. However, repeated disagreements and compromises led to a confused set of proposals (which met with only half-hearted support), and the resulting *Statement* was both complex and muddled. The whole history has been described in detail by Whittington (1983). Stamp found these developments exasperating, but he was not personally involved in the processes of the ASC, and meanwhile had plenty of other work to do.

CONCEPTUAL FRAMEWORKS

Stamp's work on *The Corporate Report* has been referred to in the previous section. This represented one aspect of his wider interests in the ways that business entities should be run, his main concern being to ensure that affairs were conducted in as open and democratic a manner as possible. He tended to draw upon a body of theory that was eclectic and complex rather than based upon one single paradigm; he was not convinced, for example, that economic competitive equilibrium analysis was very helpful in analysing the problems of financial reporting, any more than he relied upon any other single theoretical tradition. This was not due to lack of understanding on his part; his library was full of books on scientific method, in the social sciences as well as the so-called 'hard' sciences, and these books were heavily annotated in his handwriting. He read widely in economics and politics, sociology and history, and he had a particular interest in law and jurisprudence.

In the years immediately before his sudden death in 1986, he spent several months interviewing legal scholars, reading the philosophy of law, and preparing the first stages of a book on the jurisprudence of accounting. The 1980 study he wrote in Canada (see below) offers hints of the direction his thoughts were taking; indeed, it is even possible to guess from this that he was beginning to see accounting theory as driven less by a single model than by a series of procedures or processes, in which the informed judgement of experienced accountants and auditors would be drawn upon to create a form of precedent akin to case law. Unfortunately, the work was not sufficiently advanced for it to be taken over by his successors, even though he had discussed his ideas at some length with his son Philip, a research physicist who has since written about the distinctions between the philosophy of physics and that of the social sciences (Stamp 1993).

In 1980 Eddie Stamp spent several months in Canada, preparing and writing his study *Corporate Reporting: Its Future Evolution* (Stamp 1980). The background to this work was detailed in an article he wrote for *Accounting, Organisations and Society* (Stamp 1985). There he describes, with clear traces of residual anger, how the Canadian Institute of Chartered Accountants (CICA) asked him in Spring 1979 to help them out of a difficult position by writing for them a study of corporate reporting, in place of a study of their own that had foundered. Having done so, after working full-time over several months and forgoing any payment, Stamp was incensed to find that his name as author had been removed after he had left the final typescript with CICA's Research Department.

Evidently as a result of this, he was motivated to write the 1985 paper, 'The Politics of Professional Accounting Research'. Stamp was in an exceptionally good position to write such a paper. He had been involved in some measure with professional research for twenty years, in several countries. Apart from his unofficial work on the Richardson Report in New Zealand, he was one of the main authors of *The Corporate Report* in Britain and now the sole author of the Canadian equivalent. He was a close friend of several of the most experienced and highly regarded American researchers, such as Maurice Moonitz (who spent a year at Lancaster at his invitation, and with whom he wrote a study of the need for international auditing standards in 1979), and Steve Zeff (who has documented with great thoroughness and insight the history of standard setting in half a dozen countries). He had also served on technical committees of the Institute of Chartered Accountants of Scotland, as well as the research board of the Institute of Chartered Accountants in England and Wales. Moreover, he was the only person from outside North America to serve on the Council of Accounting Research Directors, which brings together a high-powered group of those responsible for research in most of the most productive and prestigious professional accounting bodies. In short, Stamp was viewed just as highly by those within the profession as he was by his academic peers.

Stamp used the article to put on record his experiences in conducting research in a number of different contexts:

> I have been involved in institutional research with a number of organisations. These involvements include membership of the Board of Research and Publications of the New Zealand professional body from 1964–1967; membership of a Commission set up by the New Zealand government to reform the country's tax system in 1966; membership of the Steering Committee that supervised the production and publication of the long-range enquiry into education and training for the accountancy profession in Britain (the Solomons Report) in the years 1971–1974; membership of the British Accounting Standards Committee's Working Party that produced *The Corporate Report* in 1974–1975; and the sole responsibility for the writing of the Canadian Institute of Chartered Accountants' Research Study entitled *Corporate Reporting: Its Future Evolution*, published in 1980. I have also been a member of the Research Board of the English Institute of Chartered Accountants since its formation in 1982; and I have had various opportunities to observe and comment upon the research activities of the American Institute of CPAs and of the Financial Accounting Standards Board.
>
> (Stamp 1985: 112)

Of course, these activities are purely those which brought him into touch with professional bodies and their research activities; the list excludes Stamp's work elsewhere, for example as an academic writer and member of editorial boards, as accounting adviser to the Treasury in Britain from 1971 until his resignation in 1976, as an expert witness in legal cases, and as a joint author of the report for Britain's National Coal Board on the uses of accounting data to justify pit closures (Custis *et al.* 1985).

Stamp's work on conceptual frameworks started from the proposition that large organisations owed a range of responsibilities to external parties far wider than conventional wisdom would suggest. It was generally alleged by the Establishment that companies existed for the benefit of their shareholders alone, with management acting merely as agents on behalf of these 'principals'. The Corporate Report Working Party could see that this model was outmoded. It came to view corporate enterprises instead as alliances of many different interests, co-ordinated to pursue certain common goals. Each of the parties made a different form of commitment, whether as employees, suppliers, bankers or shareholders; but each was entitled to receive information relevant to their interests in the enterprise. While a somewhat similar list of user groups had recently appeared in the Trueblood Report (Study Group on the Objectives of Financial Statements 1973), Trueblood tended to stress the similarities amongst user needs (for information on future entity cash flows) rather than their variety, and Stamp was himself critical of certain shortcomings in that Report – particularly its lack of illustrations and its reluctance to advocate the use of current values (Stamp 1984a, F1).

It is clear, with the advantage of hindsight, that *The Corporate Report* was a radical document, one that was probably more radical than many of the members of the Working Party suspected they would produce when they began work. In particular, the idea was to some people quite shocking that business organisations owed a duty to report to such a broad list of user groups as was set out there: government as well as share investors, the 'business contact group' as well as loan creditors, the public at large as well as employees. Moreover, extending the list beyond just the proprietary shareholders made it all the more difficult to find a general purpose system of financial reporting that would meet all user needs at once. And the more heterogeneous the group, the greater the likelihood of conflicts of interest.

By 1980, the list of user groups which Stamp had come to regard as having a right to information had become even longer. In the CICA study he listed fifteen groups: shareholders, long-term creditors, short-term creditors, analysts and advisers, employees, non-executive directors, customers, suppliers, industry groups, labour unions, government departments and ministers, the public, regulatory agencies, other companies, and an amorphous group comprising standard-setters and academic researchers (Stamp 1980: 44). Within these groups themselves there were even finer distinctions; for example, 'the public' could be divided into four sub-groups: political parties, public affairs groups, consumer groups and environmental groups. The task of satisfying all concerned parties seemed to be getting even more difficult.

In fact, in this matter as in most others, Eddie Stamp was able to explain in detail how to put his recommendations into practical effect. There was, perhaps, no single set of numbers which would achieve the complete set of goals, but multiple statements (if necessary, using more than one valuation method) would provide what was needed. Where there was a need for judgement over the extent of disclosure, he preferred to err on the side of openness rather than secrecy. But this meant that it was impractical to identify a complete range of decision needs, together with decision models, exact information requirements and a means of resolving trade-offs where conflicts arose. Some more robust way was needed to evaluate reporting rules.

Stamp believed that standard-setting could be aided by establishing a set of the desirable qualitative characteristics needed of financial reports. It might in principle be possible to count up, say, the number of trade creditors who relied on published accounts in the course of setting their credit limits. But if all the members of this group required a similar estimate of the net realisable values of the firm's assets, then their common need could be met by showing the current market selling prices of the assets in a separate column in the balance sheet. There was still, however, a need to decide how much precision was required for this purpose. This would mean trading off the costs and benefits of this particular part of the reporting process, as against using the more general data (based on historic or on current costs) which was already supplied for other purposes and hence would be a 'free good' for the purpose of trade creditors.

The use of qualitative characteristics seems to mark the 'decision usefulness' school of accounting theorists, of whom Stamp was a prominent member. He took the ideas a long way towards their logical conclusion, showing in his later writing (for example, Stamp 1981) how it would be possible to survey the strength of consensus amongst standard-setters over a set of such characteristics. There may perhaps be doubts over how far the approach will prove effective in the long term,[7] but this was an imaginative and sustained programme aimed at improving the processes of standard-setting.

The 1980 CICA paper did not merely explain the role that qualitative charac- teristics were thought to offer in the setting of standards. It also set out in detail Stamp's ideas on corporate reporting in developed economies. For example, he was able to expand his ideas on the relationship between standard-setting and the 'Accounting Court', which he had suggested some years earlier as a way of establishing a set of precedents on public record. Stamp was also convinced of the need for a conceptual framework to support accounting standards. As he wrote in the preface to the volume of his collected works in 1984:

> Most of my current thinking is directed towards these matters, and in an attempt to develop my ideas on the subject I have been led to do much reading in the fields of philosophy, law, science, and history. I am particularly grateful to Geoff Whittington and David Tweedie (who has been an Honorary Professor at ICRA for the last several years), and to Renford Bambrough, for the strong support and encouragement they have been giving me in this latest venture. All of my academic work in the last twenty years has been an attempt to marry theory to practice. The only reservations I have about the work I am doing now (and it is the most interesting work that I think I have ever done) is the danger inherent in the nature of the subject – that it will carry me too far away from the problems of the real world.
>
> (Stamp 1984a, xxv)

There is little doubt that he had a major contribution still to make at the time of his premature death in 1986.

PRIVATE BATTLES AND PUBLIC CAUSES

Earlier in this chapter, reference was made to 'the crusades that were to combine Stamp's passion and intellect throughout the rest of his life'. Some of these were matters of public interest, issues that he pursued because they served the broader goals of fair, efficient and open government. Some were private battles, often with intransigent authorities, often on behalf of friends. He enjoyed such campaigns, and was generally very good at running them. Sometimes his enthusiasms would carry him away and he would upset his adversaries inordinately. Often his campaigns would prevail, whether to secure redress for faulty goods he had bought himself, or to obtain promotion for a member of staff of the university who had been passed over, or to expose some piece of humbug or pomposity by a letter to the press.

AN ASSESSMENT

Although Eddie Stamp was impatient with the Establishment and with those who offered it their uncritical support, he was himself a man of some power and influence. He enjoyed his membership of the Reform Club, and later of the Oxford and Cambridge Club. He refused offers to return to major auditing firms that would have made him wealthy, but he was not by any standards a poor man, even as an academic. He enjoyed his luxuries – good wines, cigars, good hotels.

One of the highlights of his career was the trip he made to Canada in October 1984 to receive the honorary degree of Doctor of Laws from the University of Saskatechewan. He flew out on Concorde, and returned by sea on the *Queen Elizabeth II*. The address which he delivered to the convocation of the university on that occasion has been reprinted (Stamp 1984b); it remains a stirring reminder of the principal values of scholarship:

> In my view the most fundamental and absolute commitment of a University is its intellectual and moral dedication to the free and independent search for truth. It pursues this, its preeminent purpose, through research and teaching, and society may often be discomforted by the results. The pursuit of truth is frequently inconvenient to established authority, but a University that shrinks from its duty on that account is unworthy of the name.
>
> (Stamp 1984b: 111)

The fact that truth might be inconvenient to 'the Establishment', of course, was a matter of no regret to him. Indeed, he had earlier expressed himself forcefully on the subject:

> Generally speaking, I have little time for the Establishment, especially in Britain. All too often it seems to represent the very antithesis of leadership, and is composed of men (and occasionally women) who are smug, complacent, secretive, humourless, self-satisfied, out of date, backwards-looking, and concerned largely with protecting the vested interests that promoted them into the Establishment in the first place. In a word (and it is one that has a delightful capacity to enrage the backwoodsmen as well as the squirearchy of the profession) it is all too often composed of dinosaurs.
>
> (Stamp in Leach and Stamp 1981: 233–4)

Stamp used to describe his only hobby in successive issues of *Who's Who* as 'tormenting dinosaurs'.

It was not only the abuses of power which angered him. He was similarly scathing about academic papers that were full of clever methods, statistical or otherwise, unless they addressed a question that was of interest in its own right. He had a love for mathematics, but as a tool, rather than an end in itself. His fascination with scientific method, praxis, and epistemology always stopped short of inquisitiveness for its own sake: there had to be some useful purpose to the endeavours. This usually involved a clear social objective. He often mused what his life would have been like if he had gone into the police force: he liked the idea of being a detective. While this may be a common enough fantasy, the nature of the motivation is significant. He would have liked to apprehend villains. He would, no doubt, have been a formidable interrogator.

He was driven by a passion for getting things done. There was always a need for persistent and incisive questioning to prevent accounting standards from slipping back into the control of a cosy club, run by an oligarchy of rich and powerful partners in the big firms, in alliance with their major clients.

Stamp's inaugural lecture in Wellington, New Zealand included a significant passage:

> We might well recall the story, attributed to Arnold Toynbee, and told by a frustrated former Vice-Chancellor of the University of Adelaide (a most conservative institution in those days), of the trawler skipper whose herrings remained fresh after long days at sea whilst other trawlers landed fish as jaded as a fish can be. Asked for a solution to the puzzle the skipper said, 'For every thousand herrings in the tank I put in a catfish. He may eat a few, but he keeps the others alive.'
>
> (Stamp 1984a, B1: 22)

During his time at Lancaster, Eddie was frequently in close touch with his many friends in professional practice, in Britain and also in Canada and America. Four times he was invited to take up partnerships in different major international firms, each time on terms which would virtually have allowed him to name his own conditions. He found it flattering to receive such expressions of confidence. He spent a lot of time and thought considering these invitations, and discussing them with close friends. In the event, what persuaded him overwhelmingly to remain in academic life was his need for independence, of thought and expression, an independence he had seen demonstrated so vividly by Harry Johnson so many years earlier (Stamp 1984a: xxiv).

As a contributor to twentieth-century accounting theory, Stamp's position is rather curious. He probably did more than any other academic in Britain to change professional life and to raise the level of contribution that university teachers have come to make to the practice and administration of British accountancy. The fact that accountancy is still far from being a learned profession is certainly not his fault. Yet his contribution was not really as a theorist. Certainly, he was full of ideas, and as a critic he was able to refine and sharpen the views of others. He was impelled not so much by theoretical precepts as by strongly-held moral principles. Moreover, he would demonstrate in detail how those principles could be made to work effectively in practice. He was, in particular, passionately committed to making power open and accountable. However, such a sense of commitment operates at a level more profound than theory. While theoretical propositions often appeared in his work, they were as means to an end and not as ends in themselves.

Given the condition of accounting theory at the time he was becoming interested in it, it was probably inevitable that Stamp should belong to the 'decision usefulness' school, and he was particularly interested in extending the use of abstract qualitative characteristics as a guide to setting accounting standards (Mumford 1993: 26–7). But such an interpretation of his work fails to convey the breadth of his reading, the holist nature of his views, and the impatience with which he regarded bits of analysis that might be clever – even elegant – but which failed to get to the real point. This was always to make improvements in practical business affairs.

The number of professors of accounting in Britain who have been partners in major firms is very small. Once they have attained the level of income and standard of living that partnership in a major firm offers, there are few people who would accept the lower salary of a university professor. Even rarer are those who, having made such a break with public practice, are made welcome to return back. The most significant features of Eddie Stamp's life as a scholar and writer have been outlined in this chapter. Here was a rare academic indeed: one whose theoretical precepts were usually derived rather than original, and yet whose views were valued as highly throughout the world by financial journalists as by industrialists, by professional accountants as amongst dons.

Notes

1 The source is a set of draft working papers from this time, which were amongst Stamp's personal effects. It is, unfortunately, not clear what was meant by 'a scientific basis'.
2 I am indebted to Don Trow, a colleague of both Stamp and Richardson at the Victoria University, for this information. I had supposed that Richardson left the technical drafting of this Report to the Committee secretariate but this was evidently not so. The New Zealand Report is probably still the best study of inflation accounting. Although Eddie Stamp was now based in Britain, he corresponded with Richardson on the Report, and submitted formal evidence.
3 I recall the frisson of excitement which went round the room at a seminar at the University of Leeds in mid-1968 when Trevor Gambling rebuked Eddie Stamp for interrupting his talk: 'just a minute, laddie,' chided Gambling, 'I'll come back to you'. We expected an uproar, but Eddie just smiled and waited equably.
4 An attempt in 1970 to merge the six major professional accounting bodies in Britain failed.
5 Parker was the senior partner of Price Waterhouse in Britain; several key partners of Price Waterhouse in America had strongly supported 'general price-level accounting' ever since 1940.
6 The term CPP was not in fact yet in common usage.

7 For a critique of Stamp's research programme for using qualitative characteristics, see
   Mumford (1993).

References

Accounting Standards Steering Committee (ASSC) (1974) *(Provisional) Statement of
    Standard Accounting Practice No. 7* 'Accounting for Changes in the Purchasing Power
    of Money', London: Accounting Standards Steering Committee.

Accounting Standards Steering Committee (ASSC) (1975) *The Corporate Report*,
    London: Accounting Standards Steering Committee (shortly before it became the
    Accounting Standards Committee).

American Institute of Certified Public Accountants (AICPA) (1963) *Reporting the Finan-
    cial Effects of Price-Level Changes* (Accounting Research Study No. 6), New York:
    Accounting Research Division of the American Institute of Certified Public
    Accountants.

Baxter, W. T. (1975) *Accounting Values and Inflation*, London: McGraw Hill.

Custis, P. J., Morpeth, Sir Douglas, Stamp, E. and Tweedie, D. P. (1985) *Report of an
    Independent Committee of Enquiry on Certain Accounting Matters relating to the
    Affairs of the National Coal Board*, London: National Coal Board.

Edwards, E. O. and Bell, P. W. (1961) *The Theory and Measurement of Business Income*,
    Berkeley, Calif.: University of California Press.

Institute of Chartered Accountants in England and Wales (ICAEW) (1968) *Accounting for
    Stewardship in a Period of Inflation*, London: The Research Foundation of the Institute
    of Chartered Accountants in England and Wales.

Jones, R. C. (1955) *Price Level Changes and Financial Statements: Case Studies of Four
    Companies*, New York: American Accounting Association.

Jones, R. C. (1956) *Effects of Price Level Changes on Business Income, Capital and
    Taxes*, New York: American Accounting Association.

Leach, R. and Stamp, E. (1981) *British Accounting Standards: the First Ten Years*,
    Cambridge: Woodhead Faulkner.

Mason, P. E. (1937) *Principles of Public-Utility Depreciation* (Monograph No. 2), New
    York: American Accounting Association.

Mumford, M. J. (ed.) (1988) *Edward Stamp: Later Papers*, New York: Garland.

Mumford, M. J. (1993) 'Users, characteristics and standards' in M. J. Mumford and K. V.
    Peasnell (eds) *Philosophical Perspectives on Accounting*: 7–29.

Mumford, M. J. and Peasnell, K. V. (eds) (1993) *Philosophical Perspectives on Account-
    ing: Essays in Honour of Edward Stamp*, London: Routledge.

Parker, R. H. and Harcourt, G. C. (1969) *Readings in the Concept and Measurement of
    Income*, Cambridge, Cambridge University Press.

Richardson (Report) (1976) *Report of the Committee of Inquiry into Inflation Accounting*
    (the 'Richardson Committee'), Wellington NZ: Government Printer H. 4.

Sandilands, F. E. P. (1975) *Report of the Inflation Accounting Committee* (the 'Sandilands
    Committee'), London: HMSO Cmnd 6225.

Stamp, E. (1971) 'Income and Value Determination and Changing Price-levels: an Essay
    towards a theory', *The Accountant's Magazine*, June: 277–92.

Stamp, E. (1979) 'Financial Reports on an Entity: ex Uno Plures' (Chapter 8 in) R. R.
    Sterling and A. L. Thomas (eds) *Accounting for a Simplified Firm Owning Depre-
    ciable Assets*, Houston: Scholars Book Co. 163–80.

Stamp, E. (1980) *Corporate Reporting: its Future Evolution*, Toronto: CICA.

Stamp, E. (1981) 'Accounting standards and the conceptual framework: a plan for their
    evolution', *The Accountant's Magazine*, July: 216–22.

Stamp, E. (1984a) *Selected Papers on Accounting, Auditing and Professional Problems*,
    New York: Garland.

Stamp, E. (1984b) *Convocation Address to the University of Saskatechewan, 27 October 1984*, in M. J. Mumford (ed.) (1988) *Edward Stamp: Later Papers*, New York: Garland: 109–15.

Stamp, E. (1985) 'The Politics of Professional Accounting Research: some Personal Reflections', *Accounting, Organisations and Society* 10(1): 111–25.

Stamp, E. and Marley, C. (1970) *Accounting Principles and the City Code: the Case for Reform*, London: Butterworths.

Stamp, E. and Moonitz, M. (1978) *International Auditing Standards*, London, Prentice Hall.

Stamp, P. (1993) 'In search of Reality', in M. J. Mumford and K. V. Peasnell (eds) *Philosophical Perspectives on Accounting*: 255–314.

Study Group on the Objectives of Financial Statements (1973) *Objectives of Financial Statements* (the 'Trueblood Report', after the chairman of the Study Group, Robert Trueblood), New York, American Institute of Certified Public Accountants.

Sweeney, H. W. (1936) *Stabilized Accounting*, New York: Harper.

Whittington, G. (1983) *Inflation Accounting: an Introduction to the Debate*, Cambridge: Cambridge University Press.

16 Henry Rand Hatfield (1866–1945)

'Life and humor in the dust of ledgers'

Patti A. Mills

Abstract

Henry Rand Hatfield was one of the progenitors of modern academic accounting. Born in 1866, he had a long and distinguished academic career and was the first full-time Professor of Accounting in the US. Hatfield is remembered mainly as an author and critic. His major work, *Modern Accounting: Its Principles and Some of Its Problems*, was one of the first US contributions to the modern accounting literature. The chief concerns of Hatfield's writings were the balance sheet and asset valuation, making his work of great interest today. Hatfield was also a founder of the American Accounting Association, but came to oppose other key members on several issues, most importantly the Association's emphasis on research.

INTRODUCTION

In 1940 Henry Rand Hatfield, one of the progenitors of modern academic accounting, received an honorary Doctor of Laws degree from the University of California, seventeen years after Northwestern University had conferred upon him the same distinction. In making the presentation, President Sproul described Hatfield as a 'constant champion of the logical approach, the sane view, and the clear disclosure of the essential facts of goods and proprietorship; discoverer of scientific principles and sound philosophy in a field obscured by dogma and convention; one able to find life and even humor in the dust of ledgers' (Broad 1951: 85). Other associates largely agreed, referring at various times to the sanity of Hatfield's judgements (Cole 1909: 648), his 'keen knowledge of accounts' (Montgomery 1927: 189), his 'clarity of thought' and 'concise and vigorous style,' and finally, to his mastery of 'witty and effective satire' (Broad 1951: 85–6). While lionised mainly as author and critic, Hatfield was also known as an inspired teacher and for his critical role as a founder of the first Association of University Instructors in Accounting, later the American Accounting Association. He was elected to the Accounting Hall of Fame in 1951 (Burns and Coffman 1991: 40–1).

The man who would earn this high regard was born on 27 November 1866, in Chicago, Illinois.[1] His parents were Elizabeth Ann (Taft) and Revd Robert

M. Hatfield. He graduated from Northwestern University in 1892 with a bachelor's degree and from the University of Chicago in 1897 with a Ph.D. in political economy and political science. Apart from a few years in the municipal bond business, Hatfield made his career in academe. He began in 1894 as an instructor of political economy at Washington University, moving to the University of Chicago in 1898. There, he spent four years as an instructor, then became assistant professor and the first dean of the College of Commerce and Administration from 1902 to 1904. Hatfield never practised accounting, nor was he a certified public accountant. Nevertheless, he offered a course in Accounting while at Chicago, inspired in part by a tour of colleges of commerce in France and Germany which he had undertaken in 1899. Hatfield knew both German and French. (His abilities in this area probably contributed to his later appointment as US representative to the International Congress on Commercial Education held in Amsterdam in 1929.)

In 1904 Hatfield moved to the University of California, where he remained until his death in 1945. There, in addition to his tenure as Associate Professor, Professor, and Professor Emeritus of Accounting, he served for several years as Dean of the College of Commerce and Dean of Faculties. At Berkeley, he also devoted himself to expanding the library's accounting holdings, which became one of the premier accounting collections in the US.

During the war years, Hatfield was active in public service, as president of the Berkeley Commission of Charities from 1914 to 1918, director of the division of planning and statistics, War Industries Board, in 1918, and as an expert with the Advisory Tax Board. (In 1942, Hatfield would again answer the call and become a member of the Berkeley War Appeals Board.) His other memberships included the Beta Theta Pi and Phi Beta Kappa fraternities, and the American Economic Association, which he served as Vice-President in 1918. Hatfield also made important contributions to the American Accounting Association over many years.

HATFIELD AND THE AMERICAN ACCOUNTING ASSOCIATION

Hatfield was a founding member of the American Accounting Association, called in its early years the American Association of University Instructors in Accounting. He attended the group's organisational meeting held on 28 December 1916, in Columbus, Ohio, and sat on the committee which drafted the Association's constitution. The first year, Hatfield served as a Vice-President and in 1919 as Association President. Fourteen years later he would be one of the Association's delegates to the Fourth International Congress on Accounting, which met in London. Probably Hatfield's most critical service on behalf of the fledgling organisation was the address 'An Historical Defense of Bookkeeping', which he delivered at the 1923 annual meeting. According to Zeff (1966a: 19–22), Hatfield's 'witty and pungent defense of accounting's role in society' galvanised the membership, many of whom felt inferior to university colleagues in more established disciplines. At the time, many universities were just beginning to recognise accounting as a legitimate area of collegiate study. Indeed,

Hatfield himself was the first full-time Professor of Accounting in the US. 'An Historical Defense', which was published in the April 1924 issue of the *Journal of Accountancy* and reprinted both in Baxter and Davidson's *Studies in Accounting Theory* (1962) and Moonitz and Littleton's *Significant Accounting Essays* (1965), would become Hatfield's most famous work. Its presentation at the 1923 meeting helped to bolster confidence in the new organisation.

Although an influential figure in the Association, Hatfield found himself at odds with other key members at several critical junctures in its early history. First, he voted against publication of a quarterly journal of accounting instruction, the first issue of which was slated to appear in October 1919. Although the idea of a journal was supported by other members of the executive committee, Hatfield wanted the Association to join with the American Institute of Accountants (AIA) in publishing the *Journal of Accountancy*. Hatfield felt that it made better sense to pool a limited amount of resources and produce one worthy periodical than to divide the profession's efforts. Apparently, other members were persuaded, because the proposed October issue failed to materialise. The first instalment of *The Accounting Review* eventually appeared in 1926 (Zeff 1966a: 6–7, 9, 11–12, 15–18).

Hatfield also opposed changes in the membership and orientation of the Association, which were introduced in the mid-1930s. At about this time, Paton and other members moved to rename the organization the American Accounting Association (AAA). They hoped that the new title would broaden the constituency of the Association and also signal a new emphasis on research. Zeff relates that Hatfield took issue with these reforms, fearing that the association would abandon its focus on accounting education. For the same reason, Hatfield also objected to the proposed by-laws of the AAA, which were decidedly research-oriented. He believed that, with the exception of scholarly enquiry into accounting theory, the Association should direct its energies to pedagogy and leave research largely to practitioner organisations. Groups associated with the Institute voiced a similar view, believing the changes to be but a veiled attempt to rival the AIA for leadership of the profession (Zeff 1966a: 33–7).

Shortly after its founding in 1934, the Securities and Exchange Commission joined the Federal Trade Commission, Federal Reserve Board, and other government agencies in calling for greater uniformity in financial reporting. As part of its new direction, the Association – now the AAA – responded by sponsoring research into accounting principles. The result, 'A Tentative Statement of Accounting Principles Affecting Corporate Reports', appeared in the June 1936 issue of *The Accounting Review*. The *Journal of Accountancy* studiously ignored the piece, perhaps reflecting the view that only practitioners and the Institute should speak on such matters. Hatfield himself found the 'Tentative Statement' illogical. He co-authored, with Thomas H. Sanders and Underhill Moore,[2] the Institute's response, commissioned by the Haskins and Sells Foundation. *A Statement of Accounting Principles*, a survey and evaluation of current practice, appeared in 1938 (Zeff 1966a: 40–3).

HATFIELD'S WRITINGS

By the time he helped compose the *Statement*, Hatfield was already a renowned author in his own right.[3] In 1909, he had published his major work, *Modern Accounting: Its Principles and Some of its Problems*, a compilation and discussion of current accounting practice. It was, along with Montgomery's edition of Dicksee (1905), Sprague's *Philosophy of Accounts* (1920; originally published 1908) and Cole's *Accounts, Their Construction and Interpretation* (1908), one of the first US contributions to the accounting literature (Zeff 1966a: 4). The book was favourably reviewed in the two leading journals of the day. In the September 1910 issue of the *Journal of Accountancy*, Walton (1910) wrote regarding the book's 'excellent points' and described how he had strongly recommended the work to his advanced accounting students at Northwestern (p. 387). Cole, while generally more critical, ended his review in the *Journal of Political Economy* by praising the author for the 'sanity' of his judgements and the 'encyclopaedic character' of the text (1909: 648). Apparently, *Modern Accounting* was also a popular work, going through several editions before the author produced, somewhat belatedly, a revised and updated version eighteen years later, in 1927 (Kahle 1956: 53).

Entitled *Accounting, Its Principles and Problems*, the reissued work was more of a textbook than its predecessor, with questions and problems for each chapter. The outlines of the two books were similar, however. In the revision, Hatfield omitted chapters on double-entry bookkeeping and 'Technical Improvements in Accounting Practice', including instead a chapter on consolidations and one on interpreting the balance sheet. He also expanded coverage of depreciation, dividends and capital losses, income, surplus, and partnership accounting (Hanson 1927: 714).

Once again, Hatfield received high praise in the *Journal of Accountancy*, the reviewer writing that although it contained points with which readers would disagree, *Accounting* deserved 'the very highest commendation' (Jackson 1927: 309). Reviews in *The American Accountant* (1927) and *The American Economic Review* (Hanson 1927), while brief, were also flattering. R. H. Montgomery, one of the founders of Coopers & Lybrand and a leading author on auditing and taxation, gave the work its most thorough critique and challenged Hatfield on a number of points in the June 1927 issue of *The Accounting Review*. Overall, however, he judged that the author had produced a 'fine book' which he recommended 'without hesitation to everyone interested in accounting' (p. 193). In 1928, *Accounting, Its Principles and Problems* earned Hatfield an award of merit from Beta Alpha Psi for the year's most outstanding contribution to accounting literature (Kahle 1956: 55–6). Reflecting their abiding importance, both this work and its predecessor were later reprinted, *Accounting* in 1971 by Scholars Book Co. and *Modern Accounting* by the Arno Press in 1976. Twelve years after the appearance of *Accounting*, Hatfield authored an accounting textbook with Sanders and Burton (1940).

In 1943, Hatfield published the lectures that he gave as Dickinson Lecturer at the Harvard Graduate School of Business Administration during 1941–2.

Entitled *Surplus and Dividends*, the collection was a broad look at current problems in capital accounting.

In addition to his books, Hatfield was a prolific writer of book reviews, short notes, conference proceedings, and a lesser number of full-fledged journal articles. These pieces resound with the prodigious learning for which he was well known. They also represent the full breadth of his interests – in accounting principles and practices (see, for example, Hatfield 1928b, 1934b, 1936, 1940b), accounting history (Hatfield 1926, 1943, Hatfield and Littleton 1932), law and accounting (Hatfield 1934a), and international accounting issues (Hatfield 1966). Like other great scholars of his day, Hatfield recognised few subject limitations.

HATFIELD AS AUTHOR

In virtually all of his writings, Hatfield's basic thrust was to survey and comment upon existing thought and practice, rather than create theory *ab initio*. As Zeff has commented, 'one reads Hatfield for insights into the writings of others . . . he was more an annotator than an advocate' (1978: 5). Hatfield believed that the greatest challenge facing the young 'science' of accounting was the lack of uniformity in accounting principles, and the accompanying latitude in terminology. To develop a coherent structure, he urged accountants to become more like physicists, chemists, astronomers, and other scientists, i.e. more theoretical (1928a: 217). For Hatfield, theories were derived inductively, from practice and experience, rather than from abstract premises. Indeed, the test of a theory was its correspondence to the best customary approaches, making it important to survey accounting procedures and expert opinion on an iterative basis. This faith in theory, coupled with a lack of enthusiasm for deductive reasoning, was common among other members of the 'pre-classical school' of accounting thought, which included such luminaries as Cole, Dickinson, Esquerre, Kester, Montgomery, Sprague, and Wildman in addition to Hatfield. Accordingly, they wrote with a distinctively 'practical flavor', their theoretic formulations 'a form of explanatory justification for accepted procedure' (Previts 1980: 110).[4] In Hatfield's case at least, this pragmatic bent also fostered a commendable openness to a wide range of ideas, even some which his contemporaries found, and accountants today would find, decidedly odd.[5]

Hatfield's compendia of procedure and practice were of inestimable value at a time when both government and profession were calling for more uniform accounting principles. Nevertheless, the encyclopaedic character of his work sometimes had the unfortunate effect of occluding his own opinions. Both Cole (1909) and, later, Montgomery (1927) publicly criticised him on this account. Cole wrote that his 'chief unfavorable comment' on *Modern Accounting* was that 'the author has given so much opinion of other people and so little of his own – especially when the opinions of others are so often contradictory one of another' (p. 647). Montgomery (1927) complained that having finished *Accounting, Its Principles and Problems*, 'I am somewhat in doubt regarding Professor Hatfield's idea of an ideal balance sheet' (p. 191). Both men urged the author to greater boldness in distinguishing his own ideas.

Although undogmatic in his own writings, Hatfield was less diffident as a critic. Indeed, his activities in this regard ultimately earned him something of a reputation (Broad 1951: 86). In the numerous, elegantly written book reviews which he authored over the course of his life, he was always frank about what he considered the defects of an author's work. These usually concerned inconsistencies in argument and the careless use of terminology, weaknesses which Hatfield, throughout his professional life, considered of utmost concern to the developing discipline. While his criticism was normally confined to the major issues at hand, Hatfield could also be, in his own words, 'picayunish' (1925: 433). Typical was his expression of regret in a 1925 review of a managerial accounting text published by the University of Chicago: 'that a work bearing the imprint of one of our greatest centers of culture should fall for the phrase 'this data'" (1925: 433). To his credit, Hatfield was also generous with praise where he felt such was due, practising an equal frankness about the fine points of an author's work.

In his life-long effort to extirpate slovenly argument and loose terminology from the accounting literature, Hatfield did not confine himself to book reviews and to asides in his own scholarly writings. Later in his life, he was also an avid writer of 'letters to the editor' and other short pieces, the sole purpose of which was to criticise an author's assault on what Hatfield called 'Our Blessed Language' (1940a: 48). His favourite targets were poorly expressed statements regarding the nature of depreciation and, to a lesser extent, of inventory valuation. A two-part note in the February and December 1931 issues of *The American Accountant* was typical of the scathing wit that Hatfield brought to these critiques. Entitled 'How Can They Say Such Things', it expressed

> deep surprise, and perhaps horror, at finding in a most recent book, written by two eminent certified public accountants (both professors in a distinguished New England university), edited by the Graduate Dean of an even more famous university, and bearing the imprint of most respectable publishers

an unfortunately worded statement regarding the reserve for depreciation (1931b: 365).[6] In this case, Hatfield refrained from directly identifying the authors and the publication. His normal practice was to include such information (1940a, 1942a, 1942b).

Hatfield was known in his own day, and is remembered today, for his wicked wit. A sense of fun also suffused many of his writings. The premier example is of course 'An Historical Defense of Bookkeeping', in which he defended accounting against the snubs of more established academic disciplines and the ignorance of the public in general ('And how abysmal that ignorance!'). The following quotations give some flavour of the piece:

> Long ago Sir Roger de Coverley assumed that 'little that is truly noble can be expected from one who is ever poring on his cashbook or balancing his accounts'. Literature has maintained this attitude ever since, and the bookkeeper has reached his apogee in the gentle and pathetic figure of Tim Clerkenwell.
>
> (Baxter and Davidson 1962: 2)

and

> Perhaps I should adopt the language appropriate to the kennel and speak of bookkeeping as having been sired four hundred years ago by a monk, and today dammed by thousands of university students, and yet, despite certain questions which the frivolous might raise to a celibate paternity and the extremely puzzling biological enigma of such a multiple maternity, book-keeping is thoroughly respectable.
>
> (Baxter and Davidson 1962: 6–7)

Even in ostensibly more serious works, Hatfield was tempted to humour. The index to *Accounting, Its Principles and Problems*, for example, contains a reference to 'Mike, love of, 256' (1927: 546). A footnote in the same work regretted that Cole had apparently abandoned the colourful term 'Where-Got-Gone' for the funds statement. The note concluded that 'it hardly seems the function of this treatise to serve as an asylum for a foundling abandoned by its progenitor' (1927: 460). Hatfield was also fond of trivia (1940b), fable (1932b), paradox (1928b) and *Alice's Adventures in Wonderland* (1940b), all of which he used to enliven his exploration of accounting principles.

HATFIELD AND THE LAW

Besides these whimsical devices, Hatfield usually incorporated an impressive array of the 'best accounting authorities' (Walton 1910: 387) in examining opinion and practice. Indeed, among the early pioneers of US accounting litera-ture – Montgomery, Sprague, Cole, and Hatfield – Hatfield's mastery of the extant source material was unsurpassed, particularly of the French and German accounting literature. He confided in the preface to *Modern Accounting* that he found 'foreign authorities' necessary since in the US 'far too little attention has been given to matters of principle' (1916: vii). For many years, Hatfield's writings, and later, Henry Sweeney's work on price level accounting (1936), were among the few works that enabled non-German and non-French speakers to keep in touch with Continental developments.

Like many of his contemporaries, Hatfield drew on the existing literature and on published accounts of leading corporations to fill out his discussions. He was virtually alone, however, in his broad and imaginative use of legal sources, such as juristic commentaries and statutes from both the US and abroad, commission rulings, internal revenue regulations and most importantly, court decisions dealing with accounting matters. In *Modern Accounting* he made reference to over seventy English and US legal cases, expanding to almost twice that number in the 1927 revision. Hatfield's unique contributions to the study of accounting and law were recognised at the time. In the tribute that accompanied his 1928 award of merit from Beta Alpha Psi, Hatfield was praised 'as one of the very first to recognize, and make use of the fact, that much of value and interest to students of accounting is to be found in the decisions of the law courts' (Kahle 1956: 55).

Hatfield's interest in court decisions and the law in general was consistent with his call for greater standardisation in accounting principles, to end what he considered 'the most embarrassing confusion in terminology' that beset the profession and public (1916: vi). Faced with the unsettled nature of accounting practice in the US, Hatfield turned to the courts to discover which accounting principles, among the many available, were becoming customary, if only in the legal arena. He was particularly interested in how the courts defined 'income' or 'profits', the treatment of which in corporate accounts still varied widely, especially with regard to the deduction of depreciation. As a result of his legal research, Hatfield correctly surmised that questions regarding profits 'entered into legal disputes more than any other accounting matter', and that in legal discussions 'profits' usually meant income available for dividends (see Mills and Harmon 1993). He also saw that the legal understanding of profits considerably complicated the accountant's task in recording income. Should the accountant employ some 'economic' or 'accounting interpretation of the increment in proprietorship', or represent as income only what could be 'legally distributed' as dividends? (Hatfield 1927: 250–1, 259).

On the whole, Hatfield was disappointed in the courts' treatment of accounting matters. He found legal decisions 'discordant', 'not so conclusive as could be desired', and in many cases 'opposed to what the accountant considers fundamental principles of his profession'. Indeed, while recognising that 'the accountant is greatly influenced by the attitude of the courts', he advised the profession to 'transcend the limitations under which the courts labor', i.e. the courts' ignorance of accounting theory. 'For a more perfect rationalization of legal dicta regarding profits,' accountants would have to 'await the day when the growing dignity of the profession of accounting shall cause its principles to permeate the ranks of bench and bar' (1916: 230). Until then, court records would continue to furnish 'many other interesting illustrations of the difficulty which the legal mind finds in solving problems requiring accounting knowledge' (1916: 330).

THEORETICAL CONCERNS

'The vital question in all accounting is the value which is to be placed on existing assets . . . Closely allied to the problem of valuing assets is that of depreciation' (1966: 175, 177). This quote, from one of Hatfield's early addresses to the American Association of Public Accountants, identifies the major preoccupations of his theoretical work.

Balance sheet focus

Like other writers of the 'pre-classical' school, Hatfield's chief focus was the balance sheet. He considered the 'correct exhibit of the financial status of the concern at a given moment of time' to be the 'essence of accounting'; the 'showing of results', though important, was secondary (1976: v). Income determination assumed greater significance in his later work, as it would in accounting theory generally, but for Hatfield the determination of profit and loss was always but an outcome of the valuation process. Accordingly, he developed no independent definition of income components. Profit or loss was the difference between balance sheets, representing the change in 'net wealth' or in 'proprietorship' (1927: 243). It was both a corollary of and secondary to treatment of balance sheet accounts. Later developments in accounting theory would obscure the concept that income is anchored to the balance sheet. Eventually, however, the idea would resurface, most recently in the 'asset/liability' view of net income currently favoured by the Financial Accounting Standards Board.

Hatfield was an ardent exponent of the 'materialistic' or 'proprietary' conception of the balance sheet first championed in the US by Sprague. At the beginning of the twentieth century, it was common for accountants to conceive of the account in highly 'personalistic' terms, as representing an actual debtor–creditor relationship. Under this theory, also known as the 'entity' theory, all assets were regarded as debts owed to the business and 'liabilities' as amounts owed by the business, which included owners' equity or 'proprietorship'. Thus, the standard form of the accounting equation was 'assets = liabilities'. Sprague, influenced by Hugli, Schaer, and other Continental writers (1920: 40, Hatfield 1908: 67), considered this relation misleading and proposed an expanded expression, 'assets = liabilities + proprietorship'. Sprague argued that liabilities and proprietorship were not the same, but two distinct groups of accounts representing different financial relationships. 'Surely The Business does not stand in the same relation to its proprietors or its capitalists as its "other" liabilities. It would seem more appropriate to say that it is "owned" by than "owes" the proprietors' (1920: 49). Sprague's expanded relation, disseminated by Hatfield, Paton, and others, and with some small refinement of terminology, would become the modern form of the accounting equation.

In the years after Hatfield's death, the emphasis on the balance sheet appeared increasingly old-fashioned, as net income and earnings per share became the critical measures of performance for shareholders, managers and analysts. The balance sheet perspective endured, however, and became the subject of renewed interest in the late 1970s. Today, financial reporting in the US is in full transition – from an income statement focus back to the balance sheet (Sever and Boisclair 1990). This shift was foreshadowed in the FASB's conceptual framework (see especially *Statement of Financial Accounting Concept* Nos. 5 and 6). It is also clearly evident in recent standards on accounting for income taxes (*Statement of Financial Accounting Standard* Nos. 96 and 109), and in the Board's current project on financial instruments and off-balance sheet financing (*Statement of Financial Accounting Standard* Nos. 105 and 107).

Asset valuation and depreciation

Hatfield regarded asset valuation as generally the most 'perplexing' problem of the balance sheet. In comparison, the issue of liabilities was simple: 'the question of valuation, so perplexing in regard to assets, practically disappears when liabilities are concerned' (1916: 185). Hatfield considered the natural tendency of people to over-estimate the value of their possessions as the root of the problem. Nevertheless, he also identified two other factors which, beginning in the late nineteenth century, considerably complicated the issue: an unprecedented rise in prices and more rapid technological obsolescence. These conditions created a great deal of confusion and some debate among accountants concerning the values at which different kinds of assets were to be recorded.

To help alleviate the confusion in valuing assets, Hatfield proposed three general 'rules of appraisal': that assets or 'inventory' be recorded at their value to a 'going concern', not at liquidation value; that fluctuations in the market value of fixed assets 'may be' ignored; and finally, that depreciation always be given full recognition. By the time he wrote *Accounting*, Hatfield believed that most accountants had abandoned liquidation value and had rejected the idea of revaluing fixed assets to reflect current market values, even if below cost. They especially objected to marking up fixed assets. Hatfield attributed this aversion to fears about recognising appreciation income. He himself had no real objection to marking up land as long as the offsetting credit on the balance sheet was to a reserve for appreciation rather than to profit and loss or surplus (1927: 78–9).

However, the business community, and presumably the accountants they employed, had yet to accept the full recognition of depreciation, which vexed Hatfield no end. In 1908 'any recognition of depreciation was relatively uncommon in the accounts of American corporations'. Although the situation had greatly improved by 1927, companies were 'still apt to look upon the charge for depreciation as being an act of grace rather than of necessity and the allowance is frequently less in lean than in prosperous years' (1927: 140). For Hatfield, depreciation was nothing less than a law of nature: 'All machinery is on an irresistible march to the junk heap, and its progress, while it may be delayed, cannot be prevented by repairs' (1927: 130). Unlike fluctuations in market value, depreciation of a fixed asset could not be ignored if the aim was to list it at its value to a 'going concern'. Nevertheless, Hatfield counselled equally against charging too large a sum to depreciation. Although condoned by press and public alike as evidence of 'conservatism', this practice tended to create 'secret reserves' of profits and to understate assets, which depressed share prices.

Even where depreciation was well established, Hatfield believed that many people in a position to know better misunderstood its essential nature. It was a complaint he would make numerous times over the course of his professional life, even as late as 1940:

> For many years, at divers times and places, I have criticized current expressions regarding depreciation. But all this has been of no effect, and I am beginning to worry lest I, and not the rest of the regiment, am out of step.
>
> (1940a: 49)

For Hatfield, the most common misapprehension was that depreciation constituted a fund for asset replacement or a reservation of profits. On the contrary, depreciation was 'an expense without which profits can never be earned'. It represented a consumption of wealth, the decline in use value due to ordinary wear and tear, obsolescence or other factors. To account for this decline, Hatfield rejected earlier approaches, such as charging replacement cost of fixed assets to expense. Instead, he proposed an analogy with accounting for resources 'consumed in a single use': match the benefits received by allocating the cost of the asset over its period of service (1927: 130–1).

The allocation was charged to profits for all depreciable assets. In the case of wasting assets, however, Hatfield was willing to bypass profit and loss and carry the charge for 'depreciation' directly to some other proprietorship account. He reasoned that investors in mines, oil wells, and similar enterprises rarely expected the company to continue once the natural resource was exhausted. Thus, it made little sense to withhold from profits an amount equal to the original cost of the resource, which in more permanent undertakings would be invested in additional assets. Shareholders fully expected dividends to consist of both earnings and a return of capital, often writing such provisions into their corporate charter.

On this basis, Hatfield defended the controversial decision in *Lee v. Neuchatel Asphalte Company* (1889). In this case, the English court permitted a mining company to pay dividends without allowing for exhaustion of asphalt deposits, much to the outrage of accountants on both sides of the Atlantic. Although the decision was, admittedly, 'somewhat vague in principle, contradictory in detail, and difficult of apprehension', Hatfield considered that it applied to wasting assets only and not to fixed assets generally, as many believed. He also held that the justices fully expected the loss in capital to appear somewhere else in the balance sheet, if not in profit and loss.

For Hatfield, the moral of *Lee* was plain:

> It may be logical to claim that *all* losses or gains, however caused, should go to Profit and Loss, and not direct to some other proprietorship account. But such a claim, while logical enough, does not at all conform to accounting practice of any land or time.
>
> (1927: 264, 276)

He reasoned that instead of entering it to current income, an item might be debited to the capital account; to general surplus; established as a deferred charge and amortised over future periods; or entered as profit but excluded from the general profit and loss account (1927: 245–6). The choice depended on what the accountant wished to represent as the profits of a particular period. For example, was it to show the changes due to current operations, with unusual gains or losses excluded? In this, Hatfield presaged later debates on the merits of a 'current operating performance' approach as opposed to an 'all-inclusive' view of the income statement.

Although Hatfield remained critical of statements regarding depreciation and of depreciation practice, by 1927 he acknowledged that corporate accounting for the charge had improved. By that date, Hatfield had also become more sanguine about the progress of US courts in recognising depreciation expense. Hatfield attributed this new attitude largely to the influence of the Interstate Commerce

Commission, which had enacted rules requiring railroads to make a regular provision for depreciation in their accounts. Subsequently, public utility commissions in several states had passed similar requirements. For Hatfield, another factor in promoting the propriety of depreciation charges was the establishment of the federal income tax in 1913, which made firms 'vitally interested in showing all possible expenses' (1927: 147). He apparently had little faith that in the absence of statutory provisions, the majority of companies or judges would accept depreciation as an 'unavoidable' expense (1916: 136).

Other valuation issues

As described previously, there were certain accounting practices that Hatfield found thoroughly irritating. Foremost, of course, was the abuse of depreciation. The conservative treatment of land appreciation and the illogical aspects of goodwill accounting were others. Accounting for merchandise also fell into this category. According to the traditional view, merchandise was normally valued at cost. However, as a 'circulating' rather than a 'fixed' asset, goods were listed at 'current' or 'market' value if less than cost. Hatfield found this practice 'curiously inconsistent and illogical', and a prime example of how accountants disregarded common sense in the name of 'conservatism'. If value to the going concern was the overriding criterion, surely the most sensible approach was to list merchandise at net realisable value, i.e. selling price less costs of disposal. Despite the incongruity of practice and theory, Hatfield realised that custom in this case was probably too strong, and that merchandise would continue to be listed at cost or replacement cost, whichever was lower (1927: 99).

At the beginning of the century, there was some public resentment against the recognition of intangible assets in the financial reports of corporations. Hatfield and other pre-classical writers supported the practice, arguing that as 'a transferable right from which exceptional profits may be derived', goodwill and other intangible assets had a legitimate place in the balance sheet (1916: 118). To make recognition easier, they developed a general formula for quantifying the value of these 'immaterial' items: excess earnings capitalised at a reasonable rate. In all instances, value was to be limited to cost.

This limitation was particularly important with regard to goodwill, the vaguest of the intangibles. In effect, it meant that goodwill was excluded from recognition unless 'secured at a cost', i.e. unless purchased. Hatfield himself found it illogical that the firm that had initially created this value was unable to count it as an asset. Nevertheless, he acknowledged the practical necessity of the restriction. Another source of controversy, albeit of a more technical nature, concerned the amortisation of intangibles. In the case of goodwill, English opinion appeared to support permanent capitalisation. Hatfield, true to his belief that fixed capital declines in service value over time, advised regular amortisation for all intangibles. For goodwill, he thought a reasonable approach was to write it off over the number of years incorporated in its valuation. For other intangibles, he recommended legal life. Kester would stress the idea of useful life (Previts 1980: 143).

HATFIELD TODAY

To read Hatfield today, is to understand what accounting as a scholarly discipline has largely lost. Most contemporary accounting enquiry pales in comparison to the magnificent prose, the satirical wit, breadth of learning, and the intelligent discussion of critical issues displayed in Hatfield's work. To read Hatfield is also to appreciate his gift for prophecy. Hatfield anticipated two of the most important trends in modern US accounting. First, he correctly surmised that the AAA would abandon its focus on accounting education when it adopted a 'research' emphasis beginning in the mid-1930s. For this reason, he strenuously opposed the new orientation, believing, perhaps naïvely, that pedagogy should remain central in the lives of accounting educators. Almost sixty years later, the membership of the AAA, disillusioned by decades of research programmes and paradigms which yielded little by way of practice or pedagogy, have begun to renew their commitment to teaching. Hatfield was also a prognosticator regarding accounting theory. He saw that financial accounting derived its essential structure from the accounting equation and that income was fundamentally a creature of the balance sheet. As explained previously, the profession today is in the process of restoring the balance sheet to its place at the apex of accounting theory, again confirming Hatfield's insight.

Over the last thirty years, Hatfield's life and work have been largely ignored in the accounting literature. In light of the recent developments that he anticipated, Hatfield should become the subject of renewed interest.

Notes

1 The biographical information presented in this section is taken primarily from Kahle (1956). Other sources are Broad (1951); Burns and Coffman (1991); Mumford (1980); Previts (1980); *Who Was Who in America* (1950: 241); and Zeff (1966b, 1978). See also Zeff (1971) for an elegant and incisive overview of Hatfield's life and work.
2 Apparently, Moore was a replacement author, added to the team after one of the original co-authors bowed out to join the SEC. I am indebted to M. J. Mumford for this information.
3 For a lengthy bibliography of Hatfield's writings, see Previts (1980: 214–17).
4 In *The Philosophy of Accounts*, Sprague believed he was pursuing a different, more deductive approach: 'the principles of accountancy may be determined by a priori reasoning, and do not depend upon the customs and traditions which surround the art' (1920: iii). Nevertheless, the substance and flavour of his analysis were within the pre-classical tradition.
5 Perhaps the best example is Hatfield's view endorsing the payment of cash dividends out of premium on capital stock (1927: 290–1).
6 The authors wrote 'The Reserve [for Depreciation] account, therefore, represents profits withheld from Capital to take care of expected losses resulting from depreciation of fixed assets'. Hatfield objected that such an account could not possibly represent profits but had to be a provision for loss in asset value (1931b: 365).

References

American Accounting Association (1936), 'A Tentative Statement of Accounting Principles Affecting Corporate Reports', *The Accounting Review*, June: 187–91.

Baxter, W. T. and Davidson, S. (1962) *Studies in Accounting Theory*, Homewood, Il.: Richard D. Irwin, Inc.

Broad, S. J. (1951) 'Presentation of Distinguished Accountants to the Accounting Hall of Fame', *Proceedings of the Thirteenth Annual Institute on Accounting*, Columbus, OH.: Ohio State University Publication.

Burns, T. J. and Coffman, E. N. (1991) *The Accounting Hall of Fame: Profiles of Fifty Members*, Columbus, OH.: College of Business, The Ohio State University.

Cole, W. M. (1908) *Accounts, Their Construction and Interpretation*, Boston, Mass.: Houghton Mifflin Company.

Cole, W. M. (1909) Review of *Modern Accounting* by Henry Rand Hatfield, *Journal of Political Economy*: 647–8.

FASB (1984) *Statement of Financial Accounting Concepts No. 5*, 'Recognition and Measurement in Financial Statements of Business Enterprises'.

FASB (1985) *Statement of Financial Accounting Concepts No. 6*, 'Elements of Financial Statements'.

FASB (1987) *Statement of Financial Accounting Standards No. 96*, 'Accounting for Income Taxes'.

FASB (1990) *Statement of Financial Accounting Standards No. 105*, 'Disclosure of Information about Financial Instruments with Off-Balance-Sheet Risk and Financial Instruments with Concentrations of Credit Risk'.

FASB (1991) *Statement of Financial Accounting Standards No. 107*,'Disclosures about Fair Value of Financial Instruments'.

FASB (1992) Statement of Financial Accounting Standards No. 109, 'Accounting for Income Taxes'.

Hanson, A. W. (1927) Review of *Accounting, Its Principles and Problems* by Henry Rand Hatfield, *The American Economic Review* 17: 714–15.

Hatfield, H. R. (1908) Review of *The Philosophy of Accounts* by Charles E. Sprague, *Journal of Accountancy*, November: 67–9.

Hatfield, H. R. (1916) *Modern Accounting, Its Principles and Some of its Problems*, New York: D. Appleton. Reprinted 1976 by Arno Press, New York.

Hatfield, H. R. (1924) 'An Historical Defense of Bookkeeping', *Journal of Accountancy*, April: 241–53.

Hatfield, H. R. (1925) Review of *Managerial Accounting* by J. O. Mckinsey, *Journal of Accountancy*, May: 432–3.

Hatfield, H. R. (1926) 'Earliest Use in English of the Term Capital', *Quarterly Journal of Economics*, May: 547–8.

Hatfield, H. R. (1927) *Accounting, Its Principles and Problems*, New York: D. Appleton and Co. Reprinted 1971 by Scholars Book Co., Lawrence, Kan.

Hatfield, H. R. (1928a) 'What is the Matter with Accounting?', *Canadian Chartered Accountant*, January: 213–25.

Hatfield, H. R. (1928b) 'An Accounting Paradox', *The Accounting Review*, December: 342–4.

Hatfield, H. R. (1931a) 'How Can They Say Such Things?', *The American Accountant*, February: 50.

Hatfield, H. R. (1931b) 'How Can They Say Such Things? – II', *The American Accountant*, December: 365.

Hatfield, H. R. (1932) 'A Fable', *The Accounting Review*, September: 175.

Hatfield, H. R. (1934a) 'Accounting Principles and the Statutes', *Journal of Accountancy*, August: 90–7.

Hatfield, H. R. (1934b) 'Operating Deficit and Paid-in Surplus', *The Accounting Review*, September: 237–41.

Hatfield, H. R. (1936) 'What They Say About Depreciation', *The Accounting Review*, March: 18–26.

Hatfield, H. R. (1940a) 'Financial Aspects of Depreciation' (Correspondence), *Journal of Accountancy*, January: 48–9.

Hatfield, H. R. (1940b) 'Accounting Trivia' (Accounting Exchange), *The Accounting Review*, September: 417–19.

Hatfield, H. R. (1940c) 'An Accountant's Adventures in Wonderland', *Journal of Accountancy*, December: 527–32.

Hatfield, H. R. (1942a) 'Accounting Boners' (Correspondence), *Journal of Accountancy*, April: 355.

Hatfield, H. R. (1942b) 'On the Unreliability of Arithmetic' (Correspondence), *Journal of Accountancy*, October: 355–7.

Hatfield, H. R. (1943) 'Neither Pietra nor Flori' (Correspondence), *Journal of Accountancy*, February: 165–6.

Hatfield, H. R. (1947) *Surplus and Dividends* (1941–42 Arthur Lowes Dickinson Lectures), Cambridge, Mass.: Harvard University Press. Second printing of the 1943 edn.

Hatfield, H. R. (1966) 'Some Variations in Accounting Practice in England, France, Germany and the United States', *Journal of Accounting Research*, Autumn: 169–84.

Hatfield, H. R. and Littleton, A. C. (1932) 'A Check-List of Early Bookkeeping Texts', *The Accounting Review*, September: 194–206.

Jackson, J. H. (1927) Review of *Accounting, Its Principles and Problems* by Henry Rand Hatfield, *Journal of Accountancy*, 44: 308–9.

Kahle, J. J. (1956) *American Accountants and Their Contributions to Accounting Thought, 1900–1930*, Master of Arts Dissertation, Washington, DC: Catholic University of America.

Mills, P. A. and Harmon, M. E. (1993) 'Limitations of the Contractarian Approach to Accounting Regulation: Enforcement of Accounting Contracts, 1843–1931', *Critical Perspectives on Accounting* (forthcoming).

Montgomery, R. H. (ed.) (1905), *Auditing: A Practical Manual for Auditors* by Lawrence Robert Dicksee, New York: Authorised American Edition.

Montgomery, R. H. (1927) Review of *Accounting – Its Principles and Problems* by Henry Rand Hatfield, *The Accounting Review* 2: 189–93.

Moonitz, M. and Littleton, A. C. (1965) *Significant Accounting Essays*, Englewood Cliffs, NJ: Prentice-Hall.

Mumford, M. J. (1980) 'An Historical Defense of Henry Rand Hatfield', *Abacus*, December: 151–8.

Previts, G. J. (1980) *A Critical Evaluation of Comparative Financial Accounting Thought in America, 1900 to 1920*, New York: Arno Press.

Review (1927) of *Accounting, Its Principles and Problems* by Henry Rand Hatfield, *The American Accountant*, May: 50.

Sanders, T. H., Hatfield, H. R. and Moore, U. (1938) *A Statement of Accounting Principles*, Sarasota, Fla.: American Accounting Association.

Sever, M. V. and Boisclair, R. E. (1990) 'Financial Reporting in the 1990s', *Journal of Accountancy*, January: 36–41.

Sprague, C. E. (1920) *The Philosophy of Accounts*, New York: The Ronald Press Company. Reprint of 1908 edn.

Sweeney, H. W. (1936) *Stabilized Accounting*, New York: Harper & Brothers.

Walton, S. (1910) Review of *Modern Accounting* by Henry Rand Hatfield, *Journal of Account- ancy*, September: 387.

Who was Who in America, Vol. II, 1943–50 (1950), Chicago, Ill.: The A. N. Marquis Company.

Zeff, S. A. (1966a) *The American Accounting Association, Its First 50 Years, 1916–1966*, Sarasota, Fla.: American Accounting Association.

Zeff, S. A. (1966b) Introduction to 'Some Variations in Accounting Practice in England, France, Germany and the United States' by Henry Rand Hatfield, *Journal of Accounting Research*, Autumn: 169–70.

Zeff, S. A. (1971) 'Foreword to the Reissue' in *Accounting its Principles and Problems* by Henry Rand Hatfield, Lawrence, Kan.: Scholars Book Co. Reprint of the 1927 edition published by D. Appleton & Co., New York.

Zeff, S. A. (ed.) (1978) *Selected Dickinson Lectures in Accounting 1936–1952*, New York: Arno Press.

17 William A. Paton (1889–1991)

Theorist and educator

Gary J. Previts and Thomas R. Robinson

Abstract

William A. Paton's writings defined and advanced a classical theory of accounting for property rights in a capital market economy. His contributions derived from his own skills in reasoning and writing and trace back to immediate forebears including Sprague and Hatfield. Sprague's algebraic exposition, *The Philosophy of Accounts*, and Hatfield's *Modern Accounting* were acknowledged by Paton as the writings which attracted him to accounting.

Recognised in 1987 by the American Institute of Certified Public Accountants as the 'Accounting Educator of the Century', Paton's longevity (1889–1991), combined with his boundless intellectual energy and lasting good health, enabled him to touch and influence several generations of accountants during periods of unprecedented growth. Paton's accomplishments, his recognition and the controversy related to the joint effort with Littleton in 1940, are among the topics considered in this chapter. We portray Paton's personage and his ideas appreciatively as part of the continuum of double-entry development.

INTRODUCTION

William Andrew Paton was born near Calumet, Michigan on 19 July 1889. He died on 26 April 1991. Paton is renowned as both an accounting theorist and educator. Within his lifetime the public accounting profession in the United States was formed (1896) and grew substantially, such that by 1991 the American Institute of Certified Public Accountants (AICPA) was comprised of over 300,000 members. Paton has been called 'Mr Accounting' and the 'Sage of Ann Arbor' (Greer 1965) and was named the 'Accounting Educator of the Century' by the AICPA in 1987. Commentaries published at the time of his death note his long career as an educator and estimate that he taught more than 20,000 students, including many who became top executives in industry and public practice. An *Introduction to Corporate Accounting Standards* (1940), which he co-authored with A. C. Littleton, is considered a classic and is one of the most highly regarded expositions of accounting theory.

As part of a celebration of the 500th anniversary of Pacioli's *Summa*, this chapter describes and identifies the contributions of Paton to accounting thought.

It also assesses the influences upon Paton, as well as those communities most influenced by his writings and works. The chapter is organised as follows. The first section presents a profile of Paton, including his family, education, career, and professional activities. The second section explores the major influences on Paton's theory development. The final section examines Patonian theories and Paton's personal influence.

A PORTRAIT

Paton was born on 19 July 1889 to Andrew Paton and Mary Nowlin Paton. Andrew Paton had emigrated from Scotland as an infant in 1851, and would become superintendent of the local Michigan school district. Mary Paton, who like Andrew held a teaching certificate, was for a time local custodian of the Michigan state travelling library. With this family background it is not surprising that Paton would become an educator. Paton worked his way through the University of Michigan, earning his bachelor's degree in 1915. He then continued his studies at Michigan, earning an MA in 1916 and a Ph.D. (Economics) in 1917. Paton's dissertation, 'The Theory of Accounts', would later be substantially revised and published as *Accounting Theory – With Special Reference to the Corporate Enterprise*. Paton's academic career began prior to receipt of his BA degree by serving as a teaching assistant (1914) and instructor of economics (1915) at Michigan. Paton was an assistant professor of economics at the University of Minnesota from 1916 to 1917, after which he returned to Michigan to fill a similar position.

Government service required Paton's presence in Washington for several years during the First World War. In Washington, Paton served on the United States War Trade Board and in the Income Tax Unit of the United States Treasury. He returned to Michigan in 1919 as an associate professor and later was promoted to full professor (1921). In 1926, he formed a public accounting partnership with Francis Ross. Due to his academic obligations, he restricted his practice to consulting for public utilities and municipalities. Paton had earlier engaged in the practice of accounting during academic breaks (Paton 1981). Later, upon discontinuing his participation in the firm to concentrate on academic duties he served the profession in many ways. As a member of the Committee on Accounting Procedure he became 'well acquainted' with George Oliver May (Paton 1981). Paton was also chosen (1939–40) to follow May (1936–7) and Sir Laurence Halsey (1937–8) as the Dickinson Lecturer in Accounting at Harvard. Paton's lectures were published as *Recent and Prospective Developments in Accounting Theory*.

Paton was a member of the American Accounting Association's predecessor organisation, serving as its sixth president and as the first editor of *The Accounting Review*. He was honoured by both the AICPA (1944) and Michigan Association of CPAs (1968) for distinguished service to the profession. Paton was among the first inductees in the Accounting Hall of Fame at Ohio State University in 1950 and is the namesake of the William A. Paton Center for Accounting Education at Michigan (1976). Writing in 1987, Zeff succinctly points out that:

In 1939 when the CAP (Committee on Accounting Procedure of the American Institute) was authorized to issue ARBs (Accounting Research Bulletins) in the Institute's name, Paton was one of the three accounting academics named to the committee. He served on the committee until 1950; his name appeared on more bulletins – 33 in all – than that of any other member in the committee history. He tried on several occasions to gain the committee's support for explicit accounting recognition of . . . replacement costs, but the SEC's opposition to such a practice defeated his efforts.

(Zeff 1987: 53)

Paton retired officially in 1959 when he was holder of both the title Edwin Francis Gay University Professor of Accounting and Professor of Economics. He continued to lecture after his retirement at many universities, including the University of Chicago and the University of Florida (Taggart 1964).

Paton's long academic career was surpassed only by his career as a writer. He published 'Severity of the Trade Cycle in America' in 1915 and his first accounting article, 'Theory of the Double-Entry System', in 1917. His writing continued long after his official retirement, including his role as a frequent contributor to *The Freeman*, a conservative economic publication, and authorship of several articles reflecting on his career. Paton's writings were not limited to topics of accounting and economics. A 1962 publication professed the advantages of living underground and was an effort he considered to be one of his popular public successes. More recently, Paton's *Words! Combining Fun and Learning* (1984) provided a tool for increasing verbal skills.

THE INFLUENCE OF OTHERS

Paton was influenced by the early theoretical works of Hatfield and Sprague. Taggart (1976) describes the time when Paton was a student of David Friday at Michigan:

One of Friday's students in the fall of 1912 was a young redhead by the name of William Andrew Paton. The text then in use was an early book by William Morse Cole, called *Accounting and Auditing*. According to this student it was a very poor book. Its instructions were about on the level of 'Debit that which comes into the business; credit that which goes out'. If this book had been all that Paton was exposed to, he probably would never have entered the accounting profession. Fortunately, Professor Friday, whatever his shortcomings as an accounting scholar may have been, knew a good book when he saw one. One day he came to class waving a red-bound copy of Hatfield's *Modern Accounting*. This was a revelation to Paton: accounting did provide an intellectual challenge after all. When he later found . . . [C. E.] Sprague's *Philosophy of Accounts*, Paton was sold.

Friday placed Hatfield's text, as well as a copy of Sprague's *The Philosophy of Accounts*, on reserve in the library (Paton 1978). Paton (1978) recalls that he read both books that semester and remembers that they 'stimulated' his 'interest in accounting'. These texts provided a starting point for his own theory development which would appear in *Accounting Theory: With Special Reference to the Corporate Enterprise*. This work is based upon Paton's dissertation, which was revised substantially for publication in 1922. Zeff (1979) notes that while it is often said that *Accounting Theory* is the published form of Paton's dissertation, *Accounting Theory* is, in fact, a longer, comprehensive work of which the dissertation provided but a portion. In *Accounting Theory*, Paton argues for replacing the 'proprietorship' viewpoint with an 'entity' viewpoint. In the new world of corporate form, Paton argued that the 'doctrines of proprietorship, as propounded by Sprague, Hatfield, and others, are not an entirely adequate statement of the theory of accounts under the conditions of modern business organization' (1922: xiii).

Another influence on Paton was Sweeney's 1936 *Stabilized Accounting*, a text which he cited frequently (Zeff 1979: 92). Zeff notes that while Paton 'never preferred 'stabilized accounting' to the booking of replacement costs, he regularly recommended that reckonings on a 'common-dollar' basis be provided in supplementary disclosures'. When *Stabilized Accounting* was reissued in 1964, Paton provided the new foreword, praising the text as a 'break-through', pointing out the limitations of '"ordinary" accounting data' in dealing with an unstable dollar. Sweeney in turn gives some credit to Paton, noting in the revised edition that when he initially developed an interest in the concept of 'stabilized accounting' he was directed to a 1920 article by Paton on revising accounting numbers to reflect purchasing power changes (Sweeney 1964: xx). The earlier Paton article 'stimulated and encouraged' Sweeney in his project (p. xx).

PATON'S THEORIES AND INFLUENCE

Proprietary vs. entity orientation

One of Paton's early, significant contributions to accounting theory was the publication of *Accounting Theory*, espousing the 'entity' viewpoint. Paton (1978: 5) would later note that he 'leaned heavily on Sprague as a starting point'. Paton also evidenced the important linkage to Sprague's ideation of the discipline by borrowing Sprague's title terminology to describe the essential orientation ingredient of Patonian theory during the 1939 Dickinson lecture at Harvard (p. 2). To quote Paton:

> A first step in the development of a 'philosophy of accounts' is the taking of a position, the adoption of a point of view, the recognition of a focus or center of attention . . . In an earlier period, accounting was largely represented by the record-keeping of the particular individual or proprietor . . . With the growth of corporate organization . . . accounts have become more . . . institutional . . . I have always been a supporter of the business-entity conception of accounting.
>
> (Paton 1940: 2)

Viewing the corporate entity, and not the 'proprietor' of Sprague's orthodoxy, as the orienting focus was an essential difference between Paton and his intellectual forebears.

Income determination

If a single document can be attributed to have influenced a generation of academics to consider the primacy of the matching principle, an income determination process and earning power, *An Introduction to Corporate Accounting Standards* would have to be the most prominent candidate. Paton was the lead author, as is evidenced by the sequence in which the names appear on the work. And too, it was somewhat of a catchphrase to note that a document oriented to income statement primacy was also to be identified as the 'P&L' monograph. The persistent influence of income determination issues on the allocation of academic intellectual resources, even in most recent times, was noted by David Solomons in 1987:

> Many sophisticated accounting academics have lost patience with the income concept and have turned their backs on it . . . But, proper or not, 'earnings' (the practical embodiment of the accrual concept of income) has been the focus of a vast amount of academic empirical research in the last two decades . . . it does not look as though the concept is about to drop out of the literature any more than it seems to be about to lose interest for financial analysts.
>
> (1987: 6)

Yet the monograph's influence over the academic community may have been less important than its role in forming ideas to guide the future development of practice standards.

In 1939 in a paper at the 52nd Institute annual meeting, Paton outlined the significance of income determination as follows:

> As you know, the research department (of the Institute) is approaching its study of principles from the point of view of corporate reports, particularly those issued to stockholders. Moreover, in one of the early meetings it was proposed and agreed that we take as a 'golden text' the proposition that the most important purpose of corporate accounting is the periodic measurement of income. This emphasizes the income statement rather than the balance sheet, something of a departure from accounting tradition.
>
> (Paton 1939: 231–2)

The 1977 American Accounting Association committee that prepared *A Statement on Accounting Theory and Theory Acceptance* (SATTA) relates the following to the 1940 monograph: 'Much of the writing is Paton's but all the ideas are not. Price aggregates and the dominant "interpretation" theme of the final chapter [Chapter VII] are pure Littleton. Yet most of Paton's ideas find expression in the monograph' (AAA 1977: 29).

However, in December 1981 Paton related to one of the authors of this essay, during an interview in Ann Arbor, that he did, in fact, write Chapter VII

(Interpretation). Indeed a careful review of Paton's previous works and consideration of the details in Chapter VII supports this view. What's more it seems reasonable to take Paton at his word. In SATTA there are several other assertions:

> [T]he Paton and Littleton monograph was evidently written so as not to annoy the practitioner audience. At that time, the American Accounting Association was attempting to replace rivalry by collaboration in its relations with the American Institute of Accountants, as the AICPA was then called. Copies of the monograph were distributed without charge to members of both bodies, and the authors clearly sought to achieve a maximum favorable impact on practitioners without sacrificing their principles.

> (AAA 1977: 29)

Considering Paton's established views regarding the principle of current value, one might ask whether Paton relented on his views at this point. The SATTA committee then continues:

> Paton and Littleton enumerate measurement rules which are assertedly pre-dicated on the several concepts, conventions and assumptions set forth in Chapter 2. If there is a pervasive standard it is dependability which is frequently invoked in defense of traditional historical cost.

> (ibid.)

Other evidence of Paton's candour about his role in the monograph project indicates he later disavowed his association with the monograph, perhaps because of its historical cost posture.

In a July 15, 1991, handwritten letter to one of this paper's authors, Paton's son, William A. (Andy) Paton Jr, also a recognised accounting academic, re-emphasised a point omitted in an essay about his father which relates to Chapter VII.

> There is an error [in the June 1991 *Accounting Education News* profile] which should be noted. The correct quotation is (p. 118 of the Paton and Littleton monograph): 'Accounting sets no limits upon the supplying of *interpretive* information in financial statements through footnote, account titles, parenthetic figures, or extra columns for estimated current values' [emphasis supplied by W. A. Paton Jr]. This is an important point I believe since my Dad favored 'current value' or estimated current value – at least for much of his teaching career . . . He stated many times that he wished the Paton & Littleton monograph 'had never been written'.

Influence on accounting practice

Paton enhanced the practice of accounting beyond his contributions to accounting theory. In addition to the estimated 20,000 students whom he taught directly, his textbooks and other writings reached scores of students and practising accountants. *Essentials of Accounting* was not only used on university campuses, but was also reprinted for use by returning US servicemen in the 1940s (Paton 1978: 5). Several Paton texts were translated into other languages, including Chinese and Spanish. Paton undertook a major revision of the *Accountants' Handbook* for the 1932 edition. The book was more than just a 'second edition' according to Paton (1978) and an early review of the book by Lawton (1932). Paton rewrote 60 per cent of the second edition himself and orchestrated the work of approximately ninety contributing and consulting editors for both the second and third editions (Paton 1943, 1978). The handbook was widely used by practising accountants and served as a source of 'authoritative' guidance (Lawton 1932). Paton (1978: 6) reflected that he had undertaken the task with 'missionary zeal' and that it provided him with 'an opportunity to spread the Paton gospel more widely'.

PATON IN PERSPECTIVE

Paton was a rugged economic and intellectual individualist in its increasing institutional influence. His longevity enhanced his influence over his former students in both academe and practice, as he was first a mentor and then an adviser in a world which reflected Patonian ideas. His classical views of theory in the entity and current value sense were vital to stimulating accounting from a process-based discipline to a judgemental form. His exemplary effort as an empiricist is found in the 1935 study *Corporate Profits as Shown by Audit Reports* (National Bureau of Economic Research, Study No. 28) which foretold the increasing attention which academic members would pay to positive accounting research.

Paton contributed frequently to the *Journal of Accountancy* and in later years continued to offer his perspective on issues ranging from the elements of professionalism to the limitations of standard-setting. He championed the importance of professional judgement in the application of principles. Writing in 1971 for the *Journal of Accountancy*, Paton warned (in the context of the Accounting Principles Board), that standard setting has 'no business laying down the law', noting that it was not the role of standard setting to be dictatorial in specifying practice, but to recommend or urge (Paton 1971b: 42).

What is a proper historical evaluation of W. A. Paton as a theorist and academic in the view of the ages? He was an important inauguratory figure in several important activities – including *The Accounting Review*, for example. He was an initial inductee to the Accounting Hall of Fame. He served as an initial member of the Committee on Accounting Procedure and his involvement, as noted by Zeff, was unparalleled. His handbooks, texts, authorship, and research leadership, from his earliest works, presented his own 'philosophy of accounts' and his entity and current value interpretative views, to his criticism of the 'fogeyism' of institutional standard setting at the 1983 AAA Annual Meeting in New Orleans, all bespeak his unique commitment to the role of the individual in a society seeking to specialise and develop institutions to cope with rapid technological and demographic change.

Admittedly, the AICPA in 1987 determined the proper historical evaluation of Paton by awarding to him a special distinction as the 'Accounting Educator of the Century', but how do other major contemporary figures, including George O. May, A. C. Littleton, and Eric Kohler – the other persons which Edwards and Salmonson consider among the 'Four Accounting Pioneers' – compare in full retrospective? This chapter does not seek to answer that question. Rather, we encourage that the question be asked and the comparisons be undertaken earnestly and with as much objectivity as is possible. For if our discipline is to understand itself, comparative historical study of the development of thought as explored by each succeeding generation is as important to our discipline as it is, for example, to the field of economics.

What is lacking are definitive scholarly analyses of Paton, his forebears, his peers and their work. To appreciate the man one must more clearly understand his personal life as well, which until recently has been left as untouched ground – yet there is some evidence suggesting he faced several substantial personal difficulties, if not tragedies. An assessment of these in the process of making him more than a 'cardboard' historical figure will require much skill and effort on the part of biographers, and much trust on the part of family and colleagues.

As recent scholars assert, Paton best represents what to other countries is typical of an American creed: 'Our nation may well be exceptional not for the power of the organization, but for the persisting sense of human agency' (McGerr 1993). The matter of interest to accountants – leaders and scholars – is to understand why individuals remain a source of power in our national order.

Note

1 References used in this essay are listed below. Paton's writings are extensive and the reader is encouraged to review a collection of some of his writings by Taggart (1964), which includes a more comprehensive bibliography of Paton's work. An extensive biblio- graphy is also available in Zeff *et al.* (1979).

References[1]

Audiotape of 19 December 1981 interview with W. A. Paton conducted by Norman X. Dressel and G. J. Previts. Available for loan from The Accounting History Research Center, School of Accounting, Georgia State University (120 minutes).

American Accounting Association (1977) *A Statement on Accounting Theory and Theory Acceptance*, Sarasota Fla.: American Accounting Association.

Burns, T. J. and Coffman, E. N. (1982) *The Accounting Hall of Fame: Profiles of Forty-One Members*, Columbus, OH: College of Administrative Science, The Ohio State University: 50–1, 89.

Edwards, J. D. and Salmonson, R. F. (1961) *Contributions of Four Accounting Pioneers: Kohler, Littleton, May, Paton*, reprinted 1988, The Academy of Accounting Historians, Classics Series, New York: Garland Publishing, Inc.

Fitzgerald, J. A. (ed.) (1935) *Faculty Personnel: A Directory of the Instructional Staffs of the Member Schools*, Austin, Tex.: American Association of Collegiate Schools of Business.

Greer, H. C. (1965) 'Review of Paton on Accounting', *The Accounting Review* XL(1), January: 290–2.

Hatfield, H. R. (1909) *Modern Accounting: Its Principles and Some of Its Problems*, New York: Appleton.

Lawton, W. H. (1932) 'Review of Accountants' Handbook', *The Journal of Accountancy* 53(5), May: 392.

McGerr, M. (1993) 'The Persistence of Individualism', *Chronicle of Higher Education*, February 10: A48.

Narvaez, A. A. (1991) 'William Paton, 101, Pioneer Accountant, Theorist and Scholar', *The New York Times*, May 1: c20.

Paton, W. A. (1915) 'Severity of Trade Cycle in America', in W. H. Hamilton (ed.) *Current Economic Problems*, Chicago, Ill.: University of Chicago Press.

Paton, W. A. (1917) 'Theory of the Double-Entry System,' *Journal of Accountancy* 23, January: 7–26.

Paton, W. A. (1922) *Accounting Theory, With Special Reference to the Corporate Enterprise*, New York: The Ronald Press Co. Reprinted in 1962 by Scholars Book Co., Lawrence, Kans., 1973.

Paton, W. A. (ed.) (1932) *Accountants' Handbook*, 2nd edn, New York: The Ronald Press. Co.

Paton, W. A. (1935) *Corporate Profits as Shown by Audit Reports*, Washington, DC: National Bureau of Economic Research, Study No. 28.

Paton, W. A. (1939) 'Objectives of Accounting Research', *Papers on Auditing Procedure American Institute of Accountants Fifty-Second Annual Meeting*, 1939: 231–2.

Paton, W. A. (1940) *Recent and Prospective Developments in Accounting Theory*, Business Research Studies, Number 25, Harvard University 27(2): March.

Paton, W. A. (ed.) (1943) *Accountants' Handbook*, 3rd edn, New York: The Ronald Press Co.

Paton, W. A. (1952) *Shirtsleeve Economics; A Commonsense Survey*, New York: Commune-Century-Crofts.

Paton, W. A. (1962) ' On Going Underground,' *Michigan Quarterly Review*, January: 19–26.

Paton, W. A. (1971a) 'Accounting's Educational Eclipse,' *Journal of Accountancy*, December: 35–6.

Paton, W. A. (1971b) 'Earmarks of a Profession – and the APB', *Journal of Accountancy*, January: 37–45.

Paton, W. A. (1972) 'Can We Sustain Prosperity?', *The Freeman*, January: 33–41.

Paton, W. A. (1976) 'In All My Years – Notes on Handicapping', *Accounting Historians Journal* 3(2): 29–31.

Paton, W. A. (1978) 'Wandering Into Accounting – Notes on a Writing Career', *Accounting Historians Journal* 5(2): 1–10.

Paton, W. A. (1981) 'Recalling George Oliver May and Me', *Accounting Historians Journal* 8(2): 91–5.

Paton, W. A. (1984) *Words! Combining Fun and Learning*, Ann Arbor, Mich.: University of Michigan, Graduate School of Business.

Paton, W. A. and Littleton, A. C. (1940) *An Introduction to Corporate Accounting Standards*, Monograph No. 3, American Accounting Association.

Previts, G. J. and Robinson, T. R. (1991) 'William Andrew Paton: Patriarch and Theorist', *Accounting Education News*, American Accounting Association, June: 10–13.

Solomons, D. (1987) 'The Twilight of Income Measurement: Twenty-Five Years On', *Accounting Historians Journal*, Spring.

Sprague, C. E. (1908) *The Philosophy of Accounts*, New York: published by the author.

Sweeney, H. W. (1964) *Stabilized Accounting*, New York: Holt, Rinehart and Winston Accounting Classic.

Taggart, H. F. (ed.) (1964) *Paton on Accounting: Selected Writings of W. A. Paton*, New York: Bureau of Business Research, Graduate School of Business Administration, The University of Michigan, New York.

Taggart, H. F. (1976) 'Beginnings of Accounting at the University of Michigan', *Michigan CPA*, May–June.

Zeff, S. A. (1979) 'Paton on the Effects of Changing Prices', in S. A. Zeff, J. Demski and N. Dopuch (eds) *Essays in Honor of William A. Paton: Pioneering Accounting Theorist*, New York: Division of Research, Graduate School of Business Administration, The University of Michigan: 91–137.

Zeff, S. A. (1987) 'Leaders of the Accounting Profession: 14 Who made A Difference', *Journal of Accountancy*, May: 46–71.

Zeff, S. A., Demski, J. and Dopuch, N. (1979) *Essays in Honor of William A. Paton: Pioneering Accounting Theorist*, Division of Research, Graduate School of Business Administration, University of Michigan.

18 Carman G. Blough (1895–1981)

Maurice Moonitz

Carman George Blough,[1] the son of Silas S. and Mary Wertz Blough, was born on 11 November 1895 in Johnstown, Pennsylvania. He died in Bridgewater, Virginia on 9 March 1981. During the thirty years from 1934 to 1964, Blough played a significant role in virtually every development in the field of professional accounting. He was without doubt one of the most influential 'high priests' of the profession during the twentieth century.

Blough graduated from Manchester (Indiana) College in 1917. In his senior year, he lost his right arm in a railway crossing accident while on a basketball trip. Despite this serious accident, he played tennis well enough to make the college team. In 1922, he earned a master's degree from the University of Wisconsin. Honorary degrees were bestowed upon him by Manchester College (1944) and by Bridgewater (Virginia) College (1972). He received his first CPA certificate in 1922 from the State of Wisconsin.

From 1922 until 1929 he was employed by the State of Wisconsin on its Tax Commission (1922–7) and on its Board of Public Affairs (1927–9). For the next four years he was Professor and Head of the Accounting Department at the University of North Dakota. In 1933, he left North Dakota to go to Armour Institute of Technology in Chicago, but resigned in 1934 to join the staff of the Securities and Exchange Commission (SEC), in Washington, DC.

At the SEC, Blough served as a financial analyst for about a year, then as Assistant Director in the Registration Division, also for about a year. In December 1935, he became the first Chief Accountant of the Commission. He left the SEC in 1938 to join Arthur Andersen & Co. as a manager; in 1940, he was made a partner; he resigned in 1942 to join the War Production Board, where he served until 1944.

Blough became the first full-time Director of Research for the American Institute of Accountants (as it was then known) in 1944, a post and title he held until his retirement in 1961. After retirement, he acted as a consultant, operating in later years out of an office in Harrisonburg, Virginia, near the farm on which he and his wife, the former Katherine Flory, lived.

He was active in professional organisations, serving as a member of the AICPA's Committee on Accounting Procedure (1938–42) and of its Accounting Principles Board (1959–64). Earlier (1928–9), he was a member of the

Wisconsin State Board of Accountancy. In 1938, he served a term as Vice-President of the American Accounting Association; in 1944, he became the AAA's first non-academic president.

His honours were many, including the AICPA's Gold Medal Award in 1953, election to The Ohio State University's Accounting Hall of Fame in 1954, and the Alpha Kappa Psi Foundation Award in 1955. In 1969, the Carman G. Blough Chair of Accounting was established at the University of Virginia by the Virginia Society of CPAs.

A word or two about Blough's religious affiliation serves to round out his background. He was a member of the Church of the Brethren, the conservative arm of a German Baptist sect that evolved from the Pietist movement in Germany. This group came to the United States in 1719 and settled in German-town, Pennsylvania. The Brethren oppose war, and advocate temperance, the simple life, plain-dress, and 'obedience to Christ rather than obedience to creeds and cults'. For many years, Blough was a trustee of Bridgewater College, a Church of the Brethren school (*The New Columbia Encyclopedia*, 1975, article, 'Brethren').

Blough's published work consists mainly of articles and reports of speeches in the professional journals. Excerpts from some of them will be used below in order to set forth the contributions he made to the profession.[2] He published just one book, *Practical Applications of Accounting Standards* (1957), a compilation of 200 selected responses to readers' queries that originally appeared in *The Journal of Accountancy* in his Department entitled 'Accounting and Auditing Problems'. That Department was under his editorship from 1946 to 1963, and was a major element in solidifying his position as a moulder of professional accounting thought in the US.

I first met Carman in September 1955 at a conference of CPAs in Seattle, Washington, where we both appeared on the programme. Later, in the early 1960s, he and I worked closely together in New York at the AICPA while I was Director of Accounting Research, and later a member of the Accounting Principles Board. During that period, I came to know him fairly well.

AT THE SEC

The Commission did not have a Chief Accountant when Blough joined its staff. Chatov (1975: 103) states that two incidents seem to have led to the creation of that office. (Chatov's account, incidentally, is based on a conversation he had with Blough in Harrisonburg on 19 October 1972.) In the earlier incident, Blough wanted to issue a 'stop order' on a company but was overruled by Chairman James M. Landis. Toward the end of 1935, the company was in financial difficulties. In the later incident, Charles Sprague, head of the division within the SEC that administered the Public Utility Holding Company Act of 1935, ordered a company to change its financial statements to meet his standards. Later the company registered, using Sprague's accounting methods. Blough and his staff felt that the accounting practices being pursued by the company were wrong. The company complained to the Commission, which held a meeting with Sprague and Blough in November 1935. Blough's position was that one accountant ought to have the final authority on policy matters within the Commission. The Commissioners agreed, and Blough was appointed to the post of Chief Accountant in December 1935, a position he held for the next two-and-a-half years.

Zeff (1972: 130) reports that 'in the early years of the Commission, Blough regularly sought the counsel of senior technical partners in the large public accounting firms on novel accounting and auditing questions'. This practice persisted during the rest of Blough's career, as will be seen in his years with Arthur Andersen & Co. and the AICPA.

Even before he became Chief Accountant, Blough had been exposed to the realities of the accounting world and had become convinced that something should be done to narrow the areas of differences in practice. As Blough himself reports, the SEC occupied itself in 1934 with recruiting a permanent staff and

> in developing the forms and regulations that would provide the kind of financial data that would be most useful to investors and prospective investors in whose interests the laws had been passed.
>
> As a result, most of the forms and regulations were completed and available to prospective registrants by the beginning of 1935. During the first six months of that year probably more questions on accounting matters were raised and resolved, rightly or wrongly, than ever before or since in a like period of time . . . Never before had so much information regarding the accounting principles, methods and procedures of business concerns been made known as that which became public during the first six months of 1935.
> . . . For the first time it was possible to know of the many areas of differences that actually existed among the accounting practices followed by well known business enterprises. These differences soon became the subject of discussion, criticism, defense and analysis. From these sprang much of the impetus for the consideration that has been given to the subject of accounting principles in the years that have intervened.
>
> (1967: 4)

Blough did not waste much time in telling the profession what he thought of the state of affairs in practice. In January 1937, he addressed a meeting of the New York State Society of CPAs and made the following strong statement

> In the course of our work, we have occasion to see a wide variety of procedures followed in the treatment of almost every conceivable kind of an accounting problem. The term 'generally accepting accounting principles' has been widely used in accounting literature, particularly by the American Institute of Accountants and the Securities and Exchange Commission; yet I do not know of any satisfactory definition of the term. A principle in some fields of knowledge is a fundamental concept universally accepted by persons in the particular field; in others, it may be considered as a rule of action. When we modify principle by the words 'generally accepted', there is an inference that

there may be principles not generally accepted. This seems to place accounting in a class where principles are not immutable laws but rules of action. Accordingly, it would seem that the proper interpretation to give to the term 'generally accepted principle', in the field of accounting is that it is a procedure for handling the recording and interpretation of a particular type of business transaction so extensively followed that it may be considered to be generally accepted. If this is a proper interpretation of the term, I am very much afraid it is difficult to name very many principles that are generally accepted.

(1937: 6)

According to Carey

The cumulative effect of this speech was devastating. Mr Blough's challenge, in conjunction with the earlier challenge of the American Accounting Association [the 1936 'Tentative Statement of Accounting Principles Affecting Corporate Reports'], made it clear that if the Institute wished to maintain a position of leadership it would have to do more than it had so far done to promulgate authoritative accounting principles.

(1970: 11–12)

Blough was also in the centre of another critical development within the SEC, namely, the decision to let the private sector take the lead in establishing a set of accounting principles so that the areas of difference in practice could be narrowed. Blough himself summarises the division within the SEC in the following passage

During the latter part of 1936, 1937 and the early part of 1938 an increasingly heated controversy was taking place within the Securities and Exchange Commission among the commissioners themselves. Two of the commissioners, both lawyers, were of the opinion that the Commission itself should promulgate a set of Accounting Principles that would have to be followed by all companies required to file financial statements with the Commission. The others were either strongly opposed to that procedure or were not convinced that it was desirable. The then Chief Accountant [i.e. Blough himself] was very much opposed to the proposal. He argued that the development of accounting principles and the elimination of the areas of differences should be left to the accounting profession, whose members dealt so intimately with the problems in their day to day practice, and that the Commission should cooperate.

(1967: 5)

Blough communicated the decision of the Commission to the profession at the American Institute's annual meeting in the autumn of 1937 (Chatov 1975: 130). Using the carrot-and-stick approach of the SEC that has persisted to this day, Blough told his audience that the private sector should take the initiative, with the blessing of the SEC, but that if the private sector failed to do the job, the Commission would step in to do it. This threat of 'accounting principles by governmental fiat' has been used by the rule-making bodies ever since to stifle opposition to their activities, even when there was not the slightest evidence that the SEC was willing or able to step in. Blough himself played a leading role in keeping alive the ideological confrontation between public and private sectors, thereby inhibiting almost completely any solid and meaningful partnership between the two in the pursuit of a generally accepted set of accounting principles.

In addition to Blough's speech to the Institute in 1937, the SEC issued its Accounting Series Release No. 4 in April 1938, which stated in essence that the 'rules, regulations, or other official releases of the Commission, including the published opinions of its chief accountant', were controlling in connection with accounting practices used in financial statements submitted to it. If the Commission itself had not spoken on a particular accounting problem, then it would accept only those practices for which there was 'substantial authoritative support', a phrase that, as later quotations will show, is uniquely Blough. The concrete meaning of 'substantial authoritative support' was not spelled out.

The American Institute reacted to the challenge. In September 1938, Council enlarged the Committee on Accounting Procedure and instructed it to submit a comprehensive plan for accounting research by April 1939. The Committee carried out its charge; a year later it issued the first three Accounting Research Bulletins. Blough was a member of the Committee from 1938 to 1942; he had left the SEC in 1939 to join the staff of Arthur Andersen & Co.

Before we move on to Blough's career with a large auditing firm, one additional facet of his attitude toward the world around him is worthy of mention. Blough made a speech in 1952 during which, among other things, he reviewed the background of events leading up to the creation of the SEC. He sketched the speculative frenzy in the stock market in the late 1920s, the plummeting stock market that started to drop in late 1929, and the onset of the Great Depression. People were dumbfounded at what had happened, and looked for someone or something to blame. 'They had to blame their predicament on someone besides themselves', he said. Financial reports of corporations whose securities had gone sour were singled out by those who had lost heavily. They asserted that if they had only had adequate information they would never have made those losing investments. Then, in two paragraphs anticipating the position of the Rochester School, he said:

> In my opinion all that was a lot of nonsense. It is true there were persons who wanted more information than they received and who were entitled to more information than was given them. Some of them probably would have developed a more intelligent investment program if they had been able to get better information. But the rank and file of the persons who lost money in the securities market would have bought just as open-handedly if there had been comprehensive prospectuses available to them.

> Enough information was available to show that many of the securities they were buying were priced at a capitalization of net earnings of less than one percent. They knew that the earnings of the companies were such as to afford less than one percent return on the money they were investing but they still

bought. But human nature, being what it is, refuses to take responsibility for its own mistakes if it can find someone else to blame, and so it blamed the corporations which had failed to furnish the information. This blame would not have stuck, however, if there had not been some basic reason beyond the agitation of those who needed a scapegoat.

(1952: 5)

The last sentence of the preceding quotation leads into Blough's explanation of the reasons that made 'the Securities Act and the Securities and Exchange Act [*sic*] . . . almost inevitable' (1952: 5). He emphasised the great pressures for more information about companies whose securities were being sold to the public, pressures emanating from financial analysts, teachers of corporate finance (e.g. William Z. Ripley, of Harvard, in *Main Street and Wall Street*, published in 1926), and many accountants. Pressures of this type legitimised the complaints of those who had lost, and lost heavily, in the stock market crash, and gave Congress the direction it needed to try to prevent a recurrence of the débâcle.

AT ARTHUR ANDERSEN & CO.

During the period from 1938 to 1942, Blough learned much at first hand about some of the problems that confronted a large national auditing practice. His experience with Arthur Andersen & Co. laid the foundation for his activities later on as Director of Research for the AICPA. Two matters are referred to below for special attention.

The first is the question of the 'position' of the auditor. At the SEC, as we have already seen, Blough was occupied with several important issues. One of special importance was the question of the auditors' independence, independence with respect to clients, as a review of Accounting Series Releases Nos. 22 and 47 will amply demonstrate. The SEC deserves a great deal of credit for stiffening the backbone of the independent auditors, giving them the support they needed to be objective in their examination of their clients' financial statements.

Blough gave his views on the position of the auditor as follows:

The auditor, as an independent expert, has an obligation to the outsiders who rely for important judgements upon the statements he certifies which is peculiar among the professions. The lawyer, for example, is an advocate. He represents his client's interest to the exclusion of all others. Any opinion he renders for public consumption are usually interpretations of the law based upon a recital of facts which any lawyer may study and form a judgement upon. Not so with the auditor. His opinion relates to findings of facts which he alone has the opportunity to investigate and his opinion (except upon certain special matters) is not readily subject to check by an outsider. He is not an advocate. He must dig out the facts and state his unbiased opinion concerning what he finds. He is more nearly a judge.

Again, the doctor, other than the public health official, has very little for which he must account to anyone but his patient. His findings of fact are for his own and his patient's action only. Not so with the accountant. His findings are very much for the action of others. His certification lends much to the confidence which public investors place in corporate reports. He holds a position of trust which places a responsibility upon him for fair, dependable, and intelligent representation that is unique among the professions.

(1940: 34)

It would be well for all practising CPAs today to read and absorb the message of those two paragraphs. As recently as March 1981, I testified as an expert witness against a CPA who insisted that his only obligation was to his client, that he had not addressed his report to the outsider who was suing him in a California court, and that therefore the outsider had no cause of action against the auditor for any loss he may have suffered. The case, incidentally, was settled out of court, so we do not know how the judge would have ruled.

Blough's views on the nature of research and its purposes when conducted by a professional organisation were spelled out in *The Andersen Chronicle*:

In a firm the size that this has now become it is inevitable that some members will follow principles and procedures that conflict fundamentally with those adopted by others. It is essential that variations of this kind be kept at a minimum. Not only must we present a united and consistent front to those who come in contact with our work but it is important that our policies reflect the soundest thinking available. Practices of the firm in which there has been complete uniformity must be reconsidered from time to time in the light of our experiences, of our own changing thought, of the practices of other firms and of the attitudes of governmental bodies, in order that we may be assured that our policies are alive and progressive. *The accomplishment of these purposes is the aim of our research program.*

(1941: 36, emphasis added)

Blough then proceeded to indicate the three major parts to the research programme at Arthur Andersen & Co. that he presumably was to conduct:

1　Problems were to be brought to the attention of those who were primarily responsible for the research procedures. The agenda of the research group must not be set solely by those who were to do the research. This policy would ensure that the research group worked on real issues that had arisen in the field, and that it would receive information concerning the manner in which those issues were handled in the first instance, before any research findings were available.
2　The problems selected for consideration must then be studied and analysed and a report on the findings issued. '[T]hese studies cannot be conducted in any cloistered manner or restricted to those devoting their major attention to the task . . . [W]ithout the benefit of the experiences and judgements of those having the experience most pertinent to a particular case, the final solution lacks the soundness that our combined judgements warrant' (pp. 37–8).
3　The results of the research and any firm policies decided upon must then be disseminated effectively to all in the organisation.

This sketch of a research programme is reminiscent of Blough's practice at the SEC, previously noted, of conferring with the senior partners of the large firms for advice and counsel on novel accounting and auditing issues. It also carries over into his activities with the AICPA.

AT THE AICPA

In 1942, Blough resigned from his post as a partner in Arthur Andersen & Co. to do war work in Washington, DC. In 1944, he left government service to become the first full-time Director of Research for the AICPA in New York.

The pace of research activity quickened under Blough's leadership at the Institute (Zeff 1972: 145). In keeping with his earlier views and practices at SEC and at Arthur Andersen & Co., Blough started or strengthened liaison with a variety of organisations that had interest, knowledge, or expertise in accounting and auditing. He used various methods, such as meetings with key persons, with committees, or with research staffs. He sent out subcommittee reports, discussion papers, and interim drafts for comment and criticism. He also used his column in *The Journal of Accountancy* to good effect. True to his own expressed views, Blough kept in touch and listened to the voices of the practitioners and users of financial information.

In 1957, the Institute set up a 'Special Committee on Research Program' to study and make recommendations on the Institute's role in shaping accounting principles. The Committee was under the chairmanship of Weldon Powell, of Haskins & Sells. Blough was a member of the Committee, as were William W. Werntz, a former Chief Accountant of the SEC, and Andrew Barr, the then Chief Accountant of the SEC. (As an aside, while at the SEC, Blough had employed the three men who succeeded him in the Chief Accountant's post: William W. Werntz, Earle C. King, and Andrew Barr.)

The Special Committee recommended the phasing out of the Committee on Accounting Procedure, the creation of an Accounting Principles Board, and the establishment of a quasi-autonomous Accounting Research Division. The major recommendations were adopted by Council, and the new APB came into being on 1 September 1959 under the chairmanship of Weldon Powell. Blough was a member of the APB. Perry Mason became Acting Director of the new Accounting Research Division, and I took over as Director on 1 July 1960, with Mason as my Associate Director.

Blough's views on the nature of research were once more expressed at a meeting in Columbus, Ohio:

> In the field of accounting principles and procedures, such investigations and inquiries [i.e. research] cannot be directed primarily to the literature in the field. Accounting has been defined by the Institute's terminology committee, as 'the art of recording, classifying, and summarizing in a significant manner and in terms of money, transactions and events which are, in part at least, of a financial character, and interpreting the results thereof'. In harmony with this

definition, accounting research is directed toward an understanding of the accounting needs of all segments of business, the methods that have been tried to meet them, the development of possible alternatives, the arraying of possible arguments for and against the different proposals, the gathering together and analyzing of the viewpoints of others – all with a view to determining which alternative would be most useful.

(1960a: 7)

Blough also told an Institute meeting about the need for an underlying framework to narrow the areas of differences in accounting:

We read, from time to time, about basic assumptions or underlying postulates of accounting, yet nowhere is an authoritative statement of them to be found. Individual authors have undertaken to express them, but the organized profession has never dealt with them. Similarly, we speak freely about basic accounting principles and use the term generally accepted accounting principles. But what are they and what distinguishes them from procedures or practices? Until the groundwork is laid by solidifying these foundations, our specific day-to-day problems are likely to be resolved more by expediency than as consistent parts of a cohesive body of thought.

(1959b: 38)

As Director of Research, Blough had jurisdiction over auditing questions as well as those involving financial accounting and reporting. In an article in *The Journal of Accountancy*, he wrote about 'Responsibility to Third Parties'. Here are the headnote and first paragraph of that article, both of them reminiscent of the position he had taken previously:

It is the auditor's obligation 'to select, from all the financial information he has about the business, what is significant to formation of an intelligent judgment regarding its financial position and results of operations, and see that it is presented as informatively as possible'.

There are those who assert that the auditor has no responsibility except to his client. They believe that the accountant enters into a contract (written, oral, or implied), and that the only one he owes a duty is the party with whom he has made the contract. This has long been considered invalid both under the standards which the profession itself has established and under the decisions of the courts.

(1960b: 58)

The rise in the price level after the Second World War placed conventional accounting under tremendous strains. Blough was in the midst of the controversies swirling about the accountants as to what, if anything, should be done about the situation. Although Blough was no pioneer, no reformer with a cause, he was acutely aware of the problems involved, the solutions proposed, and the pressure groups whose interests were at stake. Here are a few excerpts from his published output to illustrate his position.

In 1948, he published an 'accountant's view' of the way to handle replacement costs and depreciation policy in a period of rising prices. Two paragraphs from his comments follow:

> Perhaps, after all, the solution to this problem is not to be found in changing accounting procedures. Maybe basic business concepts of profits are at fault and rapidly rising or falling price levels merely bring out the need for different concepts. Perhaps we should develop a system of measuring business activity in terms of index numbers. Possibly existing accounting procedures would be most effective for reporting basic data if a plan for measuring profits in terms of constant units of value were developed and supplementary statements in terms of these units were adopted.
>
> Until some basic changes in business measurement or some sound change in accounting procedure can be developed to meet these current difficulties, however, we must resist the adoption of procedures that have no basis for objective determination and are not intended to be applied consistently. Certainly the answer to our problem is not for companies to decide their procedures without regard to the need for orderly and consistent practices. Business as a whole will suffer if there should be any widespread feeling among the users of financial statements that charges to income are based on the whim of management, are not in accordance with generally accepted accounting procedures, and cannot be tested for fairness within reasonable limits.
>
> (1948: 11)

Blough had a dislike for partial solutions (such as LIFO and its cousin, replacement-cost depreciation) and a distrust of those who wished to change accounting principles for the purpose of achieving some special-interest objective. True to his legacy from SEC days, he preferred the use of disclosure in the form of notes to the financial statements and of supplementary schedules and statements. What he constantly fought against were attempts to change the underlying basis of accounting by tinkering and tampering, as though accounting itself was really not of much importance.

On one aspect of my comments in the foregoing paragraph, here is a paragraph from a paper he published in 1959 arguing against a proposal to permit depreciation charges to be increased to reflect 'inflation':

> Before going any farther, let me say that I do not disagree, in principle, with those who advocate price-level adjustments for all transactions affected by inflation, whether set forth in financial statements or not. I do seriously disagree as a matter of consistency, logic, and fairness with all those who limit their adjustment proposals to depreciation. However, though I acknowledge the soundness of complete adjustment as a matter of principle or theory, I do not feel it is practical at this time. How far must inflation go before it would be practical? I do not know but it would have to be far enough for its significance to be understood by many more than understand it today.
>
> (1959a: 49)

Blough then makes several important points:

1 Management's need to make financial decisions in a period of rising prices can be facilitated by the preparation of special-purpose reports or analyses. But most other users of financial statements are not so fortunately situated and must rely on general-purpose financial statements. To adjust for depreciation alone would probably confuse them and lead to false conclusions. The impact of changing prices on a company's financial position and results of operations can better be shown in supplementary statements or analyses (p. 51).

2 If 'price-level depreciation' were accepted for income-tax purposes, it would no doubt be good for those with large amounts of depreciable property, but only at the expense of other taxpayers. In inflation, the investor in 'productive, physical assets' benefits from rising prices. The one who lent his capital to the owner of the productive assets not only would not share in these benefits, but would receive no tax concessions and, furthermore, is repaid in dollars smaller than those he lent (p. 52).

Blough sums up his position as follows:

Please do not misunderstand me; I am just as interested in having the productive plant in this country efficiently maintained as anyone else. On the other hand, I do not want to see a plea for special consideration for one group of taxpayers at the expense of others on either accounting grounds or statistical grounds that are developed on biased bases. As the old saying goes, what is sauce for the goose is sauce for the gander.

(1959a: 54)

The paragraph just quoted brings out Blough's opposition to departures from 'neutrality', as the term is used today. He understood the 'economic consequences' that could flow both from a well-established set of accounting procedures, and from changes therein. He knew full well that pressures are great to make accounting reflect some policy or policies of special-interest groups. He also knew full well that the power of the output of the accounting process to inform a larger rather than a smaller group of users of financial data depends on its neutrality among the competing special interests. Carman Blough may have been wrong at times, but he was not subservient, venal or stupid. And he had the courage to speak his mind so that no one was in doubt as to where he stood, and why.

In a discussion of 'The Meaning of Generally Accepted Accounting Principles', Blough has a striking passage:

Now I do think that means that accounting principles are exclusive of any other accounting principle dealing with the same subject. Just to use one example with which you're all familiar is the principle of valuing inventories. The valuation of inventories on the LIFO basis is sufficiently followed; has been adopted by a sufficient number of substantial companies; has been certified to by representative and well-qualified accountants; has been accepted by the government as a reasonable method of arriving at taxable income; has been accepted by The Securities and Exchange Commission as a reasonable representation of income for filing with that Commission; and has been recognized in textbooks – *all of which, it seems to me, forces us to accept LIFO (whether we like it or not)* – forces us to accept LIFO as a generally accepted principle of valuing inventories. On the other hand, the acceptance of LIFO did not make FIFO an unacceptable method. There are still sufficient numbers of companies following FIFO and certified to by highly qualified and professionally competent accountants; and also accepted by The Securities and Exchange Commission; and by The Treasury Department; and by text-book writers. So that we have to recognize that *there is substantial authoritative support for both of those methods and yet, each is in conflict with the other.* And it seems to me that only when one of them becomes so *preponderantly* used to the exclusion of the other and the other is discredited by authoritative pronouncements and writings and discussions – both in the profession and in government and other circles – that only then will it cease to be a 'generally accepted accounting principle'.

(1956: 118, emphasis added)

Blough's distaste for LIFO shows through clearly in this excerpt; his distaste was real, as I can attest from first-hand contact with him. It also reveals his willingness to live with the consequences of 'general acceptance' and 'substantial authoritative support' as the foundation for accounting principles.

In connection with LIFO, I was told about an incident at a meeting which Blough attended. I cannot document this incident, so it will have to remain in the oral tradition for the present, but I have every reason to suppose it actually happened. At this meeting, one of the topics for discussion was the desirability of trying to convince the taxing authorities to accept the cost-or-market option with LIFO. Blough knew very well, as did the rest of those present, that one of the conditions agreed to by the profession for the privilege to use LIFO for tax purposes was that LIFO would remain strictly a cost method, i.e. not subject to the cost-or-market option. For the first time, Blough heard a highly placed and influential practitioner advocate this departure from the agreement reached in the late 1930s. When he heard this, he blurted out from the floor, so that all could hear him, 'No! No! This is immoral!'

He did not say that it was illogical, inequitable, or statistically biased, but immoral to urge a system that would exclude realised holding gains on inventories from retained earnings (and from taxation) but would take unrealised holding losses into income on a current basis, acceptable as a deduction for tax purposes. 'Immoral' was the strongest pejorative he could muster to express his deep-seated distaste for the proposal.

SOME RECOLLECTIONS

In this concluding section, I will relate some recollections I have of Blough. To get one bit of unpleasant business out of the way, I start with Blough's treatment of Perry Mason at the Institute. In the early 1950s, Blough was ill, and it was uncertain if he would be able to return to work, and if so, if he could operate at full speed. Perry Mason was asked to come to New York to serve as Blough's replacement, if one were needed, or as his assistant if he recovered fully from his illness. For family reasons, Mason resigned his position as Full Professor of Berkeley (at an above-scale salary, incidentally) to join the Institute at exactly the same salary he was making at Berkeley. When I arrived on the scene in mid-1960 to take over as Director of Accounting Research, with Mason as my Associate Director, I found that Mason was making precisely the same salary, to the dollar, as he had made when he came to New York many years before. Under the procedure in effect at the Institute, at least when I joined the staff, the division directors took the initiative to recommend salary increases for their staff to the executive director.

Why Blough treated a person of Mason's reputation and abilities in this fashion, I do not know. I realise full well that equally puzzling is why Mason put up with this treatment for so many years. At no time did he reveal anything at all about his relationship with Blough. So the puzzle remains unsolved.

Now to more pleasant things. One of the nicest memories of the early 1960s at the Institute is the manner in which Blough blended in with his staff on a natural basis. This showed up particularly at lunch-time. He and I would check with each other to see who was free for lunch. On many occasions a group of us – consisting of Blough and me, Perry Mason, Cecilia Tierney, Richard Lytle, Richard Nest, and others from the staffs of both Blough's division and mine – would go out together. These were informal sessions, and the standing rule was that the costs were borne on a 'Dutch treat' basis – everyone paid his own tab. Blough would frequently raise an issue for informal discussion – he clearly was using us as a sounding board. For example, one thing that still bothered him was the precise meaning of 'fairly' in the auditor's standard opinion.

Blough's behaviour at the meetings of the Accounting Principles Board was interesting. Except on one occasion, discussed below, he did not dominate the meeting but participated in an unobtrusive manner. In part, this followed from the manner in which the APB was staffed. It satisfied one of his necessary conditions for progress in agreeing on generally accepted accounting principles, namely, that the policy-makers keep in touch with the leading practitioners. Except for the first year of the APB's existence, all the top partners of the Big Eight accounting firms were members, so that communication among them was direct and continuous. Blough himself was in touch with others through his position on the Institute's staff and his Department in *The Journal of Accountancy*. He also performed an important service because of his deep knowledge of the SEC and the way it operated. As far as I can remember, no major issue was ever decided by the Board until someone asked the question, 'Has anyone talked to Andy?' (i.e. Andrew Barr, Chief Accountant of the SEC during that period). Usually someone had, although not always Blough himself. The point Blough was making was that the chief policy-maker in the private sector (the APB) should know what the powerful Federal Agency had in mind on the topic under discussion, not in order to be subservient, but to avoid rushing ahead only to find out too late that it was tilting at a windmill (or worse) when it had no intention of so doing. The role of 'high priest' or *éminence grise*, if you will, came easily and naturally to Blough in the closing years of his active career in the accounting world.

Blough's views and mine on the kind of research necessary to establish accounting principles collided when the Board discussed Accounting Research Study No. 3, 'A Tentative Set of Broad Accounting Principles', in April 1962. I have discussed that meeting and its background elsewhere, so I will not go into it in detail here, but here is the paragraph that tells of Blough's role:

> At the meeting the discussion was sharp and pointed. Carman Blough led the attack, so to speak, maintaining the position that the study should never have been written, let alone published. Characteristically, Blough kept his attack on the issues and not on the persons involved. My respect for Blough increased immeasurably as a result of his conduct at that meeting, and part of the reasons for his leadership in the profession became clear to me. He never let his attention wander from the central issue, even though he felt deeply about the problems involved.
>
> (Moonitz 1974: 19)

The Study did, of course, appear with the disclaimer by the APB now known as 'Accounting Principles Board Statement No. 1'. After the Board voted in effect not to oppose publication of the Study, Blough and I worked together in open meeting to iron out the procedural details: where in the publication the Board's disclaimer was to appear, the colour of the paper on which it was to be printed, the weight of the paper to be used, and the physical separation of the disclaimer from the research study itself. These details seemed important at the time to emphasise the distinction between the Board's position and that of the Director of Accounting Research.

Two and a half years later, Blough resigned from the APB. I wrote him a letter of appreciation for his efforts to build a stronger and more responsible profession. I cannot locate a copy of my letter to him, but I do have his letter to me. Below is the first paragraph from his reply. It is characteristic of the man.

> It is difficult for me to tell you how very much your letter regarding my resignation from the Accounting Principles Board means to me. It has always been my wish to deal with principles and problems without any reflection on those who disagreed with me. Sometimes my disagreement with you on technical matters was so vigorous that I have been afraid that at times you might have felt that I was reflecting on you personally, so I doubly appreciate your statement that I never indulged in personalities.

All of us who knew Carman George Blough agree that he was a man of integrity, simplicity and modesty, one who unswervingly focused on issues, not on personalities, and who was completely dedicated to his profession.

Notes

1 Biographical data were obtained from several sources, but principally from Burns and Coffman (1976: 9, 73).
2 Many of Blough's published writings have been reprinted in Shenkir (1978).

References

Blough, C. G. (1937) 'Some Accounting Problems of the Securities and Exchange Commission', *The New York Certified Public Accountant*, April: 3–14. Reprinted in Shenkir (1978).

Blough, C. G. (1940) 'The Auditor's Responsibility to the Investor', *Proceedings of the Fifteenth Annual Michigan Accounting Conference*, University of Michigan: 33–42. Reprinted in Shenkir (1978).

Blough, C. G. (1941) 'Our Program for Accounting Research', *The Andersen Chronicle*, January: 35–40. Reprinted in Shenkir (1978).

Blough, C. G. (1948) 'The Accountants View', *Replacement Costs and Depreciation Policy*, National Industrial Conference Board: 8–11. Reprinted in Shenkir (1978).

Blough, C. G. (1952) 'Trends in Financial Reporting of Private Enterprise', *Federal Accountant*, November: 3–9. Reprinted in Shenkir (1978).

Blough, C. G. (1956) 'The Meaning of Generally Accepted Accounting Principles', *Technical Papers Presented at the 1956 Mountain States Accounting Conference*, Santa Fe, New Mexico: 115–24. Reprinted in Shenkir (1978).

Blough, C. G. (1957) *Practical Applications of Accounting Standards*, New York: AICPA.

Blough, C. G. (1959a) 'Depreciation – To Measure Income or to Provide Funds for Replacement?', *NAA Bulletin*, August: 47–55. Reprinted in Shenkir (1978).

Blough, C. G. (1959b) 'Challenges to the Accounting Profession in the United States', *The Journal of Accountancy*, December: 37–42. Reprinted in Shenkir (1978).

Blough, C. G. (1960a) 'Accounting Research for Better Financial Reporting', *Proceedings of the Twenty-Second Annual Institute on Accounting*, Ohio State University: 5–14. Reprinted in Shenkir (1978).

Blough, C. G. (1960b) 'Responsibility to Third Parties', *Journal of Accountancy*, May: 58–65. Reprinted in Shenkir (1978).

Blough, C. G. (1967) 'Development of Accounting Principles in the United States', *Berkeley Symposium on the Foundations of Financial Accounting*, University of California, Berkeley: 1–14. Reprinted in Shenkir (1978).

Burns, T. J. and Coffman, E. N. (1976) *The Accounting Hall of Fame: Profiles of Thirty-Six Members*, The Ohio State University.

Carey, J. L. (1970) *The Rise of the Accounting Profession*, Vol. II, New York: AICPA.

Chatov, R. (1975) *Corporate Financial Reporting: Public or Private Control?*, New York: The Free Press.

Moonitz, M. (1974) *Obtaining Agreement on Standards in the Accounting Profession*, Studies in Accounting Research No. 8, AAA.

Shenkir, W. G. (ed.) (1978) Carman G. Blough: *His Professional Career and Accounting Thought*, New York: Arno Press.

The New Columbia Encyclopedia (1975) article: 'Brethren', Columbia University Press.

Zeff, S. A. (1972) *Forging Accounting Principles in Five Countries: A History and Analysis of Trends*, New York: Stipes Publishing Co.

19 *Truth in Accounting*
The ordeal of Kenneth MacNeal (1895–1972)

Stephen A. Zeff

Abstract

Kenneth MacNeal was the author of *Truth in Accounting*, a 1939 book known for its undiluted advocacy of 'economic value' accounting. Thus far, MacNeal's book and other writings, though cited have not been subjected to in-depth analysis. Nothing is publicly known about MacNeal's background, how he came to write the book, how it was received, and why he ceased contributing to the accounting literature a scant two years after the appearance of the book. In this article, MacNeal's work is placed in an historical frame, and the principal arguments in his book are critically examined. Finally, an incident, hitherto unreported in the accounting literature, in which MacNeal was commissioned by *Fortune* to write an article critical of the accounting profession in the wake of the McKesson & Robbins scandal, only to be told, under suspicious circumstances, that the commission had been rescinded, is related.

INTRODUCTION

Kenneth MacNeal is widely known as author of a vigorous advocacy of market-based valuations in financial statements. His *magnum opus, Truth in Accounting*, was published in 1939 by the University of Pennsylvania Press and was reprinted in 1970 by Scholars Book Co. His book continues to be cited and discussed in accounting theory seminars more than forty years after its initial appearance. MacNeal wrote three articles in *The Nation* (1939b, 1939c, 1941a)[1] and one in *The Accounting Forum* (1941b).[2] Thus, his entire published output occurred between 1939 and 1941.

Virtually nothing can be found in the accounting literature about MacNeal. What was his trade or profession? What motivated him to break into print with a book that defied the conventional wisdom of his day? How was the book received in the literature? And, finally, what became of MacNeal – and why did his published writings reach an abrupt end in 1941? This chapter throws some light on these questions and evaluates MacNeal's contribution to the accounting literature.

This chapter consists of eight parts. First, some biographical data on MacNeal are presented, followed by a brief discussion of the reason why he wrote *Truth in*

Accounting. The longest section is an examination of the main points of the argument presented in his book, and this is followed by a discussion of the major published criticism of the book. Then the source of MacNeal's well-known article, 'What's Wrong With Accounting?', is traced, including the controversy attending its publication in *The Nation* instead of *Fortune*, whose editors had originally commissioned the article. Following a brief treatment of the contributions of early valuation theorists, the influence of MacNeal's writings among professionals, policy makers and academics is reviewed. In the final section, a few concluding remarks are offered.

PERSONAL DATA

Kenneth Forsythe MacNeal (he never used his middle name) was born in Berwyn, Illinois on 20 December 1895. His father, Arthur W. MacNeal, was a physician and later founded what is today known as the MacNeal Memorial Hospital in Berwyn. He was educated in J. Sterling Morton High School in suburban Chicago and entered the University of Chicago in September 1912, majoring in commerce and administration. He took but three courses in accounting, all taught by Jay Dunne (BA, Michigan), an Instructor in Accounting: Introductory (B-), Intermediate (B), and Cost (C). Overall, his grades were a mixture of Bs, Cs, Ds and, finally, a quarter of Fs. In January 1916 he was dismissed, formally, for 'poor work', but he explained to friends that the real reason was an excess of absences from class. It was said that this brush with University authorities was a source of pride, as it was the first evidence of his independent thinking.[3] While MacNeal was at the University of Chicago, John B. Canning was taking courses and lecturing, but I have found no evidence that the two ever met. On the social side, MacNeal was active in Phi Gamma Delta fraternity.

In 1915–1916, he took three accounting courses in Northwestern University's School of Commerce, receiving a grade in only one. His courses were Accounting II and III (taught by David Himmelblau) and CPA Quiz (taught by Arthur E. Andersen, founder of Arthur Andersen & Co.) in which he received a grade of C. After two years of service with the US Army in France during the First World War (1917–19), MacNeal enrolled for a brief period in the Université de Montpellier. He then returned to the United States and took the Uniform CPA Examination in November 1919. His performance on the examination earned him the Gold Medal from the State of Illinois. He received Certificate No. 234 in April 1920. He received a reciprocal certificate from Pennsylvania in 1944.

He married Marguerite Giroud on 19 March 1921, and they later had three children: Richard Henri, Edward Arthur, and Marguerite Louise.

MacNeal began his professional career in 1916 (at the age of twenty), while attending Northwestern University. In January of that year, he joined the staff of Price, Waterhouse & Co., in Chicago, and in the Preface of *Truth* he mentions his early exposure to the conventional accounting wisdom and proceeds to state the premise of his book:

I was warned [at Price, Waterhouse] that accounting was, after all, 'only common sense'. Perhaps this warning was meant as an antidote for undigested economic theories, acquired from two universities, in which I had much faith. Be that as it may, the intervening years of experience, in both public and private work, have not tended to confirm in me the idea that accounting is only common sense. . . . Yet . . . the vital defect in present accounting practice is its disharmony with the simpler principles of economics and logic, commonly called common sense.

(1939a: xi)

He remained with Price, Waterhouse & Co. until February 1917, when he left for France. Beginning in the 1920s, MacNeal occupied a series of accounting and financial positions in a number of Philadelphia enterprises which embraced manufacturing, building construction, and hotel, real estate, and financial projects. In 1929–30, as a treasurer in an investment trust, he was immediate and directing head of a staff of five other CPAs which conducted an extensive five-year analysis of the published financial statements of all companies listed on the New York Stock Exchange. In 1944, he founded a small firm of CPAs in Philadelphia, known as MacNeal & Co., and later as MacNeal, Keetz & Allen.

MacNeal retired in the early 1960s, and he died on 16 March 1972.

BACKGROUND TO THE BOOK

According to MacNeal, the stimulus for his book arose in a dispute with Price, Waterhouse & Co. in 1930. In a long letter written on May 17, 1940 to Henry Rand Hatfield, MacNeal related that 'P. W. & Co. were at that time auditing an investment trust which we controlled, and had refused to show the portfolio at market values and to exhibit the unrealized profits in the income statement'. MacNeal drafted the 'Fable of the Two Investment Trusts', which later appeared in the first chapter of *Truth*, in an effort to persuade the auditors to his view. The 'Fable' shows how the managers of two portfolios of securities, each of which has risen in value, can elect the fiscal period in which to recognise the gain as accounting profit merely by the decision of when to dispose of the portfolio. MacNeal says in the letter that PW evidently was impressed with his argument, although George O. May, then the PW senior partner, was reported as saying that it might be some time before practice would be likely to accept MacNeal's treatment of unrealised profits. None the less, MacNeal writes, PW consented to have 'the statements . . . prepared on a strictly present value basis, with unrealized profits shown in the body of the income account and included in the total profits earned'. 'At the time', MacNeal writes, 'I can remember thinking that perhaps this was the first time a reputable firm of CPAs had ever done such a thing, and I remember feeling quite proud of myself'.[4]

The victory in his bout with PW led MacNeal to undertake a 'holy crusade' to bring about a change in accounting practice. It took seven years for MacNeal to complete the manuscript for the book that was eventually to be published under the provocative title, *Truth in Accounting*. MacNeal sent the typescript to several friends in CPA firms for their opinions, and he also sent copies to a number of publishers. It was rejected by McGraw-Hill Book Company, The Ronald Press Company, and Prentice-Hall, Inc. MacNeal then approached the University of Pennsylvania Press. (He was a resident of Philadelphia, where the Press was located.) Before reaching a decision, the Press obtained the views of an economist and an accounting academic. Both consultants reported favourably, and the Press offered to publish MacNeal's manuscript.[5]

The book was dedicated to Lawrence E. Jones. In correspondence, MacNeal explained Jones's role in the project as follows:

> Lawrence E. Jones was a Phi Gam brother with whom I was associated, off and on, for a great many years, starting with a partnership in Chicago in 1915.
>
> [He] was quite a guy. Without putting them into words, he made the 'Three Fables' [related in the first chapter of MacNeal's book] work for him all his life. I was younger than he and his contempt for accountants' figures and his understanding of their short-comings could not fail to leave its mark on me. Eventually this resulted in my effort to explain a situation that few accountants would admit existed.[6]

Jones died a millionaire in 1961 at the age of 73. He was a successful inventor, although most of his career was spent in real estate development. For a number of years, he was president and MacNeal was secretary-treasurer of various building corporations associated with the Alden Park complex, in Philadelphia.

AN EXAMINATION OF *TRUTH IN ACCOUNTING*

MacNeal's overriding concern in his writings is with the small investor. His argument is that small investors are deceived by financial statements that are predicated on the accountant's notions of 'realisation' and 'conservatism'.

In the first quarter of the book, he states the problem, examines some contradictions in a sample of major accounting treatises, endeavours to understand the reasons behind the realisation and conservatism concepts, and traces the historical evolution of accounting practice – during all of which he reiterates his main contention – that small investors are being misled by financial statements that are not based on economic values.

In his first chapter, MacNeal presents three 'Fables'. Each Fable illustrates how the notions of realisation and conservatism can be misleading. In the first Fable, a small investor, relying totally on conventional financial statements, misjudges the worth of an investment. In the second, two flour mills are being compared. One had invested most of its funds in wheat, and the other had invested a like amount in interest-bearing securities. At the end of one period, by which time the price of wheat had doubled, the second mill liquidated its holding of securities, reported interest income in its certified financial statements, and used its proceeds from the sale of the securities to purchase wheat at the higher price. Thus, the second mill had half as much wheat as the first mill. The first mill

338 Twentieth-century accounting thinkers

continued to hold its wheat, and no gain owing to the increase in market price was reported in its certified financial statements. A banker, noting that both companies had an identical number of *dollars* invested in wheat but that only the second mill had reported any profit for the period, advised a small investor to invest in the second mill. The moral is that the accountant's realisation test can mislead bankers and small investors.

In the third, MacNeal's well-known 'Fable of the Two Investment Trusts', the financiers of two trusts which hold securities that are appreciating in price succeed in 'fooling' the market by alternating the years in which each trust realises its gain. The securities market is assumed to bid up the price of the trust that has realised its gains, and to bid down the price of the trust showing no such accounting gains during the period. MacNeal characterises the market reaction as follows:

> as soon as the certified financial statements of the American Trust and of the National Trust were mailed to stockholders and printed in the newspapers, everybody learned that the American Trust had earned 23% on its capital stock during the year whereas the National Trust had earned only 3% on its capital stock. The price of the American Trust stock therefore rose sharply as many investors rushed to buy it, and the price of the National Trust stock dropped sharply due to selling by disappointed stockholders.
>
> (1939a: 12)

The financiers of the two trusts sell a portion of their shares in the American Trust and buy more shares in the National Trust. In the following year, gains accrue on the investment holdings of both trusts, and the National Trust is instructed to sell its holdings, thus recognising two years of gains in its profit and loss statement. The market reacts in like manner as in the first year, and the financiers dispose of a block of their shares in the National Trust and buy shares in the American Trust.[7]

Following the second Fable, MacNeal does not tell his readers why a banker would regard financial statements as representing the worth of a company's assets. In the third Fable, MacNeal does not explain why the aggregate securities market would be 'fooled' by financial statements known to embody the realisation and conservatism concepts, particularly when, as MacNeal indicates, the market values of the investments held by the two trusts were disclosed by each in a footnote.[8] He simply asserts that 'most of the public did not pay much attention' to the footnotes and, moreover, '[t]he few people who did see and understand the footnote disregarded it' because they knew that the unrealised gain would be wiped out prior to sale if the prices of the investments were soon to fall (1939a: 11–12). Except in his discussion of the third Fable, MacNeal confines his argument to the supposed impact on the small investor and his advisers. MacNeal offers no defence of the view that the aggregate market could be deceived, indeed systematically deceived period after period, by financial statements known to reflect the notions of realisation and conservatism, even when public disclosure were made of market prices on the balance-sheet date. It was not until the 1960s that researchers began to study the impact of accounting information on the aggregate market as opposed to the individual investor (see, e.g. Beaver 1981).

In Chapters II and III, MacNeal skilfully exposes accounting authorities[9] who, on the one hand, contend that financial statements should figure importantly in the making of economic decisions but, on the other, prescribe rules such as realisation and conservatism which would generate information of little use for economic decision making. MacNeal writes:

> although accounting authorities do at times seem to give lip service to the idea that balance sheets should exhibit real values as of the date of the balance sheet, they advocate methods which make the exhibition of such values almost impossible.
>
> (1939a: 32)

In Chapter II, MacNeal reviews the theoretical justifications for the realisation and conservatism notions, and finds them wanting. He writes, 'Conservatism will not appeal to intelligent individuals as a valid argument when it is used in defense of untruths which may cause widespread injustice' (p. 52). He believes that, while the notion of 'going value' (i.e. the use of original cost for assets) made sense when financial statements were of interest only to owner-managers, its use 'ignores all consideration of creditors and inactive stockholders' (p. 48). He adds that 'uninformed temporary stockholders are hopelessly deceived, not only as to the value of the assets behind their stock, but also as to the earnings of their company' (p. 48). Finally, he rejects May's proposal (though he does not name May, who was then the powerful senior partner of Price, Waterhouse & Co., anywhere in the book) that listed companies should publish a summary of the accounting principles and practices used in their financial statements. May believed that investors, provided with such a summary, would be in a much better position to appreciate what financial statements do and do not report about a company.[10] MacNeal saw it as 'a hopeless task to attempt to educate millions of stockholders regarding present accounting principles' (p. 56). A more feasible answer, argued MacNeal, was to bring accounting principles into line with 'simple truth as it is instinctively understood by laymen everywhere' (p. 57).

In Chapter IV, the last chapter before MacNeal begins to present his preferred concept of economic-value accounting, he lapses into an unfortunate twelve-page digression on early bookkeeping techniques and treatises – unfortunate because, first, the great majority of readers would have found it to be of no interest or relevance, and, second, at least according to Hatfield, it contains numerous errors.[11] He follows this section with a more pertinent discussion of the historical development of accounting practices against the background of the evolution of business enterprise. As MacNeal's available sources provided only thin support for this more germane historical foray, 'it seems necessary to endeavour to reconstruct conditions as they existed from medieval times and to attempt to deduce therefrom the probable development of these principles in the light of those conditions' (p. 70).

In doing so, MacNeal interpolates liberally and with an occasional dash of cynicism. He identified the eras of (1) the owner-manager, (2) the creditor, and (3) the 'small uninformed security holder' (p. 82), and concludes that the accounting practices still in use in 1939 were those suited mainly to the first two eras – and that they are woefully anachronistic in the era of broad equity capital markets. Warming to his passionate sense of mission, and perhaps remembering the successes of Lawrence E. Jones, MacNeal assailed accountants for their ineptitude in serving small investors:

> In other words, the millions of small investors who own the great industries of this country, and of other countries, are unable to learn the truth about their own properties and are left at the mercy of individuals with inside information who may care to prey on them, largely because the accounting profession sees fit to turn out reports which, in many cases, are misleading and untrue, and whose preparation is in accordance with principles suited only to conditions existing many years ago. The simple truth of the matter is that an accountant's present knowledge and training do not wholly qualify him to prepare correct financial statements. If accountants would complete their educations, to the end that they might adopt sound accounting principles and might be fitted to value those assets whose economic values are not immediately apparent, they would be so qualified. Accountants must either become valuers, or must employ valuers, if they are to prepare truthful financial statements. Financial statements purport to deal with present economic values, and they are apt to be useful only to the extent that they do. They are extremely apt to be mischievous to the extent that they do not do so.
> (1939a: 84)

This is only one of many places in the book where MacNeal 'lectures' accountants, and the effect was doubtless to rankle most of those upon whom he had hoped to make a favourable impact.

In the remaining three-quarters of his book, MacNeal methodically builds a case for accounting in terms of economic values. He devotes Chapter V to a primer on demand, supply, and the nature of value, and in Chapter VI he discourses on the nature of money as a medium of pricing and exchange. Half of the chapter on money is taken up with a critical discussion of Sweeney's 'stabilized accounting' (1936). He praises Sweeney (whose name he consistently misspells as 'Sweeny') for having 'clearly seen the glaring faults of accepted accounting principles' (1939a: 123). In like vein, MacNeal adds:

> The result is, within the limits of accuracy of the data available an exhaustive and mathematically impregnable system for displaying changes in purchasing power. Whether or not one approves the concept employed by Stabilized Accounting, he must admit that it completely achieves its announced purpose.
> (1939a: 123)

But MacNeal objects to Sweeney's general price-level concept on two grounds. First, the 'stabilized' profit and loss statement, which would be expressed in purchasing power as of the balance-sheet date and not as of the dates of the several transactions, 'may be far beyond the comprehension of the ordinary man or woman who would have to depend for financial information upon the figures presented' (pp. 123–4). Further: 'Such data would not inform the ordinary stockholder or the ordinary director. It would merely make him doubt the accountant's sanity' (p. 124). MacNeal thus reiterates his theme that accountants should present financial statements that would be readily understood by stockholders, rather than expect stockholders to learn special accounting meanings, e.g. original cost/realisation results, or purchasing-power-adjusted results. MacNeal's second objection is that stockholders and businessmen already understand intuitively that today's dollars are worth less than the dollars of a year or years ago, and it is unlikely that Sweeney's 'stabilized accounting' would, therefore, tell them any more than they already know. That MacNeal may have less than fully understood the phenomenon for which Sweeney was endeavouring to account, is suggested by the following passage:

> If the general commodity index doubled during a year, [Sweeney's] Stabilized Accounting would show both the original capital account and surplus account at twice their former amounts and would omit the amount of this increase from earnings, whereas the writer would exhibit the capital account and surplus account unchanged and would show the entire increase in net worth as earnings.
>
> (1939a: 116)

According to MacNeal, accounting must meet the common-sense expectations of the readers:

> A balance sheet and a profit and loss statement purport to state values. In order to fulfil their purpose, they must state values according to economic concepts, commonly called economic values, because these are the only values that anyone knows how to state.
>
> (1939a: 86)

'Economic value' is 'its "power in exchange" which, measured in money, is its market price. The market price of a thing is the price at which it *is actually being bought and sold*' (p. 87; emphasis in original). MacNeal makes it abundantly clear that he is not interested in 'future improbabilities, probabilities, or even certainties' (p. 146). He would reject Canning's 'direct valuation' (1929: Chapter XI), although nowhere in the book does MacNeal actually discuss the possible use of discounted present values of future cash flows. 'It is an accountant's duty to deal with the facts as he finds them, not to alter them to conform to some imaginary action on the part of his client' (1939a: 44).

In Chapter VI, 'Market Prices', MacNeal describes at some length the circumstances in which acceptable market prices could be obtained. His ideal is to have free, competitive, broad, and active markets. The key terms are defined as follows:

- 'A free market is one in which no constituted authority interferes with the free functioning of supply and demand' (p. 129).
- 'A competitive market is one where buyers and sellers compete not only with each other but among themselves' (p. 129).
- 'A market is broad to the extent that its prices represent the counteraction of world supply and demand' (p. 131).

- 'An active market is one in which transactions occur frequently or in which bid and offered quotations are available' (p. 133).

MacNeal acknowledges that ideal conditions seldom obtain, and he advises accountants how they should proceed when imperfections exist. Of particular interest is his insistence that acceptable market prices are to be used strictly and without modification to value a company's assets. If a company holds a large block of securities, for example, the prevailing market price should not be modified downward (for asset-valuation purposes) on the assumption that it would be depressed if such a large block of shares were immediately sold.[12] Nor should an estimated broker's commission be deducted from the valuation, or should a liability for estimated income taxes be reflected (p. 144).

> [T]he value of a thing is not what it *could* be sold for *if* it were offered for sale. Its value is what it *is being bought and sold for* or, if it is not being bought and sold, its logical price under the ratio of supply and demand that *actually exists*.
>
> (1939a: 143)

This advice would not have been gladly received by a profession which employed net realisable value – i.e. estimated selling prices less expected cost of carrying, selling, and delivering – in its computation of 'lower of cost or market' for inventories (see, e.g. Montgomery 1934: 209–10). MacNeal adjures the accountant not to make predictions of the unknowable future: 'Many things may happen in the future to prevent a sale, a broker's commission, or an income tax. An accountant should not act as a prophet. Creditors and stockholders can do that as well as he can' (p. 145).

As indicated above, MacNeal imposes strict conditions on what constitutes an acceptable market, and it soon becomes evident that not many assets are traded in such markets. Thus, where acceptable markets are not available for particular assets, surrogate measures must be found, and in Chapters VIII and IX MacNeal recommends candidates. Assets are classified into three kinds:

1 marketable;
2 non-marketable and reproducible; and
3 non-marketable and non-reproducible.

Surrogates apply to the second and third kinds. For non-marketable and reproducible assets, MacNeal recommends replacement cost, which is defined as

> the cost of reproducing a thing plus a profit sufficient to provide a motive for so doing. In this definition any two things are assumed to be alike if their utilities or serviceableness are identical, regardless of differences in their structural form. The cost of matching the precise physical structure of a given asset is known as its reproduction cost. The cost of matching the utility or serviceableness of a given asset is known as its replacement cost.
>
> (1939a: 161)

Owing to technological progress, the replacement cost of an asset may be less than the cost to reproduce it, in which event its reproduction would not be economically justified. For non-marketable and non-reproducible assets (such as patents, copyrights, mines and oil wells), MacNeal makes 'a big concession to expediency' (p. 188) by recommending original cost. It is a last resort, and he sees original cost as a better alternative than a zero valuation (p. 188). Here, however, MacNeal forgets his earlier logic and opens himself to avoidable criticism. He defends the use of original cost in such instances in the belief that 'the public could be educated to understand the true nature of these assets' 'and be put on notice that this part of the balance sheet, and that part of the profit and loss statement relating to the depreciation or depletion of these assets, was not to be trusted and was merely a concession to expediency' (p. 189). Practitioner critics might add the refrain that, by the same token, the public could be educated that the entire balance sheet and profit and loss statement are based on original costs, and that readers should colour their inferences accordingly. Why does MacNeal believe that education of the public might succeed for some assets (which, in some companies, constitute the lion's share), while not for all assets?

Aware that a recommendation in favour of original cost in certain cases places him on a weakened foundation, he is seen in this chapter (Chapter IX) to soften his 'lectures' to accountants. He none the less distinguishes his system of economic values from the practices used by accountants, by contending, perhaps a bit self-righteously, that he starts with an ideal and introduces concessions to expediency as necessary, while accountants 'start from a basis of expediency and . . . work toward the ideal only as expediency might dictate' (p. 175). These asides would not have endeared him to the very readers whom he sought to influence.

The next 125 pages are used to explain and defend how particular accounts in the balance sheet and profit and loss statement would be treated under his system. He goes into considerable detail, and some matters are discussed at length. Yet the section would have been shorter and more palatable if MacNeal had not continued to administer stern admonitions to accountants for their accounting practices – and the frequency of these reproofs seems to increase in the second half of the book.

MacNeal includes in profit all changes in economic value during the period, whether realised or unrealised, as the following, rather blunt passage affirms:

> There is one correct definition of profits in an accounting sense. A profit is an increase in net wealth. A loss is a decrease in net wealth. This is the economist's definition. It is terse, obvious, and mathematically demonstrable.
>
> (1939a: 295)

MacNeal recommends against separating 'speculative profits' from 'processing profits' on inventories solely on pragmatic grounds (pp. 309–11). He refers, without naming them, to practising accountants who have suggested that a company's purchasing operation should be assessed apart from its ability in processing operations (p. 309), a view which he seems to favour, but the difficulty of achieving the separation in practice leads him to merge both elements of profit in cost of sales in the 'current' section of his profit and loss statement. The final result in his 'current' section (sales less the sum of cost of sales (at market price or replacement cost, as applicable) and period expenses) is called 'net profit from business operations', and is credited to earned surplus. Net profit from business operations, by MacNeal's definition, would include the unrealised increases and decreases during the period in the market price or replacement cost of the company's inventories of raw materials, work in progress, and finished goods. The second section of his two-part profit and loss statement gathers the profits and losses on non-current assets; its final result is called net capital profit and is credited to capital surplus. MacNeal dislikes making the 'current'/'capital' separation at all, and does so only for 'legal and historical considerations' (p. 289). His reference is evidently to the definitions of earned surplus (retained earnings, in today's jargon) and other surpluses propounded by committees of the American Institute of Accountants in the late 1920s and early 1930s. These committees excluded from earned surplus the revaluations arising from the appraisal of fixed assets (which MacNeal called 'capital') but were silent on the treatment of the revaluation of inventories (which MacNeal called 'current').[13]

In principle, MacNeal prefers not to separate realised from unrealised profits. 'Under modern conditions', he argues, 'the term "realized" applied to profits means literally nothing, for such profits are continually being "derealized" by reinvestment in other assets' (p. 296).

MacNeal's position on goodwill is compatible with his view that the economic values in the balance sheet should represent 'present facts':

> The books of a business are intended to record the transactions and the possessions of a business. They are not designed to record the present speculative value of its future expectations or probabilities. Men and corporations may pay money for such expectations and probabilities, but this does not cause them to become balance sheet assets. The simple truth is that such men and corporations undergo a present sacrifice, or a present loss of capital, for the expected benefit of a future gain. A balance sheet, being merely a statement of present condition, can only exhibit things as they stand after such a sacrifice has been made.
>
> (1939a: 236)

When one corporation buys another at a price that would indicate the existence of goodwill, MacNeal's solution is to treat this amount as a reduction in stockholders' equity.[14] Even where, in rare instances, accountants are able to value the goodwill of a business, such goodwill should not be allowed to appear on the company's balance sheet, for 'such inclusion would be very apt to confuse or deceive many stockholders when they attempted to compare such a company with one whose goodwill was not susceptible to valuation' (p. 234).

MacNeal adopts a similar view of organisation costs. He looks upon the practice of capitalising such costs as a subterfuge to conceal what should properly be shown as losses incurred by companies during their formative years (p. 242).

MacNeal's position on liabilities is unexpected. He would record all discounts and premiums as capital losses or gains, respectively, and long-term liabilities would be carried at face value. He looks upon the amortisation of discounts and premiums as a 'theoretical' averaging process which results in a misrepresentation of the amount of actual interest which the corporation is legally obligated to pay (pp. 283–5). As to liabilities in general, he makes the following statement (after having disqualified goodwill and organisation costs as assets):

> Since the asset side of the balance sheet does not exhibit the total value of a business, but merely exhibits the total wealth owned by that business, neither can the liability side of a balance sheet exhibit the total value of the liabilities of that business, but can merely exhibit the status of these liabilities as legal claims on the undivided [owned] wealth of the business.
>
> (1939a: 274)

He adds:

> Furthermore, in many cases, the market values of existing liabilities and capital stock may be completely unknown. When such market values are known they are usually as available to stockholders and creditors as they are to accountants, and little additional information would be supplied by using them.
>
> (1939a: 274–5)

(From this last quotation, one evidently is to conclude that MacNeal's basis for not attempting to show liabilities at economic value is one of practicability, not principle).

As in the cases of goodwill and organisation costs, MacNeal has interposed some arbitrary (and undefended) definitions of the role of the balance sheet, and he has also made some empirical observations that may or may not be true. He talks about creditors and stockholders as if they were the class of readers to whom financial statements are directed. Yet he asserts, *pace* Paton, that 'Universal custom decrees that the profit and loss statement of a business be drawn from the standpoint of its owners, namely, its stockholders, its partners, or its sole proprietor' (p. 297). If that were so, why shouldn't the liabilities be valued (as best one can, using market prices) for the benefit of the owners?

One concludes, therefore, that MacNeal's 'truth' consists of a balance sheet showing a company's possessions at their respective economic values (or at surrogates where necessary), its liabilities at their legally owing amounts, and its stockholders' equity as the residuum; and a profit and loss statement reflecting both realised and unrealised profits and losses classified into 'current' and 'capital' sections. The 'truthful' information is intended to place small investors (and, perhaps, creditors) on a plane with insiders regarding the 'true' valuation of the company's assets. The economic valuations are to be based on actual or estimated 'facts' but not on speculations about future events.

MacNeal says nothing about footnotes or other forms of supplementary disclosure. Since the early to mid-1930s, probably owing to the passage of the Securities Acts of 1933–4 and the regulatory activities of the Securities and Exchange Commission, footnotes and other explanatory information had become commonplace in the financial statements published by listed American companies (see McLaren 1947: Chapter 18, 'Footnotes' 1939, and Daniels 1939

109–10). Other authors (e.g. Paton and Littleton 1940: Chapter VII) argued for the disclosure of some kinds of accounting information, such as replacement-cost data or purchasing-power restatements, in supplementary reports. MacNeal, however, insisted that his 'truth' be embodied in the financial statements themselves. He was impatient for reform, and he makes no reference to a possible period of transition from then-extant practice to 'truthful' financial statements.[15]

Was MacNeal an advocate of exit-price accounting? As indicated below, several authors associate MacNeal with exit-price accounting, i.e. the use of resale prices in the valuation of assets.[16] A close reading of *Truth in Accounting* does not justify such a conclusion.

In his specific discussion of the treatment of different classes of assets, MacNeal applies market prices only to marketable securities and raw materials. It was evidently his belief that the other classes of assets could not normally be found to trade in acceptable markets; therefore, he proceeds immediately to a discussion of a surrogate for these assets. He would employ a surrogate even for finished goods:

> many inventories will be found to contain items such as goods in process, or finished goods, which have no acceptable market and which must therefore be valued at the best remaining index of value, namely, present replacement cost.
>
> (1939a: 226)

Only perhaps in his choice of surrogates can one infer how MacNeal might have stood in the later controversy over entry prices and exit prices. Could MacNeal's preference for replacement cost, and his failure to suggest resale price as another option (in markets where differences between entry prices and exit prices could be expected to exist), suggest that he had more in common with the advocates of entry-price accounting? No definitive answer may be given. Since MacNeal recommends that realisable cost savings on both inventories and fixed assets be included in income, he would be regarded today as an advocate of financial capital maintenance.[17]

CRITICISM FROM REVIEWERS

In view of the strength of MacNeal's convictions, and the almost sanctimonious tone of the argument, it is perhaps not surprising that MacNeal's academic and professional critics were quick to find fault. The words 'the truth', 'the simple truth', 'the truth of the matter', 'truthful', and 'truthfully' are the standard-bearers of MacNeal's argument, and they are repeated on and on throughout the book. Such terms, when used in excess (as they are here), can offend both academic and professional alike, for different reasons. To suggest that one knows the truth may imply that others do not.

MacNeal was stung by the ferocity of the published criticism, and in an address delivered in January 1940, he catalogued some of the 'more expressive words put in print by my brother accountants to denote their appreciation of me and my ideas':

audacious	drastic	not plausible
antiquated	extreme	pugnacious
academic	excited	rambling
accusatory	exaggerated	revolutionary
bold	foolish	sensational
controversial	inadequate	thin
unnecessarily critical	impractical	unbalanced
cocky	illogical	unorthodox
combative	ineffective	unmerciful
crackpotty	light	vicious
disturbing	mistaken	worse than naïve[18]
dubious	nebulous	

As he indicates, this criticism was directed not only at MacNeal's ideas but also at MacNeal himself. Yet the invective suffered by MacNeal was caused, in some measure, by the strong and vivid language used in his book. MacNeal employs the following adjectives to describe accounting practices with which he took issue:

untruthful	demonstrably absurd	disgraceful
deceptive	deplorable	flagrant
misleading	faulty	wholly misleading
morally indefensible	seriously false and	maliciously misleading
fallacious	misleading	fraudulent
false and pernicious	misleading and untrue	indefensible
false and misleading	false	unjust and pernicious
childish	untenable	

Non-adjectival characterisations by MacNeal are as follows:

sheerest nonsense	defraud	deception
illogic and fundamental	a tool of knaves	falsify
unsoundness	misrepresented facts	erroneous ideas
grotesque humor	exhibiting a meaningless	evils
sophistry and specious	figure	fraud
reasoning		

In the preface, MacNeal writes,

> I particularly wish that I had the ability to write without the occasional appearance of ill temper and sweeping denunciation which my friends tell me is my greatest fault. Apparently, I have, in a literary sense, a low boiling point of which I am scarcely aware,
>
> (1939a: xii)

It is unfortunate that MacNeal could not have avoided the frequent use of intemperate language, for his argument was developed with great care and considerable thought. It is clearly and simply expounded, easily suited to a wide audience. Several of the chapters reflect extensive library research. Attention is given both to broad economic and philosophical questions and to the details of financial-statement presentation. Technical terms are chosen judiciously and are used consistently and with good effect. Scholars may complain that MacNeal did not relate his ideas to those of others who had written in like vein. But MacNeal was not a trained researcher, and his book – unlike Paton (1922), Canning (1929), and Sweeney (1936), with which it is often compared – was not developed from a doctoral dissertation completed under the supervision of university dons. All things considered, it was indeed an admirable work.

The major reviewers of *Truth* were John B. Canning, William A. Paton, J. Hugh Jackson, Norman J. Lenhart, Henry Rand Hatfield, and Pearson Hunt. Paton and Hatfield were accounting professors at the Universities of Michigan and California, respectively. Jackson was an accounting professor and dean of the Graduate School of Business at Stanford University. Canning was an economics professor at Stanford University, and Lenhart was a partner in the public accounting firm of Lybrand, Ross Bros. and Montgomery (and was later to become a co-author of *Montgomery's Auditing*). Hunt was an economics instructor at Yale University (and later served on the faculty of the Harvard Graduate School of Business Administration).

Canning and Paton had themselves been major advocates of current-cost or current-value accounting. In his laconic review of *Truth*, Canning confines his remarks to MacNeal's view of product markets. After summarising MacNeal's criteria for the identification of actual or imputed market prices, Canning writes: '[MacNeal] seems to regard such a procedure as uniquely correct regardless of the erratic and extreme amplitudes of price fluctuation to which such markets are subject' (1939: 757). He adds:

> In price imputation the author gives much space to replacement cost but gives scant attention to the cost analysis necessary to a determination of usefulness equivalent to that of substitutes. Moreover, truth may be both expensive and useless. One may pay too much for estimates of present replacement costs, especially if no early replacements are contemplated.
>
> (1939: 758)

Canning thus raises an important point which MacNeal (and most accounting authors prior to the 1970s) ignored; the cost of producing the information. By his reference to 'useless', Canning suggests that MacNeal did not undertake to show in a rigorous manner how the 'truthful' information would actually lead to better economic decisions.

Paton, himself an uncompromising advocate of replacement-cost measures in 1917–18, is seen to be offended by MacNeal's facile appeal to 'truth', his 'sweeping' assertions, and his heavy-handed criticism of the accounting profession (1940). This was Paton at the most 'conservative' moment of his career, having just completed, as senior author, *An Introduction to Corporate Accounting Standards* (Paton and Littleton 1940), which was to become the definitive explication (and, in large measure, defence) of conventional financial accounting (see Zeff 1979). Paton was, at best, a cautious reformer in 1939–40, and although he was in sympathy with the general direction in which MacNeal was heading, he disagreed with a number of MacNeal's specific recommendations (e.g. the treatment of organisation costs and of bond discounts and premiums) and was irritated by MacNeal's writing style.

Jackson, never the revolutionary, has nothing positive to say about the book. The closest he comes to praise is: 'There is just enough truth in some of the author's contentions to make the book dangerous' (Jackson 1939: 855). In view of Jackson's rather traditional position on accounting matters, that statement should have been welcomed by MacNeal! There is little in Jackson's review to indicate that he read the book carefully, and there is no doubt that he was opposed to MacNeal's argument from the start.

Lenhart's is a sarcastic and derisive review (1939). He questions some of MacNeal's facts about recent changes in the standard form of the auditor's report, and severely challenges the practicability of making annual revaluations of fixed assets. Lenhart shows no inclination to give MacNeal a hearing.

Hatfield's review is the most restrained and considerate (1940). As usual in Hatfield's writings, his views are stated with caution and are clothed in understatement. He refers to the 'three clever fables' (1940: 14) and avers that MacNeal 'contributes some good arguments' to the 'much-debated question' of the valuation of assets. Hatfield adds:

> But [MacNeal] is somewhat ungenerous to those who hold the other view in that he repeatedly speaks of their statements as being untrue. It is just as truthful (whether as serviceable or not) to present a statement which professedly shows unamortized costs as it is to state estimated present value. One may prefer present value to original, or cost, value, but one is as much a fact as the other. And, as in all accounting discussion, much depends on the debater's use of terms.
>
> (1940: 14)

Hatfield questions some of MacNeal's specific recommendations, e.g. his zero valuation of goodwill, treatment of bond discounts and premiums as losses and gains, and 'that amortizing discount on debentures payable falsifies the accounts; that, in this case, the effective rate of interest is "theoretical" interest, and the nominal rate is "actual" interest' (1940: 15). He praises MacNeal for his explanation of goodwill, his criticism of the cost method of carrying investments in wholly-owned subsidiaries ('By this method, a holding company may show virtually any earnings desired, whether earned or not' (MacNeal 1939a: 213)), and his recommendation that companies should not show all 'reserves' in one place in the balance sheet. As indicated above, Hatfield mentions the presence of errors in MacNeal's rendering of bookkeeping history. Hatfield sent MacNeal a draft of his review of *Truth*, and the two exchanged friendly letters for the next few years. They both were possessed of large curiosities, and they quickly discovered this mutual quality in correspondence.

Hunt's assignment was to discuss *Truth* and Gilman (1939) in the same review. He finds MacNeal to be a 'pamphleteer', while Gilman is 'ever the cautious, thorough, academician' (Hunt 1939: 168).[19] On the subject of the use of appraisals in the accounts, Hunt writes: 'Lawyers and economists who have struggled over some matter of valuation will find MacNeal's confidence in appraisals and appraisers worse than naive' (p. 169). He concludes that 'MacNeal's work is too light to do more than to stimulate controversy' (p. 170). As will be suggested below, the controversy stirred by *Truth* seems to have been principally in its published reviews. Subsequent references to the book, and to MacNeal's few articles, have largely been perfunctory, even though (or perhaps because) other writers have, in their own treatises, taken up his cause.

On the whole, the major reviews were less than encouraging. *The Accounting Review* did not even review MacNeal's book, and the reason can only be guessed.[20] MacNeal's style of argument and exposition would probably have offended most academics and accounting professionals, and his undisguised contempt for the hallowed doctrines of conservatism and realisation would have won acceptance only among the very small number of other renegades of the day. The known antipathy of the Securities and Exchange Commission to current valuation, and the recollection of corporate abuses of appraisal valuations of assets during the 1920s, hardly provided a climate in which to challenge the primacy of original cost. MacNeal was a courageous figure in his day, but if his writings succeeded in converting any of the heathen, they kept it to themselves.

Evidently, MacNeal was not prepared for the torrent of negative criticism provoked by his book. After his talks at professional meetings in Philadelphia, the opposition was sometimes bitter. He heard rumours of how he was regarded by some members of the accounting Establishment, and he was not pleased. In the end, MacNeal decided irrevocably to abandon the crusade. He withdrew from the literature two years after he had entered, a disappointed man. He refused to be drawn into controversy on the subject in later years.[21]

MACNEAL WRITES AN ARTICLE FOR *FORTUNE*

In December 1938, less than six months before *Truth in Accounting* was to be published, the McKesson & Robbins scandal broke.[22]

Fortune magazine had got wind of MacNeal's forthcoming book and approached him about writing a critical article on the accounting profession in the light of charges stemming from the Securities and Exchange Commission's enquiry into the manipulated accounts of the large drug firm. MacNeal accepted the assignment,[23] and in a matter of weeks the *Fortune* editors were reviewing a 9,000-word manuscript that was cut from the same cloth as *Truth in Accounting*. In their journalistic style, the *Fortune* editors led off the article with the following title and prefatory remarks:

Accountants Are Honest, But –

. . . their ways are hopelessly archaic. So says an author who calls upon his profession to adopt new methods which he feels would more truly portray the conditions of a business.

In a note to the article, *Fortune* introduced MacNeal as 'long a severe critic of his own profession'.

MacNeal's manuscript was a stern indictment of the profession's conception of its role. In the opening paragraphs, which were a preview of the lines of argument to be developed later in the manuscript, MacNeal veritably seizes the reader's attention with the assertion that 'The principles of accounting . . . are obsolete conventions which are inaccurate, misleading and untruthful'. He then describes the nature of an independent audit and traces the changes in wording of the audit opinion from the use of 'correct' to 'present fairly'. He cites the five 'broad principles' enumerated in *Audits of Corporate Accounts* (1934: 10–11) which underlie the 'accepted principles of accounting' referred to in the standard form of the auditor's opinion and proceeds to criticise accounting practice for its non-recognition of unrealised gains on the holding of assets. After presenting several simplified examples in which marketable securities are carried at 'lower of cost or market' and land and buildings are shown at 'going concern value' (original cost), notwithstanding major swings in the market prices of both, MacNeal writes: 'Behind these theories lies the fact that too many certified public accountants today are likely to be little more than highly-trained experts in the mechanics of bookkeeping.'

He then sketches the historical development of accounting, from service to the sole owner alone, to providing information for the creditor ('when public accounting came into existence'), and finally to serving smaller investors. He argues that the practice of understating, even grossly understating, asset values emerged during the creditor period in order to provide the banker with additional 'security'. MacNeal claims that this bias toward conservatism, which continued unabated in the 1930s, works against the interest of the small investor. After presenting an abridged version of his 'Fable of the Two Investment Trusts', where the securities market is assumed to react only to the reporting of realised profits, MacNeal concludes that 'Contemporary financial statements . . . allow insiders to enrich themselves at the expense of stock-holders in a most comfortable manner'. And:

> thanks to the principles of accounting, balance sheets and profit-and-loss statements are *not* statements of fact; they are statements of bookkeeping fact. To you as a shareholder, unless you are a fortunate insider knowing the real values behind the items reported, they offer little information upon which sound judgement can be based, even though they are certified with no qualifications.

MacNeal suggests that the same mentality that leads accountants to prefer original costs over current valuations also is responsible for deficiencies in auditing practices:

> For the most part [the public accountant] satisfies himself that the bookkeeping has been properly done, and he then uses book figures with an almost total disregard of how they may fail to reflect indisputable facts. It is this emphasis on book figures rather than on present facts that lies at the bottom of such occurrences as the McKesson and Robbins situation.

And:

> If these accountants [i.e. the auditors of McKesson & Robbins] had been concerned more with the assets and less with the books, if they had been concerned more with physical facts and less with documentary evidence, they would hardly have been deceived by such simple expedients as false book entries and supporting vouchers.

He was careful to point out that his criticisms of accountants referred to their actions, not their motives:

> The main problem is intellectual, not moral. The accounting profession is not corrupt. Its individual members are, on the whole, as honorable as any group of men in the country. The real difficulty lies in the sophistry, illogic, and untruth of present accounting principles, which produce figures deceiving accountants, business men, and the public alike.[24]

MacNeal's manuscript was edited by the *Fortune* staff, and independent reviews were secured from outside parties. It was set in page proofs, and MacNeal was told that it would run in the June 1939 issue. But the article never appeared. At the eleventh hour, the article was cancelled. MacNeal believed that the reason was pressure brought by Price, Waterhouse & Co. (the auditors of McKesson & Robbins) and the American Institute of Accountants.

Four months later, an abridged version of MacNeal's article was published in two parts in *The Nation* under the title, 'What's Wrong with Accounting?' (MacNeal 1939b, 1939c). Thus, an article that had been commissioned by a journal regarded as the trumpet of American capitalism – respected, elegantly crafted, and a serious student of the business and financial Establishment – came to appear instead in the pages of a weekly magazine of liberal opinion.

The Nation also had a go against *Fortune*. In its 20 May issue, the former reported that MacNeal's article had been cancelled by *Fortune* by order of Time Inc. Publisher Henry Luce and Treasurer Charles Stillman, following pressure 'brought on by an outstanding firm of accountants to have the article killed' ('In the Wind' 1939). In a letter to *The Nation*, *Fortune*'s Publisher and Managing Editor denied that pressure had been applied, and insisted that the magazine's decision not to run the MacNeal article had been based solely on editorial grounds ('Zounds!' 1939). 'The main controversy', they wrote, 'was around Mr MacNeal's propositions that accountants should become appraisers and that a new set of conventions should govern the writing-up as well as the writing-down of assets' ('Zounds!' 1939). As the McKesson & Robbins episode had exposed questionable auditing practices and did not turn on questions of accounting valuation and measurement, the editors of *Fortune* may have had reason to wince at a manuscript whose 'punch line' dealt with valuation. None the less, MacNeal had built the case that accountants' bookkeeping mentality, as he saw it, accounted for deficiencies in both auditing and accounting. The consequences of this mentality were, to MacNeal, inseparable.

MacNeal answered *Fortune* in the letters column of the same issue of *The Nation*. He contended that *Fortune*'s view that no pressure had been brought by an accounting firm or any other firm 'is abundantly denied by facts known to me at first hand both from within and from without the *Fortune* offices' ('You Cur!' 1939: 158). The name of Price, Waterhouse & Co. is mentioned in the MacNeal letter, and one supposes that this is the firm – an undoubted power in the affairs of the American accounting profession in the 1930s – which was suspected of bringing influence. In the letter, MacNeal asserts that the report carried in the May 20th issue of *The Nation* 'agrees substantially with my understanding of what took place . . . ' ('You Cur!' 1939: 158).

Less than a year after the MacNeal episode, *Fortune* published a recapitulation of the facts attending the McKesson & Robbins fraud, written by its editorial staff and devoid of any criticism of the principals ('McKesson & Robbins: Its Fall and Rise' 1940).

MACNEAL'S CONTRIBUTION TO WHAT WENT BEFORE – A BRIEF REVIEW

MacNeal was the first major accounting writer, at least in the English-language literature, to advocate a market-price system for financial statements. In 1918, Paton had argued for a thoroughgoing replacement-cost solution, including in income the unrealised changes in replacement cost. But he would not have abandoned the realisation concept entirely, for the margin between selling price and the replacement cost of goods sold would not be accorded accounting recognition until the period of sale (Paton 1918). In subsequent years, Paton retreated from that position, and by the close of the 1930s, when he wrote the review of *Truth*, he was recommending that replacement costs not be allowed to obscure original-cost information in the financial statements (see Zeff 1979: 111–17).

Hatfield (1927: Chapters X, XII: 366–7) showed a marked tolerance for the recognition of unrealised appreciation in the accounts and ridicules the unthinking attachment by accountants to the realisation concept. But Hatfield's is a 'balanced' presentation, and he does not engage in advocacy.

Canning (1929), in a major work that was his doctoral dissertation at the University of Chicago, recommended the use of discounted present values for the valuation of balance-sheet assets.

Schmidt (1930, 1931) recommended the use of replacement costs, but he preserved a distinction between realised and unrealised profits, crediting the latter to capital.

Sweeney, while he is best known for his argument for general price-level accounting, also favoured replacement-cost accounting, but he was even less inclined than the Paton of 1918 to ignore the realisation concept. He did, however, include the current period's instalment in unrealised profits and losses, labelled 'unrealised', in the 'final net income for the year' (Sweeney 1936; Chapter III, 1932).

Other writers, such as Montgomery (1921: 144–6), allowed inventories to be shown at replacement costs when in excess of original cost, and writers such as Castenholz (1931) welcomed fixed-asset appraisals. Rorem suggested that assets intended for sale should be valued at their selling prices, while assets intended for use be valued by reference to the present value of their future services (1928: 286–7). But until MacNeal (1939a), no one had presented an integrated proposal for the preparation of financial statements on a market-price basis. It was a daring argument to make, even among accounting reformers.

SUBSEQUENT REFERENCES TO MACNEAL'S WORK

What manner of mark did MacNeal leave in the accounting literature and on accounting practice? No definitive answer can be given to such a question, but it is possible to discern the degree of interest that his writings have attracted on the part of academics, professionals, and policy makers.

As suggested above, the reviewers of *Truth* gave MacNeal little encouragement. Moreover, Philips writes (1971: 634): 'I can detect no sign that [MacNeal's] book had a major impact or even was taken seriously to any considerable extent [by practitioners] in the years following its publication.'

Philips suggests that Editor Kohler's strong preference for original-cost accounting may explain why *The Accounting Review* did not even review the book.[25] He detects a lack of academic interest in other quarters as well, which is 'perhaps the result of both the unpopularity of the views expressed and the narrow scope of the economic and accounting theory background presented' (1971: 634).[26] MacNeal was not an academic, and his propensity for direct prose and categorical pronouncements probably grated on academic sensibilities. More to the point, there probably were few academics in the 1940s and even in the 1950s who would have aligned themselves with a movement away from the original-cost convention in accounting. It was not a revolutionary era. For academics, the late 1930s and early 1940s were a period of codification and consolidation. Such works as Sanders, Hatfield and Moore (1938), Gilman (1939), and Paton and Littleton (1940) testified to the prevailing mood, and few path-breaking tracts appeared. The appearance of Edwards and Bell (1961), Chambers (1961), Moonitz (1961) and Sprouse and Moonitz (1962) marked an awakening of accounting academics to the deficiencies of original-cost accounting, and in the decade of the 1960s the early normative arguments of Paton, Canning, Sweeney, MacNeal, and Alexander were 'discovered' time and again by academics. Doubtless the republication of *Truth* in 1970 by Scholars Book Co. and the reprinting of 'What's Wrong with Accounting?' in Baxter (1950) and Baxter and Davidson (1962; 1977) did much to place MacNeal's argument before the academic audience.

On the professional side of the literature, it is of interest that Arthur Andersen & Co., in a tract which endorses current-value accounting, praises MacNeal's recommended treatment of liabilities and stockholders' equity as 'unusually refreshing and clear' (1972: 47). Like MacNeal, Arthur Andersen & Co. would not exhibit goodwill as an asset or apply current values to creditors' and stock-holders' equities. To do otherwise would be 'to introduce concepts identified with the valuation of a business as a whole' (Arthur Andersen & Co., 1972: 47).

Yet Chambers and Sterling are of a mind in lamenting MacNeal's lack of influence among his practising brethren. Chambers places MacNeal in the same category as Paton, Hatfield, Canning and Sweeney – all being critics who failed to make an impression on the practising profession (1967: 241–2; 1969: 712–13). Sterling (1970: 254) includes MacNeal with Canning as being among 'the fringe group' of theorists, owing to 'their lack of impact on the practice of accounting and the textbook literature'.[27]

When assessing the impact of MacNeal and other critics of accounting practice in the US, one should recall that the Securities and Exchange Commission stood four-square behind original-cost accounting from its founding in 1934 to the early 1970s. The few attempts by the profession to depart from original-cost accounting were repulsed by the SEC (Zeff 1972: 155–7); hence, one must appreciate that the obduracy of the SEC would have made professional debates over value-based accounting futile indeed.

Truth is quoted twice in the chapter on assets in the Financial Accounting Standards Board's Discussion Memorandum on the Conceptual Framework (1976: paras. 133, 136), although one suspects that MacNeal would have winced at the hilarious typographical error in the FASB's footnote to the second of the two quotations. It gives the title of MacNeal's book as *'Trust in Accounting'*! (1976: 78, fn. 39).

In the writings of academics, including even those of non-North Americans, MacNeal's work is remembered. Hendriksen, in his three editions of *Accounting Theory* (1965, 1970, 1977), refers to MacNeal as a member of the school which employs the 'Ethical Approach' to formulating accounting theory. Most, in his *Accounting Theory* (1977), discusses MacNeal's ideas at greater length than does Hendriksen, although one may be surprised by Most's suggestion that MacNeal may be associated with the future-oriented Fisher/Canning school (p. 10). Most indicates how MacNeal's 'true income' approach to theory development has largely been supplanted by other theory approaches in the 1960s and 1970s, most notably that of 'decision usefulness':

> Since MacNeal wrote there have been innumerable restatements of his criticisms, but the rationale has changed subtly over the years. Although many critics still proceed from the assumption that accounting can be referred to a framework of economic theory, it has become unfashionable to call this the truth. Instead, critics direct attention to the need for information useful in making economic decisions. The desired values are not intrinsically good, but acquire their virtue from the decision models which call them forth.
>
> (Most 1977: 10)

In 1977, a committee of the American Accounting Association grouped MacNeal with Paton (1922), Canning (1929), Sweeney (1936), Alexander (1950), Edwards and Bell (1961), and Moonitz (1961) and Sprouse and Moonitz (1962) in the 'true income' school of normative theorists, and the committee summarised MacNeal's argument in *Truth* in a brief appendix (AAA 1977: Chapter 2).

Nelson (1973) includes MacNeal in his discussion of major *'a priori'* theorists, and McDonald (1972: 20) lists MacNeal among the major critics of accounting. Devine, after observing that accountants would refuse to recognise income even when a company, after having bought goods at a given cost, receives a 'firm offer' of sale at twice that cost, is sympathetic to MacNeal's stand on realisation:

> The conclusion is that accountants hold off recognition because of failure to meet the test of realization and not because the evidence is inadequate. . . . [T]he defense for omission of these gains is not always convincing, and, as MacNeal and many others have pointed out, the practical consequences may be ghastly.
>
> (Devine 1962, II: 276)

Solomons recalls MacNeal's 'Fable of the Two Investment Trusts' and notes the 'absurd result' yielded by applying the realisation concept (1961: 378).

Davidson cites MacNeal's 'Fable of the Two Investment Trusts' as the 'classic accounting objection to the market transaction test for realization' (1966: 104, fn. 24). Chatfield includes a discussion of MacNeal's argument in his chapter, 'Changing Concepts of Asset Valuation', and contributes the unexpected characterisation that 'MacNeal was only trying to do on the conceptual level what Sweeney had done with the practical problem of asset valuation' (1977: 243). Chatfield concludes that MacNeal's 'criticisms were simplistic, but diagnostically correct, and of a type which would become familiar after World War II' (1977: 243).

Belkaoui writes that 'The notion of current exit price was introduced by MacNeal and further developed by Sterling and Chambers' (1981: 160–1).

Among non-North American academic writers, Lee refers to *Truth* in several places and credits MacNeal with being the first advocate of what is known today as 'exit price' accounting (1975: 88). Scapens describes MacNeal as 'an early supporter of selling prices' (1977: 54). Barton remarks that two of MacNeal's fables 'vividly portrayed' the deficiencies of the realisation concept in accounting (1975: 30–1). Baxter (1975: 143, fn. 4) quotes approvingly from MacNeal's 'What's Wrong with Accounting?', and Gynther (1966: 164) cites the MacNeal article with favour.

Thus, it may be said that MacNeal is remembered among academics.[28] Yet the citations to his work are not nearly so frequent or substantive as are those to the writings of Paton, Hatfield, Canning, and Sweeney – most of whose major works have also been republished in recent years.

In most of the works cited above, MacNeal is mentioned once, briefly, and only in passing. Seldom is his argument treated at any length. Furthermore, MacNeal is not mentioned in quite a few places where one might have expected to see his name: Vatter (1947), Fitzgerald (1952), Edwards and Bell (1961), Mathews and Grant (1962), Sprouse and Moonitz (1962), Littleton and Zimmerman (1962), Roy (1963), Mattessich (1964), Deinzer (1965), Goldberg

(1965), Bedford (1965), Salmonson (1969), Thomas (1969), Skinner (1972), Rosen (1972), Backer (1973), Ijiri (1975), and Previts and Merino (1979). These are all substantial works that evince a commendable awareness of the genre of writings of which MacNeal's are a part, but he is not cited.

CONCLUDING REMARKS

Kenneth MacNeal was a revolutionary in a non-revolutionary time. The late 1930s were hardly a propitious time for radical change in American accounting thought. The Securities and Exchange Commission, an ardent defender of original-cost accounting, had begun to assert its authority over accounting principles, and the normally defensive accounting profession was nervously contemplating the repercussions of the McKesson & Robbins scandal (Carey 1970: Chapters 1, 2). For academics, the late 1930s and early 1940s were evidently not a period of innovation.

While MacNeal would have preferred to abandon the realisation concept *in toto*, he seemed at ease with this outcome only when discussing marketable securities and basic commodities. The markets for other assets were not acceptable to MacNeal, and he was obliged to retain the realisation concept for the margin between selling price and replacement-cost cost of sales.

MacNeal was not alone in failing to attract an immediate following. Few apparently were lured by Canning.[29] Sweeney's followers did not rise in large numbers until the 1960s. Paton had the benefit of turning out disciples at the University of Michigan, although his prolific writings have had a noticeable influence on others. MacNeal did not hold an academic post, and he discontinued his professional writing and speaking in 1941.

Although MacNeal and pioneers before him were seldom appreciated by their peers, they may have given later reformers the courage that comes from knowing that one is not alone.

Notes

The author gratefully acknowledges the useful comments and suggestions of R. J. Chambers, William W. Cooper, Roman L. Weil, G. Edward Philips, Loyd Heath, Robert J. Coombes, Frank L. Clarke, Geoffrey Whittington, and especially George Foster and Philip W. Bell.
  1 MacNeal's 'What's Wrong with Accounting?' (1939b, 1939c) became known to readers of the accounting literature when it was reprinted in Baxter (1950) and Baxter and Davidson (1962, 1977).
  2 MacNeal is also shown as author of 'Shortcomings of Some Accepted Accounting Principles Under Modern Conditions', *The Annalist* (13 July 1939: 38–9), but this article is omitted here as it appears to consist of a straight reprinting of a few pages of *Truth in Accounting*.
  3 Related in introductory comments by Harold C. Stott in 'Remarks by Kenneth MacNeal, CPA (Illinois), copied from Stenotype Operator's Report of Annual Meeting of Pennsylvania Institute of Certified Public Accountants – June 19, 1939' (Kenneth MacNeal Scrapbook).

4   I found MacNeal's letter to Hatfield both in the Kenneth MacNeal Scrapbook and in the Hatfield Papers, Accounting Area, Schools of Business Administration, University of California, Berkeley.

5   The Press's consultants were Professors Ernest Minor Patterson, the economist, and Edward Needles Wright, the accounting academic, both of the Wharton School, University of Pennsylvania. MacNeal proposed that he defray the costs of manufacture, and the Press accepted his manuscript on those terms.

6   Letters dated 2 August 1963 and 3 September 1963 from MacNeal to the writer.

7   In 1973, a committee of the American Institute of Certified Public Accountants recommended that the current market values of portfolio holdings and the resulting unrealised gains and losses be presented in the audited financial statements of investment companies (AICPA 1973: Chapter 2). This was, I believe, the first official acceptance of this position by the American accounting profession. Several works are cited in the AICPA Audit Guide, but MacNeal's book is not among them.

8   MacNeal evidently did not regard footnote disclosure as an issue, for, in his rendering of this Fable in 'What's Wrong with Accounting?' (MacNeal 1939c: 410–11), he omits mention of any footnotes.

9   In Chapter II, MacNeal quotes at length from Hatfield (1909, 1913 printing), Montgomery (1912, 1913 printing), Dickinson (1913, 1914 printing), and Esquerré (1914, 1915 printing). Why did he choose these particular works? Hatfield had revised his 1909 book in 1927, and Montgomery had since published three revisions of his 1912 volume. MacNeal is sensitive to the question. He writes:

> The four accounting works quoted in this chapter may be mistakenly assumed by some to be out of date inasmuch as the first edition of each was published over twenty years ago. In the writer's opinion, these books still constitute the most representative works on accounting in this country [and they have] exerted a dominating influence on the formation of current American accounting thought.
>
> (1939a: 25, n. 2)

I think it is more likely that MacNeal selected books that had become known to him, during his studies at the University of Chicago and Northwestern University in 1912–16 and perhaps during his brief employment with Price, Waterhouse & Co. in 1916–17. Since the period 1913–15 (the printing dates of his cited works), major treatises had been written by Kester, Paton, Finney, Saliers, Canning, Rorem, and Scott, among others, and MacNeal cites none of their writings. One is therefore dubious that the four cited works could have been said to 'constitute the most representative works on accounting' by the close of the 1930s. MacNeal does, however, discuss Sweeney (1936), as is brought out below.

10   May was the principal author of the letter dated 22 September 1932 from the Special Committee on Co-operation with Stock Exchanges of the American Institute of Accountants, to the New York Stock Exchange, in which the proposal was first formulated (see *Audits of Corporate Accounts*, 1934).

11   In a letter dated November 17, 1939, Hatfield sent MacNeal a three-page, single-spaced corrigenda, dealing chiefly with MacNeal's pp. 61–72 (the bookkeeping history). It became evident that MacNeal had relied heavily on Green (1930), one of three historical works cited in a footnote on p. 58, which is a book that Hatfield had found to be 'crudely inaccurate' (Hatfield 1940: 15). (Hatfield, 1931, reviewed the Green book in *The Journal of Accountancy*.) In a letter to Hatfield dated November 30, 1939, MacNeal admitted a number of proofreading errors and misstatements, and regretted his naïve reliance on Green (1930). Hatfield Papers, Accounting Area, Schools of Business Administration, University of California, Berkeley.

12   It is interesting to note that this position is consistent with the 'substitution hypothesis' discussed by Scholes (1972) in relation to the impact of a block sale on the price of a security. Scholes examined the price reaction to a sample of 'the largest

block distributions of securities' (secondary distributions) and concluded that 'the data give consistent and strong support to the assumptions of the substitution hypothesis' (p. 207).

13 In 1929, the Institute's Special Committee on Definition of Earned Surplus rendered a report in which it favoured the exclusion of fixed-asset revaluations from earned surplus (see Heckert (1930: 168–9). Although the committee's report failed to gain acceptance at the Institute's annual membership meeting the following year, its proposed definition was nonetheless adopted by the Institute's Special Committee on Terminology 'for purposes of [its] tentative report' in 1931 (AIA 1931: 119–20).

14 Dicksee and Tillyard (1906: 82–3) had recommended that goodwill be written off against capital 'at the earliest possible stage'. An immediate write-off against capital was later advocated by Spacek (1964) and Chambers (1966: 209–12).

15 Although nothing is said in *Truth* about a possible transition, MacNeal is on record as favouring parallel money columns in the financial statements during any such transition. He would show conventional figures in one column and the figures resulting from his recommendations in the other. His views on this transitional procedure were given in reply to a question from M. C. Conick, partner in the Philadelphia office of Main and Company, at a meeting in 1939. 'Remarks by Kenneth MacNeal, CPA (Illinois), copied from Stenotype Operator's Report of Annual Meeting of Pennsylvania Institute of Certified Public Accountants – June 19, 1939' (Kenneth MacNeal Scrapbook).

16 The terms 'exit price' and 'entry price' were coined by Edwards and Bell (1961: 75).

17 For a discussion of 'financial capital maintenance' vs. 'physical capital maintenance', see FASB (1976: paras. 283–312). The term 'realizable cost savings' is defined in Edwards and Bell (1961: 93).

18 Taken from 'Address delivered January 11, 1940 by Kenneth MacNeal to Controllers' Institute of America, at The Penn Athletic Club, Philadelphia, Pa.', p. 1 (typescript), Hatfield Papers, Accounting Area, Schools of Business Administration, University of California, Berkeley.

19 It is unfortunate that *Truth* was arrayed against Gilman (1939) in Hunt's review. The outstanding characteristic of Gilman was his comprehensive review of the accounting literature, as if it had been done as a doctoral dissertation. MacNeal's work of full-throated advocacy would have seemed shallow by comparison, and it should have been reviewed on its own ground.

20 See note 25.

21 Telephone conversation with MacNeal, December, 1963.

22 For a popular account, see Shaplen (1955). A summary of the final report of the Securities and Exchange Commission appears in its Accounting Series Release No. 19 (SEC 1940a). See SEC (1940b) for the full report.

23 By a coincidence worth noting, the auditor of McKesson & Robbins was Price, Waterhouse & Co., which was the firm for which MacNeal had worked in 1916–17 and with which he had jousted in 1929 (as a client) over the accounting treatment of the unrealised gains and losses on securities held by an investment trust.

24 A virtually identical passage appears in MacNeal (1939a: 18).

25 William W. Cooper, in a letter to the writer dated April 13, 1981, relates that Eric Kohler regarded MacNeal's book as 'superficial', which, adds Cooper, 'would have been enough to motivate such a decision by Eric [i.e. not to have the book reviewed] even for a book that entirely agreed with his position on historical cost'.

26 I can find only three citations to MacNeal in the issues of *The Accounting Review* from 1940 to 1960. MacNeal is not mentioned in the chapters on 'Income Determination' and 'Plant Appraisals' in Paton's third edition of the *Accountants' Handbook* (1943); nor is he cited in the fourth edition of the same work (Wixon 1956). MacNeal is nowhere mentioned in volume 1 of Newlove and Garner's *Advanced Accounting* (1951), which (unlike most textbooks) contains copious citations to the literature.

27   While the works of MacNeal and other critics are frequently represented in the syllabi used for accounting theory seminars (see e.g. Burns, 1967–81), one seldom sees the influence of such writings in North American introductory or 'intermediate' financial accounting courses. To be sure, the textbooks for such courses rarely engage the student in controversial debate of any kind, save for disputed methods of applying highly detailed official pronouncements.

28   In a recent article, Mumford (1980) criticises MacNeal for having characterised Hatfield as a supporter of the 'lower of cost or market' rule and as a defender of historical-cost valuation. Oddly, Mumford undertakes to refute MacNeal by citing passages from Hatfield (1927), a work that MacNeal never cites and shows no indication of having read; in fact, MacNeal cited Hatfield (1909, 1913 printing). In correspondence which I have seen, Hatfield complained to MacNeal about this misrepresentation, and MacNeal replied that, after all, on page 224 of his 1909 book, Hatfield used the term, 'wise conservatism'. MacNeal's riposte aside, I believe that Mumford's line of criticism in this regard is justified. In addition Mumford alleges (p. 153) that Hatfield had used two vivid examples (in Hatfield 1927) that 'bear rather too close a resemblance to MacNeal's [second and third fables] for this to be entirely coincidental' I find this claim to be far-fetched, at best. In Hatfield's first example, the aim was to expose the 'lower of cost or market' rule, whereas MacNeal, in his 'Fable of the Two Flour Mills', was interested in exposing realisation and 'going value'. The Hatfield example and the MacNeal fable are similar only in outline. In the second comparison, where both authors discuss the consequences of not booking unrealised appreciation on securities, Hatfield was concerned with misrepresentation, while MacNeal focused on *manipulation*. In the setting of Hatfield's example, the manipulation suggested by MacNeal could not have occurred. Finally, Hatfield's examples appeared in Hatfield (1927) and, from what I can tell, did not appear in any printings of Hatfield (1909). As indicated above, MacNeal seemed to be aware only of Hatfield's 1909 book.

29   For a contemporary view of Canning's influence, see Whittington (1980: 236–40).

References

Alexander, S. S. (1950) 'Income Measurement in a Dynamic Economy', *Five Monographs on Business Income*, American Institute of Accountants: 1–95.

American Accounting Association, Committee on Concepts and Standards for External Financial Reports (1977) *Statement on Accounting Theory and Theory Acceptance*, Sarasota, Fla.: AAA.

American Institute of Accountants (1931) *Accounting Terminology*, A Preliminary Report of a Special Committee on Terminology, New York: AIA.

American Institute of Certified Public Accountants, Committee on Investment Companies (1973) *Audits of Investment Companies*, New York: AICPA.

Arthur Andersen & Co. (1972) *Objectives of Financial Statements for Business Enterprises*, Arthur Andersen & Co.

Audits of Corporate Accounts (1934) American Institute of Accountants.

Backer, M. (1973) *Current Value Accounting*, New York: Financial Executives Research Foundation.

Barton, A. (1975) *An Analysis of Business Income Concepts*, ICRA Occasional Paper No. 7, International Centre for Research in Accounting, University of Lancaster.

Baxter, W. T. (1950) *Studies in Accounting*, London: Sweet & Maxwell.

Baxter, W. T. (1975) *Accounting Values and Inflation*, New York: McGraw-Hill.

Baxter, W. T. and Davidson, S. (1962) *Studies in Accounting Theory*, London: Sweet & Maxwell.

Baxter, W. T. and Davidson, S. (1977) *Studies in Accounting*, London: The Institute of Chartered Accountants in England and Wales.

Beaver, W. H. (1981) *Financial Reporting: An Accounting Revolution*, Englewood Cliffs, NJ: Prentice-Hall.

Bedford, N. M. (1965) *Income Determination Theory: An Accounting Framework*, New York: Addison-Wesley.

Belkaoui, A. (1981) *Accounting Theory*, New York: Harcourt Brace Jovanovich Inc.

Burns, T. J. (ed.) (1967–81) *Accounting Trends [I]–XV*, New York: McGraw-Hill.

Canning, J. B. (1929) *The Economics of Accountancy*, New York: Ronald Press.

Canning, J. B. (1939) review of *Truth in Accounting*, *Journal of the American Statistical Association*, December: 757–8.

Carey, J. L. (1970) *The Rise of the Accounting Profession: To Responsibility and Authority, 1937–1969*, New York: American Institute of Certified Public Accountants.

Castenholz, W. B. (1931) *A Solution to the Appreciation Problem*, Chicago: LaSalle Extension University.

Chambers, R. J. (1961) *Towards a General Theory of Accounting*, Australian Society of Accountants Research Lecture, The University of Adelaide.

Chambers, R. J. (1966) *Accounting, Evaluation and Economic Behavior*, Englewood Cliffs, NJ: Prentice-Hall.

Chambers, R. J. (1967) 'Prospective Adventures in Accounting Ideas', *The Accounting Review*, April: 241–53.

Chambers, R. J. (1968) 'New Pathways in Accounting Thought and Action', *The Accountants' Journal*, July. Reprinted in R. J. Chambers (1969) *Accounting Finance and Management*, Arthur Andersen & Co.: 700–14.

Chatfield, M. (1977) *A History of Accounting Thought*, Huntington, NY: Krieger.

Daniels, M. B. (1939) *Financial Statements*, Monograph No. 2, Sarasota, Fla.: American Accounting Association.

Davidson, S. (1966) 'The Realization Concept', in M. Backer (ed.), *Modern Accounting Theory*, Englewood Cliffs, NJ: Prentice-Hall.

Deinzer, H. T. (1965) *Development of Accounting Thought*, New York: Holt, Rinehart and Winston, Inc.

Devine, C. T. (1962) *Essays in Accounting Theory*, The Author.

Dickinson, A. L. (1913) *Accounting Practice and Procedure*, New York: Ronald Press.

Dicksee, L. R. and Tillyard, F. (1906) *Goodwill and Its Treatment in the Accounts*, London: Gee.

Edwards, E. O. and Bell, P. W. (1961) *The Theory and Measurement of Business Income*, Berkeley, Calif.: University of California Press.

Esquerré, P.-J. (1914) *The Applied Theory of Accounts*, New York: Ronald Press.

Financial Accounting Standards Board (1976) *Conceptual Framework for Financial Accounting and Reporting: Elements of Financial Statements and Their Measurement*, Discussion Memorandum, FASB, December 2.

Fitzgerald, A. A. (1952) *Current Accounting Trends*, Sydney, NSW: Butterworth & Co. (Australia) Ltd.

'Footnotes' (1939) Editorial, *The Journal of Accountancy*, August: 74.

Gilman, S. (1939) *Accounting Concepts of Profit*, New York: Ronald Press.

Goldberg, L. (1965) *An Inquiry into the Nature of Accounting*, Sarasota, Fla.: American Accounting Association.

Green, W. L. (1930) *History and Survey of Accountancy*, Standard Text Press.

Gynther, R. S. (1966) *Accounting for Price-Level Changes: Theory and Procedures*, Oxford: Pergamon Press.

Hatfield, H. R. (1909) *Modern Accounting: Its Principles and Some of Its Problems*, New York: D. Appleton.

Hatfield, H. R. (1927) *Accounting, Its Principles and Problems*, New York: D. Appleton.

Hatfield, H. R. (1931) Review of *History and Survey of Accountancy*, *The Journal of Accountancy*, April: 308–9.

Hatfield, H. R. (1940) Review of *Truth in Accounting*, *Review Supplement No 10* (to *The Accountant*), The Accounting Research Association, January: 14–16.

Heckert, J. B. (1930) 'Comments on the Definition of Earned Surplus', *The Accounting Review*, June: 168–74.

Hendriksen, E. S. (1965) *Accounting Theory*, Homewood, Ill.: Irwin.

Hendriksen, E. S. (1970) *Accounting Theory*, Homewood, Ill.: Irwin.

Hendriksen, E. S. (1977) *Accounting Theory*, Homewood, Ill.: Irwin.

Hunt, P. (1939) Review of *Accounting Concepts of Profit and Truth in Accounting*, *The Yale Law Journal*, November: 167–70.

Ijiri, Y. (1975) *Theory of Accounting Measurement*, Studies in Accounting Research No. 10, Sarasota, Fla.: American Accounting Association.

'In the Wind' (1939) *The Nation*, May 20: 588.

Jackson, J. H. (1939) review of *Truth in Accounting*, *The American Economic Review*, December: 853–5.

Lee, T. A. (1975) *Income and Value Measurement: Theory and Practice*, Kingston upon Thames: Thomas Nelson.

Lenhart, N. J. (1939) review of *Truth in Accounting*, *The Journal of Accountancy*, June: 395–6.

Littleton, A. C. and V. K. Zimmerman (1962) *Accounting Theory: Continuity and Change*, Englewood Cliffs, NJ: Prentice-Hall.

McDonald, D. L. (1972) *Comparative Accounting Theory*, New York: Addison-Wesley.

'McKesson & Robbins: Its Fall and Rise' (1940) *Fortune*, March: 72–5, 120, 123–6, 128, 130–1.

McLaren, N. L. (1947) *Annual Reports to Stockholders: Their Preparation and Interpretation*, New York: Ronald Press.

MacNeal, K. (1939a) *Truth in Accounting*, Pennsylvania, Pa.: University of Pennsylvania Press.

MacNeal, K. (1939b) 'What's Wrong with Accounting?', *The Nation*, October 7: 370–2.

MacNeal, K. (1939c) 'What's Wrong with Accounting?', *The Nation*, October 14: 409–12.

MacNeal, K. (1941a) 'Caveat Investor', *The Nation*, February 8: 151–3.

MacNeal, K. (1941b) 'Is Our System of Financial Reporting Sound?', *The Accounting Forum*, April: 7–11, 56.

Mathews, R. and Grant, J. McB. (1962) *Inflation and Company Finance*, Sydney: The Law Book Co. of Australasia Pty Ltd.

Mattessich, R. (1964) *Accounting and Analytical Methods*, Homewood, Ill.: Irwin.

Montgomery, R. H. (1912) *Auditing Theory and Practice*, vol. 1, New York: Ronald Press.

Montgomery, R. H. (1921) *Auditing Theory and Practice*, New York: Ronald Press.

Montgomery, R. H. (1934) *Auditing Theory and Practice*, New York: Ronald Press.

Moonitz, M. (1961) *The Basic Postulates of Accounting*, Accounting Research Study No. 1, American Institute of Certified Public Accountants.

Most, K. S. (1977) *Accounting Theory*, Columbus, Ohio: Grid.

Mumford, M. J. (1980) 'An Historical Defence of Henry Rand Hatfield', *Abacus*, December: 151–7.

Nelson, C. L. (1973) 'A Priori Research in Accounting', in N. Dopuch and L. Revsine (eds) *Accounting Research 1960–1970: A Critical Evaluation*, Champaign, Ill.: Center for International Research in Accounting, University of Illinois.

Newlove, G. H. and Garner, S. P. (1951) *Advanced Accounting*, vol. I, New York: D. C. Heath.

Paton, W. A. (1918) 'The Significance and Treatment of Appreciation in the Accounts', in G. H. Coons (ed.), *Twentieth Annual Report*, Michigan Academy of Science: 35–49.

Paton, W. A. (1922) *Accounting Theory – With Special Reference to the Corporate Enterprise*, New York: Ronald Press.

Paton, W. A. (1940) Review of *Truth in Accounting*, *Journal of Political Economy*, April: 296–8.

Paton, W. A. (ed.) (1943) *Accountants' Handbook*, New York: Ronald Press.

Paton, W. A. and Littleton, A. C. (1940) *An Introduction to Corporate Accounting Standards*, Monograph No. 3, Sarasota, Fla.: American Accounting Association.

Philips, G. E. (1971) review of republication of *Truth in Accounting*, *The Accounting Review*, July: 634–6.

Previts, G. J. and Merino, B. D. (1979) *A History of Accounting in America: An Historical Interpretation of the Cultural Significance of Accounting*, New York: John Wiley.

Rorem, C. R. (1928) *Accounting Method*, Chicago, Ill.: The University of Chicago Press.

Rosen, L. S. (1972) *Current Value Accounting and Price-Level Restatements*, Toronto: Canadian Institute of Chartered Accountants.

Roy, G. D. (1963) *A Survey of Accounting Ideas*, Calcutta: Alpha Publishing Concern.

Salmonson, R. F. (1969) *Basic Financial Accounting Theory*, New York: Wadsworth.

Sanders, T. H., Hatfield, H. R. and Moore, U. (1938) *A Statement of Accounting Principles*, New York: American Institute of Accountants.

Scapens, R. W. (1977) *Accounting in an Inflationary Environment*, Basingstoke: Macmillan.

Schmidt, F. (1930) 'The Importance of Replacement Value', *The Accounting Review*, September: 235–42.

Schmidt, F. (1931) 'Is Appreciation Profit?', *The Accounting Review*, December: 289–93.

Scholes, M. S. (1972) 'The Market for Securities: Substitution versus Price Pressure and the Effects of Information on Share Prices', *The Journal of Business*, April: 179–211.

Securities and Exchange Commission (1940a) 'In the Matter of McKesson & Robbins, Inc. – Summary of Findings and Conclusions', *Accounting Series Release No 19*, SEC, December 5.

Securities and Exchange Commission (1940b) *In the Matter of McKesson & Robbins Inc., Report on Investigation*, Washington, D.C. Government Printing Office, December.

Shaplen, R. (1955) 'Annals of Crime: The Metamorphosis of Philip Musica', *The New Yorker* I, October 22: 49–81; II, October 29: 39–79.

Skinner, R. M. (1972) *Accounting Principles: A Canadian Viewpoint*, Toronto: Canadian Institute of Chartered Accountants.

Solomons, D. (1961) 'Economic and Accounting Concepts of Income', *The Accounting Review*, July: 374–83.

Spacek, L. (1964) 'Treatment of Goodwill in the Corporate Balance Sheet', *The Journal of Accountancy*, February: 35–40.

Sprouse, R. T. and Moonitz, M. (1962) *A Tentative Set of Broad Accounting Principles for Business Enterprises*, Accounting Research Study No. 3, American Institute of Certified Public Accountants.

Sterling, R. R. (1970) *Theory of the Measurement of Enterprise Income*, The University Press of Kansas.

Sweeney, H. W. (1932) 'Stabilized Appreciation', *The Accounting Review*, June: 115–21.

Sweeney, H. W. (1936) *Stabilized Accounting*, New York: Harper & Brothers.

Thomas, A. L. (1969) *The Allocation Problem in Financial Accounting Theory*, Studies in Accounting Research No. 3, American Accounting Association.

Vatter, W. J. (1947) *The Fund Theory of Accounting and Its Implications for Financial Reports*, Chicago, Ill.: The University of Chicago Press.

Whittington, G. (1980) 'Pioneers of Income Measurement and Price-Level Accounting; A Review Article', *Accounting and Business Research*, Spring: 232–40.

Wixon, R. (ed.) (1956) *Accountants' Handbook*, New York: Ronald Press.

'You Cur!' (1939) Letters to the Editors, *The Nation*, August 5: 157–8.

Zeff, S. A. (1972) *Forging Accounting Principles in Five Countries: A History and an Analysis of Trends*, Champaign, Ill.: Stipes.

Zeff, S. A. (1979) 'Paton on the Effects of Changing Prices on Accounting: 1916–55', in S. A. Zeff, J. Demski and N. Dopuch (eds) *Essays in Honor of William A. Paton: Pioneer Accounting Theorist*, Ann Arbor, Mich.: Division of Research, Graduate School of Business Administration, The University of Michigan.

'Zounds!' (1939) Letters to the Editors, *The Nation*, August 5: 157.

Index